WEAPONS
of the
NAVY SEALs

WEAPONS

of the NAVY SEALs

KEVIN DOCKERY

BERKLEY BOOKS, NEW YORK

THE BERKLEY PUBLISHING GROUP
Published by the Penguin Group
Penguin Group (USA) Inc.
375 Hudson Street, New York, New York 10014, USA
Penguin Group (Canada), 10 Alcorn Avenue, Toronto, Ontario M4V 3B2, Canada
(a division of Pearson Penguin Canada Inc.)
Penguin Books Ltd., 80 Strand, London WC2R 0RL, England
Penguin Group Ireland, 25 St. Stephen's Green, Dublin 2, Ireland (a division of Penguin Books Ltd.)
Penguin Group (Australia), 250 Camberwell Road, Camberwell, Victoria 3124, Australia
(a division of Pearson Australia Group Pty. Ltd.)
Penguin Books India Pvt. Ltd., 11 Community Centre, Panchsheel Park, New Delhi—110 017, India
Penguin Group (NZ), cnr. Airborne and Rosedale Roads, Albany, Auckland 1310, New Zealand
(a division of Pearson New Zealand Ltd.)
Penguin Books (South Africa) (Pty.) Ltd., 24 Sturdee Avenue, Rosebank, Johannesburg 2196, South Africa

Penguin Books Ltd., Registered Offices: 80 Strand, London WC2R 0RL, England

This book is an original publication of The Berkley Publishing Group.

Copyright © 2004 by Bill Fawcett and Associates
Cover design by Steven Ferlauto
Cover photographs courtesy of Bettman/Corbis
Text design by Tiffany Estreicher

First edition: December 2004

Library of Congress Cataloging-in-Publication Data

Dockery, Kevin.
    Weapons of the Navy SEALs / Kevin Dockery.—1st ed.
        p. cm.
    ISBN 0-425-19834-0
        1. United States. Navy. SEALs. 2. United States. Navy—Weapons systems.   I. Title.

    VG87.D6325 2004
    359.9'84—dc22   2004051278

PRINTED IN THE UNITED STATES OF AMERICA

10 9 8 7 6 5 4 3 2 1

Contents

**This book is dedicated to the memory of
Dr. Edward C. Ezell, Ph.D., who encouraged me to continue
my writing, guided me, and told me I had paid my dues.**

Help from a great many individuals and organizations went into the creation of this book and the items described between these pages. Because of the nature of their work, many of these individuals did not want to see their name in print. For others, the passage of time has rendered them anonymous.

The Author's personal and heartfelt thanks are extended to both the above and the following individuals, organizations, and institutions;

AAI Corporation, Hunt Valley, Maryland
Elaine Abbrecht
ARES, Inc, Port Clinton, Ohio
Beretta U.S.A. Corp
LTCM Roy Boehm, USN (Ret.)
Michael Boynton
Richard Brozak
Colt Firearms Division, Hartford, Connecticut
Andre Dallau
Emerson Knives Inc.
   –Mr. Earnest Emerson
Federal Bureau of Alcohol, Tobacco, and
   Firearms
   –Ed Owens, Jr.
Gerber Legendary Blades
   –Mr. Mark Schindel
Great Lakes Arsenal, Ray, Michigan
   –Vincent Tessier
Heckler & Koch, Inc. Sterling, Virginia
   –Mr. Jim Schatz
Ian Hogg
Harry Humphires
Kerry N. Kinder & Family
Knight Armament Company
   –Mr. C. Reed Knight, Jr.
   –Mr. Eugene Stoner
CMDR Richard Marcinko, USN (Ret.)
CPT Ryan McCombie, USN (Ret.)
   –Mr. Greg McPartlin
LCDR Stanley "Pete" Meston, USN (Ret.)
Militec Corporation, Arlington Virginia
   –Mr. Russel A. Logan
Mission Knives, Inc.
   –Mr. Richard A. Schultz
Frank Moncrief
Naval Historical Center
   –Dr. Dean C. Allard
   –Dr. William F. Dudley

–Mr. Henry A. Vadnais, Jr.
–Dr. Norman Cary
–Mrs. Kathy Lloyd
–Mr. Mark Wertheimer
–Mr. Frank V. Thompson
Naval Sea Systems Command
–Mr. Richard E. Brown
–Mr. Homer Detrich
Naval Surface Warfare Center, Crane, Indiana
–Mr. Larry Nash
–Mr. Mike Anderson
–Mr. Jim Scott
Sage International, Ltd.
–John M. Klein
Jim Shults
CMDR Larry Simmons, USN (Ret.)
Smith & Wesson, Springfield, Massachussets
–Ken Jorgensen
Smithsonian Institution, Museum of
   American History
–Dr. Edward C. Ezell
SOG Specialty Knives, Inc.
Dante S. Stephensen
CWO4 Thomas Swearengen, USMC (Ret.)
LTCM Frank F. Thornton, USN (Ret.)
UDT-SEAL Museum, Fort Pierce, Florida
–Jim Watson QMCS, USN (Ret.)
–H.T. Aldhizer, III
–Don Balzarini
United States Special Operations Command,
   PAO
US Army Ordnance Museum, Aberdeen
   Proving Grounds
CPT Richard Woolard, USN (Ret.)
Darryl Young

**And to the men of the Teams,
past, present, and future.**

■ 1

DEATH IN THE DARK

Joe Wilkes was quietly laying in wait along the stream, just one of thousands of little waterways that crossed the Mekong Delta area of South Vietnam. SEAL Team Two had been conducting direct action operations against the Viet Cong for over two years now and they had long ago made the VC fear the men they called "the Devils in Green Faces."

The rest of Wilkes's squad were spaced out along the stream preparing to wait out the long night in less than comfortable surroundings. At least they weren't sitting in brown water up to their chins on this ambush. There was a small path next to the stream. The platoon's intelligence had indicated that a high-ranking member of the Viet Cong infrastructure would be traveling along that path. So the SEALs were lined up to cover both the path and the stream beyond.

This was their second night in the same general area. Repetition could get you killed in this business. But the intel they had was solid on this being the path of the VC. What they didn't have was the exact day they could expect their target to be traveling. So the boss—Mr. Givens, the platoon leader—had moved the ambush up about half a klick from where they had set up the night before.

The quarter moon let the SEALs see along the path and the stream beyond. It was one of those warm, wet, tropical nights the Mekong Delta was so famous for. Insects swarmed and fed on the seven SEALs lined up along the path. It was just another thing you had to accept and endure in the jungle, like the smell and the constant wet and humidity. And SEALs could endure.

Wilkes had an old friend with him in the underbrush. Besides his teammates lined up to his right, in his hands was an M3A1 greasegun, a submachine gun built during the closing months of World War II. The gun was actually older than Joe's twenty-two years. It only spotted him a year in age, but it had seen a lot of combat. He was the youngest member of the platoon, so it made sense in military humor that they gave him the oldest gun, but he didn't mind at all.

Loaded, the M3A1 weighed more than a standard M16A1. The sheet-metal receiver of the gray phosphated gun shone wetly in the dim moonlight. The sheet metal stampings that made up the receiver of the weapon helped hold the simple gun's weight down. But this M3A1 was particularly heavy. The normal thin cylindrical barrel, part of the reason the weapon resembled a mechanic's grease gun so much, had been removed. In its place was a thick cylinder of steel pipe that stepped down to a thinner cylinder—a suppressor, commonly called a silencer, that had been designed for the OSS during World War II.

The suppressor was very heavy, the pipe it was made out of seemed thick enough to drive tent stakes with if Joe had wanted to. But the perforated barrel that the pipe surrounded, combined with the wire screen rolls and washers between the barrel and the pipes, reduced the sound of firing the M3A1 to an odd series of thuds. Kind of a clap and hiss noise. Nothing that could be recognized as a gunshot at any real distance.

The big .45 caliber bullets that streamed out of the simple weapon made more noise hitting the target than the firing of the gun did. In the darkness of the night, the preferred operating environment of the SEALs, the flash of firing the M3A1 was just a dim glow at the muzzle of the weapon, and that only from the front. To see the muzzle flash meant you weren't going to be around long enough to describe it to anyone.

His position at the left flank of the squad meant that Joe would be the first to see the target as he came along the path. The main body of the squad would take out the bodyguards and snatch the target. Joe was to maintain rear security to make sure that any enemy stragglers didn't manage to come up on the SEALs as they were searching the bodies. Or that any of the enemy managed to get away and bring back help, lots of help that could overwhelm the small SEAL unit.

A string was stretched out along the length of the SEAL squad. Each man could feel the pull of a tug on the string. That was one of the silent ways they had to run messages along the squad. Simple messages only, but enough to make sure that everyone was awake and to pass a warning of danger.

The moon was blocked by passing clouds, so a dark night became darker. The soft noises of the stream could be heard, the bubble and splash of other critters in the night who stalked their prey. The buzz of insects seemed to always be around. It was a constant noise that you just had to tune out. Joe's young ears filtered out the sound of the bugs, fish, and frogs. What he heard next was the soft chatter of men talking, and they weren't speaking in English.

Pulling on the string twice, Joe sent the danger signal up the line. As each man felt the tugs, he sent the same signal up to the next man in line. Then the answering tugs came back to show that everyone had received and understood the message.

When the two tugs came back on the string to Joe, he barely felt them. His concentration was on the movement he heard in the brush—someone was coming. And no one was supposed to be out at night in the entire area. The only people who would be moving along the path would be those who thought they would use the night to cover themselves. They were about to find out just who really owned the nights in the Mekong Delta.

Here they were. Two men stepped past a curve in the path and came into plain sight. There wasn't any question that both of the men were Viet Cong. If their being out in a freefire zone at night while wearing black pajamas wasn't enough to tag them as VC, the AK-47s in their hands would have sealed the question.

The Viet Cong had never recovered their full strength since their disastrous defeat during the Tet Offensive attacks in 1968. Their weapons and supplies had gotten a little better since then, but that was as much a result of their numbers being down as an increase of supplies coming down from North Vietnam. Weapons were becoming a bit more standardized among the VC, but AK-47s were still in limited supply. They were usually found in the hands of veteran front-line troops and those men assigned to particularly important duties.

Both of the VC who Joe could see carried AK-47s and the chest-type ammunition bandoleers that carried spare magazines. These were men who were running point for someone, and that someone rated bodyguards with AK-47s. This looked like it could be the target the SEALs had been waiting for.

Earlier, as soon as he had settled into position, Joe had made sure the ejection port cover on his greasegun was in the open position. The cover also acted as a safety, locking the bolt in place. With his weapon cocked and the safety off, Wilkes was ready to pump out thirty rounds of quiet .45 caliber slugs with a pull of the trigger.

Up forward in the squad, Mr. Givens had the hush puppy, the squad's 9mm Mark 22 pistol with a suppressor attached. The quiet handgun was still in limited supply, so each deployed platoon only had one. The hush puppy was more often used to take out the noisy ducks and geese that the Vietnamese villagers kept as food and an alarm system, rather than the dogs that the weapon's nickname suggested. On some missions, the hush puppy was used against two-legged targets other than waterfowl. This was one of those missions.

The SEALs had been waiting for two nights for these people to walk along this path. Now, it was the next few minutes of waiting that seemed the longest.

Concentrating on the job at hand, Joe ignored the thudding beat of his own heart. He knew no one else could hear it. But his heartbeat sounded so loud in his own ears that the truth was hard to believe. The two VC bodyguards walked past him, not five feet away, in spite of what he could hear. In the still night air, Joe could smell the nuoc mam, the fermented fish sauce that was a staple of the Vietnamese diet, that one of the VC had been eating.

Passing where Joe lay in concealment, the two VC walked deeper into the kill zone of the SEALs' ambush. If there weren't too many of the VC escorting the target, Mr. Givens would try for a quiet prisoner snatch. The intel had said that the VCI member the SEALs were targeting was traveling with a group of five or six VC. And two of those men had just walked by.

Moving along about ten meters behind the first two VC came a group of three men, all wearing black pajamas. Two of the men were carrying AK-47s. The armed men were walking along on either side of the third individual, who carried nothing more deadly looking than a satchel and a box. This was their target, the man with the box.

If Mr. Givens thought that there were too many VC for them to handle, he would initiate the ambush with his CAR-15. The unmistakable boom of the short-barreled M16 variant would be the signal for all of the SEALs to open fire. Their automatic weapons would sweep the kill zone of the ambush clear of any living person. Then, the SEALs would have to move quickly to strip the bodies of any information or material of intelligence value. The sounds of their gunfire would have alerted any VC in the area that they were not alone in the night.

With only the men they could see right now, Mr. Givens would probably decide that the chances were good to grab up a live prisoner. In that case, it would be a suppressed pistol shot that would be heard across the kill zone. Chief Cartwright, at the other end of the ambush site from Joe, had a second suppressed M3A1. He would be in a good position to make quick work of the first two VC who had passed.

Suddenly, there he was, the sixth VC. As Joe aimed his greasegun, he heard the loud snap from up the line, Mr. Givens had decided to go for the snatch and initiated the quiet ambush. There was a series of loud hissing thuds coming from well behind Wilkes. That was the sound of Chief Cartwright's suppressed M3A1 chopping down the first pair of VC.

Pulling the trigger of his own weapon even as he heard the sound of the Chief's firing, Wilkes felt the bolt slide forward and fire the first round in the magazine as the gun vibrated in his hands.

The VC in front of Wilkes never even got his AK up and into firing position before the heavy 230-grain .45 slugs smashed into him. He was driven backward and knocked down by the onslaught of the bullets. Behind Wilkes, there was a crashing sound followed by a grunt and more brush crackling. Then a high-pitched whistling buzz sounded out in the night, fading off into the distance.

One of the .45 slugs that Wilkes fired had struck the steel receiver of the AK in front of him. Flattened and deformed from the impact, the slug had whistled off into the distance as it ricocheted off the enemy weapon.

The thrashing around and grunting behind Wilkes had stopped. The rest of the SEALs quickly got up from their concealed positions and were moving through the ambush site. While Maynard kept cover across the stream with his Stoner light machine gun, the rest of the unit either held security, stripped the enemy bodies, or dealt with the prisoner.

For Joe Wilkes, his job was to watch back along the trail that the VC had come from. The SEALs had a prisoner, and now they had to secure him and move out of the area. The loudest sound from the ambush had been the one bullet ricocheting off, but the SEALs knew that their position had been compromised and speed was where their only real safety lay now.

The slight Vietnamese prisoner had his hands pulled behind his back and shackled with a regular pair of handcuffs. A rolled triangular bandage replaced the hand that a big SEAL was holding over the prisoner's mouth while he was being searched and secured.

Bound and gagged, the prisoner could barely move along while Ness, one of the squad's automatic weapons men, held the VC by the collar of his pajama top. In his right hand, the big SEAL kept control of his chopped-down M60 machine gun, hanging from his shoulder by a wide sling made from a pistol belt.

Now the SEALs withdrew from the area. The ambush and capture had taken less than a minute. Not a word had been spoken the whole time. The only casualty appeared to be Mr. Givens, who was limping badly. Moving downstream, the squad headed for their extraction point. Keith, the squad's radioman, called in the extraction boat under orders from Mr. Givens.

Once they reached the wide river branch where they would be extracted, the SEALs set up an immediate security perimeter. There was no sound from the marsh around them other than the normal noises of nature. While waiting for the river patrol boats to come in a pull them all out, Mr. Givens sat down on the bank of the water where Nellis, the squad's corpsman, could tend to his wounded leg. There was a nasty wound on the lieutenant's left thigh, the blood gleaming blackly in the moonlight.

The fiberglass-hulled PBRs came in on their waterjet propulsion and picked up the SEALs without incident. It was only when they were safely aboard the boats and heading out into the river that the SEALs finally relaxed. A little bit of laughter could be heard rising up from one of the PBRs.

"What the hell happened?" Wilkes asked.

"Oh, it looks like a good hit," Chief Cartwright said. "The guy we snatched was a VC tax collector. That ammunition can he was carrying was stuffed full of piasters. He'll be a good source of information."

"But how did Mr. Givens get hit?" Wilkes said. "I didn't hear a shot get fired except for ours."

"Oh, he didn't get shot," Nellis said, "he was stabbed."

"Stabbed?" Wilkes said. "One of the VC pulled a knife?"

"No," Maynard, the Stonerman, said with a grin, "Ness did it."

Wilkes just stared at his Teammates while they laughed.

"What the hell do you mean, Ness did it?" Wilkes said.

"When Givens took out the guard," Maynard said, "his hush puppy had to be reloaded for another shot. The other guard was only a few steps from Keith so he jumped up and tackled the guy. Givens dove forward and knocked down the prisoner. While Ness was wrestling this little VC, the pair of them rolled over on Givens and the prisoner. Keith pulled out his Ka-bar and finally stabbed the VC. He stabbed the guy so hard he practically drove the knife right through him."

"Actually," Keith said, "he did drive the knife right through the guy. Right through him to stab Givens in the leg."

"Oh," was all Wilkes could think to say.

∎ 2
KNIVES

One of mankind's oldest tools was also the only weapon used by the Underwater Demolition Teams (UDTs) during their earliest years in World War II. To the men of the Teams, a good knife was a necessity, and one they carried with them constantly. Even when a swimmer wasn't wearing much more than his swim trunks, face mask, and fins, on a belt around his waist would be a knife in its sheath.

The first issue knife to the early UDTs was the U.S.N. Mark 1, standard throughout the Fleets. From the official drawing of the Mark 1 dated November 1943, the design called for a 5.125-inch blade with a shaped aluminum pommel over a stacked leather washer grip with a small flat steel guard. The flat-ground, single-edge blade of the Mark 1 greatly resembles the general style of hunting knife that was popular in the civilian market at the time. The shaped metal pommel was also a part of popular commercial knives during the 1940s. It may be that the design of the Mark 1 wasn't influenced by commercial knives as much as it was just much easier to make a knife for the Navy that the civilian cutlers were already tooled up for.

On the ricasso of the Mark 1's blade, the flat area on the blade between the guard and where the cutting edge begins, is stamped U.S.N. MARK 1. On the opposite side of the blade is usually the maker's name. The large number of Mark 1s produced during World War II resulted in a number of cutlers making the Mark 1, each one modifying the design slightly to meet his own manufacturing methods. But though the details of the knife may have been different— the pommels were made of aluminum, plastic, flat steel, even wood and the handles were in slightly different shapes—the general style of the knife remained the same. Two very different kinds of sheaths were found on the Mark 1, though only one was well accepted by the UDTs.

The first type of sheath on the Mark 1 was a traditional-style folded brown leather sheath with a snap-type keeper. As the Mark 1 was intended to be a general issue knife, it was thought that the leather sheath would be satisfactory throughout the Navy. This was quickly proved false as the sheath was found to rapidly deteriorate, no matter how well kept, in the hot and humid conditions of the Pacific. For the men of the UDT, the leather sheath would be quickly rendered useless by the constant and extended immersion in salt water it received on operations and during training. A fiber-reinforced gray plastic scabbard was designed and issued for the Mark 1. The new scabbard was well received by the men of the UDTs as well as many of the Fleet sailors.

A drawback of the Mark 1 was the reported weakness of the blade. Tapering from the base to the point, the Mark 1 had a light and handy blade but not the strongest design. Being issued Navy-wide, the Mark 1 was subject to some serious misuse, especially when being used as a pry-bar to open boxes and cases. The small-sized blade was also considered by many to be too short for effective use as a combat/fighting knife.

There was also the problem of wartime production to be considered. It was not the best use of material to have several types of knives made for different service units that did much the same work. The thousands of knives needed by the Navy should also have met the requirements of the Marine Corps, since the two services worked so close together.

Camillus Cutlery Company had submitted a knife to the Marine Corps in December 1942. The design was of a multipurpose tool that would also serve well as a fighting knife. The knife was adopted as USMC item #1219C2c and put into production. In general, the knife had a great deal in common with the Mark 1 design. The handles of both knives were made up of stacked leather washers with an attached metal pommel and the guard was a simple metal stamping.

The Camillus knife had a seven-inch blade with a clip point sharpened on the back edge. The metal pommel was a flat metal affair suitable for pounding, specially in the later pinned models. The leather handle was oval in cross section and had five grooves turned into it as an aid in gripping the knife.

Where the blade of the Mark 1 had a flat grind extending from the back to the edge, the Marine knife's blade had flat, parallel sides to within a few inches of the tip and an edge grind that didn't come up to the midpoint of the blade. A fuller was also ground into each side of the blade to help strengthen and lighten it.

All in all, the knife was everything the Marine Corps wanted in a combat/utility blade and was later adopted by the Navy as the Mark 2. First manufactured only by Camillus, the Marine knife was duplicated by a number of other manufacturers. Union Cutlery was one of these producers and they already manufactured a line of knives under the trade name Ka-Bar. Knives supplied to the Marine Corps from Union Cutlery were marked "U.S.M.C." on one side of the ricasso and "KA-BAR" on the opposite side. The name Ka-Bar stuck in popular use and has been used interchangeably with the Navy Mark 2 designation.

The Mark 1 (upper) and Mark 2 (lower) knives outside of their sheaths. The length of the blade and heavier construction of the Mark 2 visible in this photograph are what helped make the knife so popular among members of the UDT and SEAL Teams.
Source: Kevin Dockery

During the war, many thousands of the Ka-Bar and Mark 2 designs were produced by at least five different makers. These makers would put their own markings on the knife as well as have slight differences in the overall pattern due to their own manufacturing methods. Several design changes were also dictated by the Marines and the Navy after field experience with the weapon. The most obvious changes were the three different methods of attaching the pommel cap. The first Mark 2s and Ka-Bars had the pommel cap held on by a flush-mounted threaded nut. Later pommels were peened in place and finally held in place with a cross pin through the tang. All of the steel parts of the knives were either matte blued or, most commonly, parkerised with a dull gray phosphate coating.

The marking of the blade for the Mark 2 also changed during the war, being moved from the ricasso to the flat metal guard. The popular story is that stamping the ricasso weakened the blade, but that was not the case. According to the people at Union Cutlery, the Mark 2 design was so popular that it was eventually demanded by all the services, including the Coast Guard. Instead of putting whatever designation was required onto the blade, and scrapping a blade that was mismarked, markings were moved to the easily handled guard. Even mismarked guards could be used if necessary by obliterating the markings with chisel cuts, something that would have been excessive if done to the blades.

Except for the very earliest issue blades, the Navy Mark 2 was given out sheathed in a gray plastic scabbard similar to the model used in the later production Mark 1s. The Marine Ka-Bars, though much the same pattern, were issued with a standard leather sheath. Part of the popularity and success of the Mark 2 was due to the excellent design of the scabbard, the plastic and canvas construction proving very resistant to damage from exposure to the elements. The scabbards were not produced by the various cutlery firms that were making

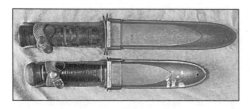

The two most common knives used by the UDTs during World War II. At the top is the Mark 2 knife with a flat-steel pommel while below it is a Mark 1 knife with a cast aluminum pommel. Both of the knives are sheathed in the gray plastic scabbards found on most of the Navy contract knives. The Mark 2 is also commonly called a Ka-Bar.

Source: Kevin Dockery

the knives. A single contractor, the Beckwith Manufacturing Company (B.M. Co. is the marking on the back of the chape), made the scabbards and supplied them to the various cutlery companies.

Though the scabbard did not suffer greatly in a moist environment, the blades of both the Mark 1 and Mark 2 were not so resistant. Being made of carbon steel, the knife blades would very soon rust after exposure to the water. Even the metal fittings on the scabbards were susceptible to corrosion. The most exposed of all the thousands of Mark 2 knives used during the war were those used by the UDTs. Even the Marine Corps with its specialty in amphibious operations only spent enough time actually in the water as was needed to get to the landing beach. The UDTs performed the missions almost constantly in the water. To help minimize the corrosion, Union Cutlery produced a modified Mark 2 especially for the UDTs, called the Bright Mark 2.

The first model of the special UDT knives had no fuller ground into the blade and all the metal parts of the knife were bright chromed. Since the UDTs were under orders not to expose themselves to direct combat with the enemy—they were considered far too valuable to risk in such a manner—the brilliant shiny appearance of the knives was not a drawback. The "flat sided" Bright UDT knife was made in very limited numbers and is quite rare today. Though still made in limited numbers, the "production" Bright UDT knife was made with a standard, fullered blade and a pinned pommel.

Another unique feature of the special UDT knife was the leather grip. Where in the standard Mark 2 and Marine Ka-Bar the leather handle had a number of grooves cut into it, the UDT knife had a smooth grip. Removing the grooves cut down on the exposed surface area of the grip and helped to limit seawater absorption into the leather. A heavy varnish was also applied to the leather during manufacture to also help protect the grip from the water.

Though several makers produced the Mark 2 during World War II and in prodigious numbers, only the Union Cutlery Company made the special UDT Bright Mark 2. In 1945, at the end of the war, Union Cutlery had made about one million Mark 2 knives. Out of that number, it is thought that only a thousand or less of the special UDT knives were made, perhaps only a few hundred.

At the war's end, no more of the plastic Mark 2 scabbards were produced, the numbers available being thought sufficient for future needs.

For the rest of the 1940s and through the 1950s, the UDTs continued using the Mark 2 and remaining Mark 1s as the general issue knife. The small number of special UDT Bright Mark 2s were quickly absorbed into the growing Teams. The rare chromed Bright Mark 2 became a cherished possession of the WWII veteran officers and senior petty officers who remained in the postwar UDTs. The vast number of WW II-manufactured Mark 2 knives in the Navy inventories were easily able to fill the needs of the UDTs for some time.

Early in the 1960s, a new knife was required for special use by the Navy. Explosive Ordnance Disposal (EOD) missions were often performed by UDT divers as part of their beach-clearing operations. Underwater mines with magnetically influenced fuzes had become much more common by the late 1950s and were an EOD problem by the 1960s. The standard clearing procedure of blowing the mines in place was complicated by the need for a swimmer to closely approach the mine to emplace the destruction charge. The equipment for such a swimmer had to be completely nonmagnetic and usually nonferrous. Special nonmagnetic breathing equipment and other diving gear was available for EOD missions that would help increase the safety of the swimmer. But the Mark 1 and 2 knives were made of carbon steel and unsuitable for specialized EOD use.

A procurement contract was issued by the Navy in February 1961 and by April 1962 a new type of knife was ready for issue. Developed by the U.S. Navy Bureau of Weapons and the Imperial Knife Company of Providence, Rhode Island, the Nonmagnetic SCUBA Swimmers Knife is made of exotic alloy and has no detectable magnetic signature.

The initial problem with making such a knife was in coming up with a material that was nonmagnetic and yet could be hardened sufficiently to hold a sharp edge without being too brittle for field use. A nonferrous alloy, Haynes Number 25, was chosen to make up the blade of the new knife. Haynes Number 25 is a mixture of copper, chromium, tungsten, and nickel. After a process that included cold rolling, machining, grinding, and a five-hour, 1,000-degree Fahrenheit heat treatment, the hardness of the finished blades were at a Rockwell-C of 53-54. The blades were able to hold a worthwhile working edge but the material was still considerably more brittle than an equivalent steel blade.

Additional fittings for the knife and scabbard were of glass-fiber plastic and 310 stainless steel. 310 stainless steel has a high chromium and nickel content, giving the alloy strong resistance to corrosion and no magnetic signature. Retaining springs inside of the scabbard were made of a copper-beryllium alloy. All the remaining components of the knife and scabbard were either nylon or reinforced plastic.

Due to the relatively high individual cost of a finished knife, over $100 in 1962, as well as the brittleness of the blade, the Nonmagnetic SCUBA Swimmers Knife was kept for special issue only. Each blade was consecutively serial numbered and marked with the year of manufacture. All production of the nonmagnetic knife was carried out by the Imperial Knife Company with the initial production lot being 280 knives and scabbards. Only about 1,100 of the nonmagnetic knives were produced in the early 1960s and the knife has remained available for issue well into the 1990s.

As the SEALs and UDTs entered into action in the Vietnam War, the Mark 2 knife remained the standard issue blade. Sufficient numbers of the Mark 1 knife remained in the supply system to issue the knife to the men who preferred the smaller blade. For diving operations, any commercially available quality stainless steel divers knife was considered interchangeable with a Team-issued blade. Operators in the UDT and especially the SEALs were given a great deal of flexibility in choosing whatever knives they preferred to carry. An individual could purchase and carry any blade that he felt comfortable with. With the level of training and professionalism in the Teams, none of the men would have carried an excessively complex blade or one that could not be counted on.

When a sheath knife was carried during a dive, its primary purpose was to cut the swimmer free of any entanglements he might run in to. Because of this, it was specified that the diver's knife be securely attached to a web belt or one of the diver's legs and not to any piece of jettisonable equipment such as a weight belt. Making certain that the knife always stayed with an operator through any situation made it an excellent place to carry another required piece of emergency gear, the day/night flare.

In many of the post–World War II photos of UDT or SEAL operators, a Mark 13 day/night flare can be seen securely taped or strapped to the scabbard of a Mark 2 knife. On some occasions, an individual may have two Mark 13s attached to his knife's scabbard. This procedure is still being followed as Mark 13s or other signals can be seen attached to the sheaths of knives carried by today's SEALs.

During the Vietnam War, a great number of nonissue knives were seen carried by the SEALs. Some operators would take little or no interest in which specific knife they carried. The issue Mark 2 was quite satisfactory for these men and the blade saw good service in their hands. Other SEALs had different tastes and some of these men would carry two or more knives on operations. In the case of men carrying multiple knives, very often one would be a folding pocketknife such as the military issue Camillus all-purpose S1760, an all-metal, four-bladed pocketknife stamped "U.S." on one side.

Blades issued by other branches of the Service were also popular with the SEALs, such as the Air Force's Camillus Pilot Survival knife. Commercial combat knives such as Randalls and Gerber Mark IIs were carried along with the occasional custom blade made to a SEALs specifications. Probably the most personal knives carried were the "used" gift blades, given to an operator from a friend or relative who had carried the knife in an earlier conflict.

The SEALs received training in

A UDT swimmer preparing to enter the water in the 1960s. Wearing a minimum of equipment, inflatable life vest, t-shirt, trunks, and canvas/rubber coral shoes, this swimmer also has a quick-release belt around his waist securing a Mark 2 knife. As is commonly done in the Teams, this swimmer has taped a Mark 13 day/night signal flare to the scabbard of his Mark 2.
Source: U.S. Navy

hand-to-hand combat that included fighting with and against a knife. Though it was rare, SEALs were much more likely to use a knife as a weapon in combat than almost any other U.S. military unit. In general, if an enemy sentry required quiet dispatching, the weapon of choice would be a suppressed firearm rather than a blade. But the SEALs were always ready to make use of the weapons that they had immediately at hand.

In 1969, during what was the high point of the SEALs involvement in the Vietnam War, a unique "pocketknife" was received at SEAL Team Two. Besides being made of exotic materials, the knife also had an unusual job to perform, that of replacing a number of basic demolition tools. The folding demolition knife could measure, cut demolition materials, and crimp blasting caps.

The design for the demolition knife came out of the Navy Research and Development Unit, Vietnam office in Saigon. Manufacturing of the knife probably took place in the United States but relatively few were made. As the demolition knife had no markings and records of its development are scarce, the manufacturer of the knife is unknown.

According to one report from the U.S. Army Limited Warfare Laboratory, dated June 30, 1968, the Demolition knife was requested by the U.S. Army Special Forces school at Fort Bragg on March 15, 1967. It may be that the Army extended its request to a design already in progress at the Navy for the Teams. This thought is reinforced by a single excerpt from the SEAL Team Two Command and Control History for 1969. On page 14, the history states:

> A demolition knife which can fulfill the job of three other basic demolition tools was also introduced during 1969. This knife is so designed that it permits the user to measure, cut, and crimp demolition materials. It was developed by Navy Research and Development Unit, Vietnam.

All other official references to the demolition knife are still in classified files and further information has yet to become available. Issue of the blades was very limited and the design did not catch on. As it was, of the 200 demolition knives reported to have been produced, 150 went to the SEAL Teams and the remaining 50 went to the Army Special Forces.

Probably the most interesting features of the demolition knife center on the main blade. As are most of the working parts of the demolition knife, the main blade is made of a nonsparking alloy. Nonsparking alloys, usually based on copper, are the normal materials of use when making tools for working with explosives. The blade has a cutting edge and, though the material is soft when compared to a steel blade, it does maintain an edge sharp enough for cutting and working explosive charges. On the handle underneath the blade are two notches. One notch, underneath the cutting edge, is intended for cutting detonating cord or time fuse. By placing the detonating cord line in the notch and squeezing the blade closed, a clean, square cut can be made.

The second notch in the handle, closer to the hinge point of the knife, has a corresponding notch in the main blade. These two notches make up a particularly unique feature on a knife. With the two notches acting together, a crimp can be made on a blasting cap to secure it to a line or firing device. By inserting the material to be secured into the cap and placing the cap in the handle notch, the blade is squeezed against the handle and the crimp made.

Also on the demolition knife's blade are deeply stamped graduations with a metric scale on one side and an inch scale on the other. A flat screwdriver blade with an integral wire stripper are next to the main blade, both of which lock in place when opened. And on the back of the knife is a nonsparking metal awl, called a demolition cap setter in the one known official illustration of the knife. The awl is dimensioned so that it can form a blasting cap–sized hole in an explosive charge.

During the 1970s and the post-Vietnam cutbacks, the SEALs and UDTs underwent the same austerity programs as the other services. As they had during the last several decades, the Mark 2 and occasional Mark 1 fulfilled the cutlery needs of the Teams. With the increase in emphasis on the SEALs and other Special Operations units in the 1980s, manpower in the Teams increased and so did the demand for new equipment.

A replacement for the dwindling stocks of Mark 2 knives was desired and a number of replacements examined. From the Naval Weapons Support Center in Crane, Indiana came a design for a new knife that was finally accepted as the Mark 1 Mod 0 Combat Knife on October 21 1982. The pattern of the Mark 3 was an adaptation of the AKM-47 bayonet design used in the Soviet Union. One result of this adaption was that the Mark 3 knife had a very deep, concave clip point giving the blade a sharp, upswept tip. The intent of the tip was to ease the penetration of the knife into a target. But the combat knife was also to be a utility blade and such blades were used for prying materials apart and digging into the ground when necessary. The tip style of the Mark 3 was very weak for this kind of work and that was a drawback of the pattern.

Part of the initial specifications for the Mark 3 included an insulated wire-cutter built into the scabbard. By inserting a stud on the scabbard tip through a hole in the blade, a scissor-type wire cutter could be made. This idea can be directly traced to the AKM bayonet in use by Soviet forces. Though considered a good idea, the wirecutter provision further complicated and weakened an already difficult knife. The final production version of the Mark 3 Mod 0 did not include the wirecutter. As produced by the Ontario Knife Company, the Mark 3 Mod 0 knife has a black oxide–coated stainless steel blade with a fine-tooth-saw back intended for rapidly cutting rope or cable.

One particularly interesting issue knife at SEAL Team Two during the early 1980s was more of a pocket toolbox than a knife. Obtained for issue to team members was a quantity of the Victorinox Explorer model Swiss Army knife. The Swiss Army knife, long noted for its versatility, was found to be a highly useful tool by many of the SEALs who carried one. Purchased as an off-the-shelf item directly by SEAL Team Two, the Explorer was basically the standard commercial model with a few requested additions. Specifically, the trademark red side covers were replaced with black covers and a small jewelers-type screwdriver inserted into the corkscrew.

SEAL Team Six issued another Swiss Army knife later in the 1980s. The knife was the SwissChamp model and it was issued in roughly the 1987 to 1990 time period. As Team Two had earlier, the knife was purchased as an off-the-shelf item with black side plates instead of the trademark red ones. The SwissChamp is almost too big to qualify as a pocketknife and can be more accurately described as a belt-pouch toolkit.

Another folding knife has been issued as a regular item by several SEAL Teams. Though it does contain a knife blade, the Leatherman tool is most obviously a pair of folding pliers. Carried in a belt pouch, the Leatherman tool unfolds into a very serviceable pair of needle-nosed pliers with a serrated nut driver section and efficient wirecutters. Issued at about the same time as the SwissChamp, the Leatherman actually became more popular with the men of Team Six than the SwissChamp. The versatility of the tool is such that a number of SEALs in the other Teams have purchased Leathermans out of their own funds rather than wait for a possible issue.

A more recent addition to the folding tool design issued by the Teams is the Gerber Multi-Plier. The Gerber design utilized a sliding pliers head to shorten the overall length of the tool to a pocket size. With a quick snap of the wrist, the pliers head of the Gerber tool will slide open and snap into place. This one-handed opening feature has helped make the tool popular among a number of Special Warfare operators. Much larger than the Leatherman, the Gerber Multi-Plier is normally carried in a nylon pouch attached to an operator's rig or belt.

During the 1980s, a number of knife designs were examined by the SEAL Teams for use as an issue knife. Because of the flexibility allowed SEAL operators in purchasing and carrying any worthwhile blade they prefer, a number of commercial knives have been used. One result of this is the quantity of commercial and custom blades on the market that are advertised as "SEAL issue." Individual qualities aside, only a very few knives have been examined and evaluated by the Teams in numbers large enough for them to be considered "issue" items.

One of these few blade designs was developed in about the mid-1980s by Phrobis International Ltd. to fit requirements put forward by SPECWAR Command. The initial design was modified for production by Buck Knives, which manufactured the blade as the Model 184 BuckMaster.

The BuckMaster was purchased in some quantity by the Navy and supplied to the SEALs. The knife itself is an all-metal design, constructed of stainless steel to minimize corrosion. The BuckMaster has several unique features, the most prominent of which are the removable guard horns.

The guard horns are two pointed steel rod sections with threads on one end. Screwed into the sockets at either end of the guard, the horns stick out from the base of the guard, spreading away from the grip. At the base of the grip, held in place by the threaded pommel, is a removable metal lug. By securing a line through the hole in the lug, the entire knife can be used as a grappling hook. Or, according to some of the people who have carried the BuckMaster, the knife can be used as a small boat anchor.

The scabbard of the BuckMaster also has some special features. On the back of the scabbard, covered by a nylon web strap, is a sharpening stone sufficient to touch up the blade when in the field. Particularly handy is the belt loop design. Holding the belt loop closed is a plastic squeeze-type buckle. By unlatching the buckle, the scabbard assembly can be removed from a combat harness or belt without requiring the operator to remove his gear.

The deeply knurled grip of the BuckMaster is hollow. By unscrewing the pommel, which is waterproofed with a rubber O-ring, a storage space is exposed where a small supply of emergency gear can be stowed.

Though interesting, the BuckMaster was not well received by the operators intended to use it. For all of its possible utility, the BuckMaster was simply too heavy and complex for acceptance. Most of the BuckMasters that did arrive at the SEAL Teams remained on the supply room shelves.

Knives continued to be evaluated and tested in the Teams. While the Mark 3 Mod 0 remained the standard issue Team knife, a replacement multipurpose blade was strongly desired by the SEALs. Modifying an in-house design called the MUK (Modular Utility Knife) according to SEAL Team suggestions, Phrobis International developed a new knife for evaluation by the SPECWAR community.

Called the CUK for Combat Utility Knife, the Phrobis design had a forged blade manufactured in Spain from modified 420 stainless steel. An addition of 5 percent molybdenum to the stainless steel alloy increased its toughness. Using forging as part of the manufacturing process adds to the overall strength of a knife. A deep fuller on the CUK blade also added to the blade's strength as well as reducing some of the overall weight of the knife.

The idea behind the CUK was for a knife that would be primarily a tool rather than a weapon. The short blade of the CUK, very close to the same length as the old Mark 1, has a fine-tooth-saw back to aid in cutting rope or thin sheet alloy such as the skin of an aircraft. A modular approach was used in the overall construction of the CUK. Six individual parts make up the knife with the components being held together by a threaded tang rod.

The CUK blade has a short threaded section, heat treated to be softer than the cutting edge for increased toughness. The blade's stub tang threads into the tang rod which in turn has a three-inch-long Allen bolt screwed into it. The Allen bolt holds the pommel cap in place, retaining the grip and guard in position on the knife. The grip of the CUK is made of DuPont Zytel plastic with deep rings and knurling cast into it. Outside of the grip and blade, all of the other components of the CUK are made from 410 stainless steel.

The scabbard of the CUK retains the knife in place with a locking plate that bears on the guard of the blade. When the lock has snapped over the guard, the blade is secured in place until the grip is intentionally pulled away from the hanger. A nylon screw on the back of the scabbard allows the tension of the blade retention to be adjusted. The screw also acts as a pivot point between the scabbard and the hanger. With the scabbard strapped in place on an operators leg, the hanger can pivot on the tension screw when the leg is bent such as when the operator is sitting down.

For all of the CUKs innovations, the knife was not accepted beyond the initial evaluation quantities. About 200 blades were sent to the West Coast and SEAL Team Three in 1989. As few as a dozen CUKs were sent to the East Coast for evaluation at roughly the same time.

After the failure of the CUK to gain acceptance with the SEALs, the Teams remained with the Mark 3 Mod 0 as their issue knife. A modified CUK design did remain with the military as the M9 bayonet, adopted for use with the M16A1/A2 rifle. As the SEALs entered the 1990s, the search for a new issue knife continued.

In August 1991, a number of different knives were examined by the Teams for possible adoption. After an exhaustive testing procedure where thirty-one different blades were tried, three finalists remained. In April 1992, a final series of examinations was begun and a single blade chosen. The final knife was the custom made ATAK (Advanced Tactical Assault Knife) submitted by Kevin McClung of Mad Dog Knives. The knife was a straightforward design with a seven-inch single edge blade, insulated grip, and Kydex plastic sheath.

In 1992 the Navy ordered 275 ATAK knifes for issue to the West Coast SEAL Teams. Problems in delivery times for the effectively custom-made blades caused the Navy to finally suspend purchase of the ATAK knife after as few as 50 were delivered. The Navy reopened the contract for a new issue SEAL knife and fourteen cutlery companies responded with submissions. The requirements put forward for the new knife were stringent and made a long list:

I. THE BLADE
  a. 6 to 7 inches in length.
  b. Choil big enough to be held with a gloved hand.
  c. A tip strong enough to pry with while still being sharp enough for penetration.
  d. Hard enough to hold a good edge without easily dulling.
  e. Corrosion resistant.
  f. Be nonreflective (have a dull finish).

II. THE HANDLE
  a. Insulated from the blade and nonconductive.
  b. Fit the hands of at least 95 percent of SEAL operators.
  c. Resistant to petroleum products (not react after a 10-minute soak in gasoline).
  d. Be heat resistant (survive a 10-second exposure to the flame of an oxyacetylene torch).
  e. Not be slippery in a wet hand.
  f. Cover the full tang of the blade.
  g. Have a lanyard hole.
  h. Have a small crossguard so that the blade can be held "choked-up" in the hand for detail work.
  i. Pommel capable of driving nails.

III. THE SHEATH
  a. Resistant to salt water.
  b. Quiet when struck against a hard object.
  c. Removable from a belt or harness without requiring a removal of the rig.

Both heavy and light lines were cut during the testing as well as crates being pried open, hammered shut, and electrical cables being severed. After the extensive testing and analysis of the personal input of a number of active SEALs, a knife was decided on. The knife chosen was the ST2SS, a modified commercial pattern of the Tech II knife produced by SOG Specialty Knives.

During the Vietnam War, a knife was manufactured specifically for issue to

The original stiffened nylon sheath of the SOG SK2000 is shown at the top of the photo, just above the knife itself. At the bottom is the hard sheath for the MPK titanium knife just above it.
Source: Kevin Dockery

the members of the 5th Special Forces group and occasionally given out to the men who operated with MAC-V SOG. The SEALs were among the personnel who worked as part of MAC-V SOG and operators would occasionally be given one of the blades. As the SOG Specialty Knife company began by making a close duplicate of the rare 5th SF knife, it is easy to see how the general lines of the Vietnam blade are in the slimmer new knife.

The SOG SEAL 2000 knife leans much more towards being a fighting knife than a general tool. The shape of the tip and back edge aid in penetration. The back edge of the knife can be easily sharpened according to the tastes of an individual operator but the knife comes as issued with a fully ground but dull back. The sheath material, being a stiffened black nylon, is not as hard and inflexible as a plastic sheath would be but is silent when the knife is drawn and makes no noise when struck. With the addition of the serrations at the blase of the cutting edge, the SEAL 2000 can quickly cut through rope, cardboard, and other harder materials.

While the SOG SEAL 2000 was being accepted as the new issue steel SEAL knife, it is important to note the term "steel knife." Another knife came forward to the SEALs attention during the tests which ran from June to October 1993. The knife noted was not of a particularly unusual design but the blade material was unique. Titanium has long been known for its lightness and strength and a blade made of titanium would be very tough, much more so than an equivalent blade made of steel. But titanium is also very difficult to work with, almost impossible to grind efficiently, and there was no treatment available that could harden a titanium blade sufficiently for it to hold a good working edge. For the 1993 SEAL knife tests, Mission Knives of California submitted their Multi Purpose Knife (MPK) with a titanium blade.

By using beta titanium alloy, Mission Knives was able to make an effective knife blade for their MPK. Though not as hard as a steel blade could be, the MPK blade is extremely tough and has several other valuable characteristics.

Titanium will not corrode easily. Salt water, humid air, moisture, chemical fumes, and even many acids will not readily affect the MPK's blade. During some jungle tests, an MPK became covered in tree sap and other sticky juices. To clean the blade, the testers washed it off with hydrochloric acid followed by soap and water and then a coating of baby oil. There were not only no signs of corrosion or other damage to the blade, the baby oil reacted chemically with the titanium, making a dark black coating. The MPK came out of the jungle testing actually looking better than it did before going in.

Another characteristic of titanium is its lack of a magnetic signature. By careful choice of materials for the handle, sheath, and fittings, the MPK package was completely nonmagnetic. The knife has since been adopted as a replacement for the earlier Imperial nonmagnetic knife. Along with the corrosion resistance and nonmagnetic aspects of the MPK, it has an additional feature—the strength of titanium when it comes to resisting abrasion and breakage.

One tester took his MPK and wedged the point of the blade some distance underneath a safe's door. Stomping on the handle finally managed to stress-crack the tip of the knife and it broke off. But this was after the handle had been stomped on several times a day, each working day, for many weeks. Under such punishment, any steel knife would break almost immediately. The blade of the MPK is soft when compared to a steel blade but it cannot be sharpened with a normal oilstone. The abrasion resistance of titanium causes the blade of the MPK to just slide across the surface of a honing stone. To sharpen the titanium blade, an EZE-Lap Model M diamond-coated sharpener is issued with each knife.

Though the MPK is hard to sharpen with anything but a diamond abrasive, the blade will still dull quickly when it is used to cut anything harder than itself. But it is rare to use a knife to cut anything harder than forty-four on the Rockwell C scale. The MPK's blade, though it will not take as sharp an edge as hardened steel, it will hold the edge it takes longer. The MPK will out-cut a steel knife when used against rope, cardboard, wood, or nylon. Even when used for digging in the sand, the MPK will not quickly dull. Along with all these features, the MPK is an amazingly light knife. Even with a blade larger than a Mark 2, the heaviest part of an MPK is the handle.

Well liked by all of the SEALs who tested it, the MPK is being purchased in quantity by the Teams. Instead of just being a special issue nonmagnetic knife, the MPK is becoming a popular underwater knife with the SEALs. The blade of the MPK cannot rust and the knife can be used for cutting, prying, and pounding without damage to the blade or handle.

The SEAL 2000 is the steel knife carried as the standard issue item by SEAL operators. For a number of the men, the large SEAL 2000 blade is too big for the more general uses a field knife is put to. A superb fighting blade, the SEAL 2000 takes up a good deal of space on an operators web gear. To meet the demand for a smaller blade, the SOG specialty knife company took the SEAL 2000 design and reduced it in size by about a third.

Both the handle and blade of the new knife was reduced in size, while still retaining the shape and characteristics of the original. Christened the SEAL Pup, the new knife has been well-accepted in the Special Warfare community with the materials and design of the blade meeting all of the physical requirements the original had to in order to be accepted. The SEAL Pup has now become an issue item in the Teams.

An active duty SEAL came up with an innovative modification of the sheath system used with both the SEAL 2000 and the SEAL Pup. The modification was a notch cut into the hard plastic of the sheath, exposing a short section of the cutting edge of the knife. While still in the sheath, the knife can be used to cut rigging and parachute shroud lines without the danger of the tip of the knife doing any damage. The idea was so new that it received a United States patent.

For all of the quality knives available for issue by the SEALs, there is still a strong desire by individual operators to carry privately purchased blades more specific to their tastes. Some men prefer a smaller, lighter blade while others like a bigger, heavier knife. During one operation, a SEAL demonstrated a further advantage of a good knife.

While wearing a Randall Bowie-style knife on his combat harness, a SEAL chief hospital corpsman was passenger in a Humvee convoy operating in Mogadishue, Somalia at the time of the Blackhawk Down incident. Struck by a sniper's bullet, the SEAL chief thought he was severely injured when he felt the

heavy impact on his right hip. Rather than remain in range of the sniper or any other Somalis in the area, the Humvee continued on without stopping to render the SEAL aid.

Once they were at a holding point with the rest of their convoy, the injured SEAL was able to receive help. What had struck the man was a 7.62mm bullet fired from an AK-47. But the bullet was not the direct

The new style of SOG sheath for the SEAL knife line allows the blade to be used to cut line without removing the blade from the sheath.

Source: Kevin Dockery

cause of the SEAL's bleeding leg wound. The projectile had been deflected by the high-quality steel of the knife on the SEAL's hip. Instead of punching deeply into his leg, the bullet shattered the steel of the knife blade.

The bullet hadn't caused the worst of the SEAL's wound, the fragments of the knife blade had cut him badly and penetrated deeply into his leg. With a bandage on the wound controlling the bleeding, the SEAL continued on with his mission. Though the SEAL was all right, his Randall needed replacement after the operation.

A number of SEALs purchase knives for their own use and carry them in the field on operations. Issue blades are satisfactory for the majority of operators, but a number of them have specific preferences that are met by a number of commercial and custom makes. The Gerber knife company took the situation a step further and had a professional knife designer sit down with a retired SEAL Chief who had extensive combat experience in Vietnam. The resultant design was put on the market as the Silver Trident, a large, fixed blade fighting knife and general tool.

In combination with the knife, the Gerber company purchased the Blackhawk Products Group Airborne Deluxe knife sheath. The knife that resulted from a SEAL Chief's suggestions was combined with a tactical sheath that was also designed and produced by retired Navy SEALs. A number of the Silver Tridents have been purchased by active-duty SEAL operators as well as the public at large. A special sterilized version of the Silver Trident, without the aggressively cutting chisel teeth on the back edge, was purchased by the military for issue in Iraq.

Folding knives have been brought up as a possible undercover or covert weapon for use by Special Warfare operators. In the early 1990s, Ernest Emerson, a custom knife maker on the West Coast, was approached by the SEAL community in Coronado to produce a folding knife design. The intent of the knife was that it could be used as a specialized tool for sentry removal. The new design was referred to as the Emerson SSDS.

Modifications were made to the existing design and the knife became the Emerson ES1-M, a slightly smaller version of the original. The final result of the design series was put into production for commercial sale as the Emerson Commander. A new and patented feature of the Commander design is the Wave, a curved hooklike protrusion on the top rear of the blade.

With the Commander carried in a side pocket, the knife can be pulled up and to the rear for removal. The wave feature catches on the edge of the pocket and pulls the blade open without any special effort by the operator. From being carried almost completely hidden in a normal pants pocket, the Commander can be drawn and locked in the opened position as quickly as a sheath knife.

Extremely popular with both the SEALs and other operators in the Special Operations community, the Emerson Commander led to the development of further tactical folding knives. The most popular design of the Emerson tactical knives has proven to be the CQC-7 series—CQC for Close Quarters Combat.

The blade of the CQC-7 has a Japanese-inspired chisel grind where only one side of the knife has the normal bevel cut into it, leading to the edge. The other side of the blade is flat, allowing for a very strong and very sharp edge geometry. The angular Tanto-style tip of the CQC-7 is also inspired by Japanese designs and had tremendous penetrating power while still having a strong point. The smaller size of the CQC-7 has made it very popular for undercover or covert carry by a number of military and civilian purchasers. Combined with the optional wave feature, the knife is light to carry and very fast to get into operation.

The Emerson designs are normally privately purchased items by the SEALs and others. Additional specialized designs have been purchased for special issue, and the designs blur the separation between a fixed and a folding blade knife.

Produced by Gerber and purchased by the Navy for issue in specialize kits, the SEAL Revolver is a fixed blade knife with a changeable blade feature. By pressing in a catch on the side of the grip, the blade is released and can rotate. One end of the blade is a normal cutting style, designed along the lines of the SEAL Pup. The other end of the blade is a deeply toothed saw blade. The saw blade can aggressively cut through wood as easily as heavy rope and plastics. The combination blade allows a single tool to do the work of both a knife and a short saw.

■ Knife Data ■

Source: Kevin Dockery

MARK 1 KA-BAR

KNIFE PATTERN Short-blade Bowie

BLADE TYPE Single edge clip point

EDGE TYPE V-grind, double edge bevel

POINT TYPE Saber

TANG TYPE Narrow full hidden tang
w/pinned shaped metal pommel

BLADE MATERIAL Carbon steel

BLADE FINISH Blued or parkerized

HANDLE MATERIAL Compressed leather
washers

SHEATH MATERIAL Gray plastic w/internal
web reinforcing, steel chape, gray canvas
hanger w/1 snap loop keeper

WEIGHTS

Knife 0.42 lb (0.19 kg)

Sheath 0.25 lb (0.11 kg)

LENGTHS

Knife 10.13 in (25.7 cm)

Blade 5.25 in (13.3 cm)

Cutting edge 5 in (12.5 cm)

Blade thickness (maximum) 0.166 in (4.22
mm)

Blade width (maximum) 1.09 in (2.8 cm)

Sheath 10.74 in (27.3 cm)

MARK 2 KA-BAR

KNIFE PATTERN Bowie

BLADE TYPE Single edge clip point w/short
back edge, shallow fuller

EDGE TYPE V-grind, double edge bevel

POINT TYPE Saber w/back edge

TANG TYPE Narrow full hidden tang
w/peened flat metal pommel

BLADE MATERIAL Carbon steel

BLADE FINISH Blued or parkerized

HANDLE MATERIAL Compressed leather
washers w/5 deep grooves

SHEATH MATERIAL Gray plastic w/internal
web reinforcing, steel chape, gray canvas
hanger w/1 snap loop keeper

WEIGHTS

Knife 0.63 lb (0.29 kg)

Sheath 0.29 lb (0.13 kg)

LENGTHS

Knife 12 in (30.5 cm)

Blade 7 in (17.8 cm)

Cutting edge (primary) 6.81 in (17.3 cm)

Cutting edge (secondary) 2.25 in (5.7 cm)

Blade thickness (maximum) 0.163 in (4.14
mm)

Blade width (maximum) 1.19 in (3.0 cm)

Sheath 13.25 in (33.7 cm)

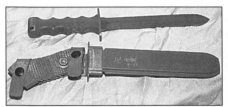

Source: Kevin Dockery

NONMAGNETIC SCUBA SWIMMER'S KNIFE

KNIFE PATTERN Long blade dagger

BLADE TYPE Double edged w/rear rake saw back

EDGE TYPE Hollow ground w/wide 0.19 in (4.83 mm) double edge bevel

POINT TYPE Double edge spear

TANG TYPE Full hidden tapered tang w/pinned flat steel pommel

BLADE MATERIAL Haynes alloy No. 25 (Copper-chromium-tungsten-nickel)

BLADE FINISH Gray oxide

HANDLE MATERIAL Molded glass fiber w/sharp 20 lpi molded checkering on flats and 4 finger grooves, all metal fittings are 310 Stainless alloy

SHEATH MATERIAL Glass fiber laminate w/nylon hanger riveted to chape extension, two 2-piece snap button nylon keepers, metal chape w/copper-beryllium alloy retainer springs, all metal fittings are 310 Stainless alloy

WEIGHTS

Knife 0.68 lb (0.31 kg)

Sheath 0.36 lb (0.16 kg)

LENGTHS

Knife 12 in (30.5 cm)

Blade 7.31 in (18.6 cm)

Cutting edge (primary) 7 in (17.8 cm)

Cutting edge (secondary) 1.38 in (3.5 cm) tip edge; 5.88 in (14.9 cm) 9 tpi saw back

Blade thickness (maximum) 0.158 in (4.01 mm)

Blade width (maximum)

Sheath 12.88 in (32.7 cm)

Source: Kevin Dockery

MARK 3

KNIFE PATTERN Short blade Bowie

BLADE TYPE Single edge deep clip point w/sharp clip and forward rake saw back

EDGE TYPE V-grind, double edge bevel

POINT TYPE Deep concave clip point

TANG TYPE Full hidden tang w/heavy flat steel pommel

BLADE MATERIAL Carbon steel

BLADE FINISH Matt blue

HANDLE MATERIAL Polycarbonate plastic w/embossed checkering

SHEATH MATERIAL Polycarbonate plastic w/nylon frog, metal belt hanger, 2-piece snap button loop keeper, metal spring clip chape

WEIGHTS

Knife 0.62 lb (0.28 kg)

Sheath 0.32 lb (0.15 kg)

LENGTHS

Knife 10.88 in (27.6 cm)

Blade 6 in (15.2 cm)

Cutting edge (primary) 5.25 in (13.3 cm)

Cutting edge (secondary) 2.5 in (6.4 cm) 11 tpi saw back edge; 1.75 in (4.4 cm) clip point back edge

Blade thickness (maximum) 0.166 in (4.22 mm)

Blade width (maximum) 1.23 in (3.1 cm)

Sheath 12.5 in (31.8 cm)

Source: Kevin Dockery

SEAL BUCKMASTER

KNIFE PATTERN Hollow grip, long blade Bowie

BLADE TYPE Single edge w/serrated edge sharp clip, saw back

EDGE TYPE Hollow ground w/double bevel edge, Flat ground partial serrated chisel edge clip, rear rake, very coarse saw back

POINT TYPE Spear point w/serrated back edge

TANG TYPE Partial stub welded to hollow handle w/removable threaded O-ring sealed flat steel pommel

BLADE MATERIAL Stainless steel

BLADE FINISH Matt

HANDLE MATERIAL Thick walled stainless steel tubing w/5 deep grooves and sharp knurling between grooves

SHEATH MATERIAL Polycarbonate plastic w/nylon frog, quick-release buckle nylon belt hanger, 1 snap button keeper strap, metal spring clip chape, removable nylon parts pouch w/Velcro strap, integral sharpening stone on sheath back, multiple belt loops on sheath body

WEIGHTS

Knife 1.39 lb (0.63 kg) w/o spikes or lanyard ring; 1.57 lb (0.71 kg)

Sheath 0.56 lb (0.5 kg) w/o pouch, compass or lanyard; 0.64 lb (0.29 kg w/pouch, compass, lanyard

LENGTHS

Knife 12.56 in (31.9 cm)

Blade 7.63 in (19.4 cm)

Cutting edge (primary) 7.75 in (19.7 cm)

Cutting edge (secondary) 2.5 in (6.4 cm) serrated clip edge 2.88 in (7.3 cm) 4 tpi saw

back; 2 in (5.1 cm) two installed knurled base guard spikes

Blade thickness (maximum) 0.287 in (7.29 mm)

Blade width (maximum) 1.5 in (3.8 cm)

Sheath 13.38 in (34 cm) w/belt loop closed

Source: Kevin Dockery

PROBIS COMBAT UTILITY KNIFE (CUK)

KNIFE PATTERN Short blade modified Bowie

BLADE TYPE Single edge w/forward rake saw back, deep fuller

EDGE TYPE Concave grind w/double bevel edge

POINT TYPE Spear point

TANG TYPE Threaded partial tang w/separate threaded rod through grip and flat knurled pommel

BLADE MATERIAL Modified 420 Stainless w/5% molybdenum

BLADE FINISH Black oxide

HANDLE MATERIAL Zytel plastic w/five deep grooves with knurling between grooves

SHEATH MATERIAL Zytel plastic w/clip-type blade keeper and rotating Zytel hanger, multiple belt loops on hanger and sheath body

LENGTHS

Knife 10.06 in (25.6 cm)

Blade 5.44 in (13.8 cm)

Cutting edge (primary) 5 in (12.7 cm)

Cutting edge (secondary) 2.5 in (6.4 cm) saw back

Blade thickness (maximum) 0.197 in (5 mm)

Sheath 10.38 in (26.4 cm)

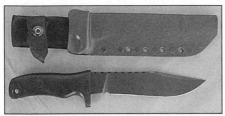

Source: Kevin Dockery

MAD DOG SEAL ATAK

KNIFE PATTERN Short blade modified Bowie

BLADE TYPE Single edge, flat clip point

EDGE TYPE Flat grind w/double bevel edge

POINT TYPE Spear point w/beveled back edge

TANG TYPE Full hidden tang

BLADE MATERIAL Starrett alloy 496-01 high carbon tool steel

BLADE FINISH Hard black chrome

HANDLE MATERIAL Flat-sided black glass/epoxy composite

SHEATH MATERIAL One-piece formed/folded kydex 0.090 in/2.3 mm thick, formed retention lips on mouth of scabbard, 1.88 in/4.78 cm wide, 3.38 in/8.59 cm long looped nylon hanger. One-piece nylon loop keeper with blacked brass snap and rivet, six blackened stainless steel rivets along edge side of sheath, bracketing four 0.25 in/0.64 cm drilled holes, formed lower leg strap loop.

WEIGHTS

Knife 0.79 lb (0.35 kg)

Sheath 0.36 lb (0.165 kg)

LENGTHS

Knife 11.56 in (29.5 cm)

Blade 6.88 in (17.4 cm)

Cutting edge (primary) 6.0 in (15.3 cm)

Blade thickness (maximum) 0.250 in (6.4 mm)

Blade width (maximum) 1.5 in (3.8 cm)

Sheath 12.38 in (31.45 cm)

Source: Kevin Dockery

SOG ST2SS (SEAL 2000)

KNIFE PATTERN Two-step, curved back bowie

BLADE TYPE Single edge clip point w/1 large-2 small serrations per 0.44 in (1.1 cm) in front of choil

EDGE TYPE V-grind, double edge bevel

POINT TYPE Concave clip point

TANG TYPE Full, insulated from grip

BLADE MATERIAL 6A Stainless

BLADE FINISH Kalgard-type powder-coated gray matt

HANDLE MATERIAL Glass fiber reinforced Zytel w/molded checkering and four finger grooves, lanyard hole

SHEATH MATERIAL A—Black formed Kydex plastic with retainer lip at mouth, stiff hanger formed w/2-snap closures at bottom, one 2-piece snap button nylon loop keeper, eight open grommets, four each along sides of sheath, two open grommets at bottom; B—Black formed Kydex plastic with solid back folded over sides with retainer lip at mouth, Sliding back, open hanger w/two-Phillips screw closures at bottom, one 2-piece snap button neoprene loop keeper, Four open grommets along edge side of sheath, two 0.85 in/2.2 cm slots cut through sheath along edge side. Open curved cutting notch, 0.375 in/1.0 cm wide, 0.835 in/2.1 cm deep, exposing edge of blade.

WEIGHTS

Knife 0.78 lb (0.35 kg)

Sheath A—0.27 lb (0.12 kg); B—0.27 lb (0.12 kg)

LENGTHS

Knife 12.31 in (31.3 cm)

Blade 7.06 in (17.9 cm)

Cutting edge (primary) 4.75 in (12.1 cm) w/o serrated portion

Cutting edge (secondary) 1.47 in (3.7 cm) serrations

Blade thickness (maximum) 0.238 in (6.05 mm)

Blade width (maximum) 1.40 in (3.6 cm)

Sheath A—12.63 in (32.1 cm); B—12.0 in (30.5 cm)

Source: Kevin Dockery

MPK (MULTI PURPOSE KNIFE)

KNIFE PATTERN Broad blade Bowie

BLADE TYPE Single edge clip point w/1 large and 3 small serrations per 0.5 in (1.3 cm) in front of choil

EDGE TYPE V-grind, double edge bevel

POINT TYPE Flat clip point

TANG TYPE Full tang insulated from grip, serrated and holed internally for secure attachment of grip

BLADE MATERIAL Beta titanium alloy

BLADE FINISH Matt finish heat-treated oxide

HANDLE MATERIAL Kevlar fiber reinforced Hytrel copolyester elastomer, textured w/multiple grooves on flats, integral guard

SHEATH MATERIAL Kevlar fiber reinforced Hytrel copolyester elastomer one piece w/integral hanger, one 2-piece snap button loop keeper, rubber slipover snubber ring, internal and external raised ribs to reduce radar signature, drain hole at base sides of sheath

WEIGHTS

Knife 0.56 lb (0.25 kg)

Sheath 0.38 lb (0.17 kg) w/o snubber ring

LENGTHS

Knife 12 in (30.5 cm)

Blade 7.17 in (18.2 cm)

Cutting edge (primary) 4.72 in (12 cm) w/o serrated portion

Cutting edge (secondary) 2 in (5.1 cm) serrations

Blade thickness (maximum) 0.247 in (6.27 mm) prototype models production blade 0.255 in

Blade width (maximum) 1.53 in (3.9 cm)

Sheath 12.6 in (32 cm)

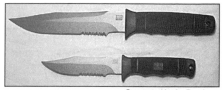

Source: Kevin Dockery

SOG SEAL PUP

The larger issue SOG SEAL 2000 knife above the smaller version of the same blade. Considered much handier to use that the larger knife by a number of operators, the SEAL Pup is simply a shortened version of the original knife, retaining all of its characteristics.

KNIFE PATTERN Two step, curved back Bowie

BLADE TYPE Single edge clip point w/1 large-2 small serrations per 0.44 in (1.1 cm) in front of choil

EDGE TYPE V-grind, double edge bevel

POINT TYPE Concave clip point

TANG TYPE Full, insulated from grip

BLADE MATERIAL 6A stainless

BLADE FINISH Kalgard-type powder-coated gray matt

HANDLE MATERIAL Glass fiber reinforced Zytel w/molded checkering and four finger grooves, lanyard hole

SHEATH MATERIAL A—Black formed Kydex plastic with retainer lip at mouth, stiff hanger formed w/2-snap closures at bottom, one 2-piece snap button nylon loop keeper, four open grommets, two each along sides of sheath, two open grommets at bottom. Open bottom plastic belt clip on front of sheath body; B—Black formed Kydex plastic with solid back folded over sides with retainer lip at mouth, sliding back, open hanger w/2-Phillips screw closures at bottom, one 2-piece snap button neoprene loop keeper, three open grommets along edge side of sheath, two 0.85 in/2.2 cm slots cut through sheath along edge side. Open curved notch, 0.375 in/1.0 cm wide, 0.835 in/2.1 cm deep, exposing edge of blade.

C—Black formed Kydex plastic with solid back folded over sides with retainer lip at mouth, sliding back, open hanger w/2-Phillips screw closures at bottom, one 2-piece snap button neoprene loop keeper, three open grommets along edge side of sheath, two 0.85 in/2.2 cm slots cut through sheath along edge side.

WEIGHTS
Knife 0.34 lb (0.15 kg)
Sheath A—0.23 lb (0.105 kg); B—0.21 lb (0.098 kg); C—0.21 lb (0.098 kg)
LENGTHS
Knife 9.13 in (23.2 cm)
Blade 4.75 in (12.2 cm)
Cutting Edge (Primary) 2.44 in (6.2 cm) w/o serrated portion
Cutting Edge (Secondary) 1.52 in (3.9 cm) serrations
Blade Thickness (Maximum) 0.157 in (3.98 mm)
Blade Width (Maximum) 1.12 in (2.8 cm)
Sheath A—10.38 in (26.4 cm); B/C—9.38 in (23.9 cm)

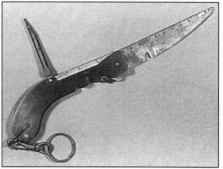

Source: Kevin Dockery

FOLDING DEMOLITION KNIFE

The rare folding demolition knife. Attached to the shackle at the end of the knife is a snap ring placed there by the last user. The blade of the knife is extended and locked into place showing the centimeter scale engraved on the right side of the blade as well as the deep notch used as part of the cap crimper. Unfolded and extending above the knife is the non-sparking punch or awl used to make blasting cap sized holes in explosive materials.

KNIFE PATTERN Multiblade nonsparking folding tool
NUMBER OF BLADES/TOOLS 1 blade, 6 tools
CUTTING BLADE TYPE Locking single edge, straight back w/crimping cut
EDGE TYPE Flat grind to edge
OTHER BLADES/TOOLS Awl/piercer, locking ¼ in flat screwdriver, wire stripper notch (in screwdriver), fuse/detonating cord cutter, cutthroat cap crimper, in/cm scale on cutting blade, locking clip on handle, lanyard shackle on handle
MATERIAL Copper/beryllium alloy, blades and springs
FINISH Black painted scaled
HANDLE/SCALE MATERIAL Aluminum
WEIGHTS
Knife 0.48 lb (0.22 kg)

LENGTHS

Overall folded/open 5.5/9.38 in (14/23.8 cm)
Cutting blade 4.44 in (11.3 cm)
Width 0.88 in (2.2 cm) blade; 1.81 in (4.6 cm) folded knife

Source: Kevin Dockery

SWISSCHAMP SWISS ARMY KNIFE

KNIFE PATTERN Multiblade folding knife
NUMBER OF BLADES/TOOLS 2 blades, 25 tools
CUTTING BLADE TYPE Single edge spear point
EDGE TYPE Flat grind w/double edge bevel
OTHER BLADES/TOOLS Corkscrew, jewelers screwdriver, wood chisel, $\frac{3}{32}$ in flat screwdriver, awl, $\frac{1}{4}$ in flat screwdriver, bottle opener, wire stripper, $\frac{1}{8}$ in flat screwdriver, can opener, #1 Philips screwdriver, magnifying glass, pliers w/serrated center, small wire cutter, scissors, wood saw, fish hook disgorger, fish scaler, inch/metric scale, fine file, nail cleaner, hacksaw, ballpoint pen, toothpick, tweezers.
MATERIAL Stainless steel
FINISH Bright polished
HANDLE/SCALE MATERIAL Black plastic scales
POUCH MATERIAL Leather
WEIGHTS
Knife 0.42 lb (0.191 kg)
Pouch 0.14 lb (0.062 kg)
LENGTHS
Overall folded/open 3.63/6.25 in (9.2/15.9 cm) (large blade open); 6.44 in (16.4 cm) (pliers open)
Cutting blade 2.5 in (6.4 cm)

Width 1 in (2.5 cm) deep, 1.25 in (3.2 cm) wide
Pouch 2.5 × 4.5 in (6.4 × 11.4 cm)

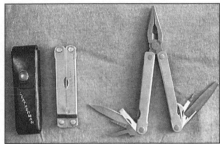

Source: Kevin Dockery

LEATHERMAN

KNIFE PATTERN Multiblade folding tool
NUMBER OF BLADES/TOOLS 1 blade, 9 tools
CUTTING BLADE TYPE Single edge clip point
EDGE TYPE Hollow grind w/double edge bevel
OTHER BLADES/TOOLS Awl, $\frac{3}{8}$ in flat screwdriver blade, $\frac{1}{4}$ in flat screwdriver blade, can/bottle opener, #1 Philips screwdriver, flat jewelers screwdriver, coarse/fine file, needle-nosed pliers w/cutters, serrated center opening, in/cm scale on handles
MATERIAL Stainless steel
FINISH Satin
HANDLE/SCALE MATERIAL Stainless w/no scales
POUCH MATERIAL Leather w/snap cover
WEIGHTS
Knife 0.33 lb (0.15 kg)
Pouch 0.0.07 lb (0.03 kg)
LENGTHS
Overall folded/open 4.0/8.0 in (10.2/20.4 cm) maximum; 6.25 in (15.9 cm) open to pliers
Cutting blade 5.13 in (13 cm)
Width 1.06 in (2.7 cm) folded; 1.84/5.13 in (4.7/13 cm) open to pliers
Pouch 4.25 × 1.25 × 1.25 in (10.8 × 3.2 × 3.2 cm)

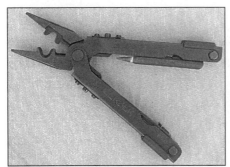

GERBER NEEDLE-NOSE

KNIFE PATTERN Multiblade folding tool

NUMBER OF BLADES/TOOLS 2 blades, 9 tools

CUTTING BLADE TYPE Single edge drop point, serrated sheepsfoot

EDGE TYPE Hollow grind w/double edge bevel

OTHER BLADES/TOOLS Lanyard, ¼ in flat screwdriver blade, ³/₁₆ in flat screwdriver blade/bottle opener, can opener, #1 Philips (cross-head) screwdriver, flat jewelers screwdriver, carbide coated coarse/fine file, needle-nosed pliers w/cutters, serrated center opening, inch/cm scale on handles

MATERIAL Stainless steel

FINISH Flat black oxide

HANDLE/SCALE MATERIAL Stainless w/no scales

POUCH MATERIAL Ballistic nylon w/Velcro-sealed cover

WEIGHTS

Knife 0.49 lb (0.222 kg)

Pouch 0.0.05 lb (0.024 kg)

LENGTHS

Overall folded 5.06 in (12.9 cm)

Open 6.63 in (16.8 cm) open to pliers

Cutting blade 2.25 in (5.7 cm)

Width 1.54 in (3.9 cm) folded

Pouch 5.75 × 3.0 in (14.6 × 7.6 cm)

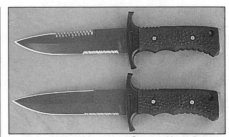

GERBER SILVER TRIDENT (STERILE)

The commercial Silver Trident knives by Gerber. The lower blade does not have the heavy chisel-toothed serrations on the top edge of the upper knife. The lower knife has a sterile blade, that is it has none of the commercial markings as are found on the upper blade.

KNIFE PATTERN Double-edged Bowie

BLADE TYPE Double edge diamond Bowie w/long back edge

EDGE TYPE Double flat V-grind, double edge bevel

POINT TYPE Clip point w/back edge

TANG TYPE Full hidden tang w/flat stainless steel pommel cap

BLADE MATERIAL 154 CM stainless steel

BLADE FINISH Black oxide

HANDLE MATERIAL Formed Hytrel with stainless steel fittings

SHEATH MATERIAL Ballistic NyTaneon nylon with hard TalonFlex plastic insert held in place with single Phillips head screw at end, plastic insert had formed retainer lug at chape, folded nylon hanger with two attachment points secured with Velcro, Velcro-closed folded nylon strap loop on back of sheath, single one-piece nylon keeper with black metal snap. Two open grommets are at the base of the sheath. A large soft pocket is on the front of the sheath, closed by a flap cover secured with Velcro.

WEIGHTS

Knife 0.71 lb (0.32 kg)

Sheath 0.38 lb (0.176 kg)

LENGTHS

Knife 11.19 in (28.4 cm)

Blade 6.25 in (15.9 cm)

Cutting edge (primary) 4.19 in (10.64 cm) w/o serrations

Cutting edge (secondary) 1.88 in (4.78 cm) serrations

Cutting edge (back) 4.63 in (11.75 cm)

Blade thickness (maximum) 0.222 in (5.64 mm)

Blade width (maximum) 1.356 in (3.44 cm)

Sheath 14.38 in (36.5 cm)

GERBER SILVER TRIDENT

KNIFE PATTERN Double edge Bowie

BLADE TYPE Double edge diamond Bowie w/back edge and chisel serrations

EDGE TYPE Double flat V-grind, double edge bevel

POINT TYPE Clip point w/back edge w/chisel serrations, 7 tpi

TANG TYPE Full hidden tang w/flat stainless steel pommel cap

BLADE MATERIAL 154 CM stainless steel

BLADE FINISH Black oxide

HANDLE MATERIAL Formed Hytrel with stainless steel fittings.

SHEATH MATERIAL Ballistic NyTaneon nylon with hard TalonFlex plastic insert held in place with single Phillips head screw at end, plastic insert had formed retainer lug at chape, folded nylon hanger with two attachment points secured with Velcro, Velcro-closed folded nylon strap loop on back of sheath, single one-piece nylon keeper with black metal snap. Two open grommets are at the base of the sheath. A large soft pocket is on the front of the sheath, closed by a flap cover secured with Velcro.

WEIGHTS

Knife 0.71 lb (0.32 kg)

Sheath 0.38 lb (0.176 kg)

LENGTHS

Knife 11.19 in (28.4 cm)

Blade 6.25 in (15.9 cm)

Cutting edge (primary) 4.19 in (10.64 cm) w/o serrations

Cutting edge (secondary) 1.88 in (4.78 cm) serrations

Cutting edge (back) 2.38 in (6.0 cm)

Cutting edge (back) 2.0 in (5.1 cm) serrations

Blade thickness (maximum) 0.222 in (5.64 mm)

Blade width (maximum) 1.356 in (3.44 cm)

Sheath 14.38 in (36.5 cm)

Source: Kevin Dockery

EMERSON COMMANDER

The upper knife is the Emerson Commander model above the CQC-7C model. The curved blade of the Commander cuts in a very aggressive manner while the tanto-point of the chisel-ground CQC-7 knife had excellent penetration capabilities.

KNIFE PATTERN Folding lock blade

NUMBER OF BLADES 1 blade

BLADE TYPE Single edge recurved clip point

EDGE TYPE Flat grind w/double edge bevel

BLADE MATERIAL 154 CM Stainless steel

FINISH black teflon

SCALE MATERIAL Black G-10 w/epoxy/glass laminate, spring steel clip on right scale.

WEIGHTS

Knife 0.3 lb (0.138 kg)

LENGTHS

Overall folded/open 5.13/8.75 in (13.0/22.2 cm)

Blade 3.75 in (9.5 cm)

Cutting edge (primary) 2.88 in (7.3 cm) w/o serrated portion

Cutting edge (secondary) 1.30 in (3.3 cm)
   serrations
Blade thickness (maximum) 0.125 in (3.18
   mm) blade; 0.382 in (9.7 mm) at knurled
   ring
Blade width (maximum) 1.38 in (3.5 cm) at
   wave
Width 1.65 in (4.2 cm) folded at wave; 1.70 in
   (4.3 cm) open

EMERSON CQC-7BW

KNIFE PATTERN Folding lock blade
NUMBER OF BLADES 1 blade
BLADE TYPE Single edge tanto point
EDGE TYPE Flat left side chisel
BLADE MATERIAL 154 CM stainless steel
FINISH Black teflon
SCALE MATERIAL Black G-10 w/epoxy/glass
   laminate, spring steel clip on right scale.
WEIGHTS
Knife 0.26 lb (0.121 kg)
LENGTHS
Overall folded/open 4.75/7.88 in (12.1/20 cm)
Blade 3.25 in (8.3 cm)
Cutting edge (primary) 2.0 in (5.1 cm) w/o
   serrated portion
Cutting edge (secondary) 1.31 in (3.33 cm)
   serrations
Blade thickness (maximum) 0.130 in (3.05
   mm) 0.382 in (9.7 mm) at knurled ring
Blade width (maximum) 1.25 in (3.2 cm) at
   wave
Width 1.44 in (3.7 cm) folded at wave
1.38 in (3.5 cm) open at wave

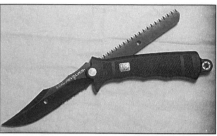

Source: Kevin Dockery

SOG SEAL REVOLVER

An unusual semi-fixed knife with a rotating
blade. Shown here with the blade rotated
partway, the SEAL Revolver has both a cutting blade, based on the SEAL Pup, and an
aggressive-cutting saw edge on the other
end of the blade. By rotating the blade, either
edge can be locked into place for use.
KNIFE PATTERN Two step, curved back
   Bowie
BLADE TYPE Single edge clip point w/1 large-
   2 small serrations per 0.44 in (1.1 cm) in
   front of choil, rotated blade is flat-ground
   round point double-tooth-saw edge,
   10 tpi
EDGE TYPE V-grind, double edge bevel
POINT TYPE Concave clip point
TANG TYPE None, stainless steel pivot
BLADE MATERIAL AUS 8 stainless steel
BLADE FINISH Blued or black titanium nitride
HANDLE MATERIAL Glass fiber reinforced
   Zytel w/molded checkering and four finger
   grooves, lanyard hole
SHEATH MATERIAL Three-piece formed
   black Kydex plastic with retainer lip at
   mouth, attached formed hanger w/two rivets at base and two open grommets at
   top, one 2-piece snap button nylon loop
   keeper, six open grommets, three each
   along sides of sheath, two open grommets
   at bottom, two 1.10 in/2.8 cm slots cut
   through sheath along sides.
WEIGHTS
Knife 0.36 lb (0.167 kg)
Sheath A—0.19 lb (0.089 kg)

LENGTHS
Knife 10.19 in (25.9 cm) w/cutting blade
Knife 10.25 in (26 cm) w/saw blade
Blade 4.5 in (11.4 cm)
Saw blade 4.5 in (11.4 cm)
Cutting edge (primary) 3 in (7.6 cm) w/o serrated portion

Cutting edge (secondary) 1.38 in (3.5 cm) serrations
Blade thickness (maximum) 0.150 in (3.8 mm)
Blade width (maximum) 1.03 in (2.6 cm)
Sheath 10.19 in (25.9 cm)

■ 3
PISTOLS

In the Navy, as in many other services, handguns, or sidearms as they are officially called, were limited in their issue. Not being considered a primary combat weapon, sidearms were usually issued to officers for self protection with other direct-combat forces using standard shoulder weapons. Personnel whose jobs prevented them from easily carrying a shoulder arm, such as radio operators or signalmen, would also often be issued a handgun. When the NCDUs (Naval Combat Demolition Units—forerunners of the UDTs) were first formed, their makeup of a single officer leading five enlisted men had the officer carrying a sidearm and the enlisted men shoulder arms, usually carbines.

Being that the primary mission of the NCDUs and UDTs did not involve direct, face-to-face combat with the enemy, small arms were rarely carried on regular missions. The limited issue of sidearms didn't result in a great hardship for the men of the Teams since in combat, fighting men who really want a handgun usually end up with one eventually. Theorists tend to agree that the handgun has no real use among modern combat forces. That same idea was put forward during World War II and is still argued today. But for a man facing the enemy, the comfort of a readily available weapon that can be carried on a hip or even stuck in a pocket is no theoretical idea, but a solid fact.

In 1911, along with the U.S. Army, the Navy accepted the M1911 .45 ACP pistol as the new standard issue sidearm. Now, for the first time, a semiautomatic pistol would be the issue handgun for all the U.S. military. The Navy sent in their initial request for 7,000 of the new pistols in July, 1911 and began issuing them soon after. After extensive use of the M1911 by U.S. forces during World War I, modifications were added to the weapon's design resulting in the M1911A1 being designated in 1922. By the 1940s and the involvement of the U.S. in World War II, the ".45," as it was commonly called, was a favorite with all the U.S. military.

No small part of the popularity of the M1911 was due to the heavy bullet it

Though pistols have always been considered a secondary weapon by the SEALs and UDTs, constant practice is given to firing them in order to maintain a high level of competency. This SEAL, a member of SEAL Team Two, is practicing with a standard issue M1911A1 during predeployment training for Vietnam.
Source: U.S. Navy

fired so dependably. The large, slow-moving, jacketed .45 caliber projectile struck hard and tended to put a target down quickly. Complaints were heard about the relative inaccuracy of the M1911 pistol, but those problems that arose could be traced to limited wartime training with a handgun. The M1911 is a difficult weapon to master without consistent practice, time for which is in very short supply during a war.

The M1911 was usually considerably more accurate than the average military shooter was able to take advantage of. The fact that the .45 has become a popular target weapon for various types of competitive shooting demonstrates the soundness of the design. And what really made the M1911 stand out as a military semiautomatic pistol was its reliability. Covered in mud, sand, or snow, the M1911 and M1911A1 would continue to function.

But with the acceptance of the M1911A1 came also the problem of limited production. World War I production of the M1911 had never matched the demand for the weapon and additional revolvers chambered for the .45 ACP round were produced to fill in the shortage. During the first years of World War II, the same situation existed. Even with the American industrial complex geared up for wartime production, available M1911A1s could not meet the demand.

In the Navy, sidearms were issued in limited numbers aboard ships and available M1911A1s could be reserved for direct-combat troops and shore police. Commercial revolvers were available in quantity and the Navy began purchasing a number of these beginning in late 1942. Though several types of revolvers were used in the Navy during World War II, the most common being the Smith & Wesson .38 Special caliber Victory model. The Victory was a variation of Smith & Wesson's Military and Police revolver but with a gray parkerized finish and much less hand fitting than the prewar weapon. A popular firearm, 900,000 of the nearly 1,000,000 revolvers produced by Smith & Wesson during World War II were Victory models.

The NCDUs and UDTs did issue M1911A1s, especially later in the war as the number of available weapons increased. But the .38 Special revolver was the standard issue sidearm to the Teams through much of World War II. There were few complaints about the stopping power of the .38 Special cartridge and those men who felt the .38 bullet was a little too anemic for their tastes could eventually find a .45. But several factors were in the favor of the revolver for use by the Teams.

In a revolver, a rotating cylinder is mechanically turned to line up a fresh cartridge with the barrel and the firing pin. In the case of a misfired round, such as one that had been watersoaked too long, just pulling the trigger again would line up a new round to be fired. In an semiautomatic pistol such as the M1911A1, a misfired round has to be cleared from the chamber by pulling back on the slide, normally a two-handed operation. Military ammunition is much more waterproof than its civilian counterpart, but in the very wet environment of the UDTs, dud ammunition due to water was a possibility.

Another advantage of the revolver over the semiautomatic pistol was particularly useful to the UDTs and has been noted by the SEALs today. Because the cylinder of a revolver has to be free to rotate, there is a small gap between the cylinder and the rear of the barrel. Because of this cylinder gap, water will immediately drain from a revolver's barrel, more quickly than water from a semiautomatic's barrel.

The safe and effective use of a revolver is generally found to be simpler to teach to recruits in the military and the NCDUs and UDTs proved no exception. Some individuals proved very competent pistol shots.

After receiving the worst individual losses of any UDT during World War II due to an enemy bomb striking their ship, UDT 15 was given a month's recreation at Saipan after leaving Iwo Jima. After having a hard time relaxing at the Officer's Club, one officer of UDT 15 returned to his quarters to get some rest. When he was awakened by an air raid signal, the officer noticed several lights were still shining in the company street. Picking up his revolver, the officer calmly shot out the offending lights. The duty officer placed the man on report. The official report of the incident stated ". . . and this officer, at 50 yards, did draw his revolver and fire at three light bulbs, hitting same (good shooting!)."

Because of limitations proscribed in The Hague Convention, standard commercial .38 Special ammunition with plain lead bullets could not be used in a combat zone. During the early part of 1943, Remington Arms began producing a copper plated, steel jacketed .38 Special round for the Navy. The round proved satisfactory enough that the other services, who also had numbers of .38 Special revolvers, adopted the round and the steel jacketed load became the most common .38 Special round produced during World War II.

After World War II ended, the M1911A1 pistol remained the standard issue sidearm throughout the U.S. forces. The UDTs retained a number of revolvers as they found the weapon had advantages for some of their operations. During the Korean War, the UDTs who operated on land found themselves equipped with the M1911A1 almost exclusively. Several years after World War II, Smith & Wesson developed a new handgun based largely on their earlier .38 caliber M&P revolver. The new weapon was a target-quality revolver, the K-38 Masterpiece. When later fitted with a four-inch barrel after numerous police requests, the weapon became known as the Model 15 Combat Masterpiece. By 1960, both the K-38 and the Combat Masterpiece had been purchased by the Navy and a number of the weapons were in the UDT inventories.

When the SEALs were commissioned in 1962, one of the weapons they asked for was a revolver, but a considerably more powerful one than that which the Navy had available. The .357 Magnum cartridge is a slightly longer version of the .38 Special round and is loaded to much higher pressures than the .38. The higher pressures of the .357 Magnum round give the bullet a higher velocity and commensurately greater energy and stopping power. During the mid-1950s, Smith & Wesson had developed the .357 Magnum Model 19 Combat Magnum revolver. The Model 19 enjoyed a high reputation with police forces throughout the United States and this was what brought the weapon to the notice of the new SEALs. But obtaining the new weapons was not an easy process.

> We asked for Smith & Wesson Model 19 Combat Magnums, a .357 magnum revolver . . . What we finally received were Smith & Wesson Model 15 Combat Masterpieces, a .38 Special revolver. The .357 is a much more powerful cartridge than the .38 Special and there is no mistaking the difference between the two calibers, or at least so we thought. . . .
>
> There was a Navy Commander supply officer somewhere in DC who had changed the order from the .357's to the less expensive .38's. As it turned out, this officer had been at a pistol range firing a .357 magnum revolver but the range officials had issued him .38 Special ammunition to use . . . This officer was convinced that he could save the government money by issuing us the regulation .38 Special Combat Masterpiece. When questioned on the subject, the Commander stated that he, "Had fired the .38 in a .357 and he could see no difference in the weapon."

The final result was that the SEALs never did receive the Model 19 Combat Magnums they had asked for. Due to the "undercover" nature of many of the

SEALs' guerrilla-warfare activities, a more concealable weapon than the Combat Masterpiece was called for. To fill this need, a number of short-barreled Colt Detective Specials were supplied to the SEALs by 1963-64. The Detective Special was available through regular supply channels as the weapon was used by the Office of Naval Intelligence. Individual SEALs who desired an even more concealable revolver purchased weapons on their own.

Two weapons that were popular among the SEALs were the Smith & Wesson .38 Special Model 38 Airweight Bodyguard and Model 36 Chief's Special. Both of these weapons were very compact revolvers, the Chief's Special having a steel frame and the Airweight Bodyguard being almost identical except for its alloy frame and shrouded hammer. The shroud on the frame of the bodyguard covered most of the hammer and prevented it from snagging on clothing when drawn. The size of both revolvers makes them very concealable but at the same time difficult to use by a large-handed individual.

Other handguns were occasionally issued to the SEALs on a trial basis. The idea of a counter-guerrilla force was still very new in the early 1960s and exactly what was needed, or even useful, in the way of weapons was still being worked out by higher command. Some weapons, such as the Colt Detective Special were reasonably well received. Other weapons, offered because they were already in the supply system, were not nearly as accepted by the Teams. While conducting combined exercises with other forces on Vieques Island in the Caribbean in latter half of 1962, a group of SEALs were issued Colt Pocket Automatic pistols left over from World War II.

> We had been issued pistols for this operation, .380 automatics (Colt Pocket
> Automatics). No ammunition, instructions or anything had come with the lit-
> tle mothers. How we ended up with these miserable weapons nobody would
> say or at least nobody ever owned up to it.

Another automatic pistol offered to the SEALs later in the 1960s was much better received. During the early 1950s, several new pistols were developed to answer complaints about the use of the M1911A1 in the Services. The primary complaint about the M1911A1 was that the heavy recoil of the .45 ACP round made the weapon difficult to handle and extended the training time needed to master the weapon. To answer this problem, Smith and Wesson submitted its new Model 39 pistol for government testing in 1954.

The Model 39 was a lightweight, alloy-framed automatic pistol chambered for the 9mm parabellum round. Among other features, the Model 39 had a double-action trigger mechanism. The pistol could be carried safely with a round in the chamber and the hammer down on the firing pin. The weapon would remain safe until the trigger was intentionally pulled, raising and dropping the hammer. After the first shot, the hammer would remain cocked in the single-action position until lowered. An advantage to the double-action system is that if a round misfired, the trigger could be pulled again in another attempt to fire the round.

The Model 39 was also a very accurate handgun as it came from the factory. A number of successful competition match pistols were brought out by Smith & Wesson based on the Model 39. The Navy examined the Model 39 in the mid-1960s as a possible issue weapon to its naval aviators. The Model 39 was considerably lighter than the issue M1911A1 and held more rounds of ammunition than a revolver. It was through this venue that the pistol was brought to the attention of the SEALs.

The SEALs liked the weapon for its mechanical features and the fact it was chambered in 9mm parabellum. The U.S. was the only major military force in NATO to use the .45 ACP round. The most common pistol ammunition in the world was, and is, the 9mm parabellum, called the 9×19mm in NATO terminology. With the Model 39 as a handgun, the SEALs could be certain of a supply of ammunition almost anywhere they might operate.

SEAL Team Two began receiving the new pistol in 1966, just prior to their first direct action platoons being sent over to Vietnam. After being allowed to try out the Model 39, the SEALs being deployed were allowed to chose which handgun they would prefer to carry, the Combat Masterpiece or the Model 39. A number of SEALs chose the Model 39, beginning a long involvement of the SEALs and 9mm handguns.

Though most of the SEALs liked the Model 39, there was one part of the design that few of them cared for. The Model 39 had a magazine safety as part of the design. In the system, if a magazine was not locked in place in the grip, the hammer would not drop if the trigger was pulled. This was considered a safety feature to prevent the accidental discharge of a supposedly empty weapon when the operator had only removed the magazine and not cleared the chamber. When possible, individual SEALs liked having the magazine safety removed from their Model 39s though this practice was officially discouraged.

Though the ratio of sidearms to men in the SEALs was much greater than it had been in the UDT, not every operator who went to Vietnam was able to have a Team-issued handgun. Model 39s and Combat Masterpieces tended to end up in the hands of the officers and senior NCOs who wanted them. M1911A1s were also available for issue and a number of these were carried by SEALs in Vietnam. An example of what could be accomplished by a competent pistol shot armed with the M1911A1 was clearly demonstrated on March 29, 1969 by RM2 Robert J. Thomas as recalled by a SEAL who had earlier operated with him.

"Later on, Thomas was to receive the Navy Cross for holding off an NVA platoon from his downed chopper. Thomas was the only person not (badly) injured in the crash and all he had for weapons were two .45 automatics. Thomas kept his cool and acted like he was back on the pistol range where he was a champion-quality pistol shot. Every time an NVA raised his head, Thomas would shoot it off, at fifty to sixty yards range! Finally extracted, Thomas had saved all the men on his bird single-handedly.

"It is the ease of carry that makes a handgun so popular with the SEALs. When going into town on official business or liberty, SEALs would almost always have a sidearm with them, either in a holster on their hip or slipped into a trouser belt and concealed under a uniform shirt. It was in the confined spaces of a bunker or tunnel that the compact size of a pistol was considered a definite asset. A handgun can be effectively used with one hand while the other hand might be otherwise engaged.

"For hooch searches I would carry the CAR-15 and a Chicom pistol. Both weapons were light and handy and the pistol was especially nice for those closed-in spaces like bunkers."

In the Viet Cong and North Vietnamese Army, such as in many of the world's armies, a sidearm is not as freely issued as in the U.S. military. Considered something of a mark of rank, pistols were only carried by officers and senior enlisted men in the VC and NVA. As these people soon became the primary target of the SEALs, enemy handguns became available in reasonable numbers.

The VC used almost any weapon they could obtain, and those they couldn't get, they tried to make. As the war progressed and supply became a little more regular, small arms became a little more standard with the VC. The most common handgun found with the VC and NVA forces was the Chicom (Chinese Communist) Type 51 and Type 54 pistols as well as the Soviet TT33 Tokarev. The Type 51 and 54 pistols were Chinese copies of the Soviet Tokarev differing only slightly from each other.

The Tokarev fires the 7.62×25mm round (7.62mm Short in SEAL parlance), a round not at all common outside of the Communist forces. Ammunition, though not available through regular supply channels, was usually found in sufficient amounts in captured ammunition caches to supply any needs the SEALs might have. Though firing a light .30 caliber bullet, until the advent of the .357 magnum round in the mid-1930s, the 7.62×25mm round was the highest velocity production pistol round in the world. Few SEALs who carried the Tokarev and its copies in Vietnam found reason to complain about the weapon.

The Central Intelligence Agency ran a number of intelligence gathering operations throughout Southeast Asia during the Vietnam War. Noteworthy among these was the Phoenix program with its goal being the elimination of the Viet Cong Infrastructure and command organization in South Vietnam. The action arm of the Phoenix program was the Provincial Reconnaissance Units (PRUs). Each province had a least one PRU made up of local citizens, Humong, Vietnamese, and ex-VC as a paramilitary force. The CIA outfitted and supplied these units and they were led by American advisors, often SEALs.

The CIA equipped many PRUs with non-U.S.-made weapons and the advisors were also able to draw weapons from the same source. One of the most prized of these weapons was the Browning High Power pistol, not available through any other military channels. The Browning High Power is every bit as reliable as its "older brother" the M1911A1, but is chambered for the 9mm parabellum round. The big advantage of the High Power was that its magazine held thirteen rounds of ammunition and a fourteenth round could be carried in the chamber. This was the highest magazine capacity of any free-world military handgun at that time. Another factor that made an Agency issue Browning popular with SEALs and other advisors was that the weapon didn't always have to be turned in after an individual's tour was over.

"The Agency (CIA) issued 9mm Browning High Power automatics to their men and I wanted one. In the Team, you couldn't get a Browning unless you bought your own and now this (Agency) man was willing to issue me one. Nice pistol, holds thirteen shots, it lets you be obnoxious longer between reloadings.

"The average guy would only count up to eight shots from a pistol. Then he would think you had to reload. Surprise, with a Browning, you had five more shots ready, something I like in a pistol."

As in the case of the Model 39, the Browning High Power had a magazine safety as part of its design. Without a magazine in place, the weapon could not be fired. Most SEALs disliked the magazine safety feature on what they otherwise considered an excellent firearm. Whenever possible, the magazine safety mechanism, only a few minor parts, was removed and the Browning continued operating dependably.

Other organizations operating in Vietnam occasionally made use of the

SEALs. The Military Assistance Command, Vietnam—Special Operations Group, later renamed the Studies and Observation Group, ran a number of intelligence-gathering operations in Vietnam including long-range reconnaissance patrols deep behind enemy lines and cross-border prisoner snatch operations. Occasionally SEALs would find themselves attached to MACV-SOG on TDY (Temporary Additional Duty) when their particular skills were needed for an operation.

Working closely with the intelligence community gave MACV-SOG access to some unusual hardware that the Teams had a hard time getting early in the war. For the kind of operations that the Teams and MACV-SOG did in Vietnam, surprise was a major weapon on the operators' side. Suppressed weapons would increase that surprise in some situations but very few weapons of that type were available during the early years of the war up to late 1967. MACV-SOG did have some of the World War II–vintage OSS weapons available to it and the SEALs were able to make occasional use of them.

One SEAL operator from SEAL Team Two who operated with MACV-SOG specifically remembered being issued a suppressed .22 pistol for his SOG missions. The pistol was the High Standard Model D Military that had been fitted with a integral barrel suppressor. The normal barrel of the pistol had been turned down slightly in diameter and four rows of eleven ⅛-inch diameter holes drilled into the bore. Encasing the barrel is a 1-inch steel tube that extends 2.5 inches past the muzzle of the barrel. Between the barrel and the tube is wrapped brass wire mesh with an additional stack of brass mesh washers between the muzzle of the barrel and the end of the suppressor tube. The end of the tube is capped with a metal disk and a front sight blade is soldered onto the tube.

The suppressed High Standard Model D military pistol was manufactured during World War II for the OSS. Mr. Warren P. Mason of the Bell Telephone Laboratories, New York, did the design work on the two-stage wire mesh suppressor found on the Model D beginning in January 1943. By November 1943, production began on the suppressed High Standard and by the war's end, several thousand had been made. It is no small complement to Mr. Mason's design that the suppressed High Standard was still in use during the Vietnam War and was even being functionally copied by other countries, including Communist China and North Vietnam.

The High Standard pistol is a semiautomatic design with an exposed hammer. The design of the suppressor is such that, even when fired with high-speed ammunition, the bullet is slowed to below the speed of sound, eliminating any sonic "crack." Though the .22 caliber rimfire round is not considered much of a military cartridge, and the slowed .22 Long Rifle round at about the same power as a .22 Short, the suppressed .22 pistol was very effective and could be fired in close proximity to troops without anyone hearing the sound and recognizing it as a gunshot.

The value to the SEALs of suppressed weapons had been noted prior to the Teams deploying for combat operations in Vietnam. Beginning in Fiscal Year 1966, the project to develop a suppressed pistol suitable for the SEALs special needs was begun at the Naval Surface Ordnance Center in White Oak, Maryland.

To satisfy the SEALs' desire for interoperability with NATO, the envisioned suppressed handgun was to be chambered for the 9mm round. The general tendency of the military to "buy American" leaned the project towards a pistol that was already headed toward the Teams, the Smith & Wesson Model 39.

A good deal of work had already been conducted in 9mm suppressor design under the direction of the CIA. As early as 1958, the CIA had a "silenced pistol kit" available for issue to their field agents under the official name of Sound Moderator, Pistol, Walther P-38. The kit consisted of a gray, hard-sided case similar to a camera case containing the suppressor, a threaded P-38 barrel, a box of subsonic 9mm ammunition, a bottle of oil, and a cleaning rod.

The Walther had been chosen because of its general availability throughout the world and its lack of connection to the United States. Mechanically, there was also an advantage to the P-38 design in that the barrel slid straight back under recoil with a separate locking block that was disengaged by a pin striking the frame of the weapon. This system allowed a suppressor to be more easily mounted on the exposed barrel of the P-38 while still allowing effective semi-automatic operation.

The suppressor was of the "wipe" type, that is a number of flexible plates were spaced inside of the suppressor body and the bullet penetrated the plates as it left the muzzle of the gun. By slowing down the passage of the propellant gases pushing the bullet, the plates helped seal off the muzzle blast of the weapon, suppressing the major sound of the gunshot. The wipe design had been developed in Austria prior to World War II and had been proven satisfactory in a number of wartime suppressed weapons.

By loading the ammunition for the suppressor with a heavy bullet, 158 grains as compared to the normal 115 or 124 grains, a subsonic cartridge could be made that had very close to the same recoil characteristics as a standard 9mm round. Because the fired bullet never broke the speed of sound, the sonic crack of the projectile passing through the air was eliminated. For more complete suppression of the noise of firing, the mechanical sound of the weapon functioning needed to be eliminated as much as possible. The easiest way this could be done was to make the firing weapon a single shot.

The advantage of the early CIA issue kit was that the suppressor could be mounted on any available P-38 by simply replacing the barrel of the pistol with the one supplied in the kit. The intent was for the operator to use the weapon for a mission and then get rid of the suppressor. This helped eliminate a problem with the wipe style suppressor in that the wipes wore away quickly under the stress of firing. This situation was reasonably satisfactory for the CIA, but the SEALs had a need for a much more permanent kind of suppressed weapon.

In the early 1960s, a new kind of P-38 suppressor was tried out and brought to the attention of the Navy designers at White Oak. Instead of having the wipes sealed inside the suppressor, a series of flexible plastic baffles were placed inside a cylindrical cartridge. The cartridge would be inserted into the body of the suppressor and held against the exit end of the suppressor by a spring. This gave the suppressor an expansion chamber just in front of the muzzle of the weapon and a set of wipes that could be easily replaced when worn.

To eliminate the mechanical noise of the weapon, a slide lock was installed on the P-38. The slide lock was a lever on the left side of the weapon, just above the trigger, that could be moved by the firer's thumb. With the slide lock pressed up, it engaged a notch in the slide of the weapon. When the gun was fired, the lock prevented the slide and barrel from moving to the rear, eliminating the noise of the action opening and closing. To reload, the firer had to pull the slide lock down with his thumb and manually pull the slide to the rear. This made for a very quiet weapon overall. If there was a need for semiautomatic fire, the slide lock could be disengaged and the weapon fired normally, but with an increase in the sound level of firing.

The general design of the suppressor was proven and the idea of a locked, single shot repeater shown to be sound. The next step in the process was to modify the Smith & Wesson Model 39 to fit the general pattern of the locked P-38. The barrel of the Model 39 was simply lengthened by one inch and the final one-half inch length threaded $\frac{1}{2}$"-32 tpi. The Model 39 uses the same locking system as the Browning High Power. When the pistol is fired, the barrel is locked to the slide by a lug in the upper surface of the barrel, engaging a matching slot on the slide. As the barrel and slide recoil when fired, a slot in the underside of the barrel engages a camming pin in the frame of the pistol. By recoiling backward some distance, the barrel and slide are locked firmly together a sufficient time to allow the bullet to leave the barrel and the gas pressure to have dropped to safe levels. At this time, the slot in the barrel cams the rear of the barrel down, disengaging the locking surfaces of the barrel and slide. Recoil continues to push the slide rearward until it is stopped by the frame. The mainspring then drives the slide forward, stripping a fresh round from the magazine and chambering it.

The moving barrel of this system not only must move backwards a short distance but also angle downward when unlocking, complicating the attachment of a muzzle suppressor. The suppressor has to be light enough so as not to interfere with the operating cycle of the weapon. For the Model 39, the suppressor was made of aluminum to help keep the weight on the barrel down. The wipe cartridge was also made of aluminum, sealed to contain the four $\frac{1}{4}$-inch-thick soft plastic wipes. The wipe cartridge, called the suppressor insert, was held against the muzzle end of the suppressor body by a wide steel spring. The threaded end cap of the suppressor body was securely sealed by the addition of a neoprene O-ring. When accepted for issue, the suppressor, developed as the WOX-1A gun silencer, was type-classified as the 9mm noise suppressor Mark 3 Mod 0.

The locking lever used to hold the slide closed on the P-38 was carried over to the Model 39 design with some modifications. Instead of being pushed up and engaging the slide behind the barrel on just the left side, as on the P-38, the locking lever on the Model 39 was pushed down at the rear, raising the front of the lever which engaged cutouts on both sides of the slide, forward of the breech and locking lug area. The locking lever was at a greater mechanical advantage in holding the slide shut in its new configuration than in the earlier P-38 system.

To clear the wide suppressor body, higher sights had to be installed. The higher, micrometer-adjustable sights of the Smith & Wesson Model 52 match pistol were installed on the production weapon, the rear sight being protected by raised wings on either side of the sight. The final mechanical change in the Model 39 pistol was the removal of the magazine safety parts and the sear release lever. In the Model 39, putting the thumb safety on while the hammer is cocked

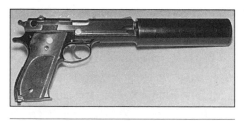

A developmental Smith & Wesson Model 39 pistol with suppressor. The suppressor on this specimen is attached to the receiver of the pistol by an extension that is secured to the slide stop by a bolt. The extension is visible just below the front portion of the slide in this photo.

Source: U.S. Navy

back locks the firing pin in place and drops the hammer. Removing the sear release lever allows the thumb safety to be put on while still retaining the hammer in the cocked position.

While the pistol and suppressor were being made ready, ammunition also had to be developed. Experiments were conducted with heavy tungsten inserts placed in the back of standard 9mm bullets. That took the weight of the bullet up to about 150 grains and made the round subsonic. The tungsten-cored rounds functioned the suppressed pistol about ninety percent of the time, but being that the intent was for the weapon to be fired single-shot, 10 percent failures to reload semiautomatically were considered acceptable.

Remington Arms assisted in adopting a fully-jacketed 158 grain .38 Special bullet to a subsonic 9mm round. Though they helped supply the initial lot of projectiles, Remington was not further interested in producing the ammunition for the new pistol. Final development resulted in a full jacketed 9mm round with a nominal muzzle velocity of 965 feet per second and a recoil impulse near that of the 9mm M1 round. The new round was suitable for use in pistols and submachine guns chambered for the 9mm round but was reserved for use in the suppressed pistol. Identified with a green bullet tip, the cartridge was given the nomenclature Cartridge, Mark 144 Mod 0, and produced by the Super Vel Cartridge Corporation of Shelbyville, Indiana as well as Industries Valcartier Inc., Valcartier, Quebec, Canada.

Additional material was designed for the weapon system to waterproof it for a marine environment. A plastic muzzle plug in the form of a flat disk could be pushed over the front of the suppressor. A back end cap plug could be inserted into the suppressor when it was not mounted on the pistol. A barrel cap fitted tightly over the threaded section of the barrel, sealing it. And a chamber plug in the shape of a plastic cartridge sealed the barrel of the pistol with a rubber O-ring. With the waterproofing seals in place, the pistol and suppressor could be transported at a depth of 200 feet safely, either with the pistol and suppressor separate or with the suppressor mounted on the barrel. With the pistol and suppressor together, an operator could ready the weapon for firing by simply drawing back the slide, ejecting the chamber plug, and chambering a live round. The muzzle disk was designed so that it could be safely shot off of the weapon without damage to the gun or firer.

Developed as the WOX-13A 9mm pistol, the new suppressed pistol received the nomenclature 9mm Pistol Mark 22 Mod 0. When fired with the special subsonic ammunition designed for it, the sound of the shot was unnoticeable at 50 yards. Since the wipe system of the suppressor only lasts for about twenty-four

This is a left side view of the Mark 22 pistol with the Mark 3 noise suppressor removed. The threaded end of the pistol barrel can be plainly seen and most of the exposed portion of the barrel would be covered when the suppressor is attached. In this photo, the Mark 3 noise suppressor is reversed above the pistol with the muzzle end of the suppressor pointing to the rear of the weapon. *Source: Kevin Dockery*

rounds of Mk 144 and about six rounds of standard velocity 9mm, additional suppressor inserts, ammunition, and materials are issued in the form of an accessory kit. The initial accessory kit contained a single suppressor insert, suppressor body O-ring, and twenty-two rounds of Mk 144 Mod 0 ammunition. When the waterproofing materials became available, a new kit was issued including these items. The new kit was given the nomenclature Accessory Kit Mark 26 Mod 0. Finally, a special holster was issued with the Mark 22 capable of holding the pistol with the suppressor installed and with an outside pocket to secure an additional ammunition magazine.

Finally available to the Teams, the Mark 22 Mod 0 was first issued late in 1967. Almost immediately, controversy began about the new weapon:

> When we originally asked for a suppressed pistol, the powers that be did not want it called a silencer, we were asked what we wanted it for. Since the idea of killing men with a suppressed handgun was somehow "unsportsmanlike" we told them the weapon was wanted to shoot dogs. Every VN village had some dogs hanging around that would sometimes bark as we approached. Since the weapon was intended to silence dogs, and any other vermin who happened to get in front of it, the pistol was named the "Hush Puppy."

An immediate success with the Teams, there never seemed to be enough of the new weapons to go around. By 1968, each deploying platoon was issued at least one Mark 22 though the weapon was far more commonly called the Hush Puppy:

> The "silent pistol shot to the head" a favorite story of the anti-Phoenix people did take place. But the target of the shot was usually a noisy village dog that could alert people that we were there. On different ops, we would carry a Hush Puppy (suppressed pistol) in the squad. Often, the point man would carry the

weapon as he would be the first to make contact where a silent shot might be needed. Not many of the weapons were available so what we had would be rotated around the squads.

There would have been times that having a Hush Puppy for each man on an op would have been great. You can't call 911 when in the bush and the element of surprise was everything sometimes. Silent rounds snapping out in an ambush could eliminate a following enemy group, without drawing attention from a larger force nearby.

The Mark 22 did suffer from some problems in the field, at least one of these was noted in the official Command History for SEAL Team Two in 1969. Mention was made in the record of an improvement in the ammunition for the Mark 22 Mod 0 pistol under the heading of Research and Development Projects:

A special 9mm down-loaded 158 grain round has been made for the Smith & Wesson 9mm pistol with silencer. the original 158 grain round lacked the essential penetration power needed for the pistol to be effective. The new round is now in-country for test and evaluation.

Production of the Mk 22 pistol and the Mk 3 noise suppressor was undertaken by Smith & Wesson at their factory in Springfield, Massachusetts. Production continued for a number of years beginning in 1967 and ending sometime in the early 1970s. Further mention of the Mark 22 was made in the 1970 Command History of SEAL Team Two which indicated that the overall design of the weapon was considered quite acceptable to the Teams:

SEAL Team Two acquired forty-five new silent 9mm Smith & Wesson Pistols (Hush Puppies). These weapons should increase the Teams' current operating capability.

Depending on how an operation was going to be conducted, a Hush Puppy may or may not be carried along. In a situation where a "sneak and peek" of deep penetration was going to be done in enemy territory, a Hush Puppy was a definite asset. Many SEALs developed a taste for the unique weapon and carried it in their own way.

The Hush Puppy was a suppressed Smith & Wesson Model 39 with a special slide lock. Though a holster was available for the weapon, I usually carried it hanging from my neck on a lanyard. From the lanyard, I could put the Hush Puppy into action faster than by pulling it from a holster and speed could be important. Others may have had different experiences but my Hush Puppy was used mostly for the very reason it had been given its name, silencing yapping village dogs. Very seldom did I used the Hush Puppy against a person, dogs and ducks raising an alarm were a much more common target. And even hitting the dog didn't always silence it right away, a few yelps would get out.

But the pistol was quiet, especially with its slide held shut during firing by the slide lock. I always used the weapon as a single-shot anyway as the subsonic ammunition we had then wouldn't work the slide reliably for semiautomatic fire.

The slide lock did cause its own problems with the weapon. Holding the slide closed during firing placed a severe strain on the slide of the Mk 22, concentrating in the notches on the slide itself. Slides would be battered or cracked at the notches, requiring replacement. Consistent semiautomatic fire was also not available in the Mk 22 given the operating system of the pistol and the weight of the suppressor. Though the lack of semiautomatic fire was not considered a major drawback by the SEALs who used the Hush Puppy in Vietnam. In fact, the weapon was so successful, the name Hush Puppy was given to any suppressed pistol used by the U.S. and its allies during the Vietnam War and for some time afterward.

When tested with and without the slide lock in operation, very little increase in noise was noticed when the Hush Puppy operated semiautomatically. It was

A left side closeup of the Mark 22 pistol showing detail of the slide lock system. The rear of the slide lock lever has been depressed, raising the front portion of the lever into the corresponding notch in the slide of the weapon. In this position, the slide cannot move when the weapon is fired.

Source: Kevin Dockery

when the slide only went partway back and then returned to battery that there was a great deal of mechanical noise with the system. Experiments were conducted to examine other ways of mounting the suppressor on the Model 39 that would increase the reliability of semiautomatic suppressed fire. The Naval Weapons Center at China Lake, California tried a very unusual experiment where the suppressor was mounted on the frame of a Model 39 pistol. In the experimental weapon, the suppressor was mounted off-center on the barrel so that the majority of the suppressor's body was below the line of the barrel. A long extension was on the bottom rear of the suppressor reaching back on either side of the pistol's frame to just above the trigger. By attaching the suppressor to the slide to lever pin of the pistol, the majority of the weight of the suppressor would not be bearing on the barrel. It is not known how well the design operated but apparently only a single experimental weapon was produced.

By 1969, the Hush Puppy was being issued as part of the Swimmer Weapons System as the 9mm Pistol and Suppressor Kit Mark 23 Mod 0. In the Mark 23 kit, two styrofoam supports hold the Mark 22 Mod 0 pistol complete with a barrel cap, chamber plug, and magazine. Along with the pistol, inside the kit was a Mark 3 Noise Suppressor complete with a muzzle plug and back end cap plug. A polyurethane plastic holster is in the kit along with a small container of grease and a humidity dessicant package and indicator. The two styrofoam supports cradle the contents of the kit and are inserted into an M19A1 ammunition box for storage.

During the development of the Mk 22 pistol, some thought was given to making a high-capacity version that would hold more ammunition. The Browning High Power was highly thought of because of its magazine capacity so the Naval Ordnance Laboratory and Smith and Wesson examined making a conversion of the Model 39 that would accept a modified Browning magazine. In 1964, Smith and Wesson had built two 14-shot 9mm automatics and these were examined by the Navy. In addition, a Model 39 frame was cut and modified to accept a Browning magazine, establishing the mechanical parameters of the proposed pistol. The weapons desired by the Navy were to be made of stainless steel to minimize corrosion. With input from a steel manufacturer on which alloys would be suitable, Smith & Wesson accepted a contract from the Navy to produce ten 15-shot, stainless steel suppressed 9mm handguns for a contact price of $33,000.

Because of the manner in which their production lines were set up, Smith & Wesson took eighteen months to produce twelve of the new pistols. Delivery to the Navy of the ten requested guns took place in early 1970. In addition to having the slide lock, extended barrel, sights, and suppressors of the Mark 22 pistol, the fifteen-shot pistols also were fitted with removable shoulder stocks. The stocks slid into a groove on the back strap of the experimental pistols and locked in place with a thumbscrew. By installing special inserts under the handgrips of the Model 39 and Mark 22 pistols, they too would accept the shoulder stock. Even though the new experimental weapons had all the improvements

Smith & Wesson had developed for the Model 39 over the course of several years, the weapons were not accepted for production by the Navy. Within a few years, Smith and Wesson issued alloy-frame versions of the Navy weapon, minus the Mark 22 modifications, for commercial sale as their Model 59 pistol.

Terrorism developed on a global scale during the 1970s and became a force to be reckoned with by the U.S. military. As part of the U.S. response to international terrorism, the Navy commissioned SEAL Team Six and tasked it with combating terrorism in the marine environment. While outfitting the new Team, thought was given to which handgun the operators would carry as their standard sidearm. There was a much greater need for powerful terminal effects on the target as a wounded terrorist was still very much a threat, more so than the average soldier. Given their penchant for attacking unarmed and vulnerable civilian targets, a terrorist would be easily able to turn his weapon on hostages if not immediately neutralized.

Experienced SEAL operators who made up the new SEAL Team had witnessed the mechanical reliability of the revolver for operating in a wet environment. Simply put, without any special waterproofing, a revolver could be pulled up out of the water and fired faster than any other handgun available. Terminal effects could be enhanced by using a more powerful caliber than a .38 Special. Smith & Wesson had developed a line of revolvers made of stainless steel and designed after their very successful K-frame weapons. The original sidearm requested by the SEAL when they were first commissioned in 1962 had been the Model 19 Combat Magnum, a K-frame .357 Magnum. For the new SEAL Team, they requested and received the S&W Model 66, a stainless steel version of the Combat Magnum.

As terrorism was considered a nonmilitary threat, the restrictions of The Hague convention were not considered applicable by the U.S. government. This meant that the restrictions on the military use of deforming ammunition was not in effect when terrorists were the target. Deforming ammunition has a much greater level of terminal effects than does the normal full-jacketed military round. Using soft-nose or hollowpoint ammunition made a handgun a much more effective weapon in terms of immediately incapacitating a target. Ammunition initially used by SEAL Team Six in their Model 66s was high-performance 158 grain jacketed hollowpoint Magnum loads. As more effective ammunition became available, it was evaluated for possible use.

A new suppressed handgun was desired by the SEALs in general by the late 1970s. The Vietnam-era Mark 22s were becoming worn and needed replacement. A German design, the Heckler & Koch (H&K) P9S pistol held a great deal

of promise as a possible basis for a
new suppressed pistol.

The H&K P9S is a double action, semiautomatic pistol with a
unique operating system common in
H&K weapons. By utilizing a roller-
locked breech system, the P9S could
fire high-pressure 9mm rounds in
complete safety without requiring a

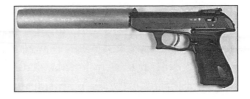

The long suppressed version of the P9S pistol. The raised competition sights can be seen to just clear the top of the suppressor
body, allowing for accurate shot placement.
Source: Kevin Dockery

moving barrel. In the roller-locked system, two rollers hold the bolt locked to
the barrel when the round is first fired. A strong mechanical disadvantage keeps
the rollers from moving inward and releasing the bolt until after the bullet had
left the barrel and pressures have dropped to a safe level. During the entire firing cycle of the P9S, the barrel remains stationary.

Using an extension barrel, the P9S was fitted with a stainless steel, wipeless,
QualaTech suppressor. Designed by Mickey Finn on the West Coast, the
QualaTech suppressor requires only periodic cleaning and minimum maintenance without needing any rebuild parts as in the case of the Mark 3 noise suppressor. Almost twice the size of the earlier Mark 3 suppressor, the QualaTech
device maintained the same level of sound suppression without an increase in
noise levels over time as would happen in the earlier suppressor as the wipes
wore away.

The slide locking feature was done away with on the suppressed P9S as the
noise level was not considered a problem. Also the mechanism of the P9S made
the weapon function semiautomatically much more reliably than the earlier
Mark 22. Higher sights were installed on the suppressed P9S to raise the sight
plane enough to clear the suppressor, otherwise the weapon was very much as
issued. The P9S became the standard 9mm suppressed pistol of the SEALs during the 1980s with the Mark 22 systems being held in reserve.

Beginning in 1979, the Joint Service Small Arms Program (JSSAP) began
what was to be a very long series of evaluations and tests to determine a new
sidearm for all of the U.S. services. The new weapon was to be a double action,
ambidextrous control pistol chambered for the NATO standard 9mm parabellum cartridge and having a minimum magazine capacity of thirteen rounds.
After three years of testing in which ten different pistols were examined, including the M1911A1 as a control weapon, a clear winner stood out and was
recommended for adoption. That pistol was the Beretta M92S-1.

The Beretta M92S-1 was a modified version of their M92S pistol which had been on the market for several years before the JSSAP tests began. Among the modifications for JSSAP was moving the magazine release from the bottom rear of the right grip to just below the trigger guard as well as making the mechanism reversible for use by left-handed firers. The original safety lever was made longer and duplicated on both sides of the slide for use by either hand. The safety mechanism also locks the firing pin in place and drops the hammer when engaged, something specifically required for the JSSAP trials.

SEAL Team Six was quick to pick up the new pistol and had Berettas available for issue in 1982. For several years the Team used its Berettas extensively, resulting in a much longer and more extensive trial than the weapon had originally received from JSSAP. The Berettas stood up to the variety of ammunition the SEALs put through them as well as passing what was in effect an endurance course considering the thousands of rounds fired by each Team Six member in the course of normal training.

Second place in the original set of JSSAP trials was held by the Smith & Wesson Model 459. Because of the showing of the Smith & Wesson pistol, the adoption of the Beretta was suspended and an additional series of trials were conducted by JSSAP. The second set of trials were due in no small part to a lawsuit brought by Smith & Wesson against the government declaring unfairness in the terms of the original tests. The second set of tests included a number of new pistols being submitted for evaluation including the Saco-Maremont (Sig-Sauer) P226. Beretta changed their Model 92S-1 slightly, incorporating a trigger-operated firing pin block as part of the safety mechanism. With the block in place, the firing pin was not released until the trigger was intentionally pulled. The new Beretta was designated the Model 92SB.

The results of the second test were much the same as the first set. The Beretta M92SB was declared the winner with second place now being held by the P226. In January 1985 the Beretta Model 92SB-F, a modified version of the test gun, was declared the new M9 service sidearm. Now the rest of the SEAL Teams would receive the Beretta.

During the JSSAP testing period, the SEALs underwent a major change in their organization. On May 1, 1983, the last UDTs were decommissioned. UDTs 11 and 20 became, respectively, SEAL Teams Five and Four. UDTs 12 and 22 became SDV Teams One and Two, respectively. With the changes in the Teams came also an increase in manpower and greater needs for new equipment and ordnance.

In an action familiar to some of the SEALs who carried suppressed High Standards in Vietnam, a new .22 caliber suppressed pistol was adopted into the

Teams during the 1980s. The new pistol was the Ruger Mark II .22 Long Rifle semiautomatic pistol fitted with an integral suppressor. The Ruger proved itself a very quiet weapon of excellent accuracy, the integral suppressor surrounding the barrel giving the weapon the appearance of a heavy-barrel target gun. The .22 caliber Long Rifle round has sufficient penetrating power and makes up for its lack of terminal energy with accuracy and slight recoil. Overpenetration with the .22 round is also not the problem it can be with other suppressed weapons, especially those in the 9mm class.

The Smith & Wesson Model 66 revolvers used by SEAL Team Six had been proving themselves a worthwhile weapon for the Teams. The Model 66, built on the stainless steel K-frame, had first become available when .357 Magnum rounds were available in only a fairly limited number of loads. With the increasing interest in handgun ammunition, and the strides taken in the 1970s in bullet performance, modern high-performance loads were increasing the amount of wear and strain on the Model 66 frame. To counter this problem, Smith & Wesson came out with a new intermediate frame size in 1981.

The largest and most powerful of the Smith & Wesson revolvers are the heavy .357, .41, and .44 Magnums built on the large N-frame. The K-frame was developed new the turn of the century as the basis for the first of the extremely popular line of Smith & Wesson .38 Special weapons. Long known to the SEALs and UDTs, the Victory Model and Model 15 Smith & Wesson pistols are both K-frame designs. Smallest in the frame sizes offered by Smith & Wesson are the diminutive J-frames used by the SEALs in the Model 36 Chief's Special.

The new frame size brought out by Smith & Wesson was the L-frame, maintaining the popular grip and trigger guard size of the K-frame but having a beefed up frame very close to the size of the N-frame. In addition to having a greater cylinder diameter, giving much more metal around the individual chambers, the barrels on the new L-frame weapons was much heavier than anything offered in the K-frame size.

The heavy barrels of the L-frame guns also had an integral under-barrel lug that extended the full length of the barrel. The result of the lug was to place extra weight forward on the gun where it would help minimize muzzle flip and hold the barrel down for a fast second shot. The first L-frame guns offered by Smith & Wesson were the blued steel Model 586 and the stainless steel Model 686. SEAL Team Six quickly picked up on the Model 686 as the weapon was proved out by a number of competition shooters throughout the United States. By January 1984, the changeover was complete and the Model 686 was the primary revolver for SEAL Team Six.

The only other revolver of note used by the Teams was the small Model 36 Chief's Special. The Model 36 had been issued during the 1970s and well into the 1980s as a personal-defense weapon for operators assigned to countries in Central America and elsewhere as the situation warranted. In several Central American countries, SEALs operated as advisors and trainers, often in plain clothes. To arm these men as unobtrusively as possible, the Model 36 was the best combination of firepower and small size available. The international availability of the Smith & Wesson line also helped the SEALs maintain a low profile by not carrying an immediately recognizable American weapon.

The small revolver could be easily carried in several convenient ways: belt holsters, ankle holsters, even slipped into a pocket. Intended for self-defense only, the Model 36 was issued as an almost throw-away weapon, the five rounds it carried being too few for any kind of protracted combat.

In spite of a number of their advantages, revolvers have too small an ammunition capacity to remain a primary weapon for modern combat. The Model 686 is used in all the Teams but is primarily a teaching aid for basic pistol marksmanship. In SEAL Team Six, the Model 686 did not go into the field but was used for a specialized form of training. The expression "you can only shoot paper so much" centered around Close Quarters Battle (CQB) and its need for quick reactions and accuracy. After marksmanship had been developed an honed on the range, a reactive target was needed to further developed skills. The very best reactive target for training is another shooter trying to get you first but this can quickly lead to an unacceptable loss in personnel. "Wax shooting" proved an effective answer to the training problem.

Since a revolver fires mechanically and does not depend on the reaction of firing in any way for its operation, the weapon will operate with any kind of projectile. By pressing a primed cartridge case, mouth first, into a slab of properly formulated wax, a cylindrical "bullet" is cut from the slab and lodged inside the case. With all participants wearing proper protective gear, primarily for the face, training can be performed where the target actually shoots back. Wax shooting was conducted by the SEALs in order to polish their skills in CQB. Training could be conducted in actual target environments, such as inside a building, ship, or aircraft, with little or no damage to the area. Wax bullets impacting on the SEALs would graphically show a mistake without costing the Team a highly trained operator.

In 1985, the Navy began receiving the Beretta Model 92F as the new M9 service pistol. Changes from the earlier Model 92SB were slight and included squaring the front of the trigger guard to facilitate a two-handed grip, a differ-

ently shaped front butt strap, a heavier magazine floorplate, chrome
plating the barrel bore and chamber,
and a matt exterior finish made of
"Bruniton," a Teflon-type of corrosion resistant coating.

The testing procedure had been
changed for the second set of JSSAP
tests and the 5,000-round limit before an allowable part breakage had
been removed from the test as well as
other factors being changed. The new
Beretta 92F was considered an improvement over the earlier 92SB and
was initially well received by the
Teams. SEAL Team Six also received
the new M9 pistol and immediately
began training with the new weapon.

It was in 1986 that a serious
weakness in the Beretta was discovered by the SEALs of Team Six. The
main incident took place during a

In the mid-1980s, this group of SEALs are range firing Beretta M9
pistols. The SEAL in the foreground has a 3-cell submachine gun
magazine pouch on his belt at his left hip. A strap is wrapped
around the lower half of the pouch, effectively shortening the individual cells to allow a 15-round Beretta magazine to be held securely without slipping in too deeply into the pouch to be easily
withdrawn. The Beretta M9 in the photo has the hammer cocked
to the single-action position.
Source: U.S. Navy

firing demonstration for a visiting political dignitary. After stating the Teams
appreciation of the new M9 pistol, a SEAL operator began firing the weapon on
the range. While firing, the Beretta had a catastrophic failure of the slide. The
rear portion of the slide broke away from the pistol and, driven by the pressure
of the fired round, struck the SEAL in the face.

The demonstration was immediately halted and first aid given to the injured SEAL. The injuries being relatively slight, the visiting dignitary wondered
if the whole incident hadn't been staged for his benefit. What had been uncov-
ered was a design flaw in the slide of the Beretta.

SEAL Team Six trained with their sidearms to a much greater extent than
any of the other services or Teams. Since this firing also involved a great deal of
high-performance ammunition, the Team Six Berettas received a correspondingly higher level of stress and wear. The fault in the Berettas design was not
able to be quickly corrected to the SEALs satisfaction. Beretta did address the
problem seriously and has since satisfactorily corrected the fault. Though the
M9 has remained the standard sidearm throughout the rest of the services,

SEAL Team Six members replaced theirs within a short time of the original range incident. Though only a very few weapons showed signs of slide cracking, the Teams wanted a replacement. In usual SEAL humor, a joke was made to cover the SEALs feelings towards the incident with the Beretta. The line "you're not a Navy SEAL until you've tasted Italian steel," has been repeated more than once, much to the embarrassment of the Beretta company.

In 1987, the Austrian Glock pistol was tested as a possible alternative to using the Beretta M9 pistol, especially in the highly corrosive marine environment. The Glock pistol, which is substantially made of plastic parts, performed better than the M9 in the Salt Fog Test, an extreme example of ocean exposure. Except for the corrosion resistance, the Glock showed itself to be significantly less reliable than the Beretta M9 in other respects. The Teams were still in the position of wanting a replacement pistol for the M9 and Team Six wanted the replacement immediately.

A replacement pistol was chosen by Team Six in early 1987, the Sig-Sauer P226, the runner up in the second JSSAP trials. Not being satisfied by the suggested changes in the Beretta, the remaining SEAL Teams followed the example of Team Six and began the process of replacing its M9s with Sig P226s. The initial request for 800 P226 weapons was put out in October 1988 with further testing and safety certification beginning on November 17. Testing included environmental tests such as exposure to sand, mud, and salt as well as drop tests and exposure to temperature extremes. In addition to the above, five pistols underwent an endurance test of 30,000 rounds fired through each weapon. Acceptance came quickly and the first weapons were in the SEAL Teams hands on January 20, 1989.

Schweizerische Industrie Gesellschaft (SIG) of Neuhausen/Rheinfalls, Switzerland, has a long record of manufacturing excellent pistols to meet the exacting standards of the Swiss military. Because of their country's export restrictions on firearms, Sig allied with the Sauer company of Germany to produce their line of weapons. Already having their P220 pistol in production as the official sidearm of the Swiss Army, Sig modified the design to meet the parameters of the JSSAP trials. The resulting pistol has since received excellent sales throughout the world as a police and military special forces sidearm. The primary reason for the P226 not surpassing the Beretta in the JSSAP trials was the overall cost per unit of the weapon as compared to the Beretta. The Sig is simply a costly handgun.

All of the SEAL Teams have stated their satisfaction with the P226 as their standard sidearm. The one major drawback with the weapon centers around the manufacturing techniques used to produce the gun. The slide of the P226 consists of a precision metal stamping with the internal components welded, dovetailed, or pinned in place. This technique allows the Sig design to be made lighter and more easily than the more common milled or forged slide. The drawback in this design noticed by the SEALs is a tendency for the P226 to rust through in spots on the slide if the weapon is not carefully rinsed after salt water exposure. Given their penchant for maintenance, the drawback is not considered a serious one by the SEALs but it does open the possibility of another sidearm coming into the Teams in the near future.

In 1991, after a number of meetings in which representatives of the Army, Navy, and Air Force Special Operations Commands discussed a number of special equipment requirements, the U.S. Special Operations Command (USSOCOM) put notification out to the firearms industry that a new handgun was desired. The Offensive Handgun Weapon System (OHWS) would be used for special operations and had to fit a specific set of criteria. Most interesting among these criteria was the requirement that the pistol be chambered for the .45 ACP round.

Some Special Operations Forces continued to use .45 ACP M1911A1 pistols, though in a customized form, well after the 9mm became the service sidearm caliber. Primary desire for the .45 centered around the rounds greater stopping power. Drawbacks of recoil, weight, and size, were not considered significant to the special operations community. Modern developments in materials and firearms technology indicated that a new weapon could be designed that would be superior to the aging M1911A1 design while still chambered for the .45 ACP round.

Additional specifications for the OHWS included a minimum ten-round magazine capacity, that it be capable of double- or single-action firing, have a dual infrared and visible laser sight, a target illuminator (flashlight) also selectable for visible or infrared light, and mount a detachable sound suppressor. Other requirements included luminous sights, ambidextrous manual safeties, and a separate decocking lever to allow the hammer to be lowered on a chambered round. On top of all this, the entire package, with ten rounds of M1911 Ball, was not to weigh more than 5.5 pounds (2.5 kilograms).

To aid in the stopping power of the OHWS, the weapon had to be capable of accepting special hot-loaded (+P in modern parlance) ammunition for enhanced stopping power. In addition to all of the above, the OHWS candidates would be subjected to the most extensive testing ever given to a Special Operations Force handgun. Each submitted unit would have to fire 30,000 rounds

The Colt .45 caliber Offensive Handgun Weapon System candidate with a KAC suppressor mounted in place on the barrel. The large dovetail mount in front of the trigger guard is for the laser aiming module (LAM). Note the square end of the slide lock protruding above the trigger and just in front of the slide stop lever.
Source: Kevin Dockery

without a parts breakage and two weapons would be fired to failure and examined for safety problems. The firing until failure was specifically put in to prevent any possibility of the Beretta slide-breaking incident to repeat itself.

In spite of the difficult parameters and stringent testing procedures, in August 1991, Phase 1 development contracts were awarded to Colt Manufacturing as well as Heckler and Koch. As part of Phase 1, thirty prototypes of each company's OHWS candidates were submitted to Naval Weapons Support Center at Crane, Indiana. The Navy facility is being used since the Navy Special Operations Command has been tasked with developing the OHWS. The OHWS program was to have three phases with the final procurement figure to be around 8,000 systems.

The Colt OHWS Phase 1 candidate is a short-recoil operated design whose barrel rotates slightly to unlock. Portions of the Colt design trace their parentage to the Colt 2000 pistol, the Double Eagle, and the M1911A1. A major number of the components for the Colt OHWS are made of stainless steel to minimize corrosion and given a matt black chrome finish. One interesting point of the Colt candidate is its use of a single-column, ten-round magazine. The single column design gives the Colt OHWS a comfortable, though very long, grip.

The Colt OHWS uses a muzzle break to reduce recoil and muzzle flip when firing the weapon without the sound suppressor. Both the muzzle break and sound suppressor mount on the frame of the pistol rather than the barrel, allowing the rotating barrel system freedom to move. Attachment to the frame is made with a spring-loaded latch allowing quick changing between the break or suppressor. The cylindrical suppressor, developed by Knight's Armament Company, uses a baffle system that gives the suppressor a long service life with minimal maintenance.

The laser aiming module (LAM), containing both a visible and infrared laser as well as a flashlight, mounts on the frame of the OHWS, underneath the muzzle with a quick release securing system. Lastly, there is a slide lock on the system to allow either unlocked semiautomatic fire with the suppressor or single shot, slide-locked fire for maximum sound attenuation.

The Heckler & Koch OHWS candidate uses technology the company developed for its Universal Self-Loading Pistol (USP) line, including a plastic polymer frame, machined steel slide, and mechanical recoil reduction system. Going with a staggered, double-column magazine gives the H&K OHWS a twelve-round magazine capacity in a slightly wider but normal length grip.

Using a modified linkless Browning system, the H&K OHWS operates on short recoil with the barrel camming down from its locked position in the slide. Instead of having separate locking lugs on the barrel matching commensurate grooves in the slide, the square-sectioned breech of the H&K design locks solidly into the ejection port opening much like the Sig-Sauer P226 weapon.

The (LAM) locks into grooves in the frame forward of the trigger guard. Created by Insight Technology Inc., the LAM contains the lasers and flashlight in an easily removed package with an IR filter for the flashlight stowed under a side cover.

Initially, the H&K OHWS was fitted with an unusual suppressor developed by H&K. The compact suppressor is an asymmetrical rectangular design with a rectangular cross section. Utilizing normal baffle technology, the H&K suppressor is shorter than a normal cylindrical suppressor while still having sufficient internal volume for effective sound suppression. By using an asymmetrical design with an off-center bullet path, the H&K OHWS does not have to have raised sights as the main portion of the suppressor body is below the sight plane.

The mechanical recoil reduction system in the H&K OHWS lowers the felt recoil of the system to significantly less than the original M1911A1 pistol. Another advantage of reducing felt recoil is a more rapid target reacquisition after a shot has been fired. Since the H&K weapon has an internal recoil reduction system, felt recoil is even less when the weapon is fired with the suppressor installed, a significant point when the OHWS is fired in its optional slide-locked configuration for maximum sound suppression.

The rectangular sound suppressor was replaced during testing on the H&K OHWS with a unit also manufactured by Knights Armament Corporation. The new suppressor is cylindrical and longer then the H&K design but still remains below the sight plane. Both the Colt and the H&K OHWS candidates met the requirement of a 30 decibel noise reduction and 75 percent flash reduction over the unsuppressed system.

In August 1992, the required thirty prototype weapons were submitted to the Navy for Phase 1 testing. After the testing was completed, the H&K candidate was the one chosen for further development under the second phase of the OHWS program. A number of refined H&K designs were delivered for further testing in November 1994. Requirements on the number of weapons and production schedules were modified by USSOCOM in October 1993. Under the new schedule, Phase 3 production commenced in mid-1995 with the initial deliveries of 7,500 pistols and 1,950 LAMs and suppressors taking place in 1996-97.

The production model of the H&K Mark 23 was essentially the same as the prototypes with some minor differences. The most major of the differences was the removal of the slide lock system from the design and the change to the Knight's Armament suppressor. The first production Mark 23 pistols were delivered to the U.S. Special Operations Command on May 1, 1996. Operational deployments of the weapon, considered a very large handgun by the operators who use it, continues throughout the Special Operations community.

In the mid-1960s, the SEALs were conducting research into what would be one of the more unique series of handguns ever issued in the U.S. military. A number of research and development projects were up and running for the SEALs and the UDTs in the field of weapons, tools, and explosive devices. One of these projects, identified as TDP 3801, was a multimillion dollar effort with products beginning to emerge into the Teams in late 1967. Among the systems and equipment being worked on as part of TDP 3801 was the underwater gun system. Identified as the Underwater Gun (WOX-5 Type), Ammunition for U/W Gun (WOX-5 Type), and Rocket Projectile for U/W Gun (WOX-5 Type), the material being investigated was designed to give an individual combat swimmer a close-in defensive capability in an easy to handle package.

Just a short time prior to 1967, a very new weapon system had been released on the civilian market and brought to the attention of the Special Warfare community. The weapon system was the Gyrojet rocket gun, a handgun that fired solid-fueled, spin-stabilized, miniature rockets instead of normal ammunition. Though the Gyrojet gun itself was not of particular interest to the SEALs or UDTs during the 1960s, at least not in its available configurations, an underwater version of the weapon, the Lancejet, did show promise.

Using the same miniature rocket systems as the Gyrojet handgun, the Lancejet fired a long, spearlike projectile from either a single-shot or repeating weapon. The standard Lancejet projectiles were about ¼ inch (6.4 mm) in diameter and 12 inches (30.5 cm) long. Weighing in at about 2 ounces (56.7 g), the Lancejet projectile was powerful enough for most underwater needs, being able to penetrate a 1-inch thick (2.5 cm) sheet of plywood at 25 feet (7.6 m), underwater. Though the loaded repeater weapon was of a manageable size and weight, about 18 inches (45.7 cm) long and 1.5 pounds (0.68 kg) loaded, the weapon had two bad drawbacks—cost and accuracy.

The Lancejet was able to put half its rockets into a 16-inch (40.6 cm) circle at 25 feet during tests. Accuracy at that level would mean that a diver would miss an average man-sized target with half of his ammunition when underwater, an unacceptable figure. In addition the cost of the ammunition was considerable, and to make it more accurate with the technology available at the time would have made it even more costly. After some examination, the idea of a rocket-powered swimmer weapon was shelved.

By the early 1970s, a piece of ordnance was available to the Teams that would give a swimmer a reasonable weapon that he could carry close to hand. Developed as part of the Swimmer Weapons System, the Underwater Defense Gun Mk 1 Mod 0 was a repeating weapon that was effective underwater while not being bigger than a large pistol.

Developed in part at the Naval Surface Weapons Center White Oak Laboratory in Silver Spring, Maryland, the Underwater Defense Gun uses the very exotic Mk 59 Mod 0 Projectile (cartridge) to launch a long, thin, fin-stabilized dart of heavy tungsten metal. As water is almost 900 times denser than air, a projectile has vastly more drag on it than an equivalent round fired in air. The tungsten alloy and extended shape of the projectile give the dart a high sectional density which aids it in penetrating the water, while also helping it maintain a sufficient velocity to give it effective terminal effects. For stabilization in flight, the Mk 59 projectile dart has four fins machined into its rear section. Each fin has a small angle cut into its leading edge allowing the water flow over the fin to give the projectile an additional stabilizing spin.

The operating system of the Mark 59 projectile prevents the Mk 1 underwater gun from requiring a normal barrel and allows the weapon to operate either underwater or in the open air. The body of the Mark 59 projectile is a steel cylinder consisting of the barrel, charge plug assembly, shear pin, projectile pusher, and tungsten dart. The charge plug assembly contains a percussion primer and a charge of smokeless powder propellant. Ahead of the charge plug assembly is the projectile pusher, a self-sealing piston that drives against the base of the tungsten dart.

The projectile pusher is secured to the front end of the plug assembly by a metal shear pin. The loaded plug assembly is threaded into the breech end of the barrel with the dart inserted into a socket in the pusher. The front tip of the dart is held centered in the barrel by a light alloy disk. The end of the barrel is

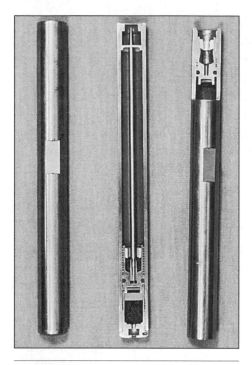

From left to right, a complete, sectioned unfired, and partially sectioned fired Mark 59 projectile.

The center round is an unfired Mk 59 showing the tungsten dart that is the actual projectile fired from the round. The breech section of the round is threaded into the stainless steel body, maintaining a gas and water tight seal. When the primer is struck, the powder (shown as the dark mass just inside of the primer end) burns until it has built up enough pressure to break the shear pin, visible as the vertical pin just behind the pusher piston. The pusher pistol has the finned end of the dart held securely and is sealed from gas leakage by the O-ring around its base. The ends of the O-ring are visible just above and below the fins of the dart. At the muzzle (upper) end of the projectile is an aluminum disc that holds the dart centered in the barrel of the Mk 59 body. Beyond the tip of the dart is the sealing disk that keeps the round water tight during transport and is shattered by the dart when the Mk 59 is fired.

The right Mk 59 has been fired and the muzzle end section to show the pusher piston at the far end of its travel. The constricted end of the Mk 59 body prevents the pusher from exiting the barrel. With the pusher pistol stopped, all of the firing gasses remain in the body of the Mark 59, releasing no bubbles into the water and reducing the sound of firing to a very low level.

Source: Kevin Dockery

left open but is constricted to keep the pusher from leaving the barrel when the cartridge is fired.

The Mark 59 projectile is fired by a normal firing pin crushing the percussion cap and igniting the powder charge. The shear pin holds the pusher in place while the propellant burns until sufficient pressure is built up in the system to force the pusher to shear through the pin, driving the dart down the barrel. As the pusher reaches the constriction at the end of the barrel, it begins to slow and collapse in on itself slightly. By this time the dart has reached its maximum velocity and it leaves the muzzle of the weapon. The constriction at the end of the barrel retains the pusher, sealing all of the propellant gases inside of the cartridge body.

Since no gasses leave the weapon when it is fired, the Mark 1 Swimmer defense gun is flashless and effectively soundless. This system also allows a normal propellant charge to be used underwater without causing a muzzle blast shock wave that could injure the operator or other swimmers around him.

The underwater defense gun is mechanically rather simple and acts as a double-action-only pepperbox revolver. A large cylinder magazine holds six of the Mk 59 projectiles and is carried completely covered by the mechanism of the gun. A large door making up much of the left side of the gun can be opened to allow the magazine cylinder to be inserted or removed.

The outside of the underwater gun has few protruding parts and shows a relatively streamlined appearance. The circular safety switch can be moved to either side of the gun to accommodate a left- or right-handed operator. In addition, the large metal clip that holds the underwater gun securely to the swimmers harness can also be moved to either side as the operator desires. No trigger guard covers the trigger to allow easy operation with a gloved hand.

By pressing a spring catch, the loading door snaps open, giving access to the cylinder magazine. The door can be operated underwater, allowing a swimmer to insert a fresh magazine and reload the weapon without surfacing. In general, the underwater gun is operated like any other pistol, the luminous sights are aligned and the trigger pulled to fire the gun.

The long trigger pull rotates the cylinder magazine and locks it place with a fresh cartridge in front of the firing pin. A metal rod protrudes from the back of the gun as the trigger is pulled showing if the firing pin has been released at the end of the trigger pull or not.

Because each dart launches from its own barrel, the underwater gun is considered a pepperbox design rather than a true revolver. In a pepperbox design, each chamber has its own barrel rather than a single barrel and multiple chambers in a rotating cylinder as is found in the true revolver. Each of the precision-made Mk 59 projectiles is retained in the cylinder magazine by its snug fit and retaining spring that sets into a small flat machine on the outside of each cartridge.

The precision aspect of the ammunition is shown in the accuracy of the weapon. To be accepted, each lot of ammunition is randomly tested and must place its darts within a 9-inch (22.9 cm) circle at 30 feet (9.1 m) range to be accepted. In addition, the standard deviation in velocity of the darts cannot exceed 25 feet per second either way or the lot is rejected. All of the acceptance tests for velocity and accuracy are conducted at a simulated depth of 60 feet of sea water also insuring the operating system of the cartridges.

The underwater defense gun is made of an aluminum frame, cylinder, door assembly, and action with all other operating parts but the trigger being made of stainless steel. The trigger is made of self-lubricating nylon. Each weapon comes packed in an ammunition can complete with two magazine cylinders, and a plastic bag of small spare parts. The Mark 59 Mod 0 projectiles come packaged in a standard ammunition can, wrapped in cardboard and packed sixty to the can.

In an emergency situation, the Mk 1 gun can be used in the open air as a covert weapon. This is not a normal use of the weapon due to the high cost of its ammunition. But when fired, the loudest sound produced is the mechanical sounds of the action and the slapping noises from the projectile pusher and buffer system. First available in late 1970, the underwater defense gun has been used by both the SEALs and the UDT throughout the 1970s and into the 1980s. As weapons became worn and ammunition stocks ran low, a replacement weapon was sought as the underwater defense gun was a unique and valuable Special Warfare asset.

Heckler & Koch designed an underwater handgun with the same general characteristics as the Mk 1 gun during the 1970s. Entering service in 1976, the H&K P11 underwater handgun is known to be in service with the SEALs but all operational information on the weapon is classified. What little information that is known has been released by other governments who also employ the P11 pistol.

In general, the P11 operates much the same as the earlier Mk 1 underwater gun. In the P11, five projectiles are held in a reusable, nonrotating barrel unit that has a set of open sights installed on the top barrel. The large projectiles are driven by pusher pistons and the system releases no propelling gas when it is fired. Each barrel is electrically fired, eliminating much of the mechanical noise found in the Mk 1. Batteries for firing are held in the grip section and the barrel unit can be replaced underwater by the operator.

Barrel units must be returned to H&K in Germany for reloading, adding to the maintenance load of the weapon but helping to keep the overall cost down at least slightly. The biggest advantage of the H&K weapon is the range of the system. The large projectile of the P11 can be used accurately in open air against a man-sized target at distances of over 98 feet (30 m). When fired underwater, the P11's range is limited to 32 to 49 feet (10 to 15 m), which is still quite reasonable given the low visibility of underwater operations in general.

Instead of having a belt clip, the P11 has a large, open holster available that is normally carried strapped around the swimmers waist. At the present time, no photographs are available of the P11 in SEAL hands and Heckler and Koch simply denies knowledge of the weapon.

■ Pistol Data ■

COLT M1911A1 GOVERNMENT MODEL

CARTRIDGE .45 ACP (11.43×23mm)

OPERATION Short recoil

TYPE OF FIRE Semiautomatic

RATE OF FIRE 35 rpm

MUZZLE VELOCITY 830 fps (252 m/s)

MUZZLE ENERGY 370 ft/lb (502 J)

SIGHTS Open, V-notch/blade, fixed, adjustable for windage only

FEED 7-round removable box magazine

WEIGHTS

Weapon (empty) 2.31 lb (1.05 kg)

Weapon (loaded) 2.80 lb (1.27 kg)

Magazine (empty) 0.16 lb (0.07 kg)

Magazine (loaded) 0.49 lb (0.22 kg)

Service cartridge M1911 Ball 331 gr (21.5 g)

Projectile 230 gr (15 g)

LENGTHS

Weapon overall 8.63 in (21.9 cm)

Barrel 5 in (12.8 cm)

Sight radius 6.5 in (16.5 cm)

Effective range 50 yds (45.7 m)

Source: Kevin Dockery

Source: Kevin Dockery

SMITH & WESSON MILITARY & POLICE REVOLVER

CARTRIDGE .38 Special (9×29mmR)

OPERATION Manual, double-action revolver

TYPE OF FIRE Repeater

RATE OF FIRE 18 rpm

MUZZLE VELOCITY 760 fps (232 m/s)

MUZZLE ENERGY 203 ft/lb (275 J)

SIGHTS Open, U-notch/blade, fixed

FEED 6-round cylinder

WEIGHTS

Weapon (empty) 1.75 lb (0.79 kg)

Weapon (loaded) 1.95 lb (0.88 kg)

Magazine (loaded) 6 rds 0.20 lb (0.09 kg)

Service cartridge Steel-jacketed ball 231 gr (15 g)

Projectile 158 gr (10.2 g)

LENGTHS

Weapon overall 9.13 in (23.2 cm)

Barrel 4 in (10.2 cm)

Sight radius 5.94 in (15.1 cm)

Effective range 30 yds (27 m)

Maximum range 1085 yds (992 m)

Source: Smith & Wesson

SMITH & WESSON K38 COMBAT MASTERPIECE MODEL 15

CARTRIDGE .38 Special (9×29mmR)

OPERATION Manual, double-action revolver

TYPE OF FIRE Repeater

RATE OF FIRE 24 rpm

MUZZLE VELOCITY 758 fps (231 m/s)

MUZZLE ENERGY 202 ft/lb (274 J)

SIGHTS Open, square-notch/blade, adjustable

FEED 6-round cylinder

WEIGHTS

Weapon (empty) 2.0 lb (0.91 kg)

Weapon (loaded) 2.2 lb (1.00 kg)

Magazine (loaded) 6 rds 0.20 lb (0.09 kg)

Service cartridge Steel jacketed ball 231 gr (15 g)

Projectile 158 gr (10.2 g)

LENGTHS

Weapon overall 9.13 in (23.2 cm)

Barrel 4 in (10.2 cm)

Sight radius 5.88 in (14.9 cm)

Effective range 40 yds (36.6 m)

Source: Kevin Dockery

COLT DETECTIVE SPECIAL

CARTRIDGE .38 Special (9×29mmR)

OPERATION Manual, double-action revolver

TYPE OF FIRE Repeating

RATE OF FIRE 18 rpm

MUZZLE VELOCITY 686 fps (209 m/s)

MUZZLE ENERGY 165 ft/lb (224 J)

SIGHTS Open, U-notch/blade, fixed

FEED 6-round cylinder

WEIGHTS

Weapon (empty) 1.31 lb (0.59 kg)

Weapon (loaded) 1.51 lb (0.68 kg)

Magazine (loaded) 6 rds 0.20 lb (0.09 kg)

Service cartridge Steel jacketed ball 231 gr (15 g)

Projectile 158 gr (10.2 g)

LENGTHS

Weapon overall 6.75 in (17.1 cm)

Barrel 2 in (5.1 cm)

Sight radius 3.5 in (8.9 cm)

Effective range 20 yds (18 m)

Maximum range 950 yds (869 m)

Source: Smith & Wesson

Source: Kevin Dockery

SMITH & WESSON MODEL 36 CHIEF'S SPECIAL
SMITH & WESSON MODEL 38 AIRWEIGHT BODYGUARD

CARTRIDGE .38 Special
OPERATION Manual, double-action revolver
TYPE OF FIRE Repeating
RATE OF FIRE 15 rpm
MUZZLE VELOCITY 691 fps (211 m/s)
MUZZLE ENERGY 167 ft/lb (226 J)
SIGHTS Open, square-notch/blade, fixed
FEED 5-round cylinder
WEIGHTS
Weapon (empty) Model 36 1.22 lb (0.55 kg); Model 38 0.88 lb (0.40 kg)
Weapon (loaded) Model 36 1.39 lb (0.63 kg); Model 38 1.05 lb (0.48 kg)
Magazine (loaded) 5 rounds 0.165 lb (0.075 kg)
Service cartridge Lead ball 231 gr (15 g)
Projectile 158 gr (10.2 g)
LENGTHS
Weapon overall 6.31 in (16 cm)
Barrel 2 in (5.1 cm)
Sight radius 3.25 in (8.3 cm)
Effective range 15 yds (14 m)
Maximum range 950 yds (869 m)

COLT .380 AUTOMATIC

CARTRIDGE .380 ACP (9×17mm)
OPERATION Blowback
TYPE OF FIRE Semiautomatic
RATE OF FIRE 21 rpm
MUZZLE VELOCITY 970 fps (296 m)
MUZZLE ENERGY 198 ft/lb (268 J)
SIGHTS Open, U-notch/blade, fixed, adjustable for windage only
FEED 7-round removable box magazine
WEIGHTS
Weapon (empty) 1.44 lb (0.65 kg)
Weapon (loaded) 1.65 lb (0.75 kg)
Magazine (empty) 0.06 lb (0.03 kg)
Magazine (loaded) 0.21 lb (0.10 kg)
Service cartridge Ball 146 gr (9.5 g)
Projectile 95 gr (6.2 g)
LENGTHS
Weapon overall 6.75 in (17.1 cm)
Barrel 3.75 in (9.5 cm)
Sight radius 5.13 in (13 cm)
Effective range 25 yds (23 m)
Maximum range 1,089 yds (996 m)

Source: Kevin Dockery

Source: Kevin Dockery

SMITH & WESSON MODEL 39

CARTRIDGE 9mm Parabellum, (9×19mm)

OPERATION Short recoil, double-action

TYPE OF FIRE Semiautomatic

RATE OF FIRE 24 rpm

MUZZLE VELOCITY 1,250 fps (381 m/s)

MUZZLE ENERGY 399 ft/lb (510 J)

SIGHTS Open, square-notch/blade, adjustable

FEED 8-round removable box magazine

WEIGHTS

Weapon (empty) 1.66 lb (0.75 kg)

Weapon (loaded) 2.03 lb (0.92 kg)

Magazine (empty) 0.16 lb (0.07 kg)

Magazine (loaded) 0.37 lb (0.17 kg)

Service cartridge M1 Ball 180 gr (11.7 g)

Projectile 115 grains (7.45 g)

LENGTHS

Weapon overall 7.63 in (19.4 cm)

Barrel 4 in (10.2 cm)

Sight radius 5.56 in (14.1 cm)

Effective range 50 yds (45.7 m)

TOKAREV TT-33 (PRC TYPE 51)

CARTRIDGE 7.62mm Short (7.62×25 mm)

OPERATION Short recoil

TYPE OF FIRE Semiautomatic

RATE OF FIRE 32 rpm

MUZZLE VELOCITY 1,378 fps (420 m/s)

MUZZLE ENERGY 367 ft/lb (498 J)

SIGHTS Open, Square-notch/blade, fixed, adjustable for windage only

FEED 8-round removable box magazine

WEIGHTS

Weapon (empty) 1.69 lb (0.77 kg)

Weapon (loaded) 2.07 lb (0.94 kg)

Magazine (empty) 0.19 lb (0.09 kg)

Magazine (loaded) 0.38 lb (0.17 kg)

Service cartridge Type-P Ball (PRC Type 50) 167 gr (10.8 g)

Projectile 87 grains (5.64 g)

LENGTHS

Weapon overall 7.8 in (19.8 cm)

Barrel 4.6 in (11.7 cm)

Sight radius 6.1 in (15.5 cm)

BROWNING HP-35

CARTRIDGE 9mm Parabellum (9×19mm)
OPERATION Short recoil
TYPE OF FIRE Semiautomatic
RATE OF FIRE 40 rpm
MUZZLE VELOCITY 1,148 fps (350 m/s)
MUZZLE ENERGY 369 ft/lb (500 J)
SIGHTS Open, V-notch/blade, fixed, adjustable for windage only
FEED 13-round removable box magazine
WEIGHTS
Weapon (empty) 1.79 lb (0.81 kg)
Weapon (loaded) 2.28 lb (1.03 kg)
Magazine (empty) 0.16 lb (0.07 kg)
Magazine (loaded) 0.49 lb (0.22 kg)
Service cartridge M1 Ball 180 gr (11.7 g)
Projectile 115 grains (7.45 g)
LENGTHS
Weapon overall 7.87 in (20 cm)
Barrel 4.65 in (11.8 cm)
Sight radius 6.26 in (15.9 cm)

HIGH STANDARD MODEL HD W/SUPPRESSOR

CARTRIDGE .22 Long rifle (5.7×16mmR)
OPERATION Blowback

TYPE OF FIRE Semiautomatic
RATE OF FIRE 20 rpm
MUZZLE VELOCITY 930 fps (283 m/s)
MUZZLE ENERGY 77 ft/lb (104 J)
SIGHTS Open, square-notch/blade, fixed, adjustable for windage
FEED 10-round removable box magazine
WEIGHTS
Weapon (empty) 2.37 lb (1.08 kg)
Weapon (loaded) 2.58 lb (1.17 kg)
Magazine (empty) 0.13 lb (0.06 kg)
Magazine (loaded) 0.21 lb (0.10 kg)
Service cartridge M24 jacketed ball 54 gr (3.5 g)
Projectile 40 gr (2.6 g)
LENGTHS
Weapon overall 14.0 in (35.6 cm)
Barrel 6.69 in (17 cm)
Suppressor 9.19 in (23.3 cm)
Sight radius 11.13 in (28.3 cm)
Effective range 20 yds (18 m) Peak sound pressure for an unsuppressed HD is 136 db, with the suppressor, 113 db

PISTOL, 9MM MK 23 MOD 0 W/NOISE SUPPRESSOR MK 3

CARTRIDGE 9mm Parabellum (9×19mm)
OPERATION Manual or short recoil, double-action
TYPE OF FIRE Manual repeater or semi-automatic
RATE OF FIRE 12 rpm
MUZZLE VELOCITY 925 fps (294 m/s) w/o suppressor; 900 fps (274 m/s) w/suppressor
MUZZLE ENERGY 300 ft/lb (407 J) w/o suppressor; 284 ft/lb (385 J) w/ suppressor

SIGHTS Open, square notch/blade, adjustable

FEED 8-round removable magazine

WEIGHTS

Weapon (empty) 1.63 lb (0.74 kg) w/o suppressor; 2.13 lb (0.97 kg) w/suppressor

Weapon (loaded) 2.04 (0.93 kg) w/o suppressor; 2.54 lb (1.15 kg) w/suppressor

Suppressor 0.5 lb (0.23 kg)

Magazine (empty) 0.16 lb (0.07 kg)

Magazine (loaded) 0.41 lb (0.19 kg)

Service cartridge 9mm Mk 144 Mod 0 ball, 223 gr (14.5 g)

Projectile 158 grains (10.2 g)

LENGTHS

Weapon overall 8.5 in (21.6 cm) w/o suppressor; 12.75 in (32.4 cm) w/suppressor

Suppressor length 5 in (12.7 cm)

Suppressor diameter 1.57 in (4 cm)

Barrel 5 in (12.7 cm); 0.5 in end length threaded ½×20 tpi

Sight Radius 5.75 in (14.6 cm)

Effective Range 40 yds (36.6 m)

9mm Pistol and Suppressor Kit Mk 23 Mod 0 consists of the 9mm pistol Mk 22 Mod 0, two magazines, 9mm Pistol Noise Suppressor Mk 3 Mod 0, a belt holster w/integral pouch for the spare magazine, and a package of replacement parts for the pistol. The replacement parts are the ejector, depressor, plunger, and spring (S&S #6013, 6014), a standard slide stop lever (S&W #6125), and a sear release lever (S&W #6103)

9MM PISTOL ACCESSORY KIT MK 26 MOD 0

CONTENTS

1—9mm Noise suppressor Mk 3 insert (10001-2504718)

Length 2.56 in (6.5 cm)

Diameter 1.125 in

Weight 0.112 lb (0.051 kg)

24 rounds—Cartridges 9mm Mk 144 Mod 0

1—O-ring (MS-29513-24)

1—Back cap plug assembly

6—Muzzle plugs

4—Chamber plugs

1—Barrel cap

Total Weight 1.03 lb (0.48 kg)

Size 4.75 × 3.25 × 1.38 in (12.1 × 8.3 × 3.5 cm)

Packing 28 kits per wooden box

Suppressor insert is a sealed aluminum can containing four equally spaced 0.25 inch (6.4 mm) thick soft plastic discs. The suppressor insert is to be replaced after every 24 rounds of Mk 144 Mod 0 fired.

Source: Smith & Wesson

SMITH & WESSON MODEL 66

CARTRIDGE .357 Magnum (9×33mmR)

OPERATION Manual, double-action revolver

TYPE OF FIRE Repeating

RATE OF FIRE 24 rpm

MUZZLE VELOCITY 1,206 fps (368 m/s)

MUZZLE ENERGY 404 ft/lb (548 J)

SIGHTS Open, white outline square-notch/blade, adjustable

FEED 6-round cylinder

WEIGHTS

Weapon (empty) 2.25 lb (1.02 kg)

Weapon (loaded) 2.44 lb (1.11 kg)

Magazine (loaded) 6 rds 0.19 lb ((0.09 kg)

Service cartridge .357 Magnum JHP 219 gr (14.2 g)

Projectile 125 gr (8.1 g)

LENGTHS

Weapon overall 9.56 in (24.3 cm)

Barrel 4 in (10.2 cm)

Sight radius 5.87 in (14.9 cm)

Effective range 40 yds (37 m)

HECKLER & KOCH P9S

CARTRIDGE 9mm Parabellum (9×19mm)

OPERATION Delayed blowback, double-action

TYPE OF FIRE Semiautomatic

RATE OF FIRE 27 rpm

MUZZLE VELOCITY 1,148 fps (350 m/s)

MUZZLE ENERGY 361 ft/lb (490 J)

SIGHTS Open, square-notch/blade, fixed

FEED 9-round removable box magazine

WEIGHTS

Weapon (empty) 1.87 lb (0.85 kg)

Weapon (loaded) 2.27 lb (1.03 kg)

Magazine (empty) 0.16 lb (0.07 kg)

Magazine (loaded) 0.40 lb (0.18 kg)

Service cartridge 9mm Ball M882, 190 gr (12 g)

Projectile 124 grains (8 g)

LENGTHS

Weapon overall 7.56 in (19.2 cm)

Barrel 4 in (10.2 cm)

Sight radius 5.78 in (14.7 cm)

Effective range 50 yds (45.7 m)

Most often issued w/suppressor

Source: Kevin Dockery

HECKLER & KOCH P9S W/QUALATECH SUPPRESSOR

CARTRIDGE 9mm Parabellum (9×19mm)

OPERATION Delayed blowback, double-action

TYPE OF FIRE Semiautomatic

RATE OF FIRE 27 rpm

MUZZLE VELOCITY 965 fps (294 m/s)

MUZZLE ENERGY 327 ft/lb (443 J)

SIGHTS Open, square-notch/blade, adjustable

FEED 9-round removable box magazine

WEIGHTS

Weapon (empty) 1.94 lb (0.88 kg) w/o suppressor; 3.24 lb (1.47 kg) w/suppressor

Weapon (loaded) 2.39 lb (1.08 kg) w/o suppressor; 3.69 lb (1.67 kg) w/suppressor

Suppressor 1.31 lb (0.59 kg)

Magazine (empty) 0.16 lb (0.07 kg)

Magazine (loaded) 0.45 lb (0.20 kg)

Service cartridge 9mm MK 144 Mod O Ball 223 gr (14.5 g)

Projectile 158 grain (10.2 g)

LENGTHS

Weapon overall 8.19 in (20.8 cm) w/o suppressor; 15.38 in (39.1 cm) w/suppressor

Suppressor length 7.75 in (19.7 cm)

Suppressor diameter 1.382 in (3.5 cm)

Barrel 4.63 in (11.7 cm)

Sight radius 6.06 in (15.4 cm)

Effective range 30 yds (27.4 m)

Source: Kevin Dockery

SMITH & WESSON MODEL 686

CARTRIDGE .357 Magnum (9×33mmR)
OPERATION Manual, double-action revolver
TYPE OF FIRE Repeater
RATE OF FIRE 24 rpm
MUZZLE VELOCITY 1,206 fps (368 m/s)
MUZZLE ENERGY 404 ft/lb (548 J)
SIGHTS Open, white outline square-notch/blade w/red insert, adjustable
FEED 6-round cylinder
WEIGHTS
Weapon (empty) 2.63 lb (1.19 kg)
Weapon (loaded) 2.82 lb (1.28 kg)
Magazine (loaded) 6 rds 0.19 lb (0.09 kg)
Service cartridge .357 Magnum JHP 219 gr (14.2 g)
Projectile 125 gr (8.1 g)
LENGTHS
Weapon overall 9.75 in (24.8 cm)
Barrel 4 in (10.2 cm)
Sight radius 5.88 in (14.9 cm)
Effective range 50 yds (45.7 m)

RUGER MARK II W/SUPPRESSOR

CARTRIDGE .22 Long rifle (5.7×16mmR)
OPERATION Blowback
TYPE OF FIRE Semiautomatic
RATE OF FIRE 20 rpm
MUZZLE VELOCITY 984 fps (300 m/s)
MUZZLE ENERGY 86 ft/lb (117 J)
SIGHTS Open, square-notch/blade, adjustable
FEED 10-round removable box magazine

WEIGHTS
Weapon (empty) 2.54 lb (1.15 kg)
Weapon (loaded) 2.91 lb (1.32 kg)
Magazine (empty) 0.29 lb (0.13 kg)
Magazine (loaded) 0.37 lb (0.17 kg)
Service cartridge Lead ball 54 gr (3.5 g)
Projectile 40 gr (2.6 g)
LENGTHS
Weapon overall 11.61 in (29.5 cm)
Barrel 6.18 in (15.7 cm)
Sight radius 9.72 in (24.7 cm)
Effective range 20 yds (18 m)

Source: Kevin Dockery

M9 PISTOL (BERETTA M92SB-F)

CARTRIDGE 9mm Parabellum (9×19mm)
OPERATION Short recoil, double-action
TYPE OF FIRE Semiautomatic
RATE OF FIRE 45 rpm
MUZZLE VELOCITY 1,280 fps (390 m/s)
MUZZLE ENERGY 447 ft/lb (606 J)
SIGHTS Open, square-notch/blade, fixed
FEED 15-round removable box magazine
WEIGHTS
Weapon (empty) 1.89 lb (0.86 kg)
Weapon (loaded) 2.53 lb (1.15 kg)
Magazine (empty) 0.23 lb (0.11 kg)
Magazine (loaded) 0.64 lb (0.29 kg)
Service cartridge 9mm Ball M882 190 gr (12 g)
Projectile 124 grains (8 g)
LENGTHS
Weapon overall 8.56 in (21.7 cm)
Barrel 4.94 in (12.5 cm)
Sight radius 6.09 in (15.5 cm)
Effective range 50 yds (45.7 m)

Source: Kevin Dockery

MARK 11—SIG P226

CARTRIDGE 9mm Parabellum (9×19mm)
OPERATION Short recoil, double-action
TYPE OF FIRE Semiautomatic
RATE OF FIRE 40 rpm
MUZZLE VELOCITY 1,132 fps (345 m/s)
MUZZLE ENERGY 350 ft/lb (475 J)
SIGHTS Open, square-notch/blade, fixed
FEED 15-round removable box magazine
WEIGHTS
Weapon (empty) 1.66 lb (0.75 kg)
Weapon (loaded) 2.28 lb (1.03 kg)
Magazine (empty) 0.21 lb (0.10 kg)
Magazine (loaded) 0.62 lb (0.28 kg)
Service cartridge 9mm Ball M882 190 gr
(12 g)
Projectile 124 grains (8 g)
LENGTHS
Weapon overall 7.72 in (19.6 cm)
Barrel 4.41 in (11.2 cm)
Sight radius 6.30 in (16 cm)
Effective range 50 yds (45.7 m)

Source: Kevin Dockery

AUGUST 1991 USSOCOM OFFENSIVE HANDGUN WEAPON SYSTEM (OHWS) SPECIFICATIONS (CONDENSED)

A closeup of the breech end of the Colt/Knight OHWS suppressor showing the quick release mechanism. The square notch at the top end of the breech indexes the suppressor with the front sight of the pistol. Pressing in on the spring-loaded plunger lines up the two semicircular notches in the suppressor locking pins with the bore of the suppressor body. Slipping the suppressor over the muzzle of the Colt OHWS candidate and releasing the plunger securely locks the suppressor in place.

Source T/K

CALIBER .45 ACP
MAGAZINE 10-round minimum
LENGTH OVERALL 9.84 in (25 CM)
LENGTH W/SUPPRESSOR 15.75 in (40 cm)
WEIGHT W/EMPTY MAGAZINE 2.86lb (1.30 kg)
WEIGHT W/12 RDS BALL, SUPPRESSOR, LAM 5.5 lb (2.5 kg)

Double-action trigger w/single action capability, decocking lever, adjustable sights w/colored or tritium (luminous) inserts, dual-mode (infrared and visible) laser sight, flashlight, removable sound suppressor providing 30 db sound reduction and 75 percent flash suppression capable of holding those characteristics after firing 15,000 rounds without maintenance. Fire 30,000 rds without a material failure and fire 10,000 rounds without a failure to function. Specialized round used in the nonsuppressed mode is envisioned to be a 200 grain truncated cone bullet loaded to +P levels minimum.

USSOCOM COLT OFFENSIVE HANDGUN WEAPON SYSTEM (OHWS) W/SUPPRESSOR

The complete Colt OHWS with laser aiming module in place underneath the barrel and the KAC suppressor locked onto the flash hider of the barrel.

CARTRIDGE .45 ACP (11.23×23mm)
OPERATION Short recoil, double action
TYPE OF FIRE Semiautomatic
RATE OF FIRE 30 rpm
MUZZLE VELOCITY 804 fps (245 m/s); Special +P 1,043 fps (318 m/s)
MUZZLE ENERGY 336 ft/lb (456 J); 447 ft/lb (606 J) w/special +P load
SIGHTS Open, square-notch/blade, adjustable for windage only, may be fitted with white plastic parts or luminous dot inserts, one front, two rear. S-tron laser aiming module with flashlight, weight (0.676 kg) w/batteries.
FEED 10-round, single-column removable box magazine
WEIGHTS
Weapon (empty) 3.34 lb (1.51 kg)
Weapon (loaded) 3.97 lb (1.80 kg) w/loaded magazine (Ball); 4.85 lb (2.20 kg) w/loaded magazine, suppressor; 6.34 lb (2.88 kg)

w/loaded magazine, suppressor, LAM w/batt
Magazine (empty) 0.16 lb (0.07 kg)
Magazine (loaded) 0.63 lb (0.29 kg)
Service cartridge 45 Ball M1911 331 g (21.4 g); Special +P JHP (Olin) 282 gr (18.3 g)
Projectile 234 gr (15.2 g)
Special +P JHP 185 gr (12 g)
LENGTHS
Weapon overall 9.80 in (24.9 cm) w/o suppressor; 16.89 in (42.9 cm) w/suppressor
Suppressor length 7.09 in (18 cm)
Suppressor diameter 1.38 in (3.5 cm)
Barrel 4.77 in (12.1 cm)
Sight radius 6.88 in (17.5 cm)
Effective range 54.7 yds (50 m)
Maximum range 1,467 yds (1341 m)

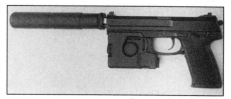

Source: Kevin Dockery

USSOCOM HECKLER & KOCH OFFENSIVE HANDGUN WEAPON SYSTEM (OHWS) W/SUPPRESSOR

CARTRIDGE .45 ACP (11.43×23mm)
OPERATION Short recoil
TYPE OF FIRE Semiautomatic
RATE OF FIRE 26 rpm
MUZZLE VELOCITY 886 fps (270 m/s); Special +P 1,142 fps (348 m/s)
MUZZLE ENERGY 408 ft/lb (553 J); 536 ft/lb (727 J) w/special +P load
SIGHTS Open, square-notch/blade, adjustable for windage only, may be fitted with white or luminous dot inserts, one front two rear. Insight Technology LAM (laser aiming module) with infrared and visible light lasers, target illuminator (flash-

light), weight 0.46 lb (0.21 kg) w/2 AA batteries.

FEED 12-round double-column removable
box magazine

WEIGHTS

Weapon (empty) 2.43 lb (1.21 kg)

Weapon (loaded) 3.24 lb (1.47 kg) w/loaded
magazine (Ball); 4.58 lb (2.08 kg) w/loaded
magazine (Ball), suppressor; 5.04 lb (2.29
kg) w/loaded magazine, suppressor, LAM;
1.34 lb (0.61 kg) suppressor

Magazine (empty) 0.24 lb (0.11 kg)

Magazine (loaded) .81 lb (0.367 kg) (M1911
Ball)

Service cartridge 45 Ball M1911 331 g (21.4
g); Special +P JHP (Olin) 282 gr (18.3 g)

Projectile 234 gr (15.2 g); Special +P JHP
185 gr (12 g)

LENGTHS

Weapon overall 9.65 in (24.5 cm) w/o suppressor; 15.71 in (39.9 cm) w/suppressor

Barrel 5.87 in (14.9 cm)

Suppressor length 6.61 in (16.8 cm)

Sight radius 7.76 in (19.7 cm)

Effective range 54.7 yds (50 m)

Maximum range 1,467 yds (1341 m)

Suppressor reduces sound signature from a
peak 169 db to 139 db (-30 db).

Source: Kevin Dockery

UNDERWATER DEFENSE GUN MARK 1 MOD 0

CARTRIDGE Projectile, underwater gun Mk
59 Mod 0

OPERATION Manual, double-action only
pepperbox revolver

TYPE OF FIRE Repeater

RATE OF FIRE 12 rpm

MUZZLE VELOCITY 740 fps (226 m/s)

MUZZLE ENERGY 186 ft/lb (252 J)

SIGHTS Open, U-notch/blade, fixed w/3-
yellow dots, 2-notch, 1-blade

FEED 6-round removable cylinder

WEIGHTS

Weapon (empty) 2.26 lb (1.02 kg)

Weapon (loaded) 4.17 lb (1.89 kg)

Magazine (empty) 0.56 lb (0.26 kg)

Magazine (loaded) 1.91 lb (0.87 kg)

Service cartridge 0.225 lb (0.102 kg)

Projectile 153 grains (9.9 g)

LENGTHS

Weapon overall 9.75 in (24.8 cm)

Barrel 4.25 in (10.8 cm)

Magazine cylinder 5.56 in (14.1 cm)

Magazine cylinder diameter 1.5 in (3.8 cm)

Projectile 4.25 in

Projectile diameter 0.10 in (2.54 mm) (1/8 in
[3.18mm] across fins)

Sight radius 7.5 in (19.1 cm)

Effective range 30 ft @ 60 ft depth (9.1 m @
18.3 m depth)

Source: Kevin Dockery

HECKLER & KOCH P11 ZUB UNDERWATER WEAPON

OPERATION Electrically fired
TYPE OF FIRE Repeater

RATE OF FIRE 10 rpm
MUZZLE VELOCITY 352 fps (107 m/s)
MUZZLE ENERGY 158 ft/lb (214 J)
SIGHTS Open, square-notch/blade, fixed w/luminous tritium dot inserts
FEED 5-round removable, disposable cylinder (cassette)
WEIGHTS
Weapon (loaded) 2.65 lb (1.20 kg)
Projectile 574 grains (31.2 g)
LENGTHS
Weapon overall 7.87 in (20.0 cm)
Projectile 4⅝ in (11.7 cm)
Projectile diameter 0.375 in (9.5 mm)
Sight radius 5.75 in (14.6 cm)
Effective range 33 to 49 ft (10 to 15 m) underwater 98 ft (30 m) in air

■ 4

SUBMACHINE GUNS
ON THE PENINSULA

When the North Koreans invaded the South, they pretty much caught the whole world by surprise. The U.S. government lost no time in moving military forces into the area to help bolster the flagging South Korean army. A handful of UDT operators in Japan were detailed with conducting ops against the North Koreans. It wasn't long before several of us found ourselves off the coast of Korea preparing to launch an inland demolition raid.

This wasn't something we had done a lot of training for in the UDTs—an inland raid. The demolitions part was no problem at all for us. In the UDTs, we had been working with explosives from our first days during World War II. Inland operations had been something that we had just started training for during the last months of the war. Now we had a brand-new war to fight and a new mission had come along with it.

Only four of us would be going in on this operation. It was a simple demolition of a railway close to the shore. Blowing the rails was one way we had to slow down the North Korean advance. There was a small bridge, not really much more than a low trestle, that we had planned as our target. I would be going in as the unit leader. Chief Conway would be my partner on the operation. And two other UDT operators, Sam McGivens and Pete Walker, would be the powdermen and carry the explosives.

Since this operation was going in behind enemy lines, we would go in armed, not the most common thing in the UDT at the time. I followed Chief Conway's suggestion and all of us had .38 revolvers in holsters on our pistol belts. The .38 isn't the most powerful handgun we could have taken with us, as we did have .45 caliber M1911A1 automatics available. But the revolver drains water very quickly and we were going to travel in rubber boats.

For heavy firepower, and that was the correct word, Chief Conway and I had M1A1 Thompson submachine guns. The Thompsons were just about the toughest weapons any of us had ever seen. They were machined out of a block of steel and felt like it. The damned guns must have weighed more than ten pounds apiece, and that wasn't including the ammunition. The thirty-round magazines weighed more than a pound and a half each.

For the two submachine guns, we had a bag of six magazines each. In addition, each man had a pair of Mark II fragmentation grenades, the traditional pineapple grenades. Neither McGivens nor Walker were intended to do any fighting on the operation. Their job was to put the demolitions in place and fire the charges. For that matter, there wasn't supposed to be any enemy contact at all. We had chosen a very isolated section of railway to attack. The guns we were taking along were just for self-defense and to put down covering fire while we withdrew if there was enemy contact.

Our transport ship, the APD Samuel Grimm, had a few light guns for anti-aircraft work mostly. She wasn't going to be able to enter the bay where the railway was, so the Grimm wasn't going to be able to cover us with her guns anyway. She would be standing offshore in open water, ready to pick us up once the mission was done.

Four haversacks of M1 demolition chain were going to be the explosives we took in to the target. Another pair of haversacks would be in the rubber boat for backups in case we needed them. If the trestle was wood, the planned charges were all we would need. If there were concrete parts to the construction, the extra charges might come in very handy.

One chain was going to be run along the rail while the other three charges were going to be packed in under the trestle. A pair of ten-minute time fuses was all we were going to use to fire the charges. That would give us enough time to pull back to the beach and get into our boats. The railway was only about fifty yards away from the edge of the water, right at the foot of a mountain range that ringed the little bay.

All of our preparations were ready well before the Grimm arrived off the target area. Now there was nothing to do but get in the water and move out.

There was a half-moon illuminating the waters of the Sea of Japan as we paddled our rubber boat in toward shore. Scattered clouds broke up the moonlight but we could still see well enough to stay on course. The black mountain range made a silhouette against the stars as we paddled along. The tide would be turning inside of about half an hour, so that would help us when the mission was completed and we were pulling out.

Looking around the rubber boat for a moment, I could see all of my Teammates paddling at their stations. Black camouflage makeup was smeared across everyone's face. And the green fatigue uniforms we all wore blended in well with the night. There wasn't a word spoken as we went in to shore. This was a real operation, there were enemy forces on the land in front of us who would shoot each one of my men dead if they caught us. This was something I thought about a bit as I paddled along. These men were my responsibility. I had to get them in and get them safely back out again, while still accomplishing the mission.

While I watched and thought about what we might be facing, Chief Conway must have felt me looking. From up front on the starboard side of the boat, he turned back to me. A big white grin broke across his face, a reassuring smile to let me know he had faith in his officer. Only the shine of his teeth and the whites of his eyes showed in his blacked-out face. They were a good thing to see right then.

The water was just about dead clam as we came in to shore. Chief Conway slipped into the water as we pulled up short of land. He went in as a scout to check out the beach before we brought the boat in.

Taking his weapons with him, Chief Conway slipped into the water and immediately sunk to the bottom. That damned Thompson was as heavy as an anchor. The weight of the magazines and grenades didn't exactly help you float either. But Conway was a hell of a swimmer and he quickly recovered and headed in to shore. It was a very long few minutes that we waited on that rubber boat. Then the soft flash of a red-lensed flashlight from the shore told us it was clear to bring the boat in.

This was it, we were on shore well behind enemy lines in hostile territory. I hoped my nervousness didn't show to any of the men as I took a position up on the beach next to Chief Conway. Both of us had our Thompsons up and ready. Now the weight of that gun felt pretty reassuring. There wasn't any movement on the shore or up by the railway. We could just see the black line of the railway against the lighter darkness of the mountain. Tunnels bracketed the length of trestle at either end.

Only a few hundred yards of the railway was along the beach before it entered the tunnels at either end. Bringing down the tunnels would have blocked the railway for a much longer time than our just blowing the tracks and the trestle would. But dropping a railway tunnel takes some very careful preparation and more explosives then we could have brought in with an entire UDT platoon.

The mountain range circling the bay is what kept the Air Force flyboys from being able to bomb the railway. So the mission had fallen to us and it looked like we wouldn't have a lot of trouble setting it up. McGivens and Walker brought up the explosives, haversacks hanging on either side of each of them as they came up with their pistols drawn. There was no sign of any North Korean patrols as we crouched there in the darkness. Now, it was time to get on with the mission and get the hell out of there.

The trestle was only a few feet above the rocky beach. The other side of the railway bed was firmly up against the side of the mountain. Taking up a position on the right end of the target area, I crouched down with my Thompson and kept watch on the north end of the tunnel in front of me as well as the rest of the northern beach area around us. At the other end of the target, Chief Conway was doing the same thing for the south tunnel and beach.

Setting the explosives was the only part of the operation that we had done over and over again during training. Laying out the long M1 chain of tetrytol blocks, McGivens rigged the uphill side of the railway for destruction. Walker was placing his haversacks where they would breach the downhill support structure of the trestle. Between the two sets of charges, a good length of the railway would be breached and unusable until the North Koreans could get it repaired.

Things went along fast and smooth as the men placed the charges and rigged up the detonating cord trunk lines that hooked everything together. Ten-minute fuzes would burn down to blasting caps and set off all of the explosives at once. Being two of the best powdermen in the Team, I wasn't worried at all that McGivens or Walker would make any mistakes in laying out the charges. As I kept watch, I would check over my shoulder now and then to see how they were coming along. Finally, I got the wave-in signal that the charges were set and we were ready to pull the fuze igniters.

Moving back to where the men were gathered around the firing assemblies hidden under the trestle, I took a fast look around and then waved them back to the beach. Pulling the igniters would be my responsibility once the men were back at the boat. That action started the delay and there was no turning back from that point. The charges would be going off and that railway was not going to be accepting its scheduled runs. Checking my watch, I took a last look around.

Things had been going along very well, which should have been a warning for me. As the men were about halfway back to the boats. A patrol of about six North Koreans came out of the tunnel I had been watching. They didn't see me where I was crouching down by the trestle, but they did see my men on the beach.

Shouting and pointing, four of the North Koreans pulled up long bolt-action rifles while the other two opened fire with Russian-made submachine guns. The burping sound of a PPsh-41 submachine gun was going to become very familiar to the U.N. Forces that would be fighting in Korea over the next several years. For me and my men, it was the first time we had ever heard one, and the first time a weapon had been fired in anger at any of us.

Standing up, I cut loose with a long burst from my Thompson. The muzzle flash of my weapon in the darkness blinded me for a moment. Firing from the shoulder, I just held the trigger back and pointed the weapon in the direction of the enemy. They were only about fifty yards away from me and I have no idea if I hit any one of them.

It was when the bolt slammed forward with a click that I knew the Thompson was empty. Dropping back down to my knee, I fumbled in the bag at my left hip to pull out a spare magazine. With my thumb, I pushed up on the catch above the trigger and dumped the empty magazine. I just knew that the North Koreans would be right on top of me when I raised my head again. It seemed to take forever to fit a loaded magazine into place and pull the bolt back.

While I felt I was fumbling in the dark trying to reload, Chief Conway was firing on the North Korean patrol, only he was putting out short, controlled bursts. Lifting my head, I could see that the patrol was pinned down and they weren't returning fire very well at all. I had no way of knowing that my first long burst had dropped the one sergeant with the patrol and the junior officer. Those had been the two men with the submachine guns.

With Conway keeping the Koreans' heads down, I grabbed up the firing assemblies and pulled the igniters. Waiting only long enough to see the glow and smell the smoke of the burning fuses, I pushed the assemblies back under the trestle and got ready to run for the boat.

We did a lot of swimming in the UDT. To help build up leg strength, we ran a lot when we weren't swimming. It was hard to keep up any kind of running training when you were aboard an APD transport. Right then, I told myself that we would increase the running training for the men, even aboard ship. My feet felt like lead as I moved them across the gravel and rock beach. Chief Conway could see me coming and he increased his volume of fire. Back in the rubber boat, McGivens and Walker already had the boat off the beach and turned around for launching.

Steady and by the numbers, Chief Conway kept up a hail of gunfire on the North Koreans. He didn't fumble with any magazines when he reloaded. Slipping on the rocks, I went down and skidded across the gravel. At least I had the presence of mind not to have my finger on the trigger of my Thompson when I went down. Chief Conway saw me go down and immediately got up and ran towards me. His weapon emptied as he kept firing at the North Koreans. Out in the boat, McGivens and Walker saw what was going on and they opened fire with their revolvers. It wasn't that they expected to hit anything at that range, and in the dark. But anything firing at the North Koreans helped keep their heads down.

Standing next to me, Chief Conway pulled up a grenade from the bag at his side, pulled the pin and threw it hard in the direction of the North Koreans. As I got to my feet, I felt the Chief's strong arm pulling me up. Then we were both running for the boat.

The grenade went off with a thump behind us. Whoever those North Koreans were, they seemed to be as scared as we were at that moment. Only they didn't know about the eighty pounds of high explosives along the railway behind us, or the fact that the fuses had been burning merrily along during the incident.

Finally reaching the boats, the Chief and I splashed through the water and started shoving on the rubber. As we scrambled aboard, the North Koreans behind us finally started firing again. Those long rifles of their had a lot more range than anything we carried with us. So all of us just crouched down on the tubes of the rubber boat and paddled for all we were worth.

Pulling out of sight of the Koreans, we kept paddling as the incoming fire petered out. Then we all heard a sound we had not planned for. It wasn't unusual, especially not after running into a North Korean patrol along the tracks, but the last thing we expected to heard was the sound of an oncoming train.

Moving slowly as it came out of the northern tunnel, a southbound steam train puffed out onto the trestle. The North Korean patrol must have been moving just ahead of the train as they came up to the tunnel. It didn't matter. All of us in the boat were stunned as we stopped paddling and watched the train come onto the tracks we had charged only a few minutes before.

In the UDT, we had all seen a lot of explosions during training. None of them had the same slow majesty of the train tracks blowing up as the steam engine passed over them. There was a bright orange-red flower of flame and smoke then bloomed on the tracks practically right under the engine. The engine wobbled a moment, then left the trestle and fell into the beach, plowing up the rocks and gravel before bursting apart. The white cloud of steam was shot through with red from the firebox as the engine just came apart. Behind the engine, the seven boxcars we could see just kept coming forward.

There must have been some munitions or ammunition aboard some of those boxcars because we suddenly couldn't see the beach for the blinding explosion that thundered out. Bits of rock, wood, and train rained down after being thrown high into the air. Some of the smaller pieces even splashed into the water near us as we just watched for a moment.

Dipping our paddles into the water, we headed back out towards the Grimm. This had been a hell of an operation. The results were a lot more successful than we could have hoped for. Of course, all that our success meant was that higher command gave us even more inland demolition raids to conduct.

■ 5

SUBMACHINE GUNS

The submachine gun is one of the few small arms that traces its history only through the 20th century. By the end of World War I, trench warfare had shown a need for a light, easy to handle, fast-firing shoulder weapon that had a high volume of fire. To fill this need, the submachine gun was developed.

Under its classic definition, a submachine gun is a shoulder- or hand-fired weapon capable of full-automatic fire and chambered for a pistol caliber cartridge. Early weapons tended to resemble shortened rifles and were fairly complex machinings. The general operating system for most submachine guns is mechanically simple but was made complicated in the application.

Most submachine guns use the blowback principle as their operating system. In the blowback principle, the gasses of firing make the cartridge case act much like a piston while in the chamber. The propellant gasses push the light bullet down the barrel while at the same time try to push the cartridge case out of the chamber. The heavy bolt used in the blowback system must have its inertia overcome by the pressing cartridge before it starts to move backward.

The delay time needed for the bolt to start moving backward allows time for the bullet to leave the barrel and pressures to drop down to safe levels. The backward momentum of the bolt completes extraction of the fired casing, ejects it, and comes to a stop as its energy had been absorbed by the mainspring.

If the trigger has been released, the bolt remains to the rear retaining the compressed mainspring. If the trigger is pulled or has been held back, the bolt moves forward under the pressure of the spring, stripping a cartridge from the feed device, chambering and then firing it. At this time the cycle continues until the ammunition is expended or the trigger released.

The blowback system requires a fairly heavy bolt and strong mainspring to operate safely. The bolt is held to the rear in the open position until the trigger is pulled, at which time it moves forward. This is called firing from the "open-bolt" position and is the major drawback of blowback operation. Each time the weapon is fired, the heavy bolt moves forward and slams against the breech face, jarring the weapon and making a precise first shot very difficult, if not impossible.

The firepower of the submachine gun and the fact it is intended to be fired on full automatic minimizes the open-bolt accuracy drawback. A multiple of bullets can be placed on a target in a very short time. Accuracy is achieved by firing short bursts of only a few rounds each which gives the firer a reasonably high hit probability.

The first submachine gun to come to the notice of the U.S. military was the M1921 model Thompson. Though a M1919 model had been completed some time earlier, the hostilities of World War I were over before it could see action in Europe. The Navy purchased a small quantity of M1921 Thompsons for trials with the Marine Corps. The weapons did see some limited combat in Nicaragua in 1927 and 1928. The results of the trials and testing was the Navy ordering a quantity of Thompsons modified to their specifications. Among the modifications to the M1921 Thompson were:

- Replacing the vertical forward grip with a horizontal forearm.
- A smaller recoil spring and pilot as well as a heavier bolt, reducing the cyclic rate of the weapon from 800 rounds per minute to about 600 rounds per minute.
- A one-piece buffer unit.
- Provisions for a sling with sling swivels on the weapons stocks.

The new weapon was designated the 1928A1 Thompson. In addition to the above changes, most of the M1928A1 Thompsons were fitted with the Cutts Compensator on the muzzle. The Cutts Compensator is a cylindrical device that fits over the muzzle of the Thompson and extends for some distance past it. On the top of the compensator is a series of four different-sized slots. Working with the reduced diameter of the compensator's muzzle, the slots direct some of the propellant gasses straight up. The force of the gasses help push the muzzle down and keep the weapon on target during a long burst. Though the Thompson had been described as "kicking like a horse," the weapon actually has relatively light recoil, much less than the average rifle. The lack of substantial recoil is due to the high weight of the M1928A1 and the relatively low power of the .45 ACP round it fires. What the Thompson does is rotate its muzzle upwards (climb) quickly on full-automatic fire as well as vibrate heavily from the force of firing.

The M1928A1 Thompson was adopted by the U.S. military just as World War II was beginning. The Navy issued the weapon in some numbers to both the Marine Corps and for use by ships' landing parties. Two feed devices were used on the M1928A1 Thompson, the Type L 50-round drum magazine and the type XX 20-round box magazine. The box magazine made the Thompson a fairly handy weapon but the sustained firepower of the 50-round drum made it quite popular with its Navy users. One drawback with the drum was its difficulty in being inserted quickly into the weapon and its tendency to rattle when carried.

The Thompson is an example of what is called a first-generation sub-

On board his APD transport in the Pacific Ocean during World War II, this UDT operator demonstrates his M1928A1 Thompson submachine gun. This weapon is set up in the classic Thompson style, being loaded with a 50-round Type L drum magazine. The cocking knob on the top of the receiver is in the forward, fired, position indicating that the drum is empty. This UDT operator is wearing rubber and canvas coral shoes and has a M1911/M1911A1 pistol in a leather M1912 holster.

Source: UDT-SEAL Museum

machine gun, an expensive, heavy, complex weapon made up of many milled and machined parts. What stood in the Thompsons favor was its very strong receiver and parts and good dependability. The weapon was very popular among many of the troops who were issued it, including the UDTs who used a small number of the M1928A1s for guard duty and self-defense on enemy islands. When possible, Thompsons would be begged, borrowed, traded for, or just picked up by individual UDT operators who felt a need for one.

The Thompson continued to see duty with the Navy and the UDTs well through the Korean War. By the 1960s, Many M1928A1s were feeling their age, the last one having been made for the Navy in 1945. During World War II, the difficulty and expense in producing the M1928A1 Thompson caused a search to begin for a simpler and easier to produce weapon. Some simplified Thompsons were produced during World War II, specifically the M1 and M1A1 models. But most of these weapons ended up in Marine and Army hands. A new style of submachine gun, the second-generation type, was first developed in the U.S. as the M3, commonly called the "greasegun."

Second-generation submachine guns have become the most common type of their class of weapon to be found in the world. This is due in no small part to the vast numbers of this type of weapon that were produced during World War II and throughout the 1950s. A second-generation submachine gun is characterized by being mechanically simple, made up of easily manufactured sheet metal stampings, tubing, and formed parts that are welded and riveted together. A minimum number of machined parts, usually the bolt and barrel, are in the second-generation submachine guns and the weapons are fitted with folding or sliding stocks to reduce bulk.

Because of its close resemblance to a well-known garage tool, the M3 and later M3A1 submachine guns were better known as the greasegun. The M3 was one of the simplest modern firearms ever produced by the U.S. government. The receiver of the M3 was made from two metal stampings welded together with the barrel being attached to the front of the weapon by a threaded collar. The General Motors Corporation Guide Lamp Division with their long experience in producing stamped car parts was the primary contractor for all of the M3s and M3A1s made during World War II.

Ease of manufacture stood out in the M3, as many parts were simple assemblies of stamped parts. The machined bolt with its guide rod assembly and driving springs was slipped into the receiver of the M3 from the front and held in place by the barrel being screwed down over it. The safety of the weapon was a stud on the inside of the ejection port cover. With the cover closed, the stud engaged a hole in the bolt, securing it in place. By just opening the cover, the safety was removed and the weapon was read to fire. First suggested in 1942, the M3 was in production and being received by troops in mid-1943. Though the UDTs would later receive M3 and M3A1 weapons after World War II, during the war the greasegun saw duty with tank and vehicle crews as well as Airborne, Ranger, and other Special Forces–type units.

The M3 submachine gun was further simplified and improved by a design study begun in April 1944. The bolt cocking handle assembly was removed and replaced with a finger hole drilled into the bolt. The ejection port was enlarged so that the bolt could be cocked by just putting a finger into the hole and pulling the bolt back. Other improvements were included, such as installing a magazine loading tool as part of the sliding metal stock. Even the stock was improved not only with the loading tool but one arm of the stock was drilled so that it could be used as a cleaning rod. Officially adopted in December 1944 as the M3A1 submachine gun, the M3 was put on limited standard status. By the end of World War II in Europe, the M3A1 was declared the submachine gun for all U.S. forces and would replace all earlier model in service.

One accessory for the M3 and M3A1 submachine guns was produced during World War II that would be of particular interest to the SEALs later. The long, exposed, and removable barrel of the M3 submachine gun made the weapon particularly adaptable to having an integral suppressor mounted on it. In 1942, Bell Telephone Laboratories in New York had already developed a suppressed .22 pistol for the Office of Strategic Services (OSS) and they were approached to perform the same action with the M3. The M3 suppressor was an adaptation of the Mason suppressor used on the OSS High Standard Model D suppressed pistol (see Pistols). By February 1944, six suppressed M3 submachine guns were supplied by Bell Labs to the OSS and the weapons were tested at Aberdeen Proving Grounds. The design was accepted and by April 1944, the OSS entered into a contract with the High Standard Company for the production of 1,000 suppressed barrels for the M3.

General Motors Guide Lamp supplied 1,000 specially drilled barrels to High Standard for the suppressor order. The barrels were drilled with four rows of 12¼-inch holes drilled into the bore of the barrel. The barrels were threaded at their muzzle end to accept a bushing for the attachment of the two suppressor tubes.

The 7.5-inch-long, 1.63-inch-diameter rear expansion tube was held at the breech end by a cut made into the barrel collar and was secured at the muzzle by a threaded reducing bushing. The expansion tube was filled with a wrapping of 16 mesh brass wire screen for its entire length. The front suppressor tube is 6 inches long and 1.13 inches in diameter. Attached at its rear end to the reducing bushing at the muzzle of the barrel, the front suppressor tube is closed by a metal cap with a 0.5-inch hole through its center. Inside the front suppressor tube is a stack of 30 mesh brass wire screen disks with a 0.5-inch hole in their centers.

The wire mesh screen roll and disks cooled and reduced the speed of the escaping gas when the weapon was fired, eliminating much of the muzzle blast–related noise. The mechanical noise of the M3 was not reduced in any way and the .45 ACP projectile was subsonic, eliminating any sonic crack.

Sound is measured in decibels (db) with the actual measurement of a suppressor's efficiency being dependent on several variables. In general, normal conversation can be rated at 65 db. Exposure to sounds over 115-120 db can cause hearing problems and sounds over 130 db can cause physical pain. An unsuppressed M16 is rated on this scale at 165 db and the unsuppressed M3 at a relatively quiet 130 db. With the OSS suppressed barrel installed, the M3 measures 107 db, a 23 db reduction.

Though the actual sound reduction of the OSS suppressor is not as good as present day weapons, the sound signature is unrecognizable as a firearm at fifty

The M3A1 showing the special suppressed barrel built for it during World War II. The suppressed barrel is in the same relation to the overall length of the submachine gun as it would be if mounted.
Source: Kevin Dockery

yards. Even when heard and recognized as a firearm, the OSS suppressor makes the firing position of the M3 very hard to locate.

High Standard manufactured 1,000 of the M3 suppressed barrels for the OSS by the spring of 1944. The weapons were so well received that an additional 4,000 units were ordered. Barrels were difficult to come by and Army Ordnance was reluctant to release the necessary numbers. By 1945, the barrels became available and High Standard manufactured an additional 4,000 suppressed M3 barrels.

Except for two flats cut into the barrel collar, allowing the wire stock to be used as a disassembly wrench, there is no difference between the barrel assemblies of the M3 and M3A1 submachine guns. The M3A1 weapon was just as easily fitted with the suppressed OSS barrel and this weapon has continued to see duty as a suppressed weapon with the U.S. forces past the Vietnam War.

The M3A1 submachine gun had seen some duty with the UDTs in Korea and was still retained in the Navy armories for use by the Teams when needed. The slow cyclic rate of fire of the M3 and M3A1 weapons allowed single shots to be fired by just releasing the trigger quickly, and the weapon was quick and easy to handle. The magazines of both the M3 and M3A1 were identical and both had their difficulties. A slight dent to the feed lips of the M3 magazine could easily cause a malfunction and jam the weapon with a misfed round. In addition to the possible feeding problem, the M3 magazines were considered just plain heavy by the weight-conscious UDTs and SEALs. When the SEAL Teams were commissioned in 1962, M3 submachine guns were included in the original allowance lists and were among the first weapons to show up at the new Teams.

> The first weapons that we received were some .45 caliber M3 greasegun submachine guns that at the Navy sent us and the AR-15 rifle. The greaseguns we considered just too heavy for our purposes, especially the loaded magazines. Though we kept some around, no one I knew really wanted the greasegun.

The greasegun remained with the Teams throughout the Vietnam War. Occasionally, an individual operator would like the firepower of the M3 and carry the weapon for a specific mission by preference. Training was continued on the

M3 and M3A1 weapons well into the 1970s, but the greasegun was considered an obsolete weapon by 1974. During the early combat tours of SEAL platoons in Vietnam, the M3A1 saw some popularity as the only easily available suppressed weapon. New weapons had been fitted with the old OSS suppressed barrels and worked just as well as when they had left the High Standard plant in World War II. During 1967, when a SEAL mission called for a suppressed weapon, the OSS M3A1 was what was available, and even they were in short supply.

During my first tour, the M3A1 greasegun with the World War Two OSS silencer was the only suppressed weapon we had been able to get our hands on. And the operation we had the suppressed greaseguns for was scrubbed.

Though some firearms training was given to the men of the UDTs during the late 1940s and through the 1950s, it was fairly limited in scope. The primary tool of the UDT operator was explosives and not small arms. When the SEALs were commissioned, this attitude changed greatly. SEALs were trained on all types of weapons, both foreign and domestic. Initial small arms training was conducted by the Teams themselves at Navy or Marine facilities. Training in depth was conducted for the first SEALs at the Army Special Warfare Training Center at Fort Bragg, North Carolina.

The whole of SEAL Team Two went to Fort Bragg in September, 1962. Among the training they received was instruction in small arms. The instruction was comprehensive, detailed, and complete, and the SEALs were an avid audience.

The course (at Ft. Bragg) was a two-week block of instruction in foreign small arms familiarization, firing, field stripping, unconventional warfare, and kitchen table demolitions (improvised munitions). . . . The instructors gave us a complete course of instruction in U.S. and foreign weapons. The French MAT-49, British STEN Mark II, German MP40 (Schmeisser) and Swedish K were among the submachine guns taught to us along with the American M3 greasegun and M1928A1 Thompson. Before then we had almost no experience with submachine guns. But once the instructors showed us how to load the weapons and which end the bullets came out of, we had little trouble qualifying as experts on the Army ranges.

Many of the SEALs developed a lasting fondness for the compact firepower of submachine guns after the Fort Bragg training. Some of the weapons taught at the course were chosen for their likelihood of appearing in guerrilla hands somewhere in the world.

The MP40, along with its earlier versions the MP38 and MP38/40 are considered among the very first of the second-generation submachine guns. The MP in their designation comes from the European naming of the submachine gun a machine pistol or "maschinen pistolen" in German. The MP40 family was the standard submachine gun of the German forces in World War II and was first issued in 1938. Made up of plastic castings and stamped metal parts, the MP38 was a far cry from the precision machined found in most German weapons prior to 1938.

Operating efficiently from a simple blowback action, the MP38 field stripped into only five major parts including its magazine. The simplicity and ease of manufacture of the MP38 family was not lost on the Allies. Captured examples of the German weapon were studied in England and the USA. In England, the MP38 led to the development of the STEN series of submachine guns. In the United States, the M3 submachine gun owes some of its development to the MP38 and MP40. Over one million of the German MP38, MP 38/40, and MP 40 weapons were manufactured in the years between 1938 and 1945. Several postwar armies outfitted their men completely with captured German weapons including the MP40. As time progressed, thousands of the World War II weapons found their way into guerrilla hands including those of the Viet Cong. A number of German MP40s were captured in Vietnam more than twenty years and half a world away from where they had been made.

Two other submachine guns the SEALs trained with first at Fort Bragg later turned up in enemy hands in Vietnam. The Danish Madsen Model 1950 was the improved model of the Madsen Model 1946. The Madsen was developed in Denmark after World War II as a possible commercial venture. The Danish Police forces picked up the Model 1950 and it did see some sales in South America and Southeast Asia. Two items in its design cause the Model 1950 to stand out: the forward bolt safety and method of field stripping.

For increased safety, the Model 1950 has a large bolt safety lever just behind the magazine well. The lever must be held in against the magazine well or the bolt will not move, whether it is in the open or closed position. Though the bolt safety requires the Madsen M1950 be held with both hands in order to be operated, the magazine well acts as a front hand grip, the safety prevents the weapon from being accidentally discharged if dropped or struck sharply on the butt.

To field strip the Madsen M1950, the magazine is first removed and then the barrel nut unscrewed. With the barrel removed and the magazine catch held back, the two stamped metal sides of the Madsen unfold like a book, hinged at the rear. This unusual system allows the Madsen to be thoroughly cleaned more easily than most other weapons of its class. The fact that the Madsen M1946 and M1950 saw sales in reasonable numbers in Southeast Asia, notably Thailand and Indonesia, allowed the weapon to make its way into VC hands in some numbers.

The French Army needed to be rebuilt after World War II with a need for a concurrent development of French small arms to equip it with. Though the French military made do with a mix of American and ex-German weapons immediately postwar, new French designs became available within a few years.

By 1949, after several other weapons had been tried, the French Military settled on the MAT (Manufacture Nationale d'Armes de Tulle) Model 1949, commonly called the MAT 49. Composed primarily of metal stampings and having a rectangular cross-section receiver, the MAT 49 operates as a standard submachine gun with only a few unusual features. On the back edge of the rear pistol grip is a grip safety. Unless the grip safety is held in by the firing hand, the sear is blocked and the bolt will not move either forward to fire or backwards to cock.

The forward hand grip of the MAT 49 is the magazine well and has a pivot on its front top edge. By pressing a catch in front of the trigger guard, the magazine well, complete with the magazine, can be pivoted forward and locked in place underneath the barrel jacket. This feature renders the MAT 49 absolutely safe against accidental discharge and also makes the weapon a very compact package.

The MAT 49 remained the standard submachine gun of the French forces up to the present day where it is still seen in both police and military hands. After the French withdrawal from Indochina, thousands of MAT 49s ended up in Viet Cong and North Vietnamese hands. So many MAT 49s were in the hands of the Communist forces in Vietnam that they found it worthwhile to convert a number of the weapons to a communist caliber. The converted MAT 49 has a longer 10.24 inch (26 cm) barrel chambered for the 7.62mm Short (7.62×25mm) round. Other than the longer barrel giving an additional 2.05 inches (5.2 cm) to the overall length of the converted MAT-49, the weapon remains essentially the same as the French model.

One submachine gun that was introduced to the SEALs at Fort Bragg remained in their inventory through the Vietnam War. The Swedish Model 45, also known in Europe as the Carl Gustav, was commonly called by the SEALs the Swedish K. The SEALs had a few Swedish Ks in their arms inventory as early as 1964 and the weapon was well liked by a number of SEALs who used them.

Though the Swedish K has few outstanding features, it is a simple and robust weapon that showed good reliability in a bad environment.

Sweden, officially neutral during World War II, saw a need for increasing its armed forces to help defend its neutrality and required a simple submachine gun designed for mass production. Actually put into production after World War II, the Model 45 is a straightforward second-generation submachine gun that was made in a number of slightly different models. The most common variation of the Swedish K seen in the U.S. military was the M45b model. In the M45b, the weapon had a removable magazine well, secured in place by a U-shaped wire clip. By removing the magazine well, the M45b could accept the earlier Suomi 50-round box magazine that had been in Swedish service prior to the M45 being adopted. Later models of the Swedish K had permanently attached magazine wells and only accepted the standard 36-round box magazine. None of the 50-round Suomi magazines were known to be in U.S. service.

The Swedish K had appeal to the SEALs for two reasons, one of which was its being chambered for the 9mm parabellum round. In addition, the Swedish K was found worldwide and had even been produced in Egypt and Indonesia. The U.S. Intelligence community issued the Swedish K as a sterile weapon with no direct ties to the USA. In addition to issuing the standard Swedish K, the CIA had a several different special suppressed versions available. Individual SEAL operators would occasionally use the suppressed Swedish K, especially when operation on intelligence missions with CIA assets.

The exposed barrel attached to the receiver by a threaded collar gives the same advantages to suppressing the Swedish K as was found on the M3 submachine gun by Bell Labs over twenty years earlier. But the Swedish K fires a supersonic round rather than the subsonic .45 ACP used by the greasegun. To prevent the need for a special ammunition to be issued for maximum noise reduction in the suppressed Swedish K, the muzzle velocity of the weapon while firing standard ammunition was lowered by porting the barrel.

In porting a barrel, sufficient gasses are bled off to reduce the velocity of a supersonic round to a subsonic level. One suppressed barrel (the production model) used on the Swedish K had four rows of twelve 0.188 inch holes drilled along its length. Later, another designing team found that by placing four 0.125 inch holes just in front of the chamber of the barrel and drilled into the bore at an angle of 10 degrees, the average velocity of a projectile was reduced below that of sound while maintaining maximum accuracy.

The most common suppressor used on the Swedish K greatly resembled the Bell Labs suppressor used on the M3/M3A1 greasegun and was referred to in a study as the production suppressor. The rear expansion tube of the production suppressor surrounded the ported barrel and contained a roll of stainless steel mesh screen. The forward suppressor tube was held to the rear tube by a reduction bushing. The forward tube was filled with stainless steel mesh washers that eliminated much of the muzzle blast.

Several different suppressors were used on the Swedish K by the U.S. forces. Any one of the suppressed Swedish Ks would be used by the SEALs when needed. The preferred model was the one described above, the production suppressor, and is identified by having the suppressor built out of two different diameter tubes. Another model suppressor used on the Swedish K can be identified by its having a group of porting holes just behind the muzzle on the side of the suppressor tube.

Prior to the Teams sending direct action platoons to Vietnam, there was little training given with submachine guns. Though the men were generally trained in how to operate a wide variety of weapons including submachine guns, little emphasis was placed on operating in direct combat. With the commitment to Vietnam changing the operations of the SEALs practically overnight, training changed to prepare the men for operations. Small arms training changed from general knowledge and marksmanship to reaction training against popup targets with a variety of weapons.

> For our submachine gun pop-up course B—set it up so that you not only learned the proper way of shooting a submachine gun, but you also became very familiar with handling a variety of weapons. On the range were a Schmeisser MP40, a Mat-49, a STEN Mark II, and a greasegun. To run the course, you were given a single magazine for each weapon. Starting the e course with, say, a Sten gun, you would walk along a trail, shooting at targets as they popped up. When the order was shouted to "change weapons" there would be another different weapon somewhere at your feet. You would have to quickly load the weapon with the proper magazine. And lord help you if you tried to use the wrong magazine, that sharp-eyed Eagle was just waiting to catch you doing something like that.
>
> Very quickly, the whole squad became proficient at using different submachine guns and loading them by feel alone.

Submachine guns soon became a favorite with a number of SEALs operating in Vietnam. The Swedish K was the most popular weapon used, especially when on "sterile" ops where Americans did not wish to be identified by their equipment. A problem arose with the Swedish K that had nothing to do with the functioning or design of the weapon.

The Swedish government, having a law stating that they would not supply weapons to either side in a conflict, refused to sell any more weapons to the United States during the Vietnam War. The Navy had been looking at purchasing a quantity of Swedish Ks for the Teams but were stopped by the Swedish law. The number of spare parts for the Swedish Ks in use was limited and the SEALs looked to U.S. companies to supply them with a replacement weapon.

Smith & Wesson saw that a possible market existed for an American-made submachine gun with the U.S. police market as well as the military. By June 24, 1968, Smith & Wesson had released their Model 76 submachine gun onto the market. Developed in part with the SEALs in mind, the Smith & Wesson Model 76 is a very close duplicate of the proven Swedish K design. The magazines are almost interchangeable between the two weapons and the overall features are very similar.

One significant change in the Smith & Wesson Model 76 over the Swedish K is the S&W weapon incorporates a selector lever. Where the Swedish K fires full-auto only, the Model 76 can be set to semi or full automatic. In the S&W weapon, the selector also can be set on safe while the safety on the Swedish K was a notch the cocking lever could be moved up into.

The receiver of the Model 76 is made of thick-walled steel tubing with the additional housing parts welded onto it. Early model weapons have a bare barrel sticking forward from the barrel collar. Later production model weapons had a distinctive perforated barrel jacket. The barrel jacket was intended to help protect an operator from the hot barrel while still allowing free circulation of air for cooling. The high cyclic rate of fire of the Model 76 helped make the weapon popular for its fast volume of fire but also quickly heated up the barrel.

The S&W Model 76 was type

During the latter part of the Vietnam War, this SEAL is armed with a production model Smith & Wesson Model 76 submachine gun (Mark 24). The bolt is forward in the uncocked (fired) position and the folding stock of the weapon is extended. At the left shoulder strap of his nylon M1967 Modernized Load Carrying Equipment (MLCE) harness this SEAL has attached an SDU-5/E strobe light in its pouch.

Source: UDT SEAL Museum

classified by the Navy as the Gun, Submachine, 9 millimeter, Mark 24 Mod 0 on 24 March 1970. In addition to having four magazines issued with the weapon, reported a suppressor and ported barrel were also issued for each SEAL Mark 24. Mounting the suppressor onto the Mark 24 just required the operator to unscrew the barrel collar and jacket from the front of the receiver, remove the barrel, insert the ported barrel, and screw on the suppressor in place of the barrel jacket.

The ported barrel of the Mark 24 has eight 0.093 inch holes drilled into the barrel one inch in front of the chamber at a 30 degree angle to the bore and reduced standard 9mm ammunition to subsonic velocities. The suppressor body was sealed and required almost no maintenance by the operator. In addition, the suppressor was made of stainless steel, minimizing problems with corrosion. The sights of the Mark 24 are both mounted on the receiver body and no sighting change was required when the suppressor was installed.

Smith & Wesson only produced about 6,000 Model 76 submachine guns before they suspended production on July 5, 1976. The weapon remained with the Teams throughout the 1970s and into the 1980s. Replacement parts were getting scarce by the early 1980s and SEAL Team One contracted with a manufacturer to produce a number of much-needed parts. By the late 1980s, the last of the Mark 24 Mod 0 submachine guns were out of the SEAL inventory.

By the early 1970s, the SEAL Teams were looking for an additional 9mm submachine gun to supplement the Smith & Wesson Model 76s on hand. A very compact submachine gun, almost a machine pistol, had been on the U.S. arms market for only a few years and was examined by the SEALs. The weapon was the Ingram Model 10 in 9mm parabellum. The weapon itself was not exactly new to the SEALs as at least two of their number had examined one in mid-1967.

"Frankford Arsenal gave R—and I the opportunity to fire the first small Ingram submachine gun. 'Nice weapon,' we said, 'But it needs a front strap to give you something to hold on to.'"

The weapon examined was probably M10 9mm gun number 2, which had been purchased by the U.S. Army and was at Frankford Arsenal in Philadelphia for further study. Gordon Ingram, the designer of the M10, did later add a web strap to the front of the compact weapon to give it an additional handhold.

Third-generation submachine guns are advances on the second-generation models with emphasis being placed on reducing overall size and weight. The main identifying feature of a third-generation weapon is its use of a telescoping bolt. In a telescoping bolt, instead of the breech face being on the end of the bolt, it is further back inside of the bolt body. With the bolt face inside of the bolt body, part of the mass of the bolt surrounds and telescopes on the barrel. With the bolt wrapping itself around the barrel, the weight of the bolt can be kept high enough for safe blowback operation while shortening the overall length of the weapon.

The Ingram is a third-generation submachine gun and a particularly compact example of the type. The single pistol grip acts as the magazine well maintaining the center of balance of the weapon just above the grip. The web strap just below the muzzle of the Ingram acts as a forward grip to keep the nonfiring hand from straying in front of the barrel. Bracing the M10 against the shoulder is possible, but not very comfortable, by using the short sliding stock attached to the back of the weapon.

The receiver of the M10 is square in cross section and made of stamped sheet metal parts. The bolt of the Ingram is an investment casting, which helps keep the overall cost of the weapon down. The short bolt travel, relatively light bolt, and small recoil spring of the M10 combine to give the weapon a very high cyclic rate of fire. The 9mm M10 cycles at 1,050 rounds per minute and the .45 ACP version, built on the same receiver, cycles at 1,145 rounds per minute.

The very high cyclic rate of the Ingram makes it a high volume of fire weapon but has a drawback in that the magazine can be emptied in under two seconds. For breaking contact with an enemy, such a high volume of fire has some distinct advantages, and this was one of the reasons the weapon appealed to the SEALs. Another reason was one of the accessories that had already been designed for the weapon.

When Gordon Ingram went to Sionics Inc. in 1969 to complete the design of the submachine gun that would bear his name, the company was already producing a line of suppressors for the U.S. government. Prior to the Ingram submachine gun being ready to go into production in 1970, the company changed its name to the Military Armament Corporation (MAC). When first marketed,

In the 1970's, a SEAL tries out a suppressed Ingram submachine gun from the assault position at the range. The weapon is an Ingram M10 chambered for .45 ACP. The SEAL has the sliding stock extended and braced under his right arm. His left hand is holding the Sionics suppressor and he has just completed a short burst, three fired casings being in the air above the weapon.
Source: U.S. Navy

the Ingram weapons were offered along with a MAC-designed suppressor specifically engineered to the different calibers of Ingrams available. Each Ingram M10 submachine gun had a short length of screw thread at the muzzle of the weapon in order to accept the MAC suppressor.

The internal design of the MAC suppressor was quite complicated. The different parts of the system had been developed and used by Sionics Inc. for a number of years and had been field tested in Vietnam on the M16 and M14 rifles. As in the Sionic rifle caliber suppressors the M10 suppressor is a muzzle blast device only and does not affect the velocity of the fired projectile.

The M10 suppressor has two chambers, much as in the earlier Bell Labs M3 OSS suppressor. The rear tube of the suppressor is a large 2-inch diameter by 3.75-inch-long expansion chamber with a perforated barrel extension running down its center. The rear portion of the barrel extension is a threaded sleeve that fits over the muzzle of the weapon. At the front of the barrel extension is a perforated reducing bushing that threads onto the extension and clamps the rear tube between itself and the rear sleeve.

Contained within the rear tube and secured by the two end pieces are several hundred "baffles," actually uncrimped lightweight metal eyelets. The eyelets act as a heat diffuser, cooling and slowing the initial blast of propellant gas. After the projectile has gone through the rear diffuser tube, it passes into the front suppressor tube. The hot gasses following the projectile are constantly expanding and, after initial passage through the diffuser tube, pass through the reduction bushing. The reduction bushing has a twelve radial 0.188-inch holes drilled around the central tube. The hot gasses are further slowed down as they bleed through the smaller radial holes as well as the large central projectile hole.

In the 7-inch long, 1.5-inch inside diameter suppressor tube is first a conical baffle and then two spiral diffuser assemblies. The baffle is a hollow disk with a conical central protrusion surrounding the projectile hole. The action of the baffle is to further trap and diffuse the propellant gasses while also absorbing some of their heat.

The two spiral diffusers in front of the baffle disk are mirror images of each other. Both diffusers are aluminum spiral helixes about 2 inches long, one having a left hand spiral and the other a right hand spiral. A hole goes through the center of each diffuser to allow for the passage of the projectile and 0.125 inch holes are spaced 90 degrees apart between each vane to aid is gas dispersion. The reason behind the spirals is that they present a very large surface area to the propellant gasses to help cool and slow them. The two different spirals theoretically cause an additional slight slowing of the propellant gasses as the change direction.

Holding the diffusers in place is an "encapsulator" containing a single flexible $\frac{1}{4}$-inch-thick plastic wipe with a central $\frac{1}{4}$-inch hole. Holding the encapsulator in place is the end cap also with two plastic wipes. The end cap wipes are spaced $\frac{1}{2}$-inch apart and are of the same material and design as the wipe in the encapsulator.

As the M10 suppressor absorbs a great deal of the heat from the propellant gasses, the exterior of the tubes becomes very hot. To protect the operator, the outside of the suppressor is covered with an insulating, heat-resistant Nomex sleeve.

Using the suppressor with the M10 submachine gun cuts down on the sound of firing considerably. At a distance, the weapon is unlikely to be noticed. If the sound of firing the suppressed Ingram is recognized for what it is, the suppressor makes the location of the firer very hard to point out. By using subsonic 9mm ammunition, the weapon is even quieter as the sonic crack of the projectile is eliminated.

Though the Ingram was a very compact and easy to carry weapon, it had the drawback of relatively poor accuracy. Jokingly called the "phone booth gun" by some Special Forces troopers, the general opinion was that you had to be inside of a phone booth, along with you target, to be sure of hitting it with the rapid-firing little Ingram. But for a SEAL scout swimmer, the size of the Ingram was what gave it an advantage. And when used with its suppressor, the little M10 could put out a fast hail of bullets, helping a SEAL break contact and withdraw from an unwanted conflict.

For most reconnaissance work, contact with the enemy is something to be avoided if at all possible. But if contact is inevitable, the SEAL philosophy is to put out the greatest volume of fire possible in the shortest time. That philosophy, along with close-in personal defense, is exactly what the Ingram was designed for.

With the end of the 1970s, a new mission for the SEALs arose, and with it a need for new hardware. Terrorism on an international scale had been building in intensity during the 1970s and a new force of counterterrorist units were needed to combat the threat. Most of the Free World's counterterrorist units were taken from the ranks of elite military services. The SAS in Great Britain, GSG-9 in West Germany, SEAL Team Six, and Special Forces Operational Detachment Delta in the United States are all examples of the military response to global terrorism.

One of the most highly visible early actions of a counterterrorist unit took place in Great Britain in 1980. The Iranian Embassy in London was seized by a number of terrorists and, when the situation was decided to warrant it, the SAS Counter Revolutionary Warfare (CRW) units were ordered in.

Plainly visible in the photographs taken by the press of Operation Nimrod on May 5, 1980 are the members of the SAS Pagoda Teams, their arms, and equipment. That the Heckler and Koch MP5A3 was the primary weapon of the CRW troops could be clearly seen in the striking videos and still photographs of the operation. Though not as widely shown, an earlier use of the MP5 weapon had shown its capabilities in a counterterrorist operation. When the German GSG-9 group attacked the terrorist-held Lufthansa airliner at Mogadishu, Somalia on October 17, 1977, it was not only the first time stun grenades were used against terrorists but it was the blooding, the first combat USC of the MP5 as well.

When the SEALs were looking to equip their new counterterrorist unit, input from many of the already established units was encouraged and accepted. The German GSG-9 group worked closely with the SEALs of Team Six and the German group highly recommended the Heckler & Koch submachine gun family. The MP5A3 was already in the U.S. inventory in small numbers by the late 1970s. A number of the H&K weapons had been purchased by the Department of Defense for Army Special Forces, Rangers, and other special operations units. SEAL Team Six ordered there weapons from the H&K facility in Oberndorf, West Germany. Assistance from the GSG-9 group expedited the delivery of the weapons to Team Six.

The Heckler & Koch MP5 submachine gun is part of a family of weapons with a commonality of operating systems. Most of the standard H&K small arms resemble each other in their general operation, controls, and sighting systems. The basic operating system of the H&K small-arms family centers around the concept of delayed blowback through roller locking.

In the closing months of World War II, the German military was developing a new assault rifle, the Stg 45(m), with the Mauser-developed Gerat 06H being the most likely contender. After the war and the fall of Nazi Germany the designers of the Gerat 06 went to the CETME arms works in Spain where the design was perfected.

The Stg 45(m) utilized much the same Stecke roller locking system of the battle proved MG-42 light machine gun but was chambered for the 7.92×33mm Kurz assault rifle cartridge. The weapon first produced by CETME was chambered for a round of ammunition that was never widely accepted and soon died out. The basic CETME design was modified and perfected for use with the new NATO 7.62×51mm round and was submitted for trials with the new German army.

The rechambering and redesign of the CETME was accomplished in Germany by the new Heckler & Koch company as their first major weapons development. The new rifle passed all tests and was adopted by the German military as the G3.

The roller locking system does not actually lock the bolt to the barrel at the moment of firing. Instead it is a form of delayed blowback that carries with it some substantial problems. Without the camming action of a rotating bolt to help initiate extraction, fired cases tend to stick in the chamber. This problem is solved in the H&K system by the chamber being cut with a series of longitudinal flutes along ⅔ of its length. The flutes allow the hot propellant gasses to flow along the body of the cartridge along the area of most expansion. This system "floats" the casing on a layer of gas and eases extraction.

The fluted chamber/gas flotation system eliminates much of the sticking case problem but the roller locking system also has a very violent case ejection. Casings ejected from a H&K weapon are often dented and have a series of very distinguishing marks on them indicating the type of weapon they were fired from. The violent case ejection is not considered a problem among operators who use the H&K weapons, as long as you're not on the right side of someone else who is firing one.

The heart of the roller locking system works is the two movable rollers in the sides of the bolt. The rollers are driven partway into locking recesses in the barrel extension by the forward movement of the wedge-shaped locking piece that carries the firing pin. When the locking piece has moved forward enough to allow the firing pin to reach the chambered cartridge, the rollers are pressing securely into their respective recesses, blocking any rearward movement of the bolt.

The rearward pressure of the cartridge being fired presses against the bolt and drives the rollers against the rear of the recesses in the barrel extension. The rear surfaces of the barrel extension recesses are slightly angled and allow the rollers to force themselves inward against the locking piece. The force of the rollers drives the locking piece backwards but at a great mechanical disadvantage to the pressure on the rollers. The disadvantage the rollers have to work against slow the opening of the breech until the bullet has left the barrel and pressures have dropped to safe levels.

Inertia of the bolt carrier continues the rearward travel of the bolt, extracting and ejecting the fired casing. As the bolt carrier continues its rearward movement, it recocks the hammer. When the bolt carrier starts to move forward under the pressure of the recoil spring, the bolt strips a fresh round from the magazine and chambers it. As the bolt carrier closes, it forces the locking piece forward, securing the system. If the trigger has remained pulled, the bolt carrier trips the hammer release as the bolt goes fully into battery.

The roller locking, delayed blowback system has been applied by Heckler & Koch to a large family of weapons including light machine guns, rifles, submachine guns, and pistols. With the roller locking system eliminating the need for the heavy bolt found in most blowback-operated submachine guns, the MP5 is lighter than many weapons of its class. But the major advantage is that the MP5 weapons all fire from the closed-bolt position.

Firing from a closed bolt eliminates the sight-jarring slam of a heavy bolt moving forward before the first round is fired as happens in an open-bolt system. This means the MP5 has excellent accuracy for the first round fired in a burst. It is the inherent accuracy in the system that makes the MP5 weapon so popular among the world's counterterrorist forces. The accuracy and reliability of the H&K MP5 submachine gun are what has made the weapon so popular with the SEALs.

Another point of appeal in the MP5's favor is all of the variations in which the basic weapon is offered. Over a dozen different variations exist, all using the same basic action and operating system. This commonality of operation allows quick familiarity with a different member of the weapons family by anyone trained in one weapon's operation. A partial listing of all of the Heckler & Koch MP5 weapons includes the following:

HK-54—This was the original designation for the first submachine gun made by H&K and was later modified to the MP5 configuration.

MP5A1—This model has a receiver cap and no buttstock giving it the shortest overall length of the standard MP5s.

MP5A2—The standard MP5 with a fixed buttstock.

MP5A3—The standard model fitted with a retractable sliding metal buttstock.

MP5A4—The newer model MP5 with a fixed buttstock and a new trigger group among other improvements. The new trigger group allows semiautomatic fire, 3-round controlled bursts, or full automatic fire to be selected.

MP5A5—The newer model MP5 with a retractable sliding metal buttstock and controlled burst trigger group.

MP5SD1—The suppressed version of the MP5 with an integral suppressor and receiver cap.

MP5SD2—The suppressed version with a fixed buttstock.

MP5SD3—The suppressed version with a retractable metal stock.

MP5SD4—The suppressed version with a receiver cap and controlled burst trigger group.

MP5SD5—The suppressed version with a controlled burst trigger group and fixed buttstock.

MP5SD6—Suppressed version with a controlled burst trigger group and retractable buttstock.

MP5K—The shortest MP5 with no buttstock and a vertical front grip as well as adjustable sights.

MP5KA1—Shortened MP5 with nonadjustable, low, nonadjustable sights for maximum concealability.

MP5KA4—Shortened MP5 with adjustable sights and controlled burst trigger group.

MP5KA5—Shortened MP5 with the small nonadjustable sights and controlled burst trigger group.

In addition to the weapons listed, Heckler & Koch make a very comprehensive line of accessories for the MP5 weapon to which they are continually adding. At the present time the list includes the following:

Magazine clips for holding two magazines together parallel to each other

Blank firing adaptors

Tear gas canister launchers

Rifle grenade launchers

Removable aiming point projectors

Removable telescopic sights

Two types of briefcases that can carry an MP5K and fire it while concealed

Removable starlight scopes

A subcaliber device firing .22 long rifle ammunition that can be fitted to any standard MP5 and allow it to fire .22s instead of 9×19mm ammunition

An infrared sighting scope

A replacement front grip with a built-in flashlight for aiming or illumination

A miniature laser sight (for use with night-vision goggles) that is built into the weapon

Only a few of the accessories listed were available when the SEAL first started receiving the MP5 weapons. As their weapons began arriving from Germany, SEAL Team Six became the first SEAL Team to use the MP5 as its standard weapon.

The first model MP5 to see service with the SEALs of Team Six was the MP5A3. With its sliding stock, the MP5A3 can make a compact package for transportation when size is a consideration. The MP5A3 was first issued with what is called the SEF trigger group. In the MP5 system, the trigger group containing the complete trigger mechanism, is removable from the weapon for cleaning. As new trigger groups have been developed, they can be added to earlier weapons in order to easily upgrade them.

The name SEF for the most common MP5 trigger group comes from the three letters imprinted on the frame sides: a white S and a red E and F. Since the H&K MP5 is originally a German weapon, the words the letters stand for are German. The S stands for Sicher (safe) with the white color indicating no fire. The E is for Einzelfeuer (single fire) and F indicates Feuerstößen (bursts of fire). Both the E and F are printed in red indicating they are live firing positions.

The SEF trigger group also holds the pistol grip. The SEF pistol grip has finger swells on the front strap and a thumbrest of the left upper side for the thumb of the right hand. The fire selector lever is on the left side of the trigger group, just above the trigger itself. The location of the fire selector lever makes it very easy to operate with just the thumb of the firing hand. On butt end of the fire selector shaft has an indicator notch cut into it where it is exposed on the right side of the trigger group. The SEF markings are duplicated on the right side of the trigger group so that the setting of the fire selector lever can be seen at a glance.

The front handguard is a slim, deeply checkered design that inserts into the frame just forward of the magazine well and is held in place by a locking pin just behind and below the front sight. Above the front handguard, on the left side of the weapon, is the cocking lever. Drawing the lever to the rear and releasing it loads the MP5 and cocks the firing mechanism.

When the last shot is fired by the MP5, the bolt does not stay locked to the rear and closes on the empty chamber. By drawing the cocking lever to the rear an pushing it up, the lever can be seated in a notch, locking the bolt open. As the MP5 is fired, the cocking lever does not reciprocate with the bolt and remains in the forward position unless drawn back by hand.

The muzzle of the standard MP5 series has three lugs running concentrically around the barrel. The lugs act as a locking surface for mounting several of the muzzle devices offered by H&K. These devices include a blank firing adaptor, a spigot-type rifle grenade launcher, and a flash hider. The only one of the muzzle devices commonly seen used by the SEALs is the flash hider, used on all the standard MP5s issued in the Teams.

On the left side of the magazine well of the MP5 is a rear-pointing spring metal hook. The hook is only used as part of the H&K multipurpose carry sling. A sliding square buckle clips into the hook on the MP5. With the sling properly adjusted, the MP5 can be carried across the chest in a "port arms" position with the muzzle tilted up and to the left. By just grabbing the weapon by the handguard and pistol grip and pushing the weapon away from the body, the sling loop pops off the clip, releasing the weapon. The MP5 can be easily carried and quickly brought to the shoulder with this method. In addition, if the weapon is dropped after being shouldered, the sling remains attached and holds the MP5 down by the operator's side.

The rear sight of the MP5 is ad-

Keeping his eyes held low, this combat swimmer is coming ashore after having just left the water during a demonstration. His weapon is an H&K MP5K with its 30-round magazine additionally secured in place with tape for the demonstration. The open ejection port shows that the bolt of this weapon was removed for the public demonstration. Hanging from around his neck, just to the side of his chin, is this SEAL's diving mask. Hanging low on his chest is the hard black casing of a Draeger LAR-V rebreather. The green-painted oxygen tank of the Draeger can be seen underneath the casing of the device with its chromed valve on the right side where it can be easily reached with the operator's hand.
Source: Kevin Dockery

justable by being loosened with a screwdriver and moved into position. Though the drum-type rear sight has several different sized holes, the all go to the same point of aim with the front sight post. The different sized holes can be changed by the operator to account for different levels of light as well as where the operator places his head on the weapon's stock. In front of the rear sight are two mounting flats on the upper part of the receiver. The two flats allow the standard H&K scope mount to be securely fastened to the weapon. In addition to the scope, other aiming devices such as lights or night-vision devices can also be mounted on the MP5.

The other full-size MP5 first used in the Teams by Team Six was the suppressed MP5SD3. The SD series of MP5s is the standard weapon fitted with an integral barrel suppressor. The designation SD stands for Schalldämpfer, the German word for silencer. A very popular weapon for covert operations with the Teams, the MP5SD weapons are considered some of the best suppressed submachine guns in the world.

The MP5SD is intended to be used with NATO standard 9mm ammunition. To eliminate the sound of the sonic crack of the bullet, the SD has a ported barrel to limit the velocity of the projectile to below the speed of sound. A series of thirty 0.118 inch (3mm) holes are drilled into the bore of the barrel a short distance in front of the chamber.

The body of the suppressor is a 12-inch-long aluminum tube, threaded at the breech end and covered over at the muzzle with a convex cap. The suppressor fits over the barrel and screws into a threaded seat at the front of the receiver. To insure a gas-tight seal, a rubber O-ring at the base of the threaded section seats itself just into the suppressor base.

The rear section of the suppressor body, the part that surrounds the barrel, is an expansion chamber for the bleed holes on the barrel. From the muzzle forward, the suppressor has an internal baffle assembly made from a section of square metal tubing. In the German patent drawings for the SD suppressor, the square tubing is shown having four baffles made up of two opposite walls of the tube cut free and folded in toward the centerline of the tube. The cut sections form a V-shape with the apex of the V pointing at the chamber. The center of the V baffle has a bullet clearance hole for free passage of the projectile.

Each baffle in the suppressor alternates in orientation 90 degrees from the one in front and behind it. Surrounding the baffle tube assembly is an open space between the assembly and the suppressor body to allow the gasses room to expand. As the propellant gasses impinge on the suppressor baffles, they are forced to change direction and cool as they move across the metal.

The rear section of the MP5SD weapons are exactly the same as the regular MP5 weapons. The only internal action change in the SD weapons being a slightly different roller assembly to operate with the reduced gas pressure from the bled-off barrel. The front of the MP5SD receivers is modified to surround and protect the long suppressor tube. The insulated handgrip surrounding the suppressor frame is cylindrical in shape and ribbed for a better grip.

The designations of the MP5SD series follow the same order as the standard MP5s with the 1 suffix indicating no buttstock, only a receiver cap, the 2 being a fixed stock and the 3 being a sliding stock. All three of the weapons utilize the standard SEF trigger group. The MP5SD1 with its receiver cap is a very concealable version of the SD series but required a new method of supporting the weapon in order to be fired accurately.

The Heckler & Koch sling assembly fits on a sling swivel at the back of the receiver cap. By placing the sling around the body and over the shoulders, the MP5SD1 can be carried slung under one arm, muzzle down, and hidden beneath a long coat or jacket. By grabbing the weapon and pushing it forward, a properly adjusted sling will allow the weapon to be pushed out to the extent of the firer's arm. Pushing the MP5SD1 hard against the sling, outwards from the body, braces the weapon for firing almost as much as pulling it back against a stock. The added weight of the suppressor also helps stabilize the weapon and hold the muzzle down on full automatic fire.

The above system of bracing the weapon with a sling has been adopted by some SEAL units as a way of quickly and accurately bringing an MP5SD3 into action from a slung position. The MP5SD3 has the sliding stock assembly which also incorporates a sling mounting point on its receiver housing.

SEALs familiarize French commandos with SEAL weapons aboard the USS *JOSHUA HUMPHREYS* while in the Red Sea during Operation Desert Storm. The men are firing both SIG P226 pistols and H&K MP5-N submachine guns. The submachine guns are loaded with double magazines and have flash hiders clipped over the muzzle of their barrels. The SEALs are teaching the French commandos a SEAL firing technique for the MP5 where the shooter pulls the weapon away from the shoulder against a shoulder strap. This technique gives good accuracy and is very fast to use in action.

Source: U.S. Navy

The third basic type of MP5 used by the SEAL Teams is the MP5K. The MP5K, K for Kurz (short) is the shortest, most concealable member of the MP5 family. First obtained for the

SEALs in Team Six, the MP5K was used for VIP protection missions where low-visibility armament was most needed.

The action of the MP5K is functionally and mechanically the same as the other MP5 weapons. The receiver of the MP5K is shorter than a standard MP5 receiver as there is no provision for the attachment of a shoulder stock. Instead of a stock assembly, the rear of the MP5K is closed off by a flush-fitting flat plate. In the center of the rear plate is a sling swivel loop for the attachment of a sling or other carrying harness. The two longitudinal guide grooves in the sides of the MP5K receiver are used on the full-sized weapon as guides for the sliding stock. To further insure that a standard stock is not mounted on the MP5K, the rear of the two guide grooves is covered with a welded section of plate.

Since the MP5K has a shortened receiver, the bolt carrier and some other internal parts are modified from those of the standard model to operate in a shorter travel length. If a standard buttstock could be attached to the MP5K, the internal portion of the stock would interfere with the action of the weapon. The trigger group is not modified from the standard and the MP5K is fitted with the SEF group.

For added concealment, the MP5K can be loaded with the optional 15-round box magazine. The shorter length of the 15-round magazine does not protrude from the bottom of the weapon past the pistol grips and gives the MP5K a very compact outline.

The main reduction in length on the MP5K is accomplished by shortening the barrel and front portion of the receiver. The very short barrel on the MP5K makes it a very real possibility that the hand of an operator could accidentally move in front of the muzzle while firing. To prevent this, the MP5K is fitted with a special short front handgrip with a vertical grip for the firer's nonshooting hand. In addition to the vertical grip, the handguard has a downward protruding lug at the very front of the guard, just below the muzzle of the weapon. The lug helps prevent a hand from slipping up on the handgrip and moving in front of the weapon when the MP5K is recoiling. The muzzle of the MP5K is flush with the front of the weapon and none of the muzzle attachments of the standard MP5 weapons can be mounted on the K model.

As the barrel of the MP5K is shortened from the standard length, the travel of the cocking lever is also shortened. As in the other MP5s, the cocking lever can be pulled to the rear and pushed up into a notch to lock the bolt open. The MP5K uses the same adjustable sights as are found on the MP5 and MP5SD weapons. In addition to the sights, mounting lugs are found on the upper portion of the receiver for the attachment of various H&K aiming devices.

Two unusual accessories are available for the concealed carrying of an MP5K and have been used by Team Six while on escort operations. The two accessories are a hard-sided document case and a soft-sided leather attache case or tool bag. Both cases are designed to hold an MP5K loaded with a 30-round magazine, a spare 30-round magazine, and a cleaning kit. The camouflage cases both allow the weapon to be controllably fired while still secured inside of the case.

The hard-sided document case holds the MP5K in place with a clamp that locks down in the same position as an aiming device at the top of the receiver. A short muzzle guide is part of the case and reaches from the side of the case to around the muzzle of the MP5K. The handle of the case contains a safety catch and trigger. A mechanical linkage connects the handle trigger to the trigger of the MP5K.

With a loaded MP5K inside of the case, with its fire selector set to one of the fire positions, the weapon can be fired with reasonable accuracy by simply bracing the case. A shell deflector inside of the case prevents any ejected brass from jamming the weapon when it is fired. The case itself can be held in any position and fired as long as the safety catch is held back and the trigger on the inside of the handle is pulled.

The soft-sided bag works in much the same way as the document case. The same clamp arrangement holds the MP5K in place, securely attached to the top cover of the bag. Instead of a trigger linkage, a slit on the side of the case allows the operator to slip his hand inside of the case and grasp the MP5K directly. A small tube connects the muzzle of the MP5K with the side of the bag, protecting the inside of the bag and the operator's hand from the muzzle blast.

A spent casing deflector inside of the soft bag protects the operator's hand by guiding the ejected brass forward and down. In addition to the weapon being fired from inside of the bag, releasing the four snap-action connectors on the outside of the bag, two to a side, releases the entire top assembly. The top assembly, with the weapon securely clamped in place, can be pulled free of the carrying bag and held with both hands.

The MP5K's dimensions are:

DOCUMENT CASE— 17.24 × 4.25 × 12.67 in (43.8 × 10.8 × 32.2 cm)
Weight (empty)— 7.72 lbs (3.50 kg)
Weight (w/MP5K w/30 rds, spare 30 rd magazine, cleaning kit)—
14.88 lbs (6.75 kg)

ATTACHE CASE (LEATHER BAG)— 15.74 × 12.20 × 5.62 in (40 × 31 × 14.3 cm)
Weight (empty)— 6.39 lbs (2.90 kg)
Weight (w/MP5K w/30 rds, spare 30 rd magazine, cleaning kit)— 13.66 lbs (6.20 kg)

Because of its sophisticated operating system, successful closed-bolt firing, and that it is offered as part of a weapons family, the MP5 is considered a fourth-generation submachine gun. Even with all of the points in favor of the MP5 series of weapons, there is considered to be room for improvement. Experimentation was sponsored by the Joint Services Small Arms Program (JSSAP) beginning in the early 1980s in order to identify what was desired in a submachine gun by all the services.

The requirements for a new submachine gun specified that the weapon should be able to be carried and used with only one hand. This would leave the operator with a free hand to control a descent rope, climb a shipboard ladder, or even simply open a door. In addition, the new weapon would accept a suppressor, be lighter and smaller than existing weapons, have improved first shot accuracy, full automatic and semiautomatic fire, be very controllable, and have a life expectancy of at least 10,000 rounds.

The Naval Weapons Support center at Crane, Indiana was tasked with guiding the development of what was now the JSSAP 6.2 Exploratory Development submachine gun project. Many of the characteristics of the desired weapon already existed in some form in the MP5 series. Because of this, Heckler & Koch received a contract for an advanced development submachine gun in April 1983. The result was designated the HK54A1.

Several unique features are found in the HK54A1 in an attempt to have a completely all-purpose weapon. Many of these features center around the suppressed use of the weapon.

The suppressor for the HK54A1 is slipped over the barrel and secured by a threaded seat near the breech end of the barrel. The expansion chamber section of the suppressor surrounds the barrel and is itself covered by the forearm and the extended portion of the receiver. In a reverse of other suppressor designs, the forward suppression portion of the device is larger in diameter than the rear expansion chamber. The large suppression section protrudes from the muzzle of the HK54A1 and contains a series of angular baffles. The nonwipe construction of the suppressor eliminates most maintenance problems with there being no parts replacement needed after extended use.

To suppress the sound of the bullets flight, the HK54A1 has a turn on/turn off porting system. A small lever is located underneath the HK54A1 on the forearm, just in front of the magazine well. By turning the lever so that it points to the open circle (O) symbol, a series of ports are opened in the barrel just on the front of the chamber. The ports bleed off the propellant gasses into the suppressor, lowering the muzzle velocity of a standard NATO 9mm round to below the speed of sound. By turning the port lever to the solid-colored circle, the gas ports are closed and projectiles travel at their designed velocity.

With the gas ports open, the rear of the suppressor acts as an expansion chamber. With the ports closed, only the front portion of the suppressor functions as a muzzle blast device. This factor is part of the reason the forward portion of the suppressor is so large.

To eliminate much of the mechanical noise of firing, a bolt lock is included in the HK54A1. By turning the safety selector lever to its rearmost position, indicated by an arrow pointing to a solid line, the bolt lock engages. With the bolt lock operating, the HK54A1 will not unlock at all when a round is fired. The weapon has to be manually reloaded by using the bolt cocking knob.

In addition to the bolt locked position, the safety selector has a safe position, indicated by a white 0. The semiautomatic position for the selector is indicated by a red number 1. The three-shot burst position is indicated by the red number 3 and the full automatic position is indicated by the red number 50. The HK54A1 fires from the closed bolt using the HK roller delayed blowback system for operating.

Additional features on the HK54A1 include a last-round bolt hold-open device. When the last round in a magazine is fired, the bolt stays open, locked to the rear, indicating the weapon is empty. By inserting a loaded magazine and pressing the bolt release, the bolt goes forward and loads the weapon. The bolt release is a square button with a forward-pointing arrowhead on it and is located on the left side of the weapon just in front of and above the trigger. Though the safety selector is duplicated on both sides of the firearm, the square buttons on either side of the mechanism in front of the selector do different actions.

The button on the left side of the receiver is the bolt hold-open release while the button on the right side of the receiver, engraved with an M is the magazine release. The magazine on the HK54A1 is also special in that it is not a box magazine but a large-capacity drum magazine.

Inside of the plastic drum magazine housing is a spiral track cast into the cover and body of the magazine. A spring-driven lever follows the spiral track in its three turns around the circumference of the magazine body. At the end of the lever is a short chain of five flexible cylinders. The cylinders drive the ammunition around the spiral track and up through the short, straight section of the magazine that inserts into the weapon.

Further characteristics if the HK54A1 include a forward bolt assist to help silently close the bolt on a chambered round. In addition there is a sliding metal stock on the weapon and integral mounting blocks on the top of the receiver to accept telescopic or electronic sighting devices.

For all of its apparent advantages, the HK54A1 did not work out well in combat. In October, 1983 U.S. forces invaded the island of Grenada to assist the official government and rescue American citizens. During the operation, several SEALs used HK54A1s as part of a field trial in combat. The general opinion of the weapons was that they were an expensive answer to a problem that could be better taken care of by other firearms systems already on the market. Reportedly, the HK54A1 also suffered from jams when used under field conditions.

The further development of the HK54A1 was suspended shortly after the Grenada operations were completed and the JSSAP 6.2 submachine gun project was considered completed. Interest was concentrated on a new submachine gun design that would incorporate some of the lessons learned in the 6.2 project. Funded by JSSAP, development of the new weapon was to be conducted as the 6.3A submachine gun project. The intent of the JSSAP 6.3A project was to stimulate private industry development of a submachine gun based on government-supplied characteristics. The end result of the 6.3A project was to complete the engineering package for a submachine gun that could be fielded as a DOD standard weapon service-wide by the mid-1990s.

As Heckler & Koch had been the prime contractor on the JSSAP 6.2 project, they continued their work as the contractor for the JSSAP 6.3A project. Though H&K had difficulty in combining all of the required characteristics supplied by JSSAP into a single firearm, they completed the project within a reasonable amount of time. What did stand out was the final program cost for the 6.3A project was below what the original estimates had allowed for. The weapon developed by H&K has been referred to by them as either SMG I or by an alternate designation HK SMG 94054.

The H&K SMG I is a compact, streamlined package with many features taken from earlier H&K designs. The major item not taken from other H&K designs is the basic operating system of the weapon. Instead of using the successful, if complicated roller-delayed blowback system found in the majority of H&K weapons, the SMG I operates using the blowback principle common to many of the world's submachine guns. What makes the SMG I stand out from other blowback operated weapons is that it fires from the closed bolt. Firing from the closed bolt gives the SMG I the same accuracy as the MP5 family of weapons while retaining the relative mechanical simplicity of the blowback system.

To prevent the possibility of an accidental discharge of the SMG I if it was dropped or jarred, a mechanical safety was built into the operating system. The firing pin of the SMG I cannot reach the primer of a chambered round unless the trigger is pulled. When the trigger is pulled, a safety catch releases the firing pin shortly before the hammer itself is released. In addition, the hammer is mechanically blocked from being released unless the bolt is within 2mm of being fully closed.

The HK54A1 locked breech system for holding the bolt closed on a suppressed shot was eliminated in the SMG I though the system was retained as a possible optional offering by the company. In addition, the selective on/off gas porting system for reducing the speed of standard ammunition used in the HK54A1 was also eliminated in the SMG I. Heckler & Koch also offered the selective on/off porting system as an option in their commercial version of the SMG I, the MP 2000.

For suppressed firing, the SMG I has a full-length suppressor available that slips over the barrel and seats on threads near the breech. Originally, a steel suppressor was issued with the SMG I but resulted in an unsatisfactory -20 decibel drop in sound signature when tested. An alternative aluminum suppressor was supplied from the manufacturer which had an acceptable -30 decibel signature drop. The final version of the SMG I suppressor was a stainless steel design incorporating the improvements for in the aluminum version.

Internally, the suppressor acts as a muzzle blast reducer with the rear tube an additional expansion chamber. A series of four angled blast deflectors a welded into an assembly inside of the suppressor body. In addition, at the rear of the baffle assembly, in front of the muzzle of the weapon, is a circular, perforated gas diverter that forces some of the muzzle blast back into the rear expansion chamber. The whole assembly is contained within the steel suppressor tube and retained by a threaded muzzle cap and the front portion of the rear expansion tube.

The overall design of the SMG I suppressor is a particularly rugged design intended for continuous use with little or no cleaning. During testing, the sound pressure of the SMG I decrease from 108.9 db at the beginning of the test to 105.8 db after 3,000 rounds had been fired.

Cook-off, the firing of a round from residual chamber heat in a closed-bolt weapon, is considered a possible problem in closed-bolt automatic weapons. Testing was conducted on the SMG I to see just how much ammunition the weapon could fire before cook-off became a problem. In the initial test, a suppressed SMG I fired 500 rounds in 5 minutes with only 3 stoppages due to feeding. The suppressed weapon cooled to ambient room temperature without firing a round intentionally left in the chamber.

In the second cook-off test, a SMG I fired 900 rounds in 4 minutes 15 seconds, again with 3 stoppages due to feed problems. The heat absorbed by the weapon was tremendous, the rear 2 inches of the suppressor glowing red hot by the end of the test. The heat was enough to soften part of the front grip and melt it off the weapon near the end of the test. Secured in a test cradle, the suppressed weapon cooked-off 5 times while cooling to ambient temperature. After the test, no physical change was noted in the suppressor beyond a heat discoloration of the breech end to a light straw color. In addition, no change in the level of suppression was noted during or after the test.

The SMG I is intended to be used with subsonic ammunition for maximum sound suppression. The rear sight, fully adjustable for windage and elevation, is operator selectable for either sonic or subsonic ammunition. When adjusted, the sight can be switched from either type of ammunition while retaining the same point of impact. In addition, the rear sight can be set to an extended M setting, raising the rear sight for easy use while the operator is wearing an M17A1 gas mask. The front sight hood has a square post machined into the top of it for use with the rear sight on the M setting.

For use in low-light conditions, both the front and rear sights have luminous inserts. In front of the rear sight, on the top of the receiver, are lugs for the attachment of standard sighting devices. The lugs are a quick-release design that will accept all standard NATO sight bases. Just in front of the lugs on the top of the receiver is the cocking handle, located so that it can be easily reached from either side of the weapon. The cocking handle has a U-shaped cutout to clear the line of sight and does not reciprocate when the weapon is fired.

The last-round bolt hold-open device tested in the HK54A1 was retained in the SMG I in a slightly modified form. On the HK54A1, the bolt release was on the left side of the trigger group, with the magazine release being on the opposite side at the same location. On the SMG I, the square bolt release button is on both sides of the trigger group, above the magazine release button. The magazine release button is also duplicated on both sides of the trigger housing.

To complete the ambidextrous use of the SMG I, the fire selector lever is duplicated on both sides of the weapon. Fire selector settings are indicated by a

The rear sight of the JSSAP H&K SMG I. The complex rear sight can be set for either supersonic or subsonic ammunition and adjusted by the operator by simply switching the indicator bar from one side to the other. The two dots on either side of the rear peep are tritium inserts that glow green for low-light aiming. At the top of the rear sight blade is a wide square notch intended for use with an alternate front sight blade when the firer is wearing an M17A1 gas mask. The small button behind the sight is the release catch for the sliding stock that is fully collapsed in this photograph.

Source: Kevin Dockery

white 0 for safe, a red 1 for semiautomatic fire, and a red 30 for full automatic fire. Enough room is left in the travel of the fire selector lever to accommodate a third setting for 3-round burst.

Above the fire selector lever on the right side of the SMG I is the forward bolt assist. The forward assist aids in chambering the first round in a very dirty environment since the bolt cannot be forced forward by the operating handle. The forward bolt assist can also be used for "silent loading" a first round. By drawing the bolt back and easing it forward, the forward bolt assist can quietly close the bolt and chamber a round. By using the silent loading system, the sound level of chambering a round is only 40 to 45 db, quieter than normal conversation.

The compact sliding stock fits snugly over the rear of the receiver when closed, making a very smooth, compact package. The sliding stock can be extended and locked into place in several different lengths to account for different-sized operators or various uniforms or equipment worn while on a mission.

To aid in reducing the overall weight of the SMG I, the 30-round magazines are injection molded of a high-strength synthetic material. The same material is found in the forward and rear pistol grips. The design of the pistol grips follows that of the MP5K series very closely and allows for accurate firing of the SMG I without using the stock.

Overall, the SMG I was considered a very acceptable design for use by all the U.S. services. The low-maintenance design was tested and proved durable and effective with the final tests being completed in 1985. A complete specification and engineering package was received and retained by the U.S. government for possible future manufacture. Since the end of the JSSAP 6.3A submachine gun project in 1987, the SMG I design has been offered as a commercial product by Heckler & Koch. The H&K weapon, designated the MP2000 has been produced in only very small numbers but offers a number of options first tested in the HK54A1 and SMG I.

While the JSSAP SMG programs were going on, SEAL Team Six was continuing its use of the MP5 submachine gun family. The other SEAL Teams were continuing their use of the Mk 24 Mod 0 and Ingram submachine guns through the first few years of the 1980s. With the planned expansion of Navy Special Warfare and the SEAL Teams beginning in 1983, the amount and quality of submachine guns available in Navy stores were considered insufficient to meet expected needs. Since a reasonably large number of new weapons would be needed, comparison testing was initiated in order to find the best commercially available "off-the-shelf" submachine gun design. The investigation was titled the Navy Near-Term SMG project and was begun in February 1983.

By July 1984, the Navy Near-Term SMG project had been completed and the MP5 weapons family was chosen to be the new SEAL basic issue submachine gun. Initial weapons purchased for the Teams were the same as those used earlier by SEAL Team Six, the MP5A3, MP5SD3, and MP5K. The first weapons to arrive at SEAL Team Two at Little Creek were twenty-five MP5SD3s followed soon by an equal number of MP5A3s.

The SEALs found the new MP5s a great improvement over earlier issue weapons. The closed-bolt action of the MP5 gave the entire line of weapons a much greater first-round accuracy than any of the open-bolt systems the SEALs had been using for years. The MP5s were also generally very compact and were a much handier weapon for using in close areas than even the CAR-15 had been. In addition, there is much less danger of overpenetration and ricochets are slightly less hazardous with the 9mm cartridge than with a .223 or 7.62mm rifle round when boarding and searching ships.

The new SEAL MP5s were slightly different in details from the earlier models. The new issue MP5A3 is fitted with the smooth, wider "tropical" handguard. The original handguard has a round cross section and four lengthwise panels of checkering to give a secure gripping surface. The tropical handguard, originally offered as an optional accessory for the MP5 by H&K, has a textured surface and a triangular cross section. The wide-bottomed shape of the handguard offers a better grip to wet or gloved hands, something the SEALs find themselves using often.

For the most part, the SEALs MP5s were all fitted with the SEF trigger group. According to an individual Team's mission, the MP5K weapons were also available. Shortly after the first MP5s arrived at SEAL Team Two, a limited number, twenty-five each, of MP5A5s and MP5SD6s for field testing and evaluation. Reportedly, SEAL Team Two was the only East Coast Team to receive the A5/SD6 configuration weapons.

Several new developments were incorporated into the MP5A5 and MP5SD6 weapon. Foremost among these changes was the addition of a controlled burst mechanism to the trigger group. According to the standard designations put out by Heckler & Koch, the MP5A5 is a standard MP5 fitted with a controlled burst trigger group and sliding buttstock. The MP5SD6 is identified by the company as the suppressed MP5 with the controlled burst trigger group and sliding buttstock. Sometime during the first procurements of the MP5s for the Teams at large, a clerical error was made and all of the MP5s have been listed in Navy documents as the MP5A5, SD5 and KA4. This misidentification has remained to this day.

Trigger groups among all of the different MP5s can be easily changed for one another. MP5A3s with the SEF trigger group can accept a controlled burst trigger group and be changed to the MP5A5 model. The only real difference in the weapons is that the controlled burst trigger group has a setting where only three rounds will be fired on full automatic for each pull of the trigger.

The internal mechanism of the controlled burst trigger group remains the same as the earlier SEF group with some additions. The burst control itself is centered on a ratchet device fitted to the trigger mechanism. With the fire selector lever set on burst fire, the ratchet holds the sear back from the hammer when the trigger is pulled. The ratchet mechanically counts the number of times the bolt carrier moves past and releases the sear after ten programmed number of rounds have been fired. If the trigger is released before the set number of rounds have been fired, the ratchet resets to 0.

Because of the arrangement of the burst control ratchet, the number of rounds in a burst can be set by the number of teeth on the ratchet. Settings for two, three, or more rounds are available on the burst control trigger group though the normal setting, and the one supplied on the SEALs weapons is for three shot bursts.

Setting indicators for the controlled burst trigger groups are pictographic in style rather than having numbers or letters. The pictographic representations of the different control settings are considerably more graphic than the original SEF letters.

The safety setting is indicated by a single white bullet in a closed rectangular box with an X superimposed over the bullet. For semiautomatic fire, the symbol is a closed red box containing a single red bullet silhouette. Three-round burst is indicated by a closed red rectangle holding three red bullet shapes. Automatic fire is at the top setting, moving up from the trigger and is indicated by an open-ended red rectangle containing seven red bullet shapes. All the bullet silhouettes point forward toward the muzzle of the weapon, an additional indicator of what the fire selector lever settings mean.

The pistol grip shape of the controlled burst trigger groups is of a considerably different shape than that of the SEF group. The finger swells found on the SEF pistol grip are removed on the new grip. The new grip has a smoother, more conical shape with an oval cross-section. A noticeable protrusion is on the bottom of the front strap of the new grip to help keep a hand from slipping off. The thumb rest found on the left side of the SEF grip is not on the new grip making it much more comfortable to use left-handed. In addition to being more ambidextrous in use, the new-style pistol grip also gives a more secure grasp to a hand covered in a leather or rubber glove.

On both trigger groups, the pistol grip is an integral part of the plastic casting that makes up the outside housing of the group. Markings, whether the letters SEF or the pictographic symbols, are deep engravings on the outside plastic housing.

In general, the controlled burst system was not accepted by the Teams. The control mechanism itself was somewhat sensitive and extra care had to be given to it during routine maintenance. For all of the Teams, it was found to be preferable to train in burst control by fast manipulation of the trigger. Experience and training would give an operator the ability to fire three-round bursts by automatically releasing the trigger as soon as the third round had been fired. Using the trigger-control system also had the advantage that full automatic fire was immediately available by just holding the trigger down if the situation arose where a high volume of fire was needed.

The MP5A3s and SD3s that had arrived at the Teams in 1984 acted as an interim measure until weapons modified to SEAL specifications became available. By mid-1985 the MP5-N and MP5K-N (Navy) became available in sufficient numbers to begin issuing them to the Teams. These weapons, which have a detachable suppressor, have remained the primary SEAL submachine gun to this day. MP5SD3s remain available in the armories of the active Teams for use in situations where subsonic ammunition may not be available.

Mechanically, the MP5-N weapons were the same as earlier models of the MP5, Changes requested by the SEALs were primarily centered around handling characteristics. The tropical handguard has been retained on the MP5-N as well as the pistol grip configuration first found on the controlled burst trigger group. The trigger group of the MP5-N weapon has settings for safe, semiautomatic, and full automatic. Heckler & Koch offers an ambidextrous trigger group fitted with a controlled burst mechanism that is virtually identical with the Navy group.

The noticeable difference in the Navy trigger group is that the fire selector lever is duplicated on both sides of the weapon. Either lever can be used to select the fire setting on the MP5-N, making the weapon able to be equally well operated from the right or left side. This ambidextrous facility makes the MP5-N even more flexible in a combat situation. Instead of a letter or number system to indicate the control settings, the Navy trigger group utilizes the pictographic system first used by the SEALs on the MP5A5.

The sights of the MP5-N weapon have been fitted with tritium inserts for use in low-light situations. The tritium insert is a small glass tube filled with a low-level radioactive isotope. The inserts glow with a pale green light, easily visible at night or in other low-light situations.

A major modification to the MP5-N is the addition of a threaded portion to the muzzle of the barrel. Normally covered with a knurled cap to protect the threads, the muzzle of the MP5-N is able to accept a suppressor built to Navy specifications. The muzzle-blast suppressor is an all-metal, nonwipe design that significantly reduces the firing signature of the MP5-N. The size of the suppressor is such that it will fit into the same pouch pocket that holds a thirty-round MP5 magazine.

The 3-lug locking system is retained on the muzzle of the MP5-N to allow the weapon to use a standard flash hider for normal use. MP5-N's are issued both with and without the detachable suppressor. In addition to the MP5-N, the MP5K-N is issued to the Teams.

The MP5K-N has the same modifications as the MP5-N consisting of the Navy trigger group with ambidextrous controls, tritium sight insert, and threaded muzzle. The standard MP5K barrel was increased by 0.47 inches (12 mm) to accept the threaded muzzle. In addition to the threaded muzzle, the MP5K-N also has the 3-lug locking system on its muzzle to accept the H&K flash suppressor.

Several accessories have been put into general use by the SEALs on many of their MP5 weapons. One accessory is the dual magazine clamp offered by H&K. The dual magazine clamp weighs 0.35 pounds (0.16 kg) and securely holds two magazines side-by-side with each other. The two magazines are held mouth up at the same height and parallel to each other, facing forward. The dual magazine clamp holds the magazines spaced far enough apart that one of the two can be loaded into the magazine well. For quick reloading, the dual magazine only has to be pulled from the weapon and quickly reinserted. The popularity and cost of the dual magazine system has resulted in a number of SEALs fielding their own version of the system.

In the SEAL dual magazine system, the two magazines are held slightly apart by a spacer and clamped together firmly with a simple pipe clamp. Though quick to reload, the dual magazine has the disadvantage of not fitting in any standard magazine pouch. In addition, the dual magazine makes the MP5 noticeably heavier and changes the handling characteristics of the weapon.

Another accessory seeing use with the Teams is a tactical lighted forearm for the MP5. The lighted forearm replaces the regular handguard of the standard MP5 or MP5-N with no other modification to the weapon. In a swelled portion of the tactical handguard, just below the muzzle of the weapon, is a lithium-powered flashlight. The flashlight produces a strong, focused beam of white light usable for searching, target acquisition, and illuminating a low-light situation. A pressure strip switch is located on the side of the forearm where it can be pressed by the operators fingers. The flashlight does not protrude past the muzzle of the weapon to protect the lens from the muzzle blast.

Some difficulties have been noted with the MP5 weapons and the ammunition they use. Though normally extremely reliable, difficulties were noted in using standard subsonic ammunition in the MP5-N. The fluted chamber, necessary to the proper operation of the MP5 roller-locking system, has some difficulty releasing the Mk 144 subsonic ammunition originally developed for the Mk 22 pistol. A program was initiated to develop a product-improved (PIP) Mk 144 round by the Naval Weapons Support Center at Crane, Indiana.

An additional requirement was put forward for a specialized round of ammunition to be developed for the MP5 and Beretta M9 that would be both subsonic and have "enhanced incapacitation" effects. Olin ordnance developed the 9mm OSP round, its commercial designation, to fill the Navy requirement. The OSP (Olin Super Match) round is a subsonic loading of a 147 grain jacketed hollowpoint projectile. The specially designed 147-grain bullet was based on technology developed by Olin for the Winchester Silvertip line of ammunition. The OSP round gives superior terminal effects over the standard NATO 9mm and even the MK 144 round while remaining at subsonic levels.

The use of the hollowpoint round, normally banned by the Geneva and other conventions, is allowed only for use in civil or counterterrorist operations by U.S. forces. The baffle-type suppression system used by the Qual-E-Tech suppressor mounted on the MP5-N and MP5K-N allows the use of hollowpoint ammunition which is difficult to use in a wipe-type suppressor such as that found on the Mk 22 pistol.

▪ Submachine Guns Data ▪

Source: U.S. Army

M1928A1 THOMPSON (1943)

CARTRIDGE .45 ACP (11.43×23mm)

OPERATION Delayed blowback

TYPE OF FIRE Selective—semiautomatic/full automatic

RATE OF FIRE Cyclic 600-725 rpm

MUZZLE VELOCITY 920 fps

MUZZLE ENERGY 432 ft/lb (586 J)

SIGHTS Open, Lyman leaf w/aperture, notch battle sight/blade or aperture/blade (later models), adjustable

FEED 20- or 30-round removable box magazine, 50 rd drum

WEIGHTS

Weapon (empty) 10.75 lb (4.88 kg) w/stock; 1.73 lb (0.78 kg) Removable wooden stock

Weapon (loaded) 12.67 lb (5.75 kg) w/30 rds

Magazine (empty) 20 rd-0.4 lb (0.18 kg), 30 rd-0.5 lb (0.23 kg), 50 rd drum 2.6 lb (1.18 kg)

Magazine (loaded) 20 rd-1.35 lb (0.61 kg), 30 rd-1.92 lb (0.87 kg), 50 rd drum-4.96 lb (2.25 kg)

Service cartridge M1911 Ball 331 gr (21.4 g)

Projectile 230 grains (15.2 g)

LENGTHS

Weapon overall 33.7 in (85.6 cm) w/compensator, stock; 25 in (63.5 cm) w/o stock

Barrel 10.5 in (26.7 cm)

Sight radius 22.3 in (56.6 cm)

Source: Kevin Dockery

SUBMACHINE GUN M3
SUBMACHINE GUN M3A1

CARTRIDGE .45 ACP (11.43×23mm)

OPERATION Blowback

TYPE OF FIRE Full automatic

RATE OF FIRE 120 rpm, 450 rpm

MUZZLE VELOCITY 918 fps (280 m/s)

MUZZLE ENERGY 430 ft/lb (583 J)

SIGHTS Open, aperture/blade, fixed

FEED 30-rd removable box magazine

WEIGHTS

Weapon (empty) [M3] 8 lb (3.63 kg); [M3A1] 7.65 lb (3.47 kg)

Weapon (loaded) [M3] 10.17 lb (4.61 kg); [M3A1] 9.82 lb (4.45 kg)

Magazine (empty) 0.75 lb (0.340 kg)

Magazine (loaded) 2.17 lb (0.98 kg)

Service cartridge M1911 Ball 331 gr (21.4 g)

Projectile 230 grains (15.2 g)

LENGTHS
Weapon overall 22.81/29.81 in
(57.9/75.7 cm)
Barrel 8 in (20.3 cm)
Sight radius 10.88 in (27.6 cm)

Source: Kevin Dockery

M3 & M3A1 SUPPRESSED BARREL
CARTRIDGE 45 ACP (11.43×23mm)
MUZZLE VELOCITY 768 fps (234 m/s)
MUZZLE ENERGY 301 ft/lb (408 J)
WEIGHTS
Suppressor 2.63 lb (1.19 kg)
Weapon (loaded) w/suppressor [M3] 11.55 lb
(5.24 kg); [M3A1] 11.2 lb (5.08 kg)
Normal barrel weight 1.25 lb (0.57 kg)
LENGTHS
Weapon overall 29.75/36.75 in
(75.6/93.3 cm)
Barrel 7.88 in (20 cm)
Suppressor length overall 14.25 in
(36.2 cm)
Suppressor diameter 1.630/1.130 in
(4.1/2.9 cm)

Source: Kevin Dockery

SWEDISH K, AKA CARL GUSTAV, M45(B)
CARTRIDGE 9mm Parabellum (9×19mm)
OPERATION Blowback
TYPE OF FIRE Full automatic

RATE OF FIRE Cyclic 550-600 rpm
MUZZLE VELOCITY 1,200 fps (365 m/s); 980
fps (298 m/s) w/AMF suppressor
MUZZLE ENERGY 368 ft/lb (499 J); 262 ft/lb
(355 J) w/AMF suppressor
SIGHTS Open, U-notch/post, adjustable, flip-
up rear for 100, 200, and 300 meters
FEED 36-round detachable box magazine
WEIGHTS
Weapon (empty) 7.6 lb (3.45 kg); 10.88 lb
(4.94 kg) w/AMF suppressor
Weapon (loaded) 9.03 lb (4.10 kg); 12.31 lb
(5.58 kg) w/AMF suppressor
Magazine (empty) 0.50 lb (0.23 kg)
Magazine (loaded) 1.43 lb (0.65 kg)
Service cartridge 9mm Ball M1-180 gr
(11.7 g)
Projectile 115 gr (7.5 g)
LENGTHS
Weapon overall 21.7/31.8 in (55.1/80.8 cm);
28.4/38.5 in w/AMF suppressor
Barrel 8 in (20.3 cm)
Sight radius 14.13 in (35.9 cm); 20.43 in (51.9
cm) w/AMF suppressor
The AMF suppressor reduces the muzzle
blast 31 decibels from 155 db to 124 db. The
design of the suppressor also reduces stan-
dard ammunition to subsonic velocities elimi-
nating the sonic crack.

MAT-49
CARTRIDGE 9mm Parabellum (9×19mm)
OPERATION Blowback
TYPE OF FIRE Full automatic
RATE OF FIRE Cyclic 600 rpm
MUZZLE VELOCITY 1,161 fps (354 m/s)
MUZZLE ENERGY 344 ft/lb (466 J)
SIGHTS Open, aperture/blade, adjustable,
flip-up rear, 100 and 200 meters
FEED 32-round removable box magazine
WEIGHTS
Weapon (empty) 8.02 lb (3.64 kg)
Weapon (loaded) 9.41 lb (4.27 kg)
Magazine (empty) 0.57 lb (0.26 kg)

Magazine (loaded) 1.39 lb (0.63 kg)
Service cartridge 9mm Ball M1-180 gr
(11.7 g)
Projectile 115 gr (7.5 g)
LENGTHS
Weapon Overall 16/26 in (40.6/66 cm)
Barrel 9 in (22.7 cm)
Sight radius 14.88 in (37.8 cm)

MADSEN M50

CARTRIDGE 9mm Parabellum (9×19mm)
OPERATION Blowback
TYPE OF FIRE Full automatic
RATE OF FIRE Practical 120 rpm Cyclic 550
rpm
MUZZLE VELOCITY 1,250 fps (381 m/s)
MUZZLE ENERGY 399 ft/lb (541 J)
SIGHTS Open, aperture/blade, fixed, zeroed
at 100 meters
FEED 32-round removable box magazine
WEIGHTS
Weapon (empty) 6.95 lb (3.15 kg)
Weapon (loaded) 8.25 lb (3.74 kg)
Magazine (empty) 0.48 lb (0.22 kg)
Magazine (loaded) 1.30 lb (0.59 kg)
Service cartridge M1 Ball 180 gr (11.7 g)
Projectile 115 gr (7.5 g)
LENGTHS
Weapon Overall 20.8/31.25 in (52.8/79.4 cm)
Barrel 7.8 in (19.8 cm)
Sight radius 13 in (33 cm)

MP 40

CARTRIDGE 9mm Parabellum (9×19mm)
OPERATION Blowback
TYPE OF FIRE Full automatic
RATE OF FIRE Practical 120 rpm Cyclic 350
to 500 rpm
MUZZLE VELOCITY 1,250 fps (381 m/s)
MUZZLE ENERGY 399 ft/lb (541 J)
SIGHTS Open, square-notch/blade, fixed,
flip-up rear blade for 100 and 200 meters
FEED 32-round removable box magazine

WEIGHTS
Weapon (empty) 8.94 lb (4.06 kg)
Weapon (loaded) 10.32 lb (4.68 kg)
Magazine (empty) 0.56 lb (0.25 kg)
Magazine (loaded) 1.38 lb (0.63 kg)
Service cartridge M1 Ball 180 gr (11.7 g)
Projectile 115 gr (7.5 g)
LENGTHS
Weapon Overall 24.8/32.8 in (63/83.3 cm)
Barrel 9.9 in (25.1 cm)
Sight Radius 15.38 in (39.1 cm)

Source: Kevin Dockery

SUBMACHINE GUN 9MM MARK 24 MOD 0, SMITH & WESSON MODEL 76

CARTRIDGE 9mm Parabellum (9×19mm)
OPERATION Blowback
TYPE OF FIRE Selective—semiautomatic/
full automatic fire
RATE OF FIRE Practical SS—40 rpm, A—
144 rpm, Cyclic 750 rpm
MUZZLE VELOCITY 1,250 fps (381 m/s);
1,000 fps (305 m/s) w/suppressor
MUZZLE ENERGY 399 ft/lb (541 J); 255 ft/lb
(346 J) w/suppressor
SIGHTS Open, aperture/blade, fixed
FEED 36-round removable box magazine
WEIGHTS
Weapon (empty) 7.25 lb (3.29 kg) w/standard
barrel and jacket; 7.93 lb (3.60 kg)
w/suppressor & barrel; 0.48 lb (0.22 kg)
standard barrel; 0.58 lb (0.26 kg) perforated barrel jacket; 1.44 lb (0.65 kg) suppressor; 0.30 lb (0.14 kg) suppressor
barrel
Weapon (loaded) 8.67 lb (3.93 kg) w/standard
barrel & jacket; 9.35 lb (4.24 kg) w/sup-
pressor & barrel

Magazine (empty) 0.49 lb (0.22 kg)
Magazine (loaded) 1.42 lb (0.64 kg)
Service cartridge M1 Ball 180 gr
(11.7 g)
Projectile 115 gr (7.5 g)
LENGTHS
Weapon overall 20.25/30.38 in (51.4/77.2
cm); 24.31/34.38 in (61.7/89.9 cm)
w/suppressor
Barrel 8 in (20.3 cm); 5.25 in (13.3 cm)
suppressor barrel
Suppressor length 11.25 in (28.6 cm)
Suppressor diameter 1.63 in (4.1 cm)
Sight radius 11.3 in (28.7 cm)
Issued w/4 magazines

Source: Kevin Dockery

9MM INGRAM M10

CARTRIDGE 9mm Parabellum
(9×19mm)
OPERATION Blowback
TYPE OF FIRE Selective—semiautomatic/full
automatic
RATE OF FIRE Practical SS 40 rpm, A 96 rpm
Cyclic 950 to 1090 rpm
MUZZLE VELOCITY 1,206 fps (366 m/s)
MUZZLE ENERGY 371 ft/lb (503 J)
SIGHTS Open, aperture/post, fixed, zeroed at
100 meters
FEED 32-round removable box magazine
WEIGHTS
Weapon (empty) 6.25 lb (2.83 kg); suppressor
1.20 lb (0.54 kg)
Weapon (loaded) 7.62 lb (3.47 kg); 8.82 lb
(4 kg) w/suppressor
Magazine (empty) 0.55 lb (0.25 kg)

Magazine (loaded) 1.37 lb (0.62 kg)
Service cartridge M1 Ball 180 gr (11.7 g)
Projectile 115 gr (7.5 g)
LENGTHS
Weapon overall 11.6/21.57 in (29.5/54.8 cm)
w/o suppressor; 21.5/31.4 in (54.5/79.8
cm) w/suppressor
Barrel 5.75 in (14.6 cm)
Suppressor length 11.44 in 29.1 cm)
Suppressor diameter 2.13 in (5.4 cm)
Sight radius 8.27 in (21 cm)

INGRAM M10

CARTRIDGE .45 ACP (11.43×23mm)
OPERATION Blowback
TYPE OF FIRE Selective—semiautomatic/full
automatic fire
RATE OF FIRE Practical SS 40 rpm, A 90 rpm
Cyclic 950 to 1,145 rpm
MUZZLE VELOCITY 919 fps (280 m/s)
MUZZLE ENERGY 431 ft/lb (584 J)
SIGHTS Open, aperture/post, fixed zeroed at
100 meters
FEED 30-round removable box magazine
(modified US M3 magazine)
WEIGHTS
Weapon (empty) 6.25 lb (2.83 kg); suppressor
1.2 lb (0.54 kg)
Weapon (loaded) 8.42 lb (3.82 kg); 9.62 lb
(4.36 kg) w/suppressor
Magazine (empty) 0.75 lb (0.340 kg)
Magazine (loaded) 2.17 lb (0.98 kg)
Service cartridge M1911 Ball 331 gr
(21.4 g)
Projectile 230 grains (15.2 g)
LENGTHS
Weapon overall 11.6/21.57 in (29.5/54.8 cm)
w/o suppressor; 21.5/31.4 in (54.5/79.8
cm) w/suppressor
Barrel 5.75 in (14.6 cm)
Suppressor length 11.44 in (29.1 cm)
Suppressor diameter 2.13 in (5.4 cm)
Sight radius 8.27 in (21 cm)

HECKLER & KOCH MP5A3 [MP5A5]

CARTRIDGE 9mm Parabellum (9×19mm)

OPERATION Roller locked delayed blowback

TYPE OF FIRE Selective—semiautomatic/full automatic, [w/three-round controlled burst]

RATE OF FIRE Practical SS 40 rpm, A 100 rpm, Cyclic 800 rpm

MUZZLE VELOCITY 1,312 fps (400 m/s)

MUZZLE ENERGY 474 ft/lb (643 J)

SIGHTS Open, aperture/blade, adjustable

FEED 30-round removable box magazine. Double magazine clip available to hold two magazines together for quick reloading. Wt 0.36 lb (0.16 kg)

WEIGHTS

Weapon (empty) 6.34 lb (2.88 kg)

Weapon (loaded) 7.53 lb (3.42 kg) w/1-30 rd magazine; 9.08 lb (4.12 kg) w/2-30 rd magazines & clip

Magazine (empty) 30 rd .375 lb (0.17 kg); Two 30-rd mags w/clip 1.11 lb (0.50 kg)

Magazine (loaded) 30 rd 1.19 lb (0.54 kg); Two 30 rd mags w/clip 2.74 lb (1.24 kg

Service cartridge M882 Ball 190 gr. (12.3 g)

Projectile 124 gr (8 g)

LENGTHS

Weapon overall 19.29/25.98 in (49/66 cm)

Barrel 8.85 in (22.5 cm)

Sight radius 13.38 in (34 cm)

HECKLER & KOCH MP5K [MP5KA4]

CARTRIDGE 9mm Parabellum (9×19mm)

OPERATION Roller locked delayed blowback

TYPE OF FIRE Selective—semiautomatic/full automatic, (w/three-round controlled burst)

RATE OF FIRE Practical SS 40 rpm, A 100 rpm, Cyclic 800 rpm

MUZZLE VELOCITY 1,230 fps (375 m/s)

MUZZLE ENERGY 412 ft/lb (570 J)

SIGHTS Open, aperture/blade, adjustable (square-notch/blade, Fixed)

FEED 15- or 30-round removable box magazine. Double magazine clip available to hold two magazines together for quick reloading. Wt 0.36 lb (0.16 kg)

WEIGHTS

Weapon (empty) 4.41 lb (2.0 kg)

Weapon (loaded) 5.6 lb (2.54 kg) w/1—30 rd magazine

Magazine (empty) 30 rd—.375 lb (0.17 kg); 15 rd—0.265 lb (0.12 kg); Two 30 rd mags w/clip 1.11 lb (0.50 kg)

Magazine (loaded) 30 rd—1.19 lb (0.54 kg); 15 rd—0.672 lb (0.305 kg); Two 30 rd mags w/clip 2.74 lb (1.24 kg)

Service cartridge M882 Ball 190 gr (12.3 g)

Projectile 124 gr (8 g)

LENGTHS

Weapon overall 12.8 in (32.5 cm)

Barrel 4.5 in (11.5 cm)

Sight radius 10.25 in (26 cm) [7.48 in (19 cm)]

Source: Kevin Dockery

HECKLER & KOCH MP5SD3 [MP5SD6]

CARTRIDGE 9mm Parabellum (9×19mm)

OPERATION Roller locked delayed blowback

TYPE OF FIRE Selective—semiautomatic/full automatic, [w/three-round controlled burst]

RATE OF FIRE Practical SS 40 rpm, A 100 rpm, Cyclic 800 rpm

MUZZLE VELOCITY 935 fps (285 m/s)

MUZZLE ENERGY 275 ft/lb (380 J)

SIGHTS Open, aperture/blade, adjustable

FEED 30-round removable box magazine. Double magazine clip available to hold two magazines together for quick reloading. Wt 0.36 lb (0.16 kg)

WEIGHTS

Weapon (empty) 7.50 lb (3.40 kg)

Weapon (loaded) 8.69 lb (3.94 kg) w/1-30 rd magazine; 10.24 lb (4.64 kg) w/2-30 rd magazines and clip

Magazine (empty) 30 rd .375 lb (0.17 kg); Two 30 rd mags w/clip 1.11 lb (0.50 kg)

Magazine (loaded) 30 rd 1.19 lb (0.54 kg); two 30 rd mags w/clip 2.74 lb (1.24 kg)

Service cartridge M882 Ball 190 gr (12.3 g)

Projectile 124 gr (8 g)

LENGTHS

Weapon overall 23.97/30.42 in (61/78 cm)

Barrel 5.73 in (14.6 cm)

Suppressor length 12 in (30.5 cm)

Sight radius 13.38 in (34 cm)

Source: Kevin Dockery

HK54A1

CARTRIDGE 9mm Parabellum (9×19mm)

OPERATION Roller locked delayed blowback

TYPE OF FIRE Selective— semiautomatic/three-round controlled burst/full automatic

RATE OF FIRE Practical SS 40 rpm, A 100 rpm, Cyclic 800 rpm

MUZZLE VELOCITY 1,300 fps (396 m/s) w/vent ports closed; 960 fps (293 m/s) w/vent ports open (subsonic)

MUZZLE ENERGY 465 ft/lb (631 J) standard; 254 ft/lb (344 J) subsonic

SIGHTS Open, aperture/blade, adjustable

FEED 50-round removable spring-loaded drum magazine

WEIGHTS

Weapon (empty) 6.57 lb (2.98 kg) w/o suppressor; 7.49 lb (3.4 kg) w/suppressor; suppressor wt 0.92 lb (0.42 kg)

Weapon (loaded) 9.42 lb (4.27 kg) w/o suppressor; 10.34 lb (4.69 kg) w/suppressor

Magazine (empty) 1.49 lb (.68 kg)

Magazine (loaded) 2.85 lb (1.29 kg)

Service cartridge M882 Ball 190 gr (12.3 g)

Projectile 124 gr (8 g)

LENGTHS

Weapon overall 16.19/24.25 in 41.1/61.6 cm) w/o suppressor; 23.5/31.5 in (59.7/80 cm) w/suppressor

Barrel 7.06 in (17.9 cm)

Suppressor length 13.13 in (33.4 cm)

Suppressor diameter 1.854 in (4.7 cm)

Sight radius 12.75 in (32.4 cm)

Source: Kevin Dockery

HECKLER & KOCH SMG 94054, JSSAP 6.3A SMG PROJECT

CARTRIDGE 9mm Parabellum (9x19mm)

OPERATION Blowback

TYPE OF FIRE Selective—semiautomatic/full automatic

RATE OF FIRE Practical SS 40 rpm, A rpm, Cyclic 880 rpm

MUZZLE VELOCITY NATO Ball 1,227 fps (374 m/s) 9mm OSP 1,017 fps (310 m/s)

MUZZLE ENERGY 414 ft/lb (561 J) NATO Ball 338 ft/lb (458 J)

SIGHTS Open, aperture/post w/3-dot tritium inserts, adjustable 0 to 150 meters in 25-meter increments. Rear sight selectable for supersonic or subsonic ammunition, M setting for mask raises rear sight and uses post machined into front sight hood

FEED 30-round removable reinforced-plastic box magazine

WEIGHTS

Weapon (empty) 6.12 lb (2.78 kg) w/o suppressor; 7.87 lb (3.57 kg) w/suppressor; final model stainless steel suppressor 1.8 lb (0.82 kg)

Weapon (loaded) 7.1 lb (3.22 kg) w/NATO Ball; 8.95 lb (4.06 kg) w/suppressor, 9mm OSP

Magazine (empty) 0.17 lb (0.08 kg)

Magazine (loaded) 0.98 lb (0.44 kg) w/NATO Ball 1.08 lb (0.49 kg) w/9mm OSP

Service cartridge NATO Ball 190 gr (12.3 g); 9mm OSP 212 gr (13.7 g)

Projectile 124 gr (8 g); 9mm OSP 147 gr (9.5 g)

LENGTHS

Weapon overall 14.31/21.38/22.69 in (36.4/54.3/57.6 cm) stock closed/open to first notch/fully open—w/o suppressor; 21.63/28.63/29.88 in (54.9/72.7/75.9 cm) stock closed/open to first notch/fully open—w/suppressor

Barrel 5.63 in (14.3 cm)

Suppressor length 10.81 in (27.5 cm) overall; 7.31 in (18.6 cm) Can length; 3.5 in (8.9 cm) Mounting tube

Suppressor diameter 1.628 in (4.1 cm) Can; 1.062 in (2.7 cm) Mounting tube

Suppressor wall thickness 0.070 in (1.78 mm)

Sight radius 12.5 in (31.8 in)

Forward bolt assist is primarily for "silent loading," by using the system the sound level of chambering a round is only 40 to 45 db.

Suppressor reduction on the normal sound signature, 137 db for NATO Ball, was -29 db to a sound signature of 108 db

Source: Kevin Dockery

HECKLER & KOCH MP5-N

CARTRIDGE 9mm Parabellum (9×19mm)

OPERATION Roller locked delayed blowback

TYPE OF FIRE Selective—semiautomatic/full automatic

RATE OF FIRE Cyclic 800 rpm

MUZZLE VELOCITY M882 Ball 1312 fps (400 m/s); 9mm OSP 1,092 fps (333 m/s)

MUZZLE ENERGY 470 ft/lb (637 J) M882 ball; 389 ft/lb (527 J) 9mm OSP

SIGHTS Open, aperture/post w/3-dot tritium inserts, adjustable

FEED 30-round removable box magazine

WEIGHTS

Weapon (empty) 6.34 lb (2.88 kg) w/o suppressor; w/suppressor 7.57 lb (3.43 kg); suppressor wt 1.23 lb (0.56 kg)

Weapon (loaded) 7.53 lb (3.42 kg) w/o suppressor, w/1—30 rd magazine M882 Ball; 8.82 lb (4.0 kg) w/suppressor, 1—30 rd magazine 9mm OSP

Magazine (empty) 30 rd .375 lb (0.17 kg); two 30 rd mags w/clip 1.11 lb (0.50 kg)

Magazine (loaded) 30 rd 1.19 lb (0.54 kg) w/M882 Ball; 30 rd 1.29 lb (0.59 kg) w/9mm OSP; Two 30 rd mags w/clip 2.74 lb (1.24 kg) w/M882 Ball; Two 30 rd mags w/clip 2.93 lb (1.33 kg) w/9mm OSP

Service Cartridge M882 Ball 190 gr (12.3 g); 9mm OSP 212 gr (13.7 g)

Projectile 124 gr (8 g); 9mm OSP 147 gr (9.5 g)

LENGTHS

Weapon overall 19.29/25.98 in (49.0/66.0 cm) w/o suppressor; 27.94/33.06 in (71/84 cm) w/suppressor

Barrel 8.85 in (22.5 cm)

Suppressor length 7.75 in (19.7 cm)
Suppressor diameter 1.385 in (3.5 cm)
Sight radius 13.39 in (34.0 cm)
  Barrel threads for suppressor are covered with a knurled cap (wt. 93 gr [6 g]) when the suppressor is not mounted

HECKLER & KOCH MP5K-N

CARTRIDGE 9mm Parabellum (9×19mm)
OPERATION Roller locked delayed blowback
TYPE OF FIRE Selective—semiautomatic/full automatic
RATE OF FIRE Cyclic 900 rpm
MUZZLE VELOCITY M882 Ball 1,230 fps (375 m/s); 9mm OSP 1,010 fps (308 m/s)
MUZZLE ENERGY M882 Ball 420 ft/lb (570 J); 9mm OSP 333 ft/lb (452 J)
SIGHTS Open, notch/post w/3-dot tritium inserts, adjustable
FEED 15- or 30-round removable box magazine
WEIGHTS
Weapon (empty) 4.4 lb (2.00 kg) w/o suppressor; 5.63 lb (2.55 kg) w/suppressor; suppressor wt 1.23 lb (0.56 kg)
Weapon (loaded) 5.59 lb (2.54 kg) w/o suppressor, w/1 30 rd magazine M882 Ball;
6.92 lb (3.14 kg) w/suppressor, 1 30 rd magazine 9mm OSP
Magazine (empty) 30 rd .38 lb (0.17 kg); 15 rd 0.27 lb (0.12 kg); two 30 rd mags w/clip 1.11 lb (0.50 kg)
Magazine (loaded) 30 rd 1.19 lb (0.54 kg) w/M882 Ball; 30 rd 1.29 lb (0.59 kg) w/9mm OSP; 15 rd 0.67 lb (0.31 kg) w/M882 Ball; 15 rd 0.72 lb (0.33 kg) w/9mm OSP; two 30 rd mags w/clip 2.74 lb (1.24 kg) w/M882 Ball; two 30 rd mags w/clip 2.93 lb (1.33 kg) w/9mm OSP
Service cartridge M882 Ball 190 gr. (12.3 g); 9mm OSP 212 gr (13.7 g)
Projectile 124 gr (8 g); 9mm OSP 147 gr (9.5 g)
LENGTHS
Weapon overall 12.8 in (32.5 cm) w/o suppressor; 21 in (53.3 cm) w/suppressor
Barrel 4.53 in (11.5 cm)
Suppressor length 7.75 in (19.7 cm)
Suppressor diameter 1.385 in (3.5 cm)
Sight radius 10.25 in (26 cm)
  Barrel threads for suppressor are covered with a knurled cap (wt 93 gr [6 g]) when the suppressor is not mounted

■ 6
SHOTGUNS

The modern shotgun is the major surviving example of the earliest smoothbore firearms. Instead of launching a single discrete projectile at a high velocity, the shotgun puts out a swarm of projectiles (shot) at a relatively low velocity. Since the shotgun fires a heavy charge of shot, on the order of an ounce or more, the low velocity keeps the weapon's recoil down to manageable levels.

The spreading swarm of shot covers a larger and larger area as its distance increases from the muzzle of the firing weapon. This spreading pattern of shot helps the shotgun make up for errors in sighting and judgments in a moving target's speed. This action is what has helped keep the shotgun popular as a sporting weapon, increasing the chance of hitting a moving target with at least some of the pellets in its load.

Smoothbore muskets and carbines aside, purpose-made fighting shotguns have been used since the early 1600s. The musketoon was short, carbine-like version of the musket noted in Europe around the mid-1600s. With a bore equal in size to today's 12 gauge, the musketoon was loaded with large shot and used for close-in fighting. Soon, the musketoon evolved into the blunderbuss, the most common fighting shotgun of the flintlock era. Though the distinctive flared muzzle of the blunderbuss had no effect on the spreading of the shot pattern, it did make the weapon easy to reload while on the move. The blasting spread of shot from the blunderbuss proved to be very effective on-board fighting ships, where it was used against crowds of men at very short range. The other well-known use of this early fighting shotgun was in protecting moving coaches from armed moving targets (highwaymen).

The U.S. involvement in World War I brought the pump- or slide-action repeating shotgun into modern warfare. The short, powerful, 12-gauge shotgun was found to be very successful in the sudden, close encounters common in trench warfare. During World War II in the Pacific, trenches were rare, but the Marines found the shotgun worked just as well in the fast face-to-face encounters so common in jungle combat. U.S. Marines would obtain short-barreled (18 to 20 inch) repeating shotguns wherever they could, and the supply never met the demand according to the men doing the fighting.

Shotguns were familiar to the men of the World War II UDTs, but primarily as guard weapons or seen in the hands of Marines. Very little direct armed combat between the UDTs and enemy troops ever took place during World War II and shoulder weapons, even light ones like a shotgun, were rarely used by the Teams. The relative long-range fighting during the Korean War relegated the fighting shotgun to guard duty, but it still proved its value in the occasional massed charges of Communist troops. Against a close-in enemy, there are few weapons as effective as a shotgun.

During the World War II years, over twenty different makes, models, and styles of repeating shotguns were used by the U.S. military. One of these guns, the Winchester Model 97, was the original trench gun used during World War I as the Model 1917. By the 1960s, many of the various World War II shotguns had long been weeded out of the supply system for lack of spare parts or other reasons. When the SEALs were commissioned in 1962, shotguns were among the weapons included in the new Teams allotment lists. The shotgun received by the Teams came from Navy stores and was the Ithaca Model 37 Featherweight.

The Model 37 Featherweight was the first true lightweight repeating shotgun with a steel receiver and was produced by the Ithaca Gun Company beginning in 1937. One reason for the success of the Ithaca Model 37 was its being based largely on the last magazine shotgun design of John Browning before his death in November 1927.

The first very noticeable feature of the Model 37 is its lack of an ejection port on the side of the weapon. Machined from a solid block of steel, the receiver of the Model 37 is rather short for its caliber with solid, flat sides. The single port in the Model 37 is in the base of the weapon, just in front of the trigger mechanism. The action of the weapon is such that the single port is used to both load the gun and clear ejected cases.

As in almost all other repeating shotguns, the tubular magazine of the Ithaca Model 37 extends underneath the barrel of the weapon. Shells are fed into the magazine nose-first through the bottom port and seated in place with the thumb. The slide handle that operates the action surrounds and lightly guides on the magazine tube. As the slide is pulled back, any fired cartridge case is extracted from the chamber and ejected downwards from the gun.

When the slide handle has reached the end of its rearward stroke, any fired casing has cleared the weapon and a fresh round is released from the magazine.

As the slide is pushed forward, a lifter moves the shell into line with the chamber and bolt. With the slide fully forward, the bolt is locked on the chamber and the weapon can be safely fired. With the slide forward, additional shells can be fed into the magazine to help keep it full.

For all the usefulness of the shotgun in combat, the SEALs did not see much practical use for the weapon in the time just after their commissioning. Some of the weapons available to the Teams had the trench gun bayonet adaptors on them. These adaptors consisted of perforated barrel guards to help keep an operator from burning his hands on a hot barrel and heavy muzzle devices than held the barrel guard in place and allowed a long rifle bayonet to be mounted on the weapon.

A bayonet was the last thing that the SEALs would put on a shotgun, but most of the shotguns they had available were the standard, five-shot, 20-inch barreled Ithacas without the added poundage of the adaptor. Few of the Ithacas were used during the first few years of the Teams except for one. Kept in a glass-fronted case on the quarterdeck at SEAL Team Two was a fully-loaded Ithaca Model 37. The weapon was intended for the use of the SEAL on watch and all he had to do was break the glass to be well armed against an intruder.

The opinion of most SEALs about shotguns took a hard turn upwards after the first platoons deployed to Vietnam. Prior to that time, the Teams had trained and exchanged information with some of the British Special Air Service (SAS) men who had combat experience in the jungles of Malaysia. It was during their jungle experience that the SAS troopers had seen first hand the efficiency of the shotgun. Semiautomatic FN-Browning shotguns loaded with 00 buckshot were a favored weapon by the SAS, particularly by their lead scouts (point men) and this was part of the information shared with the SEALs.

The Ithaca Model 37 quickly became a much-used weapon among the SEAL point men when they conducted operations in Vietnam. The design of the Ithaca minimized openings into the action and that helped keep mud and jungle debris from jamming the weapon. If a pump shotgun did get jammed up with mud or dirt, it would usually just mean the operator had to jack the slide handle harder to work the weapon. As one SEAL said, "The fact that I could take my Ithaca and just rinse it off in a muddy stream was one of the reasons I liked it."

Two common rounds of ammunition were available for the SEALs' shotguns—XM162 00 buckshot and XM257 #4 buckshot. 00 or "double-ought" buckshot has long been the favored load for the fighting shotgun and ammunition has been loaded with it since well before the turn of the century. Common paper shotgun shells were noted to swell up in water and quickly become useless. An all-brass 00 shotgun round, the M19, had been developed during World War I just to eliminate the problems with paper shells for combat. Though the M19 round was as waterproof as it could be, and would be used by the SEALs when they could get it, but it was just not available in large numbers by the 1960s.

To counter the moisture problem with shotgun ammunition, the plastic-cased XM162 and XM257 rounds were developed. Though the 00 buckshot round had been the preferred load, SEALs in Vietnam almost universally used the #4 buckshot round. 00 buckshot is a .33 caliber lead pellet with 9 pellets loaded into a normal (XM162) round. The smaller #4 buckshot, .24 caliber, made room for 27 hardened lead pellets to be loaded into the XM257 round. The triple number of pellets in the XM257 round gave a weapon firing it a very dense shot pattern, making it easier to cause a disabling shot.

The pump-action shotgun, whether loaded with #4 or 00 buckshot, only has an effective combat range of about 75 yards maximum. And at the maximum combat range, it becomes difficult to put enough shot on the target to really be effective. But at the shot ranges the SEALs tended to operate at, the range limitations of the shotgun were outbalanced by the stopping power of the gun when close in. But one limitation of the shotgun could not be as easily ignored. The 12-gauge round is very heavy and bulky for a single shot and shotguns are not ammunition-efficient. The size and weight of any load of 12-gauge shells generally makes them two to four times heavier and larger than an equal number of 7.62mm NATO or 5.56mm rounds. This bulk not only makes shotgun ammunition difficult to carry in quantity, it minimizes the number of rounds carried in a weapon's magazine.

The Ithaca Model 37 carried 4 standard 12-gauge rounds in the magazine with a fifth round able to be carried in the chamber. This amount of ammunition can be burned up very quickly in a firefight. SEALs quickly learned the trick of constantly reloading or "topping up" their shotgun whenever possible. Some SEALs would carry a few extra rounds of ammunition between the fingers of their operating hand if they were going into a situation where they might need a very fast reload. By simply letting go of the operating slide, two rounds can be quickly thumbed into the magazine with the operating hand without having to draw them from a pocket or pouch.

To help ease the magazine size problem somewhat, a magazine extension was made available for the SEALS Ithacas by late 1967. Because of the way the front magazine cap is part of the barrel retention system in the Ithaca Model 37, the magazine extension requires some permanent changes to the barrel of the weapon. These changes could be easily done in a field repair shop and the necessary kits were forwarded to Vietnam. With the extension in place, the magazine of the Ithaca could now hold 7 rounds with an 8th round in the chamber.

China Lake had designed the magazine extension first issued for the SEALs Ithacas. In addition to the magazine extension, China Lake designed an attachment for the barrel of the Model 37 that would spread the pattern of shot in a more effective manner. The shot spreader attachment was initially a 4-inch long extension brazed onto the muzzle of the weapon. A horizontal V-slot extending halfway back from the muzzle of the device separated the top and bottom halves of the extension and directed the shot pattern. Because of the shape of the spreader attachment it quickly became known as the "duckbill."

With the duckbill installed on a shotgun, the pattern of the shot changed from a circle to an oval with the long axis in line with the open sides of the duckbill. Instead of having a 44-inch circular pattern with #4 buckshot at 30 yards, the duckbill equipped weapon would have a pattern 96-inches wide and only 24-inches tall at the same distance with the same load. The duckbill equipped Ithaca with the magazine extension became a very well-liked weapon in SEAL units.

> "The shotgun with the duckbill was an Ithaca Model 37 and the duckbill was a muzzle attachment that changed the spread of shot from a circle to an oval four times as wide as it was tall. After we started to get some good hits, I picked up the shotgun as a preferred weapon for close-in, especially around hooches. With the duckbill, you didn't have to lead (aim in front of) a moving target as you did a regular shotgun. The spread of the shot made up for any target movement at the short ranges we fought at."

The duckbill attachment was an immediate success with the SEALs even though the design suffered from some drawbacks. Many of the special loads later designed for the SEALs, such as the CS and flare rounds, could be fired through the duckbill attachment. Slugs could not be used with the duckbill. Even 00 buckshot would not work as efficiently as #4 buckshot when put through the duckbill attachment. Also the open end of the duckbill tended to catch on brush and plants as well as spread apart after extensive use, greatly changing the shot patterns. To eliminate the latter problems, a redesigned duckbill with input from Frankford Arsenal was released to the SEALs by late 1968–1969. The new attachment had a ring around the muzzle, closing off the front of the side slots and eliminating the spreading apart of the "bills."

An additional combat round was tried out by the SEALs in 1967 but it did not find a great deal of favor with the operators. The flechette round was an attempt to extend the range of the shotgun shell to over 100 yards. Several different rounds were tried out, all with about the same effect. The flechettes, inch-long finned projectiles much like small modified carpenter's nails, simply did not have the shocking power found in buckshot loads. Though the flechette rounds did extend the effective range of the 12-gauge shotgun to near 150 yards, within 30 yards the rounds were very ineffective.

Because of the aerodynamics of the flechette, the projectiles tended to be unstable when first fired. For the first 20 to 30 yards, the flechette would wobble and yaw badly, having as much chance of hitting a target sideways as point-on. The sideways-striking flechettes has little penetrating power due to their light weight and the flechettes that did hit point-first would just penetrate the target, often going straight through. A through-and-through flechette wound would eventually kill a target, but there would be little immediate shock or knockdown power. Though flechette-loaded 12-gauge rounds did see some combat successes in Vietnam, work still continues to perfect the round.

> The #4 hardened buckshot was my preferred load. Double-ought buck was good, but you could hit more with the greater number of pellets in a number four load. Flechette was also good, at least I thought so. You could hit a man at longer range with it than with a regular shot load. But when a man was hit with flechettes, he would keep on running as if he hadn't been shot at all. The targets would bleed to death with a flechette hit rather than get knocked down as with a buckshot load.
>
> My favorite shotgun ammunition was the XM257 round with the hardened lead #4 buckshot. The 27 pellets in the shell would knock down any gook I aimed at, which was exactly what I wanted. The flechette shells that were sent to us later would certainly kill a man, at even longer ranges than the XM257. But the sharp pointed little flechettes, they looked like finishing nails with fins, wouldn't stop a man as quickly as a load of #4 buckshot.

For all the firepower supplied by the pump-action shotgun, even more would be available from a semiautomatic or full automatic weapon using the same ammunition. The British had developed a strong liking for the FN-Browning A-5 semiautomatic weapon during their SAS operations in Malaysia. Though the Browning was strictly a sporting weapon and had a

number of drawbacks centering around its somewhat sensitive internal workings, the firepower it produced made up for the special care it needed. Some of
the complaints against the Browning came out of the weapon's recoil-operated
action being sensitive to variations in ammunition. It was problems like these
that helped keep the pump-action shotgun the leading favorite in fighting
shotguns.

In early 1967, the Remington Arms Company put the first of a new type of
shotgun into the SEALs' hands. The weapon was a full-automatic 12 gauge, a
machine shotgun, probably the most destructive, close-in fighting weapon ever
produced.

Developed with firepower in mind, the Remington 7188 family of weapons
certainly delivered. Modified from their gas-operated Remington 1100 product
line, the Remington 7188 for the most part resembled a short-barreled sporting
shotgun. The Remington 7188 was available in six Marks; the Mark 1 was the
primary version issued by the SEALs and had a distinctive perforated barrel
shroud, extended seven-round magazine tube, bayonet mounts, and adjustable
rifle sights. The Mark 3 also had the rifle sights and extended magazine tube but
no barrel shroud. The Mark 3 had only the rifle sights with a standard-length
tubular magazine.

The Remington 7188 Marks 2, 4, and 6 were the same as the odd-numbered
marks in that the Mk 2 had the barrel shroud assembly and long magazine, the
Mk 4 just the long magazine, and the Mk 6 the standard magazine. But on the
even-numbered marks, the sights were the simple front bead of a sporting
shotgun.

What made the Remington 7188 stand out was the small switch put in place
of the push-button safety behind the
trigger guard. With the selector lever,
found on the left side of the weapon,
turned to the rear, the gun fired semiautomatically, one shot for each pull
of the trigger. With the lever pointing
down, the weapon was on safe and
the trigger would not operate. By putting the lever in the forward pointing
position, the 7188 fired full automatic.

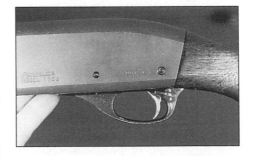

The receiver markings of a standard Remington 7188. A unique
marking rarely seen by people outside of the SEALs and a few
government agencies.

Source: Kevin Dockery

Firing on full automatic, the

7188 could spew out its ammunition at a cyclic rate of 420 rounds per minute. Using XM162 zero zero buckshot ammunition loaded with nine pellets each shell, the 7188 could empty its magazine in just over a second. This rate of fire would put seventy-two .33 caliber "bullets" out of the weapon in under a second and a half. This is heavier and faster firepower than two men firing submachine guns on full automatic in one long burst. By loading the weapon with XM257 #4 buckshot ammunition with its 27 pellets per shell, the 7188 could saturate a target with 216 projectiles in one second.

> I liked the Remington automatic shotgun (the model 7188) a lot as well as the Ithaca. It didn't have a duckbill, and the recoil of that sucker would really put a hum on you, but who cared? During a firefight, your adrenaline was pumping so hard you didn't even feel the buck and recoil of the weapon much. The only trouble was, Boom, Boom, Boom, Boom . . . eight times and whoops, you had to reload. I used the weapon on full auto a lot. It really got everyone's attention, especially the people you were shooting at.

The magazine capacity and one-round-at-a-time reloading procedure was found to be a drawback in the 7188 design, but that was not what kept the weapon from being a success. The Remington 1100, the parent design of the 7188, is a gas-operated, semiautomatic sporting shotgun. The changes for the 7188 conversion were very minor as far as the internal workings of the weapon were concerned. But these same internal workings were far more sensitive to dirt and fouling than a pump-action operating system. The 7188 was just too sensitive to dirt for the muddy conditions in Southeast Asia.

> Other weapons were in the gun shed, including the Remington 7188 full-auto shotgun. When the weapon had first arrived, B—had grabbed on to it as the best thing since sliced bread. . . . I had started carrying a shotgun, a five-shot Ithaca Model 37. B—tried to convince me that the Remington 7188 was the weapon for a point man to carry. But I considered the thing just too heavy to be worth it. Besides, my pump-gun was much more reliable than that complicated full-auto gun.
>
> B—carried the 7188 on about six patrols and finally gave up on it as just being too sensitive to dirt. During one ambush, B—used the 7188 on full auto, and the results were devastating. But the reliability problem finally caused B—to switch to either another Ithaca like mine or the CAR-15 and M16 rifle.

The gas operating system of the 7188 and 1100 allowed the weapons to operate well with a wide variety of ammunition. The gas piston of the system surrounds the magazine tube and is sealed with the barrel seal. Combat operations were hard on the 7188 weapons and their maintenance did cause some problems. In the weekly situation reports for Fifth Platoon, SEAL Team Two covering the period of June 24 to July 1, 1967 the 7188 shotgun is noted under item 2 (c):

> There is a sixty-cent part needed for the automatic shot gun. D— or M— can
> supply you with information on the part.
> The item needed was the barrel seal. Without it, the Remington action
> does not work dependably. Constant maintenance had consumed the supply
> of parts available in Vietnam.
> B—liked the shotgun [7188], even though it was a bitch to hang on to
> during full automatic fire.

In addition to the maintenance difficulties, the Remington 7188 was hard to control when fired on full automatic. The stock design and recoil forces of the 7188 forced the barrel up and back very quickly when the weapon was fired from the shoulder. Training and strength were two items the SEALs had in abundance and both were brought to bear in controlling the 7188. When fired from the hip and properly braced, the 7188 was completely controllable and would put out its swath of fire like a mowing machine. But very quickly the small magazine would be empty and the weapon was just as slow to reload as any other shotgun at the time.

But with its drawbacks, the Remington 7188 Mark 1 remained in SEAL hands through the Vietnam War. Never available in very large numbers—reportedly only a few dozen of all the marks were ever made—the Remingtons that were incountry were coveted for their awesome firepower. After Vietnam had ended, The 7188s were removed from inventory but the full-automatic shotgun question was looked at again in later programs.

A Remington 7188 selective-fire shotgun in SEAL hands in Vietnam. The perforated barrel guard and rifle-type rear sight of the 7188 Mark I can be clearly seen in this photograph. The SEAL holding the weapon is carrying his extra ammunition in a sporting-type vest normally used by duck hunters in the States.
Source: U.S. Navy

COMMAND AND CONTROL HISTORY—1968 SEAL TEAM TWO
The twelve gauge shotgun has been fitted with a specially designed muzzle to give a greater spread to the pellet pattern. Special ammunition has been delivered for shotguns in the form of CS and flare rounds.

The 12-gauge shotgun had quickly established a place for itself in the SEALs arsenal in Vietnam. To increase the versatility of the weapon, a number of new ammunition types were developed an tried out. The buckshot loads used during the first two World Wars had been made up of close to pure lead pellets. These pellets were found to deform and lose their ballistic shape under the acceleration of being fired. The popular XM257 #4 buckshot load had eliminated this problem in two ways. The 0.24-inch diameter pellets in the XM257 were made up of lead alloy containing 4 percent antimony. The alloy shot were much harder than the commercial lead shot found in the XM162 round. The open space between the #4 buckshot in the XM257 round was filled in with granulated polyethylene with the entire padded shot load enclosed in a sheet polyethylene collar.

The alloy pellets and plastic fillers used in the XM257 round gave it a much more uniform shot pattern when fired and kept the pattern from spreading as quickly as it otherwise would have. When fired from a normal 20-inch cylinder bore barrel, all of the pellets from an XM257 round impact inside of a 40-inch (101.6 cm) circle at 44 yards (40 m). This is what gives the XM257 round and the shotgun such a high hit probability which is increased with the duckbill muzzle attachment. Within 5 yards or less, the pattern of shot opens to be only a few inches wide, effectively hitting as a single, huge projectile.

Several rounds of ammunition used in the SEALs shotguns in Vietnam were not intended to be direct, casualty-producing rounds. The 12-gauge CS tear-gas round fired a small metal capsule filled with CS and a burning agent. Acting much like a miniature M7A3 tear-gas grenade, the CS round would ignite when fired and could be used to put a small amount of CS into a bunker or hooch. Several CS rounds were usually carried by most SEALs armed with a shotgun, especially when going out on search operations.

The other special pyrotechnic 12-gauge round used by the SEALs was an aerial flare cartridge. Much brighter than any small-arms tracer round, the 12-gauge flare round launched an aluminum capsule loaded with colored flare composition. Besides being usable for signaling, the flare round could also act as a small incendiary projectile for setting fire to buildings and other flammable structures.

What was probably the most unusual shotgun shell ever produced was manufactured for the SEALs in Vietnam. With the SEALs strong tastes for shotguns and suppressed weapons, the idea of a suppressed shotgun held a great deal of appeal. But the large caliber and multiple projectile load of a shotgun badly complicates any attempt to put a suppressor on the barrel or muzzle of the weapon. What was attempted was the silencing of the shotgun shell itself.

The requirement put forward by the Navy in 1967 was for a low-signature munition that could be loaded, fired, and ejected from a standard shotgun without modification to the weapon. The round was also to have the high-hit probability and lethality of a shotgun shell but could be accepted with a shortened range. The low-signature requirement not only meant the sound of the shot being suppressed but also the elimination of much or all of the flash and smoke of firing. The difficult requirements of the round were met within a year by the AAI Corporation of Baltimore, Maryland.

By using its patented telecartridge device as a base, AAI succeeded in producing what they called the Silent Shotgun Shell by early in 1968. The telecartridge was a method of producing mechanical action through the use of burning propellant. The heart of the telecartridge system was the use of an expanding metal capsule to produce the mechanical motion by retaining the expanding gasses of a suitable propellant. A byproduct of the system was the retention of the propellant gasses eliminated most of the noise of burning as well as all of the smoke and flash. Produced for the aerospace industry, the telecartridge was also able to make an effective silent round of ammunition for the military.

The Silent Shotgun Shell used the expanding metal capsule of the telecartridge system to drive a plastic pusher piston. The piston in turn drove the round's twelve #4 buckshot to a muzzle velocity of 450 feet per second. The expanding metal capsule prevented any gasses from escaping the fired round and so the only sound heard when firing the Silent Shotgun Shell was the click of the shotgun's firing pin.

The body of the cartridge was made of steel in the configuration of a 12-gauge round. The sides of the body were parallel for about two-thirds of their length and then tapered slightly into the mouth of the casing. The tapering was to help the round feed and extract after firing. The cadmium-plated steel body of the silent shotgun shell was rust resistant and waterproof. The telecartridge capsule itself was made of 1010 steel and folded into itself to reduce its overall length. An aluminum capsule at the base of the round contained the smokeless-powder propellant charge and acted as a high-pressure chamber to ensure the

This is one of the few existing photographs of the very rare silent shotgun shell produced for SEAL use during the Vietnam War. The round to the far right is a complete, unfired cartridge showing the steel case with the partial taper to aid in feeding. The center round is a cutaway showing the buckshot charge at the top of the round resting on the pusher piston. The piston is surrounded by the telescoping, folded metal component that is the heart of the "telecartridge" power system. The open chamber at the base of the round would normally hold the powder charge. The casing to the left is a fired round and shows the bulging end of the unfolded telecartridge capsule protruding from the mouth of the case.

Source: AAI Corporation / Thomas Swearengen Collection

complete burning of the powder. A standard percussion primer completed the system.

About 200 rounds of silent shotgun shell ammunition was produced overall and supplied to the Naval Ordnance Laboratory for testing. Suggestions put out by the laboratory reduced the muzzle velocity of the original rounds from 550 feet per second to around 450 feet per second. The reduction in velocity removed some of the stopping power of the round but also reduced the chances of the telecartridge capsule rupturing.

Though the silent shotgun shell was not completely silent, it made a weapon firing it very hard to hear and effectively unnoticable. The few rounds made were consumed in testing and none were known to be sent to Vietnam for field testing. The major factor that prevented the silent shotgun shell from being used in quantities by the SEALs in Vietnam was the very high cost of each round. The high cost was not considered balanced by the usefulness of the round as other suppressed weapons were becoming available and the project was shelved.

By the mid-to-late 1970s, the shotguns the SEALs had been using in Vietnam were more than showing their age and a replacement weapon was needed to supplant existing Ithaca stocks. After an exhaustive series of tests in 1966, the Marine Corps had adopted the Remington 870 as its primary issue shotgun.

The Marine model of the Remington was the 870 Mark 1 designed particularly for military use. The Mark 1 differs from the normal 870 in that it came equipped from the factory with a two-shot magazine extension, giving the Mark 1 an ammunition capacity of eight rounds. Distinctive on the Mark 1 is the long double sleeve near the muzzle that acts as a brace between the magazine extension and the barrel. The magazine cap works with a stud on the underside of the brace and allows the Mark 1 to mount the M7 bayonet.

Most Marine 870 Mark 1s have a standard wooden buttstock but some are fitted with the Remington folding stock. The Remington folding stock has a pistol grip and a square cross-section metal stock. The stock can swing over the top of the 870 and lay across the top of the receiver and barrel. Though the rifle-type sights of the Mark 1 are obscured with the Remington stock in the folded position, the pistol grip allows the weapon to be comfortably fired with the stock folded. Some Remington 870 Mark 1s are fitted with a front bead sight in place of the rifle-type sights but the bead is also blocked when the stock is folded.

The SEALs respected the testing done by the Marines and examined the Remington 870 for their own use. Instead of the Marine 870 Mark 1, the SEALs chose the standard Remington 870 in several different patterns including the 870R and 870P. The Remington 870R is a 20-inch-barreled, wooden-stocked weapon with a five-round ammunition capacity and parkerized military finish. With a bead sight, the 870R is the Mark 6, and with a set of rifle-type sights, it is the Mark 5.

The Remington 870P is much like the 870R except that the P model has the two-shot magazine extension attached. With the rifle-type sights, the designation is Mark 3 and with a plain bead front sight, it is the Remington Mark 4. The designations get even more blurred when the SEALs start attaching the various accessories and different-length barrels they prefer.

In general, the Remington 870 is a very rugged slide-action repeating shotgun. Having stood up to severe testing, the 870 is the standard shotgun issued in the Teams since the mid-1980s. The steel receiver of the Remington 870 allows the weapon to accept a great deal of abuse and wear. Individual weapons have fired thousands of rounds without requiring any maintenance beyond cleaning. The Remington folding stock, originally only found on the 870P model intended for police sales, has been used in two different configurations by the SEALs.

The regular Remington 870P with a folding stock is used where size is a major consideration. The ease with which the Remington 870 can be used with the stock folded has led to a number of weapons having the folding metal portion of their stocks removed. The short-barreled, pistol-grip 870 is used by the Teams especially as a breacher's weapon.

The breacher assignment developed from SEALs involvement in counterterrorism. Learned from their opposite numbers in the British SAS is the SEA technique for opening locked doors rapidly. Instead of targeting the lock with a shotgun blast and kicking the door open, a breacher uses his shotgun against the hinges of a closed door. With two or three quick blasts of 00 buckshot against their hinges, most doors simply fall open. In the SEALs case, the door

A SEAL Breacher member of an assault squad covers a stairway with his shotgun while undergoing ship searching drill during Operation Desert Storm. The weapon is a Remington 870 12-gage shotgun with a police folding stock and two-shot magazine extension. The metal portion of the folding stock has been removed leaving the Remington with just a plastic pistol grip. The SEAL is wearing a PRO-TEC helmet and safety glasses and has a single M1951 glove over his left hand.
Source: U.S. Navy

will usually fly open and crash to the floor as a close quarters battle (CQB) trained team of SEALs enters the room.

Special ammunition has been examined in order to open doors with minimum danger to the occupants inside. In a terrorist hostage situation, 00 buckshot can easily overpenetrate a door, becoming a danger to any hostages on the other side. Lock-buster rounds were developed to overcome the penetration problem. Using the Hatton Pattern solid round as an example, the projectile is a flat-ended 1.8-ounce composition cylinder made of pressed plastic and powdered lead. Fired from a standard 12-gauge casing, the cylindrical projectile will smash its way through a door lock or hinge easily. Once it has struck the target, the composition projectile breaks up into heavy particles and powder. Since the target has to absorb the tremendous energy of the projectile, it is usually completely destroyed with a single shot. The projectile fragments have very little power and are harmless a short distance beyond the target. The Hatton round was one of the lock-buster ammunition types examined by Navy Ordnance for use by the Teams.

To make their 870s quicker and easier to handle, minimum-length barrels would be used by the SEALs when possible. The normal 20-inch barrel is the most generally useful length for a combat shotgun used in the same manner as the Ithaca Model 37 was in Vietnam. For close-in work, a 16- or 17-inch barrel is the best trade-off between handiness and practical ballistics. A shorter barrel loses velocity and becomes very ineffective at range. In addition, the 17-inch barrel can be used on the 870P with the magazine extension with only an inch or so of the magazine protruding past the muzzle.

Though the slide-action shotgun is by far the most successful model of combat shotgun used by the SEALs, the lessons learned in Vietnam and the firepower of the full-automatic Remington 7188 were not forgotten. Research was sponsored in the early 1970s by the Defense Advanced Research Projects Agency (DARPA) into developing a 20mm Multi-Purpose Assault Weapon as part of the TRICAP program. Though no adoptable weapon design came out of the TRICAP program, the data it developed proved useful to later projects.

In 1979, the Joint Services Small Arms Program (JSSAP) Management Committee, responsible for new small arms development for the Department of Defense, initiated the sponsorship of a series of new small arms designs. The military shotgun program for JSSAP was initially titled RHINO for Repeating, Handheld, Improved, Non-Rotating Ordnance. Within a short time, the project was renamed MIWS for Multipurpose, Individual, Weapons System. For the MIWS project, all the services—Army, Navy, Marine Corps, Air Force, and Coast Guard—submitted their requirements for a military shotgun.

What the project resulted in was the search for a design that would use a whole new family of ammunition. To accomplish the range requirements, lethal over at least 150 meters, a new caliber of high-pressure shotgun ammunition would have to be developed. And to prevent the ammunition from being used in a shotgun not designed for the pressure, it would be a larger size than normal shotgun shells, 3.5-inches long and 12 or 10 gauge.

In addition to the range requirements, the new weapons were to be capable of selective fire and loaded with a box magazine. Recoil was not to be excessive and the gun was not to be longer than 39 inches. The magazine would preferably hold 20 rounds of the new ammunition. In 1983, the Navy Weapons Support Center issued two contracts for what was now called the Close Assault Weapon (CAW) system. Contracts went to AAI in Baltimore, Maryland and the Olin Corporation in East Alton, Illinois. The Olin Corporation intended to develop the new family of ammunition and subcontracted the weapon development to Heckler & Koch.

The H&K CAWS was a bullpup design, that is, the action of the weapon is behind the trigger guard. The bullpup configuration was chosen to give the shortest overall length while allowing for a long barrel. Initially intended for full-automatic fire, the requirements were changed as the project went along and the final H&K CAWS was only a semiautomatic weapon.

The overall design of the H&K CAWS made for a very quick to handle weapon with much greater capabilities than commercially available shotguns. The cocking handle of the H&K CAWS is at the top of the weapon, protected by the raised sight/carrying handle. By moving the sightline up high, the recoil force of the H&K CAWS is kept low, making the weapon more controllable when fired. The low line of recoil force helps keep the muzzle of the weapon down when fired as the force is absorbed directly by the shoulder and does not rotate the barrel upwards.

The box magazine of the H&K CAWS only held 10 rounds but was much faster to insert into the weapon than the traditional single rounds into a tubular magazine. Though the H&K CAWS could use regular 12-gauge ammunition for training, the combat ammunition developed by Olin was also found to be very effective.

The Olin ammunition is an all-metal cased round with a raised belt above the rim of the cartridge as found in belted magnum rifle ammunition. The raised rim adds strength to the base of the cartridge as well as preventing it from being chambered in any regular 12-gauge weapon. The 12-gauge caliber Olin ammunition was loaded with either 000 buckshot, #2 tungsten buckshot, or flechettes. The flechette loading was only considered experimental and development was concentrated on the two buckshot loads.

The 000 buckshot CAWS round holds eight 0.36 caliber hardened lead shot. The round proved itself lethal out to 150 meters but the density of the shot pattern did not raise the hit probability as much as desired. Another round loaded with eight #2 buck (0.27 caliber) made of heavy tungsten alloy was found to hold a tighter pattern and became the primary test round. The hard, dense nature of the tungsten alloy allowed the Olin round to penetrate 0.060 inches of mild steel plate out to 150-meters range, a vast improvement over the XM162 round.

The first H&K CAWS submitted was capable of full-automatic fire and had a 1-power optical sight on the top of the handle. Testing found that the sight could be effectively replaced with a simple open-sight arrangement. Ejection of fired cartridges could be user-selected to either side of the weapon. This feature allowed the bullpup design of the H&K CAWS to be used by both right- and left-handed firers. It was during the first round of testing that the requirement for full-automatic fire was found to be unreasonable given the ammunition range and power requirements. The full automatic capability was dropped at this time and further development desired on the H&K design.

The final H&K CAWS had open sights in the handle of the weapon with tritium inserts allowing for their use in low-light conditions. A longer barrel was on the last H&K CAWS candidate to try and increase the range and lethality of the weapon while also reducing the very high sound signature. Overall, the Navy testing that ended in 1987 found the H&K CAWS to demonstrate:

> Improved controllability, lighter recoil, reduced flash and faster reloading capabilities than the current military shotgun (Remington 870). The ammuni-

tion provides a significant reduction in shot pattern size and gave improved penetration and lethality compared to current military shotgun ammunition.

The AAI CAWS candidate followed the lines of a more conventional-appearing weapon than the H&K bullpup approach. Using work already done as part of the earlier DARPA 20mm Multi-Purpose Assault Weapon project, the AAI CAWS resembles a large assault rifle. The stock, which is removable, is the same as on an M16A1 rifle, which is also where the pistol grip was taken from. The large box magazine holds 12 rounds of ammunition and the weapon can use regular 12-gauge ammunition with an adapter.

The heart of the AAI CAWS candidate centered around the ammunition. Using a special plastic, rimless cartridge case, AAI used its past experience with flechette ammunition to have its CAWS launch 8 steel flechettes. The flechettes are stabilized with a plastic drag cone to help give them effectiveness from the muzzle out to their maximum range.

Development of the AAI CAWS candidate resulted in small changes to the weapon. The full automatic requirement was dropped as it had been in the H&K weapon and the magazine capacity was reduced by 2 rounds. The effectiveness of the flechette rounds was proven out in tests. The flechettes could penetrate 3 inches (7.6 cm) of pine boards, 0.125 inch (3.2 mm) of sheet steel, or a flak vest and 11 inches (27.9 cm) of ballistic gelatin, at a range of 150 meters.

Plastic sleeves on the flechettes would extend past the base of the projectile after firing. The drag of air on the sleeves would force the flechettes to fly point-first from the muzzle outwards, something that never worked with fin-stabilized flechettes. The stabilization system made the flechette load effective and gave the round its excellent terminal effects at range. But the flechette ammunition for the AAI CAWS could not hold consistent shot patterns. Overall, the AAI CAWS held a great deal of promise as a possible combat shotgun. But no matter how effective the terminal results of the ammunition, it does no good if it cannot hit the target.

Both of the CAWS candidates were shelved after the Navy testing was completed and few weapons spent any time in SEAL hands. the concept was proven out enough to show that a more effective combat shotgun could be produced sometime in the future and it would probably be first combat tested in SEAL hands.

■ Shotgun Data ■

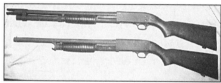

Source: Kevin Dockery

ITHACA MODEL 37

Ithaca Model 37 with magazine extension
and shot spreader (above) unmodified version (below)
CARTRIDGE 12 Ga 2¾ in (18.5×70mmR)
OPERATION Manual, slide-action
TYPE OF FIRE Repeating
RATE OF FIRE 15 rpm
MUZZLE VELOCITY 1,260 fps (384 m/s)
MUZZLE ENERGY 1,903 ft/lb (2,580 J); 70
   ft/lb (95 J) per pellet (27)
SIGHTS Front bead
CHOKE Cylinder bore
FEED 4-round tubular magazine
WEIGHTS
Weapon (empty) 6.30 lb (2.86 kg)
Weapon (loaded) 6.83 lb (3.10 kg) w/4 rds in
   mag + 1 in chamber
Magazine (loaded) 5 rds—0.53 lb
   (0.24 kg)
Service cartridge M257 #4 Buck 748 gr
   (48.5 g)
Projectile 540 gr (35 g)
Pellet 20 gr (1.3 g)

LENGTHS
Weapon overall 40 in (101.6 cm)
Barrel 20.1 in (51.1 cm)
Shot spread at 30 yds (27 m) 30 in (76.2 cm)

ITHACA MODEL 37 W/MAGAZINE EXTENSION AND DUCKBILL SPREADER MUZZLE ATTACHMENT

CARTRIDGE 12 Ga 2¾ in (18.5×70mmR)
OPERATION Manual, slide-action
TYPE OF FIRE Repeating
RATE OF FIRE 21 rpm
MUZZLE VELOCITY 1,260 fps (384 m/s)
MUZZLE ENERGY 1,903 ft/lb (2,580 J); 70
   ft/lb (95 J) per pellet (27)
SIGHTS Front bead
CHOKE Special w/horizontal to vertical
   spread of 4:1
FEED 7-round tubular magazine
WEIGHTS
Weapon (empty) 6.5 lb (2.95 kg)
Weapon (loaded) 7.35 lb (3.33 kg) w/7 rds in
   mag + 1 in chamber
Magazine (loaded) 8 rounds 0.85 lb (0.39 kg)
Service cartridge M2 #4 Buck 748 gr (48.5 g)
Projectile 540 gr (35 g)
Pellet 20 gr (1.3 g)
LENGTHS
Weapon overall
Barrel 20 in (50.8 cm)
Shot spread at 30 yds (27 m) 96 in (243.8 cm)
   horizontal, 24 in (61 cm) vertical

Source: Kevin Dockery

REMINGTON 7188 MARK 1
REMINGTON 7180 MARK 1

CARTRIDGE 12 Ga 2 ¾ in (18.5×70mmR)

OPERATION Gas

TYPE OF FIRE Selective—semiautomatic/full automatic; 7180—Semiautomatic only

RATE OF FIRE Practical SS 24 rpm, A 35 rpm, Cyclic 420 rpm

MUZZLE VELOCITY 1,252 fps (382 m/s)

MUZZLE ENERGY 1,817 ft/lb (2,464 J); 202 ft/lb (274 J) per pellet

SIGHTS Open, V-notch/blade, adjustable

CHOKE Full

FEED 7-round tubular magazine

WEIGHTS

Weapon (empty) 8.50 lb (3.86 kg)

Weapon (loaded) 9.34 lb (4.24 kg) w/7 rds in mag + 1 in chamber

Magazine (loaded) 8 rounds 0.84 lb (0.38 kg)

Service cartridge XM162 00 Buck 736 gr (47.7 g)

Projectile 522 gr (33.8 g)

Pellet 58 gr (3.8 g)

LENGTHS

Weapon overall 40.94 in (104 cm)

Barrel 20.24 in (51.4 cm)

Sight radius 13.11 in (33.3 cm)

Shot spread at 30 yds (27 m) 22.5 in (57.2 cm)

REMINGTON 870 MARK 6

CARTRIDGE 12 Ga 2¾ in (18.5×70mmR)

OPERATION Manual slide-action

TYPE OF FIRE Repeating

RATE OF FIRE 15 rpm

MUZZLE VELOCITY 20 in bbl—1,250 fps (381 m/s); 17 in bbl—1,243 fps (379 m/s)

MUZZLE ENERGY 20 in bbl; 17 in bbl—1791 ft/lb (2429 J); energy per pellet 20 in bbl; 199 ft/lb (270 J) per pellet 17 in bbl

SIGHTS Front bead

CHOKE Cylinder bore

FEED 4-round tubular magazine

WEIGHTS

Weapon (empty) 7 lb (3.18 kg) w/20 in bbl; 6.82 lb (3.09 kg) w/17 in bbl

Weapon (loaded) 7.53 (3.42 kg) w/20 in bbl, 4 rds in mag + 1 in chamber; 7.35 lb (3.33 kg) w/17 in bbl, 4 rds in mag + 1 in chamber

Magazine (loaded) 5 rounds—0.53 lb (0.24 kg)

Service cartridge XM162 00 Buck 736 gr (47.7 g)

Projectile 522 gr (33.8 g)

Pellet 58 gr (3.8 g)

LENGTHS

Weapon overall 40.5 in (102.9 cm) w/20 in bbl; 37.5 in (95.3 cm) w/17 in bbl

Barrel 20 in (50.1 cm); 17 in (43.2 cm)

Shot spread at 30 yds (27 m) 30 in (76.2 cm)

Source: Kevin Dockery

REMINGTON 870 P W/FOLDING STOCK

CARTRIDGE 12 Ga 2¾ in

OPERATION Manual slide action

TYPE OF FIRE Repeating

RATE OF FIRE 15 rpm

MUZZLE VELOCITY 1,243 fps (379 m/s)

MUZZLE ENERGY 1,791 ft/lb (2,429 J); 199 ft/lb (270 J) per pellet

SIGHTS Front bead

CHOKE Cylinder bore

FEED 4-round tubular magazine

WEIGHTS

Weapon (empty) 6.94 lb (3.15 kg)

Weapon (loaded) 7.47 lb (3.39 kg) w/4 rds in mag + 1 in chamber

Magazine (loaded) 5 rounds—0.53 lb (0.24 kg)
Service cartridge XM162 00 Buck 736 gr (47.7 g)
Projectile 522 gr (33.8 g)
Pellet 58 gr (3.8 g)
LENGTHS
Weapon overall 27/37 in (68.6/94 cm)
Barrel 17 in (43.2 cm)
Shot spread at 30 yds (27 m) 30 in (76.2 cm)

REMINGTON 870 MARK 1

CARTRIDGE 12 Ga 2¾ in (18.5×70mmR)
OPERATION Manual slide-action
TYPE OF FIRE Repeating
RATE OF FIRE 24 rpm
MUZZLE VELOCITY 1,257 fps (383 m/s)
MUZZLE ENERGY 1,831 ft/lb (2,483 J); 203 ft/lb (275 J) per pellet
SIGHTS Open, V-notch/bead, adjustable
CHOKE Modified
FEED 7-round tubular magazine
WEIGHTS
Weapon (empty) 8.0 lb (3.63 kg)
Weapon (loaded) 8.84 lb 4.01 kg) w/7 rds in mag + 1 in chamber
Magazine (loaded) 8 rounds 0.84 lb (0.38 kg)

Service cartridge XM162 00 Buck 736 gr (47.7 g)
Projectile 522 gr (33.8 g)
Pellet 58 gr (3.8 g)
LENGTHS
Weapon overall 41.75 in (106 cm)
Barrel 21 in (53.3 cm)
Shot spread at 30 yds (27 m) 26 in (66 cm)

Source: Kevin Dockery

HECKLER & KOCH CAWS CANDIDATE (SECOND MODEL— LONG BARREL)

CARTRIDGE 19.5×76mmB
OPERATION Recoil
TYPE OF FIRE Selective—semiautomatic/full automatic or semiautomatic only
RATE OF FIRE Practical SS 30 rpm A 40 rpm Cyclic 240 rpm
MUZZLE VELOCITY 1,625 fps (495 m/s) w/long barrel
MUZZLE ENERGY 2,216 ft/lb (3,005 J) w/long barrel; 277 ft/lb (376 J) per pellet w/long barrel

JSSAP RHINO (Repeating Handheld Improved Non-Rifled Ordnance) Requirements from 1979 evolved into the mid-1980's CAWS (Close Assault Weapon System) project.

CAWS requirements—A semiautomatic weapon with a 10-round box magazine. Length is not to exceed 39 inches and weight is not to exceed 9 pounds unloaded and 11 pounds loaded. The weapon is also required to have a manual safety and a sighting system usable in low-light-level conditions. Reloading time for replacing an empty magazine with a full one is to be less than 5 seconds. Magazines cannot be capable of being inserted into the weapon backwards and must be refillable in less than 30 seconds.

These requirements have changed from the original proposal put forward in 1979. Most notably, the requirement for full-automatic fire capability was dropped.

SIGHTS Open, square-notch/post w/luminous tritium dot inserts, fixed, adjustable for windage

CHOKE Special extra full

FEED 10-round removable box magazine

WEIGHTS

Weapon (empty) 8.82 lb (4.0 kg) w/long barrel; 7.62 lb (3.46 kg) w/short barrel

Weapon (loaded) 10.77 lb (4.89 kg) w/long barrel; 9.57 lb (4.34 kg) w/short barrel

Magazine (empty) 0.42 lb (0.19 kg)

Magazine (loaded) 1.95 lb (0.88 kg)

Service cartridge #2 Tungsten 1,073 gr (69.5 g)

Projectile 378 gr (224.5 g)

Pellet 47.25 gr (3.06 g)

LENGTHS

Weapon overall 39 in (99.1 cm) w/long barrel; 30.63 in (77.8 cm) w/short barrel

Barrel 26.94 in (68.4 cm)—long barrel; 18.63 in (47.3 cm)—short barrel

Sight radius 10.38 in (26.4 cm)

Shot spread at 55 yds (50 m) 22 in (55.9 cm)

■ Shotgun Ammunition ■

HK CAWS #2 TUNGSTEN

CALIBER 19.5×76mmB

LOAD #2 Tungsten buck

NUMBER OF PELLETS 8

NOMINAL MUZZLE VELOCITY 1,625 fps (495 m/s)

NOMINAL MUZZLE ENERGY 2,216 ft/lb (3,005 J); 277 ft/lb (376 J) per pellet

TEST BARREL LENGTH 26.94 in (68.4 cm)

WEIGHTS

Cartridge 1,073 gr (69.5 g)

Projectile 378 gr (224.5 g)

Pellet 47.25 gr (3.06 g)

Pellet diameter 0.27 in

HK CAWS 000 BUCK

CALIBER 19.5×76mmB

LOAD 000 Buck

NUMBER OF PELLETS 8

NOMINAL MUZZLE VELOCITY 1,601 fps (488 m/s)

NOMINAL MUZZLE ENERGY 3,141 ft/lb (4,259 J); 393 ft/lb (533 J) per pellet

TEST BARREL LENGTH 18.11 in (46 cm)

WEIGHTS

Cartridge 1,247 gr (80.8 g)

Projectile 552 gr (35.8 g)

Pellet 69 gr (4.5 g)

Pellet diameter 0.36 in (9.1 mm)

HK CAWS FLECHETTE

CALIBER 19.5×76mmB

LOAD Finned steel flechettes

NUMBER OF PELLETS 20

NOMINAL MUZZLE VELOCITY 2,953 fps (900 m/s)

NOMINAL MUZZLE ENERGY 2,246 ft/lb (3,046 J); 112 ft/lb (152 J) per flechette

TEST BARREL LENGTH 18.11 in (46 cm)

WEIGHTS

Cartridge 811 gr (52.6 g)

Projectile 116 gr (7.5 g)

Pellet 5.8 gr (0.376 g)

AAI CAWS CANDIDATE (SECOND MODEL)

CALIBER 18.5×79mm

OPERATION Recoil

TYPE OF FIRE Semiautomatic, selective fire— semiautomatic/full automatic on first model

RATE OF FIRE First model Practical SS 30 rpm, A 40 rpm, Cyclic 450 rpm

MUZZLE VELOCITY 1,794 fps (547 m/s)

MUZZLE ENERGY 1,901 ft/lb (2578 J); 229 ft/lb (311 J) per outer flechette 300 ft/lb (407 J) inner flechette

SIGHTS Optical 1-power reflex sight w/illuminated retiole, backup sight open, aperture/post, adjustable

CHOKE None
FEED 10-round removable box magazine
WEIGHTS
Weapon (empty) 8.89 lb (4.03 kg)
Weapon (loaded) 10.23 lb (4.64 kg)
Magazine (empty) 0.45 lb (0.20 kg)
Magazine (loaded) 1.34 lb (0.61 kg)
Service cartridge Flechette 623 gr (40.4 g)
Projectile 266 gr (17.2 g)
Pellet 32 gr (2.07 g) outer flechette; 42 gr
    (2.72 g) inner flechette; 27 gr (1.75 g) steel
    flechette body
LENGTHS
Weapon overall 39 in (99.1 cm)
Barrel 16 in (40.7 cm)
Sight radius 19.69 in (50 cm)
Shot spread at 55 yds (50 m) 42 in (106.7 cm)

AAI CAWS FLECHETTE

CALIBER 18.5×79mm
LOAD Drag-stabilized flechettes
NUMBER OF PELLETS 8
NOMINAL MUZZLE VELOCITY 1,794 fps
    (547 m/s)
NOMINAL MUZZLE ENERGY 1,901 ft/lb
    (2,578 J); 229 ft/lb (311 J) per outer
    flechette; 300 ft/lb (407 J) inner flechette
TEST BARREL LENGTH 16 in (40.7 cm)
WEIGHTS
Cartridge 623 gr (40.4 g)
Projectile 266 gr (17.2 g)
Pellet 32 gr (2.07 g) Outer flechette; 42 gr
    (2.72 g) inner flechette; 27 gr (1.75 g) steel
    flechette body
Flechette diameter 0.104 mm (2.65 mm)
    flechette body
Flechette length 1.62 in (4.1 cm)

12-GAUGE GUARD PAPER CASE

CALIBER 12 Ga 2¾ in (18.5×70mmR)
LOAD 00 Buck
NUMBER OF PELLETS 9
NOMINAL MUZZLE VELOCITY 1,325 fps
    (404 m/s)

NOMINAL MUZZLE ENERGY 2,035 ft/lb
    (2,759 J); 226 ft/lb (306 J) per pellet
TEST BARREL LENGTH 30 in (76.2 cm)
WEIGHTS
Cartridge 791 gr (51.3 g)
Projectile 522 gr (33.8 g)
Pellet 58 gr (3.8 g)

M19 METAL CASE

CALIBER 12 Ga 2¾ in (18.5×70mmR)
LOAD 00 Buck
NUMBER OF PELLETS 9
NOMINAL MUZZLE VELOCITY 1,125 fps
    (343 m/s)
NOMINAL MUZZLE ENERGY 1,467 ft/lb
    (1,989 J); 163 ft/lb (221 J) per pellet
TEST BARREL LENGTH 30 in (76.2 cm)
WEIGHTS
Cartridge 930 gr (60.3 g)
Projectile 522 gr (33.8 g)
Pellet 58 gr (3.8 g)
Pellet diameter 0.34 in (8.6 mm)

XM162 PLASTIC CASE

CALIBER 12 Ga 2¾ in (18.5×70mmR)
LOAD 00 Buck
NUMBER OF PELLETS 9
NOMINAL MUZZLE VELOCITY 1,325 fps
    (404 m/s)
NOMINAL MUZZLE ENERGY 2,035 ft/lb
    (2,759 J); 226 ft/lb (306 J) per pellet
TEST BARREL LENGTH 30 in (76.2 cm)
WEIGHTS
Cartridge 736 gr (47.7 g)
Projectile 522 gr (33.8 g)
Pellet 58 gr (3.8 g)
Pellet diameter 0.34 in (8.6 mm)

M257 PLASTIC CASE

CALIBER 12 Ga 2¾ in (18.5×70mmR)
LOAD #4 Hardened buckshot
NUMBER OF PELLETS 27
NOMINAL MUZZLE VELOCITY 1,335 fps
    (407 m/s)

NOMINAL MUZZLE ENERGY 2,137 ft/lb
(2,898 J); 79 ft/lb (107 J) per pellet
TEST BARREL LENGTH 30 in (76.2 cm)
WEIGHTS
Cartridge 748 gr (48.5 g)
Projectile 540 gr (35 g)
Pellet 20 gr (1.3 g)
Pellet diameter 0.24 in (6.1 mm)

REMINGTON MODEL SP-12F-20 BEEHIVE FLECHETTE

CALIBER 12 Ga 2¾ in (18.5×70mmR)
LOAD Finned steel flechettes
NUMBER OF PELLETS 20
NOMINAL MUZZLE VELOCITY 2,200 fps
(671 m/s)
NOMINAL MUZZLE ENERGY 1,620 ft/lb
(2,197 J); 81 ft/lb (110 J) per flechette
TEST BARREL LENGTH 20 in (50.8 cm)
WEIGHTS
Cartridge 750 gr (48.6 g)
Projectile 150 gr (9.7 g)
Pellet 7.5 gr (0.49 g)
Pellet diameter 0.087 in (2.21 mm)

TELESHOT SILENT SHOTGUN SHELL

CALIBER 12 Ga 2¾ in (18.5×70mmR)
LOAD #4 Hardened buck
NUMBER OF PELLETS 12
NOMINAL MUZZLE VELOCITY 450 fps
(137 m/s)

NOMINAL MUZZLE ENERGY 108 ft/lb (146
J); 9 ft/lb (12 J) per pellet
WEIGHTS
Projectile 240 gr (15.6 g) w/o plastic pusher
piston
Pellet 20 gr (1.3 g)
Pellet diameter 0.24 in (6.1 mm)

PENGUIN LONG RANGE TEAR GAS ROUND

CALIBER 12 Ga 2¾ in (18.5×70mmR)
LOAD Burning-type tear gas (CN) canister
NUMBER OF PELLETS 1
FILLER CN/Bullseye smokeless powder
(burning mixture)
NOMINAL MUZZLE VELOCITY 800 fps
(244 m/s)
TEST BARREL LENGTH 20 in (50.8 cm)
WEIGHTS
Filler 185 gr (12 g)

FLARE ROUND

CALIBER 12 ga 2¾ in (18.5×70mmR)
LOAD Red star cluster
NUMBER OF PELLETS 4
BURN TIME 5 to 6 seconds at 5,000 candle-
power
EFFECTIVE RANGE 200 ft (61 m) altitude

■ 7
RIFLES AND CARBINES

By the middle of World War II (1943) the average Navy sailor was receiving a limited amount of training in small arms while he attended boot camp as a recruit. Small arms were not a priority in the Navy, as the force fought from aboard ship with the U.S. Marines being the primary amphibious ground combat unit. In 1943, when the NCDUs began training at Fort Pierce, Florida, the primary shoulder-fired weapon in the Navy was the bolt-action M1903 Springfield rifle. The semiautomatic M1 Garand was not considered a Navy weapon at that time and all production of the M1 was going to the Army and Marines.

For the men of the NCDUs and UDTs, it was not considered a mission priority to have the men offensively armed. Little emphasis was given to small arms training in the NCDU curriculum at Fort Pierce. The men who made up the UDT operating platoons were considered to be skilled demolitionists and not people to augment ground troops. Instruction in armed and unarmed combat was given to the UDTs in order that these highly trained men would be able to effectively defend themselves if necessary.

The men who made up the Headquarters Platoon of a UDT were given training in small arms to a much greater extent than the men of the operating platoons. Headquarters personnel were expected to supply boat crews, coxswains, radiomen, and other support to the swimmers who would be doing the actual reconnaissance and demolition swims.

It was toward this end that the men of the Headquarters Platoon received hands-on experience with small arms, primarily the pistol and M1 carbine, as well as gunnery instruction for the .30 and .50 caliber machine guns. If, after the normal eight-week training period, there was a delay in sending the NCDU graduates to Maui for their UDT instruction the men would receive the same classes in small arms as the headquarters personnel.

But for all of their training, the men of the NCDUs and UDTs were still in the military. Common military jobs had to be performed such as guard duty.

Because of the highly secret nature of their mission, the men of the NCDUs and UDTs were not able to tell anyone what they did to cause all the explosions heard coming from North Hutchison Island near Fort Pierce. The locals could of course hear the blasting, but the island was off limits to almost everyone but the NCDU students.

But the ammunition and explosive magazines on North Hutchison Island had to be guarded, and it was the men of the NCDU school who pulled that duty. The same situation was repeated at the UDT training compound on Maui in the Pacific. When necessary, the NCDU and UDT men were normally armed with the M1 Carbine.

The M1 Carbine was designed early in World War II after a directive for its development was put out by the Army Ordnance Board in June 1940. The intent was to develop a shoulder-fired weapon weighing about 5 pounds and having an effective range of 300 yards. The weapon was intended as a replacement for the service pistol and submachine gun for officers and noncommissioned officers as well as being a supplementary weapon for mortarmen, machine gunners, radiomen, and other similar duty positions.

The U.S. service rifle cartridge (30-06) was far too powerful for as light a weapon as the carbine was supposed to be. And the service pistol cartridge (45 ACP) was unable to reach the range requirement. A special low-powered .30 caliber round was designed specifically for what was then called the "light rifle" trials in 1941. Several arms manufacturers submitted prototype weapons chambered for the new round. By the fall of 1941, only sixteen months after the directive had first been issued, a winner of the light rifle trials had been decided on. The Winchester Light Rifle was adopted as the M1 Carbine in October 1941.

As adopted, the M1 Carbine was a small semiautomatic rifle feeding from a 15-round magazine. It was this model carbine that was issued to the men of the UDTs as their duties required. Late in 1944, a selective-fire version of the carbine was developed. Issued as the M2 Carbine, the new weapon had a 30-round magazine available for it that could also be used in the earlier M1 Carbine. As the M2 Carbine became available, it was issued to the UDTs.

The only other shoulder weapon trained with and used in any numbers by the UDTs in World War II was at the opposite end of the small arms scale from the M1 Carbine. The Browning Automatic Rifle Model 1918A2, or simply BAR, is a very heavy and powerful rifle. Normally fired from the prone position with the weapon supported by a bipod, the BAR is capable of good accuracy at a long range. The 20-round magazine of the BAR limits its capacity for sustained fire somewhat as does its lack of a way to change a hot barrel. But the weapon was a great deal more portable that the contemporary belt-fed automatic weapons of the time.

Instead of being selective-fire, that is, firing either semiautomatic or full automatic, the M1918A2 BAR instead had two different rates of fire that could be selected by the operator. The fast rate of fire, around 600 rounds per minute cyclic, could put out a rapid volume of fire in order to engage or suppress an enemy position. The slow rate of fire, about 350 rounds per minute cyclic, allowed for single shots to be easily fired by a trained gunner and had more controllable muzzle climb when fired from the standing position.

In the Navy, the BAR would be used for shore or landing party operations. On-board ship, the Bar would occasionally be found in use to augment a ship's volume of antiaircraft fire. More important to the men of the UDT, the BAR could be used to give a reasonable amount of firepower to small craft such as a rubber boat. The BAR could be fired from such a boat by a single operator while the light machine gun of the time, the Browning M1919A4 would be very clumsy to use and take up a great deal more room.

Used by the UDT in only limited numbers, the BAR saw little if any combat duty with the Teams during World War II. Photographs of NCDUs at Fort Pierce exist showing at least one man of the six man NCDU armed with a BAR. Training was given on the M1918A2 BAR at Fort Pierce and it is likely that additional training with the weapon was conducted at Maui late in the war. The commander of the UDT school at Maui toward the end of World War II, Commander John T. Koehler, could see the mission of the UDTs expanding inland if the war continued. To account for such a situation, and to expand the capabilities of the UDTs, Commander Koehler added further small arms training and other skills to the UDT training curriculum.

During the Korean War, the land combat application of the UDTs became much more than just a possibility. Guerrilla infiltration and exfiltration, clandestine resupply ops, and behind-the-lines demolition raids all were conducted by the men of the UDT. The M1 and M2 Carbines and BARs again saw duty with the UDTs, only their use was much more serious than simple guard duty. The submachine gun was considered the favorite shoulder weapon, but the carbine, BAR, and even the M1 Garand were seen in UDT hands. Though the UDTs had few small arms of their own, the facilities of a base armory or ship's stores were available to the Teams when necessary.

A watershed event in the weapons of the UDT took place shortly after the commissioning of the SEALs in January 1962. SEAL Team Two, on the East

Coast at Little Creek, Virginia, was faced with the very real possibility of seeing combat operations in Cuba within a short time after its commissioning. Not being satisfied with what was available through Navy supply channels or in the base armory, Lieutenant Roy Boehm, the first officer-in-charge of SEAL Team Two as well as the Team's founder, sought out the best firearms on the market he could find. Desiring high-firepower, lightweight, dependability, and increased lethality over the M1 Carbine, Lt. Boehm was highly interested in a very new firearm just available commercially, the AR-15 rifle.

Early in 1962, Lt. Boehm and some of his new SEALs traveled to Baltimore, Maryland to visit the Cooper-MacDonald firm's offices. Cooper-MacDonald had been representing the AR-15 rifle to the military for several years. The original manufacturers and developers of the AR-15, the Fairchild Stratos Corporation, had sold the license to produce the ArmaLite AR-15 to the Colt Firearms Corporation in 1959. Though the AR-15 had received praise from many of the people who had fired it, the U.S. Military and especially the Army Ordnance Corps were adamantly not interested.

The Army, then responsible for small arms acquisition for the Air Force and Marines as well, had just adopted the M14 as the new service rifle in May 1957. Difficulties in production and other delays had kept the M14 from being produced in the quantities needed by the military. It was only in 1961 that productions volume had finally started reaching the numbers needed for full issue. In this atmosphere, the Army Ordnance Corps was very much against any new weapon being even remotely considered for adoption. This was particularly true for a weapon that would also add a new caliber of ammunition into the supply system.

The Army had just managed to start coming online with a new family of weapons, the M14 and the M60 machine gun, that were both chambered for the same 7.62mm NATO round. One of the selling points of the new weapons was that they would eliminate at least one caliber, the .30 Carbine, as well as several weapons—the submachine gun, M1 Carbine, M1 rifle, and BAR. The AR-15 was chambered for the unique .222 Special developed especially for it. In 1959, the new round was renamed the .223 Remington.

The lightweight .223 bullet did not seem at all a proper projectile for a military weapon according to several prominent people in the Army small arms field. These same people set out to disprove any possible advantages the .223 round might have in the military. The most obvious advantage of the new round was its light weight, at the time two loaded 20-round AR-15 magazines weighed less than a single 20-round M14 magazine.

One problem with the small bore of the AR-15 rifle was strongly pointed out by the Army board examining the weapon. During trials of the AR-15 at the Aberdeen Proving Grounds in 1958, the barrel of one test weapon split while firing during a rain test. Modifications to the barrel were completed by Gene Stoner, the AR-15's designer. But rumors persisted about the danger of the .223 bore retaining water droplets due in part to capillary action.

If the SEALs were to use the new rifle and there was a problem with water retention in the bore, it would be proved useless given the environment of their missions. Not particularly trusting anyone else's tests, Lieutenant Roy Boehm conducted his own examination of the AR-15.

... Wanting to test the AR-15 himself before making his purchase, Roy took some Team Two men up to Baltimore with him to check out the weapons the dealer had available. Roy and the guys shot the AR and fully tested it. They even tossed the weapon into the surf zone, covering it with sand, silt, and salt water, and it continued operating. With proper care, the AR-15 was able to pass any abuse Roy gave it. Team Two now could issue one of the newest weapons available on the market.

Lt. Boehm found no problem with water retention in the bore of the AR-15. He was in a unique situation where he had to outfit his men and did not have the time to wait for channels. The funds necessary for the equipping of SEAL Team Two were already at Roy Boehm's disposal in the form of open purchases he could make in any market he saw fit. The men of the SEAL Team quickly agreed with the boss's decision.

The best package of firepower and weight we had were the new AR-15 rifles. This was several years before the Army was to adopt the AR-15 as the M-16, even in limited numbers. But Roy had used his open purchase system and gotten us 66 brand new AR-15s fresh from the Colt factory.

Roy had ordered 136 of the new AR-15 rifles, the selective fire models (Colt Model 601) with green stocks. Half of the weapons were sent to Team One along with instructions, magazines, and spare parts.

As the men came in, we issued what we had. Watches, pistols, and other gear was given out. Then when Cuba calmed down, the additional men went back to their parent units, and a lot of our gear went with them. One of the items we had before any one else in the Navy were the AR-15 rifles. ... Half of the weapons went to the West Coast and SEAL Team ONE with the remainder staying with us. Those were the first rifles of their kind in the Navy and were later adopted by the military as the M-16. We had them first because we needed them.

The new weapons were well and enthusiastically received by the SEALs. For the first time, a lightweight, highly-lethal, selective-fire weapon was available. Though the M2 Carbine had been both lightweight and capable of automatic fire, the round it fired was considered underpowered and had proved itself to have less than ideal stopping power. In defense of the Carbine, it must be remembered that the weapon was designed to be a replacement for the pistol as a secondary arm generally for support troops.

Though the M-14 was the intended standard issue shoulder weapon of the early 1960s, it was considered too large and ungainly for use by the SEALs who might easily have to transport the weapon underwater. Another factor in favor of the AR-15 was its intentional design for controlled automatic fore. The M-14 could have a selector switch easily installed, but the weapon is built along traditional lines. The recoil of automatic fire in the M-14 violently pushes the muzzle up and to the right, especially when fired from the shoulder.

A group of SEAL Team Two operators in the early 1960s. They are wearing uniforms that were part of a large open-purchase of commercially-produced equipment that was made to get the newly commissioned SEAL Teams operational as quickly as possible. The groups weapons are early-model Colt AR-15 rifles. The early style fully chromed bolt carrier is readily visible through the open ejection port of the weapon held by the SEAL at the left of the picture. The smooth right side of the upper receivers show that these weapons do not have the forward bolt assist required by the Army in the later M16A1 rifle. Additionally, these weapons have the first model, stepped-down, double diameter open-prong flash hiders that were part of the early production units in the series. The SEAL at the lower right in the photo is holding the very rare AR-15 carbine with its flash suppressor mounted just in ahead of the front sight.
Source: U.S. Navy

The AR-15 has the stock in line with the barrel of the weapon. This causes the AR-15 to have less tendency to climb up and right when fired on automatic, though the weapon still takes a good deal of training to properly control. The training is considered very worthwhile as full automatic fire is very much an advantage for sudden close-in firefights or the overwhelming fire needed for an ambush. The SEALs liked the fact that the AR-15 could be fired on full automatic with just the flip of a selector switch. Sometimes, the SEALs liked full automatic fire a little too much. The first range practice with the new AR-15s for SEAL Team Two took place at a

Marine range since they had the proper firing facilities and the fledgling SEAL Teams did not.

> As we were getting down into the firing position the [Marine] Lieutenant sounded off. "There will be no automatic fire on this range," he said. "Everything will be semiautomatic fire only." That was a bit of a mistake on his part.
>
> "Lock and load one magazine. Ready on the left? Ready on the right? Ready on the firing line! Shooters, you may commence fire!" We all just raised our heads a little bit and looked up and down at each other. At the command "Commence fire" all of us switched over to automatic and let that magazine rip. The Lieutenant immediately confiscated all of the weapons and threw us off the base.

One problem that the SEALs did not have was with the lethality of the AR-15. Being the early 601 models, the AR-15s purchased directly by the Teams had barrels rifled with six grooves having a right-hand twist rate of one turn in fourteen inches. This rifling twist rate was the firearms industry standard when Gene Stoner had first designed the AR-15. Since the 55-grain .223 bullet was the same weight as commercial .22 bullets fired in high-velocity center fire rifles, the commercial twist rate was thought to be correct to stabilize the .223 bullet for accuracy.

The problem was that the commercial 55-grain bullets then in use were shorter and blunter than the full jacketed projectile designed for the .223 Remington military round. Standard M193 ball ammunition, when fired from the early AR-15, launched a projectile that was just barely stable in flight. When the bullet struck a target, or entered flesh, it began tumbling wildly, expending its energy rapidly. This rapid energy release resulted in the near-explosive wounds coming out of Vietnam in mid-1962.

Almost 1,000 AR-15 rifles, all early model 601s, and over half a million rounds of ammunition had been purchased by the Defense Department in late December 1961. These weapons and ammunition were part of Project AGILE being conducted by the Advanced Research Projects Agency (ARPA). The project intended, in part, to examine new weapons for use by "the small-stature . . . Vietnamese soldier and to evaluate the weapon under actual combat conditions."

Project AGILE resulted in the first operational tests of the AR-15 in combat being conducted by selected units of the South Vietnamese Army supported by

American advisors. The tests ran from February 1 to July 15, 1962. Besides being well-liked by the Vietnamese troops for its size and light recoil, the AR-15 had shown itself to be a very lethal combat weapon. Reports told of almost incredible wounds being caused by single .223 bullets. Amputations of limbs, massive body wounds, and decapitations had all been caused by the very high–velocity AR-15 projectiles.

But there was a drawback that came with the near-instability of the AR-15 bullets being fired in 1-in-14 twist barrels. When the ambient temperature dropped below freezing, the air density changed. In cold air, the AR-15 bullets became unstabilized and accuracy dropped off badly. In independent, unbiased tests run by the National Rifle Association, it was found to be impossible to keep ten rounds on a 3-foot by 4-foot target at 300-meters range with the air temperature below 32 degrees Fahrenheit.

Since SEAL Team Two did few operations in a cold environment during its first years, the drawback of the AR-15s rifling was not noticed as a problem. By July 1963, orders had gone out from the Department of Defense that no further AR-15s would be accepted with the old rifling twist rate. The new twist rate, which stabilized bullets in below-freezing temperatures, was 1 turn in 12 inches. All subsequent AR-15s, M-16s, and M16A1s were all made with the 1-in-12 rifling twist rate, including those used by the SEALs.

A SEAL Team Two MTT (Mobile Training Team) 10-62 went to Vietnam to continue training the Beit Hai commandos of the South Vietnamese Navy. The training program had been begun by an MTT primarily from SEAL Team One earlier in the year. Along with "3 to 4 tons" of other equipment, the Team Two MTT took along with it a number of the Team's AR-15s. At the time the AR-15 and its use by the SEAL Teams was still classified. Again, the men of the South Vietnamese military greatly liked the AR-15. In fact the MTT soon ran out of the .223 ammunition they had brought along with them. At the time, the .223 military ball was loaded by Remington Arms and came packaged in a white 20-round cardboard box. As the ammunition was gone, the MTT turned to training the Vietnamese with available weapons including the M1 Garand, M2 Carbine, and BAR. It would be some years later that .223 ammunition would be available in huge numbers in Southeast Asia.

In June, 1963, President John F. Kennedy came to Norfolk and visited SEAL Team Two. While on his tour, President Kennedy saw a number of SEALs who were demonstrating the equipment they used. One man, GMG2 A.D. Clark was holding one of the Team's AR-15 rifles. When President Kennedy approached Clark he asked, "What have you got there, son?"

"This sir," answered Clark, "is the AR-15 rifle, made by ArmaLite."

At that point, one of the officers escorting President Kennedy, an Army Colonel, interrupted, commenting about how the AR-15 was only a limited duty, special-purpose weapon as compared to the issue M-14.

The President cut off the Colonel with a curt, "I am speaking to this gentleman here," and he resumed his conversation with Clark.

That action probably did as much to endear the President with the men of the SEALs as did his signing their commissioning orders only sixteen months before. But A.D. Clark continued with his praise of the AR-15, stating that it was exactly the weapon the SEALs wanted and no other. In a way it is very proper that A.D. Clark is the SEAL who spoke to the President in regard to the AR-15 rifle. Clark had been one of the SEALs who had accompanied Lt. Roy Boehm the year before when he had gone to Cooper-Macdonald in Baltimore to first test the AR-15.

By 1965, even the UDTs had at least some AR-15s in their inventory for issue to operating platoons. By this time, the AR-15 had been purchased in some numbers by the Air Force as the M16 rifle. The Navy had purchased an additional 240 M16 rifles, announcing the contract in October 1964. In the week of January 18–22, 1965, Colt received a priority 04 MIPR from the Navy for an additional 50 M16 rifles. At the time, rifles were shipped with seven 20-round magazines, spare parts and additional materials were shipped separately. The Army was also purchasing thousands of XM16E1s at this time, primarily for use with U.S. Army maneuver battalions in Vietnam.

The AR-15 had been advertised by Colt as an almost self-cleaning weapon needing only "an occasional simple cleaning . . . (to) keep the weapon functioning indefinitely. Working parts can be cleaned by wiping with a cloth." But in the SEAL Teams and UDTs, maintenance procedures take on an importance close to that of a religion. This attitude stems from the Teams working underwater with Underwater Breathing Apparatus (UBAs). If a diver does not take meticulous care of his UBA, it will fail on him at some point, either killing him outright or causing him to drown. With something like that for a background, it is easy to see how the SEALs and UDTs keep their mania for maintenance.

In the first edition of the UDT Handbook (1965) are listed the cleaning instructions for the AR-15 (M-16) that state: ". . . all excess carbon [be] simply wiped off the working parts." But with the Team's tradition for complete maintenance, weapons, including the AR-15, were cleaned thoroughly and completely. Because of this situation, the SEALs did not suffer the large numbers of malfunctions experienced by Army personnel when the rifle was fielded in Vietnam.

Several variations of the AR-15 were also obtained by the SEALs in early 1962 in addition to a number of accessories. Very early in 1962, SEAL Team Two had at least one of the rare AR-15 carbines, the Model 605. The CAR-15 (for Colt Automatic Rifle) carbine was the same as the AR-15 rifle except that the barrel had been cut off to just in front of the front sight and the flash suppressor reinstalled. It is possible that only one of the CAR-15 carbines was ever procured as the weapon was not very successful and very few were manufactured by Colt. The AR-15 carbine was offered by Colt for situations "where stowage is a problem," that would of course hold appeal to the size-conscious SEALs. Though it shows up in a number of photographs of field exercises conducted by Team Two in 1962 and in a 1964 weapons display, the AR-15 carbine was little used and probably never fielded in Vietnam.

Several accessories for the AR-15 were experimented with by the SEALs prior to the Vietnam War. At least one removable telescopic sight was tried out by SEAL Team Two. The telescopic sight was a Delft Optics 3×25 power telescope (weight 0.875 lbs. [0.397 kg]), adapted from the earlier AR-10 rifle. Though it could be easily mounted and dismounted from the carrying handle of the AR-15, the early scope sight simply would not remain zeroed to the weapon. When mounted on the rifle, hand pressure was enough to push the sight out of alignment with the rifle. Other accessories obtained included AR-15 bayonets, clip-on bipods, and a small number of early model 30-round magazines.

In 1965, the Army had begun receiving quantities of the XM16E1 rifle and several elite Special Forces and Airborne units were equipped with the new weapon. For Army use, a number of modifications had been done to the original Model 601 AR-15. Most of these modifications had also been included in the Air Force issue M16. For the Army XM16E1, the major visible change was the addition of the forward bolt assist, a bolt closure mechanism on the upper receiver of the rifle that allowed the bolt to be pushed forward. To accommodate the new changes, Colt manufactured the M16 and the XM16E1 as their Models 602 and 603 respectively.

In the Spring of 1965, the SEALs were given the opportunity to employ their AR-15s in combat. By April, the rebels in the Dominican Republic had escalated the situation to a crisis point. U.S. Forces were finally called in to protect U.S. interests and help control the fighting in the streets. Two platoons of SEALs from Team Two arrived in the Dominican Republic complete with their equipment, including the AR-15 rifle. At the same time, components of the U.S. Army's 82nd Airborne Division were also conducting operations on the island. The airborne troops were armed with their new XM16E1s.

One drawback of the AR-15 stood out very quickly for the SEALs after their arrival. As the existence of the SEALs was still considered classified at the time and their presence in the Dominican Republic was something the military command wanted to keep secret, the SEALs moved about in civilian clothes for at least part of their duties.

But the SEALs were carrying their AR-15 rifles, a very distinctive-appearing weapon at the very least. In at least this one instance, the SEALs' penchant for camouflage didn't quite work out.

Combat employment of the AR-15 against the rebels in the Dominican Republic proved out the AR-15 to a number of SEALs' satisfaction. Incidents of combat for the SEALs was limited during the crisis, but few complaints were voiced against the new rifle.

In addition to the AR-15, the SEALs had at least one additional type of rifle with them during their deployment. Having been issued one of the new AN/PVS-2 starlight scopes for night work, the SEALs mounted the device on an M14 rifle. The power and range of the 7.62mm bullet fired by the M14 proved itself very effective, especially against snipers. Though heavy in comparison to the AR-15, the M14 had a good deal of appeal due to the added range it gave the SEALs. In one instance, the M14—AN/PVS-2 combination was able to provide security against sniper activity along a beach area at night, something no other weapon system available at the time could have done as well.

The M14 was the last "full-sized" rifle to reach standard-issue status with the U.S. military. An improved version of the M1 Garand, the M14 is chambered for the 7.62mm NATO round. The 7.62mm NATO ammunition, also identified as the 7.62×51mm or .308 Winchester (civilian), came out of the old school of thought as to what constituted and ideal battle rifle. Old-school opinion held that a military rifle must be effective at what we now consider a very long range. One thousand yards would only be considered a medium long range to earlier military planners, even though a soldier who could effectively use his rifle at that range was very rare.

Modifications to the gas system, a provision for full-automatic fire, a 20 round box magazine, and other mechanical improvements made the M14 a better overall battle rifle than the earlier M1 Garand. The long range capability and overall dependability of the M14 kept it held in reserve in the military supply system long after it had been supplanted by the M16A1 as the standard issue U.S. shoulder arm. Hand fitted and tuned to match specifications, the M14 became a highly accurate base for a later family of sniper rifles for both the Teams and the Army.

An additional AR-15 based weapon was used by the SEALs prior to their major deployment to Vietnam. The CAR-15 submachine gun was a shortened version of the AR-15, offered by Colt as its Model 607 early in 1965. Originally part of the CAR-15 weapons family, which included the Model 605 Carbine, the CAR-15 submachine gun was a very shortened version of the AR-15 rifle. Since the action of the AR-15 requires that the bolt carrier be able to recoil into the stock when the weapon is fired, a folding stock is out of the question. For the Model 607, a sliding buttstock of generally standard shape was devised.

The sliding buttstock has a switch on the buttplate to lock or unlock the stock system. Using the switch, the buttstock can be slid in or out and locked firmly into either the extended or collapsed position. With the stock in the collapsed position, the CAR-15 can be easily employed for instinctive shooting while held in the underarm position. Since the weapon was so handy when collapsed, many SEALs never bothered extending the stock.

> . . . For myself, I preferred the CAR-15, the short submachine gun version of the M16. Using the CAR, I would rarely extend the stock as most of our fighting was done close-in with instinctive firing from the hip being the norm.

The barrel of the Model 607 was cut down to only ten inches and the standard flash hider installed. The front sight was also moved back and the gas system modified as needed. The handguards of the Model 607 were of the same triangular style as those on the AR-15, only roughly half as long. Well-liked by the SEALs for its short size and fast handling characteristics, the Model 607 CAR-15 was available in very limited numbers. Those weapons that were available were used in Vietnam until they were effectively worn out.

To increase the number of possible sales of the CAR-15 to the military, especially the Army, Colt made a number of changes to the weapon while it still retained the designation CAR-15 submachine gun. The addition of the XM16E1 model forward bolt assist to the CAR-15 added about 0.2 pounds (0.09 kg) to the overall weight of the weapon. Though the forward bolt assist was not particularly desired by the SEALs, the CAR-15 certainly was. This resulted in a number of slightly different CAR-15 submachine guns being used in the Teams through the Vietnam War.

By late 1966, the Army and the Air Force had shown enough interest in the CAR-15 to have ordered several thousand from Colt. The first weapons examined for the Army were standard model 607s with the forward bolt assist added. During Army testing, one serious drawback did stand out immediately when the CAR-15 was fired. The short barrel and standard flash hider gave the weapon a tremendous muzzle blast and loud report accompanied by a large fireball. At night, the muzzle blast from the Model 607 was dazzlingly bright.

To reduce the muzzle blast and report of the CAR-15 submachine gun, Colt developed a combination flash/noise suppressor in September 1966. The first model flash/noise suppressor added only 1.3 inches (3.3 cm) to the overall length of the CAR-15 and about 0.1 pounds (0.045 kg) to its weight. The internal configuration of the combination suppressor eliminated a good deal of the muzzle flash and, when new, reduced the report of firing the CAR-15 to near that of the standard M16 rifle.

Though a number of the first-model flash/noise suppressors were made in the fall of 1966, the design was not considered completely satisfactory. In order to cut down on the sound and flash of firing, the first model noise/flash suppressor had a tight muzzle hole, only slightly larger than the .223 projectile. Though the design of the suppressor did reduce the muzzle blast of the CAR-15, it also increased the amount of fouling deposited in the barrel of the weapon. The tight exit hole also caused tracer bullets to yaw badly when fired, destroying their accuracy. To limit the barrel fouling and allow tracer bullets to be accurately fired, a new flash/noise suppressor was developed.

The second model flash/noise suppressor had an overall length of 4.25 inches (10.8 cm) and a weight of 0.14 lbs. (0.6 kg). Threading the suppressor onto the 0.635-inch-long threaded portion of the barrel muzzle, including a 0.1-inch-thick lock washer, increased the overall length of the weapon by 3.72 inches (9.4 cm). The second model flash/noise suppressor was identified by Colt as part #62370. The inside of the second model noise/flash suppressor had a small expansion chamber surrounding a ported barrel extension much the same as the first model device, but the new suppressor had a longer body that incorporated a six-slotted end piece with a large internal diameter, like a standard flash suppressor.

The second model flash/noise suppressor was fitted onto all subsequent models of the CAR-15 and retrofitted onto older weapons as parts became available. Though at least somewhat effective at cutting down the sound and flash of firing the short-barreled AR-15 variations, the suppressor was still easily clogged with fouling and would quickly lose its effectiveness in a combat environment.

The original sliding buttstock assembly of the Colt model 607 was considered too complex and costly for fielding with the Army. A new type of sliding buttstock was designed and put into production. The new stock was a more skeletal, tubular design while still retaining a full-sized buttplate. To extend or collapse the stock, a lever underneath the sliding section was squeezed with the operators fingers, unlocking the rear portion of the assembly. A spring would engage to lock the stock in the extended or collapsed position when the operating lever was released. Lastly, the triangular handguards, which were found to be somewhat fragile, were replaced with short, cylindrical handguards with raised reinforcing ribs.

The new weapon, named the Commando by Colt, began to be delivered to the military on November 7, 1966 with an initial shipment of 1,190 weapons out of a 2,815 weapon contract. By January 1967, the Commando had been tentatively type-classified as the XM177 submachine gun (Air Force version) without a forward bolt assist and the XM177E1 (Army version) with a forward bolt assist. The XM177E1 was sent to Vietnam beginning with the first shipments in November 1966 with the Army's distribution of 2,800 weapons being completed by March 1967.

SEALs had been using the model 607 CAR-15 submachine gun from the time of their first combat deployments in Vietnam, circa 1966-1967. As the XM177E1 became available, it was picked up for use with the Teams. Development of the XM177 system continued with the Army, the intention being the future replacement of all M3 and M3A1 submachine guns in service as well as the M1911A1 .45 pistol and M16A1 rifle on a selective basis.

After extensive field testing, the XM177E1 was found to not be completely satisfactory. Problems in accuracy were noted and a number of improvements made. In mid-April 1967, the new Colt model 629 Commando was type-classified as the XM177E2. A contract for 510 XM177E2s was signed with Colt with the weapons to go to the Studies and Observation Group, Vietnam (MAC-V SOG). Delivery of the new weapons was to begin in late September 1967.

Two noticeable aspects of the XM177E2 stand out in photographs of the weapon. The barrel was extended an additional 1.5 inches (3.8 cm) giving the XM177E2 a barrel length of 11.5 inches (29.2 cm). The additional barrel length was found to help cut down on the muzzle blast and increase the stability and accuracy of projectiles. Additionally, the longer barrel allows the XM148 40mm grenade launcher to be more easily attached to the XM177E2. Many elite units, including the SEALs, greatly liked the additional firepower of the XM148 launcher, but adding the weapon to the earlier CAR-15 and XM177E1 was difficult and required modifications to both weapons.

In addition to the longer barrel, the XM177E2 appears to have a third model flash and noise suppressor, one with a noticeable raised boss at the barrel end of the device. The boss is actually a stamped metal washer with an elongated cross section. The washer acts as a forward stop for the XM148 40mm grenade launcher and also allowed rifle grenades to be launched from the XM177E2, something that was rarely, if ever, done.

Since the XM177E1/E2 weapons incorporated all of the up-to-the-minute changes and improvements developed for the XM16E1/M16A1, the Commando was noticeably more reliable than many of the M16-type weapons already in Vietnam. By July 1967, thirty XM177E1 barrels with chrome-plated chambers arrived in Vietnam. Later production XM177E2s were all produced with chrome-plated chambers to help limit corrosion.

Accuracy of fire with the XM177E2 continued to be a problem throughout the life of the weapon, especially when firing tracer ammunition. In November 1968, Colt estimated that a complete ballistic and kinematic study of the XM177E2 would cost $400,000 and take six months to complete. Recommendations in December 1968 were for the XM177E2 to be reoriented to a $635,000, 29-month-long R&D program. Due to the winding down of the U.S. forces in Vietnam after 1970, no action was taken on the XM177E2 program and the weapon went out of production in 1970. Though thousands of the XM177E1/E2 weapons had been built, only a few hundred remained in use by the elite forces who strongly desired them. Cannibalization of damaged XM177s to keep the remaining weapons operational became quite common during the 1970s in the SEAL and UDT Teams.

The strong desire to keep the XM-177E1/E2 weapons operational with the SEALs is clearly shown in the mention of the production model weapons' first arrival in the Teams. The excerpt is from SEAL Team Two's Command and Control History for 1969, page 14:

> 3. (U) The XM177E1 submachine gun, better known as the CAR 15, appeared at the SEAL Team late in the year (1969). This weapon is a welcome addition to the Team's family of weapons, because it fills a size gap that had been left open by all our other weapons. Its main characteristic is its relatively short length which makes it perfect for those people in a patrol such as the patrol leader, radio man, and assistant patrol leader, who find the shorter weapon ideal for close-quarter searching and surveillance of prisoners.

On February 23, 1967 the XM16E1 was adopted by the U.S. Army as the M16A1 rifle. The weapon had received a number of improvements during its testing by the Army, some of which were necessitated by the Army changing the type of powder allowed in loading .223 ammunition. Among other changes the inside of the bolt carrier was chrome plated and the exterior parkerized with a dull finish. The chrome plating minimized corrosion while giving the carrier a non-reflective finish. Earlier bolt carriers had been entirely chromed and could be seen shining through an open ejection port.

A third model flash suppressor was added to the M16A1, this one having a closed muzzle giving it a "birdcage" appearance. The earlier open prong flash suppressors were reported by the Army to hang up on vines, tall grass, and brush, things not noticed by the SEALs. Other changes in the M16A1 included chrome plating the chamber, and later the entire bore, of the weapon. The SEALs simply liked the M16 family completely and used them interchangeably. In a single SEAL platoon in Vietnam could sometimes be seen AR-15s, M16A1s, CAR-15s (model 607s), XM177E1s, and XM177E2s. On the muzzles of the weapons could be found first, second, and third model flash hiders, on both long and short barreled weapons, as well as first and second model flash/noise suppressors on the "shorty" weapons.

The SEALs' opinion of the M16E1 shows clearly in the following quote taken from the official Command and Control History for SEAL Team Two, 1967:

> The M16E1 has proven a welcome addition to the SEAL arsenal. The weapon performs very well as long as it is kept reasonably clean.
>
> The chrome [plated] chambers and barrels should substantially lengthen the life of the barrel. It is believed that the bolt assist should be eliminated from the weapon.

For the SEALs' operations in Vietnam, surprise was as much of a weapon as any ordnance that could be carried. Specialized weapons could sometimes give an additional edge to an operating group of SEALs deep in the bush. Normally, weapon specialization extended into giving the SEALs as much concentrated firepower, in terms of volume of fire, that they could effectively carry. But other types of weapons could increase the surprise factor in the SEALs favor. And foremost among these weapons are suppressed guns where the sound of firing is eliminated as much as possible.

A suppressor, commonly called a silencer, cuts down on the noise of a weapon's firing, suppressing the sound of the shot. Usually, a suppressor does not affect the velocity of a fired projectile which, if it is moving faster than the speed of sound, causes a sonic "crack" as it passes through the air.

During the first years of the SEALs' major deployments to Vietnam, few if any suppressed weapons were available to the Teams. Those that were usually

consisted of old World War II
weapons that were in very short supply. Back in the States, the U.S.
Army's Human Engineering Laboratory (HEL) at Aberdeen Proving
Grounds was one of several places
developing suppressors for the military. The HEL M4 suppressor became available to the SEALs in the
summer of 1967. The HEL M4 suppressor was mounted as a permanent part of a modified M16A1 and
was not intended to be removed. For

These two SEALs crouch down and watch a helicopter come into
their area during a training operation. The SEAL to the left is holding an M16A1 rifle with a plastic mud cap over the flash suppressor.

Source: U.S. Navy

proper operation with the HEL M4 suppressor attached, the bolt carrier of the
designated M16A1 had an extra gas bleed-off hole drilled into it, centered and
behind the two holes already in place. The extra hole allowed the weapon to
function properly, firing in both semiautomatic and full automatic modes, but
only with the suppressor attached. With the suppressor removed, the modified
M16A1 wouldn't operate except as a manually loaded repeater.

A gas deflector shield was attached to the charging handle of the modified
M16A1 to protect the firer's face and eyes from any excess propellant gasses.
The HEL M4 suppressor made the modified M16A1 very difficult to locate by
sound when fired. At a distance of 50 meters or so, depending on the surrounding area, the sound of the shot could not be heard.

To increase the efficiency of the suppressor, the SEALs obtained a quantity
of special downloaded .223 ammunition. The special ammunition would fire a
subsonic projectile that did not break the speed of sound, about 1,100 feet per
second (335 m/s) at sea level, and yet still operate the action of the modified
M16A1. Though very quiet and effective, the subsonic ammunition still would
not operate the action as dependably as desired. Neither was the terminal effectiveness of the special ammunition as good as the standard round.

The suppressor-equipped M16A1 was used by the SEALs throughout their
operations in Vietnam and was considered a valuable asset. As noted in the
SEAL Team Two Command and Control history for 1968, page 8:

> A silencer has been produced which when used with special ammunition, has
> an undistinguishable noise level. The SEAL Team now has silencers for pistols
> and rifles.

The weapon was especially valuable on those missions that needed the longer range and accuracy of a suppressed rifle over that of a suppressed pistol or submachine gun. Off-duty SEALs sometimes found additional uses for the suppressed M16A1s they had.

> We shipped out and went on to Song Ong Doc, where we were living on a barge. At night, you'd see groups of rats swimming out from shore in a column maybe twenty feet long, trying to reach the barge and climb up to get into the potatoes that were stacked amidships. When we didn't have operations, the guys would get M-16s with silencers (suppressors) on them and sit out on deck shooting the rats. As long as they used the silencers (suppressors) the officers didn't know what they were doing.

The SEALs were constantly looking for ways to augment the firepower of their small units. This was one of the reasons that the Teams first looked at the AR-15 weapon. One item that was attractive in the AR-15 was that it came outfitted with a twenty-round magazine. Though a thirty-round magazine had been available from Colt since at least 1964, technical difficulties with the large magazines design kept it from being commonly available.

The original Colt thirty-round magazine was a "fully curved" design, that is the magazine had a slight curve to facilitate feeding rounds through its entire length. Though the original magazine fed ammunition smoothly, the magazine well of the AR-15 was a straight rectangular hole. Allowances for a curved magazine had not been designed into the weapon. Simply put, not all of the AR-15/M16/XM16E1 weapons made would accept the original thirty-round magazine. If an individual weapon's tolerances were on the large side, it could accept the curved magazine; if not, it could only feed from the standard twenty-round magazine.

The few thirty-round magazines the SEALs had were carefully hoarded and used for combat duty. Though the Teams had at least a small number of the original thirty-round magazines in 1964-65, there were never enough for general issue. The Air Force also had a limited number of the early thirty-round magazines and occasionally individual mags would be "borrowed" by enterprising SEALs.

In January 1966, a requirement was put out for a thirty-round magazine to be delivered from Colt for the M16/XM16E1 program. The late-1966 contract for the XM177E1 Commando specified that the weapon come issued with 7 thirty-round magazines. But the thirty-round magazine project was overshadowed at Colt by other problems and pushed back in priority. XM177E1s were issued with standard twenty-round magazines.

During the initial field testing of the XM177E1 by the U.S. Army in Vietnam, only 4 early model thirty-round magazines were sent over for testing. This was along with the 2800 XM177E1s being issued. The four magazines ended up with the 5th Special Forces Group. Tough the number of magazines available for testing was laughably small, 90 percent of the people asked in the survey that was part of the XM177E1 testing stated they preferred the thirty-round magazine if available.

By June 1968, Colt had signed a contact with the Army to supply 1,000 new model thirty-round magazines with delivery expected in 26 weeks. By 1969, the new model thirty-round magazines started to become available in Vietnam with the SEALs being among the first units to receive them. The new magazine has a straight top and bottom portion connected by a curved section and fit all of the AR-15/M16/16A1 weapons produced at the time of its adoption in 1969. The thirty-round magazine was enthusiastically received by the SEALs who accepted all that they could get their hands on.

SEAL TEAM TWO COMMAND AND CONTROL HISTORY, 1969, PAGE 14:

8. (U) Another favorite piece of operational gear which is now present on the SEAL TWO inventory is the 30-round magazine for the M16 and CAR 15 weapons. This gives an extra 10 rounds per magazine which is a welcome development to a unit such as the SEAL Team which constantly tries to make up for its lack of numbers with superior firepower.

In 1968, the Naval Research and Development Unit, Vietnam (NRDU/V) sent a representative to Vietnam in order to assess the needs of the Navy units there. During his four-month tour, the NRDU/V representative spent a large portion of his time with the SEALs operating in the Mekong Delta. One of the strong impressions the man came away with was of the SEALs' requirement for sustained firepower with their M16 rifles. This was needed especially to maintain the high volume of fire during the first crucial moments of enemy contact.

There was at least a year's wait before the thirty-round magazine would be available from Colt and the Naval Weapons Laboratory, Dahlgren decided to address the problem. The first model of a new fifty-round magazine was delivered from Colt in April/May 1969. The Colt magazines were made up from 3 twenty-round magazines welded together end-to-end. Inside of the magazines were a new follower mechanism designed by the engineers at Dahlgren. Thirty-five of the Colt magazines were made and forwarded to the Navy for testing.

The major engineering problem with such a long magazine is the spring pressure needed to lift the heavy column of cartridges into the rifle. Too heavy a spring and the last rounds loaded will be difficult to insert into the magazine; too light a spring and all of the ammunition will not feed into the weapon. A normal coil spring, such as is used in the twenty-round magazine, "loads up," that is, increases its spring tension as the magazine is filled. For the proposed fifty-round magazines, the pressure needed to load the final rounds against a coil spring would likely need a loading tool for assistance. In addition, the spring pressure could keep the first rounds in a full magazine from being stripped into the barrels by the weapon's bolt.

To answer this problem, the NRDU/V came up with a new method of pushing the rounds through the long magazine. The follower for the fifty-round magazines, the platform that actually pushes the ammunition itself, was made of a low-friction plastic. In the base of the follower were placed two constant-force springs, much like the coiled springs in a clock movement. The ends of the springs were attached to the mouth of the magazine rather than pressing against the magazine's bottom. The constant-force springs would unwind as the magazine was loaded, keeping the same pressure on the last rounds loaded as on the first.

The Colt manufactured (first generation) magazines were made at the special request of SEAL Team Two as an interim measure prior to a magazine becoming available from Dahlgren. Results from using the first-generation magazines in the field were poor as the magazines were particularly susceptible to mud and damage from the environment. All the first-generation magazines were replaced as new designs became available.

The Naval Weapons Laboratory, Dahlgren (NWL) made a Mod 1 magazine consisting of a twenty-round magazine body attached to a curved magazine extension. The Mod 1 magazine used the constant-force springs and follower and operated much better than the Colt magazine. A further nine Mod 1 magazines were made for testing but remained in the United States.

To eliminate some of the problems noted in testing, a Mod 2 magazine was designed. In the Mod 2 magazine, the follower remained much the same as in the Mod 1 but the body of the magazine was made up of two machined halves rather than an extension being attached to an existing magazine. In the Mod 2 design, the curve of the magazine remained the same but the angle where the curved portion met the straight section was increased. The straight section of the magazine had to be retained for easy insertion into the M16 magazine well.

The Naval Ordnance Station in Forest Park, Illinois fabricated forty-two Mod 2 magazines according to the NWL design. Testing established the viability of the magazine and the unusual follower design. Ten magazines were found to not operate properly and were removed from the test. Five of the Mod 2 fifty-round magazines were sent to other units in Vietnam and the majority of those remaining, twenty-seven units, were distributed to the members of SEAL Team Two operating in the Mekong Delta.

One difficulty with fifty-round box magazines was noted in particular by 8th Platoon in My Tho. The comment made was that the fifty-round magazine was too bulky and too long. When the platoon was operating from a defensive position, the men would have to expose 50 percent more of their bodies when firing with the fifty-round magazines from the prone position. It was also pointed out that the magazines operated best when only loaded with forty-five rounds rather than fifty.

All told, the fifty-round magazines were considered an effective and valuable piece of equipment by most of its users. A Mod 3 magazine incorporating several improvements over the Mod 2 design was developed. One improvement on the Mod 3 was the addition of a bolt stop to the follower. Now the weapon's bolt would lock open on an empty magazine when the last shot was fired. Ten of the Mod 3 magazines were made and seven were sent to SEAL Team Two elements in Vietnam.

By February 1971, a final report on the fifty-round magazine project was written as NWL Technical Report TR-2536 by Carroll D. Childers and Joseph C. Monolo. The report listed the recommendation put forward by the SEALs that the fifty-round magazine (Mod 3) be adopted for use and issued one per man as a weapon-ready magazine for deployed platoons. It was suggested that such magazines be serial numbers for positive control and not be considered a consumable item. Cutbacks in the post-Vietnam military kept any funding from being made available for the fifty-round magazine program and the project was shelved.

Other methods were used by the SEALs to extend the firepower of their firearms. The most common technique was to tape two or more magazine together, upside down to one another. This method allows for a fast reload as the magazine assembly only has to be pulled from the weapon, flipped over, and reinserted. One strong drawback of this technique is that the bottom magazine has its first cartridges exposed to the environment. It is very easy for dirt or mud to enter the exposed magazine and cause a jam when it is used. This problem keeps the technique from being as widely used as it might be.

The problem of dirt and especially mud entering their magazine was one the SEALs discovered very soon after beginning operations in Vietnam. To answer this problem, the Special Operations Branch of the Navy Weapons Center at China Lake, California came up with plastic M16 magazine caps. The caps were simple black plastic devices, one to fit on the bottom and the other over the top of any size-M16 magazine. The caps effectively sealed the magazine against dirt and mud. The top magazine cap had a tab sticking out from one end. The tab could be pulled, with an operator's teeth if necessary, tearing off the cap and clearing the magazine for insertion into a weapon.

In addition to the magazine caps to keep out the mud, China Lake came up with two items to help keep the rain and mud of Vietnam out of the bore of an M16. One device was a simple white plastic plug that could be inserted into the M16's flash suppressor. The plug was made of a soft plastic and was hollow. The tight fit of the plug into any of the three flash suppressors then in use would effectively seal the bore against rain or mud. But the plugs would not make the weapon waterproof from a full immersion, such as from an underway insertion.

Two SEALs during a training exercise. The front SEAL is carrying an M16A1 rifle loaded with a 30-round magazine and with the flash suppressor replaced with a China Lake blank adaptor. He is wearing a later-model SRU-21/P survival vest over his camouflage fatigues. The rear SEAL is armed with one of the XM177 series weapons also loaded with a 30-round magazine. He is carrying an AN/PRC-77 radio on his back with the coiled feed wire of the handset down over his right shoulder.
Source: U.S. Navy

The plugs were just large enough to be pulled from the muzzle with the fingers, or the tip of a knife. The fit was such that the weapon could even be fired with the plug still in place, blowing out the plug with no damage to the weapon.

The other device China Lake found to help keep rain and mud out of the bore of a .223 caliber weapon was a plastic cap. The cap, resembling a plastic film container, could be pressed over any standard-sized flash suppressor on any .223 caliber weapon in the SEALs inventory. The cap fit snugly, even on Stoner machine guns and XM177E1/E2s, sealing out mud, dust, and water.

Originally, the caps were made of red plastic but this was soon changed to a black material. As with the muzzle plugs, the weapon could be fired with the cap in place with complete safety to the operator and the weapon. The muzzle cap idea worked so well and had such a universal application that they were adopted by the U.S. Army as the Cap, protective, dust and moisture seal: muzzle. This simple cap is still available today as a standard-issue item.

Other materials produced by China Lake for the SEALs and their M16s predated equivalent Army items. By October 1968, a limited number of M16A1s had been modified by China Lake to have a jungle sling and integral cleaning kit. The jungle sling was simply a side-mounted sling that allowed the operator to carry his weapon hanging at his side, muzzle forward, ready for use. To accept the sling, the normal rear sling swivel of the M16A1 was moved from the toe of the buttstock to the rear upper left side. The front sling swivel was moved from below the front sight to a sliding position along a one-piece cleaning rod fitted to the upper left side of the weapon's hand guard, from the front sight to the receiver.

In addition to the sling modifications, a complete cleaning kit was made part of the weapon. A lid was added to the bottom of the hollow pistol grip allowing cleaning materials to be securely stored. In addition, a second storage place was made in the buttstock, covered by a trap door in the buttplate of the weapon. Within a few years, a larger buttstock storage area with a latched cover and a redesigned cleaning kit with a sectioned rod was made part of every M16A1 accepted for U.S. service.

Another accessory was made for the Team's M16s weapons family by China Lake. This item was particularly mundane in nature as it was simply a blank firing attachment. Using standard M200 blanks, the China Lake attachment allowed semiautomatic and full automatic functioning on the M16 and all of its variants. The unit screwed onto the weapon's barrel in place of the normal flash suppressor. The attachment would work as well on the XM177E1/E2 as it did on the M16A1. Even ball ammunition could be accidentally fired through the China Lake device without any danger to the firer or the weapon, though the attachment would be destroyed.

The China Lake blank firing attachment was much smaller and lighter than the Army's M15E1 blank firing adaptor. In addition, the China Lake device did not catch on brush and was dark in color as compared to the boxy, bright-red M15E1 adaptor.

The Teams were sold on the .223 caliber class of weapons very soon after seeing the round's terminal effects in combat. Along with the M16 family of weapons, the SEALs had a commitment in the .223 round as it was used in their

Stoner machine guns. But this commitment did not prevent the SEALs from constantly looking for additional weapons to augment their firepower. But one major requirement was that any new weapons use ammunition available in the U.S. inventory.

Other countries in the NATO alliance could see a strong future for the .223 round after its official adoption by the U.S. military. Several small arms companies developed a number of weapons chambered for the high-velocity round, known as the 5.56×45mm round in NATO terminology. Heckler & Koch of West Germany designed a version of their G3 rifle to use the 5.56mm cartridge. The new weapon, known as the HK33, was imported into the United States by Harrington & Richardson of Worcester, Massachusetts.

Marked as the H&R T 223 rifle, the weapon was submitted to the U.S. Army's Small-Arms Weapon Systems (SAWS) study for evaluation. The SAWS study ran from December 1964 to the submission of the final report in December 1966. During the study, a number of weapons were examined including the T 223, M14, M16E1, AK47, and Stoner weapons system.

One result of the SAWS study was a number of weapons being brought to the attention of the SEALs. Even though the empty H&R T 223 was 0.9 pounds (0.41 kg) heavier than an empty M16E1, the weapon had a forty-round magazine available for it and that made it attractive to the SEALs.

> Choice of weapons were left as much as possible up to the tastes of the individual SEAL. . . . For myself, I had taken a liking to the Harrington and Richardson T223 rifle. . . . One thing that immediately made the T223 appeal to me was the fact that it came with forty-round magazines. One SEAL from SEAL Team Two carried the H&R T 223 during his first combat tour in Vietnam, April to October 1968:
>
> My H&R came with four forty-round magazines which I carried in the leg pockets on my cammies for awhile. The magazines tended to rattle around and make too much noise on patrol but were too long to fit in an American ammunition pouch. I solved my problem by getting one of the chicom AK47 chest-type magazine pouches and carrying my ammo in that.

One interesting point of the H&R T 223 (HK33) is that it very much resembles a slightly smaller, 3.25 inch (8.3 cm) shorter version of the 7.62mm NATO G3 rifle. In one much published picture of a number of SEALs in Vietnam, one SEAL is holding a T 223 but the weapon can only be seen from its top side. Since the HK33 and G3 are almost identical when viewed from the top, the weapon was identified as a G3 rifle, which the SEALs did not use during the Vietnam war. In an earlier-generation copy of the same picture, the long, curved, forty-round magazine can be seen sticking out from the bottom of the weapon.

During the SEALs' time in Vietnam, a number of different rifles and carbines were used on an intermittent basis. For the most part, the men of the Teams stuck with the M16 family of weapons as their primary weapon. Unlike the other services, an individual SEAL would be assigned his weapon while still in the States, carry it with him during his deployment, and return with the same weapon after his tour was over. Other services simply issued a man a weapon when he arrived incountry and he turned it back in for reissue when he left Vietnam. The SEAL system allowed a man to care for his own weapon in such a way as to instill maximum confidence and skill with it. It was when a platoon formed-up for deployment and began predeployment training that a man was assigned his weapon and began working with it:

At (Camp) Pickett the platoon worked on ambushes, popup target courses, weapons familiarization, and zeroing in your own weapon. Each man would take his own M16 and zero the sights on the 1,000 inch range.

Carefully sandbagging his weapon, the firer would adjust his sights until he held a good three-shot group exactly 1 inch below his point of aim at 1,000 inches. For an M16, that would put the bullet's point of impact on the point of aim at 250 yards. After a man had zeroed his weapon's sights, that weapon would be assigned to him by serial number for his tour incountry.

There were times when the SEALs carried foreign weapons in order to help confuse any enemy observers. In one instance in 1968, two SEALs on patrol deep in enemy territory were reported as a pair of Russian advisors due in part to the materials they carried. Some SEALs developed a taste for the AK47 and its variants and carried that weapon as a matter of preference. Sometimes, it was the mission parameters that determined the choice of weapons. This proved particularly true during the waning years of the SEALs' combat deployments to Vietnam. The following was stated by a SEAL officer who was part of the last SEAL Team Two deployment to Vietnam:

The kind of operations we went on, it would be rare for someone to detect us, let alone fire directly at us. As rare as it would be for us to be shot at, it would be even more rare for us to return fire. With no support, we just didn't let ourselves be seen. With the few men we had, we just didn't have the firepower to take on an enemy unit. This situation greatly affected our choice of weapons. The AK47 and SKS had the same sound signature, muzzle flash and tracer color as the enemy's own weapons. An M-16, M-60, and especially a Stoner, would stand out to the VC and NVA, telling them where and possibly who we were.

The AK-47 and its variations was the primary shoulder weapon of communist forces throughout the world from 1948 until the 1980s. The SKS which preceded the AK47, is a light semiautomatic carbine that was the first production weapon chambered for the 7.62×39mm round or 7.62mm Intermediate as it was called by Vietnam-era SEALs.

The SKS, for Samozaridnya Karabina Simonova, is a relatively simple carbine with a ten-round internal magazine. The magazine can be filled with loose rounds or quickly loaded from a ten-round stripper clip. The physical characteristics of the SKS made it a very good weapon for the small-stature Asian soldier. Manufactured in several variations in at least five countries, the most common model of the SKS captured in Vietnam was the People's Republic of China (PRC) Type 56 Carbine with an integral, folding, spike bayonet.

The 7.62×39mm round was proved out in the SKS carbine and has become arguably the most common military cartridge in the world. When fired in the SKS or AK-47, the 7.62×39mm round has a unique sound signature, distinctly different from U.S. weapons. In addition, the tracer loading of the 7.62×39mm round emits a green trace when fired as compared to the U.S.'s and NATO's red trace.

By far the most popular weapon chambered for the 7.62×39mm round is the AK47. The original AK47, for Avtomat Kalashnikov, is a very robust, compact, and powerful weapon well suited for the Southeast Asian environment as well as the guerrilla tactics of the Viet Cong. The AK47 will continue to function with little or no maintenance over extended periods. Though not particularly accurate, especially after years in the jungle, the AK47 is capable of putting out a high volume of effective fire when used on full automatic.

The receiver of the AK47 was manufactured as a complex machining from a solid block of metal. The later and more common AKM47 has its receiver made up of sheet metal stampings. Several improvements are incorporated into the AKM47 and it is somewhat lighter, but every bit as rugged, as the original AK47. The AKM47, for Avtomat Kalashnikova Modernizirovanniyi, is also found in a folding stock version, the AKMS47. The earlier AK47 also had a folding stock version, the AKS47. In both versions, the folding stock swings underneath the weapon and can be locked in the open or closed position. With the stock folded, the AK makes a compact, if heavy, package of firepower.

Literally millions of AK47s have been produced in over ten countries. As found in the SKS, the most common AK47 variant found in Vietnam was the wooden-stocked PRC Type 56 assault rifle, found both with and without a folding spike bayonet.

Initially, the AK47 was available in only small numbers to the Viet Cong fighting in South Vietnam. This resulted in the AK47 being something of a prestige weapon among the VC prior to 1968 and the Tet offensive. The SEALs were very quick to notice the importance of finding AK47 armed VC:

> The AK-47 was in very short supply among the VC in 1967. Only the highest ranking VCI [Viet Cong Infrastructure], number one ichi ban, and their number one bodyguards were seen with the weapon.

Very soon after deployments began in Vietnam, AK47s were kept in stock in the armories of both SEAL Teams. The weapons acted as both training aids and as a possible source of sterile (non-U.S.) weapons if needed. AK47s and SKSs came from captures in Vietnam and elsewhere. Ammunition was also made available from supply caches captured in the field by SEALs. As the war progressed, the U.S. military had sterile (unmarked) 7.62×39mm rounds manufactured at U.S. ammunition facilities. Though the cartridges themselves were unmarked, that was not the case with the cardboard boxes the rounds came packaged in. In plain black letters is printed.

20 CARTRIDGES – AK 47 RIFLE AMMO – 7.62 × 39 MM – LOT xxx-xxx-xx

But for the Teams, the most common source of supply for 7.62×39mm ammunition was from the original people who made it, captured in Vietnam as shown in the following portion of a Barndance card. Barndance cards were short reports filled out on each SEAL field operation conducted by a SEAL platoon while deployed to Vietnam.:

BARNDANCE # 6–19 SEAL TEAM TWO; DET ALPHA; 6 PLT
DATE(S): 10 JAN 68
Located four enemy ammunition caches in vicinity of XT 270330. REMARKS
(SIGNIFICANT EVENTS, OPEVAL RESULTS, Etc.): Captured the following:

67 – 75mm rockets, 29 – 57mm recoilless rockets, 197 – B40 rockets, 30 – 81mm mortars, 28,120 rounds of AK 47, 24 hand grenades, 1615¼ lb blocks of C-3, 6 ponchos, 1 gas mask. All ammunition except 7400 AK47 turned over to Army. 7400 rounds of AK47 retained for SEAL Team 2.

The AK47 and its variations have remained part of the SEALs' training. Both the SKS and AK47 were listed as weapons a SEAL should be familiar with in the 1974 edition of the SEAL Training Handbook. It is interesting to note that one of the first weapons the SEALs faced in Vietnam, the AK47, was also one of the last weapons they carried on combat missions in Southeast Asia.

One of the last specialized weapons received by the UDTs and SEALs while they were still involved in Vietnam was a modified M16A1. The modifications done to the M16A1 were to waterproof the weapon and generally make it easier to transport underwater and prepare for immediate use by combat swimmers. Officially identified as the Rifle, 5.56mm Mark 4 Mod 0 at the time of its adoption in April 1970, modifications to the M16A1 included:

- An anti-corrosion treatment consisting of coating many of the working parts of the weapon with Kal Gard gun coating.
- Drilling a ¼ inch hole in the lower receiver extension tube and stock.
- Installing an O-ring on the end of the buffer assembly.
- Attachment of the Mk 2 Mod 0 Blast suppressor, which is considered an integral part of the Mk 4 rifle.

The changes to the basic M16A1 are to allow the weapon to be carried at a depth of 200 feet without damage. Provisions are made for the rapid drainage of water from the system and additional protection from the corrosive effects of sea water. The basic issue of materials with the weapon includes a sling, complete cleaning kit, and 6 thirty-round magazines.

The original suppressor issued with the Mk 4 was the HEL M4, identified as the Mk 2 Mod 0 blast suppressor. By the late 1970s, the HEL M4 suppressor was no longer considered adequate for the MK 4 rifle. Advances in suppressor technology had rendered the earlier design obsolete as a number of new suppressors were on the market with greater sound suppression and durability. After testing a number of available designs, the Navy chose the Knight's Armament Company's (KAC) model.

The KAC suppressor is a stainless steel, baffle-type design with a central perforated baffle tube surrounded by an annular expansion space. The suppressor, now identified as the Mk 2 Blast Suppressor, is able to be fully immersed in water and completely self-draining within 8 seconds. The advantages of this aspect of the design for the SEALs and UDTs are obvious. The KAC suppressor acts as a muzzle blast device and has a very strong barrel attachment system that is still easily removable. In addition to its being made of noncorroding materials and self-draining design, the KAC Mk 4 suppressor is able to withstand full automatic fire from the M16 at the maximum rate possible without being damaged from the heat or blast.

By the end of their involvement in the Vietnam War, the SEALs and UDTs were already experiencing cutbacks in their numbers and financing. New weapons were relatively few in number and parts difficulties were making repair of some of the Vietnam-era weapons difficult.

With the ending of the CAR-15 project by Colt in 1970, spare parts unique to the XM177/E1/E2 family were available in very limited numbers. The short barrels that helped make the CAR-15 weapons so popular were particularly rare. Most units, including the Teams, husbanded their remaining CAR-15s carefully and repaired some weapons by cannibalizing other more worn pieces for parts.

The short barrel of the CAR-15 weapons was never noted for its accuracy and when the barrels became worn, accuracy dropped quickly to unacceptable levels. When finally no more worthwhile 11.5-inch CAR-15 barrels were available, Colt offered their 14.5-inch carbine barrel. The M16A1 carbine was a new weapon from Colt that shared many features with the CAR-15 weapons. Some XM177E1 and E2 receivers were rebarreled for use with the carbine barrel and became hybrid weapons, appearing to be carbines but marked as XM177E1/E2s.

With the declaration by the BATF (Bureau of Alcohol, Tobacco, and Firearms) department of the Treasury that the CAR-15 flash/sound suppressor qualified as a silencer under the law and the State Department's out-

This SEAL is holding an XM177E2 with an XM148 40mm grenade launcher mounted underneath the barrel. Hanging from around this man's neck is a hand-held AN/PRT-4 transmitter.
Source: UDT SEAL Museum

lawing export silencer sales under the Carter administration, Colt changed the design specifications of the CAR-15 to meet market requirements. Since the flash/sound suppressor of the XM177 weapons was a major sticking point, Colt simply extended the barrel of the new carbine weapon to the point where flash and sound could be held to reasonable levels. In addition, the slightly longer barrel of the carbine made it more accurate than the earlier CAR-15 weapons as the bullets had more time to stabilize for flight.

The Colt Model 653 M16A1 carbine was eventually adopted by the SEALs and UDTs in some small numbers. The model 653 shared the same sliding buttstock and short cylindrical handguards as the XM177E2. The most visible difference between the two weapons is the longer barrel of the carbine protruding well beyond the front sight.

The longer carbine barrel is fitted with the Type 3 flash suppressor as found on the standard M16A1s of the era. Since the carbine did not require the longer flash/sound suppressor but had the shorter standard flash hider, the overall length of the Model 653 carbine was only slightly longer than the XM177E2. A favorite weapon of the SEALs is produced when the short, handy carbine is mated with the M203 40mm grenade launcher. The powerful combination of automatic rifle and high explosive grenade launcher became a common sight in SEAL hands.

More compact and powerful weapons have long been a priority with the Teams and especially the SEALs. Room is limited at best on many transports and it is at an absolute premium aboard submarines and Swimmer/SEAL delivery vehicles.

Facing much the same problem of space limitations in their armored vehicles, the Army examined fitting the then-standard M14 rifle with a folding stock during the early 1960s. Four different models of folding stock were developed by the engineers at Springfield Armory. With the winding down of M14 production, the project was abandoned by the Army.

Few of the Army folding M14 stocks were ever made and even fewer still were available for later use by the Teams. A near-duplicate of the M14/M1 Garand was produced by Italy as their BM 59 series of weapons. The Parachutists and Alpine versions of the BM 59 are fitted with folding stocks that proved to be easily adapted to fit the M14 rifle.

The modified M14 stocks with the BM 59 folding buttstock design were obtained by the Teams by the late 1970s. With the stock folded, the M14 is a more compact package, not a great deal larger than an M16A1. The added power and range of the 7.62mm NATO round and the M14 rifle, combined with the compact folding stock, gives the Teams the option of fielding the weapon as the tactical situation dictates.

Through the latter half of the 1970s, trials were being conducted by the NATO countries to locate a candidate cartridge and possible weapon for NATO standardization. Though the trials did not locate a weapon design that was acceptable to all NATO members, they did focus on a superior cartridge.

What developed out of the NATO trials was not a new cartridge but a better loading for an existing round. The loading decided on was the Belgium SS109 heavy-bulleted 5.56mm round. This loading was duplicated in the U.S. counterpart, the XM855 round. The new loading called for a steel-cored, partial armor piercing 61.7 grain (4 g) bullet to be fired from a barrel with a 1-in-7-inch (1 in 30.5 cm) twist. The new projectile held excellent accuracy and terminal effects out to ranges near that of the 7.62mm NATO round.

By late 1979, the U.S. Marine Corps was already discussing the possibility of a new issue rifle. The improved range of the XM855 round caught the Marines' attention as a possible answer to their desire for more of a "rifleman's" weapon to arm the Corps. Requirements later formalized for the Marines desired new weapon, a modified M16A1, were as follows:

- An adjustable sight good to 800 meters.
- A projectile with good accuracy to 800 meters and able to penetrate all known helmets and military body armor at that range.
- Stronger plastic and metal parts on the weapon to stand up better to the heavier demands placed on it by Marine training doctrine.
- Elimination of the full automatic position and its replacement with a controlled 3-round burst setting.

Additional tests conducted by the Navy added more parameters and suggestions to the physical changes in a possible new Marine rifle. Test weapons were ordered from Colt and examined to see if a modified M16A1 would fit the Marines desires. This led to the development of the third-generation M16, the M16A2.

The Joint Services Small Arms Program (JSSAP) approved a joint-services approach to a new and improved M16A1 by ordering fifty Product Improvement Program (PIP) M16A1s from Colt to be delivered in November 1981. Designated the M16A1E1, the new rifles were extensively tested by the Marines during the last weeks of 1981. The results of the testing gave very favorable reports on the accuracy, range, effectiveness, and handling qualities of the M16A1E1. By September 1982, the M16A1E1 was type-classified as the M16A2.

The Marines ordered 76,000 M16A2s as quickly as they were able. The Army did not have as strong a desire for the new rifle to be immediately available, stocks of M16A1s being considered sufficient to cover several years needs. By 1986, the Army contracted for the purchase of 100,176 M16A2 weapons from Colt.

The M16A2 as issued to the U.S. military is identified by Colt as their model 705. The major differences between the M16A1 and the A2 model include:

- Modification of the flash hider to a fourth type without bottom slots. The lack of bottom slots on the M16A2 flash hider prevents dust and dirt from flying up when the weapon is fired in the prone position. The flash hider also acts as a muzzle compensator, helping to hold the muzzle down when firing bursts.
- A barrel with a heavier contour from the front sight forward. In addition, the new barrel is rifled with a 1-in-7-inch twist for use with the M855 round.
- Different front and rear sights with the rear sight adjustable to 800 meters range with an easily moved elevation drum.
- New cylindrical, ribbed handguards. Stronger and more efficient at cooling that the earlier triangular M16A1 handguards, the new handguards are also ambidextrous. Either one will fit on the right or left side of the barrel.
- An angled slip ring making it easier to remove the handguards for routine maintenance.
- A strengthening of the upper receiver.
- A longer buttstock.
- A pistol grip that is slightly larger and has a single finger rest.
- All plastic parts are now made of a super-tough nylon plastic, 10 to 12 times stronger than the original M16A1 parts.
- A bulge in the upper receiver acts as a brass deflector, allowing easier left-handed firing of the weapon.
- Replacement of the full auto position with a controlled 3-round burst.

The replacement of the full automatic fire capability in the M16A2 is one of the most discussed arguments against the new weapon. Though having other good characteristics, the lack of full automatic fire limits the appeal of the M16A2 to the Teams. In addition, flaws were quickly noticed by operators who used the 3-round burst position on the M16A2.

If a 3-round burst is attempted to be fired from the M16A2, and the weapon stops or runs out of ammunition, the mechanism does not reset when the trigger is released. If the weapon runs out of ammunition on the second round of a 3-round burst, when the operator reloads and again pulls the trigger, only a single shot will be fired. If the operator releases the trigger when only a single shot of a 3-round burst has been fired, and then pulls the trigger again, 2 rounds will be fired. This fault is part of the design of the M16A2 controlled burst mechanism and cannot be changed.

As the new standard issue shoulder arm in the U.S. military, the M16A2 is issued to the SEALs as well as all the other branches of the service. A short carbine version of the M16A2 has been available to the Teams and is much preferred over the M16A2 rifle. The M16A2 carbine is identified by Colt as their model 723 weapon. Virtually identical to the earlier model 653 M16A1 carbine, the model 723 weapon has the larger pistol grip of the M16A2, the fourth model flash hider, and the 1-in-7-inch rifling twist. The full automatic capability, sights, and other characteristics of the model 653 carbine, including the thinner contour barrel, remain the same on the new model 723 carbine.

Another version of the M16A2 system is seeing duty with the SEAL teams and is being much more enthusiastically received than the M16A2 rifle. The M4 carbine is a another shortened version of the M16A2 but retains many of the new features found on the full-sized rifle.

The sights on the M4 are the same long-range adjustable model as found on the M16A2. The M4 also has the heavier barrel, fourth model flash hider, and brass deflector as on the M16A2. The heavy barrel of the

Wearing first-pattern desert camouflage uniforms, these SEALs are patrolling near Kuwait City during Desert Storm. The SEAL in the passenger seat is holding on to his M14 rifle, used in place of the M16 due to its greater range. The action of the M14 has been wrapped in a rag to keep the constant desert dust and sand from the action of the weapon. The large pouch hanging at the SEALs hip is the M17A1 protective mask carrier with spatters of light paint on the cover in order to help camouflage it.
Source: U.S. Navy

M4 carbine has a slight step in the barrel diameter roughly midway between the muzzle and the front sight. The step is so that the M203 40mm grenade launcher can be mounted on the M4 with no modifications needed on either weapon.

The M4/M203 combination is a very popular one with the Teams. Given the proper circumstances, entire platoons have been armed with the M4/M203 such as during Operation Just Cause in Panama. Two different models of the M4 are issued in the military. The Colt model 720 is an M4 carbine with the 3-round controlled burst setting and no other capability for full automatic fire. The Colt model 727 M4 carbine has the capability of full automatic fire and is the preferred model for use by the SEALs.

As of February 1994, Special Operations Command (SOCOM) awarded a contract to Colt for production of 5,000 to 6,000 M4A1 carbines. The new M4A1, Colt model 927, is intended specifically for Special Operations forces including the SEALs. Firing settings for the M4A1 will be full and semiautomatic, with the sights, barrel, and other aspects retained from the standard M4 carbine. The major change will be in the rear sight system.

The M4A1 will be equipped with the Picatinny Rail mounting located under the removable carrying handle. The carrying handle will retain the standard M16A2 rear sight but can be removed to allow different sighting devices to be mounted. Mounting on the Picatinny Rail makes for a much lower weapon outline as well as giving a more solid and accurate mounting interface than the handle of the weapon. Other modifications on some M4A1s will allow a laser sight or 12-gauge shotgun to be mounted underneath the barrel for close-quarters combat. Production of the M4A1 was planned to begin in May 1994.

To increase their available volume of fire, the SEALs and Special Forces have obtained a number of special C-MAG 100-round drum magazine for the M16 family of weapons. The C-MAG drum is a large capacity feed device that will fit any magazine well that accepts an M16 magazine.

The C-MAG weighs 2.21 pounds (1.00 kg) empty and will accept and feed a full 100 rounds of ammunition. The use of dual drums feeding from either side of the magazine extension allows the C-MAG to have a very low profile when mounted on the M16 weapon. The drums are spring driven and feed their rounds along a spiral track on the outside diameter of the drum. The rounds feed up into the magazine extension, alternating one from each drum.

As the ammunition empties onto the magazine extension, flexible feed chains move from the drums up into the magazine extension. The feed chains insure positive tension is kept on the ammunition until the last round is fed into the weapon. When the last round is fired, the C-MAG activates the bolt lock just as a standard magazine would. The design of the C-MAG is such that the weapon actually has a lower profile with the 100-round drum loaded than it does with a standard 30-round box magazine.

Army industrial experiments with the Advanced Combat Rifle (ACR) program in the mid to late 1980s resulted in a number of approaches to increase the hit probability of a weapon. Further input from other industry sources and the special operations community resulted in the creation of the SOPMOD M4 kit beginning in 1995. The SOPMOD, for M4 Carbine Special Operations Peculiar Modification Accessory Kit, is a selection of aiming, illuminating, and handling devices for attachment to the M4A1 carbine.

The Colt Model 927, originally referred to as the M16A3 Carbine, has been adopted as the primary carrier of the SOPMOD system. The primary difference between the M4 and the M4A1 is that the latter has a removable carrying handle/rear sight assembly on top of the upper receiver.

Held in place by two clamping screws, the carrying handle/rear sight assembly is secured to a machined rail mounting system built into the top of the M4A1. The grooved rail mounting on the receiver is of the Picatinny type, meeting Mil Spec 1913. The heart of the SOPMOD system is the rail interface system (RIS) That replaces the front handguard assembly of the M4A1. All of the SOPMOD accessories are able to be mounted on the four rails of the RIS, which also meets Mil Spec 1913. The very strong and ridged RIS can accept parts attached to the top, bottom, and sides of the fore end of the M4A1, while still leaving the original rail mounting on top of the receiver available for further sighting devices.

In general, four SOPMOD kits are issued for each deployed SEAL platoon of sixteen men. Each kit can modify four weapons to varying configurations. The primary advantage of the SOPMOD kit is to increase the speed of handling and target acquisition for the operator during close quarters battle situations. SOPMOD kits are developing as the program continues with different components being added or removed. In general a kit consists of:

- (4) Trijicon 4X ACOG (advanced combat optical gunsight) optical sights—weight 0.62 lbs (0.280 kg) each.
- (4) Knight Armament Rail Adaptor System (rail interface system) and (4) vertical handgrip assemblies—weight 1.55 lbs (0.70 kg) each.
- (1) M203A1 quick detachable 40mm grenade launcher with nine-inch barrel—weight 2.81 lbs (1.275 kg).

- (1) M203A1 leaf sight assembly—weight 0.35 lbs (0.159 kg).
- (2) AN/PEQ-2 Infra-red target painters—weight 0.46 lbs (0.210 kg) each w/o batteries or mounting bracket.
- (1) AN/PEQ-5 visible laser—weight 0.187 lbs (0.085 kg) with AA batteries.
- (2) Trijicon ACOG reflex sight assemblies—weight 0.51 lbs (0.232 kg) each with RX10 mounting bracket.
- (2) Knight Armament Quick Detachable sound suppressor—weight 1.0 lbs (0.454 kg) each.
- (2) Visible light illuminators (mounted flashlights).
- (4) Backup iron sights—weight 0.32 lbs (0.145 kg) each.
- (1) AN/PVS-14 Mini night vision sight—weight 0.875 lbs (1.93 kg).

Additional or alternate components of the SOPMOD M4 kit may include:

- Aimpoint Comp M red-dot reflex sight—weight 0.384 lbs (0.174 kg).
- AN/PVS-12 4 power night vision sight—weight 2.65 lbs (1.2 kg) with 2 AA batteries.
- AN/PAS-13 Thermal rifle sight—weight 4.5 lbs (2.04 kg).

The SOPMOD M4 kit has increased the lethality of an already lethal weapons system in the M4A1 carbine. By 1998, enough kits had been fielded to modify 8,000 weapons at a cost of $25 million.

■ Rifle and Carbine Data ■

Source: Smithsonian Institute

M1 CARBINE
M2 CARBINE

CARTRIDGE .30 Carbine (7.62×33mm)

OPERATION Gas

TYPE OF FIRE Semiautomatic; M2 Selective fire—semiautomatic/full automatic

RATE OF FIRE 40 rpm; M2 Practical SS 40 rpm, A 75 rpm, Cyclic 750 to 775 rpm

MUZZLE VELOCITY 1,970 fps (600 m/s)

MUZZLE ENERGY 956 ft/lb (1296 J)

SIGHTS Open, Ramp-type aperture/blade, adjustable, graduation marks at 100, 200, 250, and 300 yards

FEED 15- or 30-round removable box magazine

WEIGHTS

Weapon (empty) 5.31 lb (2.41 kg)

Weapon (loaded) 5.92 lb (2.69 kg) w/15 rd mag

Magazine (empty) 15 round 0.19 lb (0.09 kg); 30 round 0.22 lb (0.10 kg)

Magazine (loaded) 15 round 0.61 lb (0.28 kg); 30 round 1.06 lb (0.48 kg)

Service cartridge M1 Ball 196 gr (12.7 g)

Projectile 111 gr (7.2 g)

LENGTHS

Weapon overall 35.58 in. (90.4 cm)

Barrel 18 in (45.7 cm)

Sight radius 21.5 in. (54.6 cm) w/rear sight set at 100 yds

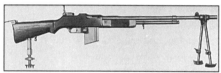

Source: U.S. Army

M1918A2 BROWNING AUTOMATIC RIFLE

CARTRIDGE 30-06 (7.62×63mm)

OPERATION Gas

TYPE OF FIRE Full automatic, fast and slow rates

RATE OF FIRE Practical (slow) 40 to 60 rpm, (fast) 120 to 150 rpm, Cyclic (slow) 350 to 450 rpm, (fast) 550 to 650 rpm

MUZZLE VELOCITY 2,800 fps (853 m/s)

MUZZLE ENERGY 2,646 ft/lb (3588 J)

SIGHTS Open, leaf-type aperture w/round-notch battle sight/blade, Adjustable, battle sight set at 300 yds, leaf graduated 100 to 1500 yds in 100 yd increments,

FEED 20-round removable box magazine

WEIGHTS

Weapon (empty) 18.96 lb (8.60 kg) w/bipod

Weapon (loaded) 20.59 lb (9.34 kg)w/bipod; bipod 2.44 lb (1.11 kg)

Magazine (empty) 0.44 lb (0.20 kg)

Magazine (loaded) 1.63 lb (0.74 kg)

Service cartridge M2 Ball 416 gr (27 g)

Projectile 152 gr (9.8 g)

LENGTHS

Weapon overall 47.8 in (121.4 cm)

Barrel 24.07 in (61.1 cm)

Sight radius 31.13 in (79.1 cm)

AR-15 (COLT MODEL 601), M-16 (COLT MODEL 602)

CARTRIDGE .223 Remington (5.56×45mm)

OPERATION Gas

TYPE OF FIRE Selective—semiautomatic/full automatic

RATE OF FIRE Practical SS 45 to 65 rpm, A 150 to 200 rpm, Cyclic 700 to 950 rpm

MUZZLE VELOCITY 3,250 fps (991 m/s)

MUZZLE ENERGY 1,313 ft/lb (1780 J)

SIGHTS Open, flip-type aperture/post, adjustable, battle aperture 0 to 300 m, long range aperture 300 to 500 m

FEED 20- or 30-round removable box magazines

WEIGHTS

Weapon (empty) 6.35 lb (2.88 kg) w/o sling

Weapon (loaded) 7.46 lb (3.38 kg) w/20 rd mag & sling; sling 0.40 lb (0.18 kg)

Magazine (empty) 20 round aluminum 0.19 lb (0.08 kg); 30 round aluminum 0.24 lb (0.11 kg)

Magazine (loaded) 20 round 0.71 lb (0.32 kg); 30 round 1.02 lb (0.46 kg)

Service cartridge M193 Ball 182 gr (11.8 g)

Projectile 56 gr (3.6 g)

LENGTHS

Weapon overall 38.6 in (98 cm)

Barrel 20 in (50.8 cm)

Sight radius 19.72 in (50.1 cm)

These weapons are among the first of their kind to be used by the Navy. A noticeable characteristic of the early AR-15/M-16 weapons is the shiny appearance of the chromed bolt carrier, visible through the open ejection port, and the green-colored plastic furniture (stocks). Later versions

of the weapon had black plastic furniture and the bolt carrier was parkerized a dull gray.

Source: Kevin Dockery

CAR-15 CARBINE (COLT MODEL 05)

CARTRIDGE .223 Remington (5.56×45mm)

OPERATION Gas

TYPE OF FIRE Selective—semiautomatic/full automatic

RATE OF FIRE Practical SS 45 to 65 rpm, A 150 to 200 rpm, Cyclic 700 to 950 rpm

MUZZLE VELOCITY 3,050 fps (930 m/s)

MUZZLE ENERGY 1,157 ft/lb (1569 J)

SIGHTS Open, flip-type aperture/post, adjustable, battle aperture 0 to 300 m, long range aperture 300 to 500 m

FEED 20- or 30-round removable box magazines

WEIGHTS

Weapon (empty) 6.0 lb (2.72 kg)

Weapon (loaded) 6.71 lb (3.04 kg) w/20 rd mag w/o sling; sling 0.40 lb (0.18 kg)

Magazine (empty) 20 round aluminum 0.19 lb (0.08 kg); 30 round aluminum 0.24 lb (0.11 kg)

Magazine (loaded) 20 round 0.71 lb (0.32 kg); 30 round 1.02 lb (0.46 kg)

Service cartridge M193 Ball 182 gr (11.8 g)

Projectile 56 gr (3.6 g)

LENGTHS

Weapon overall 33.6 in (85.3 cm)

Barrel 15 in (38.1 cm)

Sight radius 19.72 in (50.1 cm)

Source: Kevin Dockery

CAR-15 SUBMACHINE GUN (COLT MODEL 07)

CARTRIDGE .223 Remington (5.56×45mm)
OPERATION Gas
TYPE OF FIRE Selective—semiautomatic/full automatic
RATE OF FIRE Practical SS 45 to 65 rpm, A 150 to 200 rpm, Cyclic 700 to 950 rpm
MUZZLE VELOCITY 2,750 fps (838 m/s)
MUZZLE ENERGY 940 ft/lb (1,275 J)
SIGHTS Open, flip-type aperture/post, adjustable, battle aperture 0 to 300 m, long range aperture 300 to 500 m
FEED 20- or 30-round removable box magazines
WEIGHTS
Weapon (empty) 5.3 lb (2.40 kg)
Weapon (loaded) 6.01 lb (2.73 kg) w/20 rd mag, w/o sling; sling 0.40 lb (0.18 kg)
Magazine (empty) 20 round aluminum 0.19 lb (0.08 kg); 30 round aluminum 0.24 lb (0.11 kg)
Magazine (loaded) 20 round 0.71 lb (0.32 kg); 30 round 1.02 lb (0.46 kg)
Service cartridge M193 Ball 182 gr (11.8 g)
Projectile 56 gr (3.6 g)
LENGTHS
Weapon overall 26/28.7 in. (66/72.9 cm)
Barrel 10 in (25.4 cm)

M16E1 (M16A1) (COLT MODEL 603)

CARTRIDGE .223 Remington (5.56×45mm)
OPERATION Gas
TYPE OF FIRE Selective—semiautomatic/full automatic
RATE OF FIRE Practical SS 45 to 65 rpm, A 150 to 200 rpm, Cyclic 700 to 800 rpm
MUZZLE VELOCITY 3250 fps (991 m/s)
MUZZLE ENERGY 1,313 ft/lb (1,780 J)
SIGHTS Open, flip-type aperture/post, adjustable, battle aperture 0 to 300 m, long range aperture 300 to 500 m
FEED 20- or 30-round removable box magazines
WEIGHTS
Weapon (empty) 6.5 lb (2.95 kg)
Weapon (loaded) 7.61 lb (3.45 kg) w/sling & 20 rd mag; Sling 0.40 lb (0.18 kg)
Magazine (empty) 20 round aluminum 0.19 lb (0.08 kg); 30 round aluminum 0.24 lb (0.11 kg)
Magazine (loaded) 20 round 0.71 lb (0.32 kg); 30 round 1.02 lb (0.46 kg)
Service cartridge M193 Ball 182 gr (11.8 g)
Projectile 56 gr (3.6 g)
LENGTHS
Weapon overall 39 in (99.1 cm)
Barrel 20 in (50.8 cm) w/o flash suppressor; 21 in (53.3 cm) w/flash suppressor
Sight radius 19.75 in (50.2 cm). Modifications from the original AR-15 (M-16 rifle for the A1 version included:

- Chrome plating the chamber and later the entire bore
- Addition of a forward bolt-assist for forcing the bolt closed
- A heavier recoil buffer to slow the cyclic firing rate, this buffer was quickly retrofitted to all M16 rifles
- A buttstock compartment for holding a set of cleaning gear
- A closed "bird-cage" flash suppressor
- A wider charging handle
- Index lines (windage) on the rear sight

A 30-round magazine was introduced to replace the 20-shot version used in the field. This size magazine had been available since the earliest Colt manufactured weapons but had been available on a very limited basis. Prior to this (about 1968) only the Air Force had been issuing 30-round magazines as a normal item. These larger magazines were a

valued "scrounge" item among the SEALs.
Twenty-round magazines remained the norm
throughout the Vietnam War.

XM177E1 (COLT MODEL 609)
XM177E2 (COLT MODEL 629)

CARTRIDGE .223 Remington (5.56×45mm)

OPERATION Gas

TYPE OF FIRE Selective—semiautomatic/full
automatic

RATE OF FIRE Practical SS 45 to 65 rpm, A
150 to 200 rpm, Cyclic 700 to 800 rpm

MUZZLE VELOCITY 2,750 fps (838 m/s)

MUZZLE ENERGY 940 ft/lb (1275 J)

SIGHTS Open, flip-type aperture/post, adjustable, battle aperture 0 to 300 m, long
range aperture 300 to 500 m

FEED 20- or 30-round removable box magazines

WEIGHTS

Weapon (empty) XM177E1 5.2 lb (2.36 kg);
XM177E2 5.35 lb (2.43 kg)

Weapon (loaded) XM177E1 6.62 lb (3.0 kg)
w/sling & 30 rd mag; XM177E2 6.77 lb
(3.07 kg) w/sling & 30 rd mag; sling 0.40 lb
(0.18 kg)

Magazine (empty) 20 round aluminum 0.19 lb
(0.08 kg); 30 round aluminum 0.24 lb (0.11
kg)

Magazine (loaded) 20 round 0.71 lb (0.32 kg);
30 round 1.02 lb (0.46 kg)

Service cartridge M193 Ball 182 gr (11.8 g)

Projectile 56 gr (3.6 g)

LENGTHS

Weapon overall XM177E1 28.3/31 in.
(71.9/78.7 cm); XM177E2 29.8/32.5 in
(75.7/82.6 cm)

Barrel XM177E1—10 in (25.4 cm); XM177E2
11.5 in (29.2 cm); The combination
flash/noise suppressor adds about 3.5 in
to the overall barrel length

Sight radius 14.72 in. (37.4 cm)

Source: Kevin Dockery

MARK 4 MOD 0 W/MK 2 MOD 0
BLAST SUPPRESSOR

CARTRIDGE .223 Remington (5.56×45mm)

OPERATION Gas

TYPE OF FIRE Selective—semiautomatic/full
automatic

RATE OF FIRE Practical SS 45 to 65 rpm,
A 150 to 200 rpm, Cyclic 700 to
800 rpm

MUZZLE VELOCITY 3,250 fps (991 m/s)

MUZZLE ENERGY 1,313 ft/lb (1,780 J)

SIGHTS Open, flip-type aperture/post, adjustable, battle aperture 0 to 300 meters,
long range aperture 300 to 500 meters

FEED 20 or 30 round removable box magazines

WEIGHTS

Weapon (empty) 6.37 lb (2.89 kg) w/o suppressor or flashhider; 8.62 lb (3.91 kg)
w/suppressor; Mk 4 Mod 0 Blast suppressor 2.25 lb (1.02 kg)

Weapon (loaded) 7.39 lb (3.35 kg) w/30 rd
mag, w/o suppressor or flashhider; 9.64 lb
(4.37 kg) w/suppressor and 30 rd mag

Magazine (empty) 20 round aluminum 0.19 lb
(0.08 kg); 30 round aluminum 0.24 lb
(0.11 kg)

Magazine (loaded) 20 round 0.71 lb (0.32 kg);
30 round 1.02 lb (0.46 kg)

Service cartridge M193 Ball 182 gr
(11.8 g)

Projectile 56 gr (3.6 g)

LENGTHS

Weapon overall 39 in (99.1 cm) w/o suppressor; 45.38 in (115.3 cm) w/suppressor

Barrel 20 in

Suppressor length 8 in (20.3 cm)

Suppressor diameter 1.75 (4.4 cm)

Sight radius 19.75 in (50.2 cm)

Suppressor reduction on the normal sound signature of the weapon, was –32 db. The suppressor is designed to be fully self-draining within eight seconds of immersion

The Mk 4 Mod 0 rifle is a modified M16A1. The changes are to allow the weapon to be carried at a depth of 200 feet without damage. Provisions are made for the rapid drainage of water from the system and additional protection from the corrosive effects of sea water. Modifications include:

- Anticorrosion treatment by applying Kalgard coating to many of the functioning components
- Drilling a ¼-inch hole in the lower receiver extension tube and stock
- Installing an O-ring on the end of the buffer assembly
- Attachment of the Mk 2 Mod 0 Blast suppressor which is considered an integral part of the Mk 4 rifle.
- Basic issue with the weapon includes a sling, complete cleaning kit, and six 30-round magazines.

Source: Kevin Dockery

COLT MODEL 653 CARBINE

CARTRIDGE .223 Remington (5.56×45mm)
OPERATION Gas
TYPE OF FIRE Selective—semiautomatic/full automatic
RATE OF FIRE Practical SS 45 to 65 rpm, A 150 to 200 rpm, Cyclic 700 to 800 rpm
MUZZLE VELOCITY 3,020 fps (920 m/s)
MUZZLE ENERGY 1,134 ft/lb (1,538 J)
SIGHTS Open, flip-type aperture/post, adjustable, battle aperture 0 to 300 m, long range aperture 300 to 500 m

FEED 20- or 30-round removable box magazines
WEIGHTS
Weapon (empty) 5.6 lb (2.54 kg)
Weapon (loaded) 7.02 lb (3.18 kg) w/sling & 30 rd mag; sling 0.4 lb (0.18 kg)
Magazine (empty) 20 round aluminum 0.19 lb (0.08 kg); 30 round aluminum 0.24 lb (0.11 kg)
Magazine (loaded) 20 round 0.71 lb (0.32 kg); 30 round 1.02 lb (0.46 kg)
Service cartridge M193 Ball 182 gr (11.8 g)
Projectile 56 gr (3.6 g)
LENGTHS
Weapon overall 29.8/33 in. (75.7/83.8 cm)
Barrel 14.5 in (36.8 cm)
Sight radius 14.72 in (37.4 cm)

Source: Kevin Dockery

COLT MODEL 723

CARTRIDGE .223 Remington NATO (5.56 × 45mm NATO)
OPERATION Gas
TYPE OF FIRE Selective—semiautomatic/full automatic
RATE OF FIRE Practical SS 45 to 65 rpm, A 150 to 200 rpm, Cyclic 700 to 950 rpm
MUZZLE VELOCITY 2,900 fps (884 m/s)
MUZZLE ENERGY 1,158 ft/lb (1,570 J)
SIGHTS Open, flip-type aperture/post, adjustable, battle aperture 0 to 300 meters, long range aperture 300 to 500 meters
FEED 20- or 30-round removable box magazines
WEIGHTS
Weapon (empty) 5.9 lb (2.68 kg)
Weapon (loaded) 7.35 lb (3.33 kg) w/sling & 30 rd mag; sling 0.4 lb (0.18 kg)

Magazine (empty) 20 round aluminum 0.19 lb (0.08 kg); 30 round aluminum 0.24 lb (0.11 kg)

Magazine (loaded) 20 round 0.73 lb (0.33 kg); 30 round 1.05 lb (0.48 kg)

Service cartridge M855 Ball 190 gr (12.3 g)

Projectile 62 gr (4 g)

LENGTHS

Weapon overall 29.8/33 in (75.7/83.8 cm)

Barrel 14.5 in (36.8 cm)

Sight radius 14.72 in (37.4 cm)

M4 CARBINE (COLT MODEL 720)

CARTRIDGE .223 Remington NATO (5.56 × 45mm NATO)

OPERATION Gas

TYPE OF FIRE Selective—semiautomatic/full automatic

RATE OF FIRE Practical SS 45 to 65 rpm, A 150 to 200 rpm, Cyclic 700 to 800 rpm

MUZZLE VELOCITY 2,900 fps (884 m/s)

MUZZLE ENERGY 1,158 ft/lb (1,570 J)

SIGHTS Open, flip-type aperture/post, adjustable, battle aperture 0 to 200 m, adjustable long range small aperture 300 to 800 m in 100 m graduations

FEED 20- or 30-round removable box magazines

WEIGHTS

Weapon (empty) 5.65 lb (2.56 kg)

Weapon (loaded) 7.1 lb (3.22 kg) w/sling & 30 rd mag; sling 0.4 lb (0.18 kg)

Magazine (empty) 20 round aluminum 0.19 lb (0.08 kg); 30 round aluminum 0.24 lb (0.11 kg)

Magazine (loaded) 20 round 0.73 lb (0.33 kg); 30 round 1.05 lb (0.48 kg)

Service cartridge M855 Ball 190 gr (12.3 g)

Projectile 62 gr (4 g)

LENGTHS

Weapon overall 29.8/33 in (75.7/83.8 cm)

Barrel 14.5 in (36.8 cm)

Sight radius 14.72 in (37.4 cm)

M16A2 (COLT MODEL 701)

Cartridge .223 Remington NATO (5.56 × 45mm NATO)

OPERATION Gas

TYPE OF FIRE Selective—semiautomatic/three-round controlled burst

RATE OF FIRE Practical SS 45 to 65 rpm, A 150 to 200 rpm, Cyclic 700 to 950 rpm

MUZZLE VELOCITY 3,110 fps (948 m/s)

MUZZLE ENERGY 1,331 ft/lb (1,805 J)

SIGHTS Open, flip-type aperture/post, adjustable, battle aperture 0 to 200 m, adjustable long range small aperture 300 to 800 meters in 100 m graduations

FEED 20- or 30-round removable box magazines

WEIGHTS

Weapon (empty) 7.5 lb (3.40 kg) w/o sling

Weapon (loaded) 8.95 lb (4.06 kg) w/30 rd mag & sling; sling 0.40 lb (0.18 kg)

Magazine (empty) 20 round aluminum 0.19 lb (0.08 kg); 30 round aluminum 0.24 lb (0.11 kg)

Magazine (loaded) 20 round 0.73 lb (0.33 kg); 30 round 1.05 lb (0.48 kg)

Service cartridge M855 Ball 190 gr (12.3 g)

Projectile 62 gr (4 g)

LENGTHS

Weapon overall 39.6 in (100.6 cm)

Barrel 20 in (50.8 cm)

Sight radius 19.75 in (50.2 cm)

Modifications to the M16A1 to A2 configuration include:

- Changing the full automatic capability to controlled 3-shot burst
- A stronger buttstock made of new "super-tough nylon"
- Round handguards that are interchangeable with each other—no right and left guards
- A tapered slip-ring that makes it easier to strip off the handguards for cleaning

- A fully adjustable rear sight calibrated out to 800 meters
- A barrel that is thicker at the exposed muzzle end
- A rifling twist of 1 turn in 7 inches (17.8 cm) to take maximum advantage of the new NATO 62 grain 5.56mm projectile

M14

CARTRIDGE 7.62mm Nato (7.61 × 51mm)
OPERATION Gas
TYPE OF FIRE Selective—semiautomatic/full automatic
RATE OF FIRE Practical SS 20 to 40 rpm, A 40 to 60 rpm, Cyclic 700 to 750 rpm
MUZZLE VELOCITY 2,800 fps (853 m/s)
MUZZLE ENERGY 2,593 ft/lb (3,516 J)
SIGHTS Open, aperture/blade, adjustable 100 to 1200 m in 100 meter graduations
FEED 20-round removable box magazine
WEIGHTS
Weapon (empty) 8.6 lb (3.90 kg)
Weapon (loaded) 11.21 lb (5.08 kg) w/sling, cleaning kit (in buttstock), & 20 rd mag; sling 0.31 lb (0.14 kg); cleaning kit/combination tool .67 lb (0.30 kg)
Magazine (Empty) 0.51 lb (0.23 kg)
Magazine (Loaded) 1.63 lb (0.74 kg)
Service cartridge M80 Ball 393 gr (25.5 g)
Projectile 149 gr (9.7 g)
LENGTHS
Weapon overall 44.33 in (112.6 cm)
Barrel 22 in (55.9 cm)
Sight radius 26.69 in (67.8 cm)

Source: U.S. Navy

T 223 RIFLE (HECKLER & KOCH HK33)

CARTRIDGE .223 Remington (5.56×45mm)
OPERATION Roller locked delayed blowback
TYPE OF FIRE Selective—semiautomatic/full automatic
RATE OF FIRE Practical SS 40 rpm, A 160 rpm, Cyclic 650 to 750 rpm
MUZZLE VELOCITY 3,150 fps (960 m/s)
MUZZLE ENERGY 1,234 ft/lb (1,673 J)
SIGHTS Open, drum-type multiple aperture w/V-notch battle sight/blade, adjustable, battle sight 100 meters, apertures at 200, 300, and 400 m
FEED 20- or 40-round removable box magazines
WEIGHTS
Weapon (empty) 7.65 lb (3.47 kg)
Weapon (loaded) 9.04 lb (4.1 kg) w/40-round magazine
Magazine (empty) 20 round 0.25 lb (0.11 kg); 40 round 0.35 lb (0.16 kg)
Magazine (loaded) 20 round 0.77 lb (0.35 kg); 40 round 1.39 lb (0.63 kg)
Service cartridge M193 Ball 182 gr (11.8 g)
Projectile 56 gr (3.6 g)
LENGTHS
Weapon overall 36.9 in (93.7 cm)
Barrel 15.7 in (39.9 cm)
Sight radius 18.9 in (48 cm)

SKS (CHINESE TYPE 56 CARBINE)

CARTRIDGE 7.62 Intermediate (7.62×39mm)
OPERATION Gas
TYPE OF FIRE Semiautomatic
RATE OF FIRE 30 to 35 rpm
MUZZLE VELOCITY 2,410 fps (735 m/s)
MUZZLE ENERGY 1,573 ft/lb (2,133 J)
SIGHTS Open, tangent round-notch/post, adjustable 0 to 800 m in 100 m graduations
FEED 10-round integral magazine
WEIGHTS
Weapon (empty) 8.5 lb (3.86 kg)

Weapon (loaded) 8.86 lb (4.02 kg)

Magazine (loaded) 10 rds 0.36 lb (0.16 kg); 10 rds w/stripper clip 0.39 lb (0.18 kg)

Service cartridge M43 Ball 253 gr (16.4 g)

Projectile 122 gr (7.9 g)

LENGTHS

Weapon overall 40.2 in (102.1 cm)

Barrel 20.5 in (52.1 cm)

AK-47 (AKS-47)

CARTRIDGE 7.62 Intermediate (7.62×39mm)

OPERATION Gas

TYPE OF FIRE Selective—Full automatic/semiautomatic

RATE OF FIRE Practical SS 40 rpm, A 90 to 100 rpm, Cyclic 600 to 800 rpm

MUZZLE VELOCITY 2,329 fps (710 m/s)

MUZZLE ENERGY 1,469 ft/lb (1,992 J)

SIGHTS Open, tangent round-notch/post, adjustable 0 to 800 m in 100 m graduations

FEED 30-round removable box magazine

WEIGHTS

Weapon (empty) AK-47 8.53 lb (3.87 kg); AKS-47 7.65 lb (3.47 kg)

Weapon (loaded) AK-47 10.56 lb (4.79 kg) w/early steel mag; AKS-74 9.68 lb (4.39 kg) w/early steel mag

Magazine (empty) Early steel magazine 0.95 lb (0.43 kg); late steel magazine 0.73 lb (0.33 kg); aluminum magazine 0.37 lb (0.17 kg)

Magazine (loaded) Early steel magazine 2.03 lb (0.92 kg); late steel magazine 1.81 lb (0.82 kg); aluminum magazine 1.45 lb (0.66 kg)

Service cartridge M43 Ball 253 gr (16.4 g)

Projectile 122 gr (7.9 g)

LENGTHS

Weapon overall AK-47 34.25 in (87 cm); AKS-47 27.52/34.21 in (69.9/86.9 cm)

Barrel 16.30 in (41.4 cm)

Sight radius 14.8 in (37.6 cm)

Source: Kevin Dockery

AKM-47 (AKMS-47)

CARTRIDGE 7.62 Intermediate (7.62×39mm)

OPERATION Gas

TYPE OF FIRE Selective—Full automatic/semiautomatic

RATE OF FIRE Practical SS 40 rpm, A 90 to 100 rpm, Cyclic 600 to 800 rpm

MUZZLE VELOCITY 2,329 fps (710 m/s)

MUZZLE ENERGY 1,469 ft/lb (1,992 J)

SIGHTS Open, tangent round-notch/post, adjustable 0 to 1000 m in 100 m graduations

FEED 30-round removable box magazine

WEIGHTS

Weapon (empty) AKM-47 6.46 lb (2.93 kg); AKMS-47 6.90 lb (3.13 kg)

Weapon (loaded) AKM-47 8.27 lb (3.75 kg) w/late steel mag; AKMS-47 8.71 lb (3.95 kg) w/late steel mag

Magazine (empty) Early steel magazine 0.95 lb (0.43 kg); late steel magazine 0.73 lb (0.33 kg); aluminum magazine 0.37 lb (0.17 kg); plastic magazine

Magazine (loaded) Early steel magazine 2.03 lb (0.92 kg); late steel magazine 1.81 lb (0.82 kg); aluminum magazine 1.45 lb (0.66 kg); plastic magazine

Service cartridge M43 Ball 253 gr (16.4 g)

Projectile 122 gr (7.9 g)

LENGTHS

Weapon overall AKM-47 34.5 in (87.6 cm) AKMS-47 25.20/35.04 in (64/89 cm)

Barrel 16.3 in (41.4 cm)

Sight radius 14.8 in (37.6 cm)

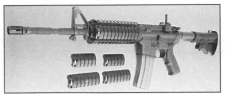

Source: Knight Armament Corporation

M4A1 CARBINE (COLT MODEL 927)

SOCOM M4A1 carbine with the forend mounting surfaces covered by grip plates. The different length grip plates below the weapon can be used to cover the forend mounting surfaces when only a portion of the mount is used by a sight or other accessory.

Source T/K

CARTRIDGE .223 Remington NATO (5.56×45mm NATO)

OPERATION Gas

TYPE OF FIRE Selective—semiautomatic/full automatic

RATE OF FIRE Practical SS 45 to 65 rpm, A 150 to 200 rpm, Cyclic 700 to 800 rpm

MUZZLE VELOCITY 2,900 fps (884 m/s)

MUZZLE ENERGY 1,158 ft/lb (1,570 J)

SIGHTS Variable from SOPMOD kit as per operator/mission requirements. Removable carrying handle/rear sight assembly with open, flip-type aperture/post, adjustable, battle aperture 0 to 200 meters, adjustable long range small aperture 300 to 800 meters in 100 meter graduations

FEED 20- or 30-round removable box magazines

WEIGHTS

Weapon (empty) 5.39 lb (2.44 kg) w/o carrying handle; carrying handle/sight assembly 0.265 lb (0.120 kg)

Weapon (loaded) 7.1 lb (3.22 kg) w/sling, carrying handle/sight assembly & 30 rd mag; sling 0.4 lb (0.18 kg)

Magazine (empty) 20 round aluminum 0.19 lb (0.08 kg); 30 round aluminum 0.24 lb (0.11 kg)

Magazine (loaded) 20 round 0.73 lb (0.33 kg); 30 round 1.05 lb (0.48 kg)

Service cartridge M855 Ball 190 gr (12.3 g)

Projectile 62 gr (4 g)

LENGTHS

Weapon overall 29.8/33 in (75.7/83.8 cm)

Barrel 14.5 in (36.8 cm)

Sight radius 14.72 in (37.4 cm) w/carrying handle/sight assembly

■ 8
KNOCK, KNOCK

The open-handed blow from the tall man with the beard rocked the other man as it landed with a loud, meaty smack. Sitting in a chair, the other man would have fallen over if his arms hadn't been tied with wire to the padded arms of the heavy wooden chair.

"Tell me who your contact is," the tall man said as he drew his hand back for another blow.

"I have no contact!" the tied man almost screamed through broken lips. "You made a mistake. I'm just an agriculture specialist. I'm not a spy! I don't know anyone, I can't tell you anything!"

Before the bearded man could land another blow, his hand was stopped by a heavyset man who stepped up to him. Talking low in Arabic, the two men stepped away from the bleeding man bound to the chair.

"Achmed," the heavyset man said, "he could be telling the truth. No one has been looking for this man since we took him from the hotel. It's been two days and he should have said something by now."

"I don't believe he's nobody, Mohammed," Achmed said. "We watched him for days. He never went to a farm or out in the country."

"The countryside around Beirut has not been a popular place for some time, Achmed," Mohammed said.

"All the more reason to question why the Americans would send an agriculture specialist here," Achmed said angrily.

"He could be here from the American DEA, their drug people," Mohammed said. "Or even from Interpol. It doesn't matter. The Doctor doesn't want this man to be found. If he is here from the drug people, he could make trouble just by people looking for him. The opium will be ready for shipment soon. You are to get rid of him. He isn't even a bargaining chip."

Two other men in very dirty fatigues stood behind the man bound to the chair. AK-47s were loosely held in their hands as they could see the man was no threat to them. The windows to the room were all covered with wooden shutters and the heavy plank door was shut tight behind a solid lock. No one was going to help the man tied up in the center of the room. He was at their mercy. And those mercies had been limited by the look of the dried bloodstains on the stocks of the AK-47s.

Throwing up his hands in disgust, the tall bearded man turned and walked to a table on the far side of the room. There was a towel there that he picked up and used to mop his face and dry his hands. Then he picked up the folding stock AKMS-47 that had been lying on the table.

Turning to the chair, Achmed pushed off the safety to his AKMS. The metallic click of the switch could be heard over the bubbling sobs coming from the man in the chair. Pulling back the bolt handle to the AKMS, Achmed let it go and the bolt slammed forward, stripping a round from the long, curved magazine and chambering it with a loud snap.

The two guards behind the bound man stepped away. It wasn't that they hadn't seen this kind of slaughter before. They had killed helpless hostages before. It was just that they didn't want to get splashed with blood or tissue, the flies in the area were bad enough as it was without drawing them in to the smell of death.

Stepping away from the table, Achmed just started to lower his AKMS when the locked wooden door suddenly opened with a smash. Two dark cylinders flew through the open door and detonated with an ear-splitting roar and blinding flash of light.

One of the flash-bangs went off only a few feet from Achmed. The light and pressure wave from the grenade shocked his system for a moment and he couldn't move. Neither could he feel the impact of the hollow-point 9mm bullets as they thudded into him. It wasn't just the fact that his ears weren't working well enough for him to hear the shots that killed him. The sound of the firing weapon was muffled and indistinct.

Coming through the doorway in a rushing martial ballet, men dressed completely in black from their boots to their masked faces entered behind black weapons that spit short tongues of flame.

The first man through the door moved immediately to the right, the second man split off to the left. The black submachine guns in their hands fired short, controlled bursts of two rounds—bursts that picked out every man standing with a gun in his hand in the room. Behind the first two men through the door came two more, dressed the same and moving in almost exactly the same way.

Spread out across the room, the four men in black made quick work of the standing men. Within four seconds of the door slamming open, three of the original five people in the room were dead. Darting forward, the last two men in the room went up to Mohammed, who was bent over and holding his ears. While his partner roughly shoved the man down, the other man in black kicked the back of Mohammed's knees. Mohammed went down hard and immediately had the silver tube screwed onto the muzzle of a proven-deadly submachine gun shoved hard into his back.

While one man held Mohammed pinned down with the muzzle of his weapon, the other jerked the prostrate man's hands behind his back and slipped a pair of plastic loops around them. With a pull, the ends of the loops made a zipping sound and snugged down. A quick snap of his hand, and an unrolled triangular bandage was pulled over the prisoner's head and tied over his mouth. Mohammed was as firmly bound as his own prisoner had been only a few moments before.

Stepping back up from where he had bound the prisoner, the man in black shouted, "Clear!"

The rest of the men in black held their weapons steady, moving them in short arcs across the entire room.

"Clear."

"Clear."

"Clear," the other men shouted out in sequence.

From outside the room and the dark alleyway beyond, another pair of men dressed in black came into the room.

"Quickly, people," the shorter of the two men said.

Two of the first men into the room stepped over to the table and quickly stuffed every piece of paper, book, or picture they could find into small sacks they pulled from inside their vests. While one man maintained watch, the other man in black stepped up to where the bleeding man sat bound to his chair.

"Henry Croft?" the man in black said.

"Yes, that's me," Henry said.

"It's okay," the man in black said as he pushed back the black balaclava hood over his head. "We're Navy SEALs and we've come to get you out."

Pulling a Leatherman tool from a pouch, the sandy-haired young looking man in the black combat suit unfolded the long-nosed pliers and started to cut away the wire binding Henry to the wooden chair.

"Seven," the man in black said, "get in here, we have a wounded Hotel."

Another Navy SEAL dressed all in black and carrying a suppressed submachine gun stepped into the room from the dark alleyway outside. In spite of his pain and shock, Henry marveled at the speed and efficiency of the men who had come to rescue him.

The rest of the men were standing guard around the room. One was taking pictures of the dead men on the floor. Seven, the man who had come in to help Henry, had pushed back the balaclava over his head. Quickly and thoroughly, the SEAL gave Henry a medical examination.

"He looks able to travel," the SEAL corpsman said.

"Then get him up," the sandy-haired SEAL said, "we're extracting now."

"What do we do with this one?" the SEAL who was standing guard over Mohammed said.

"Take him with you," Henry said.

"We're not really set up for hitchhikers," the sandy-haired SEAL said.

"He's the ringleader for this group of terrorists running drugs from the Bakaa Valley," Henry said. "He's the man the DEA sent me in here to find."

Over his green cloth gag, the eyes of Mohammed glared at Henry.

"Hey," Henry said. "I never said you guys were wrong about me."

"Fine," the SEAL who appeared to be on overall command said. "Chief, bring him along."

As if Mohammed was nothing more than a rolled carpet, the big SEAL snatched the prostrate man up from the floor and draped him over a shoulder.

"Extraction, people," the SEAL commander said, "Now. Sitrep, three tangos down, one hotel up, one tango prisoner. We are extracting."

Henry couldn't see who the other SEAL was talking to, but he noticed that there were several other SEALs in the alleyway outside the room where he had been kept prisoner. He had no idea where he was, he hadn't even known it was night outside. The SEAL in command had pulled up the black balaclava back over his head and suddenly raised a closed fist.

At the mouth of the alley, a shadow blocked the dull light from the street. There was a quiet pop and a dull thud. The shadow crumpled to the ground and lay still.

"Thorn," the SEAL commander said, "I copy, one tango down."

With hand signals that Henry couldn't understand, the rest of the SEALs lined up and moved out down the alleyway in the opposite direction the shadow had come from. The SEALs all had their weapons up and ready. Even the corpsman who was helping Henry walk along had an MP5K submachine gun in his left hand, the short submachine gun pushed out tightly against its sling.

Moving as quickly as he could, Henry stumbled along with his rescuers.

Mohammed lay still across the big SEAL's shoulder. The terrorist leader was so still that Henry wondered if the SEAL carrying him had possibly tapped the man hard enough to make certain that he lay still. If he had, Henry figured these experts knew just how hard they had to hit a man to knock him out, or kill him for that matter.

Darting along in short runs, the SEALs, their rescued hostage, and their prisoner, moved from cover to cover. They were only a block from a large open square. When they reached the square, Henry heard the SEAL leader speak softly.

"Ironman Six-Four, this is Cactus One-One. We are ready for quit the game with the chip and a dealer."

Over the sounds of a countryside that had been fighting for years came the thumping of helicopter blades. Suddenly, down a building wall behind them, another man in black slid down a rope. He had a long black rifle over his shoulder. The rifle had another black tube over the muzzle and a telescopic sight that looked much thicker and larger than any normal optical instrument.

As the helicopter came in, the SEALs tossed their prisoner aboard. Henry was helped onto the helicopter and the rest of the SEALs sat in the doorway of the bird as it lifted off. Their weapons were still pointed outward at any possible threat. Less than ten minutes earlier, Henry Martin had been an undercover DEA agent looking at the last moments of his life. Now he was going home, and with a good source of information with him. All courtesy of a group of Navy SEALs he would never know the names of.

9

HAND GRENADES

Sometimes called the pocket artillery of the foot soldier, hand grenades are the most common weapon available to the fighting man that lets him attack a target that is not in his direct sight. By being able to lob a grenade through a bunker door or over an embankment, a target can be effectively engaged without exposing the thrower to return fire. Hand grenades also affect a reasonably larger area than their immediate point of impact, allowing them to make up for the inaccuracy of throwing at an indistinct target.

In general, all hand grenades share three common characteristics. As the weapons are hand thrown, their engagement range is short. The effective casualty radius of the grenade is small, allowing the weapon to effect only its immediate area. And the delay element of the modern grenade allows them to be safely thrown, minimizing the danger to the thrower.

All hand grenades are made up of three major components. The body of the grenade contains the filler, allowing it to be transported and safely handled and employed. In addition, for some grenades, the body provides fragmentation. The filler is the chemical or explosive payload of the grenade. The use and characteristics of the grenade are normally determined by what kind of filler it contains. The fuze assembly causes the grenade to function by igniting or detonating the filler. The fuze must be safe to handle, easy to employ, and relatively uncomplicated for economic manufacture.

The U.S. employment of hand grenades in numbers only goes back to the last years of World War I. At that time millions of hand grenades of dozens of types were used by all sides of the conflict. It was during World War I that the classic pull-ring grenade fuze was developed that has become so familiar to all of the U.S. services.

In the pull-ring fuze, correctly called the Bouchon fuze, a round metal ring is attached to a cotter pin that extends through the body of the fuze. The cotter pin secures a safety lever, also called a spoon, across the top of the fuze as well as retaining the spring-loaded striker assembly inside of the fuze. The end of the cotter pin is spread where it exits the fuze body to prevent accidental removal. The legs of the cotter pin a spread in such a way as to require 10 to 30 pounds of pull to remove the pin. This much resistance effectively eliminates the Hollywood style of pin pulling with the teeth, unless the operator wants to remove his front teeth rather than the grenade pin.

When the pull ring and cotter pin are removed, hand pressure holds the safety lever down against the body of the grenade which in turn holds back the striker assembly. When the thrower releases his grip, the striker spring rotates the striker on its axis, forcing the safety lever away from the fuze. The striker rotates further and strikes the primer centered at the top of the fuze. The primer ignites the delay element, which burns for its proscribed length of time and then initiates the detonator or igniter. The detonator or igniter in its turn sets off the grenade's filler. Overseas, this type of fuze is often called the "mousetrap" fuze from the action of its rotating striker.

The Bouchon-type fuze quickly caught on with the U.S. forces as the simplest and safest fuze available. Eighty years later, it is still by far the most common grenade fuze used in the U.S. military. Two different types of Bouchon fuze are generally recognized: the detonating type and the igniting type. The detonator type of fuze is used in explosive grenades, fragmentation, white phosphorus smoke, and bursting-type chemical grenades. Igniter fuzes are generally found in burning-type chemical grenades and practice grenades.

Given their effectiveness and convenience, hand grenades have been loaded with a variety of payloads specific for different effects. As new targets developed, new grenades were designed to meet the threat. But in general, all hand grenades fall into five general categories. Two of these categories, training and practice grenades, are either simple inert bodies of the right size, shape, and weight, or have a minor reaction to simulate the actual weapon. Historically, the most important grenade family to the fighting man is the fragmentation grenade. This is the class of grenade that acts as the soldier's personal indirect fire system.

The class of fragmentation, also called defensive grenades, is the most common type of grenade used on the battlefield. This class of grenade is designed to produce casualties by the projection of high-velocity fragments. The payload or filler is high explosives and the body of the grenade is intended to shatter in some way and supply the fragmentation. The fragmentation effect will operate well against a scattered group of personnel because the effective range of the high-speed fragments is much greater then the effective radius of the blast alone. The blast effect of the fragmentation grenade may still be used to good effect in small enclosed places even though the fragmentation might not reach the intended target.

Because the fragmentation of a grenade can be projected further than the grenade can be easily thrown, especially in the case of early designs, the fragmentation grenade is also called the defensive type. The defensive type of grenade is employed when the operator is in a defensive position, that is, he's protected by cover from the effect of his own weapon. The measurement of the area of effect of a fragmentation is called the effective casualty radius. In the U.S. military, the definition of the effective casualty radius is the radius of a circular area in which at least 50 percent of the exposed personnel will become casualties.

Offensive hand grenades are the fourth general type of grenade and they are used to produce blast effects. Fragments of the grenade, especially the fuze body, may be projected over 607 feet (185 m) from the point of the explosion, but this type of grenade is not intended to produce a large number of fragments. Offensive grenades are intended to produce casualties on enemy personnel while minimizing the danger to attacking troops. They are intended for use during offensive movement, where the thrower is not able to take cover during the assault. This type of grenade has also been called a concussion grenade since the main effect of the filler is a concussive blast wave. These grenades are especially useful in built-up areas and fortified positions such as caves or bunkers. Since they tend to stun a target, they are most useful when capture of the enemy is the preferred option. Additionally, the offensive grenade can be used as a small, prepackaged demolition charge.

Chemical hand grenades are the final major category. A very broad category, chemical grenades can cause casualties, start fires, produce irritating gas, make smoke for signaling or screening, or any combination of these effects. This class of grenade is further subdivided into burning types or bursting types.

Burning-type chemical grenades cause their effect by creating a cloud of agent, either smoke or gas, by the igniting and burning of their filler. Usually a burning-type grenade is a metal canister with the fuze screwed in at one end and holes drilled into the casing to allow the agent to escape. Since this kind of grenade does not have an instant effect—the burning takes a second or two to build up volume—they are often fitted with a shorter fuze delay than casualty-producing types. Explosive grenades usually have a 4.5-second nominal fuze delay, burning-type grenades usually have a 1.5-second nominal delay.

Bursting-type chemical grenades explode and spread their agent over a wide area. This kind of grenade causes its agent to take effect quickly, whether it's a chemical agent such as powdered CS or a burning chemical agent such as white phosphorus (WP). The most commonly found loading for this type of grenade is white phosphorus. The bursting of the grenade spreads the WP over a large area where it spontaneously ignites on exposure to air creating dense white smoke.

Additional grenades come under the heading of "special Purpose." This type of grenade usually has a very specific kind of target or effect and this fact restricts its general issue. Illuminating grenades, stun grenades, and other hand-thrown devices can be included under this category.

The first type of grenade commonly issued in the U.S. military was the Mark II (Mk 2) fragmentation grenade. Commonly called the "pineapple," the Mark II had a cast iron body with external serrations formed on it, breaking the body up into eight rows of five squares each. This grenade was first issued in October 1918 and remained in the active inventory well after World War II was over.

Though the square serrations on the outside of the Mk 2 gave it a good gripping service for cold or muddy hands, and led to its colorful nickname, they did not act as their designer intended. Instead of breaking up into fragments along the serration lines, Mk 2s tended to shatter into a number of larger pieces and a quantity of iron dust. In an attempt to increase the number of effective fragments, and due to a strategic shortage of TNT in 1941 and 1942, a different explosive filler was experimented with during World War II. Instead of the 2-ounce charge of TNT, the Mk 2A1 was loaded with a 0.74-ounce charge of EC (explosive company) Blank powder and fitted with an M10A3 igniter fuze. The EC powder, a nitrocellulose propellant, was expected to break up the body of the Mk 2A1 along the designed lines but failed to meet expectations.

Mk 2 grenades were the most common grenade issued to U.S. forces during World War II an the UDTs and NCDUs were at least generally familiar with the weapon. Though the UDTs were not issued fragmentation grenades during World War II as a matter of course, it is interesting to note just how long the Mk 2 grenade remained in the Navy inventory. SEALs did carry the Mk 2 in Vietnam in limited numbers, usually just because they were available. The other services removed the Mk 2 from their inventories by the late 1960s. In SEAL ammunition manuals dated from the late 1980s, the Mk 2 fragmentation grenade is still listed as being available for issue.

The grenade that was issued to the UDTs during World War II, at least in limited numbers, was the Mk3A1 offensive grenade. In the Teams, the Mk3A1 was considered a small demolition charge, though as a concussion grenade it also had its uses in after-invasion bunker cleaning. The shock wave and over-pressure produced by the Mk3A1 when it is used in an enclosed area is much greater than the equivalent effect from a fragmentation grenade. Though the blast could drive portions of the metal ends and especially the fuze body for hundreds of yards from the point of explosion, the Mk3A1 had only a 2-yard effective casualty radius. Underwater, the Mk3A1 had a much greater casualty radius against swimmers but this effect was not used in combat during World War II. Later, in Vietnam, the underwater blast effect of the Mk3A2 was used to good effect when defending boats and shipping from enemy sappers in the water.

The Mk3A1 is a very simple grenade, not much more than a cylindrical block of explosive surrounded by cardboard and fitted with a fuze. The body of the Mk3A1 had thin metal end caps to secure the cardboard tube and threaded fuze well. Late in World War II, a new version of the offensive grenade was designed and issued. The new grenade was the Mk3A2, a larger and improved version of the Mk3A1. In the Mk3A2, the body was made up of two thick, asphalt-impregnated fiber—later fiberglass—cups that would nest one inside the other. The new body material eliminated the need for the metal end caps and could hold a slightly larger change than the earlier grenade. The two cups were water-resistant and were held together at their center seam with a piece of waterproof tape.

The Mk3A2 grenade proved to be a very popular design and saw long service with all the Teams through the Korean War, Vietnam, and today, where it is still an issue item. In Vietnam, the Mk3A2 was often used during waterborne ambushes where it could be thrown into the water. The underwater blast of the Mk3A2 could stove in the bottom of a sampan or stun a Viet Cong who had fallen into the river. Though the shock wave of the grenade could be very rough on a prisoner, it was far better than a fragmentation grenade landing in the sampan.

Fragmentation grenades in general saw a great deal of improvement in design following World War II. It had been found that if the serrations were placed on the inside surface of the grenade body, the body would break up along the lines. This was a major step in the direction of controlled fragmentation. Another fragmentation system was to surround the explosive filler with a square cross-sectioned wire, regularly notched along its length. The wire could be formed into a shaped coil and covered with a thin sheet-metal body. The fragmentation could be controlled and the burst radius designed into the system by setting the size of the individual fragments.

A large fragment had more weight and inertia when flying and would then have a correspondingly large lethal range, but there could be relatively few of these fragments due to the practical weight limit of a hand-thrown grenade. Smaller fragments would lose velocity quickly and have a relatively short lethal range, but there could be many more of them, making a dense pattern near the point of explosion. The first U.S. issue grenade to make use of the coiled, notched wire system was the M26 fragmentation grenade issued in the early 1950s.

Because the new style of grenade body was much thinner than the Mk 2 grenade, a larger explosive charge could be used as the filler. In addition, advances in explosive technology had come up with more effective explosives for use on fragmentation grenades. The M26 was loaded with Composition B, a mixture of RDX, TNT, and wax. With the Composition B filler, the fragments of the M26 had an initial velocity in the 3200 feet per second range (1000 m/s). The coiled wire fragmentation system gave the M26 nearly 1,000 fragments but because of their low weight and poor aerodynamic qualities, the majority of the fragments were lethal at 16 yards (15 m) and relatively harmless at 33 yards (30 m).

The Composition B filler of the M26 was less sensitive than TNT and in some conditions was not easily set off by the just the detonator on the M204 series fuze. To ensure complete and reliable detonation, the M26A1 fragmentation grenade was issued for service beginning in the late 1950s. In the M26A1, a small quantity of the Composition B explosive was removed surrounding the fuze well and pellets of tetryl were inserted. The tetryl act as a booster to the detonator and insure complete detonation of the explosive filler.

One problem arose from the use of the Bouchon-type fuze in U.S. grenades of almost all types. Because the safety handle of the Bouchon fuze stood out form the body of the grenade and was reasonably long, almost everyone who used hand grenades at one time or another carried them by hooking the safety lever to a convenient spot on their uniform. This made for colorful pictures of fighting men going into combat festooned with grenades, but it also led to a lot of lost ordnance. Not only could the grenade easily slip off under movement, the safety of the device was compromised by the habit. If the spoon should break off close to the fuze, there would be nothing for the operator to easily hold down for safety while pulling the pin.

To help eliminate this problem, two actions were taken. The M1956 universal ammunition pouch, which could hold M14 or M16 magazines, 40mm grenades, or other loose ordnance, had two special holders for carrying hand grenades. The holders were on either side of the pouch and consisted of a long vertical cloth tube for holding the grenade safety lever and a securing strap. The securing strap would be wrapped around the grenade's fuze, through the pull ring, and snapped to the pouch. In this carrying configuration, the grenade is safe from falling off or breaking the safety lever.

The second action taken to help secure the safety of casualty-producing grenades was an addition to the fuze. Beginning with the M26A1 grenade in 1970, a secondary safety clip was added to the body of the grenade's fuze. The safety clip is intended to retain the safety lever should the pin of the grenade come loose accidentally. The clip is simple in construction, wrapping either around an extension of the fuze below the pull ring or about the neck of the fuze where it enters the grenade. Not all grenades are fitted with the safety clip, but it is found on almost all modern U.S. manufacture explosive filled hand grenades. The safety clip is easily removed and is usually taken off just before the grenade is used. Nomenclature was changed for grenades that are issued with the safety clip. The M26A1 fragmentation grenade is known as the M61 grenade when fitted with a safety clip, and there is no other difference between the two grenades.

Later-issue carrying equipment, such as the All-Purpose Lightweight Individual Carrying Equipment (ALICE) gear available in the 1970s, have small pockets on the outside of the magazine pouches to safely carry fragmentation grenades. On the ALICE pouches, the grenades are secured in their pockets by a strap across the top of the grenade. The pocket system of carrying fragmentation and other grenades has been retained in the Teams through the 1980s and into the 1990s with new types of carrying gear designed specifically with SEAL missions in mind.

There was one type of fragmentation grenade loaded for the SEALs in Vietnam that could not be made safe for use in any normal sense. Designed by the Special Ordnance Branch of the Naval Weapons Center at China Lake, California, the grenade looked like a normal M26 fragmentation grenade except for one difference—its fuze had no time delay. In the "instant" M26A1 grenade, the delay element had been removed from the fuze so that it could be used as a boobytrap. As soon as the safety lever was released, the grenade detonated.

This type of grenade was very useful for the quick and dirty boobytrap, such as materials or equipment that had to be left behind. Placing one of the zero-delay grenades under a box, board, or other item would make the VC very wary about going back into an area that the SEALs had just left. Conveniently dropping one as "lost" when a patrol had gone through a known VC area would also make the VC think twice about using recovered U.S. ordnance. Care and

SEAL discipline helped keep accidents with the zero-delay grenade to a minimum; only one such accident took place with U.S. troops and that was caused by a non-SEAL. The incident involved the recovery of remote sensors for the replacement of the batteries. SEALs assisted the PBRs conducting the operation.

> They (SEALs) had booby-trapped one of the sensors before they implanted it with a special zero-delay hand grenade . . . Recovering a boobytrapped sensor was tricky.
>
> The PBR Lieutenant had the grenade in his hand. All he had to do was hold it or tie the spoon down and it would have been safe until we put the pin back in. . . . He threw it. The spoon came up and the thing went off just as it left his hand. He lost a good part of his hand. He had a flak jacket and helmet on, otherwise he really would have been shredded.

The lesson learned on the sensor recovery mission was a simple one—leave ordnance to the people who understood it. The PBR officer involved did know that the grenade didn't have a delay but he threw it before thinking the situation through. Though the SEALs did not have any other accidents involving the zero-delay grenade, there was the occasional problem with just using hand grenades in combat. Standard operating procedure on an ambush often entailed several members of the unit throwing hand grenades into the kill zone while other SEALs continued firing. This procedure helped ensure full coverage of the target but could backfire on occasion.

> Nobody was sure whose grenade hit the tree. . . . One of our grenades hit a tree and bounced right back at us, landing in the canal. These weren't old-fashioned Mark II pineapples. They were modern M26A1s lined with notched wire. All of our eyes were huge, watching that grenade bounce back at us. Smacking our faces down, everyone ate mud. The grenade detonated harmlessly in the canal.

One grenade accident the SEALs never contended with was one caused by using captured enemy ordnance. Though the SEALs were trained as to what the capabilities were and how to use grenades in use by the VC and NVA, combat use of such material was very rare. The Chinese communist pattern was of explosive-filled hand grenades that were either supplied to or manufactured by North Vietnamese forces along with a number of Soviet designs. The Chicom grenades are among the most dangerous given the variety of materials they are made of and

the difficult tropical environment of
Vietnam. The general pattern of the
Chicom explosive grenade was a
short wooden or bamboo handle
topped by a cast metal, usually iron,
head. The head could be a simple
blunt cylinder or egg-shaped with
deep serrations. A simple pull-
friction fuze was inserted into the

One type of Chinese stick grenade. In this model the head is cast
in a mold that forms serrations on the outside of the grenade. The
serrations do little to control the breakup of the head on detonation and the grenade is no more effective than the smooth model.
Source: Kevin Dockery

head of the grenade and the pull string passed through the handle. Fuze delays
ran from 2 to 6 seconds on the average, depending on the amount of humidity the
grenade had been exposed to and how it had been made originally.

The real danger in the Chicom grenades lay in the explosive filling. Various
fillers were used, including salvaged explosives removed from dud U.S. ordnance. Picric acid, long discarded as being too dangerous an explosive filling for
grenades, was in common use among the NVA and VC forces. The main danger
of picric acid is its tendency to form unstable salts when it comes in contact
with metals, including iron. Though their effectiveness was occasionally noted
by the SEALs, Chicom grenades were something the Teams scrupulously
avoided whenever possible.

Though the notched-wire coil was proving itself a successful design in the
M26 family of fragmentation grenades, a second method of producing controlled fragmentation was also fielded in quantity for the first time during the
Vietnam War. While external serrations had been proven not to affect the size of
casing fragments in a regular manner, internal serrations were another matter.

As early as World War I, a hand grenade had been produced with internal
serrations, the British Number 16 of 1915. But the design of the grenades themselves had proven faulty. During the 1950s, fragmentation control by internal
serrations was "rediscovered" and further developed. The M33 fragmentation
grenade became the first U.S. hand grenade to use the internal serration system
and was issued to the troops in Vietnam, including the SEALs, in the late 1960s.

The oblate spheroid shape of the M33 grenade is a more natural shaped object for throwing, especially for men from a country where baseball is a prominent sport. In addition to being better balanced for throwing, the rounder
shape of the M33 grenade gives the weapon a more regular fragmentation pattern, no matter what its orientation at detonation. The lemon-shaped grenades,
such as the M26 family, have their best fragmentation out from their sides but
the patterns are much poorer from the bottom and top areas.

The body of the M33 grenade is made up of two formed steel hemispheres welded together at their equator. Each body half is formed with an internal diamond serration pattern pressed into its inside surface. The characteristics of the M33 body allow the grenade to have a larger explosive charge than the M26 family of grenades while still having a good throwing range. The heavy charge of explosive gives the M33 grenade a very dense pattern of high-velocity fragments while the shape and weight of the fragments themselves prevent them from having too great a lethal range.

A later version of the M33 grenade, the M67, was produced as an almost identical piece of ordnance but incorporated a safety clip into the design. The M67 fragmentation grenade has proved itself the most successful design of its type coming out of the Vietnam War and it remains the standard issue fragmentation grenade in the U.S. services today.

Another fragmentation grenade was used by the SEALs in some numbers in Vietnam and it, too, made use of the internal fragmentation system. The Dutch V40 mini-grenade, manufactured by the Netherlands Weapon & Munition Company (NWM), was one of the smallest fragmentation grenades ever commercially produced and was issued to the Teams beginning in 1968. The round body of the V40 greatly resembles in size and effect the internal explosive ball assembly in the 40mm grenades, except that it is fitted with a special Bouchon fuze. The body of the V40 is internally notched into square fragments, ensuring optimum fragment size when the grenade explodes. The design of the V40 is such that the body of the grenade breaks up into about 500 fragments, over 300 of which are in the 2.3- to 3.1-grain (0.15 to 0.2 g) range. The V40's fragments give the weapon a 100 percent casualty rate at 3 meters from the point of burst and an almost 0 percent casualty rate at 25 meters range. This makes the V40 a very good grenade for close-in and house-to-house combat.

The fuze of the V40 has a safety lever than extends halfway around the grenade's body to insure solid gripping of the lever. The pull ring is teardrop-shaped and actually folds around the grenade's body for carrying. To add to the grenade's safety, the pull ring assembly is of the locking type. The pull ring has to be rotated about 120 degrees before an L-shaped extension on the pin can clear the fuze body, allowing the pin to be pulled. In general, the V40 grenade is less than half the size and weight of a regular fragmentation grenade, giving it a much greater throwing range and making it more convenient to carry in numbers.

But for all its apparent advantages, the V40's size also was a drawback. One young SEAL remembered vividly using the little grenade when he and his partner were cut off from the main body of their patrol. A VC had been shot by the two SEALs and lay out of their direct sight. The wounded VC was making considerable noise and drawing the very unwanted attention of a large body of VC near the two SEALs.

We were carrying a number of mini-grenades with us. These little frags weren't much larger than a golf ball and a man could carry several more minis for every normal-sized grenade. The little grenades (Dutch NWM V-40's) could also be thrown a lot farther than a regular M-26 frag as well, and that was the problem. . . . .Grabbing a minigrenade from my web gear, I pulled the pin and threw it where the wounded VC lay in the grass. Trouble was, with my heart pumping and the adrenalin flowing from the excitement, I put a little too much arm behind throwing the little 3 1/2 ounce mini-grenade. . . . We watched the mini-grenade whistle well over the horizon. . . . Grabbing another grenade off my rig. . . . I tried again to nail the wounded VC. Again, I was so pumped up that little grenade just sailed off into the distance. By this time, fire was starting up around us and I had enough of these little grenades. Pulling a standard M26 frag off my rig, I lobbed it into the wounded VC's position and his moaning suddenly stopped with the explosion.

The SEALs ceased issuing the V40 during the 1970s. Commercial sales had not developed enough for the V40 to satisfy NWM in Holland and production ceased in 1972.

Among the most universally useful grenades carried by the SEALs are the white phosphorus (WP) smoke grenades. The bursting-type "Willy Peter" grenade can be used for signaling, screening with smoke, target marking, incendiary purposes, and causing casualties. The screening effect of white phosphorus smoke is limited due to the high heat of burning phosphorus, causing the smoke to rise more rapidly than other types of smoke. In its favor, white phosphorus produces a smoke screen much faster than other smoke grenades. Reactive with oxygen, white phosphorus spontaneously ignites on contact with air. White phosphorus burns at a temperature of about 5,000 degrees Fahrenheit and is easily able to set fire to flammable materials as well as cause very severe burns on tissue.

Two WP grenades are used by the SEALs and UDTs, one being a World War II design, circa 1943. The M15 WP grenade was the first white phosphorus smoke grenade to be issued in the U.S. military. Externally, the M15 grenade resembles other canister-style, burning-type, smoke and gas grenades. To help prevent mixups with other types of less lethal grenades, the M15 has a seamless sheet steel body stamped out in one piece with rounded ends. With the rounded-edge end cap in place, the M15 grenade can be easily recognized by touch as being different from the canister-type grenade with its rolled metal edges.

Centered in the top of the M15 grenade is the same powerful M206A2 detonator fuze used in the Mk3A2 offensive grenade. A burster well extends down the center of the M15 grenade, containing the fuze and sealing out the WP filling. A very real danger of fire exists with all WP-filled grenades as any leakage of the filler will ignite as soon as it touches the air. This is part of the reason that the sheet steel that makes up the body of the M15 grenade is about twice as thick as the metal used to make up other canister-type grenades.

When the detonator of the M206A2 fuze goes off, it bursts the M15 casing, sending particles of WP streaming out in all directions. The WP particles burn through the air with a bright yellow-white light and leave tracks of white smoke behind them. Effectively unchanged since World War II, the M15 still remains a standard issue WP grenade with the U.S. forces.

Shortly after World War II, another type of WP grenade was designed. The M34 WP grenade is also a bursting-type grenade and shares most of the characteristics of the M15 WP grenade. The major difference between the M15 and M34 WP grenades is the size and body shape of the M34 grenade.

The body of the M34 WP grenade is a sheet steel cylinder of the same thickness as the M15 grenade. The body of the M34 grenade is serrated into 60 squares to help facilitate the body bursting and is tapered at its lower end for fitting into the M1A2 Grenade projection adaptor. The M1A2 grenade projection adaptor allows the M34 WP grenade to be launched from a rifle fitted with a spigot-type rifle grenade launcher. Though the adaptor was intended to allow the M34 grenade to replace both the M19A1 WP rifle grenade and the M15 WP hand grenade, in practice the system never worked to the operator's complete satisfaction. The UDT and SEALs used the M34 and M15 grenades interchangeably, by never accepted the rifle grenade adaptor concept.

Using the same M206A2 fuze as the M15 grenade, the M34 WP grenade has a larger burst radius due in part to the serrations in the grenade body. The scattered particles of white phosphorus from both grenades burn for about 60 seconds, spreading a thick cloud of relatively nonpoisonous phosphorus pentoxide smoke.

The WP grenades were found to have a large number of applications by SEALs operating in Vietnam. The white cloud of phosphorus smoke could readily be seen from aircraft or other support craft and was often used to mark targets for fire support. Even at night, the brilliant flare of the burning phosphorus could be seen though the smoke. This made phosphorus ideal for marking a units flanks, as was done in Vietnam by the SEALs.

> The SOP for this operation called for us to light up our flanks with WP grenades if anything was happening. The [boat] coming in would then be able to suppress any enemy fire on either side of us and know exactly where we were at.

On one operation, the SEALs involved were relative newcomers to direct combat. Mistakes are common during the confusion of war and even the superbly trained SEALs were not immune to making them. During the action, SOP (Standard Operating Procedure) was followed and WP grenades put out to mark the unit's flanks. Only while one SEAL was watching the approach area for possible enemy activity, other SEALs were hiding an Inflatable Boat, Small (IBS) the unit had brought with it as an escape route. When the action took place and the SOP was followed, the one SEAL who had been on guard never knew where the rubber boat had been placed. He soon learned his mistake when he was told to go into the brush and retrieve the boat for the units withdrawal.

> In the bushes? But that's where I threw the grenade. I found the IBS all right, and so had my WP grenade. The grenade had landed right inside the boat and completely destroyed it. The stink of the burning phosphorus had covered the smell of the burning rubber.

Other smoke grenades were used by the SEALs that had less destructive potential than the white phosphorus variety. The AN-M8 HC smoke grenade is a canister-style, burning-type grenade used to produce dense clouds of white smoke for signaling or screening purposes. The M8 grenade uses the standard-sized cylindrical sheet-metal body found on most of the U.S. burning-type grenades, Designed prior to World War II, the M8 is loaded Type C HC smoke mixture, a combination of zinc oxide, ammonium perchlorate, dechlorane, aluminum, and other materials.

When burning, HC mixture produces zinc chloride smoke, a dense white/gray heavy smoke that has excellent obscuring qualities and hugs the ground much better than white phosphorus smoke. Though the M8 grenade does not have the incendiary qualities of a WP grenade, the casing of the M8 becomes very hot while the filling burns, hot enough to ignite any flammable materials it may be in contact with.

The M8 grenade burns for at least several minutes, releasing its smoke through emission holes in the top of the grenade body. White smoke was not used in combat by the SEALs as often as in the other services as their operations generally did not call for it. Several AN-M8 HC grenades would be with a unit of SEALs as they conducted missions, scattered among the men. Though signaling, especially to aircraft and boats, could be done with the AN-M8 grenade, the white smoke could be mistaken for other kinds of explosions or ordnance, adding to the confusion of an already-difficult situation. For signaling purposes, the M18 colored smoke grenade was commonly used.

Developed in a few short weeks in 1942, the M18 colored smoke grenades met the U.S. Army requirement for a colored smoke grenade that would form smoke visible at a slant range of 10,000 feet (3,050 m) and last about one minute. Issued in four colors—red, green, yellow, and violet—the M18 quickly became and has remained the most widely used pyrotechnic signaling device in the military. The colored smoke produced by the M18 is not as dense as WP or HC smoke and is intended to have a bright color, making it easily visible against most natural backgrounds.

A selection of the colors would be carried on a SEAL mission with the colors either being chosen by SOP or simply picked at random. The most common use by far of the M18 grenade was to make the wind direction and speed for helicopter landing zones in the jungle. By tossing out a colored smoke grenade, the pilot of an incoming bird could also locate a hidden group of SEALs calling for fire support. The color of smoke used was not specified soon after combat operations began in Vietnam. The VC soon scrounged or made a sufficient supply of colored smoke that if a specific smoke was known to be used, they would release their own smoke of the same color. Most SEAL uses of M18 grenades followed a general pattern of first contacting the approaching aircraft by radio and then putting out an M18 grenade:

> "Well, you can identify me by this." And one of us would pop a colored smoke grenade. "Tell me what color you see. Yeah, that's me. All right, anybody else you see, you pop 'em."

The procedure was simple, straightforward, and kept confusion to a minimum. Yellow and red smoke were among the most popular loadings carried in

Vietnam, though the violet smoke, usually reserved for training back in the U.S., also stood out surprisingly well as did even the green smoke, it being a different shade than the jungle surroundings.

Other burning-type grenades were carried by the SEALs in Vietnam with a considerably more active filling than colored or white smoke. Tear gas riot control agents were found to be excellent means to empty out bunkers, concealed compartments, and tunnels without exposing the SEALs to the dangers of having to enter such areas first. Riot control gasses could quickly make an enclosure impossible to remain in for unprotected VC troops and when the people did emerge, they were usually in no condition to fight. This allowed the SEALs to conduct their preferred action, the taking of prisoners to gather intelligence. In addition, it gave the Teams a nonlethal way of clearing areas where civilians might, and often were, encountered.

The first tear gas used to any great extent was chloroacetophenone, widely known under its military designation CN. CN is a colorless solid when pure with a pleasant odor resembling apple blossoms. When mixed with a burning agent for fuel and vaporized, CN smoke has anything but a pleasant effect. Immediate weeping occurs on exposure to even slight concentrations of CN gas. Heavier concentrations quickly cause coughing and an itching, burning sensation to the body's moist tissues such as the eyes, nose, throat, and lungs. Though nontoxic, it is very difficult for even a trained individual to function in a CN atmosphere. Incapacitation will usually happen within 15 to 30 seconds of exposure to the gas and the painful symptoms can last for 5 to 30 minutes after removal to clean air.

For military use, CN is loaded with a burning fuel mixture into the standard canister-style grenade body. The original M7 grenade had 3 rows of 6 holes down the sides of the canister to release the CN gas. The M7 grenade was prone to "flashing," or catching flame and bursting. The later M7A1 grenade was designed to remove the problem of flashing and became widely issued due to its relative safety. The M7A1 CN grenade also has a cooler surface when burning and this helps limit the grass fires a burning-type grenade can cause.

First issued in 1935, the M7 CN grenade established the usefulness of the tear gas grenade for all of the services in general. Carried by the Teams in Vietnam, the CN grenade in general added a nonlethal weapon to the SEALs arsenal that increased the number of prisoners captured without a shot having to be fired.

A more serious chemical riot control agent was also used by the Teams in Vietnam and remains in the inventory today. Diphenylaminechloroarsine, also called Adamsite or more simply DM, is the only nauseating chemical agent loaded for general use. As the name of the agent type indicates, DM has a far more serious physiological action on the human body than simple tear gas. Initial reactions to even small concentrations of DM gas cause irritation to the eyes, nose, and throat after a few minutes' exposure. Within another minute or two if exposure, sneezing and coughing join the earlier symptoms, increasing in severity until the final stage of symptoms occur. The final stages of DM effects include severe headache, pains in the nose and chest, and finally nausea and violent vomiting. Long exposure is toxic and can result in death, but this is the exception since most people cannot stand being exposed to the earlier symptoms of DM.

The DM agent itself is a crystalline solid and is turned into a gas by burning it with an appropriate fuel similar to that used with CN gas. Since the effects of DM gas take several minutes to build up in severity, the agent is usually employed mixed with CN tear gas. The CN gas takes immediate effect and, if the individual exposed ignores the CN effects, masks the early symptoms of the DM agent. CN and DM are both loaded into a burning-type canister grenade with the same characteristics as the M7 series of CN grenades. The M6A1 CN-DM grenade was used in Vietnam by the SEALs in the same manner as the M7A1 CN grenade, though not in as large a number. The effects of DM last for three or more hours and this can make handling a prisoner affected by the agent a messy proposition. On the other hand, DM effects prevent a person from putting up any kind of real resistance no matter what their situation.

In 1960, the U.S. Army announced the adoption of a new riot control agent in the form of a super tear gas. The agent has the rather daunting chemical name Orthochlorobenzalmalononitrile, but is universally called CS. CS combines the effects of both CN and DM, but in a more powerful and safer form. Even low concentrations of CS gas produce its full range of symptoms within 20 to 60 seconds of exposure. Initial reactions include extreme burning of the eyes, a copious flow of tears, and sneezing. Further exposure to higher concentrations increases the severity of the symptoms already being experienced and adds irritation of the nose and throat, coughing, tightness in the chest, marked sinus and nasal drip, and difficulty in breathing. Further exposure to even higher concentrations add nausea, vomiting, and vertigo to the other symptoms, as well as increasing difficulty in breathing to a very frightening level and an involuntary closing of the eyes.

As fast and violent as the symptoms of CS gas are, they disappear within five to ten minutes of the victim being removed to fresh air. CS is loaded into a standard burning-type grenade canister in much the same way as CN or DM and the agent is mixed with an appropriate burning fuel for use. Issued as the M7A3 CS grenade, the CS agent quickly became the preferred riot control agent in the military and police forces. M7A3 grenades are still being manufactured and stocked since their introduction in the early 1960s.

An additional burning-type canister grenade is used by the Teams, only the burning effects of this type are extreme. The grenade is the AN-M14 TH3 incendiary grenade loaded with a TH3 thermate filler. World War II-issue versions of this grenade were filled with thermite, an mixture of 73 percent iron oxide and 27 percent fine granular aluminum. Thermate TH3 is thermite mixed with 29 percent barium nitrate, sulfur, and binders to make a superior mixture. In both mixtures, the general reaction is the same. Aluminum reacts chemically with the iron oxide when the mixture is heated enough. In the reaction, the aluminum strips the oxygen from the iron oxide resulting in aluminum oxide and free iron. The reaction is so hot and intense that the iron is released in a white-hot molten state.

Thermite reactions reach a temperature of 4,000 degrees Fahrenheit, spraying molten iron over a small area. This reaction makes the AN-M14 incendiary grenade one of the most effective devices for destroying equipment rapidly. The heavy AN-M14 grenade can burn its way through ½ inch of homogeneous steel plate and will weld together engine parts or the breech of cannons. Once ignited, the AN-M14 grenade will even burn underwater, the reaction supplying its own oxygen. To the SEALs, the AN-M14 grenade was an good way of destroying caches of rice and other burnable materials too bulky to be carried away. Even the normally hard-to-burn rice would ignite from the intense heat of a thermate grenade and continue smoldering for hours.

Though the AN-M14 TH3 grenade produced tremendous heat, it was not considered an optimum design for the SEALs use in Vietnam. The desire of the SEALs was for a lighter piece of ordnance than the issue incendiary grenade that could also cover a larger area with a burning agent. The humid conditions of Southeast Asia kept a high moisture content in many natural materials. Bunkers, VC hooches, and caches of burnable materials were all targets for an easy-to-carry-and-employ flame weapon. Instead of the high heat in a small area for a short time provided by a thermate grenade, a large amount of heat over a wide area for a longer time was needed to first dry out and then ignite most targets.

The Special Operations Branch of the Naval Weapons Center (NWC) at China Lake, California produced a number of limited-production, special-application materials for the SEALs and UDTs throughout the Vietnam War. The specialty at China Lake, as it was most commonly called, was answering the problems of Naval commands that required unique, quick-reaction, ordnance-related support. To meet the SEALs' need for a compact flame weapon, China Lake developed their Model 308-1 Napalm grenade.

To ease manufacturing problems and shorten production time, many of the items produced at the Special Operations Branch of China Lake were made of standard-issue components as much as possible. This policy extended to the Napalm grenade as well. Using a standard-size 18-gage sheet steel canister body, China Lake fitted an extended fuze neck that would accept a modified M206 series detonating fuze. The fuze was sufficient to rupture the grenade body and spread the filling over a reasonably wide area while the modifications insured ignition of the napalm.

Napalm, also called M1 thickener, is a mixed aluminum soap derived from coconut oil, naphthenic, and oleic acids issued as a light tan to brown granular powder. When mixed with gasoline, the napalm powder swells until the entire volume of gasoline becomes a homogeneous gel. The gel varies in consistency from a thick liquid to a rubbery material, depending on the amount of napalm used. Allowed to sit, napalm becomes a semirigid jelly. Sudden shock or being squirted through an opening causes the napalm to become almost liquid again. When thickened with napalm, gasoline will stick to a target rather than simply run off, greatly increasing its efficiency as an incendiary agent.

Made available to the Teams in mid-1968, the napalm grenade was issued in kit form. A SEAL unit only had to mix regular gasoline and the powdered na-palm supplied with the grenade to prepare the weapon for use. Designed specifically for use in to ignite watersoaked structures, the napalm grenade was found to be very satisfactory by the SEALs in Vietnam.

To satisfy a SEAL need for the fast production of a thick screening smoke, China Lake modified a standard AN-M8 smoke grenade. Modifications to the grenade did not change the physical or operational features but increased the burning time of the filler. With the faster burning rate, the modified AN-M8 grenade had a correspondingly greater smoke output and proportionally shorter burning time. Instead of having the up-to-150-second burning time of a standard AN-M8 grenade, the modified grenade was completely burned out in 120 seconds or less. Issued as the Model 308-1 White smoke grenade, the China Lake grenade could quickly put out a cloud of dense white smoke that would remain close to the ground, giving a SEAL unit cover to break contact or screen their movements.

In the early 1960s, a material was developed that has proved to be the most unusual filling for a hand grenade to date. Research was initiated by the Navy in July 1961 on a compound developed by the Dupont Company identified as PB-155. When exposed to air, PB-155 glows brilliantly with a blue-green light while undergoing oxidation. Different formulations of PB-155 were developed under the name TIARA (Target Illumination and Recovery Aid) for use in a wide variety of applications ranging from emergency lights to marking airstrips. The different formulations of TIARA had a duration of luminescence ranging from several seconds to hours.

As early as July 1962, 100 hand grenades (EX 1 Mod 0), 300 rifle grenades (EX 2 Mod 0), and Marstick colored crayons had been sent to Vietnam for testing. Results of the original testing samples were encouraging and further development of TIARA munitions continued. By 1968 TIARA-filled ordnance for special operations use had been made at China Lake specifically for the SEALs and UDTs. At least two different methods for the application of TIARA were made available to the SEALs in Vietnam during the war.

An aerosol spray can was filled with TIARA for use by the SEALs as a general marking agent. By spraying buildings or bunkers with TIARA, a glowing spot would be instantly made to indicate a place had been searched or to mark it as a target for air support. Though easily used, the TIARA spray can was not as popular with the SEALs as the other TIARA-filled piece of ordnance they had available, the Night Canopy marker grenade.

Designed to provide a method of marking a position at night in wooded or jungle areas, the TIARA marking grenade was developed by China Lake specifically for SEAL operations in Southeast Asia. The Night Canopy Marker, as it was officially called, was a gray-painted, canister-type bursting grenade loaded with a TIARA filler and marked with black stenciled letters—NWC MARKING GRENADE. A modified M206 series detonating fuze was used to burst the body of the grenade, spreading the TIARA agent over a wide area. As soon as it contacted the air the TIARA would begin glowing with a blue-green light that would be visible to aircraft up to 10 miles away on a clear night.

The Night Canopy Marker was issued as a rifle-fired or hand-thrown grenade. An M2A1 grenade projection adaptor would snap over the base of the grenade, allowing it to be fired from a rifle grenade launcher or the flash hider of an AR-15/M16 rifle. Rifle launching the marker grenade would put it above the trees before the fuze detonated, spraying the jungle canopy and indicating a specific area to aircraft.

By far the most popular method of employing TIARA by the SEALs was using the marking grenade as a hand-thrown grenade. Having the same handling characteristics as an M18 or AN-M8 smoke grenade, the marking grenade was easily carried as an additional item of ordnance.

By tossing the grenade into a hooch or bunker, everything within the building would be covered with the agent. The harmless, nontoxic TIARA filler of the marking grenade would cause everything it touched to glow in the dark. Anyone inside the area being searched by the SEALs would find it very hard to hide in the dark when they glowed like a giant firefly. Rubbing the TIARA agent to try and get it off would only increase the oxidation rate and cause the TIARA to glow even more brilliantly. Running away through the dark jungle would be next to impossible for a fleeing VC covered with TIARA and, if any of the agent had gotten on the man's feet, even if he did get away momentarily he would leave glowing footprints on the jungle floor.

There was another hand grenade used to provide combat illumination for the SEALs in Vietnam that was not quite as exotic as the TIARA marking grenade. The Mk 1 series of illuminating grenades act as a hand-thrown flare, brilliantly lighting an area with the blue-white light of burning magnesium. Three Mods of the Mk 1 illuminating grenade exist, all of which can still be found in use until supplies of the earlier mods are exhausted.

The basic Mk 1 illuminating grenade consists of a thin steel shell body made up in two parts. The bottom cup of the Mk 1 body contains the illuminating composition topped with an igniter charge. The illuminating composition is a hot-burning mixture of powdered magnesium, sodium nitrate, and binder agents. As the illuminating charge does not easily ignite from a fuse or quickmatch, it is topped with a first-fire composition that is itself topped with an igniter charge.

The upper half of the Mk 1 body shell is hollow and holds the fuze assembly in place and additionally gives the Mk 1 grenade a reasonably aerodynamic shape. When the fuze of the Mk 1 functions and ignites the main illuminating charge, pressure is rapidly built up inside the grenade casing. The two shells burst apart from the pressure and the burning contents are exposed. To help conceal the direction the Mk 1 grenade was thrown from, the fuze has a long 7-second delay.

Mods 1 and 2 of the Mk 1 illuminating grenade differ primarily in the may the fuze assembly ignites the illuminating composition. The Mod 2 is a much simple version of the initial Mod 1 design which has been in the inventory since World War II. The Mod 3 version of the Mk 1 uses the same fuze assembly as the Mod 2 version but has a body made from two plastic shells instead of sheet steel and has a slightly longer and thinner profile than the earlier mods.

In addition to acting as short-term illuminating charges, the high burning temperature of the illuminating composition allows the Mk 1 series to be use as an incendiary device for flammable targets.

The most recent type of hand grenades has only come into official existence within the last twenty years or so. With the advent of international terrorism and wholesale hostage taking, a new munition was needed to help give an edge to antiterrorist forces. The idea was to disorient the terrorists while not causing major harm to any hostages or the surroundings. Though the Mk3A2 Offensive grenade has the effect of stunning a target through concussion, it is generally considered far too powerful an explosion for use in a hostage situation, not even considering the danger from fragments of the fuze.

Pyrotechnic training munitions had long been recognized as having a strong effect on troops exposed to them at close range, even when out in the open. The first stun grenade was based closely on a training munition used to simulate hand grenades. The Schermuly training grenade, manufactured in the United States by the Kilgore Corporation, is a well-known example of the first model of stun grenade.

In the Kilgore/Schermuly grenade, a molded plastic casing makes up the body of the grenade. Shaped somewhat like the M26A1 grenade, the plastic body holds the fuze in place as well as containing a paper-wrapped submunition. The submunition is the heart of the system, containing a charge of pyrotechnic flash powder and bursting with no dangerous fragmentation.

When the safety lever of the Kilgore/Schermuly grenade is released, it ignites a 2-second delay train. At the end of the delay, the submunition is ejected from the base of the grenade with its own 1-second-or-less delay ignited. When the submunition explodes, it does so with a brilliant flash of light and thundering detonation.

Because of the brilliant light flash and loud explosion, a stun grenade can temporarily incapacitate or disorient a target for up to several seconds while causing little or no permanent damage. That stunned delay can give an antiterrorist unit a strong edge as they enter a hostage area and eliminate the terrorists. Drawbacks to the early style of stun grenade, such as the Kilgore/Schermuly, included releasing a large cloud of smoke obscuring the target area and hot paper fragments starting small fires. Constant development of the stun grenade system has largely eliminated these early complaints.

Also called distraction devices, stun grenades of various types are in use with all of the SEAL Teams for several different types of missions. Besides use in antiterrorist operations, stun grenades have proved useful in boarding ops against possible enemy shipping and would be very valuable in prisoner snatch operations. The exact types of stun munitions used by the SEALs today is not available for public release. One grenade that can be shown is a stun munition originally produced by the using units themselves.

The "flash crash," as it is called, is a modified M116A1 hand grenade simulator. Easily available from existing supply channels, the M116A1 hand grenade simulator greatly resembles the standard stun grenade submunition with its paper body and soft plastic end seals. To make the M116A1 simulator more effective and dependable as a flash crash, the issue pull-string igniter and fuze assembly is completely removed from the simulator. In the original fuze's place is an pull-ring bouchon fuze of the M201 series. The M201 series igniting fuze is the same model as used on the burning-type of chemical grenade such as the M18 colored smoke or the M7A3 CS grenade. The M201 fuze is simply screwed into the enlarged hole at the end of the M116A1 simulator where the original fuse was removed. With the M201 series fuze installed, the flash crash has the same standard pull ring and safety lever as the standard grenades used by the SEALs.

When the safety lever of the flash crash is released, the 1.5- to 2-second delay of the M201 fuze is ignited. When the fuze delay is over, it spits out a flame, igniting the flash powder charge inside the simulator body. The flash composition, a mixture of aluminum powder, potassium perchlorate, and barium nitrate, burns almost instantly with a bright flash, loud noise, and cloud of white smoke.

Though the flash crash has its drawbacks—the cloud of smoke and possible danger from the metal fuze body—the cost of the device is much less than for a standard stun grenade. It can also be made practically on demand when needed and other munitions may not be available. In general, the flash crash has proven itself very useful not only for training, but as an active nonlethal field munition.

One antipersonnel munition used by the Teams is more of a hand-thrown explosive device then a regular hand grenade. The Mk 40 Mod 1 high explosive depth charge is an antiswimmer device used in much the same manner as a large hand grenade. Designed to be launched from harbor patrol boats when enemy swimmers are suspected, the Mk 40 is an improvement over the use of the Mk3A2 offensive grenade in protecting boats against sabotage in Vietnam.

Instead of having a regular delay fuze assembly, the Mk 40 has a pull-ring safety electric firing mechanism with a pressure-activated switch.

To prepare the charge for use, a protective metal cap is removed from over the fuze. In the Mod 0 model, the pull ring is first removed to free a brass plunger at the top of the fuze. The plunger is then driven into the fuze by hand. The Mod 1 version of the Mk 40 charge acts in much the same way except that a spring-loaded striker is released when the pull ring is removed.

Both the plunger and the striker perform the same action, breaking a glass bulb enclosing the battery inside the perforated fuze housing. With the glass bulb broken, either fresh or salt water can enter the battery and activate it.

The charge sinks at a rate of about 3 feet per second. When the charge has reached a depth of about 13 feet (4 meters), the water pressure closes a switch starting a 6-second detonator delay. At the end of the delay time the charge detonates, usually at a depth of about 30 to 35 feet (9.1 to 10.7 meters) given clear water. When the charge is used in water less than 13 feet deep, the fuze will usually not detonate, though it could be activated by the over-pressure from another charge going off. The battery in the Mk 40 continues to function for about 30 minutes after activation. When the battery has expired, the fuze becomes inactive.

The shock and over-pressure of the Mk 40 charge exploding at a depth of 30 feet (9.1 meters) will stun an underwater swimmer at a radius of about 55 feet (16.8 meters) and will kill a swimmer within a radius of about 30 feet (9.1 meters). Surface swimmers and personnel in small boats are not in danger when 70 feet (21.3 meters) or more from the point of explosion of the Mk 40 charge. This safety distance is part of the reason for the detonator delay built into the fuze of the Mk 40 depth charge.

Basic loads for common hand grenades used by the SEALs in Vietnam usually consisted of several M26-type fragmentation grenades, one or two M18 colored smoke grenades of different colors, and either a WP grenade or a Mk3A2 offensive grenade. Personal taste and strength usually determined just how many grenades an individual SEAL would carry. A Chief or Officer might tell a particularly heavily laden SEAL to leave a number of his grenades off his load to keep him from being too burdened. But after a number of missions were under their belts, most SEALs knew what they wanted immediately available, as well as what the other members of their unit normally carried.

As SEAL operations grew more sophisticated in the 1970s and 1980s, basic loads of ammunition also became more specialized. During VBSS (Visit,

Board, Search, and Seizure) operations, the average SEAL would carry an M7A3 CS grenade, a Mk3A2 offensive grenade, and four flash crashes. For the same operation a sniper wouldn't carry any hand grenades at all while a breacher, armed with a shotgun and equipped to open locked doors, would carry an M7A3 CS grenade, a Mk3A2 offensive grenade, and only two flash-crash stun grenades.

The drawbacks of the flash-crash modifications to the M116A1 hand grenade simulator became very obvious after a serious training accident. The body of the M116A1 simulator is made of thick paper with no metallic or heavy parts in its construction. Flash-crash modifications to the M116A1 result in it having a roughly one-inch long by half-inch square M201a1 fuze body attached to the top of the simulator.

Though the body of the flash crash is cardboard, the fuze is a relatively hard and heavy item. The blast of the pyrotechnic filler can drive the fuze body over a long distance at high velocities. One SEAL operator lost the use of a thumb after training with the flash crash. The digit was almost severed from the hand when the fuze body smashed into it after being driven from an exploding flash crash.

The final replacement for the flash crash is the Mark 141 mod 0 diversionary charge. The main body of the mark 141 is made of machined, ridged polyurethane foam. The foam body of the charge is wrapped with adhesive aluminum foil that acts as an electrostatic shield for the sensitive pyrotechnic filler.

The body of the fuze system of the Mark 141 is made of 10 percent glass-filled polyethylene. The metal parts of the fuze system have been kept to a minimum in the design to eliminate dangerous fragmentation.

On release of the safety lever, after the safety pin is removed, the Mark 141 functions as a normal hand grenade. After the short (1.2 to 1.5 second) primary delay has expired, a separation charge is fired that drives the fuze assembly from the charge body. The separation charge also ignites a secondary delay of one-tenth of a second. After the secondary delay expires, the pyrotechnic charge initiates, disintegrating the main body of the device into harmless particles.

■ Hand Grenade Data ■

Source: Kevin Dockery

MARK II "PINEAPPLE"

TYPE High explosive fragmentation hand grenade

IDENTIFYING COLOR CODE Olive drab body or olive drab body w/yellow ring around top of fuze well

BODY Cast iron w/deep square serrations

FILLER TNT

FUZE M204A1 or M204A2 Bouchon-type detonating fuze w/pyrotechnic delay

FUZE DELAY 4 to 5 seconds

WEIGHTS

Round 1.31 lb (0.59 kg)

Filler 0.13 lb (0.06 kg)

EFFECTS

Effect Blast and fragmentation

Area of effect 10 yd (9 m) radius, individual fragments may be thrown as far as 200 yds

LENGTHS

Length 4.5 in (11.5 cm)

Width (diameter) 2.25 in (5.7 cm)

Average range 30 yds (27 m)

M26 (M26A1, M61)

TYPE High explosive fragmentation hand grenade

IDENTIFYING COLOR CODE Olive drab body w/yellow markings

BODY Sheet steel w/inner coil of square cross-section notched steel wire

FILLER Composition B; M26A1, M61 Composition B w/tetryl booster

FUZE M204A1 or M204A2 Bouchon-type detonating fuze w/pyrotechnic delay

FUZE DELAY 4 to 5 seconds

WEIGHTS

Round 1 lb (0.45 kg)

Filler 0.36 lb (0.16 kg); M26A1, M61 0.34 lb (0.15 kg) Comp B, 0.02 lb (0.01 kg) Tetryl

EFFECTS

Effect Blast and fragmentation

Area of effect 16 yd (15 m) radius

LENGTHS

Length 3.9 in (9.9 cm)

Width (diameter) 2.25 in (5.7 cm)

Average range 44 yds (40 m)

A very special version of the M26 grenade was made for the SEALs in Vietnam for use as a boobytrap. Outwardly, the special M26 was exactly the same as other grenades of the same model but the special fuze had been assembled without a pyrotechnic delay. As soon as the grenade's safety lever was released, it detonated.

Source: Kevin Dockery

CHICOM STICK-TYPE DEFENSIVE GRENADE

TYPE High explosive fragmentation hand grenade

IDENTIFYING COLOR CODE Wooden or bamboo handle, gray cast iron head

BODY Cast iron

FILLER Varies, has included TNT, picric acid, various dynamites, and salvaged explosives from dud U.S. ordnance (Vietcong manufacture only)

FUZE Pull-friction igniter

FUZE DELAY 2.5 to 6 seconds

WEIGHTS

Round 1.16 to 1.22 lb (0.53 to 0.55 kg)

Filler 0.06 to 0.14 lb (0.03 to 0.06 kg)

EFFECTS

Effect Blast and fragmentation

Area of effect 11 yd (10 m) radius

LENGTHS

Length 8.0 to 9.7 in (20.3 to 24.6 cm)

Width (diameter) 1.7 to 2.2 in (4.3 to 5.6 cm)

Average range 33 yds (30 m)

Source: Kevin Dockery

M33 (M67)

TYPE High explosive fragmentation hand grenade

IDENTIFYING COLOR CODE Olive drab body w/yellow markings

BODY Cast steel

FILLER Composition B

FUZE M213 Bouchon-type detonating fuze w/pyrotechnic delay (M67 grenade has additional safety clip around fuze body and safety lever)

FUZE DELAY 4 to 5 seconds

WEIGHTS

Round 0.88 lb (0.40 kg)

Filler 0.41 lb (0.19 kg)

EFFECTS

Effect Blast and fragmentation

Area of effect 16 yd (15 m) radius

LENGTHS

Length 3.53 in (9 cm)

Width (diameter) 2.5 in (6.4 cm)

Average range 46 yds (42 m)

Source: U.S. Navy

MARK 3A2 (MK 3A1)

TYPE High explosive blast (concussion) offensive hand grenade

IDENTIFYING COLOR CODE Black body w/yellow markings and band

BODY Asphalt-impregnated fiber (cardboard), Mk 3A1s have sheet metal end pieces

FILLER TNT

FUZE M206A1 or M206A2 (Mk 3A1—M6A4) Bouchon-type detonating fuze w/pyrotechnic delay, grenade may or may not have an additional safety clip around the fuze body and safety lever

FUZE DELAY 4 to 5 seconds

WEIGHTS

Round Mk 3A2—0.98 lb (0.44 kg); Mk 3A1—0.69 lb (0.31 kg)

Filler Mk 3A2—0.46 lb (0.21 kg); Mk 3A1—0.43 lb (0.20 kg)

EFFECTS

Effect Blast

Area of effect 2 yds (2 m), secondary missiles and fragments of the fuze may be projected 200 meters from point of detonation

LENGTHS

Length Mk 3A2—5.43 in (13.8 cm); Mk 3A1—5.35 in (13.6 cm)

Width (diameter) 2.13 in (5.4 cm)

Average range Mk 3A2—44 yds (40 m); Mk 3A1—50 yds (46 m)

Source: U.S. Army

AN-M14 TH3

TYPE Incendiary hand grenade

IDENTIFYING COLOR CODE Blue/gray body w/purple markings and ½ inch purple band or olive drab w/black markings (old manufacture), Red body w/black markings (new manufacture)

BODY 28-gage sheet steel

FILLER TH3 Thermate w/first-fire mixture VII

FUZE Bouchon-type igniting fuze w/pyrotechnic delay

FUZE DELAY 0.7 to 2 seconds

WEIGHTS

Round 2.0 lb (0.91 kg)

Filler 1.66 lb (0.75 kg)

EFFECTS

Effect Intense heat (4,000 degrees F.) and brilliant light w/molten iron spray. Can burn through 1.2 inch (1.3 cm) steel plate and will burn underwater after ignition

Burn time 40 seconds

Area of effect 2 yd (2 m) spray/spark radius

LENGTHS

Length 5.7 in (14.5 cm)

Width (diameter) 2.5 in (6.4 cm)

Average range 27 yds (25 m)

Source: *Kevin Dockery*

M18 COLORED SMOKE

TYPE Burning-type colored smoke hand grenade

IDENTIFYING COLOR CODE Olive drab body w/gray or yellow markings and one 1-inch wide band, top of grenade is the same color as the smoke the grenade produces

BODY 29-gage sheet steel

FILLER Red, green, yellow, or violet smoke composition

FUZE M201A1 Bouchon-type igniting fuze w/pyrotechnic delay

FUZE DELAY 0.7 to 2 seconds

WEIGHTS

Round 1.19 lb (0.54 kg)

Filler 0.72 lb (0.33 kg)

EFFECTS

Effect Produces large cloud of colored smoke

Burn time 50 to 90 seconds

Area of effect average 20 × 4 × 2 yd (18 × 4 × 2 m) cloud

LENGTHS

Length 5.75 in (14.6 cm)

Width (diameter) 2.5 in (6.4 cm)

Average range 38 yds (35 m)

Source: *U.S. Army*

M15 WP

TYPE Bursting-type white phosphorus smoke/incendiary hand grenade

IDENTIFYING COLOR CODE Gray body w/yellow markings and 1 yellow band

BODY 18-gage sheet steel

FILLER White phosphorus w/RDX burster

FUZE M206A1 or M206A2 Bouchon-type detonating fuze w/pyrotechnic delay

FUZE DELAY 4 to 5 seconds

WEIGHTS

Round 1.94 lb (0.88 kg)

Filler 0.94 lb (0.43 kg)

EFFECTS

Effect Bursting grenade spreads burning particles of phosphorus over the burst area. White phosphorus ignites spontaneously on contact with air creating a dense hot cloud of smoke while it burns at over 4,800 degrees F

Burn time 60 seconds

Area of effect 16 yds (15 m), some particles may be projected over 33 yds (30 m)

LENGTHS

Length 4.5 in (11.4 cm)

Width (diameter) 2.38 in (6 cm)

Average range 27 yds (25 m)

Source: U.S. Army

M34 WP

TYPE Bursting-type white phosphorus smoke/incendiary hand grenade

IDENTIFYING COLOR CODE Light green body w/square serrations, 1 yellow band, light red markings

BODY 18-gage sheet steel

FILLER White phosphorus w/RDX burster

FUZE M206A1 or M206A2 Bouchon-type detonating fuze w/pyrotechnic delay, new production has an additional safety clip around fuze body and safety lever

Fuze delay 4 to 5 seconds

WEIGHTS

Round 1.7 lb (0.77 kg)

Filler 0.94 lb (0.43 kg)

EFFECTS

Effect Bursting grenade spreads burning particles of phosphorus over the burst area. White phosphorus ignites spontaneously on contact with air creating a dense hot cloud of smoke while it burns at over 4,800 degrees F

Burn time 60 seconds

Area of effect 27 yds (25 m), some particles may be projected over 33 yds (30 m)

LENGTHS

Length 5.2 in (13.2 cm)

Width (diameter) 2.38 in (6 cm)

Average range 38 yds (35 m)

Source: Kevin Dockery

AN-M8 HC

TYPE Burning-type white smoke hand grenade

IDENTIFYING COLOR CODE Light green body w/black markings

BODY 28-gage sheet steel

FILLER Type C Hexachlorethane (HC) mixture (grained aluminum, zinc oxide, and hexachloroethane)

FUZE M201A1 Bouchon-type igniting fuze w/pyrotechnic delay

FUZE DELAY 0.7 to 2 seconds

WEIGHTS

Round 1.5 lb (0.68 kg)

Filler 1.19 lb (0.54 kg)

EFFECTS

Effect Creates large cloud of dense white smoke while burning

Burn time 105 to 150 seconds

Area of effect 5,551 cubic yd (4,244 cubic meter) cloud maximum

LENGTHS

Length 5.7 in (14.5 cm)

Width (diameter) 2.5 in (6.4 cm)
Average range 33 yds (30 m)

MODEL 308-1 WHITE SMOKE GRENADE

TYPE Burning-type white smoke hand
grenade
IDENTIFYING COLOR CODE Black body
w/white markings (prototype)
BURN TIME 120 seconds

This is a standard AN-M8 HC smoke
grenade modified at NWC China Lake to
have an increased burning rate and maximum smoke output. The general characteristics and operational features are the same as
the AN-M8.

Source: U.S. Army

M7A1 CN

TYPE Burning-type CN tear gas hand
grenade
IDENTIFYING COLOR CODE Gray body
w/red markings and 1 red band
BODY 28-gage sheet steel
FILLER CN (Chloroacetophenone)/pyrotech-
nic mixture
FUZE M202A1 Bouchon-type igniting fuze
w/pyrotechnic delay
FUZE DELAY 0.7 to 2 seconds

WEIGHTS
Round 1.16 lb (0.52 kg)
Filler 0.78 lb (0.35 kg)
EFFECTS
Effect Burning grenade releases a cloud of
CN gas and smoke from the four holes in
its top and single hole in its base. CN
causes a very heavy flow of tears and
strong pain in the eyes and upper respiratory passages within 15 to 30 seconds
of exposure. Higher concentrations,
such as would be inside a building or
bunker, will cause irritation to the skin,
especially moist skin, as a strong itching
and burning sensation. Symptoms last
for 5 to 20 minutes following removal
from exposure.
Burn time 20 to 60 seconds
Area of effect Approximately 20 × 4 × 2 yd
(18 × 4 × 2 m) cloud of dense gas, can
cover a much larger downwind area with a
less dense, less effective cloud
LENGTHS
Length 5.7 in (14.5 cm)
Width (diameter) 2.5 in (6.4 cm)
Average range 38 yds (35 m)

Source: U.S. Army

M7A3 CS

TYPE Burning-type CS tear gas hand
grenade

IDENTIFYING COLOR CODE Gray body
w/red markings and 1 red band

BODY 28-gage sheet steel

FILLER Pellatized CS (O-Chlorobenzal-
malononitrile) agent/pyrotechnic mixture

FUZE M202A1 Bouchon-type igniting fuze
w/pyrotechnic delay

FUZE DELAY 0.7 to 2 seconds

WEIGHTS

Round 0.97 lb (0.44 kg)

Filler 0.28 lb (0.13 kg) CS pellets, 0.46 lb
(0.21 kg) burning mixture

EFFECTS

Effect Burning grenade releases a cloud of
CS gas and smoke from the four holes in
its top and single hole in its base. CS
causes a heavy flow of tears and pain in
the eyes and upper respiratory passages
almost immediately on exposure. Further
exposure causes coughing, difficulty in
breathing, and chest tightness, along with
an involuntary closing of the eyes, itching
and stinging sensation on moist skin, a
runny nose, and dizziness. Onset of inca-

pacitation is 20 to 60 seconds. Higher
concentrations, such as would be inside a
building or bunker, will cause nausea and
vomiting in addition to the above effects.
Symptoms last for 5 to 20 minutes following removal from exposure.

Burn time 15 to 35 seconds

Area of effect Approximately 20 × 4 × 2 yd
(18 × 4 × 2 m) cloud of dense gas, can
cover a much larger downwind area with a
less dense, less effective cloud

LENGTHS

Length 5.7 in (14.5 cm)

Width (diameter) 2.5 in (6.4 cm)

Average Range 38 yds (35 m)

Source: U.S. Army

M6A1 CN-DM

TYPE Burning-type CN-DM tear/vomit gas
hand grenade

IDENTIFYING COLOR CODE Gray body
w/red markings and 1 red band

BODY 28-gage sheet steel

FILLER CN (Chloroacetophenone) and DM
(Diphenylaminochloroarsine or Adamsite)/pyrotechnic mixture

FUZE M202A1 Bouchon-type igniting fuze
w/pyrotechnic delay

FUZE DELAY 0.7 to 2 seconds

WEIGHTS
Round 1.25 lb (0.57 kg)
Filler 0.59 lb (0.27 kg) CN/DM mixture
EFFECTS
Effect Burning grenade releases a cloud of CN and DM gas and smoke from the four holes in its top and single hole in its base. CN causes a very heavy flow of tears and strong pain in the eyes and upper respiratory passages within 15 to 30 seconds of exposure. DM increases the flow of tears and pain in the respiratory tract as well as causing sneezing and coughing. Symptoms increase with exposure to include severe headache, acute pain, and tightness in the chest. After about 1 minute's exposure, symptoms include nausea and vomiting. DA symptoms last about 30 minutes after removal from exposure. Exposure to heavy concentrations of DM can cause the effects to last for up to 3 hours. DM takes about 1 minute to become effective and the CN is used to increase the immediate effects of the grenade. Exposure to very heavy concentrations of DM, such as in a closed room or bunker, can be toxic as the gas is an Arsenic salt
Burn time 20 to 60 seconds
Area of effect Approximately 20 × 4 × 2 yd (18 × 4 × 2 m) cloud of dense gas, can cover a much larger downwind area with a less dense, less effective cloud
LENGTHS
Length 5.7 in (14.5 cm)
Width (diameter) 2.5 in (6.4 cm)
Average range 38 yds (35 m)

Source: U.S. Navy

MODEL 308-1 NAPALM GRENADE

TYPE Bursting-type incendiary hand grenade
IDENTIFYING COLOR CODE Black body w/white markings (prototype) Light gray body w/white markings (limited production)
BODY 28-gage sheet steel
FILLER Gasoline thickened w/M1 thickener (Napalm)
FUZE M206A2 Bouchon-type detonating fuze w/pyrotechnic delay
FUZE DELAY 4 to 5 seconds
WEIGHTS
Round 0.75 lb (0.34 kg)
Filler 0.52 lb (0.24 kg) Napalm (12 fluid ounces [355 ml])
EFFECTS
Effect Spreads burning (2,200 degrees F) napalm over burst area
Burn time 20 to 60 seconds
Area of effect 3.3 yd (3m) burst radius
LENGTHS
Length 6.7 in (17 cm)
Width (diameter) 2.5 in (6.4 cm)
Average range 44 yds (40 m)

Source: U.S. Navy

MODEL 308-1 TIARA (TARGET ILLUMINATION AND RECOVERY AID)

TYPE Bursting-type illuminating/marking hand grenade

IDENTIFYING COLOR CODE Gray body w/black markings

BODY 28-gage sheet steel

FILLER TIARA (Dupont chemiluminescent compound PR-155)

FUZE Modified M206 Bouchon-type detonating fuze w/pyrotechnic delay additional safety clip around fuze body and safety lever

FUZE DELAY Nominal 3 seconds

WEIGHTS

Round 1 lb (0.45 kg)

Filler 0.75 lb (0.34 kg)

EFFECTS

Effect Spreads glowing TIARA compound over burst area

Burn time 20 minutes

Area of effect 17 yd (16 m) radius

LENGTHS

Length 5.7 in (14.5 cm)

Width (diameter) 2.5 in (6.4 cm)

Average range 44 yds (40 m) hand projected

Source: Kevin Dockery

NWM V-40 MINI GRENADE

TYPE High explosive fragmentation hand grenade

IDENTIFYING COLOR CODE Olive drab body w/white markings

BODY Internally notched steel

FILLER Composition B

FUZE Bouchon-type detonating fuze w/ pyrotechnic delay, special locking-type pull ring surrounds grenade body and must be rotated 160 degrees to unlock and be pulled

FUZE DELAY 4 seconds

WEIGHTS

Round 0.26 kg (0.12 kg)

Filler 0.99 oz (28 g)

EFFECTS

Effect Blast and fragmentation, produces 400 to 500 fragments

Area of effect 5 yds (5 m), some larger fragments may be projected over 27 yds (25 m)

LENGTHS

Length 2.24 in (5.7 cm)

Width (diameter) 1.78 in (4.5 cm)

Average range over 55 yds (50 m+)

MK 1 MOD 2 ILLUMINATING

TYPE Illuminating magnesium flare hand grenade

IDENTIFYING COLOR CODE White body w/black markings or unpainted body w/one white band and black markings or olive drab body w/white markings (most recent manufacture)

BODY Sheet steel

FILLER Magnesium flare composition

FUZE Mk 372 Mod 0 Bouchon-type detonating fuze w/pyrotechnic delay

FUZE DELAY 7 seconds

WEIGHTS

Round 0.58 lb (0.26 kg)

Filler 0.22 lb (0.10 kg)

EFFECTS

Effect Bright light, 55,000 candlepower

Burn time 25 seconds

Area of effect 218 yd (200 m) radius

LENGTHS

Length 4.35 in (11 cm)

Width (diameter) 2.21 in (5.6 cm)

Average range 44 yds (40 m)

KILGORE/SCHERMULY STUN GRENADE

TYPE Stun hand grenade

IDENTIFYING COLOR CODE Gray body

BODY Plastic casting

FILLER Cardboard cylinder (submunition) containing photoflash composition

FUZE M202A1 Bouchon-type igniting fuze w/pyrotechnic delay

FUZE DELAY 0.7 to 2 seconds

WEIGHTS

Round 0.50 lb (0.23 kg)

Filler 0.07 lb (0.03 kg)

EFFECTS

Effect Blast of 175 decibels and bright flash, 1,000,000 candela causing 5 to 15 seconds of disorientation when used in an enclosed area (room)

Area of effect 5.5 yd (5 m) radius

LENGTHS

Length 4.29 in (10.9 cm)

Width (diameter) 2.5 in (6.4 cm)

FLASH CRASH

TYPE Stun hand grenade

IDENTIFYING COLOR CODE White body w/olive drab fuze

BODY Cardboard

FILLER Photoflash powder consisting of aluminum powder, potassium perchlorate, and barium nitrate

FUZE M201A1 Bouchon-type detonating fuze w/pyrotechnic delay additional safety clip around fuze body and safety lever

FUZE DELAY 0.7 to 2 seconds

WEIGHTS

Round 0.33 lb (0.15 kg)

Filler 0.078 lb (0.035 kg)

EFFECTS

Effect Blast of 175 decibels and bright flash causing 5 to 15 seconds of disorientation when used in an enclosed area (room)

Area of Effect 5.5 yd (5 m) radius

LENGTHS

Length 4.75 in (12.1 cm)

Width (Diameter) 1.59 in (4 cm)

MARK 141 MOD 0 DIVERSIONARY CHARGE

TYPE Low-hazard, nonfragmentation producing device with loud report and brilliant flash with minimal smoke

IDENTIFYING COLOR CODE White body w/olive drab fuze

BODY Aluminum foil-covered polyurethane foam

FILLER Pyrotechnic charge consisting of aluminum powder, carbon, and potassium perchlorate

FUZE Plastic-bodied Bouchon-type igniting fuze w/pyrotechnic delay and separation charge.

FUZE DELAY 1.2 to 1.5 seconds (primary), 100 milliseconds (0.1 second) secondary

WEIGHTS

Filler 0.0385 lb (0.0175 kg)

EFFECTS

Effect Blast of 185 decibels and bright flash causing 5 to 15 seconds of disorientation when used in an enclosed area (room)

Area of Effect 5.5 yd (5 m) radius

LENGTHS

Length 5.00 in (12.7 cm)

Width (diameter) 1.75 in (4.44 cm)

MK 40 MOD 1 DEPTH CHARGE

TYPE Hand-launched high explosive antipersonnel depth charge

IDENTIFYING COLOR CODE Olive drab body

BODY Sheet aluminum

FILLER TNT

FUZE Electrically fired w/water-activated battery, pressure activated switch and electrical delay detonator, armed by standard pull ring

FUZE DELAY 6 seconds (initiates at 13 feet), fires at 30 to 35 foot (9 to 11 m) depth

WEIGHTS

Round 3.6 lb (1.63 kg)

Filler 3 lb (1.36 kg)

EFFECTS

Effect Underwater blast will kill or stun a swimmer

Area of effect Kill 30 ft (9 m), stun 55 ft (17 m)

LENGTHS

Length 9.88 in (25.1 cm) w/lid

Width (diameter) 3.59 in (9.1 cm)

Average Range Blast may cause hull damage to a naval vessel within 35 feet (11 m) or a merchant vessel within 70 feet (21 m). Charge sinks about 3 feet every second. Fuse arms at 8 foot (2.5 m) depth. After 6 second delay, the fuze will fire at 30 to 35 foot depth. If fuze fails to fire, the battery will expire after about 30 minutes rendering the device inactive.

10

AMBUSH IN THE DELTA

The two rivers that make up the Mekong Delta region of South Vietnam are both branches of the huge Mekong River that splits near the border of Cambodia and Vietnam. Dumping huge quantities of silt and mud over the years, the Mekong and its tributaries have built up the land at the southern end of South Vietnam into a fertile, lush area of plant growth, swamps, jungles, and marshes.

The area is covered with a network of waterways, some the size of rivers and other streams that a man can easily step across. In between these two waterways sizes are many man-made canals and natural streams that can accept the movement of small sampans, and others that have enough room for larger powered boats to travel on.

This was the area that the Navy SEALs operated most successfully. Their ability to move from land to water and back again with complete ease allowed the SEALs to infiltrate into places where no other troops besides the Viet Cong felt they could go. Along the jungle paths and waterways, the SEALs hunted the Viet Cong. No longer could the Viet Cong hide in the dark and move through areas they considered theirs in complete safety. At any time, the men with green faces, the heavily camouflaged SEALs, could move in from the surrounding dark to strike the VC down.

The most effective technique the SEALs found to conduct their operations against the Viet Cong was the ambush. As the VC did themselves, the ambush was a sudden volume of fire coming out of hidden positions and sleeting over an enemy force. For the Viet Cong and others in the area, that technique had worked for years, even decades. They had employed it against the Japanese during World War II, the French in Indochina, the South Vietnamese, and now the Americans. What the VC didn't expect was for the ambush to be used so effectively against them.

It was early in the afternoon when the SEAL detachment got the word that they had a mission for that evening. They had received their warning order about the upcoming op while sleeping in after another night mission the evening before. It was during the night that the Viet Cong preferred to move about in Vietnam, and so it was in the darkness that the SEALs liked to hunt the VC.

Attending to their personal needs and getting some chow, the SEALs gathered to receive their briefing in the bullpen, the area of a quonset hut they had set up as their headquarters. Each of the men had months of experience in-country behind them. When they rotated a SEAL detachment back to the States every six months, several of the old hands stayed back to introduce the incoming unit to the peculiarities of operating in their area.

The mission was a simple one, an ambush against a Viet Cong courier. The VC were reported to number five or six men, in up to three sampans. They would be traveling along the Rach La Gia canal in the Rung Sat Special Zone that evening. The canal was a smaller tributary of the Song Vam Sat River.

One squad of the SEAL detachment was going to be conducting another mission. So the remaining squad would go out on the ambush op. The squad consisted of six men, five enlisted and a warrant officer. Two of the men in the squad would carry M16A1 rifles with XM148 40mm grenade launchers on them. Two of the squad members were automatic weapons men. One man would be armed with a Stoner 63A light machine gun and 450 rounds of ammunition for it. The other SEAL automatic weapons man would have his chopped-down M60 light machine gun and 600 rounds. Between the four men, they could put out the firepower of a World War II infantry squad.

The Warrant officer would carry a CAR-15, the shortened variation of the M16A1 rifle. The radioman would not only have his PRC-77 radio to call for help or extraction, he would be armed with a very unusual piece of SEAL firepower.

Some months earlier, the SEALs had received a shipment of additional hardware. One of the more unusual items was a Remington 7188 shotgun, a self-loading 12-gauge shotgun capable of firing on full automatic. The SEALs had examined the weapon the year before and found they needed some special maintenance items to keep the weapon operating. Now with the special items in hand, they would give the automatic shotgun another try.

By 1600 hours that afternoon, the SEAL squad had prepared their weapons and were ready for a once-over by their patrol leader. The warrant officer didn't expect to find anything wrong with any of the men's equipment, but since he had the final responsibility for the operation, the premission inspection would go on.

All of the SEALs knew pretty much what they needed to take with them on this kind of operation in the way of weapons and ammunition. The only addition to the gear loadout was an extra four M18A1 Claymore mines. Two of the mines remained in their bandoleers to be laid out on the ambush. One of the mines was fitted with a blasting cap, pull igniter, and a thirty-second length of fuse. A second one-minute fuse delay firing assembly was also prepared and taken along. The last mine was an extra backup for the other three.

At 1830 hours, the SEALs all had a meal in the local mess hall. By 1900 hours, they were gathering aboard the two river-patrol boats (PBRs) for the long trip in to their insertion point. The PBRs were seen on the waterways all over south Vietnam and they wouldn't draw any extra attention to the SEALs' movement. The three .50 caliber machine guns, two M60 machine guns, and Mark 18 Honeywell 40mm hand-cranked 40mm grenade launcher on board each of the PBRs also made the SEALs feel good about having the little 31-foot boats on their operation. The PBRs would insert the SEALs and then remain in the general area to extract them or come in and give fire support if needed.

Gathering in the middle of the fiberglass hulls of the PBRs, none of the SEALs wanted to get in the way of the bow gun tub with its pair of .50 caliber guns. The ride went on for several hours, and several of the SEALs dozed quietly on the way in. They had been conducting operations for months and the anxieties that had kept the men awake during their first operations were long banished.

There were no incidents against the PBRs as they wound their way into the Rung Sat. The "Forest of Assassins," the Rung Sat Special Zone was mostly a thickly overgrown jungle area of marsh, swamps, creeks, streams, and canals between Saigon and the South China Sea. The area had been a haven for smugglers and pirates for hundreds of years, the Viet Cong found it suited the needs of their guerrilla war very well. Only the SEALs had been able to effectively challenge the VC about their self-styled ownership of the Rung Sat.

Approaching their insertion point, the PBR carrying the SEAL patrol moved closer to the bank of the river and slowed down slightly. With their UDT life jackets inflated, the SEALs rolled over the stern of the PBR as it continued down the river. This was the "underway insertion," a technique the SEALs had developed to hide their insertion point from enemy observation.

In the dark hours near midnight, it was the sound of the approaching PBRs that the VC would first notice. The VC would take cover from a normal PBR patrol, they had well learned to respect the firepower of the little boats. But, if the

VC heard the boats change their engine noise, such as they would if they were nosing into a bank to insert a SEAL patrol, they would be on the alert and more watchful—if not withdrawing from an area entirely.

So the PBRs continued on their patrol, not looking any different than the other boats on the rivers of the Rung Sat. The SEALs were slipping up onto the muddy river bank after their little swim. They were now in enemy-held territory and on their own for the time being. The SEALs had the fire support of the PBRs at the other end of their radio circuits. And air support in the form of Seawolf helicopter gunships were also on call for the six-man SEAL patrol. But until either the PBRs or the Seawolves arrived on station, the SEALs would be on their own.

So when the patrol came up onto the shore, they lay in the mud and just listened for ten minutes. A man's ears could tell him a lot about what was going on in the jungle around him if he only stopped to listen. The SEALs knew that rule very well and they listened to hear if there was any activity stirred up by their insertion.

When the patrol leader had decided that they were going to continue with the operation, the SEALs got up from their positions and prepared to move out. Quietly, the men drew the bolts back on their weapons, clearing the barrels of the M16s of any water they might have filled with during the insertion. The two machine guns, the Stoner 63A and the chopped M60, fired from an open-blot. So drawing the bolts back on those weapons cocked them for action.

Locked, loaded, and ready, the SEALs moved out to patrol to their ambush position. They had inserted about 400 meters upriver from the small canal that was their planned ambush site. Moving inland about 50 meters, the SEALs headed out with one of the XM148 men in front on point. Behind the point man was the Stonerman with his large volume of firepower represented by the 150-round drum his Stoner was loaded with.

Next in line in the patrol was the patrol leader, the warrant officer with his CAR-15 at the ready. Behind the patrol leader was the radioman, staying within reach of the warrant officer in case he wanted to use the element's communications. The other automatic weapons man, armed with the chopped M60 machine gun, came up behind the radio man. His heavy firepower had a longer range than any of the other SEAL weapons in the squad—even though he could only accurately aim his chopped M60 by using the tracers that were loaded in his ammunition belts, one tracer for every four rounds of ball.

Bringing up the rear of the patrol was the other grenadier. His 40mm XM148 grenade launcher was loaded with a canister (buckshot) round that would give him a greater hit probability if he fired at a fleeting target in the night. And it was a dark, warm night that the SEALs were patrolling in.

The weather was cool and clear, no moonlight, and the SEALs had inserted shortly after high tide. The terrain was partially defoliated, with clumps of nipa palm and brush all around them. For the most part, the SEALs were walking in mud, thin and shallow in some areas, thick and deep in others. This was the normal terrain for the Rung Sat and the SEALs were well experienced in moving across the exhausting and difficult ground.

After several hours of patrolling, with the point man position having been rotated several times, the patrol came up to their ambush position. Calling a halt by raising his fist in the air, the patrol leader stopped and again listened to the area. No extra sounds were heard, just the constant jungle and swamp noises of the animals and insects—not to say that the animals couldn't be a problem of their own.

Another SEAL patrol in the Rung Sat not more than three weeks earlier, had their point man run into a crocodile while laying in wait on an ambush. The SEAL had a first thought that the big, knobby form floating in the water was a partially submerged log. But when he noticed that the log was moving upstream toward him, the SEAL became concerned. That concern really hit a peak when an eight-foot salt-water crocodile lunged up at the SEAL where he was waiting on the bank.

A fast burst of 5.56mm slugs from his M16A1 quickly had the croc spinning and twisting in the brown, muddy waters of the Rung Sat. The SEAL patrol had been compromised and extracted immediately. But not before they had experienced a great story to tell their fellow Teammates in the community.

Running into a hungry reptile big enough to be a problem was not what was going through the minds of the SEAL at the ambush site that night. Several of the men did give the water an extra glance or two during their long wait. The patrol leader had the ambush set up back from the corner of the bank where the canal connected up at a ninety-degree angle to the river. The high bank of the canal and river was put to good use when the patrol leader had the men install two of the M18A1 Claymore mines they had brought with them into the side of the bank.

The thick mud and earth would protect the SEALs from the blast of their own mines when the claymores were fired, each mine sending out 700 steel pellets in a sixty-degree arc. Settling in back away from the mines, the SEALs lined up for their ambush. At the far upriver position was the point man with his XM148. Next to the point man was the Stonerman. He had taken the belt from the aluminum drum of his weapon from the feed tray of the Stoner, reserving the full drum for the SEALs extraction. Laying out a piecer of plastic he carried for the purpose, the Stonerman removed one of the belts of ammunition he carried Pancho Villa–style over his shoulders and between his shirt and life vest. Laying the belt section out on the plastic, the Stonerman loaded the end of the belt into his weapon. Now he was prepared for the ambush.

The radio operator with his Remington 7188 shotgun was in the center of the position, the patrol leader next to him. Both men were at the point of juncture between the canal and the river itself.

Up the canal slightly, but still where he could cover the river as well, was the automatic-weapons man with the M60. Next to him, covering the canal itself, was the other XM148 grenadier. He had changed the round chambered in his XM148 grenade launcher from a canister round to an M406 fragmentation grenade. The high explosive fragmentation grenade was much more efficient in taking out a sampan than the shotgun-like canister round.

Now the long wait came due. The SEALs remained alert, still, and quiet, as the jungle remained active around them. The noises they heard were just the common ones, the occasional splash in the water caused the SEALs to pay closer attention to their surroundings. At no time did they relax and let their attention wander. They were deep inside VC country, and a mistake could easily cost them their lives.

It was more than three-and-a-half hours since their insertion and patrol started, that the SEALs began hearing slow, controlled splashing coming from the canal to their left. The sound was that made by a paddle being dipped and raised from the water. But it was a fairly loud sound for such a soft action. Coming down the canal and into the ambush kill zone, the SEALs could see why the sound of the paddle was so loud.

It wasn't one sampan being paddled by one or two VC. It wasn't two sampans, it was six of the slender boats, almost all of them with three people aboard. The SEALs were outnumbered almost three-to-one. Each SEAL would have to completely eliminate a sampan during the ambush. Even with the element of surprise on their side, taking on six sampans was pushing their luck a bit.

During their long weeks of predeployment training back in the States, the SEALs had practiced the art of the ambush over and over again. There was a standard operating procedure in place for an ambush such as the one they had now set up. Each SEAL would concentrate his fire on the sector of the kill zone directly in front of him. Each man with a rifle would fire two magazines of eighteen rounds each on full automatic. The two machine gunners would each fire a full belt of ammunition across the entire kill zone. Grenadiers would each fire one grenade and then a full magazine from their weapons.

The concentration of firepower would be tremendous, especially in the relatively small area of the kill zone. But no matter how hard you planned an ambush, no matter how carefully it was executed, experience had taught the SEALs that some of the enemy always seemed to escape. With this many sampans in the water, it was easy to surmise that there might be a large body of men, maybe a VC base camp, nearby.

The ambush was planned to be initiated by the patrol leader firing the claymore mines. The warrant officer held both M57 firing devices in his hands, the safety bails back and solid pressure on the firing levers. Deciding that the VC may just be too many for the small group of SEALs, the patrol leader had planned on letting them pass and calling in an air strike on the sampans instead. That plan wasn't going to work out, either.

What one of the VC saw was never decided on by the SEALs. It could have been one of the men's faces shining in the night after the sweat had run off most of the camouflage face paint. It could have been the hole in the bank where the Claymores were hidden. Either way, one of the VC in the second sampan from the front suddenly dropped his paddle and grabbed up a weapon.

The SEAL patrol leader only watched the VC for a moment. His mind hadn't really registered the AK-47 that the VC was pulling up from the bottom of the sampan before he squeezed down hard on the M57 firing devices.

The loud clacks from the M57 firing devices were drowned out in the thundering roar of two M18A1 Claymore mines firing. The mud and earth of the riverbank absorbed much of the force of the explosions of 2 one-and-a-half pound C4 charges in the mines. But there was no such protection on the river side of the mines. The steel pellets of the mines sluiced out like a deadly waterfall, slicing across four of the six sampans.

The two sampans that were outside of the area slashed by the claymores didn't fare any better as the SEALs initiated the ambush. The 40mm grenades blooped out of their tubes, the SEALs on the triggers switching over to the M16A1 rifles before the grenades even impacted. The roar of five automatic weapons thundered out. The crashing thunder of the short-barreled M60 was only matched by the knocking boom . . . boom . . . boom of the Remington 7188 firing on full automatic.

The cyclic rate of the Remington was slow and the magazine tube only held seven rounds. One extra round in the chamber gave the weapon an eight-round burst before reloading, but eight rounds of XM257 number four buckshot meant twenty-seven quarter-inch hardened lead shot launched with each shot. The swarm of 216 pellets through the area could only be matched in ferocity by the fire of one of the belt-fed automatic weapons. And even they couldn't saturate an area as quickly as the 7188.

In less than half a minute, the fire from the SEALs' positions ceased. Now the men had to quickly try and recover whatever they could in the way of intelligence materials from the rapidly sinking sampans. Two of the SEALs went into the water while the others reloaded. Some packages and satchels were recovered, along with a pair of metal ammunition boxes. The lightweight and waterproof ammunition boxes were often used by the Viet Cong to transport papers and documents. They could also be booby trapped so the SEALs who grabbed them up did not open them.

As the men broke down the ambush site, shouting and a few random gunshots could be heard coming from the up-water side of the canal. There was a large body of Viet Cong somewhere nearby, and they had obviously heard the SEALs' ambush.

Pulling the unit together quickly, the patrol leader had the radioman call for emergency extraction. The position the SEALs were in was going to be occupied by a large number of the enemy very quickly, so the position for the extraction was indicated to be upriver of their present location. Pulling out, the SEALs could hear shouts of the enemy coming in behind them.

As the Viet Cong closed in, the patrol leader had the SEAL carrying the mine rigged with the thirty-second fuse delay pull it out and quickly set it up, aimed in the up-canal direction. As the patrol pulled out, the last thing the rear security man did was pull the fuse igniter, firing the delay.

The SEALs pulled out quickly, even as they heard enemy forces crashing through the brush behind them. It seemed like only seconds later that there was a crashing explosion behind the SEALs as the leave-behind Claymore detonated. The screams the SEALs heard immediately following the explosion told them their little surprise had been effective. Now the SEALs had a few more moments of running they could do before the enemy regathered their forces and again gave chase.

A few dozen meters upriver, and the SEAL patrol leader ordered the other Claymore left behind, this one set up with the one minute delay firing assembly. It was a matter of less than ten seconds for the M18A1 Claymore to be pulled from its bandoleer and set up pointing back the way they had come. The claymore was angled in a bit from the riverbank. The VC already knew which way the SEALs had run, they path they had left wasn't that hard to follow. With the pulling of the fuse igniter, another delay tactic was employed by the SEALs against their pursuers.

The explosion that followed a minute later did not have any screams of the wounded sound out after it. The blast did have the effect of slowing the VC down even further. The SEALs pulled out as quickly as they could while still maintaining good noise discipline. Their tricks had just about run out and they had to try hiding from the enemy as best they could while still making it to the extraction point.

Pulling up to a bend in the river, the SEALs set up a security perimeter. This was where they would meet the PBRs when the little boats showed up. Now, they had to hold position and wait. It wasn't more than a few minutes before the first VC came moving through the brush, firing their weapons to probe for the SEALs' position.

Before the SEALs could open fire, there was a loud roar from the river as the two PBR showed up with their weapons firing. The three .50 caliber machine guns on each boat ripped through the grass and brush of the riverbanks, and the VC beyond. The brown water PBR gunners were aiming at the enemy muzzle flashes. One of the PBRs continued to make a gun run along the river bank while the other practically stood on its nose to come to a sudden stop at the extraction point.

The SEALs scrambled aboard as the PBR reversed its water jet and pulled back from the bank. Adding the fire from their own weapons to that of the PBRs, the SEALs fired back at the enemy that had been pursuing them. Getting on the radio, the patrol leader called in the Seawolf helicopter gunships on the positions the SEALs had just left.

Within ten minutes of the radio call being made, a trio of armed Huey helicopter gunships made strafing runs across the area the SEALs had been operating in. Their multiple M60C machine guns and 2.75-inch-high explosive rockets ripped into the Viet Cong positions. Later reconnaissance of the area determined that the SEALs had hit the leadership cadre of a VC battalion as they left a planning meeting. The group of sampans would have broken up as soon as they reached the river. That night, the SEALs had taken on a much larger force and come out the winners.

11

MACHINE GUNS

Little more than a century old, the machine gun has done more to change the face of warfare in the 20th century than any other firearm. Designed to be able to continue firing as long as ammunition is supplied, the machine gun feeds, chambers, fires, extracts, and reloads automatically when triggered. This full automatic fire results in a stream of projectiles than can dominate a battlefield, preventing any movement from cover by an opposing force.

The consistent fire of the machine gun added greatly to the stalemate between the trenches of World War I. The masses of men who would charge across a field, consistent through millennia of warfare, had finally been stopped. Not until the further development of military technology—in the form of armored vehicles (tanks)—did the movement of large masses of troops against the firepower of emplaced machine guns again become possible.

The first machine guns were relatively heavy weapons, intended to be used from tripod or other adjustable mounts. Capable of long periods of sustained automatic fire, these weapons could rain lethal projectiles into an area, called the "beaten zone," well out of the sight of the gunners. To maintain these long periods of fire, the more successful machine guns had a cooling jacket of water surrounding their barrels. Even a water jacket was not sufficient to absorb all of the heat of firing, the several quarts of water in a .30 caliber machine gun's water jacket could begin boiling away after only a few hundred rounds had been fired. To prevent damage to the barrels, machine gunners would fire their weapons in bursts of six or more rounds per trigger pull, spacing out the firing of a hundred rounds of ammunition over a period of a minute or so depending on the weapon.

Other machine gun designs utilized heavier-than-normal barrels to absorb the heat of firing, with additional air cooling helping dissipate the excess heat. These weapons were able to be made in lighter configurations than the heavy watercooled weapons and could be operated from much simpler tripods and even bipods attached directly to the weapon. Lighter air-cooled machine guns could be carried and operated by just one man, who could then accompany assaulting troops and give automatic fire where needed.

The U.S. Military entered WWII with a shortage of machine guns of all types, but especially the most up-to-date designs. The demands of the war gave the priority for receiving new production weapons to the ground combat units, especially the Army. The Navy continued operations, especially in the first few years of the war, with the stocks of small arms they had on hand. Most of these weapons were used for arming shore parties and the smaller landing craft and saw some combat before their replacement. These weapons included machine guns no longer seen in the rest of the services. Serviceable but older designs, such as the .30 caliber Lewis light machine gun, were still listed for Navy use as late as 1943.

Developed from the McClean-Lissak design by Lt. Colonel Issac N. Lewis of the U.S. Army in 1910–11, the Lewis gun was the first true light machine gun built in the United States. Gas operated and firing from an open bolt, the Lewis gun was fed from a 47-round, pan-type magazine fitted to the top of the weapon. The magazine feed of the Lewis gun held the ammunition under positive control during loading and firing. This positive control feed allowed the Lewis to fire from any position, right or left side up or even upside down. The open bolt mechanism held the bolt of the weapon to the rear in the cocked position until the trigger was pulled. When fired, the bolt of the Lewis gun is released to move forward, pick up a round of ammunition, chamber it, lock, and fire. Though the open bolt design causes a slight delay between the trigger being pulled and the round firing, with the weight of the moving parts disrupting the sight alignment for the firer, the system has several advantages.

The chief advantage of the open bolt system for a rifle caliber machine gun is that a cartridge is not chambered until just prior to it being fired. Since a cartridge is not sitting in the chamber between shots, the excess heat from the barrel cannot fire the round in an uncontrolled manner, referred to as a "cook-off." In weapons where the round remains chambered between shots, cook-off can result in continuous uncontrolled firing until the ammunition runs out or a weapon becomes so damaged it ceases functioning.

To further aid in cooling the barrel, the Lewis gun had a unique jacket surrounding the barrel and extending past the muzzle. A longitudinally finned aluminum radiator surrounded the barrel, inside the steel jacket. When the Lewis gun was fired, expanding gasses from the muzzle pushed out of the front of the jacket, drawing cooler air in through the open rear of the jacket and moving it over the aluminum radiator fins. The small advantage to cooling the barrel was overridden by the added weight of the jacket and radiator but the odd system gave the Lewis gun a very distinctive sound when it was fired.

The operating system of the Lewis gun centered on an operating rod with a piston at the front end and a bolt attached to a protruding lug, the striker post, near the opposite end. With the operating rod drawn to the rear in the cocked position, pulling the trigger would release the op rod, allowing it to be driven forward by the main spring. The face of the bolt strips a round from the magazine and feeds it into the chamber as the bolt moves forward. With the bolt stopped by the breech of the barrel, the operating rod continues forward with the striker post on the op rod moving along a curved track in the bolt body.

The movement of the op rod and striker post forces the bolt to rotate, locking the front lugs of the bolt into the breech of the barrel. As the op rod continues forward, the firing pin, held at the top of the striker post, is driven forward and into the primer of the cartridge, firing the chambered round. Gas from the fired round is tapped off of the barrel near the muzzle after the bullet has passed. This gas acts on the piston at the end of the operating rod, driving it back to the cocked position. The striker lug on the op rod works to again rotate the bolt, this time unlocking it from the barrel. During its rearward travel, a stud on the bolt engages a feed mechanism that rotates the internal drum mechanism slightly, indexing another round into the feed way. If the trigger is held back, the op rod again moves forward and the operation is continued.

The somewhat complex operating mechanism of the Lewis gun gave the Army an excuse to declare the weapon unreliable during testing. The system was in fact fairly easy to use and far superior to a number of weapons already in U.S. Army service during WWI. There was a series of jams that could take place in the Lewis gun during operation that required some training on the part of the gunner to deal with. In the final 1943 U.S. Navy manual showing the Lewis gun, a flow chart listed twenty-four different steps to determine and deal with stoppages.

For what is generally considered political reasons, the Lewis gun was never adopted in any number by the U.S. Army. But production in Belgium and Great Britain put the weapon into the hands of a number of European armies. Combat service demonstrated the usefulness of the Lewis design and the tactical application of the light machine gun.

The U.S. Navy did not have the same constraints on it that prevented use of the Lewis gun by the U.S. Army. The Army had declared the Lewis gun unreliable, though its battle record in the trenches of Europe went directly against this statement. The Navy, satisfied with the Marine Corps testing of the Caliber .30 Model 1917 Lewis Gun, ordered a number of the weapons from the Savage Arms Co. Adopted by the U.S. Navy as the Mark VI Machine Gun, an initial 3,500-unit order was placed on April 25, 1917. Additional orders for 350, 2,500, and 3,000 weapons gave the Navy 9,350 Mark VI and Mark VI Mod 1 Lewis guns on hand by the end of WWI.

The mechanism of the Lewis gun remained unchanged during the years between WWI and WWII. For use in early aircraft, the buttstock of the Lewis gun could be removed and a short D handle, also called a spade grip, installed in its place. The D handle made the Lewis gun much easier to operate in confined areas. The aluminum radiator and barrel jacket was removed on a number of weapons with no obvious ill effects from overheating.

After the entry of the United States in to WWII, A number of Mark VI Mod 1 Lewis guns were used as armament in landing craft. A number of landing craft at Guadalcanal saw combat armed with two Lewis guns, one for each gun tub and usually fitted with the D handle. For Operation Torch, the U.S. and Allied invasion of North Africa in November 1942, Lewis guns also saw service as close in protection for Navy ships and landing craft.

One common type of U.S. Navy landing craft was the Higgins boat. Based on a workboat design used in the waters of Louisiana, the Higgins boat had a rather small bow ramp with a gun tub to either side of and just behind the ramp. These gun tubs could each hold a single gunner and mount a single machine gun in a ring mount. During Operation Torch, a number of Higgins boats were armed with a pair of Mk VI Mod 0 Lewis guns, one in each of the gun tubs.

One objective during Operation Torch was the capture of the Port Lyautey Airfield by the Western Task Force under the command of Major General George S. Patton. The entire Port of Lyautey at the mouth of the Sebou River was a target, but the airfield some miles inland was to be captured intact for immediate use if at all possible. A heavy cable boom was known to be blocking the Sebou River, protected by the guns of a fort nearby. A specially-trained group of Navy men, under the command of Lieutenant Mark W. Starkweather, were to go up the Sebou River and cut the boom with explosives.

The seventeen-man unit had been gathered at the U.S. Naval Amphibious base at Little Creek, Virginia in September and given a condensed course in demolitions, raiding techniques, and rubber boat operation for the Sebou River mission. Designated a Combat Demolition Unit (CDU), Starkweather's team first attacked the boom across the Sebou River at about 0300 hours on November 8, 1942. The first attack was forced back by heavy seas and fire from the guns of the nearby fort.

The second attack by the CDU was launched at just past midnight on the morning of November 11. On the second attempt, the CDU was carrying additional equipment in the form of special demolitions, rubber boats, and two light machine guns, reportedly Lewis Mark VI Mod 0s, to arm the Higgins boat. In spite of the heavier seas encountered, in comparison to the first attempt, the CDU managed to work its way up the river undetected and successfully attacked and cut the cable boom.

On the return trip out to the open sea, the Higgins boat again came under fire from the guns of the fort. This time, when the searchlights of the fort sought the CDU and its small craft, the Higgins boat fired back. Two of the searchlights were put out of action by the Lewis guns and the small boat continued on its run to open water.

It is suggested by written reports that one of the Lewis guns may have jammed during the outward-bound run of the Higgins boat. As the small craft again hit the heavy seas at the mouth of the Sebou River, many loose pieces of equipment and unused ordnance were ordered overboard to lighten the struggling boat. Included in the jettisoned equipment was one of the machine guns.

The mission of the first CDU was considered a success in spite of the delay between attempts and the airfield was captured intact. The men of the CDU were separated after their return to the United States with a number of them later joining the NCDU program at Fort Pierce, Florida. One of these men, Gunner's Mate William R. Freeman, went on to receive both his commission and the Navy Cross for his actions on Omaha Beach during the D-Day invasion on June 6, 1944.

As wartime production increased, the Lewis gun was removed from active Navy use and relegated to second-line duties. Many were sent as lend-lease to the British where they armed merchant craft. New production machine guns were generally those of the very prolific gun designer John Moses Browning.

In 1900, John Browning had designed a .30 caliber machine gun that used the recoil of firing to function its operating system. Shelved due to a lack of interest from the U.S. Army, the design was again worked on by Browning in 1910. The 1910 prototype, chambered in 30-06, was a water-cooled weapon and had been modified from the 1900 original to eject empty brass out of the bottom front portion of the receiver. Further lack of official interest again caused the design to be put aside a second time.

By early 1917, U.S. involvement in WWI had become a certainty, An urgent call went out for machine gun designs with which to arm the growing US military. Both the .30 caliber Browning Automatic Rifle (BAR) and watercooled machine gun were demonstrated on Congress Heights in Washington, D.C. on February 27, 1917. The demonstration, witnessed by some 300 people, resulted in the BAR being immediately recommended for adoption. The watercooled machine gun, though also enthusiastically received, was sent for a more thorough testing at the Army proving grounds at Aberdeen, Maryland.

The Browning .30 caliber watercooled machine gun worked from the short recoil principle. Browning had adopted this system of operation for the design since determining that is was the cleanest, most reliable, and generally most efficient for an automatic weapon that would be expected to fire continuously over long periods of time. During the 1917 tests at Aberdeen, the first demonstration weapon fired 40,000 rounds of ammunition in two 20,000 round firing tests without malfunction or a part breaking. These test results were so good that a second weapon was called for and tested, to insure that the first was not specially prepared just for the test. The second weapon fired continuously for 48 minutes and 12 seconds, with pauses only for reloading, at a cyclic rate of about 600 rounds per minute. The over 29,000 rounds fired on the test of the second weapon proved the design. The Browning watercooled machine gun was adopted by the U.S. Army as the M1917.

Though nearly 43,000 M1917 Brownings were produced by the end of WWI, relatively few actually saw action in combat. Some limited weaknesses were found in the design or construction of the weapon and modifications were called for during the post war years. In 1936, a modified .30 caliber Browning watercooled machine gun was adopted as the M1917A1. This weapon saw continuous use with U.S. forces during WWII and through the Korean War as well.

Additional weapons that came out of combat in WWI included the first armored fighting vehicles—the tanks—that finally broke the stalemate of trench warfare. U.S. tank development during late WWI required a different machine gun than those used by the rest of the ground forces. A more flexible weapon than the heavy watercooled weapon was needed, but it also required a greater sustained fire than the only light automatic weapon available at that time, the M1918 BAR.

In 1918, Browning had modified his M1917 design for aircraft use, removing the water cooling jacket. Instead of the light barrel and water jacket of the M1917, the new Browning modification had a heavier barrel surrounded by a protective perforated metal jacket that supported the barrel at its muzzle end. In addition to some internal changes to increase the rate of fire, the new weapon could also accept the disintegrating metallic link belt developed for the Marlin aircraft machine gun.

The modifications to the aircraft Browning were further developed by the Ordnance Department in late 1918 to adapt the basic gun for tank use. A different hand grip was attached to the weapon as well as a heavier barrel in order to better absorb the heat off-firing. Nine sample guns were ready for testing by October, 1918 and the design was approved for use. The end of WWI in November 1918 cut short the production of the tank design Browning after only about 500 guns were completed.

Post WWI development resulted in the adoption of the tank Browning as the M1919A1. To this weapon was added a small tripod and the M1919A2 Cavalry Browning was adopted. Further design work finally resulted in the M1919A4 Browning machine gun that became the standard U.S. military machine gun of WWII, the Korean War, and remained in service well into the Vietnam War.

Additional weapons and weapon systems made their first appearances during WWI and greatly affected warfare to this day. Instead of the armored knight riding to battle on an armored horse, armored vehicles appeared on, and above, the battlefields of Europe. Aircraft evolved considerably between the years of 1914 and 1918, By the middle of the war, German aircraft were being used that carried armor proof against many of the rifle caliber machine guns of the time.

To counteract this new aircraft threat, and have an additional weapon to combat the increasing numbers of enemy armored ground vehicles, General John J. Pershing requested a new weapon and ammunition development. In an urgent cable sent to the U.S. War Department in April 1918, General Pershing called for the immediate development of a high-power, large-caliber machine gun and ammunition. The weapon was primarily to be used on aircraft with a secondary antitank use. The Winchester Repeating Arms Co. was called on to design the needed new round.

Earlier attempts had been made to modify Browning M1917 machine guns to fire the new French 11mm Hotchkiss round. The French had developed the 11mm cartridge to penetrate armor and had an incendiary load used to attack hydrogen-filled German observation balloons. The experimental modifications failed to properly operate and General Pershing felt the 11mm round inadequate for U.S. needs. A second cable from General Pershing was sent to the War Department specifying a minimum projectile weight of 670 grain with a muzzle velocity of at least 2,700 feet per second.

Almost a full year earlier, in July 1917, John M. Browning had begun experiments to see about increasing the caliber of his basic machine gun design. Browning's intentions were to keep the reliability of his M1917 design as well as the manufacturing methods used to construct it. This would make the new weapon immediately fit military requirements for ruggedness while also minimizing production lead time.

With Winchester making parts to Browning's specifications, the first six new .50 caliber machine guns were assembled in Browning's shop in September 1918. Proving-ground tests of the new, water-cooled .50 caliber Browning were conducted in October 1918 and established the workability of the new design. The new ammunition still didn't meet General Pershing's specifications and underwent redesign.

Studying captured German 13mm Mauser antitank rifles and their ammunition, Winchester engineers designed a new round of .50 caliber ammunition that exceeded General Pershing's request. Frankford Arsenal then took over production of the new ammunition and continued their experiments with the basic Winchester design. WWI ended without the Browning .50 caliber machine gun or its new ammunition seeing combat, but development continued on after the war.

The new series of .50 caliber Browning weapons were accepted by the U.S. military in 1921. The first model fielded was the M1921 watercooled, effectively an enlarged version of the M1917 Browning. The single pistol grip of the .30 caliber M1917 had been replaced with twin spade grips to give the operator greater control of the much heavier and more powerful .50 caliber weapon. Minor improvements in the basic design of the new weapon resulted in the two models available being officially adopted at different times.

Both the Army and the Navy standardized the M1921 aircraft gun in 1923, with the M1921 watercooled gun being adopted a few years later in 1925. The M1921 aircraft gun had a slender barrel jacket extending from the receiver to the muzzle of the barrel. The jacket was perforated with longitudinal slots for cooling and held the relatively light 36-inch-long barrel on bearing at the front and rear of the jacket. The fixed version of the aircraft gun had a simple trigger mechanism and a cocking lever that extended out to the rear of the weapon. The M1921 flexible aircraft gun had the standard twin spade grips and central trigger lever found on most of the later ground guns.

The M1921 watercooled .50 also had a 36-inch barrel, this one surrounded with a water jacket holding 16 pints (2 gallons or 7.57 liters) of water. In 1930, the water jacket of the M1921 was enlarged and the cocking lever changed to ease the loading of the weapon. The new watercooled weapon was designated the M1921A1. Both the Army and the Navy liked the new .50 caliber machine gun family for its terminal (on target) effect.

But neither the aircraft or the watercooled weapons were completely without fault. Both weapons fed from the left side of the receiver only, complicating multiple weapon mounts used in aircraft. Additional, each weapon was distinct from the other, could not interchange many parts, and required a great deal of machine time to produce.

Though officially adopted by the Navy in 1923, none of the M1921 watercooled guns were purchased by that service until 1925. Funds for new weapons were very limited at that time for all of the services. Only around 1,000 of all of the M1921 models were purchased by the services between 1925 and 1934, the majority being bought between 1929 and 1933. During 1928, no .50 caliber machines guns were even made the entire year. The post-WWI economy had cut back on all government spending and the Army had no money to spend on developing a new weapon that they wanted, but had no immediate requirement for.

In 1930, some improvements were made on the M1921 series. The enlarged water jacket was developed for the watercooled gun, now cooling the barrel all the way to the muzzle, which had been exposed for the last two inches of its length in the original design. A more complex lever assembly was added to cock the M1921, making drawing back the heavy bolt much easier.

The new changes resulted in the M1921A1 designation being assigned to the modified weapons. But major changes were needed in the basic design to ease manufacture and allow for a greater range of use for the basic weapon. A ground-mounted, heavy-barreled, M1921 had been experimented with on a limited basis by the Army, but it was just a slightly modified flexible aircraft gun and was not fully suitable for use from a tripod or vehicle yet.

Doctor S. G. Green of the Army's Ordnance Department spent from 1927 to 1932 studying the problems with the M1921 designs. Improvements suggested by Dr. Green met with wholehearted approval in Army circles, but in 1933, there still were no funds to develop the new designs. Conferences between Army and Navy ordnance personnel resulted in the Navy paying for the new developments in the .50 caliber machine gun. These developments resulted in a new family of weapons, the M2 .50 caliber machine gun series, being adopted by the services in 1933.

The M2 .50 caliber machine gun design had a single receiver that could be assembled into any of seven different types of weapons to fit the needs of the Army or the Navy. Different backplates, cocking levers, and trigger systems could be switched about on the basic receiver to produce a flexible weapon for tripod or pintle mounting or a fixed weapon to be mounted in aircraft or vehicles. A 36-inch barrel and perforated barrel jacket could be mounted on the M2 receiver to make a basic aircraft weapon with a high rate of fire. A large water jacket and long, 45-inch barrel mounted to the M2 receiver resulted in a very effective antiaircraft weapon that could put out long bursts of fire without damaging the barrel. With a short perforated barrel jacket on the receiver and a very heavy 45-inch barrel mounted in place, the M2 became the heavy-barrel, ground-mount machine gun commonly known as the M2 HB.

The design changes in the original M1921 weapon gave the United States one of the most effective heavy machine guns used by any country in the world. During World War II, almost two million M2 weapons were produced from nine different manufacturers. The vast bulk of the WWII M2s were aircraft weapons, but almost 350,000 M2 HBs were made for use on ground mounts and vehicles. Watercooled M2s were used by the Army, Navy, and Marine forces for antiaircraft use. The Navy especially liked the watercooled M2 for general antiaircraft use on-board ships and at installations where the extra weight of the watercooled system wasn't a transportation problem.

With only minor changes, the M2 .50 caliber machine gun remains in front-line service today with both the U.S. forces as well as allies throughout the world. Production continues on the basic M2 weapon in a number of countries and the weapon is expected to last in service well into the next century. The M2 showed outstanding service from WWII through the Korean war, Vietnam, the 1970s, 1980s, and Desert Storm.

But the reliability of the M2 was first really proven during World War II. On one cruise of the Saratoga during WWII, 200,000 rounds of .50 caliber ammunition were fired, with only two serious jams being noted and only 24 stoppages of all types taking place in the M2s on board the ship. The Navy set great store by its M2 weapons, which may not have existed at all except for the Navy's support of the design some years earlier.

The Naval Combat Demolition Units (NCDU) Project was initiated on May 6, 1943 as a result of a directive by Admiral Ernest J. King Commander in Chief of the U.S. Fleet. Training for the NCDU Project was conducted at the Naval Amphibious Base at Fort Pierce, Florida. The first classes of NCDUs began training in July 1943. The primary mission of the NCDU Project was to produce highly fit naval personnel skilled in demolitions to eliminate German beach obstacles against an allied European landing. During the D-Day landings in Normandy, the men of the NCDU readily demonstrated the value of their training, and the valor of the kind of man who could pass it.

Months prior to the D-Day landings, a need was pointed out in the Pacific campaign for trained personnel to scout the waters off intended island landing sites. Not only were the men needed to measure the waters off enemy beaches, they were also to locate and be able to destroy obstacles to landing craft. All of this action was to take place in full view of the enemy just prior to any amphibious landings taking place.

The Underwater Demolition Teams (UDTs) raised to meet the demands of the Pacific Campaign were manned with graduates of the NCDU Project. By early 1944, the majority of NCDU graduates were reporting to Hawaii for further training in demolitions and underwater work. By the spring of 1944, the NCDU Project training program had been modified to produce men specifically to outfit the new UDTs. Primary demolition and physical training for the men of the WWII UDTs still took place at Fort Pierce with a second phase of more specialized training taking place off the beaches of Maui in the Pacific.

A WWII UDT consisted of 13 officers and 85 enlisted men broken down into a headquarters platoon of 5 officers and 25 men, and 3 operating platoons. The 2 officers and 15 men of each operating platoon performed the bulk of the actions for each UDT. The 15 men of an operating platoon was organized into 3 operating groups of 5 men each. Each operating group was able to conduct missions as an independent unit when necessary.

The headquarters platoon had the command responsibilities for the team and handled all of the clerical, administrative, medical, supply, repair, maintenance, and other functions for the team as a whole. Unlike postwar UDTs and the later SEAL Teams, the WWII UDT headquarters platoon also supplied the boat crews and communications personnel (radio operators) for the Teams' operational platoons.

By the fall of 1944, the five officers of a UDT HQ platoon were assigned as follows: Commanding Officer—Lieutenant Commander, Executive Officer—Lieutenant, Mine Disposal Officer—Lieutenant or Lieutenant (jg), Communications Officer—Ensign, Boat Officer—Ensign. For an operating platoon, the Platoon Leader was a Lieutenant (jg) and the Assistant Platoon Leader an Ensign.

Optimally, the enlisted men in the HQ platoon were assigned to fill the positions of: Master-at-Arms—Chief Bosun's Mate, Medical—Chief or First Class Pharmacist's Mate, Administration—Yeoman, Coxswains (4), Engineers (4), Radio Operators and Signalmen (6), Radio Technicians (1), Deck Hands (4), and Cook (1), Baker (1), and Steward's Mate (1). All of the HQ platoon's enlisted men, with the sole exception of the Pharmacist's Mate, had to be fully trained and qualified UDT operators. This last requirement was so that, in the case of an emergency, any of the men could be called on to perform reconnaissance and/or demolition work. The Pharmacist's Mate could be called on to set up and operate a sick bay on the parent ship if necessary.

The Radio Operator and Signalmen, Engineer, Coxswains, and Gunners (Deck Hands) formed the boat crews of the UDT, one crew for each of the operating platoons. Each member of a boat crew had to be competent for any position on a boat so that in case one man was wounded, another could immediately take his place. To fill this requirement, all members of the headquarters platoon received gunnery training. Members of a UDT's operating platoon were to know how to operate and maintain small arms, including light automatic weapons, but specific training for these weapons were not normally part of the required courses at Fort Pierce or Maui.

Headquarters platoon members of a UDT were trained with heavy automatic weapons so that they could take part in strafing runs on beaches, defensive actions in support of their swimmers, and in actions against low-flying enemy planes. Gunnery school included training in the use of .30 and .50 caliber machine guns. If a Team remained in training at Fort Pierce longer that the scheduled eight weeks, all the men received instruction in the use of .30 and .50 caliber machine guns and 20mm cannons at the base range.

Initial gunnery training was with the .30 caliber Browning M1919A4. Use was made of the Browning M1917A1 watercooled machine gun for training use and familiarization firing. Very few of the M1917A1 watercooled weapons would be seen aboard ship, but they were relatively common in the hands of landing Marines and Army troops. The first operational Underwater Demolition Teams, UDTs One and Two, had a smaller complement of men than later UDTs. Additionally, UDT Two had a mixed crew of Navy personnel along with a number of Marines and a handful of Army personnel.

The first two UDTs used standard LCVPs (Landing Craft, Vehicle/Personnel), 36-foot long craft with a large bow ramp and two single-man gunner's cockpits (gun tubs) at the rear of the boat. Each of the gun tubs mounted a single M1919A4 machine gun on a Mark 21 ring mount with a 300-round ammunition box provided for the weapon. The two machine guns on the LCVPs were used to provide covering fire for the UDT operators when they moved in close to the enemy beach to conduct their reconnaissance.

Later UDTs used the LCP(R) (Landing Craft, Personnel, [Ramp]), also called the Higgins boat, rather than the wider LCVPs. The large bow ramp of the LCVPs could not be as easily lowered while the boat was moving forward as could the smaller ramp of the Higgins boat. Also the two gun tubs on the Higgins boat were forward, one on either side of the ramp, which allowed them to concentrate their fire to the front without having to shoot over the heads of the UDT operators who may be working in the center of the boat. The two gun tubs of the Higgins boat were each fitted with a Mark 21 gun mount.

The limited range of the .30 caliber machine guns was noticed almost immediately during the first UDT combat operations. The dangers in shooting over the heads of swimmers in the water at long range cut back on the usefulness of the .30 caliber weapons to the UDT operators. If the boats were very far from the beach, the gunners had to be particularly careful covering the swimmers when they were at their most exposed point, close-in to an enemy beach. It is a point in the favor of the WWII UDT gunners that their were no recorded incidents of UDT swimmers being hit by friendly fire from their own boats.

During operations off of Saipan by UDT Seven on June 14, 1944, Japanese troops could be seen moving about on the beach areas and in several gun emplacements while the UDT operators conducted their reconnaissance. At ranges of 500 to 800 yards, the gunners on the LCPRs opened fire on the Japanese troops with their .30 caliber machine guns. By firing over the heads of the swimmers in the water, the guns of the LCPRs cut down on the intensity of the enemy fire that was falling among the swimmers in the water.

In addition to the two .30 caliber machine guns in the two bow gun tubs, a gunner was also positioned at the small bow ramp between the two gun tubs, armed with a Thompson submachine gun. The Thompson gunner would have been available for very-close-in defense of the swimmers but this proved unnecessary. Instead of the close-range defense provided by a submachine gun, it was decided that a longer range and greater volume of fire was needed to support the UDT swimmers. Besides developing a fire support plan with the heavier ships in the amphibious invasion fleet, the guns of the UDTs' own LCPRs were increased in number and power.

Additional .50 caliber machine guns were installed on the LCPRs of the UDTs. Mounts were fabricated as necessary for an additional weapon to be mounted at the stern of the boat. As weapons became available, the Browning .30 caliber M1919A4s on the LCPRs were replaced with .50 caliber M2 flexible aircraft weapons. The .50 caliber aircraft guns were chosen because of availability in the Navy supply system and the higher volume of fire put out by the rapid-fire weapons.

Modifications had to be made to the Mark 21 gun mounts used on the LCPRs, extensions were welded to the front of the ring mounts and cradles, locally fabricated to hold the much larger .50 caliber guns. An extended tray rack on the new cradles allowed the gun mounts to accept the standard M2 ammunition box that held 105 rounds of belted .50 caliber ammunition. At least one further gun mount was added, a tripod to hold a .50 caliber machine gun at the stern of the boat.

The stern mounts were also locally fabricated and consisted of a small tripod, much like the later Mark 16 mount, with a cradle to hold a gun and supply of ammunition. One photograph of this mount shows a salvaged flexible-type aircraft mounting, such as would have been used on a Catalina or other Navy aircraft. This type of cradle would have been available from damaged aircraft or even as a spare part. The mount also included a large container, holding over 200 rounds of ready ammunition to feed into the weapon.

The addition of the .50 caliber guns added greatly to the range targets on the beach could be effectively engaged by the UDT gunners on board the LCPRs. Additional UDT personnel received training in gunnery so that all of an LCPRs guns could be manned during an operation.

There was occasionally some friction between the crews of the ships that transported the UDTs and the members of the Teams themselves. The UDTs had no regular duties with the ship's company outside of maintaining, loading, and unloading the explosive supplies. Individual UDT operators would offer their services to areas of the ship where they could work in their original rate, the jobs they held prior to joining the UDTs. But when General Quarters sounded, the UDT operators stayed out of the way of the ship's crews.

This situation changed greatly after the U.S. Navy ran into the Japanese Kamikaze suicide planes. The Japanese had planned that the battle for the Philippines would be a decisive one for their side in the outcome of the war. Toward this end, the Japanese launched the first of the intentional, planned, operations where attacking aircraft would intentionally dive into Allied ships in order to destroy them. On October 25, 1944, Kamikaze attacks did serious damage to the Allied forces in the battle of Leyte Gulf.

Within a few weeks, the new Japanese method of attack had been demonstrated as more than a one-time assault of desperation. UDT Five, on board their transport ship, the *APD Humphries*, were part of the invasion force to attack Lingayen Gulf on Luzon in the Philippines. After passing Leyte in early January 1945, the task force had its effective strength cut in half by the constant attacks of Japanese planes, both conventional and Kamikaze. On January 5, 1945, at least thirty-five attacking planes crashed or were shot down in a attack that lasted little more than half an hour.

The warning brought by UDTs Fourteen and Fifteen when they arrived at the staging area for the upcoming operations against Iwo Jima were taken seriously by the men of the other UDTs. The guns of the UDTs LCPRs were added to the overall firepower of the transport ships. Mounts were fabricated that could accept the .50 caliber M2 flexible aircraft guns from the LCPRs and usually attached to the fantail of the transport APDs carrying the UDTs. On board the *USS Barr*, one UDT operator was killed in an accident while welding gun mounts to the rear of his ship.

By 1945, when General Quarters were sounded aboard the UDTs' transports, the men of the Teams went to their own battle stations. UDT operators manned their own .50 caliber guns and Teammates helped pass ammunition to keep the guns firing. The only real defense against the Japanese Kamikazes was to destroy them in the air, before they could strike at their targets.

Several UDTs on board their transports had close calls with Kamikaze planes. The *APD Crosley* with UDT Seventeen aboard encountered a Kamikaze plane early in the morning on March 27, 1945 while a few miles off the beaches at Kerama Retto, near Okinawa. The entire crew of the *Crosley*, along with the men of UDT Seventeen, poured fire into the oncoming Kamikaze, which crashed into the sea only a scant 30 feet off the *Crosley*'s fantail, where the guns of the UDT were concentrated.

Besides the Kamikaze planes, the Japanese also used small explosive motor boats (EMBs) built for the intended purpose of attacking Allied ships with large depth charges. The original intent of the small EMBs was for them to approach closely to the target ship and release their two 264-pound depth charges where they would cave in large sections of the target's hull and then speed away. Instead of the attack profile described, most of the EMB operators intended riding their small craft directly into the target ship to insure a hit.

The *Crosley* and UDT Seventeen also ran into at least one of these Kamikaze boats near Kerama Retto. The guns of the ship sank the small boat before it was able to carry out its mission. When the UDTs landed on the Kerama Retto islands, they found some 250 Japanese explosive motor boats, enough to have made a sizable inroad into the invasion force.

Some 3,000 Kamikaze sorties were made against the Allied ships at Okinawa, sinking 34, damaging 368, while also wounding 4,800 and killing 4,900 U.S. sailors. The guns of the UDTs were used on their LCPRs during their pre-invasion operations off Okinawa, and then added to the overall blanket of protection for all of the Allied ships in the force.

At the end of World War II, the UDTs were among the first U.S. forces to actually land on the main islands of Japan, again protected by the close-in fire-power of their own LCPRs. In addition, the UDT operators often carried small arms with them when they examined the beaches and the beach areas on Japan itself. Though there were no incidents between the UDT operators and the sur-rendered Japanese people, the cost of the planned invasions of the main islands, Operation Olympic and Coronet, were obvious to the men of the UDTs.

Due to the UDTs experience with demolitions, they were assigned the du-ties of locating and destroying stockpiles of ordnance near the beaches of Japan. The thousands of suicide weapons found by the UDTs, ranging from small mines to torpedoes and explosive boats, would have made the cost to any in-vading forces, in lives lost, higher than at any other time in history.

By 1945, the leadership of the UDTs in Maui could see that the continued operations of the UDTs would include missions on the land and not just in the water. Training was established in Maui to include small infantry tactics and the use of small arms, moreso than had been a part of UDT training up until then. The operational need for this training did not arise during WWII. The postwar UDTs were concerned with maintaining a presence in the postwar Navy and continued to increase their operational capabilities.

The watercooled .50 M2 was declared obsolete and removed from service with the Navy within a few years of the end of WWII. The flexible aircraft M2 .50 caliber machine guns remained in service with the Navy but had been re-placed with a newer postwar design, the M3 .50 caliber machine gun. The result of the M3 was that it gradually replaced the M2 Aircraft weapon in Navy ser-vice.

The guns of the UDTs were generally removed from their LCPRs and not replaced until the conflict in Korea broke out in 1950. The flexible aircraft M2 weapons were generally unavailable at the time of the Korean war and the UDT LCPRs were armed with the standard flexible M2 HB .50 caliber weapon. This was not considered a difficulty, as very few of the UDT LCPRs were armed at any time during the Korean conflict.

The M2 HB had been the US Army's standard .50 caliber weapon during WWII and continued in active service after the war. The M2 HB has a much heavier barrel than the aircraft or watercooled weapons. The additional barrel mass absorbs enough of the heat of firing to allow for a reasonable rate of con-tinuous fire as well as slowing the cyclic rate.

Though the United States military had received excellent service from the Browning machine gun designs, there was still a gap in the application of the weapons that had not been well addressed during WWII. The general heavy machine gun for the U.S. forces during WWII and into Korea remained the M1917A1 .30 caliber Browning. This weapon was considered a heavy gun for its use in the sustained-fire role. The watercooled Browning could maintain an effective rate of fire literally for hours as long as water was kept in the cooling jacket and the ammunition supply was big enough.

But the M1917A1 required a three-man crew just to move the gun about, set it up, and operate it with a limited supply of ammunition. The M1917A1 could not be effectively fired without its tripod or other mount and so could not easily move up with the troops in the assault. The M1919A4 Browning was considered a light machine gun during WWII, because it could be carried and manned by just two men. The tripod used with the M1919A4 was set up low to the ground, as compared to the relatively tall mount for the M1917A1. This low mounting allowed a gunner to lay prone behind the weapon when firing it.

The M1919A4 was light enough to be carried along on the assault or even on larger patrols. The mount and weapon could be quickly emplaced and supply close-in firepower during the early stages of enemy contact. And the relatively heavy barrel of the M1919A4 allowed it to maintain a reasonable effective rate of fire.

In spite of the relatively light weight and ease of movement of the M1919A4, it still could not move up and support the troops on a tactical level, being carried and operated by one man. On some operations, gunners carrying the M1919A4 would have a short belt of 30 rounds or so loaded into the weapon for immediate use. The M1919A4 could be fired from the hip with reasonable accuracy for close-in reactions to a suddenly appearing enemy, and a strong man could hold the weapon up and fire it while aiming along the barrel. But the last motion was difficult at best and the weapon was never intended to be fired as such.

To develop a belt-fed automatic weapon capable of being fired from a bipod and carried by one man required a new design to work well. The M1919A4 was modified in late 1942 to include a lighter barrel, muzzle-mounted bipod, carrying handle, and buttstock, later a flash hider, was also added to the modifications. The new weapon was standardized on February 17, 1943 as the M1919A6 light machine gun. Though lighter than the M1919A4 mounted on its M2 tripod, the Browning M1919A6 was several pounds heavier than the earlier weapon.

The Browning M1919A6 could be carried and emplaced by one man, and put into action very quickly from its attached bipod. But the weapon was anything but a very light machine gun and was considered clumsy to carry and use by the men assigned to operate it. In spite of these drawbacks, the M1919A6 remained in the US inventory through World War II and Korea and into the Vietnam War.

The M1919A6 was at best a stopgap measure to supply what could be considered a light machine gun to the U.S. forces. The ideal was considered to be a belt-fed machine gun that would weigh about 25 pounds and could be fired from a bipod. The belt feed would allow such a weapon to give a good rate of fire, one that could be sustained by including a quick-change barrel in the design.

The Germans had developed a series of new types of machine guns prior to and during World War II that fit the tactical requirements as seen by the U.S. military planners. The two German weapons, the MG 34 and later MG 42 both weighed less than the Browning M1919A4 and could be easily carried and operated by one man.

The MG 34 was a finely machined weapon developed prior to WWII. Weighing only about 27 pounds and being belt-fed, the MG 34 also had a quick-change barrel to keep the weapon from becoming overheated and jamming. Capable of both semiautomatic and full automatic fire, the MG 34 could be fed with flexible metal link belts, a special 75-round drum magazine, or a simple box that attached to the side of the weapon and held a 50-round section of belt. The cyclic rate of fire of the MG 34 was between 800 and 900 rounds per minute, an excessively high rate to some U.S. military personnel.

The MG 34 was the first General Purpose machine gun, capable of being carried within a squad by one man as a true light machine gun for squad fire support. On a tripod, the MG 34 could be used as a heavy machine gun for long-range sustained fire by changing hot barrels quickly. And the high cyclic rate of fire made the weapon somewhat effective in low altitude antiaircraft defense. But the MG 34 had been designed and built to prewar German standards and required excessively close machining tolerances for wartime mass production.

The Germans recognized the drawbacks of the MG 34 and designed a new weapon to be mass produced with minimum machining and maximum use of stampings and welded construction. The new weapon, the MG 42, was capable of only full automatic fire, was slightly larger than its predecessor, but weighed less than the MG 34, being only 25.5 pounds with bipod. The quick-change barrel on the MG 42 was improved over the earlier design and a hot barrel could be removed and a new one installed by the gunner within five seconds, with him remaining in a prone position.

The MG 42 did have a very high cyclic rate of fire, between 1,200 and 1,350 rounds per minute, and that gave it a distinctive "ripping cloth" sound when heard by allied troops. But both the MG 34 and later MG 42 had proved the tactical advantages of the general purpose machine gun in greatly increasing the available volume of fire from a squad-sized unit. This made the weapon of great interest to the U.S. military.

A captured MG 42 was examined at Aberdeen Proving Grounds in February 1943. Suitably impressed, the U.S. Military contracted with the Saginaw Steering Gear Division of General Motors to produce a copy of the MG 42, modified to fire the U.S. M2 30-06 round. Since U.S. car production was centered around the precision stamping and welding of sheet metal, the production design of a U.S. version of the German MG 42, test designated the T24, was expected to be a simple process. It was not.

The conversion of the MG 42 to 30-06 was flawed and the test firing of the T24 in October 1943 did not live up to expectations. Modifications were performed and the new weapon tested in February 1944. During the 10,000-round endurance test, only 1,483 rounds were fired with 50 malfunctions stopping the gun. Several parts of the T24 were made too short to handle the U.S. ammunition, including the overall receiver length. An extensive redesign was necessary to correct the problems and the project was canceled after only two weapons were built.

After WWII ended, the idea to develop a new light, or general purpose, machine gun was renewed. Another WWII German weapon, the late model Krieghoff FG 42, was examined and adopted as a base design. The FG 42 (Fallschirmjager Gewehr, or Paratroopers Rifle) was a limited-production weapon intended solely for the German paratroop forces. The FG 42 was essentially a magazine-fed light machine gun produced from stampings and welding to ease production. The bolt and operating rod system of the FG 42 was very similar to the earlier Lewis gun, but the feed was much simpler, consisting of a side-mounted 20-round box magazine.

The late model FG 42, also called the FG 42, Type II, was improved from the first model with wooden furniture, a removable trigger housing, a springloaded dust cover over the magazine well, a muzzle-attached bipod, and an efficient muzzle brake/flash hider. The stamped metal design allowed for the FG 42 to be a very lightweight weapon, weighing only 11.44 pounds empty. This light weight worked against the design of the FG 42, which was intended to fire a full-power rifle round on full automatic.

The stock on the FG 42 is set so that the barrel is in line with the point of contact at the shoulder of the firer, minimizing muzzle climb. The orientation of the stock to the barrel, raised sights, and muzzle brake were all part of the design to make the weapon controllable on full automatic fire. Accuracy when set on semiautomatic fire was considered excellent in the FG 42 and the weapon was quick to handle and get on target.

The late-model FG 42 was taken directly by the U.S. Ordnance Corps to be refined into a belt-fed weapon. Bridge Tool and Die Works of Philadelphia was given the contract to produce the new weapon, designated the T44. A standard late-model FG 42 was modified to accept the belt-feed mechanism from the MG 42 on the left side of the weapon.

The orientation of the feed mechanism of the T44 allowed for minor changes in the basic design of the FG 42, but gave the weapon unique loading characteristics. The nondisintegrating German link belt would feed up from the bottom of the receiver on the lower left side of the T44, directly above the pistol grip. The empty link belt came out of the top of the weapon, falling down on the right side. Being that the T44 remained chambered for the German 7.92×57mm round, eliminating the problems that plagued the T24 project, the weapon was considered only a test bed to try out the feasibility of the design.

By December 1946, the mechanical conversion of the basic FG 42 into the T44 prototype had been completed. Test firings proved much of what the German paratroops had found during the war, that the overall design was too light for sustained full automatic fire. The relatively light barrel of the FG 42 would overheat quickly, especially with the larger ammunition capacity given with the belt feed of the T44 conversion. In addition, the light weight of the weapon caused excessive spread of the rounds in a fired burst. But mechanically, the design had merit and a new contract was issued for further development.

The T44 itself never went beyond the prototype stage. But the basic bolt and operating rod mechanism of the FG 42 and the belt-feed system of the MG 42 were incorporated into a new design.

Initiated in April 1947, the new weapon was designated the T52. Using much the same configuration as the original FG 42, the T52 had the feed mechanism placed on top of the receiver in the usual position, feeding from the left side of the weapon. In addition, the T52 had the wooden forearm and buttstock, bipod, muzzle brake, and trigger group of the FG 42. The barrel could not be removed from the weapon and the bolt locked into lugs in the receiver.

Later models of the T52, as well as the T52E1 and E2, incorporated additional changes indicated by testing. The locking lugs of the bolt now engaged recesses on a barrel extension, allowing a quick-change barrel to be used to keep the weapon from overheating. The fixed headspace on the later designs eliminated one of the problems found in the earlier Browning designs—the time needed to adjust headspace when a barrel was changed. Both light and heavy barrels were tried out, weighing 4.5 and 7 pounds each respectively.

The gas system was changed to that of the gas-expansion-cutoff design. In the gas-expansion-cutoff system, the propellant gas is ported from the barrel directly into the gas piston sitting in the gas cylinder. The gas piston has a solid end, bearing on the operating rod, and a hollow body with the other end open. Expending gas moves through ports into the body of the gas piston, driving it back against the operating rod. When the piston has moved a short distance, the gas supply is cut off when the ports on the piston move away from the single gas port between the barrel and the gas cylinder. Excess gas pressure is then bled away though the barrel and a small bleed hole in the front of the gas cylinder.

This complicated system gives a constant push of sufficient force to operate the action while preventing excess pressure from putting wear on the moving parts. Theoretically, the piston will allow enough gas to operate the action and more when the action is dirty or sluggish. This gas cutoff system gives a smooth, even operating force on the action rather than the single sharp jolt of a standard gas piston.

The Army Equipment Development Guide dated December 29, 1950 stated that a new lightweight general purpose machine gun should be developed to replace all of the .30 caliber weapons (the M1917A1, M1919A4, and M1919A6) then in service. The new weapon was to have an effective range of 2,000 yards, a maximum weight of 18 pounds, a quick-change barrel with a flash hider, use a disintegrating link belt, and have a cyclic rate of 600 rounds per minute. In April 1951, a second series of weapons were begun, the T161 family, to meet the new requirements and accelerate the overall program to develop a new machine gun.

The T161 design was to be chambered for the standard .30 caliber M2 round, in case the developing T65 Light Rifle round did not meet requirements. The T52 series had been chambered for the different types of T65 round as it was being developed. The new T161 weapon was modeled after the T52 series but developed with improved mass-production techniques incorporated into it. In addition, the T161 series had the actuator lug for the belt-feed mechanism on the bolt rather than on the rear of the operating rod as used in the T52 series. This change in the method of operating the feed system was one of the major differences between the T52 and T161 series.

The T161E1 was the first of the new series to see firing tests, now designed to accept the T65 lightweight rifle round. By March 1953, the T161E1 was ready for firing and underwent testing against the T52E3.

In early 1953, the best features of the T52 series had been incorporated into the T52E3. The lightweight barrel had been abandoned due to the heavy barrel giving greater stability for automatic fire and having to be changed less often for sustained fire. The wooden furniture of the earlier designs had been changed to stamped metal for the buttstock and forearm. Overall, the T52E3 weighed 23.58 pounds empty, had a 22-inch barrel, and an overall length of 43.5 inches. This was a savings of over 8 pounds from the M1919A6 in a weapon over 9 inches shorter.

Drawbacks found in testing the T52E3 were that the weapon had a greater number of parts than earlier designs, was not as durable, and didn't function as reliably. The T52E4 model corrected some of the deficiencies found in the earlier weapon, with different parts used to ease its manufacture. In May 1954, a contract was issued to build the T52E5, which was to incorporate all of the best features of the earlier designs.

By August 1954, the T65 ammunition family had been officially adopted as the new NATO standard round. Both the T52 and T161 series now were chambered for the new ammunition. To feed the round into the belt-fed weapons, a new disintegrating link had been designed that allowed the round to be pushed forward, stripping it out of the link. As the ammunition left the belt, the individual stamped metal links separated and fell away from the feed mechanism.

The ammunition belt links used in the early 1950s tests, the T55 link, was heavier and less flexible than desired. The new T89 disintegrating belt link was lighter in construction, held the round firmly with a detent tab locating on the extractor groove, and made a more flexible belt. The T89 link later became the standard issue M13 belt link.

Tests on the T161E1 indicated that it needed additional changes to get the design ready for the more rugged Army user tests. The barrel assembly was redesigned, eliminating an aluminum component that deformed from the heat of firing. The feed plate was modified for smoother loading of the ammunition belt. A carrying handle was added to the weapon and the rear sight changed to one that was adjustable for range (elevation) only. The modified weapon was designated the T161E2 with 20 specimens ready for testing by the Army Field Forces (AFF) Board No. 3 in July 1953.

The AFF Board decided that the T161E2 was unsuitable for issue, citing failures to fire and stoppages due to the gas system and other faults. The 3-pound lightweight barrel was also abandoned at this point. The front sight on both the heavy and light barrels were considered too weak for field use, having bent during testing. In spite of the drawbacks, the AFF Board stated the design showed sufficient promise to warrant further considerations.

Additional modifications to meet the AFF Board's recommendations were made on the 20 T161E2 test guns, resulting in the T161E3 design. The feed mechanism was modified to operate with the new T89 links. Further changes were made in the firing pin, buffer assembly, operating rod, and some other minor parts. Besides the 20 modified T161E2 weapons, an additional 100 T161E3s were produced for testing.

Extensive testing of the T161E3 included temperate and arctic environments, where the T161E3 was well liked by the soldiers operating it. New tripod mounts for the T161E3 did not do as well in testing and modifications were recommended. Testing also demonstrated that the T161E3 did not have the durability of the earlier Browning designs, but did meet many of its design parameters.

The testing board reported its results on July 31, 1956. The T161E3 was found to be superior to the M1917A1, M1919A4, and M1919A6 in simplicity, portability, reliability under adverse conditions, barrel life, and other factors. The T161E3 was found to be very easy to use in hip and shoulder firing, a point stated by the majority of the gunners in the tests. The operators also preferred the new weapons because they were lighter, shorter, and easier to disassemble and assemble for cleaning.

In August 1956, the CONARC (Continental Army Command) Board No. 3 (now the U.S. Army Infantry Board) overlooking the T161E3 tests recommended the T161E3 for adoption. Minor deficiencies in the weapon and mount would be eliminated during production. The T161E3 gun was designated the M60 machine gun and the T89 belt link designated the M13 metallic belt cartridge link, both for standard issue, on January 30, 1957. At that time, the M1917A1, M1919A4, and M1919A6 Browning machine guns were designated as limited standard.

At the time that the M60 was accepted for issue, there were very few belt-fed machine guns in the UDTs. By the mid to late 1950s, the limited number of machine guns in a UDT consisted of M1919A4s to arm the gun tubs in the Teams' LCPRs. Further fire support would be supplied by other units that would be working with the UDTs during an operation.

By the 1960s, the machine gun situation had not changed in the UDTs, and was much the same for the newly formed SEAL Teams. The Navy BuWeps (Bureau of Weapons) didn't see any need for heavy weapons such as belt-fed machine guns for the SEAL Teams and none were supplied.

Originally, the Navy SEALs were considered to be a clandestine antiguerrilla and raiding force. For such missions, heavy weapons would be too difficult to hit and run with, so belt fed machine guns were not considered necessary to the Teams' operations. Other unit training, which the SEALs attended vigorously their first years, did expose members of the Teams to a wide variety of small arms, machine guns included. At the U.S. Army's Special Forces training center at Fort Bragg, the SEALs were taught to operate, employ, and maintain a wide variety of U.S. and foreign weapons. Included with these weapons was the Browning .50 caliber M2HB, the M1919A4, and the M1919A6. These Browning designs had become so widespread throughout the guerrilla forces in the world that they were no longer directly identified with the United States.

In other training conducted with the U.S. Army, the SEALs gained further experience with belt-fed machine guns. At the U.S. Army Jungle Operations Course taught deep in the tropics of Central America, members of the SEAL Teams carried and used the M1919A6 light machine gun. The general opinion of the M1919A6 was that it was a good weapon that operated well and no one wanted to carry it. Even big SEALs found the clumsy M1919A6 an armful to drag around, especially in the hot, humid environment of the jungle.

By the mid-1960s, the scope of SEAL operations were beginning to expand. Strategic planners had the SEAL Teams going to an active combat role in Vietnam within a few years. SEAL Team One would be sending direct action platoons to Vietnam beginning in January 1966, and SEAL Team Two would follow a year later. By 1965, SEAL Team One had received the first of their M60 machine guns and had begun training with them.

As SEAL operational capabilities evolved, the equipment used by the Teams increased. SEAL Team Two had purchased several civilian PowerCat Trimeran boats and converted them for special warfare use. Among the conversions to the 24-foot fiberglass boats were modifications for the secure installation of four weapons mounts. The mounts were each intended to be able to accept a .50 M2HB, an M60, or 40mm Mark 18 grenade launcher.

No .50 caliber machine guns were reportedly in the Teams inventories until after they arrived in Vietnam. The Boat Support Units that worked alongside the Teams in Vietnam did have heavy machine guns and were able to supply guns and ammunition to the SEAL platoons and detachments.

The M2 HB was the last of the .50 caliber Browning designs to still be in use with all of the U.S. military services. The ruggedness of the design was well proven and the power of the large round it fired would make small work of most of the enemy targets that would be engaged in Vietnam. Almost every support craft used for SEAL operations in Vietnam and since has carried the .50 M2 HB as part of their arsenal.

Both the Boat Support Unit and the Brown Water Navy used the flexible .50 M2 HB as part of their standard weapons loadout. The Mark I and Mark II PBRs (Patrol Boat, River) each carried twin mounted .50 M2s in the forward Mark 56 gun tub and an additional .50 on a tall, tripod-like Mark 26 pedestal mount at the stern of the boat.

The BSU "Mike" boat was a converted 36-foot Mark 6 landing craft that was used almost exclusively for SEAL operations starting in 1966. Though the mounted weapons on the armored Mike boat would change from time to time, along the gunwales were from four to six M2 HB .50s, each on a pintle mount and feeding from a standard 105-round M2A1 ammunition can.

One of the larger boats that commonly supported SEAL operations when the water depth allowed was the 50-foot Fast Patrol Craft or Swift boats. The Swift boats were not as heavily armed as the Mike boats, but they did carry at least three .50s, two in a Mark 56 gun tub on top of the superstructure, and one on the stern deck on one of the most unusual gun mounts of the war.

The rear deck of the Swift boats carried the Navy Mark 2 Mod 1 direct-fire 81mm mortar. Unlike a normal, muzzle-loading, drop fired mortar, the Mark 2 mortar loaded from the muzzle and then could be either drop fired or directly aimed and trigger fired like a small cannon.

On the firing range, this SEAL familiarizes himself with the M2HB .50 caliber machine gun on an M3 tripod mount. To help control the heavy recoil of the weapon, the SEAL has braced his feet up against the tripod. Both hands are on the spade grips of the weapon, the thumbs pressing down on the Y-shaped trigger bar between the grips. There is no traversing and elevating mechanism on the lower receiver of the .50 so this operator has a very firm grip on the weapon as he "free-aims' the weapon on its pintle. Fired cartridge cases are ejected from the bottom of the receiver with empty links falling off to the right on this specimen. An empty link can be seen falling from the weapon just below the carrier assembly to the barrel.
Source: U.S. Navy

To increase the already heavy firepower of the mortar, a .50 M2 HB flexible gun was mounted on top of the mortar in a piggyback style. This gave the gunner the choice of using the mortar or the machine gun, depending on what the target called for.

But the .50 caliber M2 was not the best weapon for all of the SEALs' small craft. When the SEAL Team Two first arrived incountry in Vietnam with their converted PowerCat Trimarans, now called the Mark I STAB (SEAL Team Assault Boat), the boats were to be armed with locally supplied .50s. The ten socket mounts around the sides, corners, bow, and stern of the STABs had been reinforced so that the fiberglass hull would stand up to the punishing recoil of the .50.

A difficulty arose with using the .50s on board the STABs that had nothing to do with the mechanics of the weapon. Most of the targets the SEALs would take under fire from the STABs were either too light to begin with and the overwhelming power of the .50s would go right through them and continue on for several thousand yards, or they were thick earth bunkers that the .50s would take too long to chew through. In addition, the .50s were very large weapons and so was their ammunition.

> The (STABs') .50's were dismounted and their space filled in with M60s. The 7.62mm M60s could have 800 rounds of ammunition stored in the same space that was taken up by only 210 rounds of linked .50 caliber ammo. This gave the STABs a much greater organic unit of fire.

The M60s soon became the favored heavy automatic weapon used in the SEAL platoons. At least one SEAL in each platoon was armed with an M60, and often more men carried them. The requirements were that each squad have at least one automatic-weapons man, and preferably two. The use of the M60 was a matter of taste to each SEAL, and the men who preferred the weapons normally carried them.

It was during predeployment training that the men in the Teams learned more about their weapons and developed individual preferences. Every SEAL was familiar with the M60 and .50 caliber M2 HB. Training was given on the ranges with each of the weapons as part of a SEAL's basic indoctrination. In predeployment training prior to going to Vietnam, the M60 had several hours of classroom instruction as well as several hours of range firing devoted to it and each member of a platoon attended all of the classes.

Some of the range and field training done by the SEALs were unique to them. Men were able to take the weapons they preferred and develop their skills and mechanical familiarity with them.

There were a few organized training evolutions (in early predeployment training, circa 1966/67), but they were spread pretty thin. what you spent your time
doing was learning about your weapons on the range. Taking an M60 machine
gun, you would experiment with different ways of firing it; feeding it with the
belt over your arm, your shoulder, from a bag. Holding the weapon with the
sling around your neck, your neck and shoulder, just your shoulder, no sling,
from the hip, the shoulder.

The belt-fed M60 machine gun was one of the weapons that the SEALs built their philosophy of overwhelming firepower on. The belt-fed machine gun can fire hundreds of rounds of ammunition in well under a minute, adding a constant stream of projectiles to the volume of fire that can be put out by a SEAL squad or fire team for a short period of time. The military today describes this kind of device as a force multiplier.

Force multiplier is a term used in the U.S. military for, among other things, new weapons used to increase a combat unit's effectiveness against the enemy while not increasing the size of the unit. This can mean weapons that increase the volume of fire that can be effectively put out by a limited number of men.

The M60 was a rather large weapon and it normally took a team of two men, a gunner and an assistant gunner, to operate one correctly in the other ser-vices. But the SEALs did not use the tripod, spare barrels, and other materials that were part of the M60 package, making it a crew-served weapon in the Army and Marine Corps. SEALs who could handle the M60 well were allowed to carry one, and trained with it extensively as part of their platoon during pre-deployment training. Some platoon leaders particularly liked their M60 men.

The SEALs I would take along were usually big guys who carried big guns.
These guys would carry an M60 machine gun and 600-plus rounds of ammunition. This was nice as these guys could stand up and cut trees down. You
could also stand behind them if you wanted to.

There was a drawback to the range and penetrating power of the M60. It was still a relatively heavy weapon for an individual, and the amount of ammunition carried by the average SEAL M60 man weighed quite a bit as well. The SEALs were primarily an amphibious unit. They inserted from waterways, rivers, streams, and canals. A large amount of weapons and ammunition could cause more than a little trouble for a SEAL inserting from the water.

> We were inserting from a PBR. The boat crew slipped the bow of the PBR onto the bank and we quietly got off. I slithered over the side of the boat's bow and immediately sank into the dark water. We hadn't hit the shore, the boat was nosed into a mangrove tree. As the water closed over my head I thought, Oh god, I'm going to drown on my first op.

The SEAL in the story above did not drown, though he did learn a good lesson about swimming while carrying a belt-fed machine gun. The Teams as a whole learned this lesson quickly and modified their techniques accordingly.

> A regular UDT lifejacket was worn during an underway insertion, two jackets for a man armed with a machine gun. Once on shore, the jacket was deflated and carried in a large pocket. The underway insertion technique was very much a modified version of the old UDT style of rolling off a rubber raft on the side of the boat modified to fit our situation in Vietnam.

The Mark 25 Minigun mounted in place on the Heavy SEAL Support Craft or "Mike" boat. The weapon is mounted on a complete stand-alone mount that contains an ammunition and power supply along with all of the mechanical and electrical support to operate a single 7.62mm Minigun. The large ammunition can at the front of the mount carries 3,000 rounds of linked 7.62 NATO ammunition, fed through the flexible chuting at the top of the can and into the weapon. The Minigun itself hanging from a cradle with the speed ring sight assembly attached to the top of the cradle itself. The large canvas bag just visible underneath the Minigun is attached to the cradle to capture expended brass and links.
Source: U.S. Navy

Even with the allowances made for transporting a heavy weapon by hand through the swamps of Vietnam, the M60 was still a lot to carry. The SEALs only used a tripod for .50 caliber M2s during training and didn't take the light M122 tripod for the M60 with them to Vietnam. With their access to Navy machine shop facilities on-board ship and on shore, the SEALs adapted their weapons to their own unique style of operating.

In the first year of combat operations in Vietnam, the SEALs could see that the average range of a firefight was very short. Twenty-five to thirty meters was a long range and normally an area was saturated with fire rather than a specific target. This happened due to the SEALs using the night ambush so often in their early tours. Instinctive fire was the norm in the jungles and swamps of Vietnam. Even when a weapon was shoulder fired, something a strong man could easily do with an M60, both eyes were kept open and the weapon pointed rather than aimed.

This style of shooting is discouraged in today's SEAL Teams, but during the Vietnam war, individual SEALs built up enough experience that firing a weapon effectively from the hip was second nature to them. This allowed for some very unusual modifications to be performed on the M60 in order to save as much weight as possible.

It wasn't long before we were modifying the M60 to make it lighter and easier to carry. Modifications were done according to an individual SEALs taste and ability. As long as the weapon still operated dependably, and the man could keep up with his job, SEALs in the Teams were given a lot of freedom in their equipment.

We used a lot of SEAL innovation and ingenuity in cutting down the M60 machine gun for our use. The bipod legs would be removed, saving about a pound and a half of weight. The bipod mount was removed and the barrel was cut back to the gas cylinder (in the process removing the front sight), and the flashhider then was reinstalled. Doing all of that work would take another couple of pounds weight from the weapon.

All in all, we could take the M60's weight down from about twenty-three pounds to around nineteen. That helped make the weapon much handier for one man to use on patrols. By just putting on a complete barrel assembly, the weapon would be returned to its original condition. The work we did adapted the M-60 to be an individual rather than a crew-served weapon.

Other SEALs would use the cut-down M60s and find their own preferences for how they would load them. The standard M60 by 1967 was fitted with a hanger on the side of the feed tray for 100-round bandoleers. The ammunition would come in 100-round belts, two belts to an M1A1 metal ammunition can, each belt packed in a cardboard box held in a cloth bandoleer. The bandoleers had a long strap allowing them to be easily slung from the shoulder. These handy cloth and cardboard packages would often be damaged or simply disintegrate in the water that the SEALs constantly operated in.

Some SEALs used the original heavy fabric and metal ammunition pouches

An M60E3 light machine gun on a Mk 58 gun mount aboard a light boat. The shoulder sling remains attached to this weapon allowing it to be easily carried if released from the mount. Squeezing the latch assembly underneath the receiver, directly below the rear sight, immediately releases the weapon for hand carrying. In this mount configuration, the weapon can be fed with a loose belt as shown on this specimen or a 100-round bandoleer can be hooked to the skeletonized hanger assembly. The hanger assembly can be seen just below and in front of the upper portion of the ammunition belt.

Source: Kevin Dockery

that came with the first model M60s. These strong, water-resistant pouches would attach to the side of an M60, in place of the bandoleer hanger that came later, and would hold a belt of 100 rounds. The pouches were not as fast to reload with as the later bandoleers were, but they protected the ammunition well while it was attached to the weapon.

Other operators who preferred a much larger quantity of ammunition to be available to their weapons either built or modified ammunition containers for their M60s. Later in the war and afterwards, the ammunition can and feed chuting from a helicopter door gun was sometimes modified into a backpack that fed its entire contents into a SEAL's weapon. This could give a SEAL 400 rounds ready for his M60. Other SEALs custom-built ammunition carriers for themselves.

To feed his machine gun for a good length of time, H—manufactured a U-shaped aluminum canister that would hold a 500 round belt of ammunition and feed it directly to the weapon. To carry his rig, H—fixed a harness to the aluminum belt box that would hold the whole mess around his waist like a thick belt while still feeding the ammunition belt into the left side of his M60.

With the larger quantity of ammunition available, this enterprising SEAL was able to feed his modified M60 for what he considered a reasonable amount of time. Some SEALs became very involved with the mechanics of their weapons. With this familiarity, further modifications became possible. These changes were done to increase the weapons use to the Team, while not necessarily being something the original designers would have approved of.

To modify his M60, H—took an older-style, mechanical M60 buffer and replaced some of the internal buffer pads with nickels. With the modification, H—'s M60 fired at over 800 rounds per minute, up considerably from the normal 600 rounds per minute.

Since the SEALs took meticulous care of their weapons, excessive wear was noticed before it could become a problem. The M60 had some problems with its design, the primary one that was never addressed was that the weapon wore out bolt assemblies fairly quickly. This wear problem was directly attributed to the fixed headspace, quick-change barrel system used on the weapon. But since the SEALs paid such close attention to maintenance of their weapons and equipment, even their modified weapons worked dependably.

But there was one problem with the M60 that couldn't be addressed by the SEALs with modifications or other changes. The basic weapon was still large and heavy for patrolling in a jungle or swamp. The rate of fire of the standard M60 was also considered a bit slow for the sudden encounters with the VC that were so common. For such situations, a high rate of fire, for even a short time, would saturate an area, overwhelming most opposition.

Brief experiments with the M1918A2 BAR converted to 7.62mm NATO were conducted by the Navy in the late 1950s and early 1960s. But the weight of the weapon, combined with its limited magazine capacity, eliminated it as a practical source of squad firepower, especially as compared to the M60.

The trade-off for the power of the M60 and other 7.62mm NATO weapons was in the weight of the ammunition and the basic weapon itself. A new weapons system became available to the SEALs soon after their direct involvement in Vietnam began. And this new weapon became something of a trademark of the Teams during the late 1960s and early 1970s.

In the late 1950s, firearms designer Eugene M. Stoner had completed much of his work on the AR-15 rifle. Stoner had a new idea for a family of weapons based on a single common receiver. Having served as an infantryman in the Marine Corps during World War II, Stoner knew about the needs of a fighting man while in combat.

Eugene Stoner left ArmaLite in 1961, after having spent five years with them designing and refining the AR-10 and AR-15 weapons series. ArmaLite had sold the rights for the production of the AR-10 and AR-15 to Colt, who was going to market them worldwide. Stoner had more than enough of dealing with the U.S. military, especially the Army ordnance boards who seemed determined to keep the .223 caliber AR-15 from entering U.S. service. Instead of continuing with the AR-15, Stoner moved on to develop the ideas he had for a family of weapons.

Having had discussions with Russell Bauer, then president of Cadillac Gage, Stoner joined the company at their Costa Mesa plant in California to design a new family of small arms. One of the appeals of Stoner's idea to Bauer was the less costly approach the design had to making more than one type of weapon. Instead of having to produce tooling for a machine gun and a rifle, the same receiver would be used for both types of weapons.

At that time, Eugene Stoner was raising a family of four. This did not put him in a position where he could do all of the work designing the new weapons system himself, even if he wanted to. To aid him in the new project, Stoner brought along his design team from ArmaLite. Fairchild Aircraft, the owners of ArmaLite, had decided to get out of the small arms business at that time (this decision was later changed). This made Stoner's team of James Sullivan and Robert Freemont available to work at Cadillac Gage. Sullivan and Freemont were greatly able to support and aid Stoner in the development of his new ideas as they had demonstrated with the AR-15 project.

Instead of just having appeal economically for a manufacturer, Stoner's main push for his new weapons system was from the point of view of the end user, the soldier in the field. Instead of having to learn a completely different weapon each time he changed his position in a squad, the individual trooper would only have to learn a single primary weapon to be able to take any position with a minimum of additional training.

The central part of Stoner's idea for what he called a "convertible gun" was the receiver that could be flipped over (reversed) depending on which type of weapon you wanted. In the final design, openings were on the top and bottom sides of the receiver. Attachment points where different trigger, sighting, and feed mechanisms could be secured were next to the receiver openings. A gas tube extended forward from the front of the receiver and there was a empty cartridge case ejection port on one side.

The next most ingenious part of the design was the bolt carrier and piston assembly. The carrier cap at the rear of the bolt carrier could be rotated to lock the firing pin in different positions depending on the effect desired. Used with the carrier cap rotated so that its roller was pointed to the center line of the receiver, the firing pin is free to move. The bolt carrier in this configuration is used in either the carbine or the rifle and is fired by a hammer striking the back of the firing pin when the bolt is in the forward, locked position.

For the machine gun configurations, the carrier cap is rotated and locked into position so that the roller is facing up and out from the center of the receiver. With the carrier cap in this position, the firing pin is locked into place and does not move in relation to the carrier. As the carrier-piston and bolt assembly are driven forward when the weapon is fired, the bolt enters an extension on the back of the barrel where it rotates and locks into place. As the bolt is rotated by a cam pin on the side of the carrier, the firing pin moves forward inside the bolt. When the bolt is fully rotated and locked, the firing pin has moved forward enough to strike the primer in the chambered cartridge, firing it.

The roller on the carrier cap engages a lever in the feed cover for the belt-fed machine gun versions of the weapon. The movement of the bolt carrier and piston assembly moves the roller back and forth at the top of the receiver, where it operates the belt-feed mechanism.

The primary advantage of this complicated operating system is that the Stoner design is hammer fired on a closed bolt in the rifle/carbine configurations and striker fired from an open bolt in the machine gun configurations. This puts the bolt carrier forward, and the bolt in the fully locked position, when the trigger is pulled for the rifle or carbine. At the moment of firing on a closed bolt, the only primary moving parts are the hammer and firing pin. Using this system allows for maximum accuracy with the least disruption of the sight picture for the firer.

For the machine gun, the open bolt configuration is preferred, especially for light weapons such as the Stoner design. In the open bolt system, the bolt carrier is cocked to the rear of the receiver, and held in place by the trigger mechanism. When the trigger is pulled, the bolt carrier is released and driven forward by the operating spring. The bolt strips a round from the feed mechanism, chambers it, locks into place, and then the weapon fires. This open bolt system allows air to circulate through the ejection port and barrel, helping to cool the weapon between bursts. The open bolt also prevents a chambered cartridge from accidentally firing from the residual heat of the barrel (called a cook-off) since there is no chambered cartridge until the trigger is pulled to fire the weapon.

This adjustable system of open or closed bolt gives the Stoner design appeal from an operator's standpoint. The weapon has its maximum accuracy when set to fire as a rifle or carbine. When used as a machine gun, the Stoner design can operate a belt feed system and keep a round from entering a hot chamber until the moment of firing. These parts and systems of operating were the heart of the patent Stoner applied for in March 1963 for what he called his convertible gun.

The original work for Stoner's new weapon was conducted at a small facility at the Cadillac Gage Costa Mesa Plant set up just for Stoner's work. In December 1961, the Arms Development facility at Costa Mesa was established. The first weapon produced based on the convertible receiver system was chambered in 7.62mm NATO and was marked as the Model M69W. There has been no other reason given for this designation except that it reads the same inverted as right side up.

On M69W, serial number 00001, the furniture of the weapon is entirely made of wood and there is no forend to protect the operator from a hot barrel. Intentionally "overbuilt" for development purposes, the M69W has a very heavy barrel and a milled aluminum receiver and trigger group. The M69W passed the endurance trials as a belt-fed machine gun proving out the system. The conversion parts to make the weapon a magazine-fed rifle were never completed. Built as a "tool room" gun instead of as a production weapon, the M69W was a prototype that established that the basic operating principals of Stoner's idea were sound and could be built upon.

The next two weapons built were also designed around the 7.62mm NATO round. These weapons, referred to as the Model 62, were intended to be the production version of the M69W. Using the experience he had developed with the AR-10 and AR-15 weapons, Stoner designed the Model 62 to have a forged aluminum receiver and other major components. Since the bolt of the Model 62 locked into an extension of the barrel, the other major parts of the weapon only had to support and guide the internal parts and were not subjected to heavy stress. The prototype Model 62s had milled aluminum receivers, much like the M69W, to help prove out the design prior to investing in expensive forging dies.

Set up in the rifle mode, the Stoner 62 has the gas tube above the barrel, which is a relatively light, slender unit with an integral flash hider and front sight assembly. The trigger group of the Stoner 62 slides off the bottom of the receiver with the buttstock attached as part of the assembly. The magazine well, which also contains the hammer parts, is removed from the receiver separately from the trigger group. A perforated steel handguard is attached to the front of the receiver to protect the hands of the operator from the heat of firing. The steel handguard has a wooden grip assembly that is attached to it for further operator protection.

For the machine gun version of the Stoner 62, the rear sight assembly is removed and the receiver inverted with the gas tube now below the barrel. The belt feed mechanism mounts to the front of the receiver, secured to the same point where the magazine well of the rifle version was attached. The buttstock and trigger group slides back onto the receiver, with the sear operating through the hole that was covered by the rear sight on the rifle version.

The barrel of the Stoner 62 machine gun is a particularly heavy one, with a full diameter body ending just behind the flash hider. The barrel also has a handle attached to ease the changing of a hot barrel. The front sight is mounted on a dovetail at the opposite end of the front sight post from where it would be in the rifle version.

Changes were made to the action of the Stoner 62 as compared to the M69W to allow for a smoother operating cycle. The bolt carrier assembly was made lighter to allow more power for the feeding of the ammunition belt. The entire system worked well and was demonstrated publicly. Marketing of the new system was just beginning when research changed a major concept of the weapon.

Stoner became convinced that the .223 (5.56mm) caliber that he had first fielded with the AR-15 weapon was the upcoming wave of the future. The cartridge was beginning to be noticed in military circles and some U.S. Services, notably the Air Force and U.S. Advisor groups in Vietnam. Remington had now added the new round to their official product line, identifying it as the .233 Remington. There was one large hole in the arms family represented by the AR-15 rifle, there was no belt-fed machine gun available for the round anywhere. Stoner looked to change this situation and downsized the Stoner 62 weapon system to accept the new round.

By February 1963, the first firing model of the new weapons system had been produced. Now known as the Stoner 63, the new design was of a family of six different weapons, all based on the same receiver and operating system. Using the basic receiver and a kit of parts assemblies, the Stoner 63 could be set up as a closed-bolt firing carbine with a folding stock and short barrel or a full-sized rifle with a fixed stock and long barrel.

Inverting the receiver and changing parts set up a magazine-fed, open-bolt light machine gun, referred to as the Automatic Rifle configuration in later Marine Corps testing. The mag-fed LMG used a top-loaded magazine, much like the British Bren gun, that fed down into the receiver. The sights of the mag-fed LMG were offset to the left so that the operator could aim the weapon past the magazine. The tactical advantages of such a system were that the entire squad could supply ammunition to the gun, already packaged in magazines, from their rifles. Also a very low profile could be maintained by the gunner firing the LMG from the prone position.

Changing the barrel, rear sight assembly, and magazine adapter to a different heavy barrel and adding a belt-feed mechanism top cover, which incorporated a rear sight as part of the assembly, now made the Stoner 63 a belt-fed light machine gun. A plastic box, for which design Stoner received another patent, could be hung from the side of the belt-feed tray. This assembly made the Stoner the only light machine gun at the time chambered for the .223 caliber round and it could also be carried and operated comfortably by one man.

At 11.9 pounds empty with wooden furniture and its bipod and sling at-

This SEAL is keeping watch over his Teammates during a demolition operation in Vietnam. He is armed with a Stoner 63A fitted with a 150-round drum. Additional belts of ammunition are draped over his shoulders. The right-side mounted cocking lever on the machine gun version of the Stoner 63A can be seen just above and to the rear of the operator's left hand fingers. The operating lever was extended back farther on the 63A than the earlier 63 to make it easier to pull back and clear the feed tray and feed drums such as shown here. A spring-loaded cover for the belt link ejection port was also added to the Stoner 63A and it can be seen in this photograph above the cocking lever.

Source: U.S. Navy

tached, the Stoner 63 light machine gun weighed only a few pounds more than the then-standard U.S. infantry rifle, the M14, while offering a much higher volume of fire. The standard M14, issued with six loaded 20-round magazines (120 rounds total), weighed in at 18.93 pounds. The Stoner 63 LMG weighed only 17.83 pounds with 150 rounds attached in its plastic box, a one-pound weight savings while giving the gunner an additional 30 rounds of ammunition.

There is an almost 2:1 difference in weight between the 5.56mm round and the 7.62mm NATO round. An 8-round link belt (M13 links) of 7.62mm NATO have the same weight as a 17-round link belt of 5.56mm. In addition, the smaller round allows for a much smaller and lighter weapon. This was amply demonstrated by Stoner in the new Stoner 63.

Removing the bipod and shoulder stock and attaching a tripod cradle adapter set the Stoner 63 LMG up as a medium machine gun. Ammunition could be fed into the weapon from either the plastic boxes or from a standard M2A1 ammunition can that would hold 800 rounds of belted .223 ammunition in two 400-round belts. With the cradle adapter, the medium Stoner 63 machine gun could be placed on any mount that would accept the Browning M1919A4/A6 or the M60 machine gun. In addition, the quick-change barrel system in the Stoner 63 would allow for a sustained rate of fire to be maintained that was the same as that offered by the M60 machine gun.

For its last form, the Stoner 63 could have its stock, forestock, and pistol grip (if desired) removed and an electric solenoid attached to the trigger and secured to the rear of the receiver. This made the Stoner 63 an electrically triggered fixed machine gun that could be assembled into a pod with an ammunition supply or attached to the outside of a vehicle and fired remotely at the touch of a switch.

The Stoner 63 was unique in the firearms world at the time of its introduction and caused more than a little interest in some military circles. By March 4, 1963, less than a month after the first firing model of the Stoner 63 was completed, an order was received for 25 of the weapons in various configurations. The order, SS-125, was issued from the Office of the Secretary of Defense's Advanced Research Projects Agency (OSD/ARPA). The ARPA people already had a great respect for Stoner due to his revolutionary AR-15 design, which they were pushing forward through the military system. The new Stoner 63 looked like an even more promising design with its multiple applications inherent in the system.

This SEAL operator in Vietnam has attached both a 150-round ammunition drum as well as a 150-round plastic ammunition box to his Stoner 63A light machine gun.
Source: UDT-SEAL Museum

By April 1963, Stoner was showing his new weapon to his previous service. At the El Toro Marine Corps Air Base in California, the first Stoner 63 was demonstrated for Brigadier General Walt of the Marine Corps. The Marine Corps were interested in the weapon as a complete system. The Corps felt a family of weapons with a common basis would give them the same training and tactical advantages that Stoner had considered when he had first come up with the concept of the convertible weapon.

But orders for the new Stoner 63 weapons system were very light during 1963. ARPA had ordered 25 various versions of the Stoner 63 for their tests, and that was the biggest order of the year. In early October 1963, the U.S. Air Force ordered two Stoner 63 fixed machine guns with pods holding the weapons and ammunition for trials. Later that same month, two Stoner 63 machine guns were ordered for testing at Aberdeen Proving Grounds. It wasn't until 1964 that the Stoner 63 was ordered specifically for testing and trials by one of the service branches.

On March 30, 1964, Cadillac Gage received order SS-22 for 60 rifles and 20 complete systems from ARPA, The large order was for weapons to be tested by the U.S. Marine Corps. The Marines had been suitably impressed with the Stoner system and ARPA had agreed with their request to field test the new weapon.

Marine enthusiasm for the Stoner was well received and they took in some of the earliest weapons made. Stoner 63s, serial numbers 00004 and 00005, are still maintained in the Marine Corps Museum's small-arms collection. Springfield Armory also ordered two fixed Stoner 63s during the spring of 1964 for test purposes.

In May, the Aberdeen Proving Grounds report on the Stoner was made to the Army. In July, the Office of the Chief of Research and Development made his report on the Stoner to ARPA. Neither of these reports listed the weapon in glowing terms. This situation is hardly surprising given that the Army had just recently been forced to accept a number of AR-15 rifles.

But the leadership at Cadillac Gage still thought future of the Stoner 63 looked promising. The manufacture of the weapon centered around sheet metal stamping, forming, and precision welding. The California Cadillac Gage facilities were inadequate to the task of mass producing the new weapon but the company also had a manufacturing facility in Detroit where the mechanical support for such manufacture was easily available. Detroit was the center of the automobile industry and the precision forming and welding of sheet metal was a common practice for such manufacture.

In September 1964, after some 234 Stoner 63s had been produced and serial numbered, Cadillac Gage moved the production of the weapon to their facilities in Michigan. The Arms Development and Engineering staff, Eugene Stoner among them, moved to the newly set-up Weapons Manufacturing Facilities in Roseville, Michigan, just north of Detroit. At this time, the wooden stocks and pistol grips on the Stoner 63 were changed. Grips and stocks were now made of polycarbonate plastic, though the forestock for the machine gun configuration remained black-painted wood.

General Wallace Green, the Commandant of the Marine Corps, had been impressed with the idea of the Stoner family of weapons. This may have come about in no small part due to Cadillac Gage hiring a newly retired Marine Colonel who, during the end part of his military career, spoke to General Green convincingly on the advantages such a system offered to the Corps. Colt, at the time, was offering what they called a family of weapons based on the AR-15. But the Colt weapon system, the CAR-15, was made up of specific firearms which could not be interchanged easily. This did not meet some of the advantages of the Stoner 63.

The situation did start to look very good for the future of the Stoner 63 system in 1965. On April 23, 1965, the Army Weapons Command put in an order for 861 Stoner weapons in various configurations for testing as part of the new Small-Arms Weapons Systems (SAWS) program. Within just a few days of this purchase order being issued, the Marine Corps Landing Force Development center (MCLFDC) test report was delivered to Marine Corps Headquarters.

The MCLFDC report recommended the Stoner 63 for further, more advanced, field testing. This report helped fuel the enthusiasm for the Stoner 63 among the Corps Command and Marine Corps Commandant General Wallace Greene in particular. This situation was not well received by the Army Weapons Command who strongly disliked the new AR-15 rifle over the M14 rifle. For the Army, it was now looking like the Marine Corps was going to push for another, completely different, .223 caliber weapon that also could compete with the still-new M60 machine gun.

On December 20, 1965, the Marine Corps put in an order for 1,080 Stoner rifles as well as the parts necessary to assemble other configurations of the weapon. Extensive testing of the Stoner system by the Marine Corps did indicate some weaknesses in the system that needed correction. In the first several months of 1966, these weaknesses were identified and brought to the attention of Cadillac Gage.

While the modification problem was being addressed, the Marine Corps continued their testing of the Stoner 63 system. Results from the field were varied, but in general, the weapon system was well liked by many of the men employed in testing it. Substantial tactical and logistical advantages were found in using the system by the evaluation groups. Testers included one rifle company, a platoon of the division reconnaissance battalion, and a platoon of the force reconnaissance company.

One almost immediate change to the fielding of the Stoner weapons system during evaluations was the dropping of the automatic rifle configuration. It was found that the automatic rifle was the least dependable of all of the Stoner 63 configurations. This was due to the top-loading magazine feed used in the automatic rifle. It was found during Marine testing that every time the automatic rifle was loaded, any sand, dirt, or foreign material in the magazine was poured directly into the receiver. With the open bolt of the automatic rifle configuration, this material jammed the action causing an unacceptable number of stoppages.

The remainder of the Stoner 63 weapons system was evaluated by the Marine Corps during March, April, and May 1967. A comparison testing of the new M16E1 was conducted by the same test groups during June and July of that same year. Test results were tabulated and the report made at the end of August that same year.

Testing showed the Stoner rifle had the advantages of weight, accuracy, improved ammunition, and compatibility with other weapons (the balance of the 63 system), when compared to the standard M14 rifle. The Stoner rifle was found to have a lower reliability than the M14, but this problem was considered correctable with modifications. The difference in reliability between the Stoner 63 and the M14 was not considered significant when considering the overall advantages of the entire system. When compared to the M16E1, the Stoner 63 Rifle was found to be more accurate, more reliable, and had a family of weapons that it was compatible with.

The Stoner light and medium machine gun configurations also received high recommendations by the majority of Marine testers. The Stoner light machine gun was considered a suitable replacement for the automatic rifle configuration in the Marine rifle squad. The LMG and MMG were found to be highly reliable when compared to any other machine gun in the Marine testing environment.

And the Marine testing was extensive. Boot camp trainees were issued with the Stoner and completed their training cycle with it, in the process scoring higher during weapons qualifications than any comparable Marine unit. Stoners were taken into limited combat in Vietnam, where the design was proven to be accurate and reliable in the jungle environment.

The results of the first major Marine Corps evaluation of the Stoner 63 weapons system were very positive. In the words of the evaluation committee:

> 3. The basic conclusions of the evaluation are that the Stoner family of weapons provides substantial tactical and logistics advantages. There are some relatively minor modifications required prior to acceptance but none of these appears to create any problem. The system received a high degree of acceptance from personnel involved.
>
> 4. The Stoner Weapons System is strongly recommended for adoption.

Some of the difficulties with the Stoner 63 had been addressed by Cadillac Gage prior to the evaluations being run by the Marine Corps. The order for evaluation weapons put forward by the Marine Corps in December 1965, had been filled with the available Stoner 63s. The redesign of the Stoner 63 to the

Stoner Model 63A was completed in March 1966. Changes from the Stoner 63 to the 63 A configuration include:

    a. Larger gas port opening
    b. Chromium plated chamber
    c. Stronger and better fitting dust covers
    d. A relieved breech block cam pin
    e. A gas nitrided bore
    f. Separate safety in front of trigger guard
    g. Feed tray machined casting instead of stamped metal
    h. Three position gas port valve
    i. Redesigned stock and forearm of polycarbonate material
    j. Three piece cleaning rod fitted inside of forearm
    k. Endurion metal finish on all exposed surfaces
    l. Bipod locks onto weapon or locks open for stowage
    m. Right side belt feed mechanism available, exchanges w/left side feed
    n. Over-the-shoulder assault sling available
    o. Upper sling swivel attached to front of barrel handle

The removable trigger guard of the Stoner 63, intended for using the weapon when wearing gloves or mittens and easily lost during testing, was replaced with a permanently attached trigger guard. The size of the plastic ammunition box that could be hung onto the side of the light machine gun was reduced from 150 rounds to 100 rounds. It was found that the larger box was easily struck by the user's leg when patrolling and could be knocked off the weapon.

Other changes to the system included replacing the folding stock of the carbine with a wire folding stock that had considerably fewer parts. The cocking handle of the Stoner 63 was the same for all of the weapons in the system. A perforated length of handle with an outward curved end extended along the side of the handguard, right over the gas tube. On the rifle/carbine versions of the Stoner 63, this handle was on the upper left side of the weapon, above the forestock. On the machine gun versions, the cocking handle was at the lower right side of the weapon, just behind the forestock.

For the rifle and carbine versions of the Stoner 63A, the cocking handle had been completely changed from the original. A small lug had been welded onto the operating rod, several inches behind the piston head. The new cocking handle was located on top of the receiver, over the barrel and handguard, where it could be reached by the operator with either hand easily. The new cocking lever rode along a slot cut into the receiver, just below the gas tube, and engaged the lug welded onto the operating rod. A plunger in the center of the operating handle could be pushed down by the operator and used to push the bolt forward to assist it to close.

For the machine gun versions of the Stoner 63A, the cocking lever engaged the new lug on the bottom of the operating rod, but was otherwise in the same place as in the earlier system. The machine gun cocking rod had been made longer so that it could be more easily reached.

The feed cover of the machine gun had been improved in both strength, manufacture, and function. The cap carrier had been redesigned to include a spring plunger mechanism. In the Stoner 63A, the feed cover could be closed with the bolt in any position while in the Stoner 63 the feed cover could only be closed with the bolt in the cocked position to insure no damage to the weapon.

Another change to the feed system of the Stoner 63A was the development of a drum carrier for the ammunition belt. The final drum design would hold a 150-round ammunition belt securely to the bottom of the weapon and feed the belt in smoothly while firing. The drum was made of spun aluminum to keep weight to a minimum and was securely attached to the receiver of the 63A.

To help keep the system from being jammed by excess dirt, spring-loaded covers were placed over both the ejection port of the receiver and the link ejection port on the feed cover. The ejection port cover on the receiver would spring open and remain that way as soon as the bolt carrier moved. The cover over the link ejection port only opened when a link was being ejected and otherwise remained closed.

The gas tube of the 63A was made from 17-4 PH stainless steel to minimize corrosion and giving the new tube a silver outside finish. The inside of the gas tube of the 63A was remachined to prevent carbon build up from jamming the gas piston. This allowed the 63A to fire for longer periods of time between cleanings of the gas system. From roughly serial number 2,000, all Stoners produced by Cadillac Gage were built as 63As. No changes were incorporated in the markings Cadillac Gage stamped into the receivers of their Stoners and all weapons remained marked "Stoner 63".

The large number of improvements in the Stoner 63A system made the weapon of even greater interest to the Marine Corps. On October 3, 1966, Cadillac Gage received an order from the Marine Corps to modify 286 weapons to the new 63A configuration. The new weapons were scheduled for extensive testing under combat conditions in Vietnam. This combat test series was to be completed by May 31, 1967.

On March 3, 1967, a further order was received from the Marine Corps, this one for an additional eight weapons to be converted to the 63A model. These additional weapons were intended for further testing under controlled conditions to confirm the field trial results. The tests did confirm what had been determined by most of the Marine users. The Stoner 63A was considered suitable for Marine Corps use without further testing.

Cadillac Gage received a further order from the Marine Corps on April 19, 1967, for ammunition linking systems and spare parts for the overseas support of the 286 63A systems in Marine Corps hands. But shortly after this order was received, the Army Weapons Command declared the Stoner 63 and 63A to not be acceptable for issue at the time.

Without much fanfare, all of the Stoners in Marine hands were to be turned in. The Army was still interested in the Stoner 63A as a light machine gun, but only as a low-priority project. Army tests of the Stoner to approve the system for procurement were considered extremely biased. But for whatever reason, the question of the Stoner in Marine hands was over by the middle of 1967.

Earlier in 1967, a new military unit became interested in the Stoner 63, primarily as a belt-fed light machine gun. The SEALs were entering a new stage in their direct actions in Vietnam. SEAL Team Two was just starting to deploy platoons for combat in Vietnam at the end of January 1967. Maximum firepower in a minimum package was a prime concern to the SEALs. On January 17, 1967, the U.S. Navy Test Station ordered eight Stoner 63 light machine guns for testing in combat by the SEALs.

Within a month of the new Stoners being received by the Navy, they were sent out to the SEALs in Vietnam. The limited number of weapons available resulted in only one Stoner being shipped to each deployed platoon. Though the Stoner was known for requiring regular maintenance for consistent functioning, the weapon was well received by the SEALs.

Second and Third Platoon each received one of the two Stoners that arrived from [SEAL] Team Two. The weapons we received were the early Stoner 63 model with long barrels, black wooden foregrips and black plastic buttstocks. . . .

All-in-all, we liked the Stoners for the additional firepower they gave a squad. But the weapon was temperamental, especially the first Stoner 63s we received.

You had to keep the Stoner clean and take good care of the weapon if you wanted to depend on it.

Some of the guys in the Teams didn't like the Stoner because of the amount of care you had to give it. Other operators liked the lightweight little machine gun so much that it was their primary weapon. These guys lavished care on the gun and would carry a Stoner whenever they could . . .

SEAL TEAM ONE—COMMAND AND CONTROL HISTORY—1967
SPECIAL TOPICS
(B) PERFORMANCE OF WEAPON SYSTEMS
The Stoner system malfunctioned frequently, but the problem has been eliminated to a certain extent by the proper indoctrination of personnel on the gas system of the weapon. The Stoner system performs well when properly cared for and is the most effective automatic weapon for SEAL Team operations. The weapon itself is sufficiently light that the automatic weapons-man can carry a realistic combat load of ammunition and still move with relative ease.

There were a number of difficulties with the new weapon being fielded in the Teams. But in general, the Stoner fit the need for a light weapon with high firepower nicely. One of the more unusual problems the operators had with the Stoner was a certain lack of ammunition. Though the Stoner fired the same .223 round the SEALs had in abundance for their M16s, the Stoners required linked ammunition. Though a limited supply of prelinked ammunition was supplied, packed in 150-round plastic ammunition boxes that could be hung on the Stoner, the majority of the Stoners ammunition had to be supplied "locally."

What came with our Stoner in the way of ammunition was a container of loose links. The Stonerman carried an empty sandbag to try and recover the links whenever he could. Most of the time, stopping to collect loose fired Stoner links was anything but possible, especially when someone was shooting at you and most of the guys didn't even try. But we did recover the occasional handful of links and had a fair supply of new ones. After a mission, a bunch of us would be sitting around the ready room, having a beer, swapping stories and relinking ammunition by hand. . .

The special S-63 link for the Stoner came packaged in a small cardboard drum that held thousands of links. The link was very much a reduced-size version of the M13 link used with the M60 machine gun but was unique to the Stoner weapons system. There were more problems with the Stoner 63 for the SEALs than just policing used links and loading belts. It was very much a case of one service not talking to the other that resulted in the SEALs having many of the same problems with their Stoners as did the Marine Corps when they tested the system. One of these problems centered on the plastic ammunition box used to carry rounds mounted on the weapon.

The only real problem with the side-mounted belt box was that it was in exactly the right position to get hit by your right knee as you walked along. The ammunition boxes became a real pain-in-the-ass early on. Only four boxes came loaded with belts in an ammunition can and we didn't receive very much in the way of preloaded ammunition belts in the first place. So the boxes were something you had to hang on to whenever you could . . .

In spite of the minor difficulties run in to while fielding the new weapon, the Stoner soon earned itself a solid position in the SEALs' armory.

As we said in Vietnam, the Stoner had "boo-coo" fire power and "tee-tee" weight. A lot of bullets without a lot of weight. . .

We had a Stoner light machine gun with the platoon and that was also a good weapon for us. It took some care to keep it working but the Stoner would put out a lot of fire for its weight and was well worth the extra time it took to clean and maintain. . .

In spite of this reception in the Teams, the Stoner 63 required a good deal of improvement before being fielded in quantity. When the second platoon of SEAL Team Two returned from Vietnam after their first deployment, a series of recommendations were listed by the platoon officers and men. Included in these recommendations was a very specific one directed to the Stoner;

EXCERPT FROM SEAL TEAM TWO, 2ND PLATOON'S VIETNAM
OPERATIONS, 30 JANUARY TO 30 MAY 1967
Weapons and Equipment
    8. Use of the Stoner LMG is not recommended until the drum magazine becomes available.

The plastic box used to attach a supply of ammunition was considered just too difficult to use in its available form. Hanging as it did one the side of the LMG, when the box was knocked off by an operator's knee, the ammunition belt would just trail out of the box into the mud. This was only one of several recommendations taken into account by the Navy when they ordered additional Stoners for the SEAL Teams. On May 25, 1967, Cadillac Gage received a phone call from the Naval Ordnance Test Station requesting a delivery date for 36 additional Stoners. All of these weapons were to be 63As in the light machine gun configuration and equipped with the 150-round drum magazines.

The Stoner machine gun had become a stock item in the SEAL armory by the middle of 1967. Several hours were dedicated to the weapon, its use, and its maintenance during pre-deployment training for Vietnam. Each deploying SEAL platoon now had at least two Stoners, one for each squad, with more desired. SEALs who demonstrated a penchant for the weapon were usually allowed to carry one. These SEALs were often referred to as Stonermen in later recounting of particular actions. For the weapon itself, SEAL Team One was the primary unit for developmental items and the Stoner was secure on their list for attention:

SEAL TEAM ONE—COMMAND AND CONTROL HISTORIES 1967,
ENCLOSURE 3, (J) RESEARCH AND DEVELOPMENT, PG 13–14
A listing of special procurement actions completed is summarized below:
(#22) Stoner 63A
(#28) Stoner Drum Magazine
(#29) .223 Linking Machine for Stoner Ammunition

The new drum for the Stoner made the weapon considerably more dependable while moving. An ammunition belt was secured in the drum and held underneath the receiver, close to center of balance of the weapon. Early experiments by Cadillac Gage in 1966 had resulted in a small 100-round drum, but this device was quickly dropped as impractical. The first model drums were made of spun aluminum and had a double-pinned bracket that secured them to the bottom of the receiver at the back of the forestock and front of the trigger group.

The double-pinned drums were secure, but very difficult to reload without taking them completely off the weapon. The second model drum was secured by a pin to the rear of the forestock where it was free to pivot. The rear portion of the drum mount had a lug that fit under the magazine catch on the front of the trigger group. This model drum could be unlatched and swung down for reloading without having to completely dismount the drum from the weapon.

The drum was mechanically very simple, not much more than a round container with a removable back. A 150-round belt would be coiled together in a counter-clockwise spiral and inserted into the back of the drum with the bullets forward. The loose end of the belt would be slipped up the guide located on the left side of the drum. The back of the drum would then be secured in place with its twist latch and the ammunition supply for the Stoner would be ready for use.

A stamped-metal cover was hinged at the outside, top of the feed guide on the left side of the drum. This cover could be folded back, exposing a short length of the belt. A somewhat fragile spring clip was on the side of the drum's feedway to help keep the loose belt from slipping back into the drum.

Individual SEALs developed their own manner of carrying ammunition for their Stoners. Since the drums were relatively slow to reload during a patrol, the loaded drum would be kept secured for use while moving on patrol. When set up for an ambush, another method would be used to feed the Stoner.

SEALs would often carry their extra supply of ammunition belts slung across their shoulders and crossing the chests and back like bandoleers. Sometimes, an extra T-shirt was worn over the belts, keeping them out of the worst of the dirt and mud and preventing them from shining. On getting into a fixed position, such as an ambush site, the belt in the drum of the Stoner would be taken out of the feed tray and left hanging from the drum.

A loose belt of ammunition from the SEALs "bandoleers" would be piled next to the weapon, possibly on a piece of cloth or gear to keep it out of the mud, and loaded into the weapon. In case the SEAL with the Stoner had to break cover and move out, it was a simple matter to snap the end of the drum's belt onto whatever belt was left in the feed tray.

Unlatching the magazine release allowed the empty drum to swing down until the back cover was free of the weapon. Turning the cover latch would remove the whole back of the drum. To reload the drum in the field, a SEAL could reach to his bandoleers of belts and break the link connection between any two rounds.

Keeping the loops of belts in 150-round-or-shorter lengths made the next step in reloading a drum relatively easy. The SEAL would pull out his loose belt of ammunition, wrap it clockwise around his finger, and slip it into the back of the drum. feeding the end of the belt up the feed chute, securing the cover, and snapping the drum back into place underneath the weapon allowed the fresh belt to be loaded into the receiver.

Modified standard ammunition pouches were able to carry a full 150-round plastic belt box and a Stonerman could attach as many pouches to his harness as he wanted. A number of the guys took to carrying extra Stoner belts across their shoulders like bandoleers worn by the revolutionaries in old Mexico. I found that exposed belts carried Pancho Villa–style tended to pick up jungle crud and get all crappy, possible causing a jam when you needed all of your firepower the most. I also thought the belts made a nice X for Charlie to aim at . . ."

A strap around my shoulders supported my Stoner within easy reach. For ammunition, I would feed the weapon from either a 150-round drum or with 100 round plastic belt boxes. When I carried a drum, I would drape several hundred rounds in belts around my shoulders like Mexican bandoleers. During an ambush or whatever, I would save the ammunition in the drum and feed from a loose belt. The drum would be saved in case we had to move quickly and break contact. Probably, I used the plastic ammunition boxes the most as they were the easiest to reload from.

There were 150 rounds in the drum of my Stoner and I carried an additional five hundred rounds Pancho Villa–style, in criss-crossed belts around my body . . .

Other SEALs made additional modifications to their weapons to fit them to the individual's taste. No changes were allowed that could jeopardize the dependability of the weapon, otherwise it was up to the individual SEAL. When the Stoner 63As arrived at the two SEAL Teams, they were accompanied by a number of complete systems for the weapons. Though the primary configuration of the Stoner used by the SEALs was as the belt-fed light machine gun. At least two SEALs used other configurations.

These SEALs found the carbine configuration of the Stoner to their liking. The only magazines supplied with the Stoner systems held a full 30 rounds of ammunition. This larger magazine capacity was considered a big plus by the SEALs who knew about it. The standard M16 magazine at that time (1967) held 20 rounds. The larger 30-round M16 magazines were available, but were very scarce in the SEAL Teams in 1967 and 1968. The short, handy, Stoner 63A carbine, with its folding stock and 30-round magazine was the only other configuration of the Stoner system to see any use by the SEAL Team in Vietnam.

One reason that the Stoner system didn't see wider use with the SEALs in the carbine or rifle configurations was the limited number of 63A receivers that had been purchased by the Navy. Eventually, all of the available weapons were set up as belt-fed light machine guns. But some of the conversion parts were still put to use by the SEALs. At least one Stonerman attached the vinyl-covered tubular steel (referred to as the wire type) folding stock of the carbine configuration to his Stoner machine gun. This made for a very compact package of firepower, even though the folding stock wouldn't secure properly to the side of the weapon.

STONER 63 WEAPONS SYSTEM KIT CONSISTS OF 1 EACH (MINIMUM) OF:

- Basic receiver group
- Fixed buttstock (rifle or machine guns [all but fixed])
- Folding buttstock (carbine)
- Forestock (all machine guns but fixed)
- Rear sight assembly (carbine and rifle)
- Magazine adapter and forestock assembly (carbine and rifle)
- Magazine adapter w/offset sight assembly (mag-fed LMG)
- Belt feed group w/rear sight (all belt-fed machine guns)
- Carbine barrel assembly (carbine)
- Rifle barrel assembly (rifle)
- LMG barrel assembly w/offset sight (2) (mag-fed LMG)
- Machine gun barrel assembly (2) (all belt-fed machine guns)
- Machine gun barrel assembly w/o sights or carrying handle (fixed machine gun)
- Bipod (all but carbine and fixed MG)
- (6 or more) 30-round magazine (rifle, carbine, mag-fed LMG)
- Cradle adaptor (all machine guns)
- Solenoid and trigger linkage (fixed machine gun)
- Canvas spare barrel bag w/
    - Barrel assembly (either mag or belt fed)
    - Cleaning rod
    - Barrel (bore) brush
    - Chamber and receiver brush
    - Gas cylinder brush
    - Combination tool/carbon reamer

In spite of the good reception the Stoner received from the SEALs, there were still a number of problems with the design that had to be worked out.

Most of these details developed from the SEALs' experience with the weapons. The SEALs also gave their Stoners a lot of hard usage, so even with the careful maintenance they received, weaknesses showed up faster with the Teams than they would have with other units.

> The Stoner was a particular piece that we suggested a lot of modifications for. After our return to the States, a lot of our suggestions were adopted into a new version of the Stoner. I really loved the weapon, not much heavier than a large rifle, say a fully loaded M14, but the Stoner carried lots of bullets. But the weapon was sensitive, it needed a lot of care and maintenance and there were some bugs still to be worked out.
>
> On one op, I had caught this guy just dead to rights, we're talking black pajamas and all, a bad gook without question. I was carrying the Stoner with a 150-round belt drum attached. With the VC in my sights, I pulled the trigger and click!
>
> The plastic foregrip, up underneath the barrel where it attached to the metal, had cracked from all the usage we had given the weapon. With the plastic cracked the way it was, the bolt couldn't go all the way forward and the weapon wouldn't fire. My target got away that day. But things were all right, we wrote a nice letter to Cadillac Gage saying "Hey you've got to fix this because this sucks. There's no lead coming out of the son-of-a-bitch."
>
> SEAL TEAM TWO—COMMAND AND CONTROL HISTORIES 1968,
> ENCLOSURE 1, SPECIAL TOPICS, PG 9
> The Stoner LMG has been modified due to suggestions submitted from members of SEAL Team TWO who have used the weapon in combat.

Cadillac Gage was very responsive to the SEAL requirements for modifications to the Stoner 63A. Feedback from the field resulted in a number of minor changes to the weapon. The only difficulty with the company response to the input from the Teams was the gradual changes in the parts to the Stoner system. It soon became hard for anyone not very familiar with the differences between the Stoner 63 and the 63A and the Team's requested modifications to the 63A to make sure the correct parts went into the correct model guns.

But during the Vietnam era, such problems of commonality of parts were not a difficulty for the SEALs. Operators who preferred the Stoner made sure that their weapons operated correctly. And this testing was conducted constantly during predeployment training. This made sure that any problems were corrected long before any specific Stoner went into combat.

One problem with the Stoner centered on the basic design of the weapon and took a major change to correct it. The ejection port on the Stoner was on the left side of the weapon when set up in the light machine gun configuration. Feeding from either the plastic box hanging from the feed tray or the 150-round drum caused a jam known as "spin-back."

Sometimes when firing, an ejected cartridge case would strike the box, or more often the drum, and bounce back into the receiver. The empty case would block the bolt going forward and stop the weapon from firing until it was cleared. This problem did not happen constantly, only about 1 or 2 percent of the time when the weapon was fired. This spin-back problem was serious enough to require correcting.

Moving the ejection port of the Stoner was out of the question as that would require a major change in the receiver and a number of internal parts. Instead, the direction of feeding was changed from the left side of the weapon to the right. The right-hand feed involved replacing the feed cover and feed tray but eliminated being able to use the drum magazine. SEALs who found that their individual Stoner either didn't have spin-back problems or liked the drum enough to accept the occasional jam stayed with the left-hand feed. Others used the new right-hand feed mechanism and a new method of feeding a belt.

SEAL TEAM ONE—COMMAND AND CONTROL HISTORIES
1969, ENCLOSURE (2) (C) 6, RESEARCH AND DEVELOPMENT
2. SEAL Team ONE is in the process of being supplied with a new type of feed system for the Stoner Weapon, that practically eliminates the danger of shell spinback which was one of the major causes of malfunctions.

    c. LINKING MACHINE FOR 5.56MM BALL AMMUNITION— Provides a portable linking machine for 5.56 MM Ball ammunition as used by the Stoner 63A weapon system. One unit is now in SEAL Team [ONE].

Along with the right-hand feed mechanism was a new method of loading the Stoner 63A with the 100-round plastic boxes. The hanger was a device that fit underneath the center line of the receiver, in the same position the belt drum was in. A plastic ammunition box could be slipped into the hanger where it would be held securely and the belt fed into the weapon. The box hanger system went through a number of variations with only one design seeing widespread use.

The box hanger that became standard issue was a right-hand feed system that held a single 100-round ammunition box horizontally across the underside of the receiver. The belt fed up a covered tray and into the feed cover. A spring-loaded latch was on the inside of the hanger's feed tray to keep the belt from slipping back into the ammunition box when the weapon wasn't firing. This latch helped cut back on the strain on the feed mechanism.

A new style of quick-detachable mount was used to hold the standard box hanger in place underneath the receiver of the weapon. A spring-loaded plunger was squeezed to release the front latch, which fit over the forestock holding pin. The rear of the quick-detach mount had a curved protrusion that fit over the front pin of the trigger group. This box hanger only worked with a right-hand feed top cover and feed tray. But other systems were tried.

Both China Lake and Cadillac Gage made a variety of box hangers and drums to try and come up with the best ammunition holding system for the Stoner. Some left-hand feed box hangers were made, but these had the same spin-back problems as the drum. A 250-round belt drum was made in limited numbers at China Lake for testing by the SEALs. But the Stonermen who tried the 250-round drum found it was too large and unbalanced the weapon, making it clumsy to handle.

Other box hangers were tried that held 150-round plastic ammunition boxes or secured the ammunition belt under a long cover, hinged at the bottom. None of these systems found the acceptance of the right-hand feed, 100-round belt box hanger.

But with the belt box hanger came another new problem with loading the Stoner 63A. The cocking lever for the machine gun versions of the Stoner 63A was still in the same location as the lever for the earlier 63 model. The cocking lever had been made longer on the 63A, and was more secure to use. But the box hanger and the right-hand feed interfered with the operator easily reaching the cocking handle to charge the weapon. The feed tray of the box hanger would block much of the cocking lever so that the operator could only reach the lever with one or two fingers.

To ease the cocking lever problem, a solution was taken from the carbine and rifle configurations of the Stoner 63A. The forestock for the Stoner 63A machine gun was modified with a wide, six-inch-long slot cut in the bottom center of the handguard. The protruding rod cocking lever of the carbine and rifle versions was modified by removing the center plunger and installed under the barrel of the machine gun, fitting through the slot in the bottom of the handguard.

Now a Stoner gunner could use either hand to pull back the cocking rod, easily charging the machine gun with whatever feeding system the weapon might be mounted with. Some operators found the protruding cocking rod to be a little short for their comfort. A piece of tubing forced over the rod of the cocking piece would extend it several inches and satisfy the operators who thought it too small.

The size and weight of a weapon was always a consideration in the Teams. Even with its light weight, the SEALs wanted the Stoner to be made even more compact if possible. Using the carbine configuration barrel as a starting point, Cadillac Gage designed a short, heavy machine gun barrel for the SEALs in 1968.

This short barrel was heavier and larger in diameter than the carbine barrel, but was the same overall length. To cut down on the weight of the short machine gun barrel, the outside was fluted with six deep flutes cut lengthwise into the steel. The flutes removed some weight and increased the surface area of the barrel, allowing it to radiate heat better and cool quicker.

Referring to the new barrel as their "commando" model, Cadillac Gage began supplying the new part to the SEALs in 1968. The short barrel also had a gas port selector underneath the front sight, but this selector only had two settings. The commando barrel could be slipped onto any SEAL Stoner 63A, removing 6.25 inches of length and about 1.56 pounds of weight.

A short commando barrel, right-hand feed top cover, and 150-round drum, assembles a Stoner 63A into what is considered the "classic" SEAL Stoner configuration. Most of the 63As in SEAL hands were modified with the new cocking system and the new right-hand feed mechanisms. The short commando barrel

A group of SEALs sharing a cigarette with a Vietnamese civilian, possibly a guide, at a U.S. helicopter base in South Vietnam. The SEAL to the right is armed with an XM177E2 submachine gun which he has slung across his shoulder with a length of cord. The XM177E2 is loaded with an early fully-curved 30-round magazine. Besides wearing Levi jeans and an inflatable UDT life vest, this SEAL has on a set of M1956 load bearing equipment with universal ammunition cases at each hip. The two SEALs to the left in the photo are both carrying Stoner 63A1 light machine guns with short barrels. The SEAL at the front of the picture has his Stoner loaded with a 150-round aluminum belt drum with the back of the drum secured with adhesive tape. The drum-fed Stoner has a left-hand feed mechanism. The other Stoner is set up with a right-hand feed and is loaded with a 150-round plastic belt box hanger held horizontally underneath the weapon.
Source: U.S. Navy

had some difficulties in operating the Stoner in certain environments. With the very short section of barrel, actually just the flash hider, in front of the gas port (underneath the front sight) there is very little residual gas pressure to operate the action of a Stoner fitted with the short barrel. The longer standard barrel maintained a higher gas pressure for a longer time when the weapon was fired. This allowed for a greater level of energy to be available to operate a dirty or sluggish action.

But a number of SEALs swore by the new short barrels and made sure that their Stoners remained as clean and well lubricated as possible. The advantage of the short commando barrel was that it made a compact weapon even smaller and easier to handle in the close brush and jungle. Some SEALs made the Stoner an even more compact weapon for close-in use.

> . . . my favorite configuration of the Stoner was the short barreled version with a 150-round drum attached and the stock removed. This gave me a loaded weapon that weighed only 16 pounds and was a fraction under twenty-seven-inches long. Slinging my Stoner around my neck on a piece of line, it would hang ready for use just in front of me and was very well balanced indeed. . .

The short commando barrel, right hand feed, and 100-round box hanger completed the final version of the SEAL Stoner. This weapon resulted from the input of the SEALs having used the Stoner in combat for almost two full years. In this final form, the Stoner received a nomenclature assignment by the Navy as the Mark 23 Mod 0. The original request for the nomenclature was submitted on March 14, 1969, the Mark number assigned on October 31, 1969, and the final approval made on December 4, 1969. The description of the weapon on the assignment request was:

> Gun, Machine, 5.56 Millimeter, Mark 23 Mod 0 . . . is a gas operated 5.56MM automatic weapon using disintegrating metallic belts, belt fed, fires from the open bolt position, has a quick change barrel, with right hand twist rifling (6 grooves) one turn in 12 inches, fires 700 to 1000 rounds per minute, with a muzzle velocity of 3256 feet per second. Giving a maximum range of 2895 yards (2653 meters), the maximum effective range is 1203 yards (1100 meters). The overall length is 40.25 inches. The gun empty weighs 11.68 pounds. Manufactured by Cadillac Gage Company, Roseville, Michigan. Company designation is 5.56M light machine gun, belt fed, Stoner 63A.

The nomenclature assignment fit both the long- and short-barreled Stoner, with either the right or left hand feed. All Navy purchases of the Mark 23 Mod 0 were of the short-barreled, right-hand feed versions with the 100-round box hanger. The Mark 23 was offered by Cadillac Gage to other military customers as the "Commando machine gun."

The correct nomenclature of the final configuration of the SEAL Stoner becomes difficult at this point. The Mark 23 Mod 0 Stoner was referred to as the Stoner 63A in most Cadillac Gage literature and this was the designation used by SEAL Team Two.

Receiver markings on the Stoner series had not significantly changed during the entire production run except for the address of the company. All Cadillac Gage Stoners were marked "STONER 63 .223 CAL." just in front of the serial number. All of the modifications requested by the SEALs and incorporated as a whole in the Mark 23 resulted in significant changes in the weapon. Both SEAL Team Two and Navy documentation refer to the Mark 23 as being known commercially as the Stoner 63A1.

NWM of Holland had licensed production of the Stoner weapons system for sale in Europe. Only a handful of the Dutch weapons were produced, reportedly on about 60 U.S.-made receivers. These weapons were advertised in a September 1969 booklet produced by NWM and titled the Stoner 63A1 Weapons Modifications. The machine gun configuration illustrated in the booklet, identified as the XM207, was identical to the Mark 23 except for an NWM designed bipod and mount and a long barrel.

The most numerous Stoners in SEAL hands were the Mark 23/63A1 weapons purchased by the Navy in 1969 and 1970.

SEAL TEAM TWO—COMMAND AND CONTROL HISTORIES 1969,
ENCLOSURE 1, VI NEW EQUIPMENT, PG 14
4. (U) During the year, the Team received twelve new Stoner 63A1 light machine guns which, although they are only half the operational quota requested, will help provide each platoon with greater firepower in the field.

SEAL TEAM TWO, COMMAND AND CONTROL HISTORIES 1970,
ENCLOSURE 1, VI. NEW EQUIPMENT, PG 12
3. (U) Twelve new Stoner 63A1 light machine guns were received. Each deployed platoon now has two of these weapons per squad.

Estimates according to available documents puts the number of Stoners purchased outright by the Navy at 8 Stoner 63s, 36 Stoner 63As, and 48 Stoner 63A1s (as Mk 23s). Additional Stoner receivers and systems may have been transferred into the Teams from the stocks of Marine weapons that had been turned in to storage.

With the final acceptance of the Mark 23 machine gun, no further purchases were made of parts for the Stoner 63s that were in inventory or accessories that would fit the earlier weapons. This means that drums gradually became harder to find for those SEALs who preferred that method of loading. Though the drums were simple and had few parts, the method of securing the rear cover with a twist latch was subject to wear. This resulted in an increasing number of drums being sealed with tape prior to going out on an operation. This made reloading the drums very difficult in the field.

As a field-expedient solution, a number of SEALs modified a mount for the Stoner that would accept the ammunition drum from the Soviet RPD machine gun. The Soviet RPD used a stamped steel drum to contain a 100-round nondisintegrating metal belt of 7.62×39mm ammunition. The drums were commonly found in munitions caches and were available to the SEALs in some numbers.

Each RPD drum would hold a 150-round belt of Stoner ammunition easily and feed it smoothly into the weapon. The quick-detachable mount portion of an ammunition box hanger could be removed by simply cutting away two rivets. A sheet metal extension would be locally fabricated and secured to the mount with two screws. The addition of a twist latch, such as used on a screen window, completed the mount. The RPD drum mount would fit underneath a Stoner and could be set up to feed into either a right- or left-hand feed weapon. In addition, an empty RPD drum was easily and quickly exchanged for a loaded one to reload the weapon.

Throughout the Vietnam War, the Stoners were demonstrated to be a useful addition to the SEALs arsenal. But this didn't come without a cost. Technical training on the Stoner weapons system was increased to help minimize problems with the weapon.

SEAL TEAM TWO—COMMAND AND CONTROL HISTORIES 1969,
ENCLOSURE (1) V. PREDEPLOYMENT TRAINING
Some members of deploying platoons . . . received special training in the maintenance and use of the Stoner 63A1 light machine gun and the M16A1 rifle. The machine gun instruction was administered by the manufacturer of the weapon, Cadillac Gage Company, Detroit, Michigan

Any new weapons system has to go through a development process to locate and eliminate errors in the design. Sometimes these errors were located with little more than some difficult incidents for the operator.

That [Stoner] design was good, although we did have a couple of embarrassing moments with the Stoner barrel disconnecting from the receiver when you needed it most.

The quick-disconnect barrel of the Stoner was held in place with a push-button latch just in front of the feed cover. With the bolt cocked, the only thing holding the barrel in place was the barrel latch. If the latch had been depressed accidentally, such as while moving through brush on a patrol, as soon as the trigger was pulled, the forward-moving bolt had as good a chance of pushing the barrel off of the weapon as it did of firing the cartridge it had stripped from the belt.

But some malfunctions with the Stoner had more serious results. Within a few weeks of the weapons arriving in Vietnam for the first time in early 1967, there was an accident with Second Platoon of SEAL Team Two involving a Stoner.

DET. ALFA 2ND PLATOON LOGBOOK-MY THO (30 MAR 67) PG 5
11 Apr 67—. . . . 2210H Gallagher, R—, & C—left site for pick-up. G—shot thru finger right [right ring finger] while attempting to un-jam Stoner. 6 rds. ran wild.

While on a night op on 11 April. . . . G—was the one who took the hit from the Stoner and not one of the enemy. When one of the guys attempted to un-jam the squad's Stoner, the weapon malfunctioned and ran wild, firing about six rounds uncontrollably. When the Stoner went off, G—took a bullet right through the ring finger of his right hand.

Though the accident wasn't a good one, G—wasn't hurt too badly. He still had his finger, though an infection set in and he was told to take it easy for a while until his finger healed.

The accident was a relatively simple one and involved unfamiliarity with a new weapon more than a flaw in the design. G—was not injured severely and was rejoining the platoon on operations within a relatively short time. At other occasions, there were accidental discharges of a Stoner that were never completely explained.

152045Z MAY 68 [15 MAY, 1969] GAME WARDEN SPOTREP 05/16/1/116.3.0.1/1
2. 160330H Sqd B inserted by STAB XS452426 While halted for FC check
Stoner machine gun fired one rd. 160345H extracted by STAB
    5. No US or friendly casualties. Preliminary investigation reveals that wpn
was on safe and that the bearers firing hand was clear of the trigger assembly.
Wpn being disassembled additional report will follow.

Little was learned on the accidental discharge of that single round during
that patrol. Later in that same tour, another accident took place involving a
Stoner, this one with more serious consequences. While test-firing a Stoner
aboard a small boat, one SEAL operator put an entire drum of 150 rounds
through his weapon with little difficulty. Reloading the drum and weapon with
another belt of 100 rounds, the SEAL gunner continued to fire in bursts. After
about 30 rounds had gone through the weapon, the Stoner jammed and would
not clear with simple immediate action (drawing the bolt back and recocking
the weapon).

Opening the cover of the jammed Stoner, the SEAL noticed an unfired
round stuck underneath the bolt, between the piston rod and barrel. Working
the bolt did no good in clearing the jammed round. While working the operating handle, the stuck round suddenly fired.

The SEAL was peppered with unburned propellant in his stomach, chest,
face, and right eye. Startled, the SEAL threw his hands up to his injured eye and
the unsecured Stoner went over the side of the boat. The SEAL was not seriously
hurt and was able to continue operating with his platoon within a week. The
Stoner was another question entirely. With the SEAL's test firing session taking
place in a free-fire zone, they were apparently under observation by the VC
when the accident took place. Concerned with the injured SEAL, the unit returned to base to seek aid for their Teammate. When the SEALs returned to the
free-fire zone, the lost Stoner could not be located.

The lost Stoner did turn up some months later, in a VC weapons cache
found by the Army in a sweep in I Corps on January 17, 1969. An Army Captain, Mark Gwinn, Jr., took the weapon, a long-barreled Stoner 63A with left-
hand feed, 150-round drum, and side-mounted cocking lever, and began trying
to get parts and ammunition for it. Scrounging a new barrel, links, and other
parts from the SEALs, Captain Gwinn took the corroded and pitted Stoner and
proceeded to use it in combat for some time. Eventually, the Stoner was returned to SEAL Team Two, not without some protest from Captain Gwinn who
very much liked the weapon and wanted to see it adopted by the US Army.

When we received the Stoner at Little Creek, the weapon was still fairly screwed up. Parts were rusted and it was obvious it had not been taken care of while the VC had it in spite of what Captain Gwinn had tried to do in the way of repairing the gun. After spraying the weapon with WD-40, we took it to the range and it fired fine, no problems. Probably the only reason the VC hadn't used it while they had it was that they couldn't get any linked 5.56mm ammunition. Our Stoner men were still picking up their links whenever they had the chance.

In spite of the general opinion the SEALs had about the Stoner, there had been some serious incidents with the weapon. One incident in particular almost resulted in the Navy dropping the weapon entirely. To field-strip the Stoner for cleaning, one step in the procedure is to remove a takedown pin found just above and behind the pistol grip, With the takedown pin withdrawn, the receiver can pivot up and away from the stock and trigger group. This allows the bolt and internal mechanism of the Stoner to be withdrawn.

With the Stoner machine gun operating from an open bolt and the sear which holds the bolt in the cocked position part of the trigger group, separating these parts with the bolt cocked will release it to drive forward. If there is a round in the feed tray, the weapon will fire. If there is a belt in the feed tray, the weapon will continue to fire uncontrollably until either the belt runs out, or the bolt flies out of the back of the partially opened weapon. Something very close to this situation happened to a squad of SEALs from SEAL Team One while inserting on an operation.

Mike Platoon of SEAL Team One was operating in the Kien Hoa province of Vietnam, having moved down into the Mekong Delta area from the Rung Sat Special Zone just a short time earlier. On April 29, 1968, the platoon was moving in for an insertion from a Mark 4 landing craft. The trip to the insertion point was an uneventful one up to a point. The SEALs were relaxing aboard the boat as was normal prior to an operation. One SEAL, Walter Pope, was armed with a Stoner 63A fitted with a 150-round drum. The Stoner was up, leaning against the side of the armored landing craft as the unit moved along the waterway.

It was never determined exactly what happened next, but the sudden results were that Pope's Stoner fell over on its side as it began firing wildly. According to witnesses, Pope had not been touching the weapon when the incident began, but suddenly the Stoner was firing uncontrollably.

Frank Toms, reclining nearby, was half asleep when the accident happened.

He was suddenly awakened when he was struck with an estimated 6 to 10 bullets from the runaway Stoner. Walter Pope dove onto the firing Stoner and pulled it into himself to stop the firing and protect his teammates in the boat. Pope took an estimated 40 rounds from the Stoner but prevented any one else from being struck with the ricocheting rounds bouncing around inside the armored boat.

First Class Boatswain's Mate Walter Pope was killed instantly, but saved his fellow SEALs in the boat. Frank Toms recovered from his wounds. The intense investigation that followed could only come up with the most probable reason the accident occurred. The takedown pin on the trigger group of the Stoner at that time was retained by its own friction and a small spring detent in the pin itself. It is thought that the vibration from the boat's engines and pitching of the craft in the water worked the takedown pin free of Pope's Stoner.

Sitting as it was, muzzle up, the force of gravity as well as the spring tension inside the cocked weapon would have combined to separate the two parts of the receiver, releasing the bolt to drive forward. In this situation, the weapon would have continued firing until it had jammed or run out of ammunition.

As far as Frank Toms is concerned, Pope's actions that day saved his Teammates and is deserving of the highest award that can be given. The SEALs were in immediate contact with Cadillac Gage about the incident, how it happened, and how to prevent it from ever happening again.

The pivot pin that held the feed cover to the receiver of the Stoner was secured in a different manner than the detent-held takedown pin. The pivot pin is made of two parts that screw together securely, and are further held together by a spring detent inside the body of the pin. It takes the point of a bullet to release the detent and then the two parts have to be unscrewed before the pin can be removed.

This pin was immediately supplied by Cadillac Gage to the Teams in sufficient quantities to replace all of the earlier pins in service. The field stripping procedure on the Stoners with the new pins took a little longer, but the accidental discharge of a weapon due to the receivers separating didn't happen again.

The Stoner was not the only light machine gun used by the SEALs in Vietnam, but it was the signature weapon. All production of the Stoner ceased by 1971 and Cadillac Gage closed the records on the weapon system in 1973. The Stoner remained in the SEAL inventory until the early 1980s. By 1983, the last few Stoners remaining in SEAL hands were removed from active duty due to a lack of parts and support to maintain the weapons in operating condition.

The Stoner wasn't the best weapon the SEALs have ever used, but it was the best thing available during most of the Vietnam War and we put it to some hard use.

The difficulties with the Stoner weapons system did not cause the SEALs to drop the weapon. But the Teams were constantly on the watch for new ordnance that would fit their needs.

Colt had tried to enter the market for a .223 caliber light machine gun in 1964–65 with their CMG-1 (Colt Machine Gun 1). Only prototype quantities of the CMG 1 were ever produced. The design was considered to have too many faults to be corrected economically and the design was dropped without extensive testing by any of the Services.

By 1967, Colt's interest in a belt-fed .223 machine gun was renewed with the desire for such a weapon being voiced by the U.S. military. Henry J. Tatro and George F. Curtis at Colt set about designing a new weapon in November 1967, drawing on the CMG-1 program and the Army SAWS tests for guidance. An 18-pound test fixture was ready for firing by June 1968. A total of some 40,000 rounds were expended through the test fixture during development.

A prototype model of the new CMG-2 was begun in August 1968 and test firing from the new weapon were able to begin in March 1969. The test model of the CMG-2 incorporated all of the basic design features demonstrated in the test fixture but in a lightweight and handy weapon. No military proposals voicing a need for such a weapon as the CMG-2 had been issued by the military and Colt had absorbed the entire R&D costs in hopes of starting a new market.

Firing demonstrations of the CMG-2 prototype were conducted by Colt for the U.S. Army, Marines, Air Force, and Navy, running from March 1969 to May 1970. International demonstrations were also conducted after the weapon had been shown to U.S. agencies. In March 1970, the Navy Ammunition Depot people at Crane, Indiana informed Colt that they were interested in testing the CMG-2 in their own facilities.

Colt supplied Crane with several weapons and they conducted extensive tests for endurance, functioning, accuracy, and dependability in various climates. Some minor modifications were suggested to Colt by Crane and were incorporated into three CMG-2s built by Colt for the Navy for use by the SEAL Teams.

The design of the Colt CMG-2 is a relatively simple and straightforward one. The weapon is gas operated with a quick-change barrel and feeds from a flexible disintegrating metallic link belt as is used in the Stoner 63A weapons system. The CMG-2 is ambidextrous, ejection of empty brass being straight down from the receiver, making it suitable for right- or left-handed shooters or firing positions. A modified M14 bipod could be attached to the gas tube of the weapon for firing in a supported, prone position.

The most unusual feature of the GMG-2 was the method of cocking the weapon. Above the rear pistol grip of the CMG-2, part of the fire control group, are two levers. The front lever, just above the trigger, is the safety lever which locks the sear into position, preventing the bolt from being released. The rear lever, above the back of the pistol grip, is the fire control group latch.

Depressing the fire control–group latch releases the entire mechanism so that the group can be pushed forward along the bottom of the receiver with the firing hand. When the fire control group has reached the fully forward position, it can be drawn back, bringing the bolt and operating rod with it. When the fire control group reaches its rearmost position, the release latch snaps back into position and the bolt remains in the cocked position, ready to fire.

The CMG-2 fires from the open bolt position. The bolt and operating rod have a long travel in the weapon, eliminating the need for an extensive buffer mechanism and making the recoil of the CMG-2 very light. A second, forward handgrip gives the operator a solid, two-handed grip on the weapon. The light recoil, combined with the inline recoil design and twin pistol grips, makes the Colt CMG-2 one of the most accurate and easy-to-control weapons of its type ever.

A total of three CMG-2 weapons were provided to Crane over the time period of June to August 1970. The weapons were modified according to Crane's suggestions and turned over to the SEALs for testing in combat. At least one CMG-2 in SEAL Team Two hands did go over to Vietnam for at least one deployment. On April 26, 1971, the CMG-2 was submitted for a nomenclature assignment. Identification of the CMG-2 and the Gun, Machine, 5.56 Millimeter, EX 27 Mod 0 received final approval on May 7, 1971. The item description was as follows;

> This weapon is identified by the manufacturer as the Colt Machine Gun, Model 2 (CMG-2). It is a light weight gas operated; air cooled machine gun utilizing the 5.56 Millimeter cartridge in disintegrating metallic links. The cyclic rate of fire is approximately 650 rounds per minute. It may be fired from the shoulder or the hip. By either right or left hand gunners. The weapon is equipped with a quick change barrel and a detachable bipod for ground firing.

The weight of the weapon without bipod is 13.5 pounds. The bipod weighs 1.56 pounds and the magazine "empty" weighs 1.57 pounds.

The magazine, or belt drum, of the CMG-2 was of an unusual design. Fitting under the center point of the weapon, the drum magazine had a long helical feed chute spiraling up and back out of the left rear side. The cover of the drum magazine was held by a sliding snap catch that positively locked into place. The feeding end of the belt would be slipped down the helical feed chute into the body of the magazine. Slipping the end of a link into the arbor at the center of the drum and turning it would draw a belt smoothly into the teflon-lined drum. This involved loading method insured the feeding belt would leave the drum correctly but was far too difficult to be done in combat. Also, the helical chute from the back of the drum magazine made carrying spare drums very awkward.

In spite of these relatively minor drawbacks with the drum, the EX 27 was well liked by the few SEALs who used one in combat. But the Colt weapon had been supplied at a time when the war in Vietnam was just winding down. Only a few SEAL platoons were even deployed to Vietnam while the EX 27 was available. After the war, no funds were available for the purchase of new weapons by the SEALs. Colt ceased manufacture of the CMG-2 after only 25 were ever built. On 16 November, 1982, the nomenclature assignment of the EX 27 was canceled.

Only the Stoner and the M60 machine guns were used in any large numbers by the SEALs in the field. Other machine guns were in use for close-in support, firing from various boats, small craft, and ground mounts. The .50 caliber M2 HB was the most common of these support machine guns, being mounted on every kind of small craft and vehicle. Besides the M60, there were several other 7.62mm NATO caliber machine guns commonly encountered by the Teams.

With the U.S. Military switch from the .30-06 round (.30 M2) to the 7.62mm NATO round in the late 1950s, stocks of the old .30 caliber rounds were no longer updated. The U.S. Navy investigated converting a number of its small arms on hand, notable the M1 Garand, to using the new round without a major remanufacture. The Browning M1919A4 was also examined and converted to the new caliber. Along with the caliber conversion, the feed system of the Navy M1919A4 was altered to operate with the M13 link as used in the M60 machine gun.

The Navy 7.62mm NATO conversion of the Browning M1919A4 was assigned the nomenclature, Gun, Machine 7.62 MM, Mark 21 Mod 0. The only visible external difference between the Mark 21 and the earlier M1919A4 was the long, slotted, flash hider mounted at the end of the perforated barrel jacket on the Mark 21. The Mark 21 served as the last of the Browning .30 caliber designs in frontline service with any U.S. military. The most common place the SEALs ran across the Mark 21 was as one of the gunwale mounted machine guns on the BSU "Mike" boat.

On board the Mike boat was a number of .50 caliber M2s and several of the Mark 21s lining the sides of the craft. Between the first missions of the Mike boat in 1966 and the last ops in the early 1970s, the armament of the Mike boats changed. Mounted small arms varied but usually included a number of .50 caliber and one or two 7.62mm machine guns. In 1970, the #1 Mike boat mounted two .50 caliber M2s in a gun tub, six more .50s lined the sides of the craft, and two M60 machine guns were mounted at the stern of the boat.

The M60 gradually replaced the Mark 21 in all Navy ships, including the small boats used by the SEALs. A new type of M60, the M60D, had been developed for use in helicopter gunships as door guns. The M60D was modified by having its front handguard removed, the rear sight replaced with a folding circular "speed" ring. And a new rear grip mounted in place of the shoulder stock.

The rear grip of the M60D resembles that of a .50 caliber M2 HB in that it has two vertical "spade" grips. In front of each grip is a curved trigger bar that is connected by a linkage to the modified trigger mechanism. The M60D could be fired like a .50 caliber, with the operator directly behind the weapon. Quick to bring on target and easy to aim, though less accurate due to the open rear sight than a standard M60, the M60D would mount in any pintle socket that would accept the earlier 7.62mm/.30 caliber guns.

M60 helicopter door guns were gradually completely replaced by the M60D, which could be converted from a standard M60 though the use of a simple kit. The later model STAB Mark II would mount a number of the M60D guns as well as other arms. STAB Mark IIs, now known as Strike Assault Boats, carried as many as five or more M60Ds, feeding from 1,500-round ammunition cans. The M60D has remained in the SEAL inventory, as used by the Special Boat Squadrons, to this day.

One unique aspect of the mounted M60 as used by the Navy was feeding the weapon from a large ammunition container. Helicopter door guns would also be fed from as large a container of ammunition that could be handled by the gunner. To help feed the M60s with these long belts, an interesting field modification was done. A small green C-ration can, 2.5 inches in diameter and a little over 3 inches long, would be attached to the left side of the M60, secured to the receiver, just below the feed tray. The empty can was found to straighten and level a belt of ammunition just prior to entering the weapon. This simple modification greatly increased the reliability of the M60 when used with long ammunition belts.

Another 7.62mm machine gun was used by the SEALs in Vietnam, one with probably the longest pedigree of any machine gun in the U.S. inventory. Shortly after the Civil War had begun in 1861, Doctor Richard J. Gatling invented a mechanical repeating weapon that he thought would be so efficient, it would eliminate the need for large armies. Without the large army, so many men wouldn't have to suffer during a war.

Gatling's idea was to take a series of complete weapon actions and assemble them around a central axis. The use of a hollow cylindrical receiver body surrounding the actions with a cam cut into it to guide the bolts would serve to move the bolts back and forth. The lateral motions of the bolts would complete the steps of loading, locking, firing, unlocking, and ejecting as the central axis turned, carrying the barrels and bolts with it. The motive power for this system would be provided by the gunner turning an out side crank.

This revolutionary weapon quickly became commonly known as the Gatling Gun. Though few Gatlings were used during the Civil War, the design was considerably changed and refined by Dr. Gatling during the postwar years. The Gatling Gun soon became known throughout the world of the late 1800s as a very destructive weapon that could mow down attacking troops like so much wheat.

When the fully automatic machine gun first appeared, it was not considered as reliable as the Gatling. As the designs of new machine guns

By the looks of the well-worn camouflage face paint and dirty uniform, this SEAL is coming back in from a combat patrol. He is wearing an M1 steel helmet and an M69 flak jacket. These items were not normally worn on a patrol by the SEALs as they did not float and could quickly weight a man down when crossing water. Under the M69 armor, this SEAL is wearing a standard UDT inflatable life vest.

Across his lap is a Mark 23 light machine gun in the most standard configuration.

Source: U.S. Navy

progressed, they soon superseded the Gatling in front-line use. Well prior to WWI, the Gatling had been moved to second-line service. By 1911, the Gatling Gun was declared obsolete by the U.S. Army.

It was in the post-WWII years that the idea of the Gatling Gun was resurrected. The speed of modern jet aircraft had quickly become so fast that pilots had barely seconds at best to fire at an enemy aircraft before it moved from their sights. Modern automatic weapons did not have a high enough rate of fire to put out many projectiles in the split seconds of air-to-air jet combat. A new type of weapon was required.

In the early 1890s, Gatling Guns with electric motors were experimented with by the U.S. Navy and other interested parties. With an electric motor, Dr. Gatling was able to fire at rates approaching 1,500 rounds per minute. This high rate of fire was not needed at the time and the electric Gatlings were soon dispensed with. But ordnance engineers in the 1940s remembered these experimental weapons. In early 1946, a Model 1903 45-70 Gatling Gun borrowed from a museum was set up with an electric motor drive and test-fired. The 90-year-old design reached speeds of 5,000 rounds per minute for a short time.

Further studies of the action determined the Dr. Gatling's original operating principals could reach even higher rates of fire than the tests had already proved. In June 1946, a contract was issued to the General Electric Corporation to design a weapon based on the Gatling multibarrel design that would reach a minimum rate of fire of 1,000-rounds-per-minute per barrel.

The designs were studied and worked on for several years. In the interim time, several design parameters were changed including adding another barrel to the original five-barrel requirement. A firing model of the new T45 was ready by April 1949. The prototype fired at rates of 2,500 rounds per minute for short times. Further work resulted in fire rates of 4,000 rounds per minute by June 1950. By 1952, the original caliber of the weapons, an experimental .60 caliber round, was changed to 20 millimeters. The new 20mm gun multibarrel was to be identified as the T171E1.

Thirty-three 20mm T171E1 weapons were produced by General Electric between 1953 and 1955. The T171 weighed in at 365 pounds and fired 20mm ammunition at a rate of 4,000 rounds per minute. Further design changes geared toward a production weapon were incorporated in the new model, the T171E2, in 1954. Problems with the breech of the T171E2 resulted in more changes to stiffen certain portions of the weapon. In April 1956, the T171E3 had been completed which had all of the improvements of the earlier designs. Development of the new weapon was considered complete by December 1956 and production was begun at a low rate. By December 1957, the T171E3 was designated the M61 Vulcan cannon and production speeded up.

The M61 Vulcan could fire 20mm explosive ammunition at rates of 6,000 rounds per minute. The basic design of the system was still centered on Dr. Gatling's multiple barrels and actions revolving around a central axis. A helical cam path operated the bolts throughout the cycle. As long as the barrel turned, the bolts moved back and forth in their rotor tracks (slots). Feeding of ammunition was accomplished by an external feeder attached to the receiver of the Vulcan and driven by a gear arrangement connected to the main drive system.

The Vulcan was considered one of the most dependable and safe 20mm cannons in existence. If a round misfired, it would be extracted and ejected outboard, away from the weapon. No interruption in the cycle of the weapon would take place since the system was not dependent on the firing of a round to operate. Other designs followed the success of the Vulcan, with the new weapons increasing and decreasing in caliber.

In 1960, General Electric began looking into adapting the Vulcan design into a .30 caliber externally powered machine gun. Models of the new weapon were developed at GE's cost, with the thought that the new weapon would have good military potential. One major change centered in the design of the bolts.

The bolts of the Vulcan lock directly into the end of the barrels for various mechanical reasons. The smaller version of the Vulcan didn't require such a locking system. The bolts to the new weapon were made in two parts, one (the bolt body) camming a twisting motion into the other (the bolt head). As the bolt head rotates and locks into place, the firing pin is cammed and released, firing the percussion primer of the ammunition.

The U.S. Air Force became interested in the new design and issued a contract for prototype guns and aircraft gun pods to be developed. By December 1962, the new weapon, christened the Minigun, was ready for test firing. The first gun pod (the SUU-11/A) was ready within a year and was demonstrated to the Air Force in November 1963. Extensive testing of the new Minigun was conducted by the Air Force and Springfield Armory. Redesigns were completed by General Electric to eliminate problems in 1964.

The final design of the Minigun was of a six-barreled weapon that could fire at various rates up to 6,000 rounds per minute. The rates of fire were modified by either changing the motor which drove the Minigun, or by changing the gear ratio in the drive train between the electric motor and the weapon. The Minigun has fixed-headspace, quick-change barrels and the entire weapon could be stripped down to its essentials easily.

An external feeder takes standard, M13 linked 7.62mm NATO (M60) ammunition and strips the rounds from the links. The feeder dumps links outboard and loads the incoming rounds into the receiver. The feeder can also stop feeding rounds into the Minigun before the barrels have stopped rotating. This allows any ammunition in the weapon to be cleared from the gun when the trigger is released.

A new application of the Minigun was soon tested after the final design was completed. Mounting three Minigun pods in the body of a C-47, pointing out the left side of the aircraft, created a new kind of attack aircraft. The new AC-47 Gunship could fly over a target on the ground, bank and turn the aircraft, and fire the Miniguns into the target. The new application of the Minigun was devestating in tests.

By December 1964, the new AC-47 gunship design was in combat in Vietnam. The new gunships were nicknamed "Puff the Magic Dragon" after the popular song of the period. The Viet Cong likened the aircraft to dragons breathing fire at the ground and simply called them Dragon ships. For many SEALs, their first introduction to the Minigun was due to a Dragon ship.

When that AC-47 gunship banked over the target on her left side, I could see why the VNs held the craft in almost superstitious awe. The three 7.62mm Miniguns pointing out of the side of the plane poured out their fire with a thrumming roar. The Miniguns fired so fast that the sound wasn't recognizable as a weapon. It sounded more like a long, deep note from a gigantic bass fiddle, or maybe the roar of a flying dragon.

Each of the Miniguns would spin its six barrels, spew ing out steel-jacketed death at a rate of 6,000 rounds a minute. Eighteen-thousand rounds a minute would pour from the side of the plane, every fifth round a tracer. The tracers would burn out before hitting the ground from Spooky's altitude of 3,000 feet.

Looking up from the ground, all you could see in the darkness was a moving black shape against the stars, licking down at the ground with three long fuzzy red tongues of flame. In a single pass, Spooky could cover an area the size of a football field in three seconds, putting at least one bullet into each square foot of ground.

. . . we arrived at Da Nang, Vietnam, just in time for a fire fight. The fight was going on all around us and the Cobra gunships and Spooky were working the area near the base . . .

Watching from a distance, the effect was neat. You would see this red light extend down from the sky and lick at the ground and then disappear as its tail left the plane and went down. Then you would hear the noise of the guns firing. Not the sound of a regular machine gun. The Miniguns fired so fast the sound blended together into one long WHAAAAAAA. It looked like some kind of laser tag was being played with the VC. It was strange and a very strong first impression of Vietnam.

The SEALs were impressed from early on as to what a Minigun could do from an aircraft. By the summer of 1967, the Teams were receiving some Miniguns to use in a more direct manner. Two Miniguns were supplied to the SEALs in mid-1967 for installation in SEAL support boats in Vietnam.

G—, F—and I took some training on a new weapon that we were going to take with us [on deployment]. The minigun is a six-barreled 7.62mm machine gun that could fire at very high rates of fire. A manufacturers rep from General Electric showed us the weapon and made sure G—and I knew how to take care of it. Changing the motor would give us different rates of fire, [2,000 or 4,000 rounds a minute]. . . . .Taking it out to the Bay, we fired the Minigun at some floating oil drums in the water. Didn't hit anything but it sure looked impressive. The plan was to mount the weapon on the Mike boat working out of Me Tho. The Minigun's firepower would do well for covering our withdrawals."

The Miniguns were placed in modified gun tubs in the two converted Mike boats used by the Boat Support Unit in Vietnam. The Miniguns gave the Mike boats a major force multiplier for the close-in support of SEAL units. The gun tub on the Mike boat was elevated enough to fire over the heads of deployed SEAL patrol. When a SEAL patrol came under enemy fire, the Minigun had an effect on the enemy unlike any other weapon available.

At our direction, the [Mike] boat's Minigun opened up and that was all she wrote. That Minigun just hosed down the countryside, chopping down small trees and cutting grass like a lawnmower.

The psycological effect of incoming fire from a Minigun was devestating on the Viet Cong, or anyone who was on the receiving end. Reports had come out of Vietnam that enemy snipers would ignore incoming .50 caliber machine gun fire and would continue firing on U.S. forces. As soon as a Minigun opened up on those same snipers, they immediately broke contact and moved away as fast as possible.

The bright red streak of the tracers from the Minigun, coming in at such a fast rate they appeared as a fuzzy line, also added to the mental impact of the weapon. SEAL and BSU gunners who used the Minigun developed a strong confidence in their weapon; the enemy who faced the Minigun feared it just as strongly.

The SEALs had a great deal of respect for the firepower the Minigun gave them. But the supply requirements for the Minigun in terms of ammunition, electric power, and secure mounting prevented the weapon from being as available as the Teams would have liked.

> The little six-barreled GE Minigun could put out a whopping 6,000 rounds per minute, that's one hundred rounds per second, when firing on its maximum rate. When mounted in a gun tub with a useful amount of ammunition, such as was put into the Mike boat, the Minigun was a major firepower multiplier. But the ammunition and power supply requirements of the Minigun just made it too impractical for us to put it aboard the STABs

The Brown Water Navy also liked the Minigun and modified the forward gun tubs of several Mark II PBRs to accept the weapon. Field tests of the Minigun on board a PBR gave the weapon high marks for firepower. But the heavy punch and range of the twin .50 caliber M2s normally mounted in the bow of the PBR were found to be generally more useful in knocking down bunkers and other targets. Relatively few PBRs received the Minigun mountings in Vietnam. The weapons remained popular and were officially accepted by all of the services. The 7.62mm Minigun was adopted by the Air Force as the Gun, Automatic, Universal (GAU) 2-B/A. The Army adopted essentially the same weapon as the M134 and the Navy gave the Minigun the nomenclature Machine Gun Mark 25 Mod 0.

In February 1970, the Navy took steps to develop a mounting system for the Minigun that could be supplied to the new Medium SEAL Support Craft being deployed to Vietnam. Nine systems were to be made by the summer of that same year. The Minigun weapons system was to consist of four major units: the weapon with a drive motor and delinking feeder, a suitable ammunition storage system that could deliver a large quantity of ammunition to the weapon, a secure and flexible mount, and the power and control system.

By early June 1970, the new Minigun mounting systems were ready for testing. No difficulty with the system was found, but a new problem unique to the use of the Minigun was found. The large amounts of ammunition fired though a Minigun resulted in an equally large amount of empty 7.62mm brass and a equal number of links. Collectors for the ejected brass and links were designed and added to the system. By July 29, 1970, the nine Minigun systems were shipped out to Vietnam.

The Minigun systems were mounted on the stern of the MSSCs. The idea was that the firepower of the Minigun would be most useful when breaking contact with the enemy. The system was very successful in combat, all components working satisfactorily and the weapon providing a major piece of firepower.

On December 12, 1971, the new Minigun mount was put in for a nomenclature assignment which was approved by March 13, 1972. The new mount was referred to as the Mount, Machine Gun, Mark 77 Mod 0. The mount would carry a single Mark 25 machine gun and a 3,000-round belted ammunition supply. Batteries included with the mount would not only power the weapon, they would also drive a booster motor that helped move the large quantity of ammunition to the gun.

The firepower of the Minigun was not matched by any other weapon in the post-Vietnam years. Mark 25 Mod 0 Miniguns remain in active use in the SEAL Teams and as part of their support in the Special Boat Squadrons. Additional members of the multiple-barrel weapon family have been developed in larger calibers, including .50 caliber and 25mm and 30mm cannon. A number of Miniguns had been produced in almost miniature form as the 5.56mm XM214 Microgun. The Microgun was found of limited application when examined by the Teams, and only twenty or so of this model Minigun were ever built. The larger caliber weapons have been used by supporting forces working with the Teams. All of these weapons were developed from the same basic source, the M61 Vulcan cannon and the Gatling Gun before it.

After the SEALs removed their last operating platoon from Vietnam in 1972, the entire U.S. military went into a draw-down of forces. Few funds were available for necessary training exercises and cut backs were taking place throughout the military, including the Navy SEALs. Few new weapons were available to the Teams in the middle to late 1970s. Vietnam-era issue weapons were maintained and kept in operational condition, though the end of many of the small-arms manufacturing programs made parts increasingly hard to find. This was part of the cost of the SEALs using nonstandard weapons.

The basic machine gun of the SEALs remained the M60 with the Stoner Mark 23 as a backup during the balance of the 1970s. The M60 was still modified by the Teams to make a lighter and handier package, but these modifications primarily consisted of removing the bipod. By the end of the 1970s, a new mission had begun developing for the SEALs which would have a great deal of impact on its arms and equipment.

International terrorism and attacks on U.S. interests abroad increased during the 1970s and into the 1980s. The military was tasked with developing new units and methods of combating terrorism. With the country under the guidance of a new administration, funding for the military was increased allowing some of the new counterterrorism units to be able to obtain new weapons and equipment that was unavailable to the military at large.

SEAL Team Six was the new SEAL Team commissioned specifically to combat terrorism. The U.S. Army Unit, Special Forces Operational Detachment Delta, commonly known as Delta Force, had been in existence for several years before the new SEAL Team was fully operational. Delta Force had already been working with foreign counterterrorist forces, most notably the British Special Air Service and the West German GSG-9 group. Feedback from these organizations influenced both the U.S. Army and Navy counterterrorist units as to training, equipment, and weapons.

The general family of weapons preferred by the majority of the world's counterterrorist units center on those produced by Heckler & Koch of West Germany. The basic operating system of the majority of the H&K weapons is the roller-delayed blowback system pioneered in Germany during World War II. The MG 42 machine gun was the first fielded weapon to use the roller-locking system in which two rollers on either side of the bolt are forced into recessed in the receiver as the bolt come up to its fully forward–firing position.

The rearward thrust of the firing round in the chamber of a roller-locked system drives the bolt backwards, where it is delayed by the rollers held in the receiver cutouts. The rollers work at a mechanical disadvantage, where the force of the bolt has to first push the rollers against an incline and back into the bolt carrier body. The disadvantage the rollers have to move at allows the projectile of the fired round to leave the barrel and pressure to drop to safe levels before the rollers have cleared their locking recesses. From this point back, the weapon acts as a normal blowback system.

This roller-delayed system was further refined in another wartime German weapon, the Stg 45(m) produced by Mauser in 1945. After the war ended, the design of the Stg 45(m) was taken to Spain where it evolved into the CETME assault rifle. Having been returned to West Germany in the 1950s, the CETME design was rechambered for the new 7.62mm NATO round by the new Heckler & Koch company. The new rifle was tested and adopted by the West German Army as the G3.

Further weapons were based on the proven G3 design, notably a family of 9mm submachine guns, the MP5. Other designs included the HK21 light machine gun, developed in 1961 as a companion weapon to the G3. The HK21 fired from the closed bolt and was selective fire, one of the few belt-fed machine guns in the world with this capability. In addition, the HK21 would accept all of the major accessories developed for the G3 including removable telescopic sight mountings. Changing the belt-feed mechanism, barrel, and bolt assembly would change the HK21 from a 7.62mm NATO weapon to one firing the 5.56mm round.

The barrel change on the HK21 was very fast, based much on the earlier MG 42 barrel-change system, and could be done without protective gloves by the gunner without changing his firing position. But it was the basic accuracy built into the HK21 that gave it appeal to first the Delta Force and later to SEAL Team Six.

The Teams had been familiar with one of the HK machine guns since the mid-1970s. The HK23A1 was a dedicated, 5.56mm light machine gun specifically produced by H&K for the U.S. Squad Automatic Weapons (SAW) trials in the early 1970s. The HK23A1 was eliminated from the competition early on, but not due to any major flaws in the design according to H&K.

Changes in the quality of ammunition and damage caused by excessive disassembly and incorrect reassembly had caused the HK23A1 to fail a number of the SAW competition's tests. H&K did take the HK23A1 to additional military units in the United States after correcting the problems caused by the SAW tests. One of these units was SEAL Team Two who examined the weapon in the mid-1970s but had to turn it down as there were no funds for new weapons purchases.

The new SEAL Team Six did not have the same restrictions placed on its equipment purchases that had plagued the other Teams in the late 1970s. The HK21 was fielded by SEAL Team Six in very limited numbers during the first years of its existence. A later version of the weapon, the HK21A1, which had a removable feed mechanism that could be switched from a belt-fed to a magazine-fed system, was also examined. A later design, the HK23A1, chambered for the 5.56mm round only was tested but not fielded. The primary difficulty with the HK21 and HK23 weapons were their weight and lack of accuracy when fired on full automatic.

The high rate of fire of the HK weapons, combined with their fairly abrupt recoil impulse, took away much of the accuracy that was otherwise inherent in the system. SEAL Team Six maintained some of the weapons in its inventory throughout the 1980s, but continued to look for other machine guns to fit its needs. Several members of SEAL Team Six preferred the HK21 and continued to use it even when other weapons were available.

The M60 machine gun remained the standard belt-fed machine gun in the U.S. forces throughout the 1980s. Hard usage in Vietnam had demonstrated some drawbacks to the M60. The weapon was heavier than it had to be and some parts were more prone to break than others. Built for production, the M60 just hadn't proven itself as tough as earlier designs. An official product-improvement program was begun in the early 1980s, funded from both the Navy and the Marines.

The basic objective of the upgrade program was to increase the reliability and durability of the M60 while also decreasing its weight. All changes and new parts were to be acceptable to weapons that were already in service as well as new production. Saco Defense, the prime contractor for the M60, took the offered contract and began the redesign program.

New developments in metallurgy and design allowed the new parts to the M60 upgrade to be stronger and have more wear resistance than the original. Design features of the M60 which had been long questioned were either changed or done away with entirely. The new barrel was lighter in cross section, had a smaller flash hider much like the version used on the M16A1, and has an adjustable front sight. The new barrels could be zeroed at the front sight so that each barrel issued with a weapon would shoot to the same point from the same rear sight setting.

The gas system which had given so much trouble with inexperienced users had been redesigned so that it could not be assembled incorrectly. In the original design of the M60, the gas piston could be put in backwards and the weapon would shoot, but only a single shot and the bolt would remain forward. The new gas piston could be installed either-end first and still operate correctly. In addition, the new gas system took less volume of gas to operate and was much simpler in overall design.

The bipod was removed from the barrel and mounted to the receiver, just in front of the handguard. A carrying handle now on the barrel instead of the receiver allowed a gunner to change a hot barrel without needing an insulated glove. Two different lengths of barrel were made available, one the same length as a standard barrel and the other a shortened barrel close to the same length as the Vietnam-era "chopped" M60 barrels.

The wide forestock of the M60 was replaced with a pistol grip stock that was smaller and lighter than the original. The rear buttstock and trigger group were also replaced with lighter versions made of reinforced Zytel plastic. The feed cover was redesigned as was the bolt and operating rod. Parts now had an operational life of up to 150,000 rounds.

The new upgraded M60 was designated the M60E3 and was adopted by both the Navy and the Marines in 1983. By 1985, all of the Marine Corps M60s had been converted over to the M60E3 configuration. The Navy purchased numbers of the new M60E3s including 1,384 in 1986, 1,807 in 1987, and 257 in 1988. First priority for the new weapons went to the SEAL Teams. The SEAL M60E3s were used almost exclusively with the short barrel for ease of handling though some long barrels were included in the inventory. A simple kit of thirteen parts was available to convert a standard M60 over to the new M60E3 configuration.

In the last half of the 1980s and into the 1990s, the SEALs have continued to look for a 5.56mm machine gun to replace the Stoner. A number of weapons were examined, both foreign and domestic designs. One production weapon from CIS of Singapore did show considerable promise. In mid-1986, the Weapons Department at the Naval Weapons Support Center Crane, Indiana issued a safety statement for the CIS Ultimax 100 Mark III. This was a modified version of the original Mark II weapon with the primary change being the addition of a quick-change barrel.

The Ultimax is a gas-operated light machine gun using a multi-lug rotary bolt much like that of the M16 series and the Stoner weapons system. Firing from the open bolt position for cooling purposes, the Ultimax uses a straight-line design to minimize recoil forces from lifting the weapon off target while firing. The quick-change barrel system allows the Ultimax 100 to use two different lengths of barrel, a standard 20-inch model and a short 14-inch version. With no movement of the bolt or carrier past the rear of the receiver, the buttstock on the Ultimax can be removed to make a very compact weapon.

Two pistol grips are on the Ultimax, one under the forend and one at the trigger. This arrangement gives a very firm hold for an operator and allows the relatively light weapon to be handheld and fired accurately even without the buttstock. Instead of feeding from a belt, the Ultimax uses either slightly modified

M16 magazines or special ammunition drums. The drums held the most interest to the Teams as they would give a reasonable unit of fire to the Ultimax while still being handy to use and easy to reload. The magazines were also the major source of trouble during testing.

After the 1986 safety statement was issued, the Ultimax underwent some operational testing with the Teams. During these tests, about 25 percent of all stoppages happened because the 100-round drum simply fell out of the weapon. In addition, the drums were found to wear out fairly quickly after about 30 loadings and firings.

The contractor for the Ultimax 100 addressed the problems with the weapon and its feed system as pointed out by the SEALs. Due to a change in marketing representatives, the new weapons did not arrive at Crane for testing until mid-1989. Further testing was conducted and the problems with the 100-round drum magazine appeared solved. A special 14-inch suppressed barrel had been supplied with the Ultimax during the original testing period, giving the SEALs the possible option of a suppressed 5.56mm light machine gun. The test program was completed and a final report issued on the matter in late September 1990.

With the quality assurance problems corrected, the Ultimax was recommended to be kept available as an off-the-shelf design. Only six weapons have been known to be procured at Crane and no further action has been taken to obtain additional weapons.

Though the Ultimax 100 Mark II had been shown to be an acceptable 5.56mm light machine gun, it was not what the SEALs had been wanting. In general, the Teams were still looking for a belt-fed 5.56mm weapon for light weight and longer sustained fire. The M60 and its variations were still the only belt-fed weapon available to the Teams in general in the late 1980s and into the 1990s. The same ammunition weight arguments between the 7.62mm NATO and the 5.56mm that had brought the Stoner to the SEALs some 30 years earlier were still considered legitimate.

The U.S. Army had conducted extensive tests during their SAW program in the late 1970s and early 1980s. Out of that weapons competition had come the FN-manufactured Minimi light machine gun. Chambered in 5.56mm, the Minimi could be fed from a disintegrating metal link belt, very close to the Stoner belt in design, or from standard M16 magazines in an emergency.

For ease of ammunition handling in the field, the Minimi can be loaded with a 200-round plastic belt box that attached to the underside of the weapon. Folding bipod legs lock together underneath the front handguard, giving the Minimi a reasonably sleek line.

Adopted by the U.S. Army in 1982 as the M249 SAW, some 50,000 weapons were planned for purchase between 1982 and 1991. The SEALs have examined and used the M249 SAW on occasion, but have not found the weapon to meet their needs. A later, shortened version of the M249, referred to as the para-trooper or "para" model, was also developed and offered to the SEALs as well as the U.S. military in general. A simple conversion kit with a short barrel and folding buttstock can be attached to the M249 to convert it to the para configuration. The Teams found the shortened barrel reduced the reliability of the M249 Para when used in their particular environment. Mud and water would simply cause the M249 to jam up too easily for acceptance by the Teams.

During the latter half of the 1980s and into the 1990s, the Saco Defense company maintained its program of upgrading and improving the overall M60 design. By the mid 1990s, two new enhance M60 variants, the M60E4 and M60E5, were available for evaluation by the armed forces. Rather than accept either weapon as they stood, the SEALs preferred certain improvements from both. A hybrid M60E4/E5 was produced for the Teams and examined for possible adoption. In 1995, the M60E4/E5 received the nomenclature assignment of Machine Gun, 7.62MM, Mark 43 Mod 0 in 1995.

Modifications incorporated into the Mark 43 include a heavier barrel with an improved gas system and a new, horizontally slotted, open-end flash hider. The folding bipod was made stronger and easier to deploy. The sling swivel was improved, now preventing the sling from contacting a hot barrel. The heat shield/forward grip assembly was made noticeably larger, extending up both sides to further protect the operator from a hot barrel. The bandoleer hanger was securely attached to the side of the receiver rather than hanging from the feed tray and it was strengthened and improved to accept a wider variety of mount-oriented belt-feed mechanisms.

The Mark 43 was the final evolution of the M60 series. With the final production of M60E3 to Mk 43 conversion kits in the late 1990s Saco Defense ceased manufacture of the weapon which they had been continually producing since 1960.

In the mid to late 1980s, another 5.56mm light machine gun was being developed, this one from a name well known to the Teams. Eugene Stoner was working with Ares Inc. in Ohio on a number of weapon designs during the 1980s and into the 1990s. The Ares LMG, also called the Stoner 86 or the New Stoner, was ready for its first test firing in 1986.

Designed from the base up as a rugged light machine gun that could be adapted to special operations use, the Stoner 86 had a machined aluminum receiver for both strength and lightness. Stoner was of the opinion that with modern computer-aided design and machinery, a fully machined receiver could be produced as easily and cheaply as a stamped metal one could be some decades earlier. The Stoner 86 reflected this philosophy and proved Stoner's point.

The first prototype of the Stoner 86 demonstrated a high reliability when firing with very little felt recoil to the operator. Taking note of the popularity of the final SEAL Stoner 63A1 design, the Mark 23 Mod 0, Stoner designed the 86 to accept either a standard length barrel or a special short version. The buttstock could be removed entirely, putting the Stoner 86 into a very compact Assault version when fitted with the short barrel.

Several of the components and operating systems in the Stoner 86 were taken directly from the proven Stoner 63 system including the sights, bolt components, extractor, and barrel extension. The multi-lugged bolt locking up to the barrel extension prevented the need for a heavy receiver. The use of modern machining methods eliminated the cost of dies and other dedicated materials to produce the receiver.

The ammunition supply for the Stoner 86 is contained in the same 200-round plastic belt box used with the Army M249 Minimi light machine gun, eliminating any special ammunition requirements. For night-vision devices or other aiming system, an integral scope mounting rail is part of the upper receiver of the Stoner 86.

The Stoner 86 has been marketed by Knight's Armament Company of Vero Beach, Florida. Prototype and limited production versions of the Stoner 86 have been made and were evaluated by the Navy SEALs and other Special Operations Units. With the increased use of the 5.56mm M249 light machine gun in Army and other units, as well as the success of the SOPMOD M4 kit being fielded, a further search for a 5.56mm light machine gun for use in Special Operations was continued though the 1990s.

On June 8, 2000, FN manufacturing was notified that its Special Purpose Weapon, a modified M249, had been selected as the new lightweight machine gun for the Special Operations Command. The first six weapons, now designated the Mark 46 Mod 0, were delivered in September 2000. The first delivery orders were for 406 weapons with production beginning at 100 weapons a month in February 2001. The contract called for a quantity of 2,506 Mark 46 light machine guns to be delivered over a four-year time frame.

The Mark 46 was designed to be able to accept all of the accessories offered in the SOPMOD M4 kit. A new-style lightweight barrel was developed for the weapon to reduce weight and size. To further reduce the weight of the M249 design to meet the Mark 46 specifications, the receiver was modified and the magazine well was removed. In addition, the mounting lugs for vehicular applications were taken off of the weapon. Extreme reliability was the desire for the new Mark 46 and the weapon has a projected mean-rounds-between-failure rate of 18,000 rounds.

Further development of belt-fed automatic weapons took place in the Special Operations community with the allotment of $1.5 million by Congress to convert and repair 1293 M60 light machine guns to the Mark 43 configuration. The 2000-2001, fiscal year also required the screening of existing M60E3 and Mark 43 weapons in inventory. An overhaul of 698 guns was funded for fiscal year 2000-2001 with an additional allotment to allow the overhaul of another 55 guns in fiscal year 2002.

The upkeep of the Mark 43 weapons kept the basic M60 design in place sufficiently to meet the needs of naval Special Warfare through 2003. The long-term outlook for the support of the Mark 43 was considered difficult as the rest of the services were converting over to the M240 designs as a 7.62mm belt-fed weapon. The needs of the Special Warfare community were not easily met by the heavy design of the M240 weapon and a request was put out for a new lightweight 7.62mm machine gun in 2001.

The result of the upkeep programs was to keep the Mark 43 operational until the new lightweight 7.62mm gun could be made operational in the 2003 fiscal year. That weapon was the FN design adopted as the Mark 47 light machine gun.

The Mark 47 machine gun is a 7.62×51mm weapon utilizing the same links and ammunition as the M60 and M240 family. The Mark 47 is lighter and more easily handled than the Mark 43 which it is intended to replace. In addition to its handling properties, the Mark 47 is completely interoperable with the SOP-MOD M4 kit, giving it a high hit probability out to 1,000 meters.

Additional weapons are constantly being examined by the Special Operations community as they become available. Even without an immediate demand for a specific weapon, new designs are examined and considered for adoption if they particularly fill a need not otherwise met.

Not quite a light machine gun and more than a simple rifle, the Ares Inc. Shrike is a belt-fed conversion system for the M16 family of weapons. Capable of being mounted on any acceptable M16-style receiver, the Shrike converts the rifle into a sustained-fire light machine gun. The weapon can utilize loose belts or the standard issue 200-round SAW boxes which can mount underneath the host weapon. In the case of the ammunition belt running out, the Shrike can also fire effectively from the normal box magazines used with the M16 design.

A very new design that could become an addition to the SOPMOD system or a special purchase item, the Shrike demonstrates the kind of unique and inventive weapons systems that the Special Operations community is always on the lookout for.

■ Machine Gun Data ■

Source: Smithsonian Institute

LEWIS .30 CALIBER MARK VI MACHINE GUN (MODEL 1917)

CARTRIDGE 30-06 M2 (7.62×63mm)

OPERATION Gas

TYPE OF FIRE Full automatic

RATE OF FIRE (A) 150-200 rpm Cyclic 550 rpm

MUZZLE VELOCITY 2,800 fps (853 m/s)

MUZZLE ENERGY 2,646 ft/lb (3,588 J)

SIGHTS Open, leaf-type aperture/blade, adjustable, 0 to 2,100 yards in 100-yard increments

FEED 47-round removable pan magazine

MOUNT TYPE Shoulder fired, bipod, various shipboard mounts

WEIGHTS

Weapon (empty) 26.5 lb (12.02 kg) w/full stock; buttstock 1.48 lb (0.67 kg); D-handle 0.93 lb (0.42 kg)

Weapon (loaded) 30.66 lb (13.91 kg)

Weapon (mounted and loaded) 32.41 lb (14.70 kg) w/bipod

Feed device (empty) 1.5 lb (0.68 kg)

Feed device (loaded) 4.16 lb (1.89 kg)

Service cartridge .30 M2 Ball 396 gr (25.7 g)

Projectile 152 gr (9.8 g)

LENGTHS

Weapon overall 51 in (129.5 cm) w/buttstock, 44 in (111.8 cm) w/spade grip

Barrel 26.63 in (67.6 cm)

Sight radius 32.2 in (81.8 cm)

Source: U.S. Army

BROWNING .50 CALIBER M2 WATERCOOLED FLEXIBLE MACHINE GUN

CARTRIDGE .50 Browning (12.7×99mm)

OPERATION Short recoil

TYPE OF FIRE Full automatic

RATE OF FIRE Practical 300-400 rpm, Cyclic 450-600 rpm

MUZZLE VELOCITY M2 Ball 2,935 fps (895 m/s)

MUZZLE ENERGY 13,349 ft/lb (18,101 J)

SIGHTS Open, leaf-type aperture w/u-notch battle sight/blade, adjustable, 200-2,600 yards in 200-yd increments, may also be found w/o integral sights, sights used varying w/mount, antiaircraft speed ring most common

FEED 110-round M7 fabric belt or flexible metal disintegrating M2 link belt carried in an M2 ammunition box or M2 spring-loaded ammunition chest, selectable left or right-side feed

MOUNT TYPE Various twin or single gun mounts, Mk 26, Mk 30 single pedestal antiaircraft mounts

WEIGHTS

Weapon (empty) Flexible 100.5 lb (45.6 kg) w/o water; w/spade grip, trigger back plate and retracting slide group 121.5 lb (55.1 kg) w/10 quarts (9.46 l) water; spade grips (only) 0.5 lb (0.23 kg)

Weapon (mounted and loaded) Mk 21 Naval pedestal mount 725 lb (56.7 kg), w/200 rd M2 chest and water—936.9 lb (425 kg) Mk 30 mount set up for ground use 380 lb (172.4 kg) gun w/o spade grips, w/200 rd M2 ammunition chest, M3 water chest, water—730.9 lb (331.5 kg)

Feed device 110 rd M7 fabric belt 28.35 lb (12.86 kg) loaded w/M2 Ball; 105 rd M2 link belt 30.64 lb (13.9 kg) loaded w/M2 Ball; 110 rd M7 belt w/M2 ammunition box 32.75 lb (14.86 kg); 105 rd M2 link belt w/M2 ammunition box 35.04 lb (15.89 kg); 200 rd M2 Ammunition chest (empty) 32 lb; loaded w/200 rd M2 link belt 90.37 lb (40.99 kg)

Service cartridge M2 Ball 1,776 gr (115 g)

Projectile 698 gr (45.2 g)

LENGTHS

Weapon Overall 66 in (167.6 cm)

Barrel 45 in (114.3 cm)

Effective range 2,000 yards (1829 m) surface targets, 800 yards (731 m) antiaircraft

Maximum range 7,600 yards (6949 m)

Notes on mounts Mark 21—This is a deck-mounted, pedestal type shielded mount for a single .50 caliber M2 machine gun fitted with a spade grip trigger back plate and retracting slide group assembly. Two rigid shoulder braces and a seat/back harness aid the gunner in rapidly moving and aiming the weapon, especially during anti-aircraft use. An aperture/speed ring cross hair sight is provided with the mount and is separate from the weapon. The mount will accept a weapon set up with a spade grip, trigger back plate, with the retracting slide group assembly for the weapon on the right side and feeding from the left-hand side from a 200-round ammunition chest. A ½ inch (12.7 mm) Mk 13 armor shield is provided for the protection of the gunner. Mount weight, complete w/sights, w/o weapon or ammunition 725 lb (328.9 kg), Mk 13 shield wt 298 lb (135.2 kg)

Mark 30—(Army M3 .50 caliber Machine gun mount, AA) This is a large pedestal mount with an wide three-legged base used for antiaircraft fire. The pedestal and gun carriage both have removable armor shield plates The gun can be rotated in a 360 degree circle, raised 90 and lowered -15 degrees for full antiaircraft coverage. A separate speed ring/post sight is issued with the mount that can be clamped to the water jacket of the M2 watercooled .50. The legs of the mount can be removed and a pedestal base bolted to a deck that will accept the mount, securing it with three quick-release buckles. A counterweight is attached to the front of the carriage when an M2 Aircraft or HB machine gun is mounted to offset the missing weight of the water jacket. The Mk 30 mount can accept any M2 .50 caliber machine gun set up with a horizontal buffer back plate and right side retracting slide group assembly. Weight, complete, set up for ground use w/legs, without gun or ammunition is 380 lb (172.4 kg); Weight, complete, set up for pedestal use, without gun or ammunition, 317 lb (143.8 kg); Pedestal armor plate wt. 39 lb (17.7 kg); Carriage armor plate wt. 18 lb (8.7 kg); Legs wt 81 lb (36.7 kg); Removable sight wt. 10 lb (4.5 kg); Counterweight 41.5 lb (18.8 kg)

M3 water chest—This is a cubic metal chest with handles containing a hand-operated, chain-driven water pump, water tank, hoses, and connections to be hooked up to a watercooled .50. The pump is operated by an assistant gunner to circulate water in the barrel jacket during firing, increasing the cooling efficiency of the weapon. Weight, complete w/hose assemblies (empty) 74.5 lb (33.8 kg); Weight, complete (full) 139.5 lb (63.4 kg); Weight, hose assemblies (2) 13.5 lb (6.1 kg); Capacity, 8 gallons (30.28 liters); Size 15.94 × 14.13 × 14.13 in (40.5 × 35.9 × 35.9 cm).

BROWNING .50 CALIBER M2 AIRCRAFT FLEXIBLE MACHINE GUN

CARTRIDGE .50 Browning (12.7× 99mm)

OPERATION Short recoil

TYPE OF FIRE Full automatic

RATE OF FIRE Practical 150 rpm, Cyclic 750-800 rpm

MUZZLE VELOCITY M2 Ball 2,845 fps (895 m/s)

MUZZLE ENERGY 12,543 ft/lb (17,008 J)

SIGHTS None, sights used vary w/mount

FEED Flexible metal disintegrating M2 link belt, selectable left or right side feed

MOUNT TYPE Aircraft fixed or flexible installations, shipboard on Mk 21, Mk 26, Mk 30 mounts

WEIGHTS

Weapon (empty) 61 lb (27.67 kg) w/horizontal buffer assembly flexible w/back plate w/spade grips, trigger and retracting slide group assembly—65.33 lb (29.63 kg) Component weights; Back plate w/horizontal buffer assembly wt 2.68 lb (1.22 kg); Back plate w/spade grips, trigger, and buffer wt 4.01 lb (1.82 kg); Spade grips (only) 0.5 lb (0.23 kg); Retracting slide group assembly wt 3.00 lb (1.36 kg); Operating slide group assembly wt 1.62 lb (0.73 kg); Side plate trigger assembly wt 0.44 lb (0.20 kg)

Weapon (mounted and loaded) Mk 26 pintle mount w/shield 155 lb (70.3 kg) w/105 rds;

M2 ammunition box and flexible gun 255.37 lb (115.84 kg); Mk 21 Naval pedestal mount 725 lb (56.7 kg), w/200 rd M2 chest—880.7 lb (399.5 kg); Mk 30 mount set up for ground use 421.5 lb (191.2 kg), w/counterweight, 200 rd M2 ammunition chest, gun w/o spade grips—576.7 lb (261.6 kg)

Feed device 105 rd M2 link belt 30.64 lb (13.9 kg) loaded w/M2 Ball; 105 rd M2 link belt w/M2 ammunition box 35.04 lb (15.89 kg); 200 rd M2 ammunition chest (empty) 32 lb; loaded w/200 rd M2 link belt 90.37 lb (40.99 kg)

Service cartridge M2 Ball 1,776 gr (115 g)

Projectile 698 gr (45.2 g)

LENGTHS

Weapon overall 56.125 in (142.6 cm)

Barrel 36 in (91.4 cm)

Effective range 2,000 yards (1,829 m) surface targets, 800 yards (731 m) antiaircraft

Maximum range 7,200 yards (6584 m)

Notes on mounts Mark 21—This is a deck-mounted, pedestal-type shielded mount for a single .50 caliber M2 machine gun fitted with a spade grip trigger back plate and retracting slide group assembly. Two rigid shoulder braces and a seat/back harness aid the gunner in rapidly moving and aiming the weapon, especially during anti-aircraft use. An aperture/speed ring cross hair sight is provided with the mount and is separate from the weapon. The mount will accept a weapon set up with a spade grip, trigger back plate, with the retracting slide group assembly for the weapon on the right-hand side and feeding from the left-hand side from a 200-round ammunition chest. A ½ inch (12.7 mm) Mk 13 armor shield is provided for the protection of the gunner. Mount weight, complete w/sights, w/o weapon or ammunition 725 lb (328.9 kg), Mk 13 shield wt 298 lb (135.2 kg).

Mk 26 Mod 0—This is a lightweight, shielded socket-type mount for a .50 caliber M2 Aircraft or HB flexible machine gun. The mount can be bolted to the side rail of a ship or boat. A built-in stop prevents the mount from being depressed past ½ 15 degrees and the weapon can be elevated to 80 degrees. Rotation of the mount is unlimited and a securing latch is provided to lock the weapon in the vertical or horizontal position. A removable shield is provided for the gunner. A standard M2A1 ammunition box can be attached to the left side of the weapon. No sights are provided with this mount. Mount weight, complete, w/o weapon or ammunition 155 lb (70.3 kg), shield wt 38 lb (17.2 kg).

Mark 30 (Army M3 .50 caliber machine gun mount, AA)—This is a large pedestal mount with an wide three-legged base used for antiaircraft fire. The pedestal and gun carriage both have removable armor shield plates The gun can be rotated in a 360 degree circle, raised 90 and lowered - 15 degrees for full antiaircraft coverage. A separate speed ring/post sight is issued with the mount that can be clamped to the water jacket of the M2 watercooled .50. The legs of the mount can be removed and a pedestal base bolted to a deck that will accept the mount, securing it with three quick-release buckles. A counterweight is attached to the front of the carriage when an M2 Aircraft or HB machine gun is mounted to offset the missing weight of the water jacket. The Mk 30 mount can accept any M2 .50 caliber machine gun set up with a horizontal buffer back plate and right side retracting slide group assembly. Weight, complete set up for ground use w/legs, without gun or ammunition is 380 lb (172.4 kg). Weight, complete, set up for pedestal use, without gun or ammunition, 317 lb (143.8 kg), Pedestal

armor plate wt. 39 lb (17.7 kg), Carriage armor plate wt 18 lb (8.7 kg), Legs wt 81 lb (36.7 kg). Removable sight wt 10 lb (4.5 kg), Counterweight 41.5 lb (18.8 kg)

Source: Kevin Dockery

BROWNING .50 CALIBER M2 HB (HEAVY BARREL) FLEXIBLE MACHINE GUN

CARTRIDGE .50 Browning (12.7×99 mm)

OPERATION Short recoil

TYPE OF FIRE Selective

RATE OF FIRE (SS) 40 rpm, (A) 150 rpm, Cyclic 450—550 rpm

MUZZLE VELOCITY M8 API 3,050 fps (930 m/s)

MUZZLE ENERGY 13,672 ft/lb (18,539 kg)

SIGHTS Open, leaf-type aperture w/aperture battle sight/blade, adjustable 100 to 2600 yards in 100 yard increments

FEED Flexible metal disintegrating M2 link belt, 105 rd w/M2 ammunition can, selectable left or right side feed

MOUNT TYPE M3 Tripod, Deck mounts Mk 21, Mk 26, MK 30, Mk 46, Mk 50, Mk 56, 81mm Mortar Mk 2 Mod 1

WEIGHTS

Weapon (empty) 82 lb (37.2 kg); barrel wt 27 lb (12.25 kg)

Weapon (loaded) 117.5 lb (53.3 kg) w/105 rd belt & M2 ammunition box

Weapon (mounted and loaded) 161.5 lb w/M3 tripod & 105 rds w/box; M3 tripod 44 lb (20 kg) w/e

Feed device 100 rd belt 29.71 lb (13.48 kg); 105 rd belt w/M2 ammunition box 35.5 lb (16.15 kg)

Service cartridge M8 API 1813 gr (117.5 g)

Projectile 662 gr (42.5 g)

LENGTHS

Weapon overall 65.13 in (165.4 cm)

Barrel 45 in (114.3 cm)

Sight radius 20 in (50.8 cm)

Effective range 2,000 yards (1,830 m)

Maximum range 7,076 yards (6,470 m)

Notes on mounts Mark 21—This is a deck-mounted, pedestal type shielded mount for a single .50 caliber M2 machine gun fitted with a spade grip trigger back plate and retracting slide group assembly. Two rigid shoulder braces and a seat/back harness aid the gunner in rapidly moving and aiming the weapon, especially during antiaircraft use. An aperture/speed ring cross hair sight is provided with the mount and is separate from the weapon. The mount will accept a weapon set up with a spade grip, trigger back plate, with the retracting slide group assembly for the weapon on the right side and feeding from the left-hand side from a 200-round ammunition chest. A ½ inch (12.7 mm) Mk 13 armor shield is provided for the protection of the gunner. Mount weight, complete w/sights, w/o weapon or ammunition 725 lb (328.9 kg), Mk 13 shield wt 298 lb (135.2 kg).

Mk 26 Mod 0—This is a lightweight, shielded socket-type mount for a .50 caliber M2 Aircraft or HB flexible machine gun. The mount can be bolted to the side rail of a ship or boat. A built-in stop prevents the mount from being depressed past -15 degrees and the weapon can be elevated to 80 degrees. Rotation of the mount is unlimited and a securing latch is provided to lock the weapon in the vertical or horizontal position. A removable shield is provided for the gunner. A standard M2A1 ammunition box can be attached to the left side of the weapon. No sights are provided with this mount. Mount weight,

complete, w/o weapon or ammunition 155 lb (70.3 kg), shield wt 38 lb (17.2 kg).

Mark 30 (Army M3 .50 caliber Machine gun mount, AA)—This is a large pedestal mount with an wide three-legged base used for antiaircraft fire. The pedestal and gun carriage both have removable armor shield plates The gun can be rotated in a 360 degree circle, raised 90 and lowered -15 degrees for full antiaircraft coverage. A separate speed ring/post sight is issued with the mount that can be clamped to the water jacket of the M2 watercooled .50. The legs of the mount can be removed and a pedestal base bolted to a deck that will accept the mount, securing it with three quick-release buckles. A counterweight is attached to the front of the carriage when an M2 Aircraft or HB machine gun is mounted to offset the missing weight of the water jacket. The Mk 30 mount can accept any M2 .50 caliber machine gun set up with a horizontal buffer back plate and right side retracting slide group assembly. Weight, complete set up for ground use w/legs, without gun or ammunition is 380 lb (172.4 kg). Weight, complete, set up for pedestal use, without gun or ammunition, 317 lb (143.8 kg), Pedestal armor plate wt 39 lb (17.7 kg), Carriage armor plate wt 18 lb (8.7 kg), Legs wt 81 lb (36.7 kg). Removable sight wt 10 lb (4.5 kg), Counterweight 41.5 lb (18.8 kg)

Mark 46 Mods 0, 1 & 2—Earlier model pedestal-type deck mount holding 1 .50 caliber machine gun w/105 rds and 1 Mark 18 or Mark 20 40mm grenade launcher w/24 rds 40mm. Mount has a 28-inch-wide by 30-inch-tall armor shield in front of the weapons with a 4-inch-wide slot in its center. Weight without guns and ammunition is 167 lb (75.7 kg)

Mark 50 Mod 0—Pedestal-type deck mount holding one .50 machine gun w/125 rds and one Mark 18 or Mark 20 40mm grenade launcher w/25 rds 40mm. Weight without guns and ammunition 2,275 lb (1032 kg).

Mark 56 Mods 0 & 1—Sunken deck tub-type mount holding two .50 caliber M2HB Fixed machine guns set up one w/right-hand feed, one w/left-hand feed, each w/500 rds per gun ready and 105 rds reserve. Mount extends 35 inches below deck and operator sits between the guns. Mount is electrically (24 volts 10 amps DC) or manually operated. Weight without guns and ammuniton is 370 lb (167.8 kg).

81mm Mortar Mark 2 Mod 1—81mm direct fire mortar w/pedestal-type deck mount and provisions to mount a .50 caliber machine gun w/160 rds ammuniton above mortar. Weight without ammunition 728 lb (330 kg).

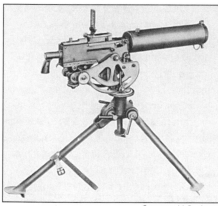

Source: U.S. Army

BROWNING .30 CALIBER M1917A1 WATERCOOLED MACHINE GUN

CARTRIDGE 30-06 (7.62×63mm)

OPERATION Short recoil

TYPE OF FIRE Full automatic

RATE OF FIRE Practical 250 rpm, Cyclic 450-600 rpm

MUZZLE VELOCITY 2,800 fps (853 m/s)

MUZZLE ENERGY 2,646 ft/lb (3,588 J)

SIGHTS Open, leaf-type aperture w/aperture battle sight/blade, adjustable 0 to 2,600 yards

FEED 250 round M1917 fabric belt or flexible metal disintegrating M1 link belt, left side feed

MOUNT TYPE M1917A1 tripod w/cradle

WEIGHTS

Weapon (empty) 32.63 lb (14.80 kg) w/o water; 39.93 lb w/7 pints (3.31 l) water

Weapon (loaded) 54.47 lb (24.71 kg) w/water & 250 rd fabric belt

Weapon (mounted and loaded) 112.13 lb (50.86 kg) w/tripod, 250 rd fabric belt and wooden ammunition chest; M1917A1 Tripod w/cradle 53.2 lb (24.13 kg)

Feed device 250 rd M1917 fabric belt 14.54 lb (6.60 kg); 250 rd M1 metal link belt 16.61 lb (7.53 kg); 250 rd M1917 belt w/wooden ammunition chest 19 lb (8.62 kg); 250 rd metal belt w/M2 ammunition box 21.01 lb (9.53 kg)

Service cartridge .30 M2 Ball 396 gr (25.7 g)

Projectile 152 gr (9.8 g)

LENGTHS

Weapon overall 38.5 in (97.8 cm)

Barrel 24 in (61 cm)

Sight radius 26 in (66 cm)

Effective range 2,500 yds (2,286 m)

Maximum range 3,500 yds (3,200 m)

Source: Kevin Dockery

BROWNING .30 CALIBER M1919A4 FLEXIBLE MACHINE GUN

CARTRIDGE 30-06 (7.62×63mm)

OPERATION Short recoil w/muzzle booster

TYPE OF FIRE Full automatic

RATE OF FIRE Practical 150 rpm, Cyclic 550-650 rpm w/booster, 400-550 rpm Cyclic w/o booster

MUZZLE VELOCITY 2,800 fps (853 m/s)

MUZZLE ENERGY 2,646 ft/lb (3,588 J)

SIGHTS Open, leaf-type aperture w/U-notch battle sight/blade, adjustable 0 to 2,600 yards in 200-yard increments

FEED 250-round M1917 fabric belt or flexible metal disintegrating M1 link belt, left side feed

MOUNT TYPE M2 or M1917A1 tripod, various shipboard pintle mounts

WEIGHTS

Weapon (empty) 31 lb (14.06 kg); barrel 7.31 lb (3.32 kg)

Weapon (loaded) 47.61 lb (21.60 kg) w/250 rd M1 link belt

Weapon (mounted and loaded) 66.01 lb (29.94 kg) w/250 rd M1 link belt, M2 box, M2 tripod; M2 Tripod w/T&E mechanism and pintle 14 lb (6.35 kg)

Feed device 250 rd M1917 fabric belt 14.54 lb (6.60 kg); 250 rd M1 metal link belt 16.61 lb (7.53 kg); 250 rd M1917 belt w/wooden ammunition chest 19 lb (8.62 kg); 250 rd metal belt w/M2 ammunition box 21.01 lb (9.53 kg)

Service cartridge .30 M2 Ball 396 gr (25.7 g)

Projectile 152 gr (9.8 g)

LENGTHS

Weapon overall 48 in (121.9 cm)

Barrel 24 in (61 cm)

Sight radius 14 in (35.6 cm)

Effective range 1,100 yds (1,000 m)

Maximum range 3,500 yds (3,200 m)

Mark 21 Mod 0—This is a scarf-ring type mount for a single .30 caliber machine gun, The weapon is mounted in a Mk 16 Mod 0 carriage which can be run through a full 360 degree circle. The gun cradle can accept the Browning M1919A4 or M1917A1 and mount a standard ammunition box on the left side of the weapon. The weapon can be depressed down to -15 degrees and elevated to +70 degrees making it suitable for both ground targets and antiaircraft use. A ¼ inch

(6.4 mm) armor plate shield is provided for the gunner on the cradle with a separate shield on the carriage. Mount weight (complete w/o gun) 178 lb (80.7 kg), carriage shield wt. 26 lb (11.8 kg), cradle shield wt. 38 lb (17.2 kg).

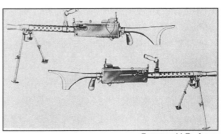

Source: U.S. Army

BROWNING .30 CALIBER M1919A6 LIGHT MACHINE GUN

CARTRIDGE 30-06 (7.62×63mm)

OPERATION Short recoil w/muzzle booster

TYPE OF FIRE Full automatic

RATE OF FIRE Practical 150 rpm, Cyclic 600-675 rpm

MUZZLE VELOCITY 2,800 fps (853 m/s)

MUZZLE ENERGY 2,646 ft/lb (3,588 J)

SIGHTS Open, leaf-type aperture w/U-notch battle sight/blade, adjustable 0 to 2,600 yards in 200 yard increments

FEED 250 round M1917 fabric belt or flexible metal disintegrating M1 link belt, left side feed

MOUNT TYPE Removable bipod, M2 or M1917A1 tripod, various shipboard pintle mounts

WEIGHTS

Weapon (empty) 33.5 lb (15.2 kg) w/shoulder stock, bipod, carrying handle, M7 flash hider; barrel wt 4.63 lb (2.10 kg); bipod wt 3.32 lb (1.51 kg); shoulder stock wt 1.75 lb (0.79 kg); M7 flash hider wt 1.37 lb (0.58 kg)

Weapon (loaded) 54.55 lb (24.74 kg) complete w/250 rd M1 link belt, M2 box

Weapon (mounted and loaded) 52.76 lb (23.93 kg) complete less shoulder stock, w/250 rd

M1 link belt, M2 box; M2 tripod w/T&E mechanism and pintle 14 lb (6.35 kg)

Feed device 250 rd M1917 fabric belt 14.54 lb (6.60 kg); 250 rd M1 metal link belt 16.61 lb (7.53 kg); 275 rd M1 metal link belt 18.27 lb (8.29 kg); 250 rd M1917 belt w/M2 ammunition box 18.94 lb (8.59 kg); 250 rd metal belt w/M2 ammunition box 21.01 lb (9.53 kg); 275 rd metal belt w/M2A1 ammunition box 23.05 lb (10.46 kg)

Service cartridge .30 M2 Ball 396 gr (25.7 g)

Projectile 152 gr (9.8 g)

LENGTHS

Weapon overall 53 in (134.6 cm) w/shoulder stock; w/shoulder stock, M7 flash hider

Barrel 24 in (61 cm)

Sight radius 14 in (35.6 cm)

Effective range 1,100 yds (1,000 m)

Maximum range 3,500 yds (3,200 m)

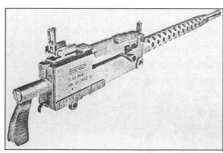

Source: U.S. Navy

7.62MM NATO MACHINE GUN MARK 21 MOD 0

CARTRIDGE 7.62mm NATO (7.62×51mm)

OPERATION Short recoil

TYPE OF FIRE Full automatic

RATE OF FIRE Practical 150 rpm, Cyclic 600-650 rpm

MUZZLE VELOCITY 2,750 fps (838 m/s)

MUZZLE ENERGY 2,502 ft/lb (3,393 J)

SIGHTS Open leaf-type aperture w/U-notch battle sight/blade, adjustable 0 to 2,400 yards in 200-yard increments

FEED Flexible metal disintegrating M13 link belt, left side feed

MOUNT TYPE M2 tripod, Mk 26 gun mount and various shipboard pintle mounts

WEIGHTS

Weapon (empty) 36 lb (16.33 kg)

Weapon (loaded) 42.54 lb (19.30 kg) w/100 rd belt

Weapon (mounted and loaded) 70.02 lb (31.76 kg) w/250 rd belt, M19 ammunition box, M2 tripod

M2 tripod w/T&E mechanism and pintle 14 lb (6.35 kg)

Feed device 100 rd belt 6.54 lb (2.97 kg) 250 rd belt w/M19 metal ammunition box 20.02 lb (9.08 kg)

Service cartridge 7.62mm M80 Ball 393 gr (25.5 g)

Projectile 149 gr (9.7 g)

LENGTHS

Weapon overall 46.75 in (118.7 cm) w/flash suppressor

Barrel 24 in (61 cm)

Sight radius 14 in (35.6 cm)

Effective range 1,200 yds (1,100 m)

Maximum range 3,500 yds (3,200 m)

Notes on mounts Mark 26—Pintle-type tripod (pedistal) gun mount able to be bolted to the deck holding 1 Mk 21 Mod 0 machine gun w/300 rds. Weight of mount without gun and ammunition is 205 lb (93 kg).

Source: U.S. Navy

7.62MM MARK 25 MOD 0 MINIGUN

CARTRIDGE 7.62mm NATO (7.62×51mm)

OPERATION External power (electrical)

TYPE OF FIRE Full automatic

RATE OF FIRE Variable, Cyclic 4,000 or 6,000 rpm

MUZZLE VELOCITY (M80 Ball) 2,750 fps (838 m/s)

MUZZLE ENERGY 2,502 ft/lb (3,393 J)

SIGHTS Dependent on mount, usually simple speed ring/post

FEED Flexible, metal disintegrating M13 link belt, right side feed

MOUNT TYPE Navy self-contained pintle mount

WEIGHTS

Weapon (empty) 56 lb (25.40 kg); gun 35 lb (15.88 kg); motor, 22 VDC electric 2.5 horsepower 8 lb (3.63 kg); recoil adapter 3 lb (1.36 kg); delinking feeder 10 lb (4.54 kg); control package 25 lb (11.34 kg); battery package 35 lb (15.88 kg); saddle assembly 11 lb (4.99 kg); yoke assembly 11 lb (4.99 kg); connecting cables 2 lb (0.91 kg); ammunition container 4,000 rounds (empty) 37 lb (16.78 kg); chuting 4 lb (1.81 kg); brass disposal bag 5 lb (2.27 kg); mount assembly 64 lb (29.03 kg)

Weapon (mounted, empty) Minigun w/saddle and yoke assembly 78 lb (35.38 kg); Pintle mount assembly 250 lb 113.40 kg)

Weapon (mounted and loaded) 511.71 lb (232.12 kg) w/full mount installation and 4,000 rds

Feed device 750 rd belt, linked 4 M80 Ball, 1 M62 Tracer 48.86 lb (22.16 kg); 4,000 rd belt 261.71 lb (118.71 kg); 2 × 750 rd belts (1,500 rds) linked 4 M80 ball, 1 M62 tracer w/M548 metal ammunition box 118.72 lb (53.85 kg)

Service cartridge M80 Ball 393 gr (25.5 g), M62 Tracer 383 gr (24.8 g)

Projectile M80 Ball 149 gr (9.7 g), M62 Tracer 141 gr (9.1 g)

LENGTHS

Weapon overall 31.5 in (80.0 cm)

Barrel 22 in (55.9 cm)

Effective range 1,650 yds (1,500 m)

Maximum range 3,500 yds (3,200 m)

Mark 25 Mod 0 Minigun—This is the 1971 standardized version of the 7.62mm GAU-2B/A Minigun first used by the SEALs in 1967. The full pintle mount system listed is completely self-contained and can power the weapon as well as contain the ammunition. The system can also be powered by a boat's 24 volt DC supply which can also supply a slight charging current to keep the battery pack charged. With the saddle and yoke, the system can be mounted on a standard Navy Mk 56 gun mount with the ammunition storage held on the mount or remotely feeding through additional chuting.

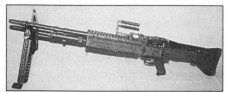

Source: Kevin Dockery

7.62MM M60 MACHINE GUN

CARTRIDGE 7.62mm NATO (7.62×51mm)

OPERATION Gas

TYPE OF FIRE Full automatic

RATE OF FIRE Practical 200 rpm, Cyclic 500-650 rpm

MUZZLE VELOCITY (M80 Ball) 2,800 fps (853 m/s)

MUZZLE ENERGY 2,593 ft/lb (3,516 J)

SIGHTS Open, leaf-type square-notch/blade, adjustable 300 to 1,200 meters in 100-meter increments

FEED Flexible metal disintegrating M13 link belt held in a magazine pouch (early) or bandoleer, left side feed

MOUNT TYPE Shoulder fired, integral bipod, M122 tripod, Navy mounts, Mk 26, Mk 58, Mk 78

WEIGHTS

Weapon (empty) 24.5 lb (11.11 kg)

Weapon (loaded) 31.3 lb (14.20 kg) w/M60 bandoleer & belt

Barrel assembly 9.19 lb (4.17 kg)

Weapon (mounted and loaded) 46.3 lb (21.0 kg) w/M122 tripod, M60 bandoleer; M122 Tripod w/pintle and T & E gear 15 lb (6.8 kg)

Feed device 100 rd belt linked 4 M80 Ball, 1 M62 Tracer (standard) 6.51 lb (2.95 kg); M60 bandoleer w/box & 100 rd standard belt 6.8 lb (3.08 kg); M60 magazine bag (canvas) w/standard belt 7.55 lb (3.42 kg); M60 magazine bag (nylon) w/standard belt 7.04 lb (3.19 kg)

Service cartridge M80 Ball 393 gr (25.5 g), M62 Tracer 383 gr (24.8 g)

Projectile M80 Ball 149 gr (9.7 g), M62 Tracer 141 gr (9.1 g)

LENGTHS

Weapon overall 43.5 in (110.5 cm)

Barrel 22 in (56 cm)

Sight radius 21.15 in (54 cm)

Effective range 1,200 yds (1,100 m)

Maximum range 4,075 yds (3,725 m)

Notes on mounts Mark 26—Pintle-type tripod (pedestal) mount able to be bolted to the deck holding one M60 or M60D machine gun w/100 rds. Weight without gun and ammunition is 205 lb (93 kg)

Mark 58 Mods 0 through 9—Pintle-type mount able to be rail or hull mounted w/bolts holding one M60 or M60D machine gun w/200-600 rds depending on Mod configuration. Weight without gun and ammunition is 33 lb (14.97 kg)

Mark 78 Mods 0 & 1—Pintle type cradle mount, Mod 0 is rail or hull mounted using the Mark 16 Mod 0 stand, Mod 1 is deck mounted using the Mark 16 Mod 2 stand and tripod. Mk 78 mount holds two M60 or M60D machine guns each w/600 rds (1,200 rds total) of ammunition. Weight without guns and ammunition is (Mod 0) 125 lb (56.7 kg), (Mod 1) 158 lb (71.7 kg)

60mm Mortar Mark 4 Mod 0—60mm direct fire mortar w/pedestal-type deck mount. Adaptor w/ammunition box allow the Mk 4 to mount an M60 or M60D machine gun w/200 rds ammunition above the mortar. Weight without machine gun or ammunition 145 lb (65.77 kg)

7.62MM M60 "CUT-DOWN" (FIELD MODIFIED)

MUZZLE VELOCITY 2,715 fps (828 m/s)

MUZZLE ENERGY 2,438 ft/lb (3306 J)

SIGHTS None

MOUNT TYPE Hip (assault) w/sling or shoulder fired

WEIGHTS

Weapon (empty) 20.29 lb (9.2 kg); barrel assembly (complete) 9.19 lb (4.17 kg); buttstock assembly 1.52 lb (0.69 kg); M60C receiver cap 0.20 lb (0.09 kg); removal of bipod assembly—1.98 lb (0.90 kg); cut back barrel @ 4.5 inches (11.4 cm), rethread muzzle and replace flash hider—0.66 lb (0.30 kg); remove front and rear sights—0.25 lb (0.11 kg); remove buttstock, replace w/M60C receiver cap—1.32 lb (0.60 kg) and—0.5 in (1.3 cm)

Weapon (loaded) 27.84 lb (12.63 kg) w/M60 magazine bag (canvas) w/standard belt

Weapon (mounted and loaded) 28.17 lb (12.78 kg); padded nylon M60 sling 0.33 lb (0.15 kg)

Feed device 100 rd belt linked 4 M80 Ball, 1 M62 Tracer (standard) 6.51 lb (2.95 kg); M60 bandoleer w/box & 100 rd standard belt 6.8 lb (3.08 kg); M60 magazine bag (canvas) w/standard belt 7.55 lb (3.42 kg); M60 magazine bag (nylon) w/standard belt 7.04 lb (3.19 kg);

Service cartridge M80 Ball 393 gr (25.5 g), M62 Tracer 383 gr (24.8 g)

Projectile M80 Ball 149 gr (9.7 g), M62 Tracer 141 gr (9.1 g)

LENGTHS

Weapon overall 38.5 in (97.8 cm)

Barrel 17.5 in (44.5 cm)

Effective range 750 yds (686 m) Tracer burnout

Source: Saco Corporation

7.62MM M60D MACHINE GUN

CARTRIDGE 7.62mm NATO (7.62×51mm)

OPERATION Gas

TYPE OF FIRE Full automatic

RATE OF FIRE Practical 100 rpm, Cyclic 550 rpm

MUZZLE VELOCITY (M80 Ball) 2,800 fps (853 m/s)

MUZZLE ENERGY 2,593 ft/lb (3,516 J)

SIGHTS Open, speed ring/blade, fixed

FEED Flexible metal disintegrating M13 link belt, left side feed

MOUNT TYPE Bipod, M122 tripod, Navy mounts Mk 26, Mk 58, Mk 78, 60 mm Mortar Mk 4 Mod 0

WEIGHTS

Weapon (empty) 24.3 lb (11.02 kg)

Weapon (loaded) 31.1 lb (14.11 kg) w/bandoleer and standard belt

Feed device 100 rd belt linked 4 M80 Ball, 1 M62 Tracer (standard) 6.51 lb (2.95 kg); M60 bandoleer w/box & 100 rd standard belt 6.8 lb (3.08 kg); M60 magazine bag (canvas) w/standard belt 7.55 lb (3.42 kg); M60 magazine bag (nylon) w/standard belt 7.04 lb (3.19 kg)

Service cartridge M80 Ball 393 gr (25.5 g), M62 Tracer 383 gr (24.8 g)

Projectile M80 Ball 149 gr (9.7 g), M62 Tracer 141 gr (9.1 g)

LENGTHS

Weapon overall 44.9 in (114 cm)

Barrel 22 in (56 cm)

Sight radius 21.15 in (54 cm)

Effective range 1,200 yds (1,100 m)

Maximum range 4,075 yds (3,725 m)

Notes on mounts

Mark 26—Pintle-type tripod (pedestal) mount able to be bolted to the deck holding one M60 or M60D machine gun w/100 rds. Weight without gun and ammunition is 205 lb (93 kg)

Mark 58 Mods 0 through 9—Pintle-type mount able to be rail or hull mounted w/bolts holding one M60 or M60D machine gun w/200—600 rds depending on Mod configuration. Weight without gun and ammunition is 33 lb (14.97 kg)

Mark 78 Mods 0 & 1—Pintle type cradle mount, Mod 0 is rail or hull mounted using the Mark 16 Mod 0 stand, Mod 1 is deck mounted using the Mark 16 Mod 2 stand and tripod. Mk 78 mount holds two M60 or M60D machine guns each w/600 rds (1200 rds total) of ammunition. Weight without guns and ammunition is (Mod 0) 125 lb (56.7 kg), (Mod 1) 158 lb (71.7 kg)

60mm Mortar Mark 4 Mod 0—60mm direct fire mortar w/pedestal-type deck mount. Adaptor w/ammunition box allow the Mk 4 to mount an M60 or M60D machine gun w/200 rds ammunition above the mortar. Weight without machine gun or ammunition 145 lb (65.77 kg)

Source: Kevin Dockery

7.62MM M60E3 LIGHTWEIGHT MACHINE GUN

CARTRIDGE 7.62mm NATO (7.62×51mm)

OPERATION Gas

TYPE OF FIRE Full automatic

RATE OF FIRE Practical 150 rpm, Cyclic 500-650 rpm

MUZZLE VELOCITY 2,800 fps (853 m/s) w/long barrel; 2,700 fps (823 m/s) w/short barrel

MUZZLE ENERGY 2,593 ft/lb (3516 J) w/long barrel; 2,411 ft/lb (3269 J) w/short barrel

SIGHTS Open, leaf-type square-notch/blade, adjustable 300 to 1,200 meters in 100-meter increments

FEED Flexible metal disintegrating M13 link belt held in a bandoleer, left side feed

MOUNT TYPE Shoulder fired, integral bipod, M122 tripod

WEIGHTS

Weapon (empty) 19.5 lb (8.85 kg) w/long barrel; 19.2 lb (8.71 kg) w/short barrel

Weapon (loaded) 26.3 lb (11.93 kg) w/long barrel, 100 rd bandoleer; 26.0 lb (11.79 kg) w/short barrel, 100 rd bandoleer

Weapon (mounted and loaded) 41.3 lb (18.73 kg) w/M122 tripod, long barrel, 100 rd bandoleer; 41.0 lb (18.60 kg) w/M122 tripod, short barrel, 100 rd bandoleer; M122 Tripod w/pintle and T & E gear 15 lb (6.8 kg)

Feed device 100 rd belt linked 4 M80 Ball, 1 M62 Tracer (standard) 6.51 lb (2.95 kg); M60 bandoleer w/box & 100 rd standard belt 6.8 lb (3.08 kg)

Service cartridge M80 Ball 393 gr (25.5 g), M62 Tracer 383 gr (24.8 g)

Projectile M80 Ball 149 gr (9.7 g), M62 Tracer 141 gr (9.1 g)

LENGTHS

Weapon overall 42.38 in (107.6 cm) w/long barrel, 36.88 in (93.7 cm) w/short barrel

Barrel Long—22.0 in (55.9 cm), Short—16.5 in (41.9 cm)

Sight radius 21.75 in (55.2 cm) w/long barrel; 16.95 in (43 cm) w/short barrel

Effective range 1,200 yds (1,100 m)

Maximum range 4,075 yds (3,725 m)

Source: Kevin Dockery

7.62MM MK 43 MOD 0 MACHINE GUN

CARTRIDGE 7.62mm NATO (7.62×51mm)

OPERATION Gas

TYPE OF FIRE Full automatic

RATE OF FIRE Practical 150 rpm, Cyclic 500-650 rpm

MUZZLE VELOCITY 2,800 fps (853 m/s) w/long barrel; 2,650 fps (808 m/s) w/short barrel

MUZZLE ENERGY 2,593 ft/lb (3,516 J) w/long barrel; 2,323 ft/lb (3,150 J) w/short barrel

SIGHTS Open, leaf-type square-notch/blade, adjustable 300 to 1,200 meters in 100-meter increments

FEED Flexible metal disintegrating M13 link belt held in a bandoleer, left side feed

MOUNT TYPE Shoulder fired, integral bipod, M122 tripod

WEIGHTS

Weapon (empty) 21.1 lb (9.57 kg) w/long barrel; 20.8lb (9.4 kg) w/short barrel

Weapon (loaded) 27.9 lb (12.66 kg) w/long barrel, 100 rd bandoleer; 27.31 lb (12.35 kg) w/short barrel, 100 rd bandoleer

Weapon (mounted and loaded) 42.9 lb (19.46 kg) w/M122 tripod, long barrel, 100 rd bandoleer; 42.31 lb (19.5 kg) w/M122 tripod, short barrel, 100 rd bandoleer; M122 Tripod w/pintle and T & E gear 15 lb (6.8 kg)

Feed device 100 rd belt linked 4 M80 Ball, 1 M62 Tracer (standard) 6.51 lb (2.95 kg); M60 bandoleer w/box & 100 rd standard belt 6.8 lb (3.08 kg)

Service cartridge M80 Ball 393 gr (25.5 g), M62 Tracer 383 gr (24.8 g)

Projectile M80 Ball 149 gr (9.7 g), M62 Tracer 141 gr (9.1 g)

LENGTHS

Weapon overall 42.2 in (107.1 cm) w/long barrel; 37.7 in (95.8 cm) w/short barrel

Barrel Long—22.0 in (55.9 cm), Short—16.5 in (41.9 cm)

Sight radius 21.75 in (55.2 cm) w/long barrel, 16.95 in (43 cm) w/short barrel

Effective range 1,200 yds (1,100 m)

Maximum range 4,075 yds (3,725 m)

Source: Kevin Dockery

STONER 63 LIGHT MACHINE GUN

CARTRIDGE .223 Remington (5.56×45mm)

OPERATION Gas

TYPE OF FIRE Full automatic

RATE OF FIRE Practical 150-200 rpm, Cyclic 650-850 rpm

MUZZLE VELOCITY 3,250 fps (991 m/s)

MUZZLE ENERGY 1,288 ft/lb (1,747 J)

SIGHTS Open, leaf-type aperture w/aperture battle sight/post, adjustable, battle sight 200 meters, leaf 200 to 1,000 meters in 100-meter increments

FEED Flexible metal disintegrating S-63 link belt carried in a 100 or 150 round removeable plastic box, left side feed

MOUNT TYPE Shoulder fired, removeable bipod

WEIGHTS

Weapon (empty) 11.13 lb (5.05 kg)

Weapon (loaded) 17.06 lb (7.74 kg) w/150 rd box

Weapon (mounted and loaded) 17.31 lb (7.85 kg) w/sling, 150 rds; barrel 4 lb (1.81 kg); sling 0.25 lb (0.11 kg); bipod 0.50 lb (0.23 kg)

Feed device 100 rd belt 3.04 lb (1.38 kg); 100 rd ammunition box w/belt 3.31 lb (1.50 kg); 150 rd ammunition box w/belt 5.93 lb (2.69 kg); 2 × 400 rd belts (800 rds) in M2A1 ammunition box 30 lb (13.61 kg)

Service cartridge M193 Ball 182 gr (11.8 g)

Projectile 56 gr (3.6 g)

LENGTHS

Weapon overall 40.25 in (102.2 cm)

Barrel 20.0 in (50.8 cm)

Sight radius 22.25 in (56.5 cm)

Effective range 875 yds (800 m)

Maximum range 2,833 yds (2590 m)

STONER 63A LIGHT MACHINE GUN

CARTRIDGE .223 Remington (5.56×45mm)

OPERATION Gas

TYPE OF FIRE Full automatic

RATE OF FIRE Practical 200 rpm, Cyclic, variable 700-1000 rpm

MUZZLE VELOCITY 3,250 fps (991 m/s)

MUZZLE ENERGY 1,300 ft/lb (1,763 J)

SIGHTS Open, leaf-type aperture w/aperture battle sight/post, adjustable, battle sight 200 meters, leaf 200 to 1,100 meters in 100-meter increments

FEED Flexible metal disintegrating S-63 link belt carried in a 100 or 150 round removeable plastic box or 150 rd aluminium drum, left side feed, right side feed mechanism also available

MOUNT TYPE Shoulder fired, removeable bipod

WEIGHTS

Weapon (empty) 11.68 lb (5.30 kg); barrel 3.35 lb (1.52 kg); buttstock 0.68 lb (0.31 kg)

Weapon (loaded) 14.99 lb (6.80 kg) w/100 rd box; 17.23 lb (7.82 kg) w/150 rd drum w/belt

Weapon (mounted and loaded) 15.30 lb (6.94 kg) w/sling, 150 rd box; sling 0.31 lb (0.14 kg); bipod (locking type) 0.88 lb (0.40 kg)

Feed device 100 rd belt 3.04 lb (1.38 kg); 150 rd belt 4.56 lb (2.07 kg); 100 rd ammunition box w/belt 3.31 lb (1.50 kg); 150 rd ammunition box w/belt 5.93 lb (2.69 kg); 150 rd drum—empty (left side feed only) 0.99 lb (0.45 kg); 2 × 400 rd belts (800 rds) in M2A1 ammunition box 30 lb (13.61 kg)

Service cartridge M193 Ball 182 gr (11.8 g)

Projectile 56 gr (3.6 g)

LENGTHS

Weapon overall 40.25 in (102.2 cm); overall w/o buttstock 30.63 in (77.8 cm)

Barrel 20 in (50.8 cm)

Sight radius 22.25 in (56.5 cm)

Effective range 1,203 yds (1,100 m)

Maximum range 2,895 yds (2653 m)

NOTE: Changes from the Stoner 63 to the 63A configuration (circa 1967)

a. Larger gas port opening

b. Chromium plated chamber

c. Stronger and better fitting dust covers

d. A relieved breech block cam pin

e. A gas nitrided bore

f. Separate safety in front of trigger guard

g. Feed tray machined casting instead of stamped metal

h. Three position gas port valve

i. redesigned stock and forearm of polycarbonate material

j. three piece cleaning rod fitted inside of forearm

k. Endurion metal finish on all exposed surfaces

l. Bipod locks onto weapon or locks open for stowage

m. Right-side belt-feed mechanism available, exchanges w/left side feed

n. Over-the-shoulder assault sling available

o. Upper sling swivel attached to front of barrel handle

Source: Kevin Dockery

STONER 63A1

CARTRIDGE .223 Remington (5.56×45mm)

OPERATION Gas

TYPE OF FIRE Full automatic

RATE OF FIRE Practical 200 rpm, Cyclic variable 650-850 rpm

MUZZLE VELOCITY 3,250 fps (991 m/s)

MUZZLE ENERGY 1,300 ft/lb (1,763 J)

SIGHTS Open, leaf-type aperture w/aperture battle sight/post, adjustable, battle sight 200 meters, leaf 200 to 1,100 meters in 100-meter increments

FEED Flexible metal disintegrating S-63 link belt carried in a 100 or 150 round removeable plastic box or 150 rd aluminium drum (left side feed only), right side feed, left side feed mechanism also available

MOUNT TYPE Shoulder fired

WEIGHTS

Weapon (empty) 11.68 lb (5.30 kg) w/box hanger, RH feed, w/o bipod; buttstock 0.68 lb (0.31 kg); barrel 3.35 lb (1.52 kg); sling 0.31 lb (0.14 kg)

Weapon (loaded) 14.99 lb (6.8 kg) w/box hanger, RH feed, 100 rd belt box w/belt, sling

Feed device 100 rd belt 3.04 lb (1.38 kg); 150 rd belt 4.56 lb (2.07 kg); 100 rd ammunition box w/belt 3.31 lb (1.50 kg); 150 rd ammunition box w/belt 5.93 lb (2.69 kg); 100 rd ammunition box hanger (right side feed only) 0.95 lb (0.43 kg); 150 rd drum—empty (left side feed only) 0.99 lb (0.45 kg); 2 × 400 rd belts (800 rds) in M2A1 ammunition box 30 lb (13.61 kg)

Service cartridge M193 Ball 182 gr (11.8 g)

Projectile 56 gr (3.6 g)

LENGTHS

Weapon overall 40.25 in (102.2 cm); overall w/o buttstock 30.63 in (77.8 cm)

Barrel 20 in (50.8 cm) w/o flash hider

Sight radius 22.25 in (56.5 cm)

Effective range 875 yds (800 m)

Maximum range 2,898 yds (2,650 m)

Source: Kevin Dockery

MK 23 MOD 0 (STONER 63 A1 COMMANDO)

CARTRIDGE .223 Remington (5.56×45mm)

OPERATION Gas

TYPE OF FIRE Full automatic

RATE OF FIRE Practical 200 rpm, Cyclic variable 650-850 rpm

MUZZLE VELOCITY 3,000 fps

MUZZLE ENERGY 1,119 ft/lb (1,517 J)

SIGHTS Open, leaf-type aperture w/aperture battle sight/post, adjustable, battle sight 200 meters, leaf 200 to 1,100 meters in 100-meter increments

FEED Flexible metal disintegrating S-63 link belt carried in a 100 or 150 round removeable plastic box or 150 rd aluminium drum (left side feed only), right side feed, left side feed mechanism also available

MOUNT TYPE Shoulder fired

WEIGHTS

Weapon (empty) 10.77 lb (4.99 kg) w/box hanger, RH feed; buttstock 0.68 lb (0.31 kg); barrel 2.44 lb (1.12 kg); sling 0.31 lb (0.14 kg)

Weapon (loaded) 14.08 lb (6.39 kg) w/box hanger, 100 rd box w/belt, sling

Feed device 100 rd belt 3.04 lb (1.38 kg); 150 rd belt 4.56 lb (2.07 kg); 100 rd ammunition box w/belt 3.31 lb (1.50 kg); 150 rd ammunition box w/belt 5.93 lb (2.69 kg); 100 rd ammunition box hanger (right side feed only) 0.95 lb (0.43 kg); 150 rd drum—empty (left side feed only) 0.99 lb (0.45 kg); 2 × 400 rd belts (800 rds) in M2A1 ammunition box 30 lb (13.61 kg)(13.61 kg)

Service cartridge M193 Ball 182 gr (11.8 g)

Projectile 56 gr (3.6 g)

LENGTHS

Weapon overall 35.75 in (90.8 cm); 26.13 in (66.4 cm) w/o buttstock

Barrel 15.75 in (40 cm) w/o flash hider

Sight radius 22.25 in (56.5 cm)

Effective range 766 yds (700 m)

Maximum range 2,651 yds (2,424 m)

Source: Kevin Dockery

COLT CMG-2 LIGHT MACHINE GUN

CARTRIDGE .223 Remington (5.56×45mm)

OPERATION Gas

TYPE OF FIRE Full automatic

RATE OF FIRE Practical 150 rpm, Cyclic 650 rpm

MUZZLE VELOCITY 3,250 fps (991 m/s)

MUZZLE ENERGY 1,313 ft/lb (1,780 J)

SIGHTS Open, leaf-type aperture/post, adjustable 200 to 1200 meters in 200 meter increments

FEED Flexible metal disintegrating link belt carried in a 150 rd belt drum

MOUNT TYPE Shoulder fired, attachable bipod

WEIGHTS

Weapon (empty) 13.0 lb (5.90 kg)

Weapon (loaded) 19.12 lb (8.67 kg)

Weapon (mounted and loaded) 20.99 lb (9.52 kg) w/150 rd drum and belt, bipod, sling; bipod 1.56 lb (0.71 kg); sling 0.31 lb (0.14 kg)

Feed device 100 rd belt 3.04 lb (1.38 kg); 150 rd drum (empty) 1.56 lb (0.71 kg); 150 rd drum w/belt 6.12 lb (2.78 kg); 2 × 400 rd belts (800 rds) in M2A1 ammunition box 30 lb (13.61 kg)

Service cartridge M193 Ball 182 gr (11.8 g)

Projectile 56 gr (3.6 g)

LENGTHS

Weapon overall 42 in (106.7 cm)

Barrel 20 in (50.8 cm)

21.15 in (54 cm) w/flash hider

Sight radius 21.38 in (54.3 cm)

Effective range 660 yds (600 m)

Maximum range 2,898 yds (2,650 m)

Source: CIS Incorporated

ULTIMAX 100 MARK III

CARTRIDGE .223 Remington (5.56×45mm)

OPERATION Gas

TYPE OF FIRE Full automatic

RATE OF FIRE Practical 200 rpm, Cyclic variable 400-600 rpm

MUZZLE VELOCITY 3,100 fps (945 m/s)

MUZZLE ENERGY 1,323 ft/lb (1,794 J)

SIGHTS Open, Slide-type aperture/post, adjustable 100 to 600 meters in 100-meter increments or 100 to 1,000 meters in 100-meter increments (calibrated for the SS109 [M855] round)

FEED Removable 20 or 30 rd box magazines (modified M16 magazines), 60 or 100 round drums

MOUNT TYPE Shoulder fired, removable bipod

WEIGHTS

Weapon (empty) 9.68 lb (4.39 kg)

Weapon (loaded) 13.65 lb (6.19 kg) w/100 rd drum

Weapon (mounted and loaded) 14.64 lb (6.64 kg) w/100 rd drum, bipod

Bipod 0.99 lb (0.45 kg)

Feed device 20 rd box magazine (empty) 0.20 lb (0.09 kg); 20 rd box magazine (loaded) 0.74 lb (0.34 kg); 30 rd box magazine (empty) 0.26 lb (0.12 kg); 30 rd box magazine (loaded) 1.07 lb (0.49 kg); 60 rd drum (empty) 0.56 lb (0.26 kg); 60 rd drum (loaded) 2.19 lb (0.99 kg); 100 rd drum (empty) 1.26 lb (0.57 kg); 100 rd drum (loaded) 3.97 lb (1.80 kg);

Service cartridge M855 Ball 190 gr (12.3 g)

Projectile 62 gr (4.0 g)

LENGTHS

Weapon overall 40.6 in (103.1 cm); 31.5 in (80 cm) w/o buttstock

Barrel 20 in (50.8 cm)

Sight radius 18.58 in (47.2 cm)

Effective range M193 Ball 500 yds (460 m); M855 Ball 1,422 yds (1300 m)

Source: FN USA Corporation

MINIMI M249 LIGHT MACHINE GUN

CARTRIDGE .223 Remington (5.56×45mm)

OPERATION Gas

TYPE OF FIRE Full automatic

RATE OF FIRE Practical 150 rpm, Cyclic 750 rpm

MUZZLE VELOCITY 3,034 fps (925 m/s)

MUZZLE ENERGY 1,247 ft/lb (1,691 J)

SIGHTS Open, Drum-type aperture/post, adjustable 300 to 1,000 meters in 100-meter increments

FEED 20 or 30 rd removable box magazine (M16) or flexible metal disintegrating M27 link belt held in a 200 rd plastic belt box, left hand feed

MOUNT TYPE Shoulder fired, attached bipod, M122 tripod

WEIGHTS

Weapon (empty) 16.5 lb (7.48 kg)

Weapon (loaded) 23.46 lb (10.64 kg) w/200 rds in belt box

Feed device 100 rd belt linked 4 Ball M855, 1 Tracer M856 3.17 lb (1.44 kg); 20 rd box magazine (empty) 0.20 lb (0.09 kg); 20 rd box magazine (loaded) 0.74 lb (0.34 kg); 30 rd box magazine (empty) 0.26 lb (0.12 kg); 30 rd box magazine (loaded) 1.07 lb (0.49 kg); 200 rd belt box (empty) 0.61 lb (0.28 kg); 200 rd belt box (loaded w/standard belt) 6.96 lb (3.16 kg)

Service cartridge M855 Ball 190 gr (12.3 g), M856 Tracer 191 gr (12.4 g)

Projectile M855 Ball 62 gr (4.0 g), M856 Tracer 64 gr (4.1 g)

LENGTHS

Weapon overall 41.0 in (104.1 cm)

Barrel 18.34 in (46.6 cm)

Sight radius 19.5 in (49.5 cm)

Effective range 1,094 yds (1,000 m)

Source: FN USA Corporation

M249 PARATROOPER MODEL

CARTRIDGE .223 Remington (5.56×45mm)

OPERATION Gas

TYPE OF FIRE Full automatic

RATE OF FIRE Practical 150 rpm Cyclic variable 750 rpm

MUZZLE VELOCITY 2,841 fps (866 m/s)

MUZZLE ENERGY 1,093 ft/lb (1,482 J)

SIGHTS Open, drum-type aperture/post, adjustable 300 to 1,000 meters in 100-meter increments

FEED 20 or 30 rd removable box magazine (M16) or flexible metal disintegrating M27 link belt held in a 200 rd plastic belt box, left hand feed

MOUNT TYPE Shoulder fired, attached bipod

WEIGHTS

Weapon (empty) 15.95 lb (7.23 kg)

Weapon (loaded) 22.91 lb (10.39 kg) w/200 rds in belt box

Feed device 100 rd belt linked four Ball M855, one Tracer M856 3.17 lb (1.44 kg);

20 rd box magazine (empty) 0.20 lb (0.09 kg); 20 rd box magazine (loaded) 0.74 lb (0.34 kg); 30 rd box magazine (empty) 0.26 lb (0.12 kg); 30 rd box magazine (loaded) 1.07 lb (0.49 kg); 200 rd belt box (empty) 0.61 lb (0.28 kg); 200 rd belt box (loaded w/standard belt) 6.96 lb (3.16 kg)

Service cartridge M855 Ball 190 gr (12.3 g), M856 Tracer 191 gr (12.4 g)

Projectile M855 Ball 62 gr (4.0 g), M856 Tracer 64 gr (4.1 g)

LENGTHS

Weapon overall 30.5/35.8 in (77.5/90.9 cm)

Barrel 13.66 in (34.7 cm)

Sight radius 19.5 in (49.5 cm)

Effective range 1,094 yds (1,000 m)

Source: Kevin Dockery

HECKLER & KOCH HK21A1 LIGHT MACHINE GUN

CARTRIDGE 7.62mm NATO (7.62×51mm)

OPERATION Roller locked delayed blowback

TYPE OF FIRE Selective fire

RATE OF FIRE Practical (SS) 40 rpm (A) 150 rpm Cyclic 900 rpm

MUZZLE VELOCITY 2,624 fps (800 m/s)

MUZZLE ENERGY M80 Ball 2,278 ft/lb (3,089 J)

SIGHTS Open, drum-type aperture/post, adjustable 200 to 1,200 meters in 100 meter increments, provision for accepting 4 power optical sight, sight wt 1.43 lb (0.65 kg)

FEED Flexible metal disintegrating M13 or nondisintegrating DM1 link belt in 100 rd attachable belt box, left side feed

MOUNT TYPE Shoulder fired, attached bipod

WEIGHTS

Weapon (empty) 18.30 lb (8.30 kg)

Weapon (loaded) 26.24 lb w/100 rd belt box, standard belt

Feed device 100 rd belt linked w/M13 links 4 M80 Ball, 1 M62 Tracer (standard) 6.51 lb (2.95 kg); 50 rd DM1 belt linked 4 M80 Ball, 1 M62 Tracer 3.11 lb (1.41 kg); 100 rd belt box (empty) 1.43 lb (0.65 kg); 100 rd belt box (loaded) 7.94 lb (3.60 kg)

Service cartridge M80 Ball 393 gr (25.5 g), M62 Tracer 383 gr (24.8 g)

Projectile M80 Ball 149 gr (9.7 g), M62 Tracer 141 gr (9.1 g)

LENGTHS

Weapon overall 40.58 in (103 cm)

Barrel 17.71 in (45 cm)

Sight radius 23.22 in (59 cm)

Effective range 1,312 yds (1,200 m)

Source: Ares Corporation

ARES 86 (STONER 86)

CARTRIDGE .223 Remington NATO (5.56×45mm NATO)

OPERATION Gas

TYPE OF FIRE Full automatic

RATE OF FIRE Practical 150 rpm Cyclic 600 rpm

MUZZLE VELOCITY 3,100 fps (945 m/s) long barrel; short barrel 2,850 fps (869 m/s)

MUZZLE ENERGY 1,323 ft/lb (1,794 J); short barrel 1,118 ft/lb (1,516 J)

SIGHTS Open, leaf-type aperture w/aperture battle sight/post, adjustable, battle sight 200 meters, leaf 200 to 1,100 meters in 100-meter increments

FEED 20 or 30 rd removable box magazine (M16) or flexible metal disintegrating M27

link belt held in a 200 rd plastic belt box, left hand feed

MOUNT TYPE Shoulder fired, removable bi-pod, M122 tripod

WEIGHTS

Weapon (empty) 10.83 lb (4.91 kg) w/long barrel, w/o bipod; 8.54 lb (3.87 kg) w/short barrel w/o buttstock, bipod; 10.97 lb (4.95 kg) setup for magazine feed w/magazine adapter, long barrel, w/o bipod; barrel wt (long) 3.82 lb (1.73 kg); bipod wt 1.23 lb (0.56 kg)

Weapon (loaded) 17.79 lb (8.07 kg) w/long barrel & 200 rds in box w/o bipod; 19.02 lb (8.63 kg) w/long barrel, 200 rds in box, bi-pod; 15.5 lb (7.03 kg) w/short barrel & 200 rds in box, w/o bipod or stock

Feed device 100 rd belt linked 4 Ball M855, 1 Tracer M856 3.17 lb (1.44 kg); 20 rd box magazine (empty) 0.20 lb (0.09 kg); 20 rd box magazine (loaded) 0.74 lb (0.34 kg); 30 rd box magazine (empty) 0.26 lb (0.12 kg); 30 rd box magazine (loaded) 1.07 lb (0.49 kg); 200 rd belt box (empty) 0.61 lb (0.28 kg); 200 rd belt box (loaded w/stan-dard belt) 6.96 lb (3.16 kg)

Service cartridge M855 Ball 190 gr (12.3 g), M856 Tracer 191 gr (12.4 g)

Projectile M855 Ball 62 gr (4.0 g), M856 Tracer 64 gr (4.1 g)

LENGTHS

Weapon overall 38.25/42.25 in (97.2/107.3 cm) w/long barrel; 26.44 in (67.2 cm) w/short barrel, w/o buttstock

Barrel 21.69 in (55.1 cm) long barrel w/flash hider; 15.69 in (39.9 cm) w/short barrel, w/o buttstock

Sight radius 22.25 in (56.5 cm)

Effective range 1,094 yds (1,000 m)

Maximum range 3,937 yds (3,600 m)

MARK 46 MOD 0 LIGHT MACHINE GUN

CARTRIDGE .223 Remington (5.56×45mm)

OPERATION Gas

TYPE OF FIRE Full automatic

RATE OF FIRE Practical 150 rpm, Cyclic 750 rpm

MUZZLE VELOCITY 2,841 fps (866 m/s)

MUZZLE ENERGY 1,093 ft/lb (1,482 J)

SIGHTS Open, drum-type aperture/post, ad-justable 300 to 1,000 meters in 100 meter increments, picatinny rails on top of feed cover and four sides of fore end to accept SOPMOD M4 aiming and handling de-vices.

FEED Flexible metal disintegrating M27 link belt held in a 200 rd plastic belt box, Left hand feed

MOUNT TYPE Shoulder fired, attached bi-pod, M122 tripod

WEIGHTS

Weapon (empty) 13.0 lb (5.90 kg)

Weapon (loaded) 19.96 lb (9.05 kg) w/200 rds in belt box

Feed device 100 rd belt linked 4 Ball M855, 1 Tracer M856 3.17 lb (1.44 kg); 200 rd belt box (empty) 0.61 lb (0.28 kg); 200 rd belt box (loaded w/standard belt) 6.96 lb (3.16 kg)

Service cartridge M855 Ball 190 gr (12.3 g), M856 Tracer 191 gr (12.4 g)

Projectile M855 Ball 62 gr (4.0 g), M856 Tracer 64 gr (4.1 g)

LENGTHS

Weapon overall 36.5 in (92.7 cm)

Barrel 14.0 in (35.7 cm)

Sight radius 19.5 in (49.5 cm)

Effective range 549 yds (600 m)

7.62MM MK 48 MOD 0 LIGHT MACHINE GUN

CARTRIDGE 7.62mm NATO (7.62×51mm)

OPERATION Gas

TYPE OF FIRE Full automatic

RATE OF FIRE Practical 100 rpm, Cyclic 675 rpm

MUZZLE VELOCITY 2,715 fps (828 m/s)

MUZZLE ENERGY 2,438 ft/lb (3,306 J)

SIGHTS Open, leaf-type square-notch/blade, adjustable 300 to 1,200 meters in 100-meter increments, picatinny rails on top of feed cover and four sides of fore end to accept SOPMOD M4 aiming and handling devices.

FEED Flexible metal disintegrating M13 link belt held in a bandoleer, left side feed

MOUNT TYPE Shoulder fired, integral bipod, M122 tripod

WEIGHTS

Weapon (empty) 18.64 lb (8.46 kg)

Weapon (loaded) 25.15 lb (11.41 kg) w/100 rd bandoleer

Feed device 100 rd belt linked 4 M80 Ball, 1 M62 Tracer (standard) 6.51 lb (2.95 kg); M60 bandoleer w/box & 100 rd standard belt 6.8 lb (3.08 kg)

Service cartridge M80 Ball 393 gr (25.5 g), M62 Tracer 383 gr (24.8 g)

Projectile M80 Ball 149 gr (9.7 g), M62 Tracer 141 gr (9.1 g)

LENGTHS

Weapon overall 39.5 in (100.3 cm)

Barrel 19.75 in (50.2 cm)

Effective range 730 yds (800 m)

Source: Ares Inc.

ARES SHRIKE

CARTRIDGE .223 Remington (5.56×45mm)

OPERATION Gas

TYPE OF FIRE Selective fire

RATE OF FIRE Practical 150 rpm Cyclic variable 650-800 rpm

MUZZLE VELOCITY 2,950 fps (899 m/s) w/14.25 inch barrel

SIGHTS Open, aperture/post, adjustable, M1913 picatinny rail on top cover accepts optical and electro-optical sighting devices.

FEED 20 or 30 rd removable box magazine (M16) or flexible metal disintegrating M27 link belt held in a 200 rd plastic belt box, left hand feed

MOUNT TYPE Shoulder fired

WEIGHTS

Weapon (empty) 7.5 lb (2.95 kg) w/14.25 inch barrel

Weapon (loaded) 14 lb (6.35 kg) w/200 rds in belt box

Feed device 100 rd belt linked 4 Ball M855, 1 Tracer M856 3.17 lb (1.44 kg); 20 rd box magazine (empty) 0.20 lb (0.09 kg); 20 rd box magazine (loaded) 0.74 lb (0.34 kg); 30 rd box magazine (empty) 0.26 lb (0.12 kg); 30 rd box magazine (loaded) 1.07 lb (0.49 kg); 200 rd belt box (empty) 0.61 lb (0.28 kg); 200 rd belt box (loaded w/standard belt) 6.96 lb (3.16 kg)

Service cartridge M855 Ball 190 gr (12.3 g), M856 Tracer 191 gr (12.4 g)

Projectile M855 Ball 62 gr (4.0 g), M856 Tracer 64 gr (4.1 g)

LENGTHS

Weapon overall 29.25/32.4 in (74.2/82.3 cm) w/14.25 inch barrel

Barrel 14.25 in (36.2 cm)

Sight radius 16.5 in (41.9 cm)

Effective range 550 yds (600 m)

■ 12

SHOTS IN THE SANDBOX

"What the hell is that?" Boatswain's Mate First Class Mike Grange said.

The SEAL element that Mike Grange was in charge of had been manning a forward observation post in the Jaji mountain range of southeastern Afghanistan for over a day now. They were working with a pair of men from the Air Force Special Operations community, Airman Keith Adair and sergeant Lionel Thomas. The two Air Force men made up a Combat Controller Team (CCT). With their tactical laser designator (TLD) mounted on a small tripod, the CCT had been "painting" targets with laser light. The coherent light reflecting off a target would draw in a laser-guided bomb like a fly to a lamp.

Navy and Air Force aircraft overhead had been striking at targets in the mountains in preparation for a U.S. assault team to come in and clear the area of Taliban and al-Qaida forces hiding in the caves and valleys of the mountains. Fighting had been going on in the distance and all of the men had heard the sound of heavy gunfire just a few minutes earlier. As the men had been preparing to guide in a bomb strike on a valley not 500 meters from their position, a helicopter trailing smoke and in obvious trouble had flown in on the scene.

The helicopter, a Bell OH-58D Kiowa, was heading in to the mouth of the valley the SEALs had been about to bomb. Whoever the pilot was, he had to work hard just to keep his bird in the air and under control. He wasn't going to get very far and looked to be lucky if he didn't just crash and burn.

"Horseman four, Horseman four," Lionel Thomas said into his radio. "This is Texas One-Niner. Wave off. I repeat, wave off. We have a broken wing on the target."

In spite of the encryption equipment on the radio that made listening in on the conversation almost impossible for the al-Qaida or Taliban, Thomas still was very careful about what he said over the air. He clicked the radio over from his headset to the speaker so that everyone in the position could hear what was being said.

"Roger Texas One-Niner," came back from the pair of F-14B Tomcats overhead. "We read a broken wing on the target. Waving off."

"Okay," Thomas said, "the Tomcat has canceled its run. Where the hell is that helicopter?"

"It went in to the mouth of the valley," Machinist Mate Second Class Ed Harmon said.

"Shit," said Quartermaster Second Class Richard Kodak, "that's where those al-Qaida are!"

"They'll be out from undercover fast enough," Gunner's Mate Third Class Steve Marstairs said. "Anyone alive in that bird will be just so much dead meat."

All of the Special Operations men had been watching a small group of al-Qaida moving through the mountain area. Inside the valley was a small cave complex. Now that the observation post was certain that there were al-Qaida inside the cave, they had been about to destroy the target.

"Texas One-Niner," came over the radio, "this is Horseman-Four. I just queried Sunshine-Three on that broken wing. That's Iguana-Seven. They just took heavy fire from a hilltop position about three klicks from your present position. There are two men aboard. They have been in contact with Sunshine-Three up to a few minutes ago. Support is delayed. I repeat, support is delayed."

"Roger that, Horseman-Four," Thomas said.

Sunshine-Three was the AWACS plane circling far overhead. The airborne warning and control system aircraft, a Boeing E-3A Sentry, had been the command, communications, and control center for most of the aircraft in the entire Afghan theater of operations. They had known about the helicopter being hit from the moment it had taken fire. Now the bird was down in enemy-held territory and the chances were that there were men alive, and probably hurt, on board that helicopter.

"We can't just to wait for someone to come in to help," Grange said. "Those al-Qaida will get to that helicopter and pull any survivors out as soon as they realize they aren't under fire. Then we'll have a hostage situation on our hands."

"I don't see anything else we can do," Kodak said, "we'll have to go and pull them out."

"Roger that," Harmon said.

"Thomas, inform Rainbow that we're going in to pull out any survivors," Grange said. "You and Adair are going to remain here and give us cover when support finally comes in. The rest of you, gear up, we're pulling out ASAP."

The men in the observation post had been living from their packs. Every time they removed and item, they resealed their packs so that they could move out at a moment's notice. In the time it took for Thomas to communicate with Rainbow, the special operations local command headquarters, the rest of the men were ready to move out on a fast rescue operation.

They were the men on the ground, and the only ones who had a chance to get to the downed helicopter before the al-Qaida people took it. As the SEALs moved out from the observation post, they did so under the watchful eyes of the Air Force CCT men. The two M4A1 carbines of the CCT men would have been an addition to the SEAL element's firepower. But the amount of fire two shoulder weapons could bring to the fight was nothing compared to the massed hell the two CT men could bring down from above by directing air strikes.

Neither Thomas nor Adair were happy about being left behind. But both of the men knew it was the best way they could support the rescue. While Thomas maintained contact with higher command, Adair kept watch on the valley nearby through the optical sights on his TLD.

Even for men in as superb physical condition as the SEALs, running along the rocky slopes of the Afghanistan mountains was a rough way to go. The fact that there were men who may not live another five minutes kept the SEALs moving quickly but carefully. The men had been watching the area for the better part of a full day. They knew all of the smaller hills and valleys in front of them. It was less than fifteen minutes since the helicopter had augered in to the valley when the SEALs arrived on the far side of the last rise.

Now, the SEALs moved in unison, each man covering the other. One shooter pair would cover the other as they moved into final position. As Grange and Harmon came up to the last rise, they could hear the sounds of gunfire not two hundred meters away. Both SEALs were carrying M4A1 carbines mounted with a SureFire torch on the front handgrip. To accurately aim the flat-topped M4A1s, the men had ACOG optical sights mounted in place on top of the weapons. These were fairly minimal additions from the SOPMOD kits available to each man. The normal black coatings of their weapons had been painted over in a mottled tan to better blend in with the surrounding area.

Kodak and Marstairs were more heavily armed than their Teammates up ahead. Kodak was an automatic weapons man and he was carrying a Mark 43 light machine gun, the last of the M60 series to still see active use. The heavy 7.62mm NATO slugs the Mk 43 fired could carry a long way across the Afghan mountains, covering men at a much greater range than the AK-47s normally used by the Taliban or al-Qaida.

Also armed with an M4A1, Marstairs was a grenadier and he had an M203A1 40mm grenade launcher mounted on his weapon. The half-pound rounds for the M203A1 were a handful to carry around the Afghan countryside. But the ability of the grenades to take out targets behind cover made them very useful indirect-fire weapons.

Every SEAL also carried his preferred knife or knives, M67 fragmentation grenades, M18 colored smoke grenades, and a Mark 11 pistol. The Mk 11 was the adopted designation for the SIG P-226 9mm handgun the SEALs had been using for years now. All of the men were carrying heavy loads of ammunition to feed all of their weapons.

Back at the observation post, Adair could see some very limited movement along the ridgeline of the valley. The al-Qaida terrorists that had been holed up in a cave in the valley were coming out and trying to move across the ridge. It looked like they intended to flank the downed helicopter and move in on the crew under the cover of the ridge. From close in, they could then rush over the ridge and down onto the crash site. What the terrorists didn't know was that they were under observation by people who knew how to use the very big gun they had at their command. The original pair of F-14Bs that had been circling overhead had to leave the area as they were running low on fuel. But there were other aircraft available in the sky.

"Any available Horseman, any available Horseman," Thomas said into the radio, "this is Texas One-Niner, I have a fire mission for you."

"Texas One-Niner, this is Horseman-Ten, go ahead with your mission," came back from the pair of F-14Bs overhead.

"Horseman-Ten," Thomas said, "I need a gun run up the valley at coordinates one-seven-four-three. We have tangos about to overrun the broken wing. Danger close, we have troops to the west of that position."

"Roger that, Texas One-Niner," came over the radio, "I read a gun run up the valley at one-seven-four-three. Danger close."

As the SEALs approached the valley where the stricken helicopter lay, the al-Qaida in the area began to move in. High overhead, a pair of F-15B fighter bombers tilted their wings to the side and slipped down into a dive.

The F-14B aircraft couldn't use their heavy punch, the 500-pound bombs they carried underneath the fuselages and wings. But they did have the M61A1 Vulcan 20mm cannons set into the lower port side of their aircraft. The six-barreled cannon fired at a rate of 6,000 rounds per minute. The 675 rounds of M56A3 high explosive incendiary ammunition for the M61A1 Vulcans gave them less than seven seconds of firepower from the cannons. But at the speed the F-14Bs traveled over the target area, they could only fire safely for a few seconds each anyway.

The SEALs looked up to see the two F-14Bs come in on a gun run up the valley. The pilots were moving very close and very fast before they opened fire. They had to pull up hard to avoid the mountains beyond the valley. But for their few seconds over the target, they made the upper part of the valley a raging hell for anyone on the ground.

The shotgun-shell sized slugs from the Vulcans plowed into the ground and exploded. Each shell held only a small charge of explosives, but there were hundreds of them. The screams of the al-Qaida caught in the open were drowned out by the roar of the F-14B General Electric F110-GE-400 engines, and by the explosions of the 20mm Vulcan ammunition.

As the jets passed, the SEALs reached the last hill that led up to the valley. Dropping to lay prone on the ground, Grange and Harmon slipped up to the ridgeline overlooking the mouth of the valley. There, they waited until Kodak and Marstairs joined up with them. The valley mouth was small, more of a gully than a true valley. Only about twenty meters wide, it moved up into the foot of the mountains—a scattering of brush and scrub grasses growing in clumps.

Past the first curve of the valley, the SEALs could see the top of the helicopter's rotor. The bird had hit on the ridgeline and slid into the valley by the looks of the scars in the ground. The sound of gunfire had died out as the SEALs came up on the valley. As the echoes bounced off the rock faces around them, they prepared to move forward.

Up on the ridgeline, Kodak would have the best position to cover the SEALs advance up the valley with his Mk 43. Unfolding the bipod legs on his weapon, Kodak settled in to protect his Teammates. Laying prone next to his shooting partner, Marstairs made certain his M203A1 was loaded with a high explosive fragmentation grenade. The most generally useful round the SEALs used in their 40mm grenades launchers was the M433 high-explosive dual-purpose round. The cartridge launched a grenade that not only spread fragmentation throughout its impact area, it could punch through two inches of steel with its shaped charge warhead.

Very familiar with the capabilities of his weapon, Marstairs laid out two more of the green-bodied, gold-tipped eggs next to his weapon, ready for a quick reload. Looking to their Teammates, Grange and Harmon saw that the other SEALs were ready to put out whatever fire was needed to cover their approach. Looking at each other, Harmon acknowledged the quick nod from Grange.

The two SEALs had been working together with each other for long months. Each man knew how the other would react in just about any situation.

Their almost intuitive knowledge about each other was a result of the constant emphasis on Teamwork among the SEALs.

Never passing directly in front of Kodak or Marstairs up on the ridgeline, Grange and Harmon moved out. Their weapons were loaded, rounds in the chamber, and the selectors' switches were set to full automatic. The SEALs emphasized safety above everything else during training. Both men knew to keep their fingers off the triggers and they rushed down the small hillside into the valley. Their weapons wouldn't fire until they wanted them to, and that moment was fast approaching.

As Grange and Harmon reached the floor of the small valley, an al-Qaida fighter who was in a small notch in the valley saw them and opened fire. The knocking booms of the AK-47 were quickly answered by the heavier thunder of Marstairs's Mark 43. The big machine gun couldn't be swung around or depressed enough to take the al-Qaida gunner under direct fire. But the rain of steel-jacketed projectiles passing right over his head did make the terrorist duck down and cease his own firing.

Both Grange and Harmon saw the movement of the terrorist even as he opened fire on them. Breaking to either side, the two SEALs snapped off short bursts from their M4A1s as they moved. Keeping the buttstock of their weapons tight up against their shoulders, the SEALs' fire was considerably more accurate than that of the terrorist. The two trios of steel-cored 5.56mm M855 projectiles ripped into and through their target. That was now one al-Qaida fighter who would never again subvert Islam for his own ends.

Since they had opened fire, the situation had changed for the SEALs. The single gunman may have been an odd scout, or he could be the pointman for an al-Qaida column. Either way, they had to move even faster now. Stealth made way for speed as Grange and Harmon move up to the small indentation in the side of the valley where the gunman had been hidden.

As soon as they could see that their Teammates had reached a good position and were prepared to cover them, Kodak and Marstairs got up and quickly moved down into the valley. Marstairs was only slowed for a moment as he picked up his two loose rounds of 40mm ammunition and quickly stuffed them into his left hip pocket.

With his 100-round bandoleer of ammunition attached to the side of his Mark 43 machine gun, Kodak handled his big weapon as if it were nothing more than a rifle as he got up and moved out. The biggest SEAL in the element, Kodak resembled his nickname "Bear" even more as he lumbered down the side of the valley. A big man could carry a large weapon, and Kodak was strong enough to pack along more than 600 rounds of ammunition for his Mark 43 as well.

Just as they reached the floor of the valley, Kodak and Marstairs heard their Teammates opening fire from thirty meters in front of them. Around the bend in the valley were coming a number of al-Qaida gunmen. The terrorists were oblivious to the fire being put out by the two SEALs on the small rise. But they couldn't ignore the sudden hail of fire that was put out by Kodak and his machine gun.

A belt-fed weapon such as the Mark 43 could put out sustained fire for as long as it held ammunition. Looking like a great bear charging forward, Kodak was putting out fire from his Mk 43 with each step he took. The rain of steel-jacketed 7.62mm projectiles cut through the ranks of the al-Qaida and thinned them considerably. None of the terrorists wanted to face the lethal spray of the heavy weapon and they broke and ran before the onslaught.

Seeing the terrorists hesitate in their charge, Marstairs popped off a 40mm grenade to help them on their way. He had to place the deadly grenade carefully. Marstairs didn't want to drop a grenade in on the helicopter that was just beyond the bend, even if the al-Qaida coming from that direction told him that the chances of finding any of the crew alive was very slim. The golden-tipped grenade arced through the air and landed just beyond the terrorists in their flight. Fragmentation tore through their ranks even as the rounds fired by Grange and Harmon knocked down their numbers even further.

Under the cover of his Teammates, Kodak stopped and quickly reloaded a second belt of ammunition into the smoking feed tray of his Mark 43. In only seconds, his weapon was back up and knocking out fire. The SEALs carried the firepower to overwhelm a much larger force, which was what they were doing. But they could only put out such a high volume of fire for a short time. While the al-Qaida terrorists were still stunned by the SEALs' ferocious onslaught, the men had to move quickly to reach the helicopter.

Coming up to where their Teammates were laying, Marstairs and Kodak fell into the prone position and started to put out fire. Neither pair of men had to speak to the other about what to do next. Not twenty meters away lay the smoking hull of the Kiowa OH-58D. Kneeling in the doorway of the downed bird was a disheveled crewman holding an M4 carbine. The SEALs now knew that one man was alive, and they were there to get him out.

While their Teammates kept up a constant fire to cover their approach, Grange and Harmon went over the rise and headed out to the helicopter. Their tan desert camouflage uniforms would have to be enough to identify them to the armed crewman. It would be a really stupid way to die for either SEAL to get shot by the man they came to rescue. But there had been no radio communications with the helicopter at all on the part of the SEALs or their CCT partners. Looking up at the bird, Grange could see how the radio antennas on the hull and tail had been ripped apart in the crash.

On the rise, Marstairs popped off round after round of 40mm grenades, aiming the rounds to land in the valley beyond the helicopter. There was a second bend in the valley that kept the SEALs from seeing the mouth of the cave they knew was there. But the 40mm M203A1 had an easy time putting out high explosive rounds in a high arc, an arc that took them over the rise beyond and down into the valley they couldn't see.

"We're Navy SEALs come to get you out!" Grange shouted as he ran up to the helicopter.

The crewman in the doorway turned and started to raise the M4 before recognizing what Grange was shouting. The SEAL was astonished to see that the crewman wasn't a man at all. Slumping down in the bird was a woman, streaked with blood and wearing a helmet and torn jumpsuit, but a woman nonetheless.

"Thank God," the woman said. "I thought those Afghans were going to have us for sure until those jets came. I'm Iguana-Seven, Captain White. My copilot is injured."

"Not a problem ma'am," Grange said as he shook off his surprise. Harmon quickly ducked into the hull of the helicopter and pulled out the almost unconscious copilot. The man groaned and moved weakly as the SEAL pulled him up and carefully as he could.

"We have no time," Grange said loudly. "We have to pull out quickly before those tangos can regroup."

Leading the way, he headed back to where Marstairs and Kodak were still putting out covering fire. Captain White was standing on the other side of her injured copilot, helping Harmon move the man out of the area. Passing by the foot of the hillside where Kodak was still firing his Mark 43, Grange waved an arm signal to Marstairs.

The two SEALs maintained covering fire while the rest of their Teammates and the two crewmen pulled back. As the others reached safety and turned to cover their withdrawal, Marstairs fired a last 40mm grenade into the hull of the downed helicopter. The blast of the grenade combined with the penetrating power of its shaped charge ripped open the hull and ignited the fuel that had been soaking into the ground. With a sudden whoomp, the helicopter was engulfed in a ball of flame. No al-Qaida would recover anything of use from that downed bird. And the flame would help cover the SEALs withdrawal.

As the group pulled back from the valley. Grange got back on the radio to Thomas and Adair back up at the observation post.

"Texas One-Niner, this is Texas One-One," Grange said. "We have the package. Continue with the run. Paint that sucker and lay one in on them."

"Roger, One-One," came back over the radio. "I copy, paint and paste coming up."

As the rescued helicopter crew and SEALs pulled back from the valley, they couldn't see the invisible laser from the TLD illuminating the upper part of the valley. That cave was about to be closed. Though they couldn't see the target, the laser seeker heads in the guided bomb units (GBU) attached to the Mark 84 bombs overhead had no trouble following the path of the coherent light. The 2,000-pound bombs shattered the quiet of the valley as they ripped apart the al-Qaida position.

FORTY-MILLIMETER GRENADE LAUNCHERS

In general, a grenade is any small, short-range, explosive munition intended to be hand thrown or projected towards the enemy. Though a relatively old weapon of war, pottery grenades filled with black powder were reportedly used in 1536, it was in the first World War of the 20th century in which the modern grenade made an appearance. In the trench-to-trench fighting of WWI, the ability to throw a hand grenade from under cover and attack a target that was behind more cover was immediately valuable.

One immediate limitation of the grenade was obvious, even the strongest man could only throw one so far. To increase the range of a grenade through chemical rather than muscle means, the rifle grenade was also brought forward during WWI. Though another old weapon idea, rifle grenades were developed into a considerably more accurate weapon between 1914 and 1918 than their flintlock predecessors had been.

In World War II, hand and rifle grenades became much more refined during the course of the war. Adopted for the U.S. Services in September 1941, the primary type of rifle grenade attachment was a spigot-type launcher that fit on the end of a service rifle. The tail of U.S.-issue rifle grenades was hollow and would slide snugly over a grenade launcher attached to a rifle. A special blank cartridge would be loaded into the weapon to launch the rifle grenade up to several hundred yards away. All U.S. rifle grenades were fin-stabilized and the rather small surface area of the fins, combined with the short overall length of the grenade launcher spigot, made the weapon system relatively inaccurate.

The rifle grenade filled the space between the maximum range a hand grenade could be thrown and the average minimum range a mortar could be used for close-in fire support. Infantry units during World War II that had been pinned down some distance from an emplaced machine gun were often too far to reach the target with a hand-thrown grenade and too close to call in artillery fire support. The elimination of such infantry obstacles required the development of a more efficient and accurate individual weapon that could be carried and operated by one man.

Mortars, both 60mm and 2-inch, were modified with small baseplates and simple sight systems for hand-held operation by one or two men in an infantry squad. But the simplified mortar systems did not deliver the greatest accuracy and effectiveness on target in a really portable weapon.

A 60mm US M19 mortar, essentially a stripped down M2 mortar with a trigger firing control, weighed 20.5 pounds (9.3 kilograms) with an M1 baseplate attached. Each 60mm M49A2 HE round weighed 2.96 pounds (1.34 kilograms). The effective range of the M19 when hand-held was considered to be only 200 yards and relatively few of the large rounds of ammunition could be carried by the gunner.

In the post-WWII years, the problem of increasing the range of a grenade, while increasing the accuracy and cutting back on the weapon weight, was studied more closely. At the height of the Korean War in 1952 the project received a priority push to develop both the ammunition and a new weapon to launch it. Several different avenues of approach were taken simultaneously by the military ordnance community to develop the new weapons system.

The U.S. Army Ballistic Research Laboratories (BRL) at Aberdeen Proving Grounds had established by 1951 that a small explosive package could be made that delivered controlled fragmentation that would be effective within a limited radius. By using small fragments that could be consistently produced in a grenade-type munition, the BRL came up with the parameters that the new round should be designed to fit.

Picatinny Arsenal in Dover, New Jersey, became the central controller for the development of the new round of ammunition. The most effective caliber was determined to be 40mm to fit the BRL guidelines. Initial designs to control the fragmentation of the grenade centered on using a hollow-walled projectile with the space filled with small ball bearings. This idea was soon dropped when it was determined that an excessively large number of ball bearings would be needed to match the estimated production quantities of ammunition desired by the army.

Fragmentation for the new round would be accomplished by internally segmenting the grenade body so that it would break up according to established lines. The Stanford Research Institute came up with an efficient way of making engraved sheet stock that could be formed into a spherical grenade body that would produce fragmentation very close to that of the ball bearing design. The engraving process, called "roll coining," made a sheet of steel that could be formed into a ball and filled with high explosive. When detonated, the steel body would break up along the engraved lines creating hundreds of small, 2-grain (0.13 gram), square fragments. The fragments would be traveling at an initial velocity of 5,000 feet per second from the point of detonation. But the low weight of the fragments, combined with their poor aerodynamic shape, caused them to lose velocity quickly. This gave the new grenade a casualty radius of only 5 meters.

The Chamberlain Manufacturing Corporation came up with an even simpler and lower-cost version of the grenade body. The Chamberlain fragmentation body was formed from notched square steel wire copper-brazed together into the form of a ball. This wire ball would form the same quantity, size, and type of fragments as the coined steel Stanford version, giving the design the same casualty-producing radius.

Working with outside companies such as Honeywell Incorporated, Picatinny came up with a fuze system for the new grenade that was considered a marvel of miniaturization at the time. Even with the small size of the fuze, it was as large as the fragmentation body itself and made up over 50 percent of the complete projectile. Further studies of the new projectile centered on determining which would be the best way to launch and stabilize it in flight.

Colonel Rene R. Stutler, Chief of Small Arms Research and Development for U.S. Army Ordnance, at his office in the Pentagon had decided that a shoulder-fired launcher dedicated to launching the new grenade would be the way the project would go forward. A deputy to Colonel Stutler, Jack Bird, became interested in the grenade launcher project and investigated the idea on his own time.

Taking a piece of pipe that would accept a golf ball, Bird capped off one end and drilled several small holes through the tube's side. With a spring placed in the tube and a golf ball dropped down over the spring, a stick was used to push the ball down against the pressure of the spring. A nail slipped through one of the holes in the side of the tube held the ball in place on the compressed spring.

Demonstrations of Bird's "launcher" took place in the central courtyard of the Pentagon. The high-arcing trajectory of the golf ball when the cross nail was pulled out demonstrated remarkable accuracy for such a crude device. The high-lobbing arc of the ball reminded a number of the onlookers of a nine-iron stroke on a golf course. Bird suggested the program for the new weapon be named after the popular term for a nine-iron at the time, a niblick. Stutler agreed and Project Niblick was so named.

Once the basic projectile had been established, both a launcher and a means of propelling the grenade were needed.

Springfield Armory received funds in June 1952 for its Research and Development Division to conduct a study of various devices to launch the new grenade design. A number of designs were established, built, and tested at Springfield Armory using the various forms of ammunition, now known as the Niblick projectile, coming from Picatinny.

Launchers for the Niblick projectile at Springfield Armory from 1952 into 1955 concentrated on muzzle attachments for the M1 Garand service rifle. These launchers used a blank cartridge to propel a Niblick projectile much like a standard rifle grenade. Designs ranged from a simple tube to a complex 8-round semiautomatic launcher attachment that had a circular magazine holding the projectiles. None of the designs had much advantage over the standard rifle grenade and did not show enough promise for further development.

The Niblick projectile used in most of the muzzle launcher attachments was a drag-stabilized round with an extending skirt that spread out behind the fired projectile. A spin-stabilized Niblick projectile, resembling a fat bullet, was found to have much more promise in terms of accuracy. A cartridge design with a self-contained propellant was needed to further develop the potential of the Niblick projectile.

To fire the very large Niblick projectile from a cartridge case, the standard method of simply filling the case with propellant would not fit the needs of the project. When a standard small-arms cartridge is fired, the projectile receives a very violent push from the rapidly burning propellant that gradually lowers in pressure as the projectile moves up the barrel. Using the standard cartridge system with the Niblick projectile would create several recoil problems, eliminating the possibility of a shoulder-launched weapon. Lowering the velocity of the Niblick projectile to allow a shoulder-fired weapon would cause most propellant powders to burn erratically at best, ruining accuracy from round to round, and badly cut back on the effective range of such a system.

During World War II, the Germans had faced a similar question, but for different reasons. The German question was how to build a worthwhile antitank weapon that would be lightweight, use few critical materials, and still have range, accuracy, and lethality. The use of a rocket projectile was ruled out due to an inherent lack of accuracy at long range and a very high consumption of fuel when compared to projectile weight.

A new internal ballistics principle, the "Niederdruck" or high-low pressure system, was developed in Germany during WWII and was used by

Rheinmetall-Borsig to solve the antitank weapon question. In the high-low pressure system, a relatively small amount of propellant is burned in a high-pressure chamber until it reaches a threshold pressure and ruptures a seal. With the seal ruptured, propellant gasses bleed through small holes in a metal plate into the low pressure chamber where they bear on the projectile. When fired, pressures in the high pressure chamber reach the 30,000–40,000 psi range while the low pressure chamber maintains a reasonably steady 3,000 psi. The high-pressure chamber allows the propellant to burn completely and efficiently. The low-pressure chamber gives the projectile a steady push with the pressure curve having a flat, almost optimal, line.

The steady push of the low-pressure portion of the high-low system gives a useful velocity to the projectile but also allows for a more fragile projectile to be used than that of a regular cannon. The low pressure also gives a low recoil impulse but is very consistent for accuracy. The major stress of firing is in the high-pressure chamber so the barrel and resulting support equipment for the weapon can be made much lighter.

The German weapon that fielded the high-low pressure system was the Rheinmetall 8cm Panzerabwehrwerfer 600, or PAW 600. The PAW 600 fired a fin-stabilized, hollow-charge round that would penetrate 5.5 inches (14 cm) of steel, out to an effective range of 600 meters. The smoothbore weapon had a light barrel with only the breech section requiring heavy walls to withstand firing. Set up for action, the PAW 600 only weighed some 1,389 pounds (630 kilograms) while a conventional 5 cm Pak 38 cannon weighed 2,205 pounds (1,000 kilograms) and only had some 400 meters additional range with much less penetration.

Though considered revolutionary in concept and the only major ballistics advance of the war, the high-low pressure principle was not developed further in the years following World War II. In the 1952-53 time period, Picatinny Arsenal revived the high-low pressure system to propel the Niblick projectile in a self-contained round of ammunition.

The high-low pressure cartridge case was made of aluminum and was unique in its design. The center of the cartridge case was the high-pressure chamber, a thick-walled extrusion in the center base of the case. Spaced around the side of the high-pressure chamber are six precise vent holes. The inside of the high-pressure chamber is sealed with a thin brass cup that contains the powder charge and closes off the vent holes. The bottom of the cartridge is closed off with a thick base plug that holds a percussion primer.

When the 330 milligram (5 grain) propellant charge of M9 smokeless powder is ignited by the percussion primer, it builds up a pressure of 35,000 psi while burning. When the 35,000 psi point is reached in the high-pressure chamber, the brass seal ruptures and the propellant gasses bleed out into the low-pressure chamber where they are reduced to a pressure of 3,000 psi. The 3,000 psi pressure moves the projectile up the barrel at a relatively slow rate, maintaining close to full pressure throughout a 14-inch barrel length. The Niblick projectile left a 14-inch barrel with a muzzle velocity of 250 feet per second and a right-hand spin of 3,700 rpm due to the rifled barrel.

The self-contained Niblick round kept a relatively low bore pressure in the launchers when compared to standard ammunition. The only point of high-pressure stress when firing the round was taken up by the high-pressure chamber itself. These facts allowed the barrels of the various Project Niblick launchers to be made of aluminum. The low muzzle velocity also prevented any of the launchers from having excessive recoil, even though a very large and heavy projectile was being launched for a hand-held weapon.

A number of launchers for Project Niblick were produced at Springfield Armory in 1953 under the direction of the project director, Cyril Moore. Two specific designs of launchers for the Niblick round showed considerable promise. One device was a simple shotgun-like fixture for determining ballistic data for the complete Niblick round. The other launcher was designed to fire six rounds semiautomatically. This was the first of the Project Niblick weapons that was a dedicated, shoulder-fired system. With a large rotating cylinder, the device acted much like a shoulder-fired revolver. Though the idea of semiautomatic fire held promise, the first device was found to be unsuitable for military use.

In the 1954–55 time period, the focus at Springfield Armory was on utilizing the complete Niblick round, though there was still some experimentation with the earlier types of projectiles. At this time, the S-3 launcher, a single-shot, break-open, shoulder-fired device with a rifled barrel was produced. This device greatly resembled the Federal Laboratories tear-gas gun that was popular with police departments at the time, but with a more complex sight and a forward hand grip.

A more complicated launcher that had semiautomatic capability was developed and under study by 1955. Identified as the S-6 strip-type shotgun, this was the first weapon to use a semiautomatic capability built into a conventional shotgun format. The S-6 used a harmonica-like strip of three Niblick rounds, each held in its own firing chamber, and feeding through the side of the receiver to give a semiautomatic-fire capability. As each round was fired, a spring would drive the strip clip through the receiver until it indexed on the next loaded chamber. This form of launcher met with high approval in the conferences between Springfield Armory and Army Ordnance personnel and effort was put into refining the design.

A second-generation semiautomatic S-6 launcher was available within a few months of the first model being accepted for development. Shortcomings from the first S-6 were eliminated in the second-generation design. Further work was needed to meet the military needs of such a weapon system and study continued on the design. Other launchers were examined, including large, flare gun—like pistols to use the Niblick round, but none of the designs met with much success.

Later in 1955, the experimental Project Niblick weapons were due to be tested by the Army Infantry Board. Lieutenant Colonel Roy E. Rayle, the Small Arms R&D Chief at Springfield Armory, suggested further development go into another single-shot launcher like the earlier S-3 design. Instead of developing a new design, Rayle suggested an already existing pattern, such as the Stevens Model 220 hammerless shotgun with a top-mounted safety and release lever, be modified to fire the Niblick round. The advantages of such a design would be the simplicity of operation and ease of training to recruits.

Lieutenant Colonel Rayle's suggestion was followed and a second launcher was developed along the lines of the S-3, this one identified as the S-5 shotgun. The S-5 was the first attempt to build a Niblick launcher that followed the lines of a conventional, single-shot, sporting shotgun. The lines of the S-5 remained simple and the mechanism straightforward. Further development continued on the design especially on the shoulder-stock and sight configurations. An immediate drawback to the S-5 that limited its appeal to the Army personnel was that the system was single-shot only.

During testing, the S-6 repeating grenade launcher was found to have problems with accuracy and was considered awkward to handle and operate. These problems were quickly traced to the harmonica magazine. A lack of a positive seal between the mouth of the magazine and the rear of the barrel caused propellant gasses to slip though the gap. This caused irregular muzzle velocity in the S-6 weapon and greatly limited the firing accuracy of the system. The much simpler S-5 launcher was favored by the Infantry Board testers. A decision was made to try and correct the problems with the S-6 launcher in order to retain the semiautomatic capability while retaining the S-5 design in reserve.

By 1958, the S-6 design had evolved into the T148E1 and T148E2 launchers. The T148E2 design was more complicated than the E1 as it incorporated a break-open design to help seal off the barrel/magazine gap. The greater number of components in the T148E2 design eliminated it from further development in favor of the simpler T148E1 pattern. A limited pilot-line production of 200

T148E1 launchers was conducted between January 1 and June 30, 1958 to supply a number of the weapons for field testing and further evaluation. The gas bleed-off at the chamber/barrel gap still caused an unacceptable loss of accuracy and the T148 project was terminated after July 1, 1960.

A conference of Army and Springfield Armory personnel decided the S-5 design, now known as the XM79, should be reactivated. U.S. Army Infantry Board testing determined that a new sighting system should be designed and a few shortcomings of the XM79 should be corrected before acceptance. The new sight design was ready by October 1959 and all XM79 launchers produced up to that point were refitted with the correction. On December 15, 1960, the M79 was officially type-classified and adopted by the U.S. Army. Further difficulties in producing the complicated rear sight limited weapon availability for some years after adoption.

By 1965, the M79 grenade launcher was in full production and available for issue to all of the services. SEAL Team One began receiving the M79 in 1965 to arm their direct action platoons in preparation for deployment to Vietnam early the next year. The M79 was well received by the Teams and quickly became a major source of firepower.

Initially with the Teams, the primary round of ammunition used with the M79 was the M406 high explosive round. The large, heavy, projectile of any of the 40mm rounds could be easily seen by the gunner as they lobbed through the air. Being able to actually see the projectile in flight was a bit disconcerting at first, as the projectile's large size and low muzzle velocity made it appear the wobble through the air without the ability to hit anything accurately. Confidence with the new weapon came with training. SEALs during predeployment training would practice extensively with their weapons, M79s among them. Even with its high, arcing trajectory and apparently slow travel, grenadiers soon learned that the 40mm grenade could be almost amazingly accurate.

Experience with the weapon is what developed skill in an M79 grenadier, and the Teams made certain some of that experience was with their men right from the start. As part of their combat preparation, SEALs would spend hours on the range practicing with their chosen weapons. A skilled M79 grenadier could often drop a grenade right onto a target that was 150 meters away by simply pointing his weapon and looking along the barrel. This kind of shooting was considered instinctive, very quick, and didn't employ the fairly complex rear sight of the M79 at all. When using the sights and aimed carefully, the accuracy of the M79 was such that a good operator could consistently drop grenades into a garbage can at 150 meters.

If you wished you could take an entire 72-round case of 40MM ammunition over to the range and fire it all. The idea was for the men to get comfortable with their weapons. . . . You would practice with your chosen weapon until you became proficient with it. Instinctive fire, point and shoot style, was what took the most practice.

Working against the accuracy and effectiveness of the M79 was the fact that it was a dedicated, single-shot weapon. Any SEAL who carried an M79 was very limited in what he could do with the weapon during a close-in encounter of less than 15 meters. The minimum arming range of the grenade, combined with its bursting radius, made the round ineffective and dangerous when used close-in during a sudden eyeball-to-eyeball encounter with the enemy.

There were occasions where an M79-armed SEAL came into close contact with a VC who was about to fire on him. In such situations, safety becomes a nonissue and the SEAL would open fire with whatever he had in his hands. When a 40mm grenade struck a target in an unarmed condition, it would still act as a very large bullet. A dead VC struck with an unexploded 40mm grenade might become a problem for explosive ordnance disposal, but the SEAL would still be around to report the incident.

Prior to the SEALs sending direct action platoons to Vietnam, Marine and Army units had been in combat in Southeast Asia and had reported the drawbacks of the M79 for close-in combat. New rounds were developed for the M79 and sent over to Vietnam for combat testing. The first of the close-combat rounds for the M79 was a flechette round loaded with 45 finned steel flechettes carried in a plastic sabot. The 10-grain flechettes resembled sharp finishing nails with fins stamped into the head and were effective immediately after leaving the muzzle of the launcher.

When fired, the plastic sabot holding the bundle of fletchettes would break away soon after the projectile left the muzzle of the weapon

Two Navy crewmen man their weapons aboard a PBR. The man to the left, in the foreground, is holding a 40mm M79 grenade launcher with the rear sight folded down against the barrel. Behind him and to the right in the photograph is another man ready to operate an M60 machine gun. The machine gunner has his right hand at the pistol grip of the weapon while he is bracing the buttstock against his shoulder with his left hand. Just underneath and forward of his right hand can be seen the barrel and bipod of another M60 machine gun. Both men are wearing WWII M1 steel helmets and have on M69 fragmentation protective body armor vests with ¾ collars.

Source: U.S. Navy

and the flechettes themselves would spread into a widening pattern. But, as with most of the small-arms flechette loads used in Vietnam, the little finned needles were not stable at the muzzle of the weapon and usually weren't flying straight and point-first until they had traveled about 15 to 30 meters through the air. Close-in, as many as half the flechettes would hit a target sideways or back-wards as point-on, severely limiting the effectiveness of the round.

Two types of buckshot round were developed for the M79 in the 1965–1966 time period to replace the fletchette load. The XM576E1 and XM576E2 rounds were both loaded with #4 (0.24 inch) hardened buckshot. The two cartridges differed in the plastic sabots that were used to launch the buckshot payloads. These rounds began arriving in Vietnam during the SEALs' first deployments but were not widely available.

> DET/ ALFA 2ND PLATOON LOGBOOK—SITUATION REPORT FOR 10 TO 16 APRIL [1967]
> Mon. 10 . . . T— and G— scrounged star clusters for M79 . . . Thurs. 13 Arr. My Tho 0130 . . . . . . Saigon won't reisse canister rounds for M79 due to 50 yd. range on round.

Though the higher command thought the new rounds for the M79 may have too short a range and be ineffective because of that, the operators in the field thought highly of the new ammunition. The XM576E1 round was not as effective as the E2 design, which was later adopted as the M576 multiple-projectile round, but both rounds turned the M79 into a very large shotgun. One of the reasons shotguns were so popular among the SEALs was that the buckshot loads had a great deal of stopping power, especially at close range. Flechette loads, though lethal, didn't transfer their energy into the target effi-ciently and never had the knock-down power of buckshot.

> In an earlier op, I had used a canister round on a gook not more than three yards away from me. That was what the canister rounds were intended for and they sure worked. The twenty or so number four buckshot in the 40mm can-ister tore this one VC's shoulder and arm clean off. The flechette rounds for the 40mm or the shotgun were like shooting needles at the guy, no stopping power although they were lethal.

With the new multiple-projectile rounds, the M79 became effective at close range. But the basic weapon was still a single-shot design. Once the M79 had fired its round, the grenadier was out of the action until he had reloaded. In the sudden combat environment of the SEALs, this situation could easily lead to men being killed because they had an empty weapon. Without there being any way to speed up the reloading of an M79, SEAL grenadiers simply took to carrying more than one weapon. In the U.S. Army and Marine Corps, grenadiers were normally armed with an M1911A1 pistol in addition to their M79, SEALs preferred considerably more firepower.

> . . . we went in heavily armed. For myself, I was carrying a CAR-15, a 40mm
> M-79 grenade launcher, and a 7.62mm Chicom pistol, along with two knives.
> For the 40mm, I had both canister and high explosive rounds.

Ammunition counts were always high when SEAls went into combat. The larger the SEAL, the more ammunition he would carry. Though the individual round count for 40mm ammunition might be low, the rounds themselves were fairly large and each weighed about half a pound. Depending on the mission, a SEAL grenadier might carry a very heavy load of 40mm grenades along with his additional equipment.

EXCERPT—PERSONAL LOG, SEAL TEAM ONE, DETACHMENT GOLF, 22
JANUARY 1968, SECURITY ELEMENT FOR DEMOLITION TEAM

- Personal Gear
- M79
- M79 vest [ammunition]
- 54 rds. H.E. 40 m.m.
- 11 rds. Canister 40 m.m.
- 2 CS (Gas) Grenades 40 m.m.
- 5 Mk 26 Frag. Grenades
- 2 Mk 13 Flares
- 3 Ammo pouches
- 1 Claymore bag . . .

[Along with an individual loadout of standard equipment and web gear]

Development of new ammunition types was considered a primary means of increasing the usefulness of the M79 in general. Literally dozens of new rounds were experimented with during the course of the Vietnam war. Some of the rounds, such as the XM576E2, eventually reached standardization, others never went to combat and were only produced in small number for testing. From the very earliest operations of the SEALs in Vietnam, new types of 40mm ammunition was desired and obtained whenever possible.

EXCERPT FROM SEAL TEAM TWO, 2ND PLATOON'S VIETNAM
OPERATIONS, 30 JANUARY TO 30 MAY 1967

Weapons and Equipment

6. If flare rounds and canister rounds were available for the M-79, the
weapon's versatility would be increased tremendously.

7. Mk 8 Very pistol rounds can be fired from the M-79.

The primary mark against the M79 was still the fact that the weapon was
single-shot. That had been a concern back in the mid-1950s when the design
was first considered. The relatively low recoil of the 40mm ammunition family,
combined with its low firing pressure, allowed another approach to solving the
single-shot problem.

In September 1964, Karl Lewis and Robert E. Roy applied for a patent on a
grenade-launcher attachment they had designed for Colt Firearms. By October
1966, the patent was granted but Colt had already been marketing the new
weapon since 1965 as the CGL-4 (Colt Grenade Launcher), part of their CAR-
15 weapons system. The CGL-4 could be mounted underneath the barrel of an
AR-15 (M16E1) and operated independently of the rifle. The CGL-4 had its
own controls and sighting system and used the rifle solely as a support and to
supply a buttstock for firing.

To mount the CGL-4 on a rifle, the standard handguards would be removed and the CGL-4 clamped in place on the barrel. A new handguard would
be placed on the barrel of the rifle to protect the operator and the grenade
launcher would be ready for use. As long as there was sufficient barrel length, a
CGL-4 could be mounted on any of the AR-15/M16 weapons including the
short CAR-15.

A small pistol grip underneath the CGL-4 allowed an operator to unlock
and slide the 40mm barrel forward, automatically extracting and ejecting any
fired casing that might be in the chamber. Slipping a loaded round into the barrel and using the pistol grip to pull the barrel shut and lock it in place was all
that was necessary to load the CGL-4.

A large knob on the rear of the CGL-4 receiver would be drawn back with
the fingers to cock the weapon. A trigger bar extended down the right side of
the supporting rifle and ended just in front of the trigger guard. Extending the
end of the trigger and rotating it in place put the trigger of the CGL-4 just below
the trigger of the supporting rifle. The dual trigger allowed the operator to fire
either the M16 or the CGL-4 by simply moving his finger to the proper trigger.

The U.S. Army found the CGL-4 a possible "off-the-shelf" answer to the limited firepower of the M79 in 1966. With minor modifications, the CGL-4 went into limited production in November 1966 as the XM148. Both the U.S. Army units in Vietnam and the Navy SEALs received the new launchers in early 1967. Now for the first time, a weapon was available that had both a point target effect (the rifle) and an area target effect (the grenade launcher). The concept was new and reactions from the men in the field were carefully examined. For the SEALs, this reaction was enthusiastic.

". . . I had found a weapon I particularly liked, the XM-148 grenade launcher. Looking like quite a complicated piece of hardware, the XM-148 was designed to be fitted underneath the barrel of an M16 rifle. The XM-148 fired the same round of 40mm ammunition as the M79 grenade launcher. Only, unlike the M79, once you had fired the XM-148, you still had the M16 in your hands, ready to go. This was a lot better than the single-shot M79 . . .

The trigger of the XM-148 stuck out a bit where it could hang up on brush and the weapon was a little more fragile than I cared for. But outside of that, I liked the additional firepower it gave me . . .

Though the XM148 was well received by the SEALs, they were not blind to the drawbacks of the weapon. The XM148 was a lot more fragile than the simple M79, and had a great deal more parts to get out of order. There was no guard for the XM148's trigger bar that extended down the right side of the carrying rifle. Any piece of brush, equipment, or even a finger that got between the trigger bar and the receiver of the rifle would push the bar out and jam the XM148 so that it couldn't be cocked. In addition, the bare trigger bar could hang up on some material during a crawl and fire the XM148 if the weapon was cocked and the safety off. It was this drawback that caused the recommendation to go out that the XM148 could be carried with a round in the chamber, but that the weapon should not be cocked until just before use.

On my first op armed with an XM148. . . . The op was a little three-man canal ambush. We had to crawl up to the ambush site about 100 meters or so through brush and vegetation. . . .

They had just come out with a new flechette round for the 40mm launchers and I had some. The new round didn't fire round shot but a bunch of thin, finned, steel needles. This looked pretty neat . . . the VC centered in my sights, I raised up, pulled the trigger, and nothing.

Instead of setting up to fire, I had put the XM148 on safe. All during that

A close-up of the sight bar mounted to the left side of the XM148 grenade launcher. On the left side of the rear of the sight bar is the windage knob for adjusting the rear aperture sight horizontally. The off-center front post sight is also adjustable to allow the sight to be zeroed to the weapon. The range scale on the disk between the sight rail and the support post allows the sight bar to be set for different ranges. This complicated and fragile sight assembly was found to be one of the weak points of the XM148 design during field trials in Vietnam.

Source: Kevin Dockery

crawl through the brush, my loaded and cocked launcher had been ready to fire. And the trigger on an XM148 is an exposed bar on the right side of the weapon, it could have caught on brush and gone off at any time.

The final Army report on the XM148 was written in May 1967. A number of the Army users liked the XM148 but the weapon was found to be too fragile and unsafe for general issue. The reporting team concluded that "the XM-148 in its present configuration is unsatisfactory for further operational use in Vietnam." Recommendations were that the XM148 be removed from service until another design was available. By the fall of 1967, all of the Army's XM148s had been turned in. The SEALs found the effectiveness of the weapon offset the bad parts of the design and retained theirs until the end of the Team's involvement in Vietnam.

The XM148 had some unusual aspects to its action that were discovered and used by many of its operators. The sear lever of the XM148 was exposed at the rear of the receiver to the weapon. Operators in both the Army and the SEAL Teams found that you could fire the cocked launcher by pressing on the upper part of the sear lever with the thumb of the left hand without letting go of the pistol grip to the M16 with the right hand. Though not officially recommended, gunners found they could move through the undergrowth with one finger on the trigger of the rifle and the thumb of the other hand on the sear bar of the grenade launcher. Either weapon could be fired immediately without changing hands. This situation was dangerous and caused difficulty during at least one patrol.

> While charging along, I had my fingers on both trig gers of my weapon. When I clenched my hands, both weapons went off. I had been carrying the weapon with a 45 degree down slant while I had been running. The roar of the CAR-15 didn't quite drown out the THOOP . . . SMACK of the 40mm going off. . . . The round impacted into the mud not six feet from where I was standing.

Those (M406) 40mm High Explosive rounds have to spin over 150 times before the impact fuse will arm. The grenade travels at least 14 meters in that time. This safety is designed into the weapon so that operators have a harder time killing themselves when they make a mistake like the one I had just made. I watched the grenade smack into the mud right in front of me and not go off. . . .

The Teams liked the XM148, but still wanted the firepower of the grenade launcher system increased. SEAL Team One examined at least one of the Springfield Armory produced T148E1 repeating grenade launchers for possible adoption early during their Vietnam war commitment.

SEAL TEAM ONE—COMMAND AND CONTROL HISTORY—1967
NWC ORD TASKS. . . . A listing of special procurement actions completed is summarized below:
[item 9] 40 M Grenade Launcher T148[E]1

It has not been reported that the T148E1 launcher examined by SEAL Team One was ever tested in combat in Vietnam. Though an interesting approach to the semiautomatic grenade launcher problem, the action of the T148E1 was too open and vulnerable to dirt to operate well in the jungle/mud environment of Vietnam. The sliding harmonica magazine has several open chambers that would pick up dirt and debris like scoops as the weapon was moved through the jungle. The sliding operation of the magazine, along with its coil-type driving spring, would also be easily put out of action from dirt and debris. Lastly, the accuracy problem from the shot-to-shot difference in muzzle velocity had never been completely corrected and varied not only from weapon to weapon in the T148E1, but also from magazine to magazine in the same launcher.

The Navy Special Warfare Groups (Pacific and Atlantic), which included the SEAL Teams and UDTs, had been recognized as having unique problems in the field of weapons and equipment by the Navy command. The Special Operations Branch of the Naval Weapons Center at China Lake, California, was structured to address the equipment needs of the SEALs and UDTs on a very rapid basis. Nonstandard ordnance and hardware required by the Teams would be acquired by China Lake, modified if necessary, and shipped out to the users as quickly as possible. When a necessary item was not available in any form "off-the-shelf," China Lake was set up to design, develop, and put into limited production such items as necessary. In three years of operations during the Vietnam War, China Lake put out some 375 items on a quick-reaction basis for the Teams.

China Lake looked into the question of increasing the firepower of the 40mm grenade launcher. Taking the direct approach, the China Lake engineers applied the pump-action operating principles from civilian sporting shotguns to the problem. Production of a tool-room prototype weapon was completed rapidly and the design was ready for testing and examination. The general design was considered acceptable and a small production quantity was produced at the China Lake facilities. Development of the pump-action grenade launcher was so rapid that it reportedly took longer to make a set of production drawings from the tool-room gun than it did to produce the first weapon.

The China Lake pump-action grenade launcher resembled a very large, short-barreled shotgun and retained the same range and accuracy of the M79. Considered one of the most significant small arms produced as part of the Naval Special Warfare Projects at China Lake, the pump-action grenade launcher was ready to be issued to the SEAL Teams for combat in Vietnam by mid-1968.

SEAL TEAM ONE—COMMAND AND CONTROL HISTORIES 1968, ENCLOSURE 3, SPECIAL TOPICS, (A) PERFORMANCE OF WEAPONS SYSTEMS
The 40MM grenade pump weapon has proven to be a good weapon and is being used by SEAL detachments in Vietnam . . .

Though a fairly large weapon, the 40mm pump-action grenade launcher was very well received by some of the SEALs in the Teams. Reports on the actual number of China Lake pump-action grenade launchers made are difficult to confirm. Between 20 and 30 weapons were put into SEAL hands during the Vietnam War with only one or two additional launchers going to the Marine Corps Force Recon units and Army 5th Special Forces Group. A receiver with the serial number "50" has been located but it was found in a stripped condition and may never have been assembled as a complete weapon.

Back in California, China Lake had a special section where they would build different weapons for us. One of the things they made for the SEAL was a pump-action 40mm grenade launcher. The weapon was a repeater that would fire four grenades. A good operator could get all four grenades in the air before the first one hit. The pump-action was made of aluminum, so it was very light to carry for its size.

The pump-action grenade launcher was one of the most successful of the shoulder-fired 40mm designs, but it was not the only one to come out of China Lake. During the calendar year 1966-1967, NWC China Lake designed and built several prototypes of a 3-barrel 40mm grenade launcher. Instead of developing a multishot grenade launcher that would be a dedicated weapon such as the M79, China Lake went with a much smaller design that could be mounted underneath an M16 in the same manner as an XM148. To minimize the size of the 40mm repeater, each round was given its own barrel.

SEALs insert into a village as part of a raid on a Viet Cong base in the Kien Hoa province of South Vietnam in January 1968. Just off the bow of the Assault River Patrol Boat (ASPB) is a SEAL wearing a tiger-strip camouflage uniform and carrying a shotgun. The two SEALS moving along the bow of the ASPB are both armed with M16A1 rifles as well as a variety of hand grenades seen attached to their load-bearing harness. The leading SEAL moving along the superstructure of the craft is carrying a Stoner 63A fitted with a 150-round aluminum drum. The last SEAL in the photograph on the far right is armed with an M16A1 rifle fitted with an XM148 40mm grenade launcher.
Source: U.S. Navy

The double-action firing mechanism has a trigger that fits underneath the trigger guard of the M16 in a sliding mount. The trigger bar extends along the right side of the M16 receiver in the same manner as the XM148 but with the trigger in a firm mount, there is much less probability of jamming up the bar with brush as could happen with the XM148. The fairly complex firing mechanism cocks, advances the hammer in a circular motion to the next barrel, and fires the round when the trigger is pulled once. This allows the operator to fire up to three grenades as fast as he can pull the trigger.

To keep the 3-barrel compact enough to fit underneath a CAR-15, the barrels are only six inches long. The short barrels are long enough for the fired grenade to pick up enough velocity and spin to arm and stabilize in flight. But the short barrels also reduced the effective range of the 3-barrel at least 15 percent less than that of an M79. A large housing covered the rear of the 3-barrel to protect the firing mechanism with the entire package ending up being about 4.25 inches wide.

At least one of the two or three prototype 3-barrel 40mm launchers was sent to the Marines to be tested by the Force Recon units in Vietnam. All of the other examples were sent on to the SEAL Teams for field testing. One grenadier from SEAL Team One carried an M16 with the 3-barrel launcher to test and

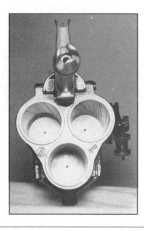

A down-the-muzzles view of the experimental tri-barrel 40mm grenade launcher mounted underneath the barrel of an early M16 weapon. The muzzle of the M16 has the second-type conical, open-prong flash suppressor. Underneath the barrel of the rifle can be seen the gaping muzzles of the three 40mm barrels of the grenade launcher. The small dot at the bottom of each 40mm barrel is the opening for the firing pin of that barrel. The lands and grooves of each barrel, set to a 1 turn in 48 inches rate, can be seen along the sides of each 40mm barrel. On the left side of the launcher, center right in this photograph, is the square-notch/post bar of the grenade launcher's sight assembly.

evaluate it under combat conditions. The one operation where a SEAL carried the weapon took place on April 13, 1968 and was the only operation where this individual carried the weapon. To put it simply, the SEAL reported that the weapon was heavy, unbalanced the rifle badly, and simply did not work.

The complex firing mechanism of the 3-barrel could not stand up to the dirt and mud of the Vietnam environment. When the trigger was pulled, the weapon had as good a chance of not firing as of going off. The wide open muzzle of the three barrels were also very hard to keep free of debris when crawling through the jungle. The weapon was not adopted by the Teams and only the few original prototypes were ever made.

The very short barrels cut down on the muzzle velocity of the 40mm grenades so much that the 3-barrel only had two-thirds the range of either the M79 or XM148. The open mouths of the barrel could quickly clog with jungle crap, mud, muck, leaves, and all the assorted gunk we found our selves crawling in on almost every op in Vietnam. The single open barrel of the XM148 was trouble enough to keep cleared, the three open muzzles of the 3-barrel were like walking around with a small bucket underneath your weapon.

The failure of the Colt and China Lake underbarrel grenade launcher attachments did not eliminate the idea for combining the point fire of a rifle with the area effect of the 40mm grenade launcher. The U.S. Army put out the information to the firearms industry that they were interested in another underbarrel grenade launcher design. Seventeen different firms were spoken to during a conference on July 18, 1967. Seven of the contacted firms reported a serious interest in the project.

AAI (Aircraft Armaments Inc.) had experience in developing a number of underbarrel grenade launchers as part of the Special Purpose Individual Weapon (SPIW) Program. AAI already had an idea in the mockup stage for a new grenade launcher in July 1967, but the Army felt their estimated production schedules may not be possible to meet. By September, three companies, AAI, Philco-Ford's Aeronutronics Division, and Aero Jet General had all received contracts to develop grenade launchers as part of the Army's new Grenade Launcher Attachment Development (GLAD) Program.

The Aero-Jet design for a delayed blowback operated grenade launcher was declined by the Army and dropped from the competition. Twenty each of the Philco-Ford and AAI designs were set for testing on May 1, 1968. "Unanimously selected based on superior performance and predicted lower cost in production," the AAI design was awarded a contract for further development on August 2, 1968. By early November of that same year, the AAI design was officially identified as the XM203 40mm Grenade Launcher.

A contract for 500 XM203 grenade launchers was awarded almost immediately after AAI received the designation for their design. By December, the XM203 launcher itself was considered complete by the U.S. Army, though further work had to go forward on a selection of sight designs. This work was quickly completed and the construction of the first 600 XM203s finished by AAI. In April 1969, 500 XM203 grenade launchers were sent to Army units in Southeast Asia for a 3-month combat evaluation.

The XM203 grenade launcher is a single-shot, manually operated, pump-action grenade launcher intended to be installed underneath the barrel of an M16 rifle. The barrel of the XM203 does not extend much past the front sight assembly on a standard M16 and so can be mounted underneath the barrel of any of the CAR-15/XM177 versions of the same weapon. A flip-up ladder-type leaf sight is attached to the handguard of the M16 so that the normal front sight of the rifle can be used to aim the grenade launcher. In addition, a complex quadrant sight is attached to the carrying handle of the mounting weapon for more precise long-range use of the grenade launcher.

To load the XM203, the unlocking lever above the barrel on the left side of the weapon is pressed in with the thumb and the barrel slid forward. Any empty cartridge case will be automatically ejected and the operator can load a single round of any of the standard 40mm grenades. Pulling the barrel shut locks the breech and completes loading the grenade launcher. There is no pistol grip for the XM203, the operator grabs the magazine of the M16 with his firing hand and pulls the trigger of the grenade launcher just in front of the magazine well.

The safety of the M203 is a curved metal flap that will extend in front of the trigger when on. The operator can easily move the safety forward with his trigger finger when ready to fire. One drawback of the M203 is that the spring metal trigger guard, which locks against the front of the magazine well of the carrying weapon, can be slipped up excessively during assembly and block the trigger so that the weapon cannot be fired. This is a minor but common error that can be corrected quickly by the operator.

The XM203 was well received by all of the units who used it. AAI was unable to build production quantities of the XM203 and Colt received the contract to produce the accepted M203 grenade launcher for all of the U.S. services. By 1986 Colt had manufactured over 250,000 M203 grenade launchers. The SEALs began receiving the M203 grenade launcher by 1970 and have continued using the weapon to this day. After the end of the Teams' involvement in Vietnam, the XM148 grenade launcher was phased out of use and replaced with the M203. In the Teams the M203 was usually mounted underneath the barrel of an XM177E2, replaced today with the M4A1 carbine.

. . . what everyone really liked was when the engineers put a grenade launcher underneath the barrel of an M16. That over/under weapon really became popular with the Teams, especially later when the improved (M203) model came out. The way you could use the M79 in combat was a lot like flushing birds when hunting. When that little 40mm grenade went off, those Viet Cong "birds" sometimes broke cover. Now with the 40mm sitting under an M16, when the "birds" took off, you still had that M16 to take them down with.

SEAL TEAM TWO COMMAND AND CONTROL HISTORY, 1970 ENCLOSURE 1, VI. NEW EQUIPMENT, PG 12

1. (U) During the year, SEAL Team TWO received ten new XM203 grenade launcher attachments for the M16 rifle. The XM203 replaces the XM148.

In some combat situations today, whole 16-man SEAL platoons, less automatic weapons men and snipers, have been armed with M4/M203 grenade launchers. The flexibility of the weapon, combined with its firepower, has made it one of the most successful weapons developments to come out of the Vietnam War.

To increase the versatility of the 40mm grenade launcher, work was also constantly done in developing new rounds of ammunition. The high-low propulsion system allowed for a very large payload to be launched from a shoulder-fired weapon, and this gave the ordnance designers great latitude in coming up with new applications for the system.

You have to appreciate how the M-79 operates in order to understand what a great weapon it was. The 40mm grenades were large, fat cartridges, about the size of an orange juice can. Each round would lob a high explosive grenade out to about 400 meters, without kicking the operator on his can with the recoil. There were all sorts of ammunition for the 40mm, high-explosive fragmentation rounds, canister rounds like large shotgun shells, and some other rounds even more exotic.

A fair number of rounds were made that never existed in much more than test quantities. Some rounds were literally handmade and proved a bad idea. Others applied a number of different techniques to reach the same objective. The primary round of ammunition for the 40mm remained the high-explosive fragmentation round. The basic notched wire-wrapped ball of explosive was the basis of the grenade, but a number of different ways to get the ball to the target were experimented with.

To make the 40mm grenade more effective against personnel, an airburst some feet above the ground was considered the best way to increase fragmentation efficiency. The M397A1 Airburst round did not use an exotic fuze to detonate the grenade some distance above the ground. Instead, the airburst round would impact with the ground where an ejection charge was fired by the grenade's fuze. The charge would pop the grenade body into the air several feet where a burning pyrotechnic fuze would detonate the main charge.

Various kinds of smoke projectiles were loaded, most intended to be used for signaling during daylight when a burning flare could not be as easily seen. Flare rounds were developed in numbers—both parachute flares and clusters of flares were used, some for signaling, others to provide illumination. The need for pyrotechnic 40mm ammunition was noticed almost from the very first days of use by the SEALs in Vietnam. One very unusual round of ammunition employed the standard HE projectile from the M406 round, but the cartridge case was far from the normal design.

SEAL TEAM ONE-COMMAND AND CONTROL HISTORY 1967
—(J) RESEARCH AND DEVELOPMENT
4. GUERRILLA AND COVERT WARFARE
20 Silent Weapons, projectiles 40 mm (waterproof)

The M463 Smokeless/Flashless High Explosive round utilized the same folding steel capsule "teleshot" technology that was used in the experimental silent shotgun shell. The teleshot capsule was developed by AAI and consisted of a steel tube with a sealed end that was collapsed inside itself, folded down to less than half its length. The propellant charge was burned inside this capsule when it was ignited by a normal percussion primer. The expanding capsule drove the projectile up the barrel with a sudden push, but held all of the propellant gasses inside itself. With no gasses expanding into the atmosphere suddenly to make a bang, or even a "bloop" in the case of the 40mm, there was no flash or smoke and very little sound. To identify the exotic round, the projectile was colored green and black.

> Have you ever seen how you make Jiffy-Pop popcorn? You start out with the flat pan and it just expands—the gas never escapes. They made us an M-79 round like that, the XM463 flashless/smokeless round. When the powder went off the gas remained in the aluminum shell and just popped out the little green and black egg (grenade) down-range. It had no noise except for the thump, and usually no flash coming out of the barrel. So you could have bad guys down in an area, and you could be hidden where they couldn't see you. With the pump action (grenade launcher) and the flashless/smokeless round you could fire four rounds on the other side of them, and they'll run towards you because they don't know where the fire came from.

Occasionally, the teleshot capsule ruptured and the gasses would leak out, giving the weapon a noticeable sound signature when fired. The technology of the teleshot round never caught on well enough for general issue. The few SEALs who had experience with the XM463 round thought highly of it for its surprise effect. Experimentation was done with a buckshot version of the teleshot round, based on the M576E2 round. The velocity of the smokeless/flashless buckshot rounds was so low that they were too ineffective at any reasonable range for combat use.

SEAL TEAM ONE—COMMAND AND CONTROL HISTORY—1967
A list of special developments completed is summarized below:
[item 14] 40 MM 3 barrel Grenade Launcher
[item 15] MK 18 Grenade Launcher 40 MM

Other items requested pending development or procure ment include:
40 MM Canister Round
40 MM Illumination (parachute type) round

40 MM Incendiary round
40 MM Grenade Launcher, Pump, semi-automatic, and single shot

Other avenues of research had been going forward since the first adoption of the M79 in 1960. The idea of an automatic weapon firing the 40mm family of grenades had been brought forward and examined by a number of civilian companies. The Honeywell Corporation first introduced the concept of a rapid-fire grenade launcher to their designers in 1962. Honeywell had been heavily involved in the design of the fuzes for the 40mm grenades and the concept of a mechanical grenade launcher was proposed during an in-house meeting on fuzes.

Instead of developing a fully-automatic grenade launcher, the Honeywell engineers suggested that a mechanical repeater be done instead. Instead of trying to adapt a standard automatic-weapons design to the characteristics of the 40mm grenade, a hand-cranked repeater would be much simpler to produce in a very short time. The idea was moved forward as an in-house development with no government contract pending. By 1965, the first launcher was ready for demonstration.

In place of a normal chamber, the new launcher had two rotors the length of the cartridge case. Each rotor had six semicircular grooves cut in its length, each half the circumference of a 40mm round. The two rotors were geared together so that a 40mm round would be held in a complete chamber made up from the two rotor halves. Since the chamber formed around the cartridge, the normal functions of chambering and extracting didn't have to happen. This gave the Honeywell a very simple operating system with relatively few parts.

The two rotors were driven by a side-mounted crank handle, much the same as an old Gatling gun. The rotors were locked into place by a cam-driven rod as the firing pin was cocked and dropped by another cam. Rotating the crank handle fired the Honeywell when the handle was at the top or bottom of a rotation, launching two grenades for each full revolution. Depending on how fast the operator turned the handle, the Honeywell would fire at rates of 1 to 250 rounds per minute.

When Honeywell was designing their 40mm hand-cranked grenade launcher, we (SEAL Team Two) tested the prototypes right on the beach at Little Creek around mid-1965. . . .

Ammunition for the Honeywell was placed in a plastic belt, spaced out at proper intervals. The initial belts were nothing more than fiberglass-reinforced sticky tape, with the rounds stuck between two lengths of the tape. Spacing of the rounds in the tape belt was done with two tape-clinching wheels (large gears) in a special loading machine. The tape belt gave a great deal of trouble when the weapon was introduced and were quickly replaced by a stronger system.

The new belts for the Honeywell were made of Mylar-backed Dacron fabric with pockets between heat-sealed sections of the belt. The fabric belts were supplied in 24- or 48-round lengths and could be reloaded about five times before they wouldn't hold the 40mm round firmly enough. Old fabric belts sometimes were seen in Vietnamese and other hands being used as 40mm bandoleers.

The Honeywell was examined by the Navy in 1965 for possible adoption as a small boat weapon. Testing proved the system and the Honeywell received the nomenclature assignment of Gun, Rapid Fire, 40mm Mark 18 Mod 0 on December 10, 1965. Between 1965 and 1968, when production ceased, about 1,200 Mk 18 launchers were produced, almost all production going to the U.S. Navy.

Though the Mk 18 could produce a good deal of firepower, it was considered a temporary, stopgap weapon until a self-powered design could be developed. There wasn't a secure seal between the cartridge case and the barrel so propellant gases leaked out, limiting the muzzle velocity. Accuracy suffered as a result. Volume of fire was considered the Mark 18's main advantage.

The Mk 18 was able to fire an entire belt of 48 rounds as fast as a man could turn the handle. By carefully sweeping the weapon back and forth, starting at the longest range (400 meters) and working back, a football-field-sized area could be covered with one 48-round belt of ammunition. Properly done, all of the grenades would impact at roughly the same time due to the high lobbing arc of the 40mm grenade.

SEAL TEAM ONE—COMMAND AND CONTROL HISTORY—1967
The performance of the MK 18 Honeywell has proved unre liable. The quality control must have been lacking since the engineering of certain vital parts is sub-standard. At the present time the MK 18 is unsuitable for SEAL Team operations.

Further testing and development of the Mk 18 continued on a limited basis. The introduction of the Dacron fabric belts helped eliminate many of the earlier complaints about the weapon.

The Honeywell weapon, eventually called the Mark 18 rapid fire grenade launcher, was the shoebox-sized weapon that we fit these belts into and turned a crank to operate. It was a lot like the old Gatling gun only it fired the same 40mm grenades as our M79 grenade launchers. We experimented with all kinds of belt feeds for the darn thing. Fabric belts and then plastic ones, even a machine that made up belts with the grenades loaded between two rolls of sticky tape. The Honeywell, as everyone took to calling it, worked fairly well in Vietnam from what I was told and it was only one of a number of weapons that we used that all fired the 40mm grenades.

The SEALs used the Mk 18 primarily from PBRs and other river boats. The Mk 18 could be fitted to the standard .30 caliber machine gun tripod for ground use, but the weapon was difficult to operate in such a manner. The SEALs only used the ground mount tripod when introducing trainees to the Mk 18 for familiarization.

Probably one of the most unusual mounts for the Mk 18 was also its most common one. The Mark 46 Mod 0 gun mount would cradle an M2 HB .50 caliber machine gun on a tall, tripod-like Mk 16 stand. This mount was often seen at the stern of the Mk II PBRs as they patrolled the rivers of Southeast Asia. The Mk 46 mount would also hold a Mk 18, or later Mk 20, grenade launcher above the rear of the .50 cal[iber] [could] switch from th[e] [.50] caliber to the [grenade] launcher by [the] grips he hel[d].

The M[k 18 was] still a manually o[perated weapon] considered not completely satis[fac]tory by the U.S. Navy. In August 1966, the Naval Ordnance Station in Louisville, Kentucky, was ordered to develop a 40mm machine gun, capable of semiautomatic and full automatic fire, as quickly as possible. Henry Watson, the Engineer in

[...] [ab]oard a Mark II PBR mans an amidships-mounted [Ra]pid Fire Gun. The operator is holding the rear grip of [...] in his left hand to aim and direct it. To fire the gun, the [operator w]ould turn the crank handle in his right hand. The crank [han]dle of the Mark 18 is just past the bottom (6 o'clock) FIRE position. As the crank handle is rotated on a loaded weapon, the gun will fire as the handle passes the top (12 o'clock) and bottom (6 o'clock) positions. The handle would have to be rotated to the 9 or 3 o'clock position in order for the top of the weapon to be opened and a belt of ammunition loaded into place. This specimen is not loaded and there is no ammunition box on the left side of the weapon. To the right, front of the grenade launcher can be seen the receiver of an M60 machine gun also set up on an amidships mount.

Source: U.S. Navy

Charge, Colonel George Chinn, and William Schnatter attacked the problem of the new design vigorously. By May 1967, only nine months later, the first three weapons of the new design were ready for testing.

On August 6, 1968, the new grenade launcher received the nomenclature assignment of Gun, Machine, 40MM (Grenade) Mark 20 Mod 0. The item description on the assignment request read:

> This is a lightweight, automatic, low-velocity, reciprocating barrel-operated 40mm weapon. It is 31" long, 9" wide and 9" high and fires M381, M382, M387, M406, or M407 40mm grenades belted with the M16 metallic links, at a rate of 200–250 rounds per minute in either full or semiautomatic modes. It was designed for pedestal mounting, however, because of its recoilless action, it is adaptable for multiple mounting systems such as tripods and bipods.

The Mk 20 has a sheet metal receiver over a framework that holds the operating parts. A set of twin spade grips are at the rear of the weapon with a push-button trigger that can be depressed with the thumb of the right hand. A sliding safety switch is to the left of the trigger button. The cycling of the weapon is so slow that the trigger button is just quickly released for semiautomatic fire.

The operation of the Mk 20 is a unique combination of blow-forward and recoil. To cock the weapon prior to firing or loading, the cocking knob at the top rear of the receiver is pushed forward. Pushing the cocking handle forward moves the barrel forward, extending it out from the front of the receiver, where it locks into place. When the trigger is pushed, the barrel slides back over the 40mm round in the feed tray. The rifling in the barrel presses back on the rotating band of the grenade, driving the round back onto the firing pin which sets off the propellant charge.

The force of the grenade going down the barrel drives the barrel forward against the barrel spring. A lug on the barrel engages a ratchet cam underneath the barrel that rotates the feed mechanism to move the ammunition belt forward one round. The bolt also recoils from the force of firing, moving against several springs. As the bolt reaches the end of its travel, it moves forward under the power of the bolt springs and a mechanical connections helps the barrel rotate the ratchet cam.

The balance of forces in firing the Mk 20 results in the weapon having very little felt recoil. Though designed to be fired from mounts, the Mk 20 can be handheld and fired for short bursts with no real difficulty. Accepted by the Navy and in limited production by 1970, the Mk 20 replaced the Mk 18 grenade launchers still in service. The Mk 20 could be mounted on any standard pintle mount or piggyback above a .50 caliber machine gun on the Mk 46 mount. Some 1080 Mk 20 launchers were reported as being made before production was suspended in April 1971.

At the same time that the Mk 20 was being developed, another project was begun for a different type of grenade launcher. In July 1966, several members of the Mk 20 design team, William Schnatter, Engineer in Charge, and Colonel George M. Chinn, joined with Project Engineer Walter Cashen to design the new weapon at the Naval facility in Louisville. The new launcher was intended to be a self-powered, fully-automatic, belt-fed weapon chambered for the high-velocity, M384/M386 family of 40mm grenades.

The high-velocity family of 40mm grenades had been developed during the last years of the 1950s. The Army had been impressed with the low-velocity family of grenades and were interested in harnessing the relatively low recoil and large projectile of the high-low pressure system to a longer range weapon that could be mounted in helicopters. The new Army Aircraft Armament program looked to the 40mm grenade as part of an arms package for the UH-1 series helicopter to provide fire suppression and short duration air-to-ground fire support.

The M169 cartridge case of the new high-velocity grenade was made 7 millimeters longer than the M118 cartridge case used with the low-velocity grenades. The longer length was one step to prevent the chambering of the high-velocity ammunition in one of the shoulder fired low-velocity weapons which could not stand up to the pressure of firing. The base of the M169 case had a greatly enlarged powder chamber, also with six propellant-gas bleed holes and a sheet brass liner. The propelling charge in an M169 cartridge case is 71.6 grains (4.64 grams) of M2 smokeless powder, more than 14 times the size of the charge in a low-velocity M118 cartridge case.

The powder charge of the M169 cartridge case burns in a high-pressure chamber until it ruptures the brass seal. The propellant gas bleeds into the low-pressure chamber of the high-velocity round and drives the projectile down the barrel. The high-velocity projectile leaves the barrel spinning at 12,000 rpm with a muzzle velocity of 795 feet per second (244 meters/second).

Where the low-velocity M118 cartridge case can drive a 0.393 pound (0.178 kilogram) projectile to a muzzle velocity of 249 feet per second (76 meters/second), the M169 cartridge case, with its higher chamber and barrel pressure, drives a 0.54 pound (0.24 kilogram) projectile to a muzzle velocity of 795 feet per second (244 meters/second). This gives the high-velocity grenade an effective range of about 1,750 yards (1,600 meters) and a maximum range of 2,400 yards (2,200 meters), depending on the firing weapon.

To help contain the pressure of firing the high-velocity grenade, the M169 cartridge case was designed with a solid base (head) surrounding the powder chamber and extending up an inch (24.5 mm) from the base of the round. This almost-solid case head allows the M169 cartridge case to safely withstand the pressure of firing without having the last ¾ inch of the case being supported in a chamber.

Projectiles for the high-velocity 40mm round have a copper alloy rotating band as compared to the soft aluminum bands on low-pressure 40mm rounds. The hard copper rotating band combines with the longer cartridge case of the high-velocity grenades to help prevent one of the rounds being inadvertently loaded into a low-velocity 40mm weapon. The M533 fuze of the M383 and other high-velocity explosive grenades was made strong enough to withstand the stresses of a high-velocity launch and used the setback and rotation of launch to arm itself at a safe distance from the weapon.

The success of the high velocity family of 40mm grenades with Army helicopter gunships influenced the Navy when they ordered a new grenade launcher to be designed. The Navy design team in Louisville was able to make good use of the strong high-velocity cartridge case design in developing its weapon. Instead of using a complex locking and unlocking system for the bolt, or an excessively heavy bolt, the new grenade launcher was able to operate using the advanced primer ignition/blowback principle.

In an advanced primer ignition system, the bolt is still moving forward with the cartridge entering the chamber as the round is fired. The blowback pressure of firing has to stop the forward motion of the bolt before it can begin to drive the bolt backwards. With the intent to place the new grenade launcher on ridged mounts, firing from an open bolt, as required by the advanced primer ignition system, was not considered a problem for such a large weapon.

Using the advanced primer ignition system, the designers were able to make a bolt for the new grenade launcher that only weighed in the neighborhood of 17 pounds instead of the near-50 pounds a standard blowback bolt would require. When the new grenade launcher fired a high-velocity round, over ¾ of an inch of the cartridge case never entered the chamber.

A fixed vertical cam or "curved rail" was the heart of the operating system for the new grenade launcher. The curved rail would force a cartridge down the face of the bolt as it traveled back from the point of firing. The major advantage of the curved rail was that it would positively prevent "stubbing" of the high-explosive grenade. Stubbing is where the bolt of an automatic weapon closes on an improperly placed round of ammunition, smashing the round between the bolt and the breech of the weapon. For most automatic weapons, this can be little more than a difficult jam. In a weapon using high-explosive projectiles, stubbing can have catastrophic consequences. The curved rail prevented stubbing from being possible.

By January 29, 1967, only 7 months and 22 days from the beginning of the project, three tool-room grenade launchers chambered for the high-velocity 40mm grenade were ready for firing tests. By October 12, 1967, production quantities of what was now identified as the Mark 19 Mod 0 grenade launcher were being produced. By January 1968, the new grenade launcher was in Vietnam and being mounted on PBRs and Huey helicopters. Reports from the field were very positive on the Mk 19 Mod 0 weapon, though some modifications were required for better operation.

The great majority (583 of 600 weapons) of Mk 19 Mod 0 launchers in use in Vietnam were converted over to the Mod 1 configuration in a product improvement program begun in 1971. The Mk 19 Mod 1 nomenclature was approved on June 30, 1971, and modifications included a riveted receiver, steel feed system parts, and modifications to the firing sequence. All of the converted weapons were found to have a greater reliability and were more easily maintained than the earlier Mod 0 version.

A highly modified Mark 19 Mod 2 version was produced by December 1978. Only two prototypes of the Mod 2 weapons were produced as it was found they differed so greatly from the original design that they simply didn't work. By October 1978, a Mod 3 version of the Mk 19 was ready for production. The Mk 19 Mod 3 design is of all-steel construction and has 60 percent fewer total parts that the Mk 19 Mod 1 weapon. On January 1, 1980, production of the Mark 19 Mod 1 ceased and the Mk 19 Mod 3 became the standard U.S. Navy 40mm (Grenade) machine gun. In the 1980s, both the Marine Corps and the U.S. Army adopted the Mk 19 Mod 3 grenade launcher as standard issue. This weapon has remained in front-line use to the present day in SEAL and other military hands.

To increase the versatility of the 40mm grenade launcher family, new rounds were designed in the late 1960s that have replaced almost all other high-explosive 40mm grenades. To meet the threat of mechanized infantry light-armored vehicles, the shaped-charge principle was adapted to the 40mm low velocity grenade.

In the M430 and M433 40mm grenades, a steel grenade body holds an explosive charge surrounding a conical copper liner. When the grenade detonates, the explosive charge collapses the copper liner, forming a jet of metal that will force its way through over 2 inches (5.08 centimeters) of steel. To increase the fragmentation effect of the steel grenade body, the inside of the body is engraved to produce much the same fragmentation pattern as a standard 40mm HE round. This double-action, armor-piercing, fragmentation effect was accounted for in the name of the new rounds, HEDP, for High Explosive, Dual Purpose.

One of the major design points that made the HEDP rounds practical was the new M550 (low velocity) and M549 (high velocity) Point Initiating, Base Detonating (PIBD) fuzes. Using the "spitback" principle, the new fuze design was able to fulfill the job done previously only in larger projectiles with much larger fuze systems. The spitback fuze contained, at its heart, a very small version of a shaped charge. When the detonator of the spitback fuze functioned, it sent a jet through the main bursting charge where it acted much like a base detonator.

The HEDP design was proven with the M430 round for the high-velocity 40mm grenade launchers. The design was immediately adapted to the low-velocity 40mm grenade. The M433 low-velocity HEDP round uses the same system for operating as the high-velocity M433 round but has a slightly simpler M550 PIBD fuze. The HEDP rounds were both type-classified as Standard A for issue by the U.S. Army in 1971. The Teams picked up on the new rounds almost immediately, but the standard M406 HE round remained in use for most of the remaining combat in Vietnam. Today, the HEDP rounds are the most commonly issued combat ammunition for both the Mk 19 Mod 3 and M203/M79 weapons.

Due to its greater inherent accuracy, the M79 is still found in the SEAL Teams today. The M79 is issued primarily for backup use by a SEAL who is armed with another primary weapon that cannot accept an M203 launcher.

For the SOPMOD M4 kit, a simple modification of the M203 resulted in the M203A1. Intended only for the M4A1 carbine, the M203A1 has its barrel cut back to nine inches. The shorter length of the M203A1 barrel could result in a fired round striking a part of the weapon or the sling if it were used on a standard-length M16-series weapon.

■ Forty-Millimeter-Grenade Launcher Data ■

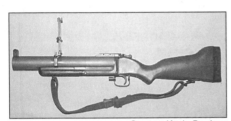

Source: Kevin Dockery

M79 GRENADE LAUNCHER

CARTRIDGE 40×46mmSR
OPERATION Manual, break open
TYPE OF FIRE Single shot
RATE OF FIRE 6 rpm
MUZZLE VELOCITY 247 fps (76 m/s)
SIGHTS Open, leaf-type, square-notch/blade, adjustable 75 to 375 meters in 25-meter increments
FEED Single round
MOUNT TYPE Shoulder fired
WEIGHTS
Weapon (empty) 5.95 lbs (2.7 kg)
Weapon (loaded) 6.45 lbs (2.93 kg)
Service cartridge M406 HE 0.50 lbs (0.23 kg)
Projectile 0.38 lbs (0.17 kg)
EFFECTS
Effect Ground-burst blast and fragmentation
Area of effect 5.5 yd (5 m) burst radius
LENGTHS
Weapon overall 28.78 in (73.1 cm)
Barrel 14 in (35.7 cm)
Sight radius 6.14 in (15.6 cm)

Minimum (arming) range 45 to 90 ft (14 to 27 m)
Effective range 383 yd (350 m)
Maximum range 437 yd (400 m)

Source: Kevin Dockery

XM148 GRENADE LAUNCHER (COLT CMG-4)

CARTRIDGE 40×46mmSR
OPERATION Manual, slide action
TYPE OF FIRE Single shot
RATE OF FIRE 12 rpm
MUZZLE VELOCITY 247 fps (76 m/s)
SIGHTS Open, aperture/post, adjustable, graduation marks at 50, 100, 150, 200, 250, 275, 300, 325, 350, 375, and 400 meters
FEED Single round
MOUNT TYPE M16/AR-15 series weapons
WEIGHTS
Weapon (empty) 3.1 lbs (1.41 kg)
Weapon (mounted and loaded) 10.3 lbs (4.67 kg) w/M406 HE & 20 rds, less ½ foregrip (0.15 lbs) CAR-15 (XM177E2) w/20 rds 6.85 lbs (3.11 kg)
Service cartridge M406 HE 0.50 lbs (0.23 kg)
Projectile 0.38 lbs (0.172 kg)

EFFECTS

Effect Ground-burst blast and fragmentation

Area of effect 5.5 yd (5 m) burst radius

LENGTHS

Weapon overall 13 in (33 cm)

Barrel 10 in (25.4 cm)

Sight radius 7.56 in (19.2 cm)

Minimum (arming) range 45 to 90 ft (14 to 27 m)

Effective range 383 yds (350 m)

Maximum range 437 yds (400 m)

Source: Kevin Dockery

40MM M203 GRENADE LAUNCHER

CARTRIDGE 40×46mmSR

OPERATION Manual, slide action

TYPE OF FIRE Single shot

RATE OF FIRE 8 rpm

MUZZLE VELOCITY 235 fps (71 m/s)

SIGHTS Two sights issued w/weapon. open, folding ladder type short range indicator/post, adjustable graduated to 250 meters, secured to handguard. open, folding long range quadrant aperture/post, adjustable graduated to 400 meters, secured to carrying handle of rifle

FEED Single round

MOUNT TYPE M16/AR-15 series weapons

WEIGHTS

Weapon (empty) 3.6 lbs (1.63 kg)

Weapon (mounted and loaded) 12.85 lbs (5.83 kg) w/M406 HE, 30 rds

Mount 8.75 lbs (3.97 kg) (M16A1 w/30 rds)

Service cartridge M406 HE 0.50 lbs (0.23 kg)

Projectile 0.38 lb (0.17 kg)

EFFECTS

Effect Ground burst blast and fragmentation

Area of effect 5.5 yd (5 m) burst radius

LENGTHS

Weapon overall 15.3 in (38.9 cm)

Barrel 12 in (30.5 cm)

Minimum (arming) range 45 to 90 ft (14 to 27 m)

Effective range 383 yds (350 m)

Maximum range 437 yds (400 m)

Source: U.S. Navy

NAME 3-BARREL 40MM GRENADE LAUNCHER

CARTRIDGE 40×46mmSR

OPERATION Manual, double-action

TYPE OF FIRE Single shot repeater

RATE OF FIRE 9 rpm

MUZZLE VELOCITY 215 fps (66 m/s)

FEED One round per barrel

MOUNT TYPE M16/AR-15 series weapons

WEIGHTS

Weapon (empty) 4.5 lbs (2.04 kg)

Weapon (mounted and loaded) 13.73 lbs (6.23 kg)

Mount 7.72 lbs (3.5 kg) (M16A1 w/20 rds)

Magazine (loaded) 3 rounds 1.5 lbs (0.68 kg)

Service cartridge M406 HE 0.50 lbs (0.23 kg)

Projectile 0.38 lbs (0.17 kg)

EFFECTS

Effect Ground burst blast and fragmentation

Area of effect 5.5 yd (5 m) burst radius

LENGTHS

Barrel 6 in (15.2 cm)

Minimum (arming) range 45 to 90 ft (14 to 27 m)

Effective range 328 yds (300 m)

Maximum range 372 yds (340 m)

Source: U.S. Navy

40MM PUMP GRENADE LAUNCHER

CARTRIDGE 40×46mmSR

OPERATION Manual, pump-action

TYPE OF FIRE Single shot repeater

RATE OF FIRE 15 rpm

MUZZLE VELOCITY 247 fps (76 m/s)

SIGHTS Open, leaf-type, square-notch/blade, adjustable 75 to 375 meters in 25-meter increments, nonadjustable, square-notch battle sight (leaf folded)

FEED Three round tubular magazine

MOUNT TYPE Shoulder fired

WEIGHTS

Weapon (empty) 8.2 lbs (3.72 kg)

Weapon (loaded) 10.21 lbs (4.63 kg)

Magazine (loaded) 4 rounds 2.0 lbs (0.91 kg) w/1 round in chamber

Service cartridge M406 HE 0.50 lbs (0.23 kg)

Projectile 0.38 lbs (0.17 kg)

EFFECTS

Effect Ground burst blast and fragmentation

Area of effect 5.5 yd (5 m) burst radius

LENGTHS

Weapon overall 34.5 in (87.6 cm)

Barrel 14 in (35.6 cm)

Sight radius 5.69 in (14.5 cm)—battle sight; folding sight raised, set at 50 m—6.19 in (15.7 cm); folding sight raised, set at 375 m—7.31 in (18.6 cm)

Minimum (arming) range 45 to 90 ft (14 to 27 m)

Effective range 383 yds (350 m)

Maximum range 437 yds (400 m)

Source: U.S. Navy

40MM MARK 18 MOD 0 RAPID FIRE GUN (HONEYWELL)

CARTRIDGE 40×46mmSR

OPERATION Manual, hand cranked

TYPE OF FIRE Full automatic

RATE OF FIRE 1-250 rpm

MUZZLE VELOCITY 215 fps (66 m/s)

SIGHTS Open speed-ring/post, fixed, graduated 50, 100, 200, and 300 meters

FEED Flexible plastic or cloth belt

MOUNT TYPE M3 or M122 (M2) tripod, deck mounts Mk 46, Mk 50, Mk 55

WEIGHTS

Weapon (empty) 19 lbs (8.62 kg)

Weapon (loaded) 31.8 lbs (14.42 kg)

Weapon (mounted and loaded) 46.8 lbs (21.22 kg) M122 tripod 15 lbs (6.8 kg)

Magazine (loaded) 25 round belt 12.79 lbs (5.8 kg)

Service cartridge M406 HE 0.50 lbs (0.23 kg)

Projectile 0.38 lbs (0.17 kg)

EFFECTS

Effect Ground-burst blast and fragmentation

Area of effect 5.5 yd (5 m) burst radius

LENGTHS

Weapon overall 22 in (55.9 cm)

Barrel 6 in (15.2 cm)

Sight radius 5.13 in (13 cm)

Minimum (arming) range 45 to 90 ft (14 to 27 m)

Effective range 383 yds (350 m)

Maximum range 437 yds (400 m)

Notes on mounts M3 and M122 (M2) tripods—Standard machine gun ground mount folding tripods. M3, for the M2 HB .50 caliber machine gun—weight 44 lbs (20 kg), M122 for the 7.62mm M60 and the .30 caliber Browning M1919A4 (M2)—15 lbs (6.8 kg)

Mark 46 Mods 0, 1 & 2—Earlier model pedestal—type deck mount holding one .50 caliber machine gun w/105 rds and one Mark 18 or Mark 20 40mm grenade launcher w/24 rds 40mm. Mount has a 28-inch-wide by 30-inch-tall armor shield in front of the weapons with a 4-inch-wide slot in its center. Weight without guns and ammunition is 167 lbs (75.7 kg)

Mark 50 Mod 0—Pedestal-type deck mount holding one .50 caliber machine gun w/125 rds and one Mark 18 or Mark 20 40mm grenade launcher w/25 rds 40mm. Weight without guns and ammunition 2,275 lbs (1,032 kg).

Mark 55 Mods 0 & 1—Pintle-type mount able to be bolted to gunwales and decks holding 1 Mk 18 or Mk 20 40mm machine gun. There is no direct provision on the mount for attaching an ammunition container. Weight without gun 18.5 lbs (8.39 kg)

Source: U.S. Navy

MARK 20 MOD 0 AUTOMATIC 40MM GRENADE LAUNCHER

CARTRIDGE 40×46mmSR

OPERATION Blow-forward combined with blowback

TYPE OF FIRE Selective, semiautomatic/full automatic

RATE OF FIRE Practical SS 24 rpm, A 48 rpm, Cyclic 425 rpm

MUZZLE VELOCITY 240 fps (73 m/s)

SIGHTS Open, ladder-type multiple square notch/blade, fixed, graduated for 100, 200, 250, and 300 yards

FEED Flexible metal nondisintegrating Mk 8 Mod 0 (M16) link belt

MOUNT TYPE M3 or M122 (M2) tripod, deck mounts Mk 46, Mk 50, Mk 55

WEIGHTS

Weapon (empty) 26 lbs (11.8 kg)

Weapon (loaded) 35.9 lbs (16.29 kg)

Weapon (mounted and loaded) 50.9 lbs (23.09 kg) M122 tripod 15 lbs (6.8 kg)

Magazine (loaded) 9.9 lbs (4.49 kg) (24 round belt)

Service cartridge M406 HE 0.50 lbs (0.23 kg)

Projectile 0.38 lbs (0.17 kg)

EFFECTS

Effect Ground-burst blast and fragmentation

Area of effect 5.5 yd (5 m) burst radius

LENGTHS

Weapon overall 31.2 in (79.2 cm)

Barrel 13 in (33 cm)

Minimum (arming) range 45 to 90 ft (14 to 27 m)

Effective range 383 yds (350 m)

Maximum range 437 yds (400 m)

Notes on mounts M3 and M122 (M2) tripods—Standard machine gun ground mount folding tripods. M3, for the M2 HB .50 caliber machine gun—weight 44 lbs (20 kg), M122 for the 7.62mm M60 and the .30 caliber Browning M1919A4 (M2)—15 lbs (6.8 kg)

Mark 46 Mods 0, 1 & 2—Earlier model pedestal—type deck mount holding one .50 caliber machine gun w/105 rds and one Mark 18 or Mark 20 40mm grenade launcher w/24 rds 40mm. Mount has a 28 inch wide by 30-inch-tall armor shield in front of the weapons with a 4-inch-wide slot in its center. Weight without guns and ammunition is 167 lbs (75.7 kg)

Mark 50 Mod 0—Pedestal-type deck mount holding one .50 machine gun w/125 rds and one Mark 18 or Mark 20 40mm grenade launcher w/25 rds 40mm. Weight without guns and ammunition 2,275 lbs (1,032 kg)

Mark 55 Mods 0 & 1—Pintle-type mount able to be bolted to gunwales and decks holding one Mk 18 or Mk 20 40mm machine gun. There is no direct provision on the mount for attaching an ammunition container. Weight without gun 18.5 lbs (8.39 kg)

MARK 19 MOD 0

CARTRIDGE 40×53mmSR

OPERATION Advanced primer ignition blowback

TYPE OF FIRE Selective—semiautomatic/full automatic

RATE OF FIRE Practical SS 30 rpm, A 60 rpm, Cyclic 500 rpm

MUZZLE VELOCITY 800 fps (244 m/s)

SIGHTS None integral, added as needed according to mount

Normal iron sight—Open, leaf-type square-notch/blade, adjustable 300 to 1500 meters in 100-meter increments, adjustable for windage in 1-mil increments, 300 meter fixed battle sight when folded.

FEED Flexible metal disintegrating M16 link belt

MOUNT TYPE M3 tripod w/Mark 64 Mod 4 gun mount, deck mounts Mk 48, Mk 63, Mk 64

WEIGHTS

Weapon (empty) 39 lbs (17.69 kg)

Weapon (loaded) 78.66 lbs (35.68 kg) w/50 rd belt

Weapon (mounted and loaded) 213.66 lbs (96.92 kg); Mk 64 Mod 2 mount 135 lbs (61.2 kg)

Magazine (loaded) 39.66 lbs (17.99 kg) 50 round belt w/o box

Service cartridge M384 HE 0.76 lbs (0.34)

Projectile 0.54 lbs (0.24 kg)

EFFECTS

Effect Ground burst blast and fragmentation

Area of effect 16 yd (15 m) radius

LENGTHS

Weapon overall 32 in (81.3 cm)

Barrel 12 in (30.5 cm)

Sight radius 14.4 in (36.5 cm) w/iron sight

Minimum (arming) range 59 to 118 ft (18 to 36 m)

Effective range 1,750 yds (1,600 m)

Maximum range 2,406 yds (2,200 m)

Notes on mounts M3 Tripod w/Mk 64 Mod 0 mount—This is the standard .50 caliber machine gun tripod fitted with the Mk 64 cradle-type mount to accept the Mk 19 40mm machine gun. A bracket can be attached to the mount that accepts a M2A1 ammunition can (.50 caliber) that will hold a 24-round 40mm belt. A cradle is also available to hold the M548 ammunition can or the can may be used while placed on the ground. Mk 64 Mod 4 carriage and cradle assembly weight 21 lbs (9.53 kg)

Mark 48 Mod 0, 1, 2, and 4—This is a turret-type armored mount that accepts the Mk 19 40mm machine gun as one of the several weapons used. In the Mod 0 is the Mk 19 with 50 rds of 40mm and the Mk 16 Mod 4 20mm cannon w/500 rounds. The Mod 1 turret has the Mk 19 and two Mk 21 7.62mm machine guns w/1000 rounds. The Mod 2 has the Mk 19 and two M2 HB .50 caliber machine guns w/1000 rounds. All weapons are internally mounted. On the outside of the turret in the Mod 4 version is two, one on either side, Mk 47 Mod 0 rocket launchers. Each of the launchers holds one 3.5 inch "Bazooka" rocket. Mount weight without guns or ammunition is 1900 lbs (862 kg)

Mark 63—This is a tub-type mount adapted from the Mk 21 gun mount. The mount is manually operated and holds one Mk 19 40mm machine gun and 300 rounds of ammunition with a powered belt booster. The tub is armored against .50 caliber machine gun fire and is intended for use on the LCM boat. The single operator stands in the tub operating the weapon manually. Mount weight 2,600 lbs (1,179 kg) without gun or ammunition.

Mark 64 Mods 1, 2, and 3—This is a cradle-type mount on various supports. All Mods accept a single Mk 19 40mm machine gun and a 50-round belt of ammunition held in a container that is part of the mount. The Mod 1 mount used the Mk 16 Mod 1 stand only for attachment to gunwales or decks. The Mod 2 uses the Mk 16 stand and tripod and the Mod 3, the Mk 16 stand, tripod, and shield. Weights without gun or ammunition are: Mod 1—56 lbs (25 kg), Mod 2—135 lbs (61.2 kg), Mod 3—180 lbs (81.6 kg)

Source: U.S. Navy

MARK 19 MOD 1

CARTRIDGE 40×53mmSR

OPERATION Advanced primer ignition blow-back

TYPE OF FIRE Selective—semiautomatic/full automatic

RATE OF FIRE Practical SS 30 rpm, A 60 rpm, Cyclic 450 to 500 rpm

MUZZLE VELOCITY 800 fps (244 m/s)

SIGHTS None integral, added as needed according to mount. Normal iron sight—open, leaf-type square-notch/blade, adjustable 300 to 1,500 meters in 100-meter increments, adjustable for windage in 1-mil increments, 300 meter fixed battle sight when folded.

FEED Flexible metal disintegrating M16/M16A1 link belt

MOUNT TYPE M3 tripod w/Mark 64 Mod 4 gun mount, Deck mounts Mk 48, Mk 63, Mk 64

WEIGHTS

Weapon (empty) 53 lbs (24 kg) w/o M10 charger

Weapon (loaded) 92.66 lbs (42 kg) w/50 rd belt

Weapon (mounted and loaded) 227.66 lbs (103.26 kg) Mk 64 Mod 2 mount 135 lbs (61.2 kg)

Magazine (loaded) 39.66 lbs (17.99 kg) 50 round belt w/o box

Service cartridge M384 HE 0.76 lbs (0.34)

Projectile 0.54 lbs (0.24 kg)

EFFECTS

Effect Ground burst blast and fragmentation

Area of effect 16 yd (15 m) radius

LENGTHS

Weapon overall 32.5 in (82.6 cm)

Barrel 12 in (30.5 cm)

Sight radius 14.4 in (36.5 cm) w/iron sight

Minimum (arming) range 59 to 118 ft (18 to 36 m)

Effective range 1,750 yds (1,600 m)

Maximum range 2,406 yds (2,200 m)

Notes on mounts M3 Tripod w/Mk 64 Mod 0 mount—This is the standard .50 caliber machine gun tripod fitted with the Mk 64 cradle-type mount to accept the Mk 19 40mm machine gun. A bracket can be attached to the mount that accepts a M2A1 ammunition can (.50 caliber) that will hold a 24-round 40mm belt. A cradle is also available to hold the M548 ammunition can or the can may be used while placed on the ground. Mk 64 Mod 4 carriage and cradle assembly weight 21 lbs (9.53 kg)

Mark 48 Mod 0, 1, 2, and 4—This is a turret-type armored mount that accepts the Mk 19 40mm machine gun as one of the several weapons used. In the Mod 0 is the Mk 19 with 50 rds of 40mm and the Mk 16 Mod 4 20mm cannon w/500 rounds. The Mod 1 turret has the Mk 19 and two Mk 21 7.62mm machine guns w/1000 rounds. The Mod 2 has the Mk 19 and two M2 HB .50 caliber machine guns w/1,000 rounds. All weapons are internally mounted. On the outside of the turret in the Mod 4 version is two, one on either side, Mk 47 Mod 0 rocket launchers. Each of the launchers holds one 3.5 inch "Bazooka" rocket. Mount weight without guns or ammunition is 1,900 lbs (862 kg)

Mark 63—This is a tub-type mount adapted from the Mk 21 gun mount. The mount is manually operated and holds one Mk 19 40mm machine gun and 300 rounds of ammunition with a powered belt booster. The tub is armored against .50 caliber machine gun fire and is intended for use on the LCM boat. The single operator stands in the tub operating the weapon manually. Mount weight 2,600 lbs (1,179 kg) without gun or ammunition.

Mark 64 Mods 1, 2, and 3—This is a cradle-type mount on various supports. All Mods accept a single Mk 19 40mm machine gun and a 50-round belt of ammunition held in a container that is part of the mount. The Mod 1 mount used the Mk 16 Mod 1 stand only for attachment to gunwales or decks. The Mod 2 uses the Mk 16 stand and tripod and the Mod 3, the Mk 16 stand, tripod, and shield. Weights without gun or ammunition are: Mod 1—56 lbs (25 kg), Mod 2—135 lbs (61.2 kg), Mod 3—180 lbs (81.6 kg)

MARK 19 MOD 2

CARTRIDGE 40×53mmSR

OPERATION Advanced primer ignition blowback

TYPE OF FIRE Selective—semiautomatic/full automatic

RATE OF FIRE Practical SS 30 rpm, A 60 rpm, Cyclic 350 rpm

MUZZLE VELOCITY 800 fps (244 m/s)

SIGHTS None integral, added as needed according to mount

FEED Flexible metal disintegrating M16A1 link belt

MOUNT TYPE M3 tripod w/Mark 64 Mod 4 gun mount, Deck mounts Mk 48, Mk 63, Mk 64

WEIGHTS

Weapon (empty) 75 lbs (35.02 kg)

Weapon (loaded) 114.66 lbs (52.00 kg) w/50 rd belt

Weapon (mounted and loaded) 348.66 lbs (158.15 kg); Mk 64 Mod 2 mount 135 lbs (61.2 kg)

Magazine (loaded) 39.66 lbs (17.99 kg) 50 round belt w/o box

Service cartridge M384 HE 0.76 lbs (0.34)

Projectile 0.54 lbs (0.24 kg)

EFFECTS

Effect Ground burst blast and fragmentation

Area of effect 16 yd (15 m) radius

LENGTHS

Weapon overall 36.1 in (91.7 cm)

Barrel 12 in (30.5 cm)

Minimum (arming) range 59 to 118 ft (18 to 36 m)

Effective range 1,750 yds (1,600 m)

Maximum range 2,406 yds (2,200 m) Prototype guns only produced by NOS/L, mid-1970s

Source: Kevin Dockery

MARK 19 MOD 3 40MM MACHINE GUN

CARTRIDGE 40 × 53mmSR

OPERATION Advanced primer ignition blow-back

TYPE OF FIRE Selective—semiautomatic/full automatic

RATE OF FIRE Practical SS 30 rpm, A 60 rpm, Cyclic 325-375 rpm

MUZZLE VELOCITY 800 fps (244 m/s)

SIGHTS Open, leaf-type square-notch/blade, adjustable 300 to 1,500 meters in 100-meter increments, adjustable for windage in 1-mil increments, 300-meter fixed battle sight when folded

FEED Flexible metal disintegrating M16A2 link belt

MOUNT TYPE M3 tripod w/Mark 64 Mod 4 gun mount, Deck mounts MK 48, MK 64

WEIGHTS

Weapon (empty) 75.6 lbs (34.29 kg)

Weapon (loaded) 115.26 lbs (52.28 kg) w/50 round belt

Weapon (mounted and loaded) 180.26 lbs (81.77 kg); M3 tripod 44 lbs (19.96 kg); MK 64 Mod 7 mount 21 lbs (9.53 kg)

Magazine (loaded) 39.66 lbs (17.99 kg) 50 round belt w/o box; 60.66 lbs (27.51 kg) 50 round belt w/M548 box

Service cartridge M384 HE 0.76 lbs (0.34)

Projectile 0.54 lbs (0.24 kg)

EFFECTS

Effect Ground burst blast and fragmentation

Area of effect 16 yd (15 m) radius

LENGTHS

Weapon overall 43.1 in (109.5 cm)

Barrel 16.25 in (41.3 cm)

Sight radius 14.4 in (36.5 cm)

Minimum (arming) range 59 to 118 ft (18 to 36 m)

Effective Range 1,750 yds (1,600 m)

Maximum range 2,406 yds (2,200 m)

Notes on mounts M3 Tripod w/Mk 64 Mod 7 mount—This is the standard .50 caliber machine gun tripod fitted with the Mk 64 cradle-type mount to accept the Mk 19 40mm machine gun. A bracket can be attached to the mount that accepts a M2A1 ammunition can (.50 caliber) that will hold a 24-round 40mm belt. A cradle is also available to hold the M548 ammunition can or the can may be used while placed on the ground. Mk 64 Mod 7 carriage and cradle assembly weight 21 lbs (9.53 kg)

Mark 48 Mod 0, 1, 2, and 4—This is a turret-type armored mount that accepts the Mk 19 40mm machine gun as one of the several weapons used. In the Mod 0 is the Mk 19 with 50 rds of 40mm and the Mk 16 Mod 4 20mm cannon w/500 rounds. The Mod 1 turret has the Mk 19 and two Mk 21 7.62mm machine guns w/1,000 rounds. The Mod 2 has the Mk 19 and two M2 HB .50 caliber machine guns w/1,000 rounds. All weapons are internally mounted. On the outside of the turret in the Mod 4 version is two, one on either side, Mk 47 Mod 0 rocket launchers. Each of the launchers holds one 3.5-inch "Bazooka" rocket. Mount weight without guns or ammunition is 1,900 lbs (862 kg)

Mark 64 Mods 1, 2, and 3—This is a cradle-type mount on various supports. All Mods accept a single Mk 19 40mm machine gun and a 50-round belt of ammunition held in a container that is part of the mount. The Mod 1 mount used the Mk 16 Mod 1 stand only for attachment to gunwales or decks. The Mod 2 uses the Mk 16 stand and tripod and the Mod 3, the Mk 16 stand, tripod, and shield. Weights without gun or ammunition is: Mod 1—56 lbs (25 kg), Mod 2—135 lbs (61.2 kg), Mod 3—180 lbs (81.6 kg)

■ Forty-Millimeter Ammunition ■
LOW VELOCITY 40MM GRENADES

M381 HIGH EXPLOSIVE

CALIBER 40×46mmSR

TYPE Low-velocity ground burst high-explosive fragmentation

IDENTIFYING COLOR CODE Green cartridge case w/yellow markings, projectile body is olive drab w/yellow markings, long, flat-pointed ogive (nose) is gold

MUZZLE VELOCITY 249 fps (76 m/s)

FILLER Composition B

FUZE TYPE M552 (T333E1) Point detonating

WEIGHTS

Round 0.503 lb (0.228 kg)

Projectile 0.393 lb (0.178 kg)

FILLER 1.129 oz (32 g)

EFFECTS

Effect Ground burst blast and fragmentation

Area of effect 5.5 yd (5 m) burst radius

LENGTHS

Overall length 3.89 in (9.9 cm)

Width (diameter) 1.72 in (4.4 cm)

Minimum (arming) range 7 to 10 ft (2.4 to 3 m)

Maximum range 437 yds (400 m)

This is the original 40mm combat round. The projectile body is made of aluminum with a soft aluminum rotating band just above the case mouth. The fragmentation effect from this round comes from the grenade body which is made up of square cross-section steel wire, regularly notched along its length, then formed and welded into a round ball. The ball makes up the rear half of the 40mm projectile.

The construction of the fragmentation system results in over 300 small fragments traveling at over 5,000 fps (1,524 m/s) initial velocity from the point of detonation. The light weight of the fragments cause them to loose velocity quickly, giving the round a 5.5 yard (5 meter) burst radius. For training purposes, there is considered to be a 142 yard (130 meter) danger radius around the point of detonation of a 40mm HE round. During combat, no targets should be engaged with HE rounds within 34 yards (31 meters).

This round was no longer manufactured after January 1961 when the M406 round became available and was classified Standard A. The short arming range of the M552 fuze was considered too dangerous for field use by combat troops where overhead cover, such as branches or leaves, could accidentally detonate the round over friendly forces.

M382 PRACTICE

CALIBER 40×46mmSR

TYPE Low-velocity ground burst practice

IDENTIFYING COLOR CODE Green cartridge case w/yellow markings, projectile body is olive drab w/yellow markings, long, flat-pointed ogive (nose) is blue (ogive is gray on early production rounds)

MUZZLE VELOCITY 249 fps (76 m/s)

FILLER Yellow dye, RDX booster

FUZE TYPE M552 Point detonating

WEIGHTS

Round 0.503 lb (0.228 kg)

Projectile 0.393 lb (0.178 kg)

Filler 0.160 oz (4.54 g) Dye, 5.9 grains (0.38 g) RDX booster

EFFECTS

Effect Ground burst of yellow dye marker cloud

Area of effect 11 yd (10 m) danger area radius

LENGTHS

Overall lengths 3.89 in (9.9 cm)

Width (diameter) 1.72 in (4.4 cm)

Minimum (arming) range 7 to 10 ft (2.4 to 3 m)

Maximum range 437 yds (400 m)

This is the first practice round available for the low-velocity 40mm weapons family. Ballistically matched to, and using the same fuze as, the M381 round, this round could be used for target practice more safely and less expensively than the HE round. The M552 fuze has an RDX booster pellet that ruptures the hollow, steel, grenade body, spreading the yellow dye over the target area. Though the yellow dye is inert, the RDX pellet makes this round dangerous due to some fragmentation of the grenade body. This round also has the short arming distance as the M381 HE round and was replaced at the same time.

M386 HIGH EXPLOSIVE

CALIBER 40×46mmSR

TYPE Low-velocity ground burst high explosive fragmentation

IDENTIFYING COLOR CODE Green cartridge case w/yellow markings, projectile body is olive drab w/yellow markings, long, flat-pointed ogive (nose) is gold

MUZZLE VELOCITY 249 fps (76 m/s)

FILLER Composition B

FUZE TYPE M551 Point detonating

WEIGHTS

Round 0.50 lb (0.227 kg)

Projectile 0.39 lb (0.177 kg)

Filler 1.129 oz (32 g)

EFFECTS

Effect Ground burst blast and fragmentation

Area of effect 5.5 yd (5 m) burst radius

LENGTHS

Overall length 3.89 in (9.9 cm)

Width (diameter) 1.72 in (4.4 cm)

Minimum (arming) range 45 to 90 ft (14 to 27 m)

Maximum range 437 yds (400 m)

The fragmentation body of this grenade is formed from coined (engraved) sheet metal formed into a ball. The grooves on the interior of the grenade body formed by the coining process control the fragmentation pattern in the same manner as the coiled, notched wire body used in other HE grenades. Production quantities of this grenade have been made but it is slightly more expensive to produce than the notched steel wire ball grenades. Except for the fuze, this grenade is nearly identical with the M441 HE grenade.

M397/M397A1 HIGH EXPLOSIVE

CALIBER 40×46mmSR

TYPE Low-velocity, ground impact air burst high-explosive fragmentation

IDENTIFYING COLOR CODE Green cartridge case w/yellow markings, projectile body is olive drab w/yellow markings, long, flat-pointed ogive (nose) is gold

MUZZLE VELOCITY 247 fps (75 mps)

FILLER Octol

FUZE TYPE M397—M536 point detonating w/pyrotechnic auxiliary; M397A1—M536E1 point detonating w/pyrotechnic auxiliary

FUZE DELAY M397 w/M536 fuze, 120 milliseconds (auxiliary); M397A1 w/M536E1 fuze, 80 milliseconds (auxiliary)

WEIGHTS

Round M397—0.507 lb (0.230 kg); M397A1—0.510 lb (0.231 kg)

Projectile M397—0.397 lb (0.180 kg); M397A1—0.400 (0.181 kg)

Filler 1.13 oz (32 g)

LENGTHS

Overall length 4.05 inches (10.28 cm)

Width (diameter) 1.72 in (4.4 cm)

EFFECTS

Effect Air burst blast and fragmentation

Area of effect 5.5 yd (5 m) burst radius

Arming range 45 to 90 ft (14 to 27 m)

Maximum range 437 yds (400 m)

The M397 round, also known as the "jump up," uses the air burst effect to give a more efficient fragmentation pattern over the burst radius as compared to a standard ground burst. After the fuze is armed, the round will function on impact. On striking the ground, the fuze fires a black powder separation charge in the body of the projectile. The separation charge ejects the fragmentation ball out behind the impact of the projectile while also arming and igniting the auxiliary delay fuse. The auxiliary fuse detonates the fragmentation charge when the ball assembly is about 5 feet above the impact point.

The M397A1 uses a slightly different fuze with a shorter pyrotechnic delay in the auxiliary fuse. In addition, the M397A1 has a thicker ogive on the front of the projectile. The thicker nose helps cut back on the incidence of premature detonation when the round is fired through trees and brush. The shorter pyrotechnic delay also give the M397A1 round better performance when fired onto snow or other soft surfaces.

Source: Kevin Dockery

M406 HIGH EXPLOSIVE

Cutaway 40mm M406 High Explosive This specimen also has the M118 cartridge case cut away, showing the high- and low-pressure chambers.

CALIBER 40×46mmSR

TYPE Low-velocity ground burst high-explosive fragmentation

IDENTIFYING COLOR CODE Green cartridge case w/yellow markings, projectile body is olive drab w/yellow markings, long, flat-pointed ogive (nose) is gold

MUZZLE VELOCITY 249 fps (76 m/s)

FILLER Composition B

FUZE TYPE M551 Point detonating

WEIGHTS

Round 0.503 lb (0.228 kg)

Projectile 0.393 lb (0.178 kg)

Filler 1.129 oz (32 g)

EFFECTS

Effect Ground burst blast and fragmentation

Area of effect 5.5 yd (5 m) burst radius

LENGTHS

Overall length 3.89 in (9.9 cm)

Width (diameter) 1.72 in (4.4 cm)

Minimum (arming) range 45 to 90 ft (14 to 27 m)

Maximum range 437 yds (400 m)

This is the present issue Standard A 40mm combat round for the U.S. military. The same wrapped wire sphere as used in the earlier M381 H.E. round is used in the M406 but with an M551 fuze to give a longer arming range for the round. The longer arming distance of the M551 fuze prevents the projectile from prematurely detonating near friendly troops when fired in heavily wooded or jungle areas.

Source: Kevin Dockery

M407A1 PRACTICE

CALIBER 40×46mmSR

TYPE Low velocity ground burst high-
explosive fragmentation

IDENTIFYING COLOR CODE Green cartridge
case w/yellow markings, projectile body is
anodized green or blue w/yellow markings,
long, flat-pointed ogive (nose) is blue (gray
ogive on older production) with white
markings

MUZZLE VELOCITY 249 fps (76 m/s)

FILLER Yellow dye smoke pellets w/RDX
booster

FUZE TYPE M551 Point detonating

WEIGHTS

Round 0.50 lb (0.227 kg)

Projectile 0.39 lb (0.177 kg)

FILLER 0.160 oz (4.54 g) dye, 5.9 grains
(0.38 g) RDX booster

EFFECTS

Effect Ground burst of yellow dye marker cloud

Area of effect 11 yd (10 m) danger area radius

LENGTHS

Overall length 3.894 in (9.89 cm)

Width (diameter) 1.72 in (4.4 cm)

Minimum (arming) range 45 to 90 ft
(14 to 27 m)

Maximum range 437 yds (400 m)

This practice round is ballistically
matched to the M406 HE round and can be
used for marksmanship training and practice
in place of the more dangerous and expensive fragmentation round. The body of the
projectile is made of a plastic ball containing
the smoke pellets and fuze well. Upon impact, the detonation fuze ignites the smoke

charge while shattering the plastic grenade
body, simulating the explosive impact of the
M406 round. The small RDX charge does
give the round some dangerous fragmentation within a short distance from the point of
impact.

Source: Kevin Dockery

M433 HIGH EXPLOSIVE DUAL PURPOSE

CALIBER 40×46mmSR

TYPE Low-velocity high-explosive shaped
charge antiarmor/ground burst fragmentation round

IDENTIFYING COLOR CODE Green cartridge
case w/yellow markings, projectile body is
olive drab w/white markings, short, round-
nosed ogive is yellow

MUZZLE VELOCITY 250 fps (76 m/s)

FILLER Composition A5

FUZE TYPE M550 Point initiating, base detonating

WEIGHTS

Round 0.51 lb (0.23 kg)

Projectile 0.39 lb (0.18 kg)

Filler 694 gr (45 g)

EFFECTS

Effect Penetrates 2 in (5.1 cm) steel with
fragmentation around the point of impact
(approximately equal to the M406 HE)

Area of effect 5.5 yd (5 m) burst radius

LENGTHS

Lengths 4.05 in (10.3 cm)

Width (diameter) 1.72 in (4.4 cm)

Minimum (arming) range 45 to 90 ft
(14 to 27 m)

Maximum range 437 yds (400 m)

The most commonly used combat round for the 40mm family of weapons is the M433 HEDP round. The projectile of this round can both penetrate armor and has a reasonable antipersonnel fragmentation effect. On impact, the M550 fuze fires an explosive spitback element that drives an explosive wave to the rear of the main charge.

Detonation from the rear allows the main charge to collapse the copper cone liner within the round into a high-velocity jet of molten metal that can pierce over two inches (5 cm) of armor plate, 12 inches (30 cm) of pine logs, 16 inches (41 cm) of concrete blocks, or 20 inches (51 cm) of sandbags.

The steel body of the grenade that contains the explosive shaped charge is also internally segmented (engraved) so that it breaks up into a fragmentation pattern only slightly less efficient than that of the M381/M406 wire wrapped grenade.

M441 HIGH EXPLOSIVE

CALIBER 40×46mmSR

TYPE Low-velocity ground burst high-explosive fragmentation

IDENTIFYING COLOR CODE Green cartridge case w/yellow markings, projectile body is olive drab w/yellow markings, long, flat-pointed ogive (nose) is gold (yellow)

MUZZLE VELOCITY 249 fps (76 m/s)

FILLER Composition B

FUZE TYPE M552 Point detonating

WEIGHTS

Round 0.50 lb (0.227 kg)

Projectile 0.39 lb (0.177 kg)

FILLER 1.129 oz (32 g)

EFFECTS

Effect Ground burst blast and fragmentation

Area of effect 5.5 yd (5 m) burst radius

LENGTHS

Overall length 3.89 in (9.9 cm)

Width (diameter) 1.72 in (4.4 cm)

Minimum (arming) range 7 to 10 ft (2.1 to 3 m)

Maximum range 437 yds (400 m)

The fragmentation body of this grenade is formed from coined (engraved) sheet metal formed into a ball. The grooves on the interior of the grenade body formed by the coining process control the fragmentation pattern in the same manner as the coiled, notched wire body used in other HE grenades. Production quantities of this grenade have been made but it is slightly more expensive to produce than the notched steel wire ball grenades. Except for the fuze, this grenade is nearly identical with the M386 HE grenade.

Source: Kevin Dockery

M463 HIGH EXPLOSIVE SMOKELESS, FLASHLESS

CALIBER 40×46mmSR

TYPE Low-velocity ground burst high-explosive fragmentation w/encapsulated propellant charge

IDENTIFYING COLOR CODE Green cartridge case w/yellow markings, projectile body is olive drab w/yellow markings, long, flat-pointed ogive (nose) is black

MUZZLE VELOCITY 247 fps (75 m/s)

FILLER Composition B

FUZE TYPE M551 Point detonating

WEIGHTS

Projectile 0.38 lb (0.17 kg)

Filler 494 gr (32 g)

EFFECTS

Effect Ground burst blast and fragmentation

Area of effect 5.5 yd (5 m) burst radius

LENGTHS

Overall length 3.89 in (9.9 cm)

Width (diameter) 1.72 in (4.4 cm)

Minimum (arming) range 45 to 90 ft
(14 to 27 m)
Maximum range 437 yds (400 m)

The projectile of this round is the same as that launched by the M406 HE round and has the same limitations and effects. The cartridge case utilizes the "teleshot" system developed by Advanced Aircraft Armaments Inc. for the U.S. space program. The teleshot system uses a folded metal capsule to contain the propellant gasses of a fired cartridge. The folded teleshot capsule expands and unfolds suddenly, driving the projectile at near the same muzzle velocity as a standard round, but with a much greater and shorter duration initial push.

Since the teleshot capsule contains all of the propellant gasses, there is no flash or smoke to indicate the point of firing. Containing the propellant gasses also cuts back considerably on the sound of firing, resulting in a much more difficult to identify or locate sound than the discharge of a standard round.

Source: Kevin Dockery

M576/M576E1 MULTIPLE PROJECTILE

CALIBER 40×46mmSR
TYPE Low-velocity antipersonnel shotshell
IDENTIFYING COLOR CODE Green cartridge case w/white markings, black plastic projectile (sabot)
MUZZLE VELOCITY 883 fps (269 m/s)

MUZZLE ENERGY 640 ft/lb (868 J); 32 ft/lb
(43 J) per pellet
FILLER 20 #4 Buckshot 0.24 in (6mm) diameter
WEIGHTS
Round 0.269 lb (0.122 kg)
Projectile 0.13 lb (0.059 kg) (sabot w/pellets)
Filler 0.85 oz (24 g)
Pellet 18.5 gr (1.2 g)
EFFECTS
Effect Multiple projectiles on target
Area of effect 39 in (99 cm) circular pattern at
15 yds (13.7 m)
LENGTHS
Overall length 2.64 in (6.7 cm)
Width (diameter) 1.72 in (4.4 cm)
Effective range 33 yds (30 m)
Maximum range 55 yds (50 m)

This was the most successful of the various nonexplosive antipersonnel rounds developed for the low-velocity 40mm family of weapons during the mid-1960s. Acting like a low-pressure shotgun shell, the M576/XM576E1 launches a single projectile that quickly breaks away from its payload of smaller buckshot. The buckshot continues in a spreading pattern toward the target.

The projectile of the M576/XM576E1 is a molded polyethylene sabot holding a shot cup in a center cavity. The shot cup has a snap-on cap, much like the cap on plastic 35mm film canisters and there is room for the cup to move backward in the sabot. Upon firing, the shot cup moves back in the sabot due to setback. The rearward movement of the shot cup causes the cap to be pushed off the cup by the sabot.

Leaving the muzzle of the weapon, the deep air scoop cavities in the sabot around the central cavity slow the sabot down quickly from air resistance. The pellets, continuing on from inertia, begin dispersing from the shot cup within four to five feet of the muzzle of the firing weapon.

M576E2 MULTIPLE PROJECTILE

CALIBER 40×46mmSR

TYPE Low-velocity antipersonnel shotshell

IDENTIFYING COLOR CODE Green cartridge case w/white markings, green plastic cap at mouth

MUZZLE VELOCITY 880 fps (268 m/s)

MUZZLE ENERGY 837 ft/lb (1135 J); 31 ft/lb (42 J) per pellet

FILLER 27 #4 Buckshot 0.24 in (6mm) diameter

WEIGHTS

Round 0.287 lb (0.130 kg)

Projectile 0.148 lb (0.067 kg) (sabot w/pellets)

Filler 1.14 oz (32.3 g) (pellets)

Pellet 18.5 gr (1.2 g)

EFFECTS

Effect Multiple projectiles on target

LENGTHS

Overall length 2.1 in (5.3 cm)

Width (diameter) 1.72 in (4.4 cm)

Effective range 38 yds (35 m)

Maximum range 55 yds (50 m)

This was the next most successful of the various nonexplosive antipersonnel rounds developed for the low-velocity 40mm family of weapons during the mid-1960s. Also a low-pressure shotgun shell, the XM576E2 has a greater number of shot in its pattern but was less efficient at range. The shot spread quickly to the point where a man-sized target could be completely missed because of the holes in the pattern.

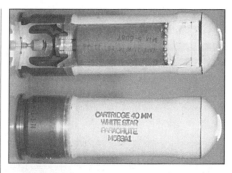

Source: Kevin Dockery

M583/M583A1 (WHITE), M661 (GREEN), M662 (RED), XM695 (ORANGE) STAR PARACHUTE FLARES

CALIBER 40×46mmSR

TYPE Pyrotechnic illumination and signal flares

IDENTIFYING COLOR CODE (All) Green anodized cartridge case, white projectile with black stenciling, colored plastic ogive with raised letter. M583/M583A1—White ogive w/raised letter W; M661—Green ogive w/raised letter G; M662—Red ogive w/raised letter R; XM695—Orange ogive w/raised letter O

MUZZLE VELOCITY 250 fps (76 m/s)

FILLER Magnesium/Nitrate based flare composition

FUZE TYPE Pyrotechnic delay

FUZE DELAY 5 seconds

WEIGHTS

Round 0.487 lb (0.221 kg)

Filler M583 2.29 oz (65 g); M583A1 3.28 oz (93 g); M661 3.0 oz (85 g); M662 3.0 oz (85 g);

LENGTHS

Overall length 5.268 in (13.38 cm)

Width (diameter) 1.72 in (4.4 cm)

EFFECTS

Effect Ejects a burning parachute flare at altitude, illuminating an area with 45,000 cp (M583), 90,000 cp (M583A1), 8,000 cp (M661), 20,000 cp (M662)

Area of effect 109 yd (100 m) illumination radius (M583 White)

Burn time 40 seconds

Effective range 550 ft (168 m) altitude at an 85 degree firing angle

Maximum range 700 ft (213 m) maximum altitude at a 90 degree firing angle

These are long pyrotechnic cartridges generally identical except for the flare composition of the filler. The M195 cartridge case is a very short aluminum assembly with the body of the projectile being made of aluminum tubing with a snap-on plastic ogive. The center tip of the ogive has the raised letter indicating the color of the flare composition. Upon firing, the delay element is ignited and begins its burn. When the 20 grain (1.30 gram) black powder ejection charge is fired after the fuse delay, the charge ignites the illuminant candle and ejects the candle and parachute through the plastic cap on the carrier. The burning flare is attached to the 20-inch (50.8 cm) diameter cloth parachute by a short chain and descends at about 7 fps (2.1 m/s).

M585 (WHITE), XM663 (GREEN), XM664 (RED) STAR CLUSTER

CALIBER 40×46mmSR

TYPE Pyrotechnic illumination and signal flares

IDENTIFYING COLOR CODE (All) Green anodized cartridge case, white projectile with black stenciling, colored plastic ogive with raised letter and five raised dots along the outer circumference.

M585—White ogive w/raised letter W;
    XM663—Green ogive w/raised letter G;
    XM664—Red ogive w/raised letter R

MUZZLE VELOCITY 250 fps (76 m/s)

FILLER Magnesium/Nitrate based flare composition pressed in five pellets

FUZE TYPE Pyrotechnic delay

FUZE DELAY 5 seconds

WEIGHTS

Round 0.449 lb (0.204 kg)

Filler 3.00 oz (85 g)—0.60 oz (17 g) per pellet

LENGTHS

Overall length 5.268 in (13.38 cm)

Width (diameter) 1.72 in (4.4 cm)

EFFECTS

Effect Ejects five flare pellets at altitude burning with an intensity of 55,000 cp (M585)

Burn time 7 seconds

Effective range 550 ft (168 m) altitude at 85 degrees firing angle

Maximum range 700 ft (213 m) maximum altitude at 90 degrees firing angle

These are long-bodied pyrotechnic cartridges, generally identical except for the flare composition of the filler. The M195 cartridge case is a very short aluminum assembly with the body of the projectile being made of aluminum tubing with a snap-on plastic ogive. The center tip of the ogive has the raised letter indicating the color of the flare composition. Along with the raised letter on the nose are five raised dots along the ogive's outer edge to help identify the round by touch in the dark.

Upon firing, the delay element is ignited and begins its burn. When the 20 grain (1.30 gram) black powder ejection charge is fired after the fuse delay, the charge ignites the kraft paper wrapped illuminant pellets and ejects them, blowing off the plastic cap on the carrier in the process. The burning flare pellets freefall though the air, normally burning out before reaching the ground. The green pyrotechnic mixture can be mistaken for white when burning in bright sunlight.

Source: Kevin Dockery

M651/M651E1 TACTICAL CS

CALIBER 40×46mmSR

TYPE Penetrating burning type chemical agent (CS) gas round

IDENTIFYING COLOR CODE Green anodized cartridge case w/black markings, gray projectile w/one 1/4-inch-wide red band around body above rotating band and red stenciling. Six evenly spaced notches are cut into the circumference of the cartridge rim for identification by touch.

MUZZLE VELOCITY 250 fps (76 ms)

FILLER Pyrotechnic CS gas composition

FUZE TYPE XM651E1 point detonating

FUZE DELAY None

WEIGHTS

Round 0.63 lb (0.29 kg)

Filler 2 oz (57 g)

LENGTHS

Overall length 4.5 in (11.4 cm)

Width (diameter) 1.72 in (4.4 cm)

EFFECTS

Effect Penetrates barrier material (up to 3/4 inch [1.9 cm] pine at 218 yds [200 m]) and initiates, releasing a white cloud of CS gas

Area of effect Two properly placed rounds will incapacitate 95 percent of the personnel within a 15 × 30 foot (4.5 × 9.1 m) enclosure within 60 seconds of functioning

Burn time 25 seconds

Arming range 30 to 100 feet (10 to 30 m)

Effective range 220 yds (200 m)

Maximum range 435 yds (400 m)

This is a highly accurate CS round for all of the low velocity 40mm grenade launchers. The nose of the projectile contains an impact fuze and a slight change in the internal fuze arrangement differentiates between the two rounds. On impact with a target, the fuze ignites the filler, which burns and builds up internal pressure within the projectile. When sufficient pressure is built up, the plastic plug in the 3/8 inch vent hole in the base of the projectile blows out, releasing a white cloud of CS gas with a hissing sound.

The round will function against earth, brush, sandbags, and bamboo and is suited for driving out the occupants of enclosed areas such as rooms or bunkers. To protect the plastic blow out plug in the base of the projectile, the cartridge case used with the XM651 rounds is a special one with a folded metal driver cup, much like a simplified version of the teleshot capsule used with the XM463 HE round. The driver cup retains enough of the propellant gasses to prevent damage to the blowout plug with heat or abrasion when the round is fired.

XM674/M674 CS "HANDY ANDY"

CALIBER 40mm

TYPE Burning type chemical agent (CS) gas round

IDENTIFYING COLOR CODE Gray body and cap, both with 1 red band, red stenciling on body or body has an attached gray label with red printing, white plastic adapted sleeve

MUZZLE VELOCITY 250 fps (76 m/s)

FILLER Pyrotechnic CS gas composition

FUZE TYPE Pyrotechnic delay

FUZE DELAY 2 to 7 seconds

WEIGHTS
Round 0.75 lb (0.34 kg)
LENGTHS
Overall length 8.81 in (22.3 cm)
Width (diameter) 1.45 in (37 mm)
EFFECTS
Effect Releases white cloud of CS gas on
   burning
Burn time 12 to 36 seconds
Area of effect 133 square yards (120 square
   meters)
Effective range 74 yds (70 m)
Maximum range 437 yds (400 m)

Adapted externally from the body of the M128A1 hand-launched ground illumination signal, this round is too long to be chambered in the M203 grenade launcher and is intended to be fired from the M79 (w/adapter), AN-M8 pyrotechnic pistol, or by hand. The round comes packaged in its own launcher, the body of the round acting as the barrel for the projectile contained inside. A removable firing-cap assembly is slipped over the muzzle of the round for shipping and has to be removed for use.

A white plastic launcher adaptor is on the barrel of the round, secured to the firing end. The adapter acts as a cartridge rim, allowing the M674 round to be properly chambered in an M79 grenade launcher, which is the most accurate way to use the round. With the plastic launcher adapter removed, the round can be chambered in the AN-M8 pyrotechnic (flare) pistol. The launcher adaptor also has to be removed or slipped up on the barrel of the M674 for hand firing.

The firing cap is slipped over the opposite end of the M674 to prepare the round for hand firing. By holding the body of the round in one hand and striking the firing cap with the opposite hand, the internal projectile is fired downrange. The projectile contained within the body of the round is a rubber cylinder with a blunt end containing the CS gas

composition. The rear of the projectile has a pyrotechnic delay element that ignites when the round is fired. At the end of the 3 to 6 second delay, the CS gas filling ignites and internal pressure blows out the gas emission holes at the base of the round. The rubber projectile of the M674 is somewhat unstable in flight and has an unreliable range so the round is generally intended to be used to disburse or control crowds or mobs of people.

XM675 RED SMOKE TRAINING (CS)
CALIBER 40mm
TYPE Burning type smoke round
IDENTIFYING COLOR CODE Light green
   body and cap, body has 1 brown band,
   white stenciling on body or body has an
   attached light green label with white print-
   ing, white plastic adapted sleeve
MUZZLE VELOCITY 250 fps (76 m/s)
FILLER Red smoke pyrotechnic composition
FUZE TYPE Pyrotechnic delay
FUZE DELAY 2 to 7 seconds
WEIGHTS
Round 0.75 lb (0.34 kg)
LENGTHS
Overall length 8.81 in (22.3 cm)
Width (diameter) 1.45 in (37 mm)
EFFECTS
Effect Releases red cloud of smoke on burn-
   ing
Burn time 12 to 36 seconds
Area of effect 133 square yards (120 square
   meters)
Effective range 74 yds (70 m)
Maximum range 437 yds (400 m)

This munition was produced as a practice round to train troops in the use of the XM674 CS gas round. As such, it is ballistically and functionally identical to the XM674. The fired rubber projectile produces a cloud of harmless red smoke when burning. Adapted externally from the body of the M128A1 hand-launched ground illumination signal, this round is too long to be chambered in the M203 grenade launcher and is intended to be fired from the M79 (w/adapter), AN-M8 pyrotechnic pistol, or by hand.

M676 (YELLOW), M679 (GREEN), M680 (WHITE), XM681 (VIOLET), M682 (RED) SMOKE CANOPY

CALIBER 40×46mmSR

TYPE Pyrotechnic daylight signal round

IDENTIFYING COLOR CODE Green anodized cartridge case w/black markings, light green projectile body w/black stenciling, colored plastic ogive. The nose section is noticeably larger than the body of the projectile to aid in identification by touch.

M676—Yellow ogive; M679—Green ogive; M680—White ogive; XM681—Violet ogive; M682—Red ogive

MUZZLE VELOCITY 250 fps (76 m/s)

FILLER Pyrotechnic smoke composition

FUZE TYPE Pyrotechnic delay

FUZE DELAY 2 seconds

WEIGHTS

Round 0.48 lb (0.21 kg)

Filler M676—2.08 oz (59 g); M680—2.08 oz (59 g); M682—2.8 oz (80 g)

LENGTHS

Overall length 5.212 in (13.2 cm)

Width (diameter) 1.7 in (4.4 cm)

EFFECTS

Effect Produces cloud of colored smoke on functioning

Burn time 90 seconds

Effective range 100 yds (91 m) altitude at 85 degrees launch angle

The projectile of this round is of the standard design as the other parachute-type pyrotechnic rounds. Firing the round ignites the delay element and drives the projectile from the launcher. After the delay has burned, it in turn ignites the 18.5 grain (1.2 gram) black powder ejection pellet which ignites the smoke pellet and drives the payload of the projectile through the plastic nose cap.

The parachute is of the ribbon style, formed into an X to aid in entangling the round in the jungle canopy. The round is intended to be fired through the dense foliage of a jungle and then eject a smoke candle. The parachute of the burning smoke candle will spin when opened, aiding in tangling it in the top of the trees. The colored smoke marks the position of a man or unit located beneath the thick foliage to an overhead aircraft.

Source: Kevin Dockery

M713 (RED), XM714 (WHITE), M715 (GREEN), M716 (YELLOW) GROUND SMOKE MARKER

CALIBER 40×46mmSR

TYPE Pyrotechnic ground signal/spotting round

IDENTIFYING COLOR CODE Green anodized cartridge case w/black markings, green anodized projectile body with colored ogive tip

M713—Red ogive tip; XM714—White ogive tip; M715—Green ogive tip; M716—Yellow ogive tip

MUZZLE VELOCITY 250 fps (76 m/s)

FILLER Pyrotechnic colored smoke composition

FUZE TYPE M733 pyrotechnic impact

FUZE DELAY 8 to 10 second pyrotechnic delay

WEIGHTS

Round 0.49 lb (0.22 kg)

Projectile 0.38 lb (0.17 kg)

Filler 2.65 oz (75 g)

LENGTHS

Overall length 3.91 in (9.9 cm)

Width (diameter) 1.72 in (4.4 cm)

EFFECTS

Effect Releases cloud of colored smoke initiating on impact

Burn time 25 seconds

Arming range 49 to 147 ft (15 to 45 m)

Maximum range 437 yds (400 m)

This series of rounds is used both for signaling and marking ground targets for aircraft and other units. The ground smoke marker rounds are pyrotechnic rounds but are the same size and shape as the high explosive and practice 40mm rounds. The M733 is a very unusual fuze that has no mechanical parts but operates on impact with the target as well as having a backup delay system.

When the ground smoke marker round is fired, the first fire mixture at the base of the round ignites from the propellant gasses. The first fire mixture in turn initiates a high-temperature transfer mixture contained in a steel cup. As the transfer mixture burns, the projectile travels for a minimum of 49 feet (15 meters). When the transfer mixture has reached a high enough temperature, when the round is between 49 to 147 feet from the launcher, the transfer mixture has heated the steel cup sufficiently for it to ignite the delay mixture.

When the round impacts, the casing of the delay mixture breaks and the burning portion flies forward, out of the fuze casing, and ignites the smoke composition payload. If the fuze fails to function on impact, the burning delay mixture will again ignite the smoke composition 8 to 10 seconds after launch. If the round impacts prior to the delay mixture being ignited by the transfer cup, the round will dud and not function. Early rounds had a smoke emitting hole in the nose of the ogive, sealed by a pressed-in

rivet. Present production rounds have the smoke emitted from the fuze hole in the base of the projectile only.

Source: Kevin Dockery

XM781/M781 PRACTICE

CALIBER 40×46mmSR

TYPE Low-velocity ground burst nonexplosive practice round

IDENTIFYING COLOR CODE White plastic cartridge case w/white markings, blue projectile w/white stenciling, some production rounds have green or brown/gold plastic cartridge cases

MUZZLE VELOCITY 250 fps (76 m/s)

FILLER Orange dye powder

FUZE TYPE None

WEIGHTS

Round 0.452 lb (0.205 kg)

Projectile 0.366 lb (0.166 kg)

LENGTHS

Overall length 4.05 in (10.3 cm)

Width (diameter) 1.72 in (4.4 cm)

EFFECTS

Effect Releases puff of yellow-orange "smoke" on impact

Area of effect Several meter burst radius depending on wind

Maximum range 437 yds (400 m)

This round ballistically matches the M406 round and can be used for training on ranges that limit the use of explosives. The M781 projectile has no explosive components being made up of a plastic body containing a steel weight, dye powder, and flat steel leaf springs in the nose. One of the leaf springs retains the weight core and the other bears against the nose of the projectile. On impact with the target, the frangible plastic nose shatters and the dye powder is driven out-wards by the impact and the action of the two steel leaf springs.

HIGH VELOCITY 40MM GRENADES

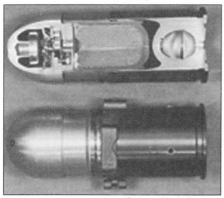

Source: Kevin Dockery

M383 HIGH EXPLOSIVE

CALIBER 40×53mmSR

TYPE High-velocity ground burst high-explosive antipersonnel fragmentation

IDENTIFYING COLOR CODE Green anodized cartridge case w/yellow markings, green projectile body w/yellow (gold) ogive and yellow stenciling

MUZZLE VELOCITY 795 fps (244 m/s)

FILLER Composition A5

FUZE TYPE M533 point initiating

WEIGHTS

Round 0.75 lb (0.340 kg)

Projectile 0.53 lb (0.24 kg)

Filler 1.92 oz (54.5 g)

LENGTHS

Overall length 4.415 in (11.2 cm)

Width (diameter) 1.72 in (4.4 cm)

EFFECTS

Effect Ground burst blast and fragmentation

Area of effect 16.4 yd (15 m) burst radius

Arming range 19 to 39 yds (18 to 36 m)

Maximum range 2,406 yds (2,200 m)

This is the first of the family of high-velocity 40mm rounds intended originally for the helicopter mounted M75 weapon system. Based on the M406 HE round, the projectile of the M383 is longer and heavier that those of the low-velocity 40mm series and can carry a correspondingly larger payload.

The body of the projectile is steel and is internally embossed to control fragmentation. The rotating band on the outside of the projectile body is hard copper and this, combined with the 7mm (0.276 in) longer high-velocity case, prevent the high-velocity round from being chambered in low-velocity weapons. To assist in using this round, and to additionally prevent accidents with low-velocity weapons, this round and others like it are normally only issued in linked belts.

Source: Kevin Dockery

M384 HIGH EXPLOSIVE

CALIBER 40×53mmSR

TYPE High-velocity ground burst high-explosive antipersonnel fragmentation

IDENTIFYING COLOR CODE Green cartridge case w/yellow markings, projectile body is olive drab w/yellow markings, rounded ogive (nose) is yellow

MUZZLE VELOCITY 795 fps (244 m/s)

FILLER Composition A5

FUZE TYPE M533 Point Detonating

WEIGHTS

Round 0.76 lb (0.34 kg)

Projectile 0.54 lb (0.24 kg)

Filler 841 gr (54.5 g)
Belt of 50 39.66 lb (17.99 kg)
EFFECTS
Effect Ground burst blast and fragmen-
tation
Area of effect 16 yd (15 m) radius
LENGTHS
Overall length[4.42 in (11.2 cm)
Width (diameter) 1.72 in (4.4 cm)
Minimum (arming) range 59 to 118 ft (18 to
36 m)
Maximum range 2,406 yds (2,200 m)

This round is effectively identical to the
M383 HV HE round. The fragmentation body
of the M384 round is also internally embossed to control fragmentation but is designed slightly differently for ease of
manufacture and greater efficiency.

M385 PRACTICE

CALIBER 40×53mmSR
TYPE Solid shot target practice
IDENTIFYING COLOR CODE Green anodized
cartridge case w/yellow markings, Blue
anodized projectile w/black stenciling
MUZZLE VELOCITY 800 fps (244 m/s)
FILLER Aluminum
FUZE TYPE None
WEIGHTS
Round 0.77 lb (0.35 kg)
Projectile 0.55 lb (0.25 kg)
LENGTHS
Overall length 4.415 in (11.2 cm)
Width (diameter) 1.72 in (4.4 cm)
EFFECTS
Effect Impact at target site
Maximum range 2,406 yds (2,200 m)

This round is made for target practice and
live fire function testing with high velocity
grenade launchers. The projectile is a solid
aluminum shot with a copper rotating band.
The projectile body has a noticeably smaller
diameter body with a full diameter "cap" at
the nose of the round. The double diameter

helps identify the projectile and prevent it being mixed up with live warhead rounds.

M430 HIGH EXPLOSIVE DUAL PURPOSE

CALIBER 40×53mmSR
TYPE High-velocity high-explosive shaped
charge anti-armor/ground burst fragmen-
tation round
IDENTIFYING COLOR CODE Green cartridge
case w/yellow markings, projectile body is
olive drab w/yellow markings, long
rounded ogive (nose) is yellow
MUZZLE VELOCITY 795 fps (244 m/s)
FILLER Composition A5
FUZE TYPE M549 Point initiating, base deto-
nating
WEIGHTS
Round 0.75 lb (0.34 kg)
Projectile 0.53 lb (0.24 kg)
Filler 586 gr (38 g)
EFFECTS
Effect Penetrates 2 in (5.1 cm) steel with
fragmentation around the point of impact
(approximately equal to the M384 HE)
Area of effect 16 yd (15 m) radius
LENGTHS
Lengths 4.42 in (11.2 cm)
Width (diameter) 1.72 in (4.4 cm)
Minimum (arming) range 59 to 118 ft (18 to
36 m)
Maximum range 2,406 yds (2,200 m)

The M430 HEDP has become the standard round of combat ammunition for the
Mark 19 Mod 3 grenade launcher. Developed
from the same design that resulted in the
M433 low-velocity HEDP grenade, the M430
is intended to attack light armored vehicles,
such as the Russian BMP, while still having
an effective antipersonnel capability.

On impact, the M549 fuze fires an explosive spit-back element that sends an explosive wave to the rear of the main charge.
Detonation from the rear allows the main

charge to collapse the fluted copper cone liner within the round into a high-velocity jet of molten metal that can pierce over two inches (5 cm) of armor plate, 12 inches (30 cm) of pine logs, 16 inches (41 cm) of concrete blocks, or 20 inches (51 cm) of sandbags.

The steel body of the grenade that contains the explosive shaped charge is also internally segmented (engraved) so that it breaks up into a controlled fragmentation pattern along with significant explosive blast.

NAME HIGH VELOCITY CANISTER CARTRIDGE (FLECHETTE)

CALIBER 40×53mmSR
TYPE High-velocity, close-in antipersonnel
IDENTIFYING COLOR CODE Green anodized cartridge case w/yellow markings
FILLER 115 17 grain (1.1 g) 2 in (5.1 cm) flechettes
FUZE TYPE None
WEIGHTS
Filler 4.47 oz (127 g)
LENGTHS
Overall length 4.42 in (11.2 cm)
Width (diameter) 1.72 in (4.4 cm)

EFFECTS
Effect Releases multiple projectiles on target
Area of effect 34 foot (10.4 m) wide pattern at 55 yds (50 m)
Effective range 100 yds (91 m)

This under-development high-velocity round is intended to give the Mark 19 grenade launcher a close-in defensive capability. The design of the high-velocity canister cartridge is such that the round will give sufficient rearward force to operate the action of the Mark 19. When fired, the HVCC releases a swarm of 2-inch long (5.1 cm) fin-stabilized steel flechettes.

The flechettes are contained within the body of the projectile, stacked alternately nose-to-tail. When the HVCC round is fired, propellant gas bleeds into the projectile, blowing off the sheet metal ogive and driving the flechettes and their pusher cup forward. On leaving the muzzle of the weapon, the pusher cup quickly falls away from air drag, allowing the flechettes to break up as a pack and the reversed flechettes to stabilize in a point-first orientation.

CARTRIDGE CASES

NAME M118 CARTRIDGE CASE

CALIBER 40×46mmSR
TYPE Low-velocity 40mm grenade cartridge case
IDENTIFYING COLOR CODE Green anodized body with black or yellow stenciling
MATERIAL Aluminum
STANDARD PROPELLANT M9 double-base flake mortar powder
STANDARD PRIMER M42 percussion
WEIGHTS
Cartridge Case (Empty) 1.76 oz/771.6 gr (50 g)
Cartridge Case (Loaded) 1.78 oz/776.7 gr (50 g)

Standard Propellant Load 5.09 grains (0.33 grams)
LENGTHS
Overall Length 1.816 (4.61 cm)
Width (Diameter) 1.718 in (4.36 cm)
Rounds Used With M381 HE, M382 TP, M386 HE, M397/M397A1 HE Airburst, M406 HE, M407A1 TP, M433 HEDP, M441 HE, M713 GSM (R), M715 GSM (G), M716 GSM (Y)

M169 CARTRIDGE CASE

CALIBER 40X53MMSR
TYPE High-velocity 40mm grenade cartridge case

IDENTIFYING COLOR CODE Green
anodized body with black or yellow stenciling
MATERIAL Aluminum
STANDARD PROPELLANT M2 double-base
flake cannon powder
STANDARD PRIMER Federal No. 215 percussion
WEIGHTS
Cartridge Case (Empty) 3.39 oz/1,481.4 gr
(96 g)

Cartridge Case (Loaded) 3.55 oz/1, 553 gr
(100.6 g)
Standard Propellant Load 71.6 grains (4.64 g)
LENGTHS
Overall Length 2.086 in (5.3 cm)
Width (Diameter) 1.718 in (4.36 cm)
Rounds Used With M383 HE, M384 HE,
M385 TP, M430 HEDP, HVCC
flechette

FUZES

The fuze of the 40mm HE grenade was considered one of the major accomplishments of
post-WWII ammunition design in miniaturization. Not only did the 40mm fuze have to be
reliable and safe to use, it had to be inexpen-
sive enough to be worth adoption.

M551 POINT DETONATING FUZE
ROUNDS USED IN M386 HE, M406 HE,
M407A1 TP, M463 HE
This is the second generation of low-
velocity 40mm grenade fuzes. The more
complex internal workings of the M551 is
needed to extend the arming range of the
fuze, giving a greater safety margin for the
weapon. A rotor at the center of the M551
body keeps the detonator out of line with the
firing pin and the explosive train until the fuze
is fully armed. The rotor is locked in place by
the firing pin, a centrifugal lock, and a setback pin. When the round is fired, setback
forces move the rotor locking pin rearward,
unlocking part of the arming rotor.

As the projectile rotates at 3,600 rpm from
the rifling of the launcher barrel, three inertial
weights at the top of the fuze pivot outward.
The inertial weights move the centrifugal lock
away from the rotor while at the same time
moving the spring-loaded firing pin out from
its detent in the rotor. Now free to move, the

rotor is slowed in its rotation by a geared es-
capement mechanism. The rotor moves the
detonator into firing position after the round
has traveled at least 45 to 90 feet (14 to 27
meters) from the launcher.

On impact or graze with the target, the
spring-loaded firing pin is driven into the detonator. The detonator in turn ignites the RDX
booster pellet which detonates the high-
explosive burster charge.

M552 POINT DETONATING FUZE
ROUNDS USED IN M381 HE, M382 TP,
M441 HE
This is the original fuze design intended
for the low velocity 40mm HE grenades. A
first-generation design, the M552 fuze uses
the forces of firing to remove the built-in
safety and arm the fuze. The setback (inertia)
of firing the round causes the firing pin of the
fuze to be withdrawn from the detent of the
rotor ball in the center of the fuze body. With
the detent released, the rotor ball is free to
move under centrifugal force.

On firing, the rifling of the barrel causes
the 40mm grenade to be spinning at a rate of
3,600 rpm by the time it leaves the barrel.
The centrifugal force caused by the spinning
of the projectile forces the rotor ball assembly to turn, aligning the detonator contained

in the rotor ball with the explosive train. This fuze arms in a very short distance from the muzzle of the firing weapon.

On impact with the target, an inertial ring moves forward, pushing two pins which drive levers onto the firing pin, forcing it into the detonator. In case of only a brushing graze with the target, two spring-loaded hammers, that were driven outwards against their springs by centrifugal force, move forward against the levers which drive the firing pin into the detonator. When the detonator ignites, it in turn sets off the RDX booster charge, which detonates the main charge.

M533 POINT DETONATING FUZE
ROUNDS USED IN M383 HE, M384 HE

This fuze is mechanically similar to the M551 low-velocity fuze but is designed to utilize the stronger firing forces of the high-velocity 40mm round. The internal mechanism is much the same as the M551 fuze but includes some additional safeties to delay arming. A rotor at the center the fuze keeps the detonator out of line from both the firing pin and RDX lead, breaking the explosive train. The rotor is locked in place by the spring-loaded firing pin, a setback pin, and a controlled centrifugal lock.

When the round is fired, setback forces move the fuze setback pin back to unlock the rotor. At this point, the centrifugal lock keeps the rotor from turning further. The force of firing and rifling in the barrel of the launcher spins the projectile to 12,000 rpm by the time it has left the barrel. The spin rate is sufficient to force three bracket weights at the nose of the fuze outwards from the center. As the bracket weights move, they release a push pin that unlocks the firing pin. The firing pin spring lifts the firing pin from its detent slot in the rotor.

As the firing pin is being raised, the centrifugal lock releases a star wheel in the fuze timing mechanism. Springs on the now-released rotor initiate its movement which is accelerated by the centrifugal force from the round's spin. The timing mechanism controls the movement of the rotor, slowing its locking into the armed position for 0.07 to 0.16 seconds. That delay is sufficient time for the projectile to have traveled 59 to 118 feet (18 to 36 meters).

Impact or graze of the projectile causes the bracket weights to pivot inward, forcing the firing pin into the detonator. The detonator in turn ignites the RDX lead which initiates the main charge. The entire mechanism of the M533 fuze is contained in the screw-on ogive at the nose of the projectile, measuring 1.6 inches (4.1 cm) in diameter and 1.6 inches (4.1 cm) tall.

BELTS

TAPE BELT

This was the original style of belt only used with the Mark 18 Rapid Fire Grenade Launcher. A special loading machine was developed that took advantage of the fact that the round fed into the Mk 18 didn't have to be chambered, instead, the split breech, two-piece chamber closed over a belted round before it was fired.

The loading machine fed 25 rounds of 40mm into a chain belt that had spring clips properly spaced along its length. The rounds fed into the clips and between two rolls of fiberglass fabric tape. Two tape clinching wheels pressed the sticky side of the tape to the cases of the clipped 40mm rounds. Between the rounds, the two tapes were pressed together, where they adhered firmly.

A feed wheel would count 25 rounds into the mechanism and then stop. A heavy leader strip would be attached to the beginning of the belt to aid in loading. Fired casings remained in the belt as it was ejected from the Mk 18. The tape belt of ammunition would be used once and then discarded.

MYLAR FABRIC BELT

The Mylar-backed, Dacron fabric belt was a replacement for the original Mk 18 fiberglass sticky tape belt which proved unsatisfactory in use. The fabric belts were supplied in 24- and 48-round lengths, each belt having pockets for 40mm rounds between heat-sealed sections of the belt. New belts had to have the pockets opened by hand and stretched slightly with the thumbs.

A round of 40mm ammunition would have the belt slipped over the nose of the projectile and pressed down until it contacted the rim of the cartridge case. Fired belts could be reused and loaded more easily by pressing the spent cartridge case in the belt over the nose of a fresh round sitting base down on a flat surface. The loaded round would push the expended case from the belt and the belt would then be again pressed onto the cartridge rim.

Belts could be reused about five times. When the loaded rounds were no longer firmly held in the fabric belt, the used belt would be discarded. Occasionally, discarded Mark 18 belts could be seen being used as ammunition carrying devices, acting as bandoleers or waist belts.

LINKS

M16 LINK

Developed by Philco Ford as the primary feed device for the M75 high-velocity grenade launcher, the M16 link is hexagonal in shape. Early production links were made from a single stamping, welded together on one flat. Later production links were made from a two-piece, welded assembly. The pieces of the link are spot welded together at the large flats on their top and bottom portions. The four flats, one on each side of the welded sections, are slightly curved to fit the diameter of the 40mm cartridge case.

Four small indents in the link body seat up against the rotating band of the round, helping hold the link in place when the round is detached from the belt during the feed cycle. One side of the link has a deep notch on a raised section at its center. The opposite side of the link has a flat-sided, mushroom-headed swivel that slips into the corresponding notch on the next link in the belt. Though it detaches from the remainder of the belt when it is fed, the link remains with the cartridge case throughout the cycle of operation and is ejected with the casing.

M16A1 LINK

By the late 1960s, difficulty with feeding in some Mark 19 and other weapons caused a modification to be required on the M16 Link. Made from two stampings welded together on the outside long flats, the M16A1 link has six indents, spaced at the center of six flats along the top edge of the link. The six indents hold the cartridge case more securely and brace against the rotating band of the projectile.

The same mushroom-head pin and slot arrangement as used in the M16 link is retained in the M16A1. On the outside of the two welded flats are shallow V-notches on the bottom side of the link for identification. An identification number is stamped on the upper rounded flat next to the notched side.

M16A2 LINK

This is the present production link, made up as a 2-piece welded assembly. The detents used in earlier model links have been done away with in the M16A2 link. Instead, there are two notches cut into the four rounded flats of the link. The square projection between the two notches is bent inward, where it can solidly brace against the rotating band of the projectile. The M16A2 link holds itself firmly against the rotating band and cannot move forward in a loaded round.

Identification of the M16A2 link is made by the two shallow V-notches on the welded flats and the two deep spot welds also on the same flats. A shallow M16A2 is stamped in the upper rounded flat next to the notched side.

MARK 8 MOD 0 LINK

This is a modified version of the M16A1 link. Externally identical to the M16 link, the Mk 8 link was originally made by having four of the six indents found on the upper edge of the M16A1 link hammered flat. The additional detents of the M16A1 link were found to increase the stripping power needed to move the cartridge case through the link during the firing cycle. This stripping force was more than could be supplied by the low velocity Mark 20 grenade launcher.

The initial production of the Mk 8 link was 3,000 units, modified by hand, at the Louisville naval facility in the late 1960s. Later production of the Mark 8 link was machine produced without the additional detents found on the M16A1 link. The Mark 8 Mod 0 link is colored green to distinguish it from the M16 series of links used with high-velocity grenade launchers.

■ 14
EXPLOSIONS IN THE PHILIPPINES

It had been a long day preparing for our upcoming mission, and it was going to be a much longer one actually conducting the operation. Our actual time in the water at the target could be measured in just a few hours at most. But those hours were going to be spent with us all within just a few hundred yards of an enemy-held beach.

Beyond the high-tide line, only a few dozen yards away across the sand, were Japanese fortifications holding machine guns, mortars, cannons, and hundreds of enemy soldiers. The situation was something we were absolutely sure of—we had seen the emplacements for ourselves only a few days earlier.

Our Underwater Demolition Team had conducted a recon swim off the planned invasion beaches in order to gather intelligence on the area, and conduct a hydrographic recon of the waters. Third platoon, my platoon, had swum across several hundred yards of beach frontage in broad daylight. With fishlines and lead weights, each man had measured the depth of the water. The lines had a series of knots on them that made using them pretty easy, But counting knots and making marks on a piece of plastic with a crayon is not as easy as it sounds, not when the enemy is shooting at you from onshore.

The gunners aboard our LCP/Rs (landing craft, personnel/reconnaissance) came in close to fire over our heads directly at the targets onshore. The .50 caliber machine guns spoke with real authority as they blasted the hell out of the jungle. They were a lot more powerful and had better range than the .30 caliber machine guns we had used on the boats earlier. Those aircraft .50s poured out ammunition almost twice as fast as the .30 caliber guns had. But we still took fire in spite of the hail of steel our people put out.

Japanese snipers would pop off rounds at us, even though they had little more than a swimmer's head as an aiming point. The rounds would snap through the air or splash up water near us as they hit.

The rifle bullets would only penetrate a couple of feet down into the water before they lost power and just started to sink. If you were more than four or six feet under the surface, you could just see them drifting down, not even going point-first, just kind of sinking sideways. A lot of the guys would catch the bullets in nothing more than their hands, keeping them as souvenirs or trading them to the sailors back on the transports.

It was the mortars and small cannons that really gave us the worst trouble, the big stuff that the Japanese usually kept hidden until the actual invasion force showed up. A small mortar shell could kill a man in the water, even if the fragmentation never reached him. The shock from the blast of the round could just turn a swimmer's insides to jelly if it was too close when it went off. A lot of guys had their eardrums damaged from explosions that happened a good distance from where they were swimming.

Whenever something big came out of hiding and did open up on us, it would draw the attention of spotters in the air or our people back in the boats. They would get on the radio and call in naval gunfire support. So while we were being covered, we kept up our mission in the water close-in to the enemy.

From the high water mark on the beach out to the 3.5 fathom line, where the water is 21 feet deep, we measured and noted. The Navy made sure we had a lot of preparatory fire before the operation. They had been standing off-shore and pounding the little chunk of coral and sand for days. Palm trees and plants flew into the air every time a big naval shell pounded into the jungle and exploded. The 14-inch shells of the big cruisers were neat. But it was the massive 16-inchers from the battleships that were really something to see.

You could look up from the water and actually see those one-ton shells flying through the air. They were these big black dots you could see way up in the sky. And where those dots hit, the geography was rearranged. I was awfully glad those big bruisers were on our side. They could hit a hill and turn it into a valley, or at least a smoking crater.

For all of the steel and explosives the Navy threw into the enemy positions, we still had to swim in and look around armed with nothing more than a sharp knife, a fish line and weight, plastic slate, and a crayon. What was just as important to note down as the water's depth was the location type, size, and number of obstacles we saw—both natural and man-made.

The obstacles were a big deal. My platoon's chief petty officer, Chief Parks, had been with the Naval Combat Demolition Units (NCDU) in France on D-Day. Chief Parks had told us that they had set charges on and blown thousands of obstacles all up and down both Utah and Omaha beaches that day. And for days afterwards, the expert demolitioneers of the NCDU had blown up

more obstacles and even gone inland to try their hand at some enemy bunkers
and pillboxes.

Explosives didn't care what they blew up and they would be quick to take us
out if we didn't handle them with respect. But after months of training, Parks
and his fellow NCDU men didn't feel like packing it in after just one day of operations, even if that had been a very long day.

From somewhere Chief Parks had scrounged up an M1928A1 Thompson
submachine gun and he had actually gone in on missions with the Army troops.
Explosives were the normal weapon we used in combat, that was something
they had drummed into out heads from day one at Fort Pierce in Florida and
again at the advanced UDT training base in Maui. What Parks told me was that
sometimes it was nice to also hold a chunk of wood and steel that would convince anyone shooting at you that it was a good idea to go somewhere else for a
while. Besides, he liked shooting a Thompson, and who was I to argue with a
Navy Chief?

For now, there weren't any guns available to the regular swimmers in the
UDTs. The officers had .38 caliber revolvers issued to them, but they rarely took
such a thing along with them on a swim. Only one officer that I knew of even
used his pistol for anything better than shooting targets. Back on Maui, he had
gotten pissed at a street light that was shining through his officers' quarters
window. When he couldn't convince anyone else to put the light out, he did with
one well-placed shot from his .38. It was a good thing that we were shipping out
for the Philippines only a few days later.

Now, we had completed our recon swims and the information we had gathered was put together to make accurate charts of the offshore waters of the invasion beaches. The obstacles we had found had been counted, measured, and
planned for. The plan for dealing with the obstacles was for the men who had
found them, namely us, to go back and blow them up—clearing the way for the
landing craft to make it to the beaches where the Marines and Army troops they
transported could start to do their jobs.

A lot of obstacles took a lot of explosives to clear. It was a good thing the explosive magazines of our APD high-speed transport ships carried tons of explosives for us to do our jobs with. We had spent the day before preparing
hundreds of individual explosive charges as well and a number of bigger demolition charges.

Our primary explosive was tetrytol, a mixture of TNT and tetryl. The explosive was cast into blocks and eight of them were spaced out along a length of
detonation cord. We had to cut the blocks apart and waterproof the open ends

of the detonating cord. Then we tied longer detonating cord leads to the 8-inch-long stub ends of cord that were sticking out of the tetrytol blocks. Finally, we wrapped a length of wire around the blocks, leaving about 2 feet of wire loose to attach the charge to the target.

Chief Parks had been a hard-rock miner and a powderman in civilian life. He had joined up with the Seabees early in the war and had kept on working with explosives. When the NCDUs were looking for volunteers, Parks had stepped right up and kept on going from them into the UDTs. He had been working with explosives all his adult life. He had an easy, safe way of working around explosives and everyone pretty much felt the same way whenever they were working with him.

We had hundreds of pounds of explosives sitting around on the deck of the APD as we made up charges. The sailors who were watching us probably thought we were crazy as hell and wanted to be anywhere but on that boat as we cut and wrapped blocks. But the job had to be done and we were the only ones around who could do it.

We were making tropical versions of what were called Hagensen packs. Chief Parks told us that those were the charges they had used to blow open Normandy Beach. But the Composition 2 explosives the Hagensen packs were loaded with didn't like the tropical heat we had to deal with every day. The oils that made the C2 explosive soft like clay, leached out in the heat and left some very nasty and sensitive crystals of explosive behind. Tetrytol didn't care about the heat and was waterproof to boot, so in the UDTs, we used it a lot.

And we would be placing a lot of charges on our demolition swim the day before Love-Day, L-1, the actual day of the invasion. The four LCP/Rs on board the APD each carried one UDT platoon in to the beach. I was in the boat along with my swim buddy Jim Harriston. Jim was originally from Chicago, Illinois and had spent most of his life swimming in Lake Michigan. Those days were a long way behind him as we got ready to hit the water off the shore of a Philippine island.

The boats took us in to our assigned stretch of beach underneath a huge bombardment of the shore from naval gunfire. We just watched the jungle get churned into black dust and smoke as the explosions went off. For all of the destruction, we knew that the Japanese would be riding out the bombardment in their bunkers, blockhouses, and hidden fortifications. There would be plenty of the enemy to face the incoming waves of invasion troops, if they didn't get out of their holes earlier and open up on us.

The barrage lifted and it was time for us to go in. Our boat started making its run while still about 400 yards offshore. There was a rubber boat tied to the side of the LCP/R. Two swimmers would get into the rubber boat while another swim pair got ready at the side of the LCP/R. As soon as we got the signal, we would roll off the rubber boat and into the water. Then the next pair of swimmers would scramble to get into place for their turn in the water.

As soon as we hit the water, we swam over to the shore side of where the LCP/R had passed. The rest of the crew onboard the LCPR had been busy tossing demolition charges, marker buoys, and whatever other gear we needed over the shore side of the boat. Once we gathered up our explosive packs, we struck out for shore.

Jim and I had been assigned to load a line of wooden posts that were about 100 yards offshore. The posts were just barely awash at high tide, but they would block and maybe capsize or hole the plywood landing craft that would be coming in with the invasion troops. Even if the posts didn't damage the landing craft, they would hang them up long enough for the emplacements on shore to make short work of them.

So each of us would swim up to a post and attach a single tetrytol block. Taking the wire from the block, it was a simple matter to wrap it around the post and give it a hard twist to lock it in place. Jim and I would each do a post, then swim on to the next target. While we were doing our part of the mission, flank swimmers were swimming the length of the assigned demolition target, towing a big reel of detonation cord.

The flank swimmers were laying out the main trunk line of detonating cord that all of the rest of us swimmers would tie in the leads from our individual demolition charges. Pulling over the trunk line, it was a simple, practiced matter to tie the long detonating cord leads into the trunk line. We had practiced the right-angle knot that we used until we could do it in our sleep. You almost didn't have to look to know the double loop, crossover, and loop-through tie of the detonating cord. We had all done it hundreds of times, and we would be doing it a few dozen more times today.

There were a few palm-log crib obstacles in the area, boxes made of palm logs and filled with broken coral and rocks. The cribs were about 4 feet square and 2 feet deep. Blasting one of those obstacles took two full M1 chain demolition charges. The big charges had inflated rubber bladders on them to make it easier to tow them through the water. When the swimmers who were assigned to load the cribs got to their targets, a quick stab with a knife let the air out of the flotation bladder and sank the 20-pound charges.

One of the nastier jobs was given to the really experienced men in the

Team. Chief Parks and his swim buddy went in with Mark 136 demolition outfits strapped around their waists to take out the big Type JE antiboat mines. The big mines were large domes, about a foot tall and nearly 2 feet across at the base. Each mine was filled with nearly 100 pounds of high explosives. On top of the mines were two lead horns that each held a glass tube of acid. Bending or denting a horn broke the acid tube and set up an electric current detonating the mine. If a mine went up with you nearby, there wouldn't be anything to send back home.

To attack the mines, the Navy had come up with these Mark 1 destructors. The destructors weren't much more than a blasting cap with a spring clip and a time pencil attached to it. The spring clip went around the horn of the mine and you crushed the time pencil with your fingers to initiate the chemical delay. After a delay of up to 7 hours, depending on the destructor and the temperature of the water, their blasting cap went off, denting the lead horn and detonating the mine.

Of course, swimming around the mine while clipping a destructor to the horn wasn't that great a time for the swimmer. You had to make good contact with the horn, then pinch the time pencil. And it was a real good idea not to let the waves push you against the mine. And you had to do all of this right up under the guns of the enemy.

By this time, some of the Japanese had crawled out of their holes and were sniping at those of us in the water. Again, our LCP/R gunners would come in and strafe the beaches to give us cover. Finally, we were ready to make the swim back out to sea and get ready for our pickup. Only the last part of the demolition operation still had to be done and we always had the fastest swimmers assigned to it.

A line of detonating cord had been laid out from the main line out to the seaward side of the obstacles. That line of cord was tied in to the main line at a right angle. The other end of the detonating cord line was attached to a floating board with two firing assemblies on it. Each assembly—there were always two in case one didn't work—was a 10-minute time fuse delay with blasting caps crimped on and waterproofed. The fuse igniters were also heavily waterproofed.

The UDTs used so many rubber prophylactics to seal up the caps and igniters on our firing assemblies that the supply people back in Hawaii at first thought we were way too oversexed to be allowed out on liberty. When the people finally found out just what we used all the pro kits for, they just decided to leave us alone and let us get on with our work. We all preferred things that way anyway.

Those 10-minute time delays on the firing systems were selected to be as short as they could be for safety, and not too long to help prevent a lucky Japanese shot from breaking the detonating cord line. A broken line and we would have to go back in and charge the obstacles again, not a job anyone wanted to do.

Being the last guys picked up from the water wasn't the most popular position to be in, either. But that's what the fuse pullers had to do. When they pulled the igniters, the swimmers stayed around that floating board just long enough to see that each fuse was smoking, then they took off for the pickup line.

Back offshore, we were all spaced out singly, each swimmer about 25 yards away from the next man. It was about as far as you ever intentionally got from your swim buddy—a man you never, ever, left the side of. The LCP/R would come buzzing in along the swimmer line, with the rubber boat back on the seaward side, away from exposure to enemy fire from the island.

Leaning way over the side of the rubber boat was the snare man. He had this big figure-8 of looped rubber. As the pickup boat zoomed in on you, you gave a really hard kick with your legs and stuck your arm up high. The snare man would loop the snare over your arm, and you would snap the arm down and catch the snare in the crook of your elbow and grab your hand. If everything went right, you were snatched up from the water and rolled into the rubber boat. You only had a few seconds to scramble out of the rubber boat and into the LCP/R before the next man would be snared.

The last two swimmers snared were the fuse pullers. With everyone safe on board the LCP/R, it was time to head back to the transports. Watching the water rise up behind us in a huge curtain of white foam and smashed obstacles was a great sight to see. That meant there was another beach open to our forces—and another step taken to the eventual liberation of the Philippines and the Pacific.

■ 15

EXPLOSIVES AND EXPLOSIVE DEVICES

To a SEAL or UDT man, a weapon is something you use to kill people or destroy material, simple as that. A tool is something you use to get a job done. To the men of the Teams yesterday and today, explosives are a tool, one they are very accomplished with.

Whether it is as the filler in a grenade or shell, the propellant in a round of small arms ammunition, or in bulk as a demolition charge, explosives have been used by special warfare personnel more often than any other single item. Beginning with the first Naval Combat Demolition Units in World War II, training with explosives has been an important part of the indoctrination and development of every special warfare operator. During Hell Week, the most famous portion of basic UDT training, men are exposed to large and small explosions during one long day. The constant barrage of blasts is calculated to expose any latent fear of explosions the men might have.

At (that) time (circa 1952), the instructors didn't have limitations put on the size of the charges they would fire during "So Solly" day, the last day of Hell Week. Without the buildup of houses and other construction that's all around the base today, the instructors didn't have to worry about breaking windows, just breaking us.

A twenty-pound charge of explosives going off near you can pick you right up off of the ground, and then slam you down with your teeth rattling and ears ringing.

This training gives the men of Naval Special Warfare a healthy respect for the power of explosives while eliminating any nervousness or fear of the powerful materials. The result of all this allows the men of the NCDUs, UDTs, and SEALs to apply the power of explosives in a controlled and precise manner. Refresher training and regular requalifications ensure that the skill with explosives that was hard taught during BUD/S or its earlier equivalent remains high with each active specwar operator.

An explosion is a violent bursting or expansion caused by the sudden release or creation of a high pressure wave. A pressure release explosion is common and can be as innocuous as the popping of a child's toy balloon or as shattering as the bursting of a large steam boiler.

An explosive is a material that reacts chemically at an extremely fast, almost instantaneous, rate and in doing so creates a pressure wave by the release of large volumes of gas combined with heat and noise. The chemical reaction of an explosive is caused by the sudden addition of high energy to the material in the form of a shock and/or heat. The chemical reaction in an explosive is self-sustaining once initiated and normally consumes the entire mass of material. The rate at which the reaction takes place determines the power and grade of the explosive as well as the amount of work it can be expected to do. These characteristics have led to explosives being referred to as "energetic materials" in modern parlance.

The rate of reaction in an explosive material is measured by the length of a column of the explosive that would react completely in one second. This rate is called the detonation velocity, or speed of burning in the case of some low explosives or propellants, and is stated as feet or meters per second. Low explosives are those materials whose detonation velocity ranges from just an inch or so per minute to about 1,300 feet per second (400 m/s). Low explosives are rarely encountered in the military today except in the form of pyrotechnic delay elements, time fuze, and propellants.

Those energetic materials referred to as high explosives react so quickly they detonate rather than burn. Reaction rates for high explosives range from over 1,300 fps to 27,000 fps (8,230 m/s) or greater with a correspondingly powerful shock wave producing a shattering effect on a target. A high explosive can be either a pure compound or a close mixture of several compounds along with additional additives. Though explosive materials can be found as solids, liquids, or gasses, practical considerations limit most military explosives to being made of solid materials.

High explosives are further divided into three classes of explosives: primary or initiating, booster, and bursting or main charge explosives. The three subclasses of high explosives are separated primarily by their differences in sensitivity. Initiating explosives are the most unstable in terms of the amount of energy needed to initiate their reaction. Heat, spark, impact, friction, or flame are all capable of firing initiating or primary explosives. Though sensitive, initiating explosives also have sufficient power to detonate stronger but more stable and inert materials.

Booster explosives are somewhat less sensitive than initiating explosives but tend to have higher detonation velocities and greater power. A booster explosive is used as part of an explosive train to increase the shock wave from an initiator sufficiently to insure the detonation of a main charge. Booster explosives themselves are too sensitive or have other drawbacks that prevent them from being used as larger main charges or bulk explosives.

Main charge or bulk explosives are powerful with a reasonably high detonation velocity. For safety in handling, main charge explosives are relatively insensitive and require a good initiator for detonation. Safety in handling is not the only reason for bulk explosives needing to be insensitive. The main charges of shells or rockets need to withstand the forces of firing or launching and sometimes even the shock of impact without detonating prematurely. For bulk explosives used as demolition charges, they need to withstand the rigors of combat including rough handling, gunfire and possible bullet impacts, and nearby explosions. At the same time, demolition explosives and fillers have to be capable of positive detonation, preferably with a minimum of special preparation or materials.

The power of an explosive is measured by more than its detonation velocity. For military purposes, the shattering effect or brisance of an explosive is of primary importance in a bursting charge or demolition explosive. The brisance of a specific explosive is an effect measured by a number of laboratory tests. In general, brisance is referred to as the relative efficiency or RE of a particular explosive. Because of its almost universal use and availability in a very specific purity, TNT is normally used as the standard for measuring the RE of an explosive. With TNT having and RE of 1.0, another explosive might have an RE of 1.25. With an RE of 1.25, it would only take 4 pounds of that explosive to attack the same target that would require 5 pounds of TNT.

Other characteristics of explosives that are important are the material's stability in storage. If heat decomposes a material or makes it unstable, it would be a poor choice for use in tropical climates or for storage aboard non-air conditioned ship's magazines. Sensitivity to water would also tend to rule out a particular explosive's military use, especially with the Teams. Of the hundreds of explosive materials known to modern chemistry, only a small handful meet the requirements necessary for their safe use in the military.

EXPLOSIVES
TNT

TNT is the most common military explosive and has been such since before World War II. Used alone or as a component of explosive mixtures, TNT is found in use as booster charges, main fillings in shells and other munitions, and in bulk form as a demolition charge.

Economical to make, TNT in its refined form is extremely stable chemically in storage, samples having lasted for 20 years without noticeable change. The explosive is a brittle solid when cast and small pieces of TNT can be shaved off a larger block and ignited. Unconfined burning TNT releases a toxic black smoke and the explosive becomes very unstable and sensitive while burning.

Under normal circumstances, TNT is insensitive, cast blocks of the material being able to withstand a rifle bullet impact without exploding. Because of its stability, general characteristics, and low cost, TNT is the most common material included in explosive mixtures.

RDX

The name RDX was coined from the British Research Department explosive which was the identifier used by that department which developed RDX for military use. One of the most powerful explosives known, RDX is rarely used in its pure form in any large quantities. Though chemically very stable, RDX is too sensitive to impact and friction for use in its pure state. When used as a filler in delayed action bombs and shells RDX is prone to premature detonation or to breaking up and failing to fully detonate. Where RDX demonstrates its great importance is as a primary component of explosive mixtures.

Most of the common plastic explosive compositions presently use RDX as their main active ingredient. Many of the widely used explosive compositions in circulation also include RDX as an active ingredient. Certain of these explosive mixtures are particularly suited for use underwater. As part of Composition B, RDX is also found in many hand grenades, artillery shells, aircraft bombs, and land mines. Small quantities of desensitized RDX are used as booster charges and fillers for special munitions. Both the M6 electric and M7 nonelectric blasting caps use RDX as their base charges.

PETN

PETN is also one of the most powerful military explosives, only slightly less powerful than RDX. Chemically stable in storage, PETN is also one of the most sensitive explosives in wide use with the military. Uses for PETN include booster charges, in blasting caps as a base charge, as part of explosive mixtures, and in detonating cord. The last two uses are the primary ones for PETN in the military and the Teams. As part of the explosive mixture pentolite, PETN is very effective in forming shaped charges for penetrating hard targets. But by far the greatest use of PETN is as the explosive filler for detonating cord.

When loaded in detonating cord, PETN loses a great deal of its sensitivity to heat, shock, and friction. The small cross-section of the PETN core found in detonating cord requires the shock of a blasting cap to insure its detonation. Almost insoluble in water, PETN has been found useful in underwater operations by the Teams.

AMMONIUM NITRATE

Ammonium nitrate (AN) is the least sensitive military explosive in use and requires a good-sized booster charge to insure its complete detonation. In spite of its insensitivity and low power, ammonium nitrate is very useful when employed for earthmoving or as a cratering charge. The low detonation velocity of ammonium nitrate causes the explosive to have a heaving effect on a target rather than a shattering one. This characteristic also prevents ammonium nitrate from being used as a cutting or breaching charge.

Normally very stable in storage, ammonium nitrate has the drawback of being hygroscopic in nature. Unsealed containers of ammonium nitrate will draw moisture directly from the air, quickly becoming a soggy and useless mess. Wet or moist ammonium nitrate cannot be detonated by any normal means and the explosive is considered to have no water resistance whatsoever. When its sensitivity to moisture is taken into account, ammonium nitrate can be very effectively employed in bulk charges for earthmoving.

Ammonium nitrate is also one of the cheapest explosives available and is widely used in agriculture. Available as a common fertilizer, ammonium nitrate is often used in expedient or improvised explosive charges. ANFO, an ammonium nitrate/fuel oil mixture, is a common improvised explosive used by guerrillas and terrorists. ANFO is a roughly 94 percent ammonium nitrate, 6 percent number-2 diesel fuel mixture that is slightly more powerful than ammonium nitrate used alone.

TETRYL

Tetryl is normally found in its pure state as a finely divided white powder. Exposure to light gradually turns tetryl yellow and loaded tetryl in munitions is gray due to graphite being added as a lubricant. Reasonably stable chemically in storage, tetryl is toxic when taken internally and handling tetryl will stain the skin brown and cause dermatitis.

The sensitivity of tetryl to shock and heat, roughly midway between PETN and TNT, prevents the explosive from being easily used in large charges. Compressed tetryl loses enough of its sensitivity to be used in pellet form as the main charge in 20mm and 37mm projectiles. Pellets of tetryl are also used as booster charges and have been loaded as the base charge in blasting caps. Tetryl has been most used by the Teams, especially the UDTs during World War II in the Pacific, as part of the explosive composition Tetrytol.

TETRYTOL

Tetrytol is a powerful and brisant explosive mixture with slightly less sensitivity than straight tetryl. The addition of TNT to tetratol helps lower the sensitivity of the tetryl while the tetryl itself helps raise the detonation velocity and brisance of the mixture. Tetrytol can be melted and cast loaded into ordnance or forms to produce demolition blocks. Cast tetrytol demolition blocks are formed around booster pellets of tetryl to insure detonation of the charge.

Chemically stable enough for satisfactory storage properties, tetrytol reacts slightly with most metals and must be protected from such contact. The solid tetrytol explosive is considered toxic to handle or ingest and the fumes of detonated tetrytol are considered dangerous to breathe. Most commonly used as a demolition explosive, tetrytol is also found cast into shaped charge munitions as well as being used as the bursting charge in chemical munitions such as white phosphorus shells.

PENTOLITE

Pentolite is a family name for a number of composition explosives made up of a mixture of PETN and TNT. The most commonly used blend of pentolite consists of a 50/50 mixture of PETN and TNT. Additional mixtures of 75/25, 40/60, 30/70, and 10/90 PETN/TNT have been used occasionally. In terms of sensitivity, brisance, and suitability for melt loading, 50/50 pentolite is superior to all of the other mixtures of its family.

Pentolite was the most common explosive used as the filler for shaped charges during World War II, its explosive efficiency for such charges being very high. The PETN in pentolite has the tendency to separate from the TNT in the mixture if improperly stored and the material is not considered as chemically stable as TNT. In sensitivity, pentolite is at the same level as tetryl.

COMPOSITION A-3 (A-4)

Composition A explosives are RDX mixtures desensitized by the addition of wax or oils. The addition of wax not only coats and desensitizes the RDX crystals to friction and impact, it also acts as a binding agent allowing Composition A explosives to be press loaded. The lack of sensitivity and loading procedures available for Composition A material makes them a primary explosive for loading shells and other ordnance.

Though Composition A explosives are less sensitive to shock and friction than TNT, they are slightly easier to initiate than TNT. Though other mixtures are available in the family, the most common Composition A explosives used are A-3 and A-4. These compositions are used as booster charges and as the main charge in armor piercing and some High Explosive, Plastic (HEP) shells.

COMPOSITION B

Composition B is a desensitized mixture of RDX and TNT that has wide applications as an explosive filler. Originally developed by the British prior to World War II for use as a filler for large aircraft bombs, Composition B has since been loaded in shells, grenades, land mines, and shaped charges.

Less sensitive than tetryl, Composition B is more sensitive than TNT. Because of its power and brisance, Composition B is used where it would be of tactical advantage and the slight increase in sensitivity over TNT is not a drawback. Chemically stable in storage, unconfined Composition B will burn when ignited without exploding. Composition B is the most commonly used member of the cyclotol family of explosives, all mixtures of RDX and TNT combined with wax and stabilizers.

COMPOSITION C-2

The Composition C family of explosives is commonly referred to as "plastic" explosives due to their special characteristics. All of the Composition C explosives are more powerful and brisant than TNT while remaining just about as insensitive. The most important feature of the Composition C explosives is their ability to be formed and shaped by hand and be tamped down for intimate contact with a target.

The initial mixture, Composition C, or C-1 as it is also called, uses RDX as the base explosive and was developed by the British early in World War II. The mixture for Composition C was 88.3 percent RDX and 11.7 percent plasticizing oil. Though Composition C proved out the viability of the plastic explosive mixture, it suffered from some serious drawbacks.

Below 0 degrees Fahrenheit, Composition C would freeze, becoming hard, brittle, and difficult to use or detonate. Above 110 degrees Fahrenheit, the mixture would become soft and almost liquefy after further exposure.

The plasticizing oils in Composition C tended to sweat (leak) out of the mixture, especially when the material was stored at a warm temperature. When the oils had left the mixture, what was left behind was pure RDX crystals, far too sensitive for use in the field.

To eliminate the sweating problems encountered with Composition C, Composition C-2 was developed by late 1943. The mixture of Composition C-2 is 80 percent RDX and 20 percent explosive plasticizer. The plasticizer mixture is made up of 10 percent DNT (Dinitrotoluol), 5 percent MNT (Mononitrotoluol), 4 percent TNT, and 1 percent Nitrocellulose. The DMT and MNT are both oily liquids and plasticize the mixture.

The plasticizing mixture turned the RDX explosive into a brown, putty-like material able to be formed and molded over a target. More powerful than TNT, Composition C-2 soon proved itself a valuable explosive for breaching and especially steel cutting operations. With C-2's flexibility, it can be shaped around a steel target such as a rail or I-beam. The closer the contact between the explosive charge and the material to be cut, the greater the chance of the cut being successfully made and wasting explosive can be held to a minimum.

For all of its positive aspects, C-2 still suffered from some drawbacks. Though not as serious as the problem with Composition C, some of the volatile oils in Composition C-2 would evaporate after long storage aboard ship. The explosive remainder after evaporation had lost much of its flexibility and was more sensitive to impact and shock.

Though Composition C-2 was usable underwater, the material had to be wrapped and protected against the abrasive effect of wave action. Long exposure underwater would leave Composition C-2 waterlogged and difficult to detonate.

COMPOSITION C-3

By 1945, Composition C-3 was available for use by the military and the Teams. The general mixture of C-3 is very close to that of C-2 but the ratio of explosive to plasticizer is 77 percent RDX to 23 percent plasticizer. The main difference chemically between C-2 and C-3 is that tetryl was substituted for 3 percent of the RDX.

As an explosive C-3 is slightly less powerful than Composition B but is much less sensitive than TNT as far as handling goes. It was not uncommon for troops in the field to pinch off small portions of C-3 and burn them to heat their rations. Though C-3 will burn hot and quiet, it is very unstable while burning and shock can set it off. In addition, the fumes from burning or detonated C-3 are toxic as is the explosive itself.

A yellowish, putty-like material, C-3 remains flexible from −20 degrees to 125 degrees Fahrenheit. At high temperatures, C-3 exudes an oil which does not affect the explosive properties of the material. Handling C-3 with bare hands does cause a yellowish discoloration of the skin that is difficult to remove.

Slightly hygroscopic, C-3 is suitable for underwater use but has to be protected from erosion and long submersion prior to detonation. C-3 remained in the U.S. inventory as a primary demolition explosive from the end of World War II well through the Vietnam War. Most major militaries in the world produce their own version of C-3 with either RDX or PETN as the base explosive.

COMPOSITION C-4

Developed in the years immediately following World War II, C-4 gradually supplanted C-3 as the primary plastic explosive in the U.S. military. A dirty white semiplastic solid, C-4 has the putty-like consistency that characterizes all of the Composition C explosives. Very powerful and brisant, C-4 retains its plastic consistency over a much wider range of temperature than the earlier Composition C explosives. Pliable from −70 to 170 degrees Fahrenheit, C-4 is less volatile than C-3 at elevated temperatures though it will exude oils at temperatures above 170.

Similar to TNT in sensitivity, C-4 is very stable chemically and may be stored for extended lengths of time. Nonhygroscopic, C-4 acts as an excellent underwater explosive when protected against the physical action of the water though it is less subject to erosion than C-3. While only slightly toxic itself, C-4 does produce dangerous toxic fumes when burned or detonated. C-4 is one of the most powerful explosives available for bulk demolition purposes and is insensitive enough to be used as a burster charge in some munitions.

HBX-1

HBX-1 is the first of the High Blast Explosives to be fielded primarily for underwater use. A mixture of RDX and TNT explosives. HBX-1 also contains powdered aluminum which enhances the blast effect of the two explosives, especially when used underwater. Used in underwater ordnance such as depth charges, mines, and torpedoes, HBX-1 is also loaded as a general demolition charge for use by the Teams. To prevent gas buildup in warheads, a problem when aluminum is used, wax, and calcium chloride are added to the overall explosive mixture. The original World War II HBX mixture did not initially include the calcium chloride. Later HBX mixtures that included the anti-gassing agent were designated HBX-1.

HBX-3

This is a modified formulation of the high blast explosives with a much higher percentage of aluminum than HBX-1. Though the HBX-3 mixture has a lower detonation velocity than HBX-1 it is 10 to 15 percent more effective as an underwater explosive due to the higher aluminum content. The additional aluminum adds slightly to the gassing problem of HBX mixtures when they are improperly stored.

The wax used in both HBX-1 and HBX-3 is referred to as composition D2, a nonexplosive desensitizer and emulsifier developed in the years just after World War II. Composition D2 is made up of 84 percent paraffin wax, 14 percent nitrocellulose, and 2 percent lecithin.

H-6

H-6 is a relatively new member of the family of high blast explosives with much of the data on the material still unavailable. Generally, H-6 consists of a mixture of RDX, aluminum, and composition D2. The higher detonation velocity of H-6 over HBX-1 or HBX-3 gives the explosive a high shearing effect when cutting metal. This effect is demonstrated in the underwater limpet mines whose explosive component is made up of H-6.

LEAD AZIDE

Lead azide is a primary explosive used to initiate booster or base charges in blasting caps. Much more easily detonated by a flame than the earlier mercury fulminate, lead azide replaced the earlier fulminate in military blasting caps just prior to World War II. More powerful than earlier initiators, a smaller amount of lead azide is needed than mercury fulminate to detonate an equal amount of TNT.

Dextrinated lead azide is a mixture of 93 percent lead azide, 4 percent lead hydroxide, and 3 percent dextrin and is much easier to handle than the pure azide. Only used in blasting caps and other initiators, lead azide is the most sensitive explosive used in the military. Very stable chemically in stowage, lead azide is able to withstand elevated temperatures without breaking down.

DETASHEET C

Detasheet C was developed by DuPont Explosives Specialties beginning in the mid 1960s. The original material, designated EL 506 by DuPont, showed great promise and was further refined by the Engineer Research and Development Laboratory at Fort Belvoir, Virginia. Detasheet is a PETN-based explosive mixture consisting of 63 percent PETN, 8 percent nitrocellulose, and 24 percent binders formed into a rubberlike flexible sheet. Other manufacturers offer an RDX-based Detasheet equivalent.

Water and moisture proof, Detasheet can be cut to any desired shape with a straight-edge knife. To build up thicker charges, individual sheets of Detasheet can be bound together. Detasheet is also offered in different thicknesses so that any-sized charge can be quickly and easily made up.

Very stable in storage, Detasheet retains its flexibility over a wide range of temperatures. Insensitive, Detasheet can withstand impacts from .50 caliber rounds without detonating. Easily used for general demolition work, Detasheet is very accurate when used for metal cutting applications. Brisant and powerful, Detasheet is able to be detonated with military special blasting caps or detonating cord.

Besides its almost unique properties of flexibility and toughness, Detasheet is also extremely durable. The material is very resistant to water erosion and will withstand high hydrostatic pressures while remaining relatively unchanged. All of these characteristics are combined in an explosive material with a very uniform detonation velocity and a degree of safety rarely found in high explosives. The only real drawback of Detasheet is that it is expensive when compared to other types of high explosives.

DEMEX 400

Demex 400 is an extrudable form of RDX-based plastic explosive. A mixture of 86 percent RDX and 14 percent plasticizer/binder agent, Demex 400 is intended for the fast application of controlled amounts of explosive.

The high power and brisance of Demex 400 make it an excellent cutting explosive. For its fast application to a target, Demex 400 is available packaged in caulking-gun cartridges. By simply squeezing a pistol-grip handle, an operator can apply Demex 400 to a target with only one hand. Besides filling in difficult to load targets, Demex 400 is well suited for cutting through doors or walls rapidly with little prior preparation. Available in either a caulking-gun cartridge or two sizes of collapsible "toothpaste" tubes, Demex 400 is a pale green, semisolid material able to be detonated by blasting cap or detonating cord.

DEMOLITION CHARGES

Demolition charges have been the most common way of employing all the different types of explosives used by the Teams over the years. In general, demolition charges provide packaged units of high explosives for destroying or altering man-made or natural objects and obstacles.

These charges are used for general demolitions, cutting, breaching, cratering, and the destruction of abandoned equipment and ammunition. In addition, the Teams use demolition charges to clear obstacles in the water, open channels, remove coral, destroy mines and other ordnance, and eliminate hazards to navigation. All of these different tasks use explosives in one form or another, some being more suitable for a specific task than others.

The most general issue unit of an explosive is as a block demolition charge. These charges are measured units of high explosive of a known strength and are used for the calculated employment of an explosive. Almost all of the high explosives used by the Teams are available in some form of explosive block. TNT, Tetrytol, Composition C-2, C-3 and C-4, HBX-1, and even ammonium nitrate are or have been made in some form of rectangular explosive block. The exception to this is the ammonium nitrate demolition block which is made in the form of a 40-pound cylinder.

TNT BLOCKS

The first and most common charge of explosive used by the Teams during World War II was the ½-pound TNT block. Even today, this charge of explosive is the one SEAL candidates are first exposed to, not during demolition training, but intermittently throughout the last long, searing day of Hell Week.

The compressed ½-pound TNT block is formed with an activator (blasting cap) well about $2\frac{7}{8}$ inches (7.3 cm) deep in one end. The entire block is wrapped with a heavy fiberboard (cardboard) paper wrapper. The wrapper is waterproofed and coated. World War II and later production blocks were in olive drab colored containers. Since the 1950s, ½-pound TNT blocks have been packaged in yellow containers.

The two square ends of the ½-pound block are covered with lacquered sheet metal caps, crimped onto the fiberboard wrapper. The cap over the end with the activator well has a central hole on the well. The well hole is protected by a paper cover that is easily pierced by the user. When used for training explosions, care has to be taken by the operator that the metal end caps will not cause a hazard as they fly off at a high velocity.

For combat demolitions throughout World War II, the standard charge was

the 1-pound TNT block. As the majority of demolition calculations are
designed to give the weight of TNT
needed for a specific charge, most
other packaged explosive charges are
measured in part by the number of
TNT blocks they represent.

The 1-pound TNT block consists
of two ½-pound blocks enclosed end
to end in the same type of fiberboard
wrapper as used on the ½-pound
TNT blocks. The water-resistant
fiberboard container has always been
olive drab for the 1-pound TNT
charge.

These UDT combat swimmers are loading concrete and steel
horned scully obstacles with demolition charges. The size and
strength of the obstacle requires two demolition haversacks each
to insure their destruction. Strung between the charges is a detonating cord lead that will detonate all of the obstacles simultaneously.

Source: Kevin Dockery

The two end caps are also the same as on the ½-pound TNT block except
that the activator well cap has a central threaded hole. The 9/16-12 NC
threaded metal cap will accept a priming adaptor or the standard coupling base
of a firing device. This allows the activator to be secured into the charge easily
and also allows the charge to be quickly emplaced as a booby trap. The fiberboard container of the 1-pound TNT charge can be cut in half to provide two
unprotected ½-pound TNT blocks.

The 8-pound TNT block is simply a large, flat rectangle of explosive
wrapped with a waterproof barrier material. Originally, the 8-pound TNT
block was intended as an auxiliary charge for the M6A1 and M6A2 antitank
mines. The block has since been used as a general source of TNT explosive for
any suitable demolition work.

TNT being insoluble in water, all of the above demolition blocks may be
used underwater without special preparation. TNT is slightly difficult to detonate and all of the military charges are intended to be detonated by a military
special blasting cap or several wraps of detonating cord. The 8-pound TNT
block does not have an activator well and is either detonated by detonating cord
or sympathetically by another explosive charge.

40-POUND AMMONIUM NITRATE CRATERING CHARGE
The ammonium nitrate demolition charge is primarily used for postassault demolitions or the preparation of earthen obstacles for defense. Other targets that
can be effectively destroyed with the cratering charge include buildings, fortifi-

cations, and bridge abutments. To protect the moisture-sensitive ammonium nitrate explosive, the charge is contained in an airtight metal can and is emplaced as a complete unit.

The ammonium nitrate explosive is difficult to detonate. To insure the complete detonation of the 40-pound charge, the center section of the canister contains a large TNT booster charge. The central booster charge takes up about 25 percent of the interior of the canister with the main charge of ammonium nitrate divided evenly at the top and bottom of the can. Even with the central booster charge, a 1-pound priming charge is recommended to be placed at the side of the canister to dual-prime the charge.

To maintain the airtight integrity of the canister, there is no actuator well penetrating the sides into the booster charge. Instead a cleat is firmly attached to the side of the canister directly over the TNT booster. The cleat has two tunnels, one the correct size to accept a blasting cap and the other, longer tunnel intended for a strand of detonating cord.

At the very top of the canister is a steel lowering ring. Normal emplacement of the charge involves setting it down into the base of a borehole. The size of the canister is such that it will fit into a borehole dug out with a standard post hole auger.

MARK 8 DEMOLITION HOSE
The Mark 8 demolition hose is one of the demolition charges used by the Teams that is unique to the Navy. The long, flexible Mark 8 charge is intended for clearing paths, being wrapped around obstacles, and opening channels through sandbars and coral reefs. This charge was later renamed a flexible-linear demolition charge due to its length being so much greater than any of its other dimensions.

The Mark 8 charge is a length of 2-inch rubber hose filled with TNT (Mod 0) or modified Composition A-3 (Mods 2, 3). Each end of the hose is provided with a coupling fitting for the attachment of a tow ring, bail, or other hoses. The tow ring on the Mark 8 Mod 0 charge is a male fitting that threads into the female coupling on one end of the hose.

The end of the Mk 8 Mod 0 charge that has the female coupling also has the actuator well for a blasting cap or firing device. The female coupling end of the Mk 8 Mod 0 charge is also where the Mark 8 Mod 0 booster charge of TNT is located. At the other end of the charge is a male coupling that is issued with a removable bail loop for towing or anchoring a charge. The male end of the Mk 8 Mod 0 charge also contains a booster element, a Mk 12 Mod 0 booster. The

Mk 12 and Mk 8 boosters are both small charges of TNT with the Mk 8 booster differing only by having an actuator well cast into it.

The main charge of the Mk 8 Mod 0 hose is made up of flexed (broken) TNT. In the Mk 8 Mods 2 and 3 flexible charge, the main filling is a mixture of Composition A-3 and 30 percent aluminum powder. The boosters and physical arrangement of the Mods 2 and 3 charges are the same as on the Mk 8 Mod 0 charge.

The Mk 8 Mods 2 and 3 charges differ mainly in the type of coupling fittings they are issued with. The couplings on the Mk 8 Mod 2 charge are of the slip ring/locking ball type. The type of fitting found on the Mod 2 charge can be quickly connected or disconnected without the use of special tools or wrenches. The slip ring is drawn back on the female fitting, freeing the locking balls inside. When the male fitting is inserted and the slip ring released, the locking balls securely hold the male fitting against removal.

Though a good idea, the slip ring system was found to be too sensitive to mud, silt, and sand jamming the rings or locking balls. The Mk 8 Mod 3 charge went back to an improved system of threaded fittings, much like those used on modern fire hoses which the Mk 8 charge greatly resembles.

The main advantage of the Mk 8 linear charges lay in their flexibility and capability of being connected together in whatever length is desired. One unique charge that can be built with Mk 8 hoses is the mat weave pattern.

The mat weave pattern is a net made of five lengths of Mk 8 hose with an additional five lengths of hose laid out perpendicular to the first set. The hoses are woven one over the other and lashed in place, making a 25-foot-square net able to be placed over large areas of coral in order to blast shipping channels.

The most often used feature of the Mk 8 hose is its ability to be connected together into long lengths of continuous explosive. Literally thousands of feet of channel have been blasted by lengths of Mk 8 hose, widths being determined in part by the number of hoses lashed together into a bundle.

In one memorable incident in Vietnam, UDT-12 performed a massive demolition project using Mk 8 Mod 2 hose. The project was to blast a navigable channel between the Co Tay and Co Dong rivers, a distance of slightly less than 6 miles. The operation used five lengths of Mk 8 hose pyramided together and attached to other five-hose pyramids. One thousand feet of hose would be fired in a single shot and about thirty shots were fired. The completed project consumed 60 percent of the free world's supply of Mk 8 hose, was the largest combat demolition job in Navy history, and was conducted within plain sight of VC and NVA positions in Cambodia.

M1 CHAIN

The M1 chain demolition charge is even more flexible than the Mk 8 hose while being much easier to transport and emplace by a single person. The explosive charge itself in the M1 chain demolition charge consists of eight blocks of tetrytol strung together by being cast onto a 16-foot length of detonating cord. The detonating cord goes through the center of each 11-inch long explosive block which also has a tetryl booster pellet straddling the detonating cord cast into each end.

The entire charge is packaged in a canvas haversack. Some of the haversacks made for the Navy have been constructed of gray cloth but most of the M1 charges encountered are found in olive drab bags.

The M1 charge can be applied as a whole unit to any obstacle or target as a single, large charge or the chain can be wrapped around an irregularly shaped object. The chain itself can be easily cut apart into separate blocks, each with a detonating cord lead, and used as individual charges.

The tetrytol is more sensitive than TNT and the charges need to be protected against heat, flame, and severe drops or jolts. Water has little effect on the M1 chain and the charge may remain in the water for 24 hours without having its explosive characteristics weakened.

The blocks of tetrytol each weigh 2.5 pounds and are the equivalent to six ½-pound TNT blocks for the purposes of calculating charges. Though the M1 chain demolition charge is easy to carry, the haversack itself has no provision for adjusting buoyancy. The M1 charge was very popular among the UDT Teams in the Pacific during World War II due in part to the explosive being able to be stowed in conditions that would render the Composition C explosives useless or even dangerous.

MARK 133 DEMOLITION CHARGE

To answer some of the problems in using the M1 chain demolition charge by combat swimmers, the Mk 133 demolition charge assembly was developed. The Mod 0 charge used by the UDT during World War II had as its main explosive component the Mk 23 Mod 1 chain-type charge of TNT blocks.

The TNT blocks in the Mk 23 Mod 1 charge (chain) are 2.5 pound blocks each cast around a central line of detonating cord. The eight TNT blocks are each 12 inches long and contain a booster charge pellet of 50/50 pentolite. The center detonating cord line is 25 feet long with the blocks spaced along its center at 1-foot intervals. For tying the charge off to another charge or firing line, a 5-foot tag end of the detonating cord line is left free at each end of the chain.

The main use of the Mk 133 charge assembly is for general demolitions especially in or under the water. Because of the explosives used, the Mk 133 charges should not remain submerged for more than 3 hours before firing. The design of the Mk 2 Mod 0 haversack containing the Mk 133 charge is such that it can be easily towed through the water by an experienced combat swimmer. A flotation bladder inside of the haversack can be adjusted by the swimmer for the amount of buoyancy desired. Once at the target, the flotation bladder can be deflated or simply pierced with a knife.

As many as five charges have been connected and towed by individual swimmers during combat operations in World War II. As in the M1 chain, the Mk 133 charge can be used as a single large charge, a flexible chain of explosives, or a source of individual demolitions as the mission dictates. To facilitate attachment of the entire haversack to an obstacle, the charge is equipped with a 10-foot length of sash cord. On the end of the sash cord and on the opposite side of the haversack are two flat metal hooks. The hooks have been found to be the fastest way of securing demolition lines by a swimmer underwater. The cotton sash cord is simply slipped into the sharp V-notch in the hook and pulled tightly into the notch.

The Mod 2 variation of the Mk 133 charge is different only in its explosive content. Contained within the Mk 133 Mod 2 charge assembly is one Mk 23 Mod 2 demolition charge (chain) consisting of eight blocks of HBX-1 explosive cast onto a detonating cord line. Except for the use of HBX-1 instead of TNT, the Mod 0 and Mod 2 versions of the Mk 133 charge assembly are exactly the same in construction and operation.

MARK 20 DEMOLITION CHARGE

The Mark 20 demolition charge is one of the first demolition charges designed specifically for use by the Naval Combat Demolition Units (NCDUs or CDUs), the forefathers of the UDTs. The main mission of the NCDUs was the destruction of obstacles on the beaches of Europe. Though they didn't know it at the time, the men of the NCDUs would be the first on the beaches, blowing open the way to Hitler's Germany at Normandy.

The primary and most difficult of the obstacles the NCDUs would face was referred to as "Element C," popularly called the "Belgian Gate." This obstacle was a large, heavy construction of steel beams bolted together to form a 10-foot high by 10-foot wide flat-faced section of "picket fence."

Each Belgian Gate section was 14-feet deep with a steel brace to support the $2\frac{1}{2}$-ton structure. Sections could be attached together to form long rows of obstacles. These rows could be moved into deeper water by means of muscle (conscripted labor) and the rollers attached to each section's base and support.

As a whole, the Belgian Gates formed a very formidable defensive obstacle especially as mines were discovered attached to the tops of the "pickets." Installed at the low-tide mark, they would impale or sink any landing craft attempting to cross over them while still allowing defensive fire to be directed through the "pickets" against any infantry hiding behind them.

It was the discovery of these obstacles as well as their numbers and effect that influenced Admiral Ernest J. King, Chief of Navy Operations, to issue the orders authorizing the CDUs on May 6, 1943. After arriving in England, the teams finally met the object they were created to destroy. The difficulty of the job was obvious.

The simple size and strength of the gate, combined with its complex construction, ruled out using any demolition technique then known. The gates didn't just have to be knocked down, they had to be destroyed quickly by men under fire on an enemy-held beach. Other obstacles also stood in the way of the Allied forces. New demolition techniques had to be developed practically on the spot.

Initial attempts at blasting mock-ups of the Belgian Gates resulted in twisted masses of wreckage as impassable as the original obstacle. Using greater amounts of explosive to completely flatten the gates caused an unacceptable hazard from the size of the blast and the amount of flying steel fragments it caused. A new style of explosive charge was needed. The new charge would have to be quickly attached to strategic points on a target in known amounts and then the necessary number of charges all be simultaneously detonated.

If the above requirements weren't enough, all of this had to be done using the simplest method possible. This was to prevent mistakes happening during the heat of battle, mistakes that could get many men killed.

An officer of the CDUs, Lieutenant Carl Hagensen developed a type of explosive charge that combined the newly developed plastic explosive Composition C-2 with a second new item, the explosive detonating cord. Detonating cord could be used as the explosive line to detonate an unlimited number of charges at the same time. A method of attaching the charges was then needed.

The first experimental charges were simple blocks of Composition C-2 formed onto a knot at the end of a length of detonating cord. The prepared charge was placed in a cloth container and the open end of the bag tied shut with a length of line. Through the tied end of the container was led the detonating cord lead. The tag end of the line used to close the cloth bag was used to secure the entire charge to the target. The first charges developed used old socks as the containers and clothesline to tie the ends shut. The new charge showed promise and was quickly improved on.

A 2-pound block of C2 was placed inside of a rectangular canvas container and was primed for detonation by a length of detonating cord inserted into the block with an additional length of the cord wrapped on the outside of the case. A length of sash cord with a flat metal hook was also attached to the canvas case to secure the charge to an obstacle. The flat metal hook had a sharp V-notch cut into it that the sash cord could be quickly jammed into, preventing the need for a knot to be tied.

Referred to as the "Hagensen Pack," the new type of charge quickly proved that is could solve the demolition problem of the Belgian Gates. Sixteen of the packs could be quickly attached to strategic points on the gate's structure by using their attached sash cords and hooks. By connecting all of the pack's detonating cord lines to a master detonating line any number of obstacles could be instantly reduced to a flat pile of rubble.

The charges proved so successful and generally useful that they became a standard-issue demolition item to Navy units. Designated the Mark 20 Mod 0 demolition charge, the only major change between the charge used today and that used on Normandy Beach is an upgrade in explosives from Composition C-2 to Compositions C-3 and C-4. In the new charges, the Mk 20 Mod 0 charge is loaded with Composition C-3 and the Mk 20 Mod 3 charge is loaded with Composition C-4.

To many of the men of the UDTs who used them over the years, the Mark 20 demolition charge is still called the Hagensen Pack.

MARK 127 DEMOLITION CHARGE

Once the Hagensen pack had been developed, a method of carrying a supply of them was then needed. The CDUs and very early UDTs did not swim to their targets. Instead, these demolition specialists worked either standing in the water or on dry land. At Normandy Beach, the men of the CDUs worked on dry land but had a racing tide to contend with.

To carry the Hagensen pack, the men of the CDUs "borrowed" a number of M2 ammunition vests from the Army. The M2 vest is a long rectangle of olive drab canvas, reinforced on the edges. At the center of the rectangle is a hole so that the soldier can place the carrier over his head. The long flaps hanging at the front and back of the carrier have large pockets sewn into them. The M2 carrier was issued to carry ammunition for 60mm mortar teams but the men of the CDUs quickly found another use for them.

Though the carrier is very difficult to swim with, this was not considered a drawback at the time. By using the M2 ammunition carrier, a CDU operator could carry up to twenty Hagensen packs, ten in front and ten in the back. This amount of explosive would allow a man to continue working rather than run back and forth to a powder supply for his basic tool.

After D-Day and the Normandy Invasion, the pack idea used to carry the Hagensen packs was formalized into the Mk 127 Mod 0 demolition charge assembly. In the Mk 127 charge, twenty Mk 20 Mod 0 charges are carried in a Mk 1 Mod 0 haversack.

The Mk 1 haversack is made of treated gray cotton canvas. Two large pockets are sewn one each into the front and back of the haversack. On one side of each pocket is a 10-foot length of sash cord secured under retaining web straps. On the opposite side of the pocket is a flat metal securing hook. Laces are at the top of each pocket to secure the cover. In addition, lashings are at the sides of the pockets so that the entire charge can be secured to the individual carrying it.

By the end of World War II, Mk 20 charges were being loaded with Composition C-3 instead of C-2 explosive. Both of these explosives had the same restrictions and the Mk 127 charge was not to be used on operations where it would remain underwater for over 3 hours without being fired. Though the Mk 127 demolition charge assembly is next to impossible to swim with without considerable additional buoyance aids, the charge is a very convenient way to carry 40 pounds of explosive easily.

MARK 135 DEMOLITION CHARGE

The Mk 135 demolition charge is a combination of the flexibility of the Mk 20 charge system with the ease of transportation found with the Mk 133 demolition charge. The haversack used with the Mk 135 charge, designated the Mk 3 Mod 0 Canvas Field Pack, is the same general configuration as the one used with the Mk 133 charge.

The main pocket of the Mk 3 field pack is sized to hold ten Mk 20 demolition charges. The pocket on the back of the pack holds one inflatable rubber flotation bladder that can have its size adjusted by the operator. The flotation bladder can hold the Mk 135 charge fairly high in the water for low drag or can be adjusted so that the pack is just barely awash.

The long, adjustable shoulder strap on the top of the pack can be slipped through the tow ring secured to the bottom of another Mk 135 charge. In this manner, any number of packs can be connected for towing through the water by a single swimmer. The main advantage of the Mk 135 charge is the ease at which it can be carried through the water. This was the preferred method of transporting the Mk 20 charge used by the UDT when they were operating as combat swimmers.

The Mk 135 Mod 1 Demolition Charge Assembly is identical to the Mk 135 Mod 0 charge except for the explosive content. The Mk 135 Mod 1 is loaded with ten Mk 20 Mod 3 demolition charges that are filled with 2-pound blocks of Composition C-4. The Mk 135 Mod 1 charge is somewhat more water resistant than the Mod 0 version but both charges are not recommended for demolition operations where they would be submerged for over three hours before firing.

This UDT operator is securing the cover to the flotation bladder pocket on a Mark 135 demolition charge. The inflated flotation bladder will make transporting the twenty-pounds of plastic explosive in the haversack much easier. A simple stab with a knife will deflate the bladder allowing the charge to sink. The length of cotton sash cord used to secure the charge to a target is visible on the side of the charge, seen held in place by cloth loops.

In the background, a man is inflating a Mark 1 flotation bladder for use with another Mk 135 demolition charge. In the foreground is a pair of Duck-Feet style swim fins laying across a UDT life jacket. The very simple round face mask between the fins and the demolition charge date this photograph as having been taken in the mid-1950s.

Source: U.S. Navy

MARK 34 DEMOLITION CHARGE

The Mk 34 demolition charge is simply a slightly improved version of the earlier Mk 20 charge. The design changes in the charge are primarily to facilitate its manufacture and application. Loaded with a 2.5-pound block of Composition C-3, the Mk 35 Mod 0 charge is contained in a cotton duck bag, rectangular in shape with a square cross-section.

A 9-foot length of detonating cord acts as both the initiator for the charge and a connecting lead. Three feet of the detonating cord is looped to make a booster charge. The composition explosive is formed around the detonating cord booster with the remaining length acting as a lead.

The bag the charge is placed in has been simplified somewhat from that of the Mk 20 charge. The detonating cord lead is looped and secured under two webbing straps on one side of the charge with the opposite side holding a length of sash cord and a flat hook secured under a webbing strap. The flap ends of the Mk 34 charge can be easily torn open and the explosive inside removed. The freed charge of explosive can be formed into any shape and packed into direct contact with irregularly shaped targets.

The Mk 34 Mod 1 charge is exactly the same as the Mod 0 charge except that the explosive has been changed to Composition C-4. The Mk 34 demolition charge is a component of the Mk 137 demolition charge assembly and is not issued separately.

MARK 137 DEMOLITION CHARGE ASSEMBLY

The Mark 137 demolition charge assembly is an updated version of the Mk 133 charge assembly first developed during World War II. The Mk 137 incorporates improvements learned over the years by the Teams. One of the main changes in the Mk 137 charge is found in the Mk 4 Mods 0 and 1 Canvas Field Pack it is assembled in. The Mk 4 pack has the flotation bladder located in a pocket in the cover flap rather than on the rear of the charge as in earlier designs. A simple bladder valve allows the flotation device to be inflated or deflated to the swimmer's desire.

With the flotation device in the cover flap, the charge floats face up rather than down. If the flap is opened in order to use the Mk 34 charges individually, the pack will hang down from the flap with its open mouth facing up. In this orientation it is less likely that the charges will spill out as the pack is used.

Vent holes are located in the bottom of the pack to allow water to drain out if the charge is carried onto dry land. On one side of the pack is a length of cot-

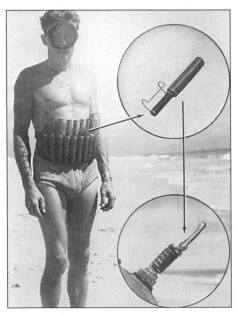

ton sash cord with a flat hook attached to the pack just above the cord. The cord is secured under webbing straps where it can easily be removed. On the opposite side of the pack is the traditional flat hook secured to the top of the pack and a snubber assembly down near the bottom of the pack.

The snubber assembly is a metal strap with a notch cut into it and a piece of spring steel riveted over the notch. The end of the spring piece has a V-notch cut into it. The sash cord can be slipped under the spring and pulled through the notch. When the cord is released, it is secured by the spring strip clamping down on it.

Source: U.S. Navy

The Mk 137 Mod 0 charge assembly consists of the Mk 4 Mod 0 pack holding ten Mk 34 Mod 0 charges loaded with C-3. The Mk 137 Mod 1 charge assembly utilizes the Mk 4 Mod 1 pack and Mk 34 Mod 1 charges loaded with C-4.

MARK 35 MOD 1 DEMOLITION CHARGE

The Mark 35 demolition charge is the most recent version of the World War II Hagensen pack. The only noticeable difference between this charge and the Mk 34 is that the Mk 35 has only been loaded with Composition C-4 explosive. The Mk 34 demolition charge is part of the Mk 138 demolition charge assembly and is not issued separately. This charge is presently standard issue with the SEAL Teams today.

MARK 138 MOD 1 DEMOLITION CHARGE ASSEMBLY

The Mark 138 Mod 1 demolition charge is visibly little different than the Mk 137 charge assembly except in terms of contents. The Mk 138 charge uses the same Mk 4 Mod 1 field pack as used with the Mk 137 Mod 1 charge assembly. The Mod 1 field pack has the plastic flotation bladder sewn into the cover flap to help prevent its loss while being used in the field.

The Mk 138 Mod 1 demolition charge assembly is loaded with Mk 35 charges containing Composition C-4 explosive. The use of C-4 explosive extends the time that the Mk 138 charge may be immersed underwater without materially affecting its explosive effects. The overall design of the Mk 138 charge is primarily intended for use in underwater demolition operations but it may be adapted for other uses as well. The Mark 138 demolition charge assembly and its component Mk 35 demolition charges carry forward the tradition of the Hagensen pack developed over fifty years earlier.

M112/M183 DEMOLITION CHARGE

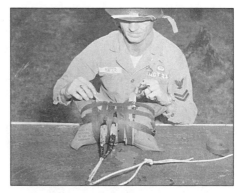

Source: U.S. Navy

The M112 C-4 demolition charge was originally developed for use by the U.S. Army. The general usefulness of the charge soon brought it to the attention of the UDTs and SEAL Teams who adopted it for their own use.

Designed roughly in the mid-1960s, the M112 demolition charge is used for general combat demolitions and is particularly well suited for cutting steel and timber as well as breaching concrete. The charge itself is a simple 11 × 2 × 1-inch block of composition C-4 explosive enclosed in a plastic bag.

The bag containing the C-4 charge has differed slightly over the years. The Composition C-4 in some charges has been colored a dull gray and was packaged in a clear mylar film bag. Blocks more recently manufactured have been placed in olive drab mylar film containers and the C-4 is white in color. The bags have been sealed with a knot or small metal clip over the open end.

On the back of the M112 bag is a strip of pressure-sensitive adhesive tape. The tape is securely fastened to the bag itself and is covered by a peel-off cover strip. The adhesive backing allows the charge to be attached to any relatively clean, dry, flat surface above freezing.

Limitations of the M112 demolition charge center around its weight and adhesive strip. The odd 1.25-pound explosive weight of the M112 charge makes charge calculations involving it difficult. In addition, the adhesive strip will not adhere to wet surfaces without additional treatment. The additional treatment involves coating the target surface with a supplementary adhesive. With the use of additional adhesive, the M112 charge can be emplaced even underwater.

The M112 demolition charge is available in bulk amounts packaged in wooden crates or contained in the M183 demolition charge assembly. The M183 assembly consists of an M85 olive drab canvas case which can hold sixteen M112 demolition charges. Eight of the M112 charges are placed in one of two M5 charge bags that fit inside of the M85 carrying case.

In addition to the M112 explosive charges, the M183 demolition charge assembly includes four M15 priming assemblies. The M15 priming assembly is used to connect several charges of M112 blocks for simultaneous detonation. A 5-foot length of detonating cord with RDX booster charge capsules crimped on each end makes up the M15 priming assembly. Each booster contains 13.5 grains (0.9 g) of RDX or PETN. Two M1 detonating cord clips are also included with each M15 assembly. The M1 clips allow the priming assembly to be easily attached to additional detonating cord lines without any knots or tying being needed.

The M183 demolition charge assembly is intended for use by assault demolition teams in combat. The charge can be used for reducing small obstacles, cutting, breaching, and cratering. A single M183 demolition charge assembly, employed as a simple satchel charge, can destroy a 3-foot high, 3-foot wide at the base, concrete dragon's tooth obstacle.

DETASHEET

One of the problems in producing a number of the more sophisticated demolition charges is in maintaining the density of the explosive being used. Using plastic explosives such as Composition C-3 or C-4 to produces charges such as the diamond, saddle, and ribbon charge require the explosive to be cut, shaped, and formed to exacting sizes. The manipulation of the explosive invariably produces cracks, voids, indentations, and bumps that can be held to a minimum but almost always appear, especially if the explosive is transported as a prepared charge.

The use of Detasheet flexible explosive removed many of the problems in using advanced demolition techniques. With Detasheet, it is relatively easy to conduct pinpoint metal cutting demolition operations with a minimum explosive loading. Keeping the explosive loading down also helps in cutting down the amount of weight that a generally overloaded specwar operator has to carry.

Because Detasheet is completely waterproof as it is issued, the explosive is also of great use in conducting underwater demolition operations. For maximum flexibility in producing charges, Detasheet is supplied in rolls or sheets of varying thickness. Sophisticated charges can be either premade prior to a mission or quickly produced on the spot by using Detasheet. In general it takes less than one third of the time to manufacture a charge from Detasheet as it does when using conventional plastic explosives.

MARK 36 MOD 1 DEMOLITION CHARGE

The Mark 36 demolition charge is the main part of the Mk 1 Limpet mine family. The pan-shaped metal body of the Mk 36 charge contains the explosive components of the Mk 1 limpet mine. The body of the Mk 36 charge consists of a welded, cylindrical aluminum case with a wide flat flange around its outside circumference.

The main explosive load, about 4 pounds of H-6, is cast in place through a hole located in the top of the case. Two cavities in the case accept firing devices and are both fitted with internal booster charges. A cylindrical cavity inside the explosive charge is not accessible from the outside of the case but is open on the lower (target) side of the charge. The cylindrical cavity accepts an antidisturbance fuze and firing device.

On the rear end of the case is an activator well assembly protected by a screw-on shipping cap. The activator well extends into the main charge where it is surrounded by a booster charge. The exterior activator well is threaded to accept the Mk 39 Mod 0 safety and arming device as well as any additional fuzing called for by a particular mission.

Around the circumference of the charge, underneath the flange, are six permanent magnets for holding the charge to a steel target. The magnets are oriented so that their north and south ends abut each other alternately. The magnets are quite powerful and hold the charge securely in place on a target.

The H-6 explosive loaded into the Mk 36 charge is among the most brisant and sensitive used by the Teams. The size of the charge is sufficient to blow a 4 × 2-foot or greater hole in the bottom of the average ship. Properly placed, a single charge can break the back (keel) of a medium-to-small-sized warship.

MARK 70 MOD 0 EXPLOSIVE CHARGE

The Mk 70 Mod 0 charge is the active explosive component of the Mk 5 Mod 0 Modular Limpet Assembly (LAM). As part of the Mk 5 LAM, the Mk 70 charge is referred to as the explosive module during assembly and employment. The body of the Mk 70 charge is a cylindrical metal canister with four annular rings for reinforcement.

Inside of the body of the Mk 70 is a central area containing the charge of 50 pounds of cast H-6 explosive. Surrounding the charge is an annular flotation chamber. The flotation chamber is designed to make the Mk 70 charge neutrally buoyant when it is immersed in seawater. In fresh water, the Mk 70 charge is negatively buoyant and additional flotation is needed.

For shipment and handling, two Mk 70 charges are encased in a cradle contained by a steel drum. The filled drum makes up the Mk 70/Mk 71 Explosive Charge Kit portion of the Mk 5 LAM. During shipment, each Mk 70 charge is equipped with a cover that is held in place by a vee-band coupler (clamp assembly). The cover protects the exposed explosive face of the H-6 charge inside the Mk 70 body.

The vee-band coupler is used to connect multiple Mk 70 charges together once the protective cover is removed. In addition, at least one vee-band coupler is used to attach a control unit to the explosive charge. When the modules are assembled and the clamps tightened, the entire unit becomes a ridged assembly.

The clamp assembly of the vee-band coupler is equipped with a special breakaway nut that can be tightened and the hex portion broken off. With the band tightened and the hex nut broken away, the clamp assembly cannot be easily loosened. Not being able to remove the clamp assembly prevents the explosive charge from being removed from the Mk 5 LAM if the device is discovered by the enemy.

Each Mk 70 explosive charge is designed to be able to attack roughly 1,500 tons of displacement per ship. In planning a swimmer attack, this would mean that targeting a 4,000 ton ship would mean assembling a Mk 5 LAM with 3 Mk 70 explosive charges.

EXPLOSIVE DEVICES

Explosive devices are manufactured weapons or tools that use explosives to complete their designed action. This can range from a detonator (blasting) cap for setting off explosive charges to a mine or specially engineered charge. This is not actually an "official" designation but is used as a convenience in describing the materials listed here.

M7 SPECIAL NONELECTRIC BLASTING CAP

The M7 military special nonelectric blasting cap will detonate all military explosives when properly used. The cap originally was a lacquered copper tube but is now made of thin aluminum. Three layers of explosive are pressed into the tube. The top layer consists of an ignition charge of lead styphnate. The next layer is an intermediate or priming charge of lead azide. The base charge is approximately 13.5 grains of PETN or RDX.

The base charge gives the M7 special cap sufficient power to detonate any standard military explosive charge. The open end of the cap is flared to facilitate inserting the nipple of a base coupling, time fuse, or detonating cord. The explosive load of the cap fills about two-thirds of the body length, leaving sufficient room for the insertion of fuze or other material. Once the firing method is inserted into the cap, the open end is crimped down securely with an M2 cap crimper.

The spit of flame from a time fuze or firing device or the blast from detonating cord is sufficient to fire the ignition charge which in turn sets off the intermediate charge. The power of the intermediate charge is magnified by the further detonation of the base charge. The blasting cap is probably the most sensitive item used in demolition operations. In general, blasting caps are sensitive and can be set off by a strong blow or being dropped just a few inches onto a hard surface. To protect the caps and the operator, a number of special carrying boxes and cases are available for transporting blasting caps during operations.

M6 ELECTRICAL BLASTING CAP

The M6 electrical blasting cap has much the same physical makeup as the M7 Special cap. The body of the cap is an aluminum alloy cup containing three different explosive charges. The M6 cap is provided with two plastic-covered copper lead wires that extend out from a rubber plug in the mouth of the cap. The two lead wires are contrasting colors and their bared ends are tinned for the last 1.75 inches. The ends of the wires are shorted with an easily removable shunting clip to protect the cap against stray electrical currents.

The ends of the lead wires that extend into the cap pass through the rubber plug that holds them separated. The rubber plug is secured in the mouth of the cap by two circumferential crimps. In some caps, the rubber plug is in addition to a sulfur plug that fills the interior of the cap. The ends of the lead wires are held apart and connected by a thin bridge wire. When an electric current of about ½ ampere minimum passes through the wires, the bridge wire heats and initiates the ignition charge.

The ignition charge on some earlier M6 caps consisted of a lead styphnate/barium chromate mixture. In more recent caps, the ignition charge is a special mixture of smokeless powder, potassium chlorate, and the lead salt of dinitro cresol. The ignition charge sets off the lead azide intermediate charge which in turn detonates the RDX base charge. The power of the M6 cap is sufficient to detonate all standard military explosive charges.

The M6 electric blasting cap is used for initiating explosive charges when a source of electricity such as a battery or blasting machine is available. The use of an electrical firing system gives the most positive control as to exactly when an explosive charge will detonate. The electric blasting cap has weaknesses unique to it that increase the complexity of using the electric firing system.

The most notable weakness of an electric cap is to radio frequency transmissions taking place near it. When an electrical firing system is fully prepared to fire, with all shunts removed, the long lead wires can act much like a radio antenna. Care has to be taken that all radio transmissions be kept away from the firing system to prevent induced electrical current from prematurely firing the blasting cap. Radio transmissions that must take place have to be kept to a minimum and the transmitter power kept below maximum safe limits.

In spite of these restrictions, the electrical firing system using the M6 blasting cap is safe and effective. The construction of the M6 cap is such that the interior of the cap is waterproof and the system can be used underwater. The M6 cap is also used in some command-detonated mine systems such as the M18A1 Claymore mine.

TIME BLASTING FUZE

This is a burning-type fuze that burns at a steady rate of 30 to 45 seconds per foot. To be sure of the burning rate, each spool of fuze is tested by timing a given length before it is used. The fabric-covered fuze has a black or orange wax outer coating and a core of black powder. The construction of the fuze leaves it reasonably flexible and waterproof, though it cannot be left underwater for extended lengths of time without a risk of failure.

Time fuze is used as the delay element in a nonelectric firing system. As long as the outer covering has remained intact, the fuze is sufficiently waterproof for underwater use. Because of its corrugated surface, safety fuze does not make a waterproof seal when crimped into a blasting cap. Sealing compound for additional waterproofing is needed on the cap for underwater use.

The construction of safety fuze is such that a spit of flame comes out of the end of the fuze when the core burns out. This spit of flame is sufficient to ignite most blasting caps including the M7 special cap. To insure the detonation of a charge when using a nonelectric firing system, dual-priming is normally used. In a dual-primed system, the entire firing system, from the igniter to the cap, is duplicated. At the moment of initiation, both fuzes of a dual-primed system are ignited one after the other.

DETONATING CORD

Detonating cord, or primacord/detcord as it is also called, is a flexible fuze-like line resembling normal time blasting fuze. Instead of having black powder as a core, like safety fuze, detonating cord has a core of PETN high explosive. The PETN charge in detonating cord has a rate of detonation of from roughly 21,000 to 23,000 feet per second. A 4-mile length of detonating cord would all explode in just 1 second. It is this characteristic that makes detonating cord valuable as an instantaneous fuse.

The power of detonating cord is such that it can be used as a cutting charge for small operations. Several wraps of detonating cord as sufficient to cut small trees, cables, or lines. The main use of detonating cord is to detonate a number of explosive charges simultaneously. An unlimited number of charges can be tied into a main detonating cord line for initiation. During combat operations in the Pacific during World War II, men of the UDTs would connect hundreds of charges to a detonating cord main line. When the bulk of the Team had been recovered, the fuze puller, usually the fastest swimmer in the Team, would ignite the nonelectric firing system. After a safe delay, all of the detonating cord connected charges would detonate in one massive shot.

Detonating cord will detonate explosive charges when attached by several wraps around an explosive block or tied in a knot and the explosive wrapped around it. Detonating cord usually has a yellow or yellow/black outer skin covered in wax over a fabric tube. The slippery skin of some types of detonating cord have made knot tying difficult, but this mild problem has since been eliminated. Detonating cord is particularly useful for initiating charges placed in wet boreholes or underwater. Even after 24 hours of immersion, detonating cord will still function provided the free ends have been protected or the initiator is at least 6 inches in from the end of the line.

Detonating cord is detonated by a blasting cap or detonating cord initiator attached anywhere along the line. A blasting cap is usually used to initiate detonating cord by being taped along the length of the cord, parallel to the explosive core. Branch lines to charges are tied to the trunk line at 90-degree angles with a girth hitch knot.

The girth hitch starts by taking the branch line over the main line, to the side then under the main line and across to the other side, then under the main, back over, and through. Over, under, over, around, and through. This knot is practiced by the men of the Teams until they tie it almost instinctively.

SHAPED CHARGES

A shaped charge is generally a cylindrical explosive charge formed so as to have a conical top and a conical or hemispherical cavity at the bottom. Detonating the explosive charge at the top center of its conical peak causes the detonation wave to move downward through the explosive mass. As the detonation wave in the explosive moves along the cavity, it causes a shock wave to leave the wall of the cavity and move directly away from the explosive surface.

The shock wave of the explosion meets at the center of the cavity and is reflected off of itself approaching from the opposite side. The reflecting shock wave moves downward, forced along by the detonation wave following the angled wall of the cavity. This reflection and focusing of the shock wave creates an explosive jet of energy that moves away from the mouth of the charge at a right angle to the center of the original cavity. This entire phenomenon is called the Munroe Effect after the man who first noted it.

Because of the physics of the Munroe Effect, the velocity of the explosive jet is several times faster than the detonation velocity of the explosive charge used to form it. In the M3 shaped charge, the explosive jet has a velocity of 73,000 feet per second (22,250 m/s). The 73,000 fps jet velocity is roughly three times the detonation velocity of the M3's explosive filler. The jet is focused on a very small area in relation to the diameter of the original charge. The power of the focused jet is such that any material it meets is literally forced away from the point of contact.

If the cavity in the explosive charge is lined with a variety of materials—soft metals such as copper have advantages—the penetrating power of the explosive jet is greatly increased. Maximum penetration for a shaped charge, lined or unlined, takes place when the charge is held away from the surface of the target at the charge's optimum stand-off distance. The optimum stand-off distance varies from charge to charge and is directly related to the diameter of the mouth of the charge.

The metal liner of a shaped charge inverts as the explosive detonates and precedes the explosive jet in the form of a slug of hot metal. The slug so formed is called a carrot due to its long shape. The power of the jet drives the carrot into and possibly through the target material. If the target is an armored vehicle or concrete fortification, and the carrot penetrates the wall of the target, it adds to the casualty-producing effect of the charge.

Shaped charges can blast boreholes into steel and concrete or similar materials. When used against a concrete obstacle, a shaped charge can open a borehole that can be packed with explosives to completely destroy the obstacle. Some shaped charges are made so that they retain their effectiveness underwater. Others are formed so as to produce a cut line rather than a hole in a target.

M3 40-POUND SHAPED CHARGE

This is a large shaped charge that will penetrate 55 inches of reinforced concrete with a hole tapering from 5 inches to 1.75 inches. The charge will also penetrate at least 20 inches of steel armor plate with an average hole diameter of 2.5 inches.

Developed during the early part of World War II, the original explosive filling for the M3 charge was 50/50 pentolite. More recently manufactured charges use a Composition B filler with a large pentolite booster. The explosive charge is contained in an olive drab steel casing about 9.5 inches in diameter and 14.5 inches tall. The container resembles a deep metal funnel set with the open end down into a short cylinder. At the top of the funnel is a threaded activator well to accept any standard demolition firing device or a blasting cap and adaptor. The 60-degree cavity in the base of the charge is lined with a pressed steel liner for added penetration.

To give the charge its optimum standoff distance, three steel legs are welded to a round band that will attach to the bottom of the charge body. The band clamps to the base of the M3 charge with a simple thumbscrew and when reversed, the legs will go over the body of the charge, telescoping the system for easier storage.

The M3 shaped charge will bore a hole into earth, ice, masonry, concrete, and paved or unpaved roads. It is especially useful for punching holes into thick reinforced concrete pavements laid on dense, high-strength bases. This type of material is found on the better roads and airport runways. By using the shaped charge to open up the target for heavier charge emplacement, a runway or modern roadway can be quickly made impassable.

The M3 shaped charge can also be used as a antipersonnel weapon, as can any shaped charge. By laying the charge down on its side, the M3 can clear a 30 by 100 foot (9 by 30 m) area of all jungle vegetation except large trees. The blast will also throw loose materials and fragmentation for long distances from the point of the explosion.

M2A3 15-POUND SHAPED CHARGE

The M2A3 shaped charge was designed specifically for attacking targets made of reinforced concrete. The charge can easily carried and emplaced by one man and will quickly open up a concrete fortification for follow-up demolitions.

The body of the M2A3 shaped charge is molded from an olive drab, moisture resistant fiber. At the top of the conical body is a flat apex with a threaded activator well. The explosive charge has been improved since the first introduction of the M2A3 charge in mid–World War II. Early production charges were filled with 50/50 pentolite. Later charges were loaded with Composition B with a large 50/50 pentolite booster. The design of the M2A3 shaped charge has been improved further with the introduction of a different charge arrangement in the M2A4 charge.

The M2A4 shaped demolition charge is the same in effect and dimensions as the M2A3 charge. The main change in the M2A4 charge is in the explosive filling. By replacing the 50/50 pentolite booster with a 0.11 pound (50 g) Composition A3 booster, the M2A4 shaped charge is less sensitive to gunfire than the M2A3 charge. The main charge of Composition B in the M2A4 is increased to 11.39 pounds (5.17 kg) to maintain the same total weight as the M2A3.

A standoff sleeve is issued with the M2A3 charge made of the same pressed fiber material as the body of the main charge. The standoff sleeve fits snugly into the bottom of the charge body. The scalloped base of the standoff sleeve is intended to allow the charge to be emplaced on irregular surfaces.

The cavity liner of the M2A3 shaped charge is unique and specially designed for demolition use. The 60 degree conical liner is made of a special high-density glass rather than the usual metal. Because of the glass cone, the M2A3 charge produces a hole of greater volume, though slightly less in depth, than the same charge would with a steel cone.

The use of the high-density glass cone has another advantage in that a second demolition charge can be used immediately after the first. The material of the cone forms a glass slug in the hole, which can be shattered and removed, leaving the hole cool enough for the second charge.

MARK 1 MOD 0 CABLE AND CHAIN CUTTER

The Mark 1 cable and chain cutter was one of the first special demolition devices ever used by the units that eventually became the Navy SEALs. In November 1942, Operation Torch, the invasion of North Africa took place. A small contingent of specially trained Navy demolitionists were tasked with cutting a steel boom blocking the advance of an amphibious force up the Wadi Sebou river. To cut the cable boom, the men of the first Combat Demolition Unit used the then new Mk 1 Mod 0 cable and chain cutter.

The Mk 1 is an explosive cutter using a shaped charge to sever steel cable or anchor chain. The charge has a U-shaped sheet metal case with a removable cover. The U-shaped case resembles a large, thick, horseshoe magnet. Inside of the casing, underneath the cover and facing in toward the center of the U, is a 80-degree metal V-liner with a built-in standoff. The container is shipped empty and is filled with Composition explosive by the unit in the field prior to use. With the cover removed, the pliable Composition explosive is packed by hand entirely around the circumference of the U. The metal cover can then be replaced and secured with cotter pins.

A securing hook, resembling an inverted question mark, is spring loaded and will hold the target in place in the center of the U. A wooden handle is placed at the apex of the U to hold the charge and give the operator's hand leverage when working the spring-loaded securing hook.

Next to the base of the handle, at the apex of the U, is a threaded activator well. The activator well will accept any standard firing device or blasting cap with adaptor. Simple and easy to use, the M1 cable and chain cutter was one of the first uses of the linear shaped charge. In the linear shaped charge, the V-liner runs along the long axis of the charge, which is rectangular rather than circular. Reasonably waterproof, the Mk 1 cutter can operate underwater to a depth of 20 feet (6.1 m). Once in place, the Mk 1 cutter should be fired within 3 hours depending on the specific explosive composition used.

FLEXIBLE LINEAR SHAPED CHARGE

The flexible linear shaped charge is a specialized application of the Munroe Effect used when a cutting rather than a perforating action is desired. The charge is intended to produce a linear cutting action in a situation where remote, fast, and reliable cutting is a primary requisite.

The charge has a continuous explosive core of PETN, much like that in detonating cord, enclosed in a seamless lead sheath. The sheath itself, and the explosive it contains, is shaped in the form of an inverted V. The continuous liner and explosive make a shaped charge that produces a linear cutting action.

The optimum stand-off distance for this particular charge is [5ST] of an inch (7.9 mm). Since the charge itself does not come with any kind of stand-off, it has to be supplied by the operator. Several materials can be used to supply a stand-off distance such as foam rubber strips or thin plastic hose. When used with a proper stand-off, the charge will cut a minimum of 0.25 inches (6.4 mm) into a 2-inch (5.1 cm) steel plate.

This cutting action also take place on wood and other target materials. Detonation of the linear shaped charge can be accomplished with blasting caps, detonating cord, or other firing devices. In general, any system that will detonate detonating cord can be used with the linear shaped charge.

By using prepared strips of the linear shaped charge, holes of any needed size can be blasted through wooden walls and metal bulkheads that are made of sheet steel. This technique has been advanced even further since the introduction of the flexible linear shaped charge and new developments are being tested by the Teams on a regular basis.

MARK 136 DEMOLITION OUTFIT

The Mk 136 outfit and its Mk 1 destructors are an application of the special abilities of a combat swimmer to clear mines. The horn-type mine fuze is a chemical battery encased in a soft metal sheath. When the metal casing of the horn is flexed or dented, such as when struck by a ship, a glass ampule of electrolyte is broken. Once the ampule is broken, the horn acts as a battery, detonating the attached explosive charge electrically.

The careful design of the M1 destructor allows the controlled crushing, but not rupturing, of a chemical horn after a safe time delay. The nature of the mines that use the chemical horns as fuzes prevents the approach of any kind of transport or boat. The very flexible UDT swimmer is easily able to safely approach a mine, attach one or more of the M1 destructors, and safely leave the area well before the mine detonates. Once the ten destructors in the Mk 136 outfit have been used, the remaining belt can be easily jettisoned, freeing the swimmer.

Though originally designed to be used against Japanese type JE and JG antiboat mines during World War II, the Mark 136 demolition outfit has been used since. Particular use of the Mk 136 outfit and its Mk 1 destructors was made during mine clearing operations during the Korean War. The overall usefulness of the Mk 136 outfit and its materials was such that the item remained in the special warfare inventory well into the 1970s.

LIMPET MINES

During the first and second World Wars, attacks were made against shipping by individual and small teams of underwater swimmers. Though primitive by modern standards, use was made of the limited underwater breathing equipment available at that time by a number of the world's navies. Successful antiship operations did take place and proved the worth of the swimmer attack idea.

Though the United States Navy did not conduct swimmer attacks against shipping during World War II, the idea was brought forward to Navy officials and was examined in some detail. Experiments were conducted using UDT personnel as attack swimmers during the war but no combat operations in the field were undertaken.

The Office of Strategic Services (OSS) had a Maritime Unit during World War II and these men also conducted swimmer attack experiments. Though mission-specific Navy ordnance was not available at the time, the OSS had a number of pieces of ordnance developed specifically for attacking ships. The British Royal Navy had been conducting operations and experiments for some time prior to the OSS entering the field and had developed explosive charges intended to be hand emplaced against a ship's hull. The British named these explosive charges "limpet mines" after the small shellfish that clings to hulls, rocks, and pilings so tenaciously. The OSS also took to calling their antiship charges limpet mines after the British system.

World War II limpet mines tended to be small, self-contained charges designed to be easily carried and emplaced. Antiship attacks would often be conducted as part of a sabotage campaign in enemy-held territory so the mines had to be quickly used by agents passing in small boats or swimming by. Successful attacks took place even with the limitations of technology and personnel. In the years after World War II, part of the impetus behind developing underwater breathing systems for the UDTs was to advance the idea of swimmer attacks against shipping. Limpet mines were developed that were larger and much more powerful than the World War II models.

Until the men of the UDT had proved the idea of swimmer attacks by actually placing mines on Navy ships that were under alert, many of the senior officers of the Fleet Navy did not believe just a tiny handful of men could cripple or sink a capital ship. This situation has not changed greatly even to the present day.

MARK 1 MODS 2, 3, AND 4 LIMPET MINE

The heart of the Mk 1 limpet mine family is the Mk 36 demolition charge. Using the Mk 36 charge as a base, several different mods of limpet mine are assembled by using any of three different firing devices. Each mod of the Mk 1 limpet family has its own characteristics in terms of time delay, antidisturbance capability, and arming.

The Mk 1 Mod 2 limpet is made up of the Mk 36 Mod 1 demolition charge with the Mk 39 Mod 0 Safety and Arming device fitted with the Mk 23 Mod 1 Firing device. Inside the Mk 36 charge is placed the Mk 24 Mod 2 antidisturbance firing device. The Mk 39 safety and arming device provides the Mod 2 limpet with a positive safety system incorporating an arming delay. The Mk 23 firing device is a mechanical clockwork time delay of from 15 to 180 minutes in pre-set increments. The Mk 24 antidisturbance fuze prevents the Mod 2 limpet from being removed if discovered. Since the Mk 24 fuze cannot be seen from the outside of the casing of the Mk 36 charge, it cannot be determined by observation if the mine is boobytrapped against removal or movement.

The Mk 1 Mod 3 limpet is made up of the Mk 36 Mod 1 Demolition charge and the Mk 39 Mod 0 Safety and Arming device fitted with the Mk 48 Mod 0 Firing device. Inside the mine is fitted the Mk 24 Mod 2 antidisturbance firing device. The Mk 48 firing device provides the Mod 3 limpet with an electronic delay system with settings from 15 minutes to 72 hours. The Mk 39 safety and arming device provide a positive safety to the system and the Mk 24 fuze prevents removal.

The Mk 1 Mod 4 limpet is the simplest member of the family being made up of the Mk 36 Mod 1 Demolition charge with just the Mk 39 Mod 0 Safety and Arming device fitted with the Mk 23 Mod 1 Firing device.

A black foam-plastic float is issued that fits snugly over the Mk 1 limpet covering all but the base of

Source: Kevin Dockery

the mine and the fuze assembly. With the float attached and strapped in place, the limpet has neutral or slightly positive buoyancy for ease in underwater transportation by a combat swimmer.

One Mk 1 limpet may be transported by a combat swimmer using the Mk 46 Mod 0 backpack kit. The backpack is outfitted with an optional pouch for accessories used in emplacing the mine such as stud drivers or other tools.

An additional trailer can be attached to the Mk 46 Mod 0 backpack at the bottom of the pack in place of the tool pouch. The flat board of the trailer rides on the swimmer's rump and is held in place by a cross strap going around in front of the swimmer. Two Mk 1 limpets can be easily transported by a single combat swimmer using the Mk 46 backpack and trailer. The mines are held to the backpack base by their integral magnets where they can be easily detached by the swimmer or his partner.

MARK 5 MODULAR LIMPET

The Mark 5 limpet mine is a group of modules that can be assembled in the field according to the size of the projected target. This versatile modular mine is capable of seriously damaging or destroying an enemy ship at anchor. The Mk 5 can also be used effectively against other maritime targets such as dams, underwater pipelines, piers, and bridges. The assurance of target destruction is the reason behind the mine's modular construction, allowing the limpet to be tailored to produce a desired explosive force.

The explosive component of the Mk 5 is the Mk 70 Mod 0 Explosive charge with an active element of 50 pounds of H-6 explosive. Any reasonable number of Mk 70 charges can be assembled to attack a target. To aid in handling the Mk 5, a concave-dished end fairing with integral handles is placed on both ends of the assembled mine. The end fairings have internal flotation chambers with water-flood valves that allow the mine to be trimmed for neutral buoyancy by the operators.

Source: Kevin Dockery

Between one end fairing and the explosive module(s) is the Mk 126 Mod 0 control unit. The control unit contains the Mk 47 Mod 1 Timer device and the Mk 156 Mod 0 power supply. Also part of the control unit is the arming handle and target sensing probe. When the arming handle is activated, the target sensing probe is released and the power supply begins charging the system 15 minutes after the arming cycle begins. When the arming cycle is completed, the sensing probe will detonate the charge if there is any movement between the mine and the target.

The Mk 47 Mod 1 timer is made up of solid-state timing and firing circuits with two settings for detonation, CONTACT and STANDOFF. The firing mode is set by the operators before the mine is emplaced. At the time the firing mode is selected, the delay time is also selected, ranging from 1 to 99 hours.

If the CONTACT firing mode is used, the charge fires after the expiration of the delay time. In the STANDOFF mode, a separation bolt is fired at the end of the delay time. The separation bolt allows the unit to sink to a proper standoff depth. Four seconds after the separation bolt is fired, the detonators are initiated setting off the main charge.

A wing-and-yoke assembly is used to stabilized the weapon for underwater handling by the swimmer. The assembly is formed of aluminum filled with polyurethane foam and has 25 pounds (11.34 kg) of positive buoyancy in seawater. The wing-and-yoke assembly is attached to the control unit by the explosive separation bolt controlled by the Mk 47 timer. The two wings of the wing-and-yoke assembly fold in against the body of the mine for ease in transport. When extended, the inflatable bladders that are part of the wings are filled with CO_2 by the operator at the target. The positive buoyancy of the wing bladders hold the limpet firmly to the target.

The Mk 5 may also be used as a modular demolition charge. In the demolition charge mode only the end fairings and explosive modules are used in the assembly. Fuzing is accomplished by using a firing assembly consisting of the Mk 114 Mod 0 firing device adapter along with the Mk 39 Mod 0 safety and arming device as well as a proper timer. Once the Mk 114 Mod 0 firing device adapter is inserted into the fuze well of the end fairing it cannot be easily removed.

Theoretically, there is no limit to the number of Mk 70 charges that could be assembled as part of a Mk 5 limpet mine. Even a ship as large as the aircraft carrier Enterprise could be attacked by a single Mk 5 mine and a group of swimmers to place and arm it. The size of a Mk 5 set up to sink the Enterprise would be difficult to use as a practical matter. The 95,100 tons loaded displacement of the Enterprise would require 64 Mk 70 modules or a Mk 5 limpet 66 feet (20.1 m) long and weighing 4,441 pounds (2,014 kg) with 32 wing-and-yoke assemblies, a large weapon even for a team of SEALs.

The Teams use a number of standard manufactured explosive munitions produced originally for the U.S. Army. Among these munitions is the full family of land mines issued to both the Army and the Marine Corps. Although the Navy's specwar demolition training course covers the safe application and use of land mines, they are not employed by the Teams on a regular basis. The static land mine, whether a small antipersonnel or large antitank model, does not normally fit into the dynamic offensive style of most specwar operations.

One mine in particular has seen a great deal of use in the Teams both in the past and still today. The mine is of the directional fragmentation type and is designated the M18A1 Claymore.

M18A1 CLAYMORE MINE
The M18A1 Claymore mine is a directional, controlled fragmentation weapon easily described as acting like a giant shotgun. The M18 Claymore mine was developed from an original concept by Norman A. MacLeod of Los Angeles as an answer to massed human wave attacks such as had been faced by U.S. forces in the Pacific during World War II and again in the Korean War some time later. The name Claymore was chosen by MacLeod after the Scottish broadsword of his homeland, a sword that has been described as a scythe cutting a path through massed enemies.

Type classified by the Army in 1959, the M18 Claymore was found to have a number of shortcomings when used by the troops. With a short time a modified weapon, the M18A1 Claymore became standard issue. The Claymore has remained relatively unchanged since then and is still an efficient and popular weapon today.

The body of the M18A1 Claymore is a glass-filled polystyrene plastic molding produced in two parts. The rectangular mine body is curved outwards towards its front in order to control the spread of the fragmentation when the mine is fired. Inside the front portion of the mine body is the fragmentation matrix consisting of 700 steel balls held in place with a plastic resin.

The rear of the mine body holds the charge of C-4 explosive. Detonation of the C-4 blasts the fragmentation outwards in an expanding arc with a velocity of about 3,000 feet per second (914 m/s. The design of the Claymore's body is such that the spread of the fragmentation remains in a 60-degree fan-shaped beaten zone 2 meters high and 50 meters wide at a distance of 50 meters from the point of detonation. This area of maximum effectiveness is called the killing zone of the mine.

Within the killing zone of an M18A1 Claymore, the fragmentation has a high-enough velocity to penetrate a U.S. Army M69 armored vest. An additional area of moderate effectiveness extends outward from the mine to a distance of 250 meters. The area of moderate effectiveness is also wider than the killing area and covers an arc 90 degrees to the right and left of the center of the killing zone.

Because of the blast of explosive when a Claymore is fired, all personnel must be undercover when within 100 meters of the mine and no one should be within 16-meters of the point of detonation. With the 16-meter danger area of a Claymore, the backblast of the explosive can cause concussion injuries of personnel, even when they are under cover. Even when friendly personnel are undercover and at a proper distance, the power of a Claymore going off can be staggering. In a large ambush, where a number of Claymores are fired at one time, the effect is incredible, even when the operators know what is coming. During one PRU ambush operation in Vietnam, the SEAL advisor had over a dozen M18A1 Claymores laid out, and fired them all in a single shot.

The mines going off sounded like an ARC LIGHT strike (B-52s w/500 lb bombs). Then my PRUs opened up, covering the entire area with a swath of fire. As the firing stopped, there was only dust and a ringing kind of silence.

SEALs in general quickly came to like the Claymore mine a great deal, and use it whenever its sudden blast of firepower would work to their advantage. The primary use of the Claymore for the SEALs was as an ambush weapon. When properly laid out and aimed, the Claymore could literally sweep an area clear of vegetation, and any personnel who might be there.

The Claymore comes complete in a bandoleer (Claymore bag) with everything necessary to employ it. The firing system supplied is electrical and includes an M4 blasting cap, an M6 special electric cap attached to 100 feet of firing wire, and a squeeze-type M57 firing generator intended to fire a single cap.

The Claymore can be set up with the M4 blasting cap inserted into either of the cap wells at the top of the mine's body and secured in place with the screw plugs provided. The 100 feet (30.48 m) of firing wire attached to the cap is unwound from its spool out to the firing position. At the position, the shorting plug is removed from the firing wire and the wire's end plugged into the M57 firing device, also called the "clacker."

The M57 clacker has a safety bale that prevents the operating handle from being depressed unintentionally. Moving the safety bale on the firing device allows the handle to be squeezed, firing the mine. To test the firing circuit of the Claymore without firing it, an M40 test set is supplied, one per case of mines. The bandoleer of the mine kit containing the M40 test set is marked by a green tag on the shoulder strap of the bag.

The M40 test set itself is a simple green box that has a socket to accept the M57 firing device at one end and a plug intended for the M4 blasting cap assembly at the other end. By placing the M40 test set into the circuit, the firing system can be tested by squeezing the firing device. If the circuit is sound, a visible light will flash in the test set without setting off the cap. Simply removing the test set and plugging the M4's wire into the M57 firing device readies the Claymore for firing.

In the humid and corrosive environment of Vietnam, even testing a setup M18A1 Claymore didn't guarantee the mine would go off. Even mines that tested positive seemed to have a mind of their own on occasion. During one operation in the T-10 area of the Rung Sat Special Zone, a squad of SEALs had laid out an ambush for a number of VC thought to be operating in the area. As a group of 10 to 15 armed VC walked into the kill zone of the ambush, the SEAL officer in charge prepared to trigger the ambush.

> Whispering, I said, "Claymore!" The VC were right there, 30 feet away. We would have had them cold. We wouldn't have had to fire a shot. Only the damned Claymores didn't go off. We cranked them two or three more times and they still didn't go off. I couldn't believe it. Still on all fours, I said, "Open up," to the Stoner man and the whole squad started shooting . . .
>
> . . . we called in slicks and left in style, guns blazing and the Seawolves hosing the place down. We tried the Claymores one last time before the helos came in. The damned things went off. Lesson: Explosives can be unreliable so you'd better have a backup plan.

Even with the occasional disappointment, the M18A1 Claymore mine earned itself a solid place in the SEALs arsenal. Use of the mine was only limited by the operator's imagination. Claymores were used as booby traps, base defense, and as a counter-ambush device when a group of SEALs were trying to break contact with an pursuing enemy force. For this kind of use, a prepared Claymore would be carried by the squad, outfitted with a nonelectric firing system and a 30-second time delay.

The SEAL squad could quickly emplace the Claymore to cover the path behind them. Pulling the fuse igniter on the Claymore would start the delay and the squad would pull out. As the pursuing VC would come after the squad, they would often run right into the killing area of the mine as the Claymore detonated. The simple act of setting up the Claymore and pulling the fuse actually takes longer to describe than to do.

MARK 57 MOD 0 EXPLOSIVE SHEET CHARGE KIT

In the years since the Vietnam War, the Teams have taken the idea of the Claymore mine even further and tailored it to fit their unique needs. Intended for both surface and underwater use, the Mk 57 Mod 0 explosive kit uses the Mk 56 explosive sheet to supply the SEALs with an antipersonnel weapon even more flexible than the M18A1 Claymore.

The Mk 56 charge is a lightweight fragmentation composite sheet with an explosive core of sheet explosive. Glued with rubber cement to the back of the explosive sheet charge is a layer of 0.25 in (6.4 mm) foam rubber. On the front surface of the explosive sheet is glued a single layer of steel fragments. The fragments are cut from cold-rolled steel sheet and each one measures 0.063 in (1.6 mm) thick by 0.25 in (6.4 mm) square. The fragments are glued to the explosive sheet with rubber cement and are additionally secured with an outside layer of nylon mosquito netting.

As supplied in the kit, the Mk 56 sheet charge is not susceptible to sympathetic detonation in air or underwater. The waterproof charge can be cut to shape or size with a knife without changing its explosive characteristics. Though the supplied M4 (M6 special electric) blasting caps are sufficient to detonate, the Mk 56 sheet charge, detonating cord, or other firing devices can be used if the situation dictates it.

When fired, the Mk 56 charge blows out a swarm of projectiles, covering as large an area as desired by the operator. The charge can be wrapped around a 6-inch-or-greater-diameter tree, rock, vehicle, or other available object, and taped in place to cover the desired field-of-fire. No size or shape limits the application of the charge and there is no optimum size or shape.

BOOBY TRAPS

Among the least-liked of all explosive devices are booby traps. A booby trap is an explosive charge set up to detonate when an apparently harmless object is disturbed or a presumably safe act is performed. The average military booby trap is made up from materials available in a combat area. To aid in the safe setup of booby traps, a number of specialized fuzes are available as standard issue items.

All of the booby trap fuzes issued to the general military react when disturbed in a specific manner. These disturbances include, but are not limited to: Pressure—adding a weight, Pressure-Release—removing a weight, Pull—adding tension such as pulling a trip wire, Pull-Release—adding or relieving tension such as pulling or cutting a trip wire. Some fuzes can use only a single kind of triggering disturbance while others can be set up to utilize a number of different triggering disturbances.

In addition to the above simple mechanical triggers, a number of sophisticated electronic fuzes are available that react to vibration, magnetic fields, or capacitance changes. These last fuzes tend to be very classified and only available to some elite forces, such as the SEALs.

In general, booby traps are an outgrowth of the nuisance mine technique. Just a few active booby traps in the proper area can slow and severely hamper an advancing force. Men of the Teams have been instructed about booby traps, their construction, and effects, since the earliest days of the NCDUs of World War II. The primary reason for the training during World War II was to prevent casualties among the Navy men due to their encountering enemy booby traps. Later NCDU and UDT training included setting up booby traps.

Applying booby trap fuzes and munitions is limited only by the creativity of the operator. Supplied fuzes and standard explosives can be assembled into a bewildering array of improvised booby traps by men familiar with their use and application. By the time the SEALs were heavily involved in Vietnam, a number of SEAL operators had developed a skill in setting up booby traps.

The skills the SEALs had were augmented by a number of specially made, manufactured booby trap items. These items could be innocuous in themselves or actual military munitions modified in a deadly manner. The proper application of these manufactured items could have an effect far out of proportion to the number of actual booby traps set.

By 1968, the fielding of booby traps by the SEALs had become something of a standard operating procedure. In particular, prepared booby traps could be used to disrupt enemy supply lines in an area. These actions were highly classified at the time in order to maximize their effect on the enemy forces. Even today, the type and nature of the booby trap program used by the SEALs is just becoming declassified. VC supply caches were a favored target of the SEALs, moreso because ammunition stocks were very suited to a kind of in-place destruction the SEALs had prepared for.

. . . Blowing the stuff [supply cache] in place would just deny it to the enemy until they brought in a resupply. What we did was far more devious than any of those answers.

At that time there was a program going on back in the States to take care of these little caches we would find. I think the program was called POOR BOY but I may be mistaken about that. What the program did was manufacture enemy ordnance modified to explode when it was used. All sorts of things were made and packaged in regular Chicom and Russian packaging, B-40 rounds, mortar rounds, grenades, even small arms ammunition filled with explosives instead of propellant powder. By salting the caches with these materials we denied them to the enemy and screwed up his supply system at the same time.

Not all of the ammunition in the cases we placed was doctored. What the ratio was I don't know. But the VC could use the hidden supplies and suddenly notice that things were exploding when used. Rumors of that sort of thing happening would spread through the VC ranks like a disease. Personally, I thought it was a great way of attacking the problem.

Even if you took the stuff out in Chinooks, it seemed that all we did was store it for Charlie's later use. They would steal it back as they could. But salting the cache in place would frighten the VC into not using what they had. And the supply record keepers up in Hanoi or wherever would receive the requests from areas like the Seven Mountains and have supply dumps on their books. That would hold up any replacement material from coming in as soon as it could. Instead the supplies would be held as a "last resort" by the local commanders.

We had checked out the materials we were placing earlier. Setting up a VC mortar tube and dropping a salted round with a remote rig was all it took to convince us of the efficiency of the program. There was nothing left of the tube after the explosion which would have wiped out the crew and any VC who might have been nearby. Careful records had to be kept by us as to which caches we salted, but the results were worth the trouble.

CHINESE 82MM TYPE 53 HE (BOOBY TRAPPED)

This mortar round is an example of how munitions can be booby trapped and what their effect is. The Type 53 HE round is a Chinese produced copy of the Soviet Model 0-832DU 82mm fragmentation projectile. A pre—World War II design, the Type 53 is a simple, drop-fired mortar round with an impact fuze. When the round is dropped down the tube of the mortar, it strikes a fixed firing pin at the base of the tube. The firing pin sets off the round's ignition cartridge which in turn ignites any propellant increments. The sudden stop and reversing of direction of the mortar round when it is fired produces an action known as setback.

Setback takes place when inertia forces the moving parts of a fuze to effectively "stand still" while the rest of the fuze moves forward. Normally, this action is utilized to unlock the safety portions of the fuze. Since setback only occurs normally when a round is fired, using it to arm a fuze prepares the round to detonate on impact. Some form of pull-ring safety is manually removed before the round is fired, removing a mechanical safety that makes the round safe to transport and handle.

This is an oversimplification of what is a complex mechanism, but the modified Type 53 rounds planted by the SEALs used setback in a different way. Removing the manual safety pin would fully arm the fuze of a modified Type 53 round. When the booby trapped Type 53 round was fired, setback would detonate the round rather than simply arm it.

Quantities of the communist Type 53 round were found in supply caches in sufficient numbers to make their booby trap conversion a relatively simple thing. By using communist packaging and original ammunition, the conversion would be impossible to detect by simple examination. When the booby trapped round would be fired, it would not only fragment the body of the mortar round, the mortar tube would add its share of fragmentation to the explosion.

CHINESE TYPE 56—7.62MM INTERMEDIATE (BOOBY TRAPPED)

Early in the Vietnam War, the technique of booby trapping small arms ammunition was used by the SEALs to shake the VC's faith in their own supplies. The actual procedures used to booby trap the ammunition were simple and several SEALs made something of a production of it.

> We made all kinds of stuff to mess with the enemy. Such as taking the bullets out of 7.62 intermediate rounds [7.62×39mm] and replacing the powder with C4. After packing the casing full, we would replace the bullet. Leaving rounds like this in enemy ammunition caches could cause Charlie to distrust all of his ammo.

Ammunition thus treated could be taken out into the field with a SEAL squad and be salted into ammunition caches. A round of the booby trapped ammunition could even be placed inside of a magazine for an AK-47 or a ten-round clip for an SKS. The booby trapped feed devices would be left where VC scavengers would be able to find them and take them back into the supply system.

When one of the booby trapped rounds were fired in a weapon, the C-4 charge would detonate. Even a low-order detonation would far exceed the pressures acceptable to any small arm. Not only would the weapon be wrecked, but the man who pulled the trigger would be dead or at least very seriously wounded.

The booby trapped ammunition became so successful that it began to be produced in very limited numbers back in the United States. Careful control of such dangerous munitions kept them out of the hands of most troops. Even the knowledge of such ammunition was limited for security reasons.

Other booby trap items were produced for the SEALs back in the United States. A number of such items were designed and manufactured at the Naval Ordnance Center at China Lake. At China Lake, a number of kits were produced for use by the SEALs in Vietnam. The kits consisted of an otherwise innocuous item that had been modified for use as a booby trap. Modifications included fitting a fuze assembly into the device and making a cavity for the addition of an explosive charge. The kits were complete except for the addition of the explosive filler which was normally Composition C-4 explosive added by the user in the field.

A variety of fuzes were used in the booby trap kits. In some cases, the device had an option to use a special trembler fuze, sensitive to any movement whatsoever. When the device was left in place on a operation, a delay in the arming system allowed the safe withdrawal of the SEALs before the booby trap was fully armed. Very often when the trembler switch was used, there was no way to disarm the booby trap once the arming delay had expired.

Very little information is available on an unclassified level as to the extent of manufactured booby trap materials produced by China Lake during the Vietnam War. Enough anecdotal information is available to allow two of these devices to be described here.

FLASHLIGHT KIT—INSTAMATIC CAMERA KIT

On January 21, 1968, ADR2 Eugene Fraley of Seventh Platoon, SEAL Team Two, was killed when a booby trap he was assembling exploded in his hands. Fraley had been preparing a flashlight booby trap using a China Lake antidisturbance (trembler) switch. For safety, the booby trap was being assembled in a sandbag enclosure within the SEAL compound at My Tho. For some unknown reason, the booby trap exploded in Fraley's hands just after he had removed it from the enclosure.

It is possible that the trembler switch had been accidentally activated during assembly and, while it was being moved, detonated as soon as it armed. Use of a number of the China Lake devices was suspended after the incident pending a full investigation. The SEALs receive demolition pay for performing hazardous duties, sometimes the pay is earned at a very high level.

MODEL 308-5 FIRING DEVICE

China Lake also designed several booby trap firing devices for the Teams using an electrical system to initiate an explosive. The Model 308-5 firing device used several different types of trigger disturbances to activate the device including the breaking of a fine wire, opening a circuit (trigger switch), or disturbance of the system. The disturbance trigger is initiated by what is called a trembler switch.

A trembler switch is very sensitive to the slightest movement. Adjustable in design, trembler switches can be so sensitive that simply walking nearby can fire the system. Most often, a trembler is built to fire if the device containing it is moved or disturbed in any way after the system is armed. This sensitivity to movement makes it very important that a trembler system have an arming delay to give the operator a safe time to leave the area.

The arming delay in the Model 308-5 device is from 75 to 85 seconds, after which the device cannot be disarmed until the batteries run down. The batteries in the Model 308-5 have an operational life of about 2 months when fresh. High humidity and temperature both can cut the battery life significantly. When set up, the Model 308-5 device can fire up to four M6 blasting caps wired in series or in parallel.

Though waterproof for transport at a depth of down to 70 feet (21.3 m), the Model 308-5 firing device must be used in a dry condition. Several different types of pressure switches were issued with the Model 308-5, with the most unusual being the bathmat. The bathmat switch resembles a small green mat that contains a pressure switch effective through most of the surface of the mat. When properly placed and camouflaged, the green colored mat would trigger the Model 308-5 firing device as soon as it had been stepped on with sufficient pressure. This type of trigger was found most useful for paths and areas around known supply caches. Limited numbers of the Model 308-5 firing device were produced by China Lake during the Vietnam War and their effectiveness in the field was well established by the SEALs.

MODEL 308-6 FIRING DEVICE

Another firing device for setting booby traps in Vietnam was the Model 308-6 firing device. The Model 308-6 had all of the features of the Model 308-5 firing

device and worked in exactly the same way. The major difference in the two firing devices was that an optional clock timer was available for the Model 308-6.
An additional difference was in their effective life in the field. The self-
contained battery of the Model 308-5 had an operational life of only 2 months
or less. The Model 308-6 has an operational battery life of approximately two
years, depending on temperature exposure.

Though very long-lived, the battery output of the Model 308-6 will still fire
a maximum of four M6 blasting caps wired in series or parallel.

The clock timer option for the Model 308-6 has a variable delay of from 5
minutes to 23.5 hours. The arming delay of the Model 308-6 device is also 75 to
85 seconds as the Model 308-6 also has an antidisturbance trembler fuze.

The Model 308-6 was the most successful of the China Lake booby trap
fuzes developed during the Vietnam War. Several hundred of the fuzes were
produced and used not only by the SEALs and UDTs, but were also supplied to
the Army Special Forces. Limited production of the Model 308-6 firing device
was underway by late 1968.

DEMOLITION EQUIPMENT AND FIRING DEVICES

Many tools and equipment used for demolition work are of a very prosaic nature. Folding pocket knives, pliers, and other items are used on a constant basis.
Some tools are made of special nonsparking alloys to prevent accidents when
working with volatile explosives. One special tool is used only for demolition
operations and for working with explosives in general—the cap crimper.

M2 CAP CRIMPERS

M2 cap crimpers resemble a pair of pliers with one leg having a point and the
other a flat screwdriver end. The jaws of the crimpers have two openings. The
outer opening will not close completely and will crimp a blasting cap around
time blasting fuse or detonating cord.

The crimp formed by the M2 tool is a completely circular type which is
water-resistant. The circular crimp identifies the M2 crimper as the "cutthroat"
style of crimpers known to civilian pre–World War II blasters. The rear opening
in the jaw is for cleanly cutting time fuze or detonating cord. Using the cutters
results in a clean, squared-off cut on the end of the line, best suited for insertion
into blasting caps or igniters. The pointed leg of the crimpers is used to punch
holes in explosive charges sized to accept a military blasting cap.

Cap crimpers are made of a relatively soft, nonsparking metal alloy which
conducts electricity. Early World War II manufactured M2s were made of steel

but they have been purged from the supply system and replaced with nonsparking models. The M2 crimpers are only used for cutting fuze and detonating cord or crimping caps. The same M2 crimper design has been in use with the Teams and the military in general since the first days of World War II. The simple and effective design of the tool will probably keep the M2 crimpers in the hands of SEALs well into the next century.

One of the problems Naval Special Warfare has with operating in a marine environment is in attaching explosive charges to a target in the water. In the case of large obstacles, charges could be simply tied or even hung on the target with a strap. In the case of limpet attacks on ships and other targets, the use of magnets has proven to be the easiest approach. But not all ships' hulls are built of magnetic materials. In the past, wooden hulls would prove the occasional problem and today these same problems show up in the fiberglass and occasional ferroconcrete hulls in use.

Adhesives have proven to be something of an answer. But many adhesives lose much of their advantage in the water. Just a wet target surface can defeat many of the adhesives in use. Some special demolition adhesives have proven very valuable. But even these had difficulty adhering to a slick fiberglass hull. One innovative solution to an underwater adhesive came about from a suggestion put forward by an operator to an explosives engineer.

The idea was that since the problem was making a charge adhere to a slick hull while in the water, why not use an adhesive designed just for use in the water? An adhesive that also held firmly to slick porcelain surfaces. The material in question was a commercial dental adhesive used to secure dentures. Advertising suggested the adhesive would work in an aquatic environment, even in extremes of temperature.

The engineer considered the suggestion and purchased a popular product at a local drug store. Several charges were stuck to a test hull with the adhesive and left in the water for an extended time. Twenty-four hours later, the charges were still stuck in place. This is not a product endorsement likely to be used by the manufacturer. But the SEALs were satisfied with a very creative answer to a rather sticky problem.

During World War II, limpet attacks by saboteurs dictated that a simple and quick method was needed to attach the explosive charges to a target hull with as little noise as possible. Maritime units would operate from small boats and slip up to a target ship's hull in the darkness. The limpet would be prepared and emplaced quickly before the small boat could be noticed. Magnets proved satisfactory against most steel hulls but wooden hulls needed another form of attachment. Badly corroded or barnacled steel hulls also did not accept the magnetic limpets very strongly.

A limpet attachment device called the "pin-up" was developed and put into production by mid-1944. The pin-up device would fire a nail-like projectile into a wooden or steel hull when a safety ring was pulled. Pin-up worked well with two models being available, one loaded for wooden targets, the other for steel targets.

Pin-up operated by a striker assembly being released and firing a small propellant charge. The charge would launch a steel pin into thetarget like a projectile. Placed at the end of a long rod, pin-up could secure a limpet against a ship's hull quickly and covertly. The sound of firing the pin-up was not noticeable by crewmen aboard the target ship, but concern was voiced about possible damage to a swimmer's ears. It was decided that the danger of damage to a swimmer's ears was small, especially if the swimmer wore earplugs. Pin-up was accepted and put into full production.

MARK 22 DRIVER

Well after World War II had ended, the problem of attaching demolitions underwater remained. The idea of having swimmers wear earplugs had been completely abandoned, water pressure alone could drive earplugs into the ear canal dangerously deep. The idea of the pin-up device was combined with captured-piston technology and the Mk 22 power actuated projectile unit driver was developed.

The Mk 22 driver is a single-shot explosive-driven fastener. The Mk 2 Mod 0 powder actuated stud cartridge that the Mk 22 is loaded with contains all the active material needed for use. The Mk 2 stud cartridge contains a pusher piston, stud, primer, and propellant powder contained within a steel case that also acts as the barrel of the launcher. The firing pin assembly is held in place by a trigger mechanism that is locked in place with a safety pin and arming tab.

To use the Mk 22, the safety pin and arming tab must first be removed. When the trigger button in depressed, the firing pin is released, setting off the propellant charge. The propellant gasses drive the pusher piston to the end of the barrel where it is retained in place. The trapped piston holds the propellant gasses in place within the barrel. Since the gasses cannot leave the barrel, there is little noise and no injuring muzzle blast to contend with.

The projectile is driven out of the barrel by the propellant charge and drives itself deeply into steel, wood, or concrete. The driver is designed to operate on land or at depths of up to 200 feet (61 m) underwater. The main purpose of the

Mk 22 driver is to fasten demolition charges to a variety of targets and obstacles. The Mk 22 is not reloadable and is discarded after being fired.

MARK 12, MARK 15 FIRING DEVICES

An emplaced demolition charge needs a dependable time delay to give the combat swimmers who armed it time to withdraw to a safe distance. Designed during World War II, the Mark 12 and Mark 15 demolition firing devices are clockwork timers with spring-driven firing pins. By screwing a coupling base onto the bottom of the firing devices, a nonelectric blasting cap, time fuze, or detonating cord initiator can be fired with a mechanical delay. After the adjustable time delay has expired, the firing pin is released by the internal mechanism of the Mk 12 and 15 devices. The firing pin in turn sets off the primer cap in the coupling base, sending a spit of flame out the coupling's snout.

Both the Mk 12 and Mk 15 firing devices have a cylindrical body with a knurled cap. The cap can be rotated by hand to line up the desired time delay according to the increments marked on the cap. Once the time delay has been set and the coupling base and initiator installed, the Mk 12 and Mk 15 firing devices are ready for use.

The only difference between the Mk 12 and Mk 15 devices is in the amount of time delay offered by each device. The Mk 12 has a time delay from 5 to 92 seconds and the Mk 15 delay is adjustable from 15 minutes to 11 hours. Both firing devices can be used underwater to a depth of 25 feet (7.6 m) and are expected to operate with 5 percent of their time setting. Once the device is set, pulling the safety pin is all that is required to start the delay. When the pin is pulled, an arming pin protrudes outward from the body of the Mk 12 and 15. Once the arming pin has moved, the timer cannot be stopped or the time setting changed.

MARK 23 MOD 1 FIRING DEVICE

The Mark 23 Mod 1 firing device is a clockwork delay nonelectric firing device with a operator variable time setting. A wide base on the Mk 23 has a knurled edge and is easily removable. In the center of the removable base is a standard threaded firing device base with a crimping snout. A short piece of rubber tubing over the snout helps ensure a watertight seal when a blasting cap is crimped onto the device.

The entire action of the Mk 23 is mechanical except the final firing of the Mk 125 percussion primer. The Mk 23 is effectively a very improved version of the World War II vintage Mk 12 and Mk 15 timers. The fairly large body of the

Mk 23 has a small window at one end where the internal delay settings can be seen. The settings are drawn in luminous paint so they can be seen in very low-light conditions.

At the same end of the Mk 23 as the window is the time selector knob and the arming pin and ring. The selector knob has detents inside the device that allows the operator to hear and feel the number of clicks he is setting the delay to. The time delay on the Mk 23 ranges from 15 minutes to 12 hours in twenty-five different settings. Once the time is set and the charge is in place, removing the arming pin sets the delay into motion. Once the arming pin has been removed, the shaft the time selector knob is on retracts into the casing a short distance. When the shaft is retracted, the arming pin cannot be reinserted or the delay setting changed.

Completely waterproof, the Mk 23 firing device can be operated on dry land or at depths of up to 200 feet (61 m). The Mk 23 firing device is a component of the Mk 1 limpet mine and is also available as a separate item for use in general demolitions.

MARK 48 MOD 0 DEMOLITION FIRING DEVICE

The Mk 48 firing device has an electronic delay system that electrically fires a Mk 96 detonator when the delay has expired. The Mk 48 is the same diameter but slightly longer than the Mk 23 firing device. The general operating characteristics of the two firing devices is the same with the adjustable time delay able to be set by the operator at the target.

Prior to employment, a fresh battery has to be installed inside the Mk 48. Once the body of the device is tightly sealed, the entire system is protected from stray electromagnetic radiation causing a premature firing of the detonator. At the base of the Mk 48 is a standard coupling covered by a protective cap. A blasting cap or another initiator can be crimped onto the coupling base or the Mk 48 can be screwed onto another device.

The delay settings on the Mk 48 are visible at the top of the device as four large dots each marked with the delay for that setting in hours or fractions of an hour. A large knob at the top of the Mk 48 is rotated to choose the delay setting desired and the knob retainer pushed in. Prior to deployment, the Mk 48 can be time-tested to insure its proper functioning.

To arm the Mk 48, the lanyard assembly at the top of the device is removed along with the attached arming pin. Once the arming pin is removed, a spring-loaded shaft retracts into the casing and the delay begins. Once armed, the Mk 48 cannot be disarmed or the delay setting changed.

The Mk 48 is normally used with the Mk 39 safety and arming device as the explosive initiator. Completely waterproof, the Mk 48 can be used on dry land or underwater to initiate explosive charges, pyrotechnics, or other devices. The Mk 48 is a component part of the Mk 1 limpet mine system and the Mk 5 modular limpet mine assembly (LMA).

MARK 39 MOD 0 SAFETY AND ARMING DEVICE

The Mark 39 safety and arming (S&A) device is designed to add a positive safety system to an explosive train that would otherwise not have one. The cylindrical body of the Mk 39 has a threaded well at one end to accept a standard firing device such as the Mk 23 or Mk 48. Inside of the Mk 39 is an explosive train with a detonator held out of line by a mechanical cam.

Even if the firing device screwed into the activator well of the Mk 39 should fire, if the detonator inside the Mk 39 is out of line, the explosive train is broken and will not fire. The detonator inside of the Mk 39 is a Mk 43 model and the explosive lead is a charge of Composition H-6. The Composition H-6 lead extends outward from the base of the Mk 39 for 2.5 inches. The head of the explosive lead is threaded for insertion into a standard activator well.

On the side of the Mk 39 is a large safety plug and pull ring. The safety plug is a positive safety and is colored red for easy identification. Once the safety plug is removed, the arming pin can be pulled. When the arming pin is pulled, the system is activated and cannot be disarmed.

Removing the arming pin releases the spring-loaded piston that holds the Mk 43 detonator. The piston moves inward enough to initiate the mechanical delay but not far enough to line up the detonator with the explosive train. The 10 to 15 minute arming delay is controlled by a mechanical timer. Once the delay has expired, a cam moves the Mk 43 detonator in line with the explosive train and the train is no longer safe.

Though waterproof, the Mk 39 is sensitive to water pressure. The device has to be armed at a depth of less than 60 feet (18.3 m) to assure proper functioning. After actuation, the Mk 39 can be used at depths of down to 240 feet (73.1 m). This requirement allows the Mk 39 S&A device to be released and functioned before another firing device is actuated. The Mk 39 S&A device can be used with a number of firing devices and is a component part of the Mk 1 limpet mine family and the Mk 5 modular limpet mine assembly.

The most recent and sophisticated firing system used by the Teams involves a radio controlled command detonation system. It was not until the Vietnam War that a dependable radio controlled remote firing device became a practical matter. Major difficulties with a radio system center on making the system small enough to be transportable, have enough range to be practical, and be safe enough for field use.

The last problem has some unique characteristics when using a radio firing device. A firing order transmitted as a simple signal does not have the security needed to be safe for use. Any stray radio signal in the same frequency could detonate an unsophisticated receiver firing device. Circuitry developments in the 1960s helped eliminate this problem.

MODEL 3801-308-4 REMOTE FIRING DEVICE

The Model 3801-308-4 system is a development from the China Lake Naval Ordnance Center intended for the SEALs and UDT units operating in Vietnam. The purpose of the remote firing device is to give the operators a stand-off capability when firing explosive charges. By using a radio signal rather than a hard-line system, the explosive charge can be detonated on command at a much greater range than would be practical to lay a wire.

The remote firing device consists of a radio transmitter and receiver system using a pulsed code as a firing signal. The number of pulsed codes available for the system, which uses two frequencies, is 2,048 possible combinations. The broad number of possible pulse combinations greatly eliminates the possibility of a stray signal detonating the charge. The pulse codes also prevent any easy detonation of the system by any unauthorized personnel.

The Model 3801-308-4 system has a range of 5 miles (8 km) ground-to-ground with a clear line of sight over normal open terrain. Any vegetation or other blockages to the line of sight limits the range of the transmitter just as in any other radio system. Firing the system with the transmitter in an aircraft greatly increases the effective range. To simplify operator use, a code plug furnished with the firing receiver must be inserted into the transmitter for the proper signal for that particular receiver to be generated.

As an additional safety, the receiver has a variable arming time able to be set by the operator. The arming time can range from 1 to 60 minutes. After the delay has expired, the system is armed and the receiver will detonate the charge upon reception of the proper signal. The receiver can fire up to ten electrical blasting caps wired in series. Batteries in the receiver give it an active field life of 14 days.

Though the system is not itself waterproof, the transmitter and receivers come packaged in a watertight container for transport. Twelve receivers and four transmitters were sent to Vietnam in 1968 and were well received by the men in the field. A limited pilot production program of the system was initiated in late 1968.

MARK 30 RADIO FIRING DEVICE

Several new firing systems using radio signals were developed in the post-Vietnam period specifically for use by the SEALs and UDTs. The Mark 30 radio firing device is a receiver unit used with the Mk 100 radio firing device control (transmitter). Distances and safety have been improved in the Mk 30 system over the earlier units used in Vietnam. The Mk 100 transmitter, which should be at least 600 feet away from the Mk 30, has a range of at least 5 miles under normal circumstances.

The receiver of the Mk 30 is a crystal-controlled superheterodyne system that accepts one of the 32 available coded signals put out by the Mk 100 transmitter. The complexity of the coded signal is such that it is very difficult for any accidental triggering of the receiver from any possible stray signal.

The Mk 30 itself is a cylindrical device with a 5-foot flexible wire antenna. The circuitry of the Mk 30 is solidly contained inside the cylinder body and is completely waterproof and sealed from outside contamination. The device is powered by four standard D-sized alkaline batteries that give the system an operational life of 14 days. The power output of the firing circuit is sufficient to fire ten series-connected M6 blasting caps through 1,000 feet of No. 18 AWG blasting wire.

For added safety, the Mk 30 has a delay arming system with a variable delay that can be set by the operator. The safety system blocks the firing circuit from receiving any signal until the arming delay has expired. The ten different delay times have an accuracy of 0 and 20 percent of the time indicated.

The Mk 30 is not itself waterproof when set up for firing. Sealed in its aluminum transport cylinder, the Mk 30 is waterproof to a depth of 240 feet (73 m). Though the system cannot be set up for use below the surface of the water, the firing lines leading from the Mk 30 can be led underwater to a properly prepared explosive charge. The Mk 30 receiver/Mk 100 transmitter system is one of the older systems in use by the Teams and is already being supplanted by even more sophisticated technology.

EXPLOSIVES (ENERGETIC MATERIALS)

DEXTRINATED LEAD AZIDE

TYPE Primary explosive

COLOR White to buff

STATE Crystalline powder

INITIATOR Flame or shock

DETONATION VELOCITY 17,700 fps (5,400 m/s) at a density of 4.68 g per ml

COMPOSITION 93% lead azide, 4% lead hydroxide, 3% dextrin

SENSITIVITY Extremely sensitive to heat, friction, and shock

USE Primer charge in blasting caps over a base charge of RDX or PETN

TNT

TYPE High explosive

COLOR Straw yellow to yellowish brown

STATE Flaked granular or crystalline solid

INITIATOR 0.26 g lead azide (minimum)

DETONATION VELOCITY 22,200 fps (6,767 m/s) at a density of 1.6 g per ml

COMPOSITION Trinitrotoluene

SENSITIVITY Very insensitive to heat, friction, and shock, melts and burns when heated, less than 2% chance of detonation when struck by a .30 caliber rifle bullet

RELATIVE EFFECTIVENESS [TNT = 1.0] 1.0

USE Demolition blocks, common general explosive filler

RDX (RESEARCH DEPARTMENT FORMULA X)

TYPE High explosive

COLOR White

STATE Crystalline solid

INITIATOR 0.05 g lead azide (minimum)

DETONATION VELOCITY 27,000 fps (8,230 m/s) at a density of 1.6 g per ml

COMPOSITION Cyclotrimethylenetrinitramine

SENSITIVITY Sensitive to heat, friction, and shock in its pure state, 100% chance of detonation when struck by a .30 caliber rifle bullet

RELATIVE EFFECTIVENESS [TNT = 1.0] 1.60

USE Very powerful military explosive. Primarily used as a component of explosive mixtures. Also used as a base charge in blasting caps

PETN

TYPE High explosive

COLOR White (when pure) Light gray w/wax and impurities

STATE Fine crystalline or granular powder

INITIATOR 0.03 g lead azide

DETONATION VELOCITY 26,000 fps (7,925 m/s) at a density of 1.6 g per ml

COMPOSITION Pentaerythrite tetranitrate

SENSITIVITY Very sensitive to heat, friction, and impact, 100% chance of detonation when struck by a .30 caliber rifle bullet,

becomes insensitive to heat when loaded in Primacord
RELATIVE EFFECTIVENESS [TNT = 1.0] 1.45
USE Primacord

AN

TYPE High explosive
COLOR White
STATE Crystalline powder
INITIATOR Requires TNT or other high explosive booster to detonate
DETONATION VELOCITY 9,200 fps (2,800 m/s) at a density of 1.0 g per ml
COMPOSITION Ammonium nitrate
SENSITIVITY Very insensitive to heat, friction, and shock, less than 1% chance of detonation when struck by a .30 caliber rifle bullet, difficult to initiate
RELATIVE EFFECTIVENESS [TNT = 1.0] 0.42
USE Cratering charge, component in explosive mixtures.

TETRYL

TYPE High explosive
COLOR Colorless when fresh, turns yellow when exposed to light, gray when loaded due to graphite lubricant
STATE Fine crystalline powder
INITIATOR 0.10 g lead azide
DETONATION VELOCITY 24,600 fps (7,498 m/s) at a density of 1.6 g per ml
COMPOSITION Trinitrophenylmethylnitramine
SENSITIVITY Somewhat sensitive to heat, friction, and shock, 70% chance of detonation when struck by a .30 caliber rifle bullet, may be ignited by a spark
RELATIVE EFFECTIVENESS [TNT = 1.0] 1.28
USE Base charge in detonators and boosters, component in explosive mixtures

TETRYTOL

TYPE High-explosive mixture
COLOR Yellow
STATE Solid

INITIATOR 0.23 g lead azide
DETONATION VELOCITY 23,900 fps (7,285 m/s) at a density of 1.6 g per ml
COMPOSITION 70% Tetryl, 30% TNT
SENSITIVITY Slightly more sensitive to heat, friction, and shock than TNT, 30% chance of detonation when struck by a .30 caliber rifle bullet
RELATIVE EFFECTIVENESS [TNT = 1.0] 1.22
USE M1 Chain demolition charge, filler for shaped charges

PENTOLITE

TYPE High-explosive mixture
COLOR White, gray, or yellow
STATE Solid
INITIATOR 0.13 g lead azide
DETONATION VELOCITY 24,300 fps (7,402 m/s) at a density of 1.62 g per ml
COMPOSITION 50% PETN, 50% TNT
SENSITIVITY Somewhat sensitive to heat, friction, and shock, 80% chance of detonation when struck by a .30 caliber rifle bullet
RELATIVE EFFECTIVENESS [TNT = 1.0] 1.26
USE Cast in shaped charges for demolitions, rockets, and shells

COMPOSITION A-3 (A-4)

TYPE High-explosive mixture
COLOR Buff
STATE Soft granular semisolid
INITIATOR 0.25 G lead azide
DETONATION VELOCITY 26,600 fps (8,100 m/s) at a density of 1.59g per ml
COMPOSITION A-3—91% RDX, 9% petroleum wax; A-4—97% RDX, 3% petroleum wax
SENSITIVITY Very insensitive to heat, friction, and shock, 0% chance of detonation when struck by a .30 caliber rifle bullet
RELATIVE EFFECTIVENESS [TNT = 1.0] 1.35
USE Mk 8 Mod 2 Explosive hose filler (mixed w/aluminum), primary filler for HEP projec-

tiles. Composition A-4 is the explosive filler for the Mk 211 .50 caliber projectile

COMPOSITION B

TYPE High-explosive mixture
COLOR Yellow-brown
STATE Solid
INITIATOR 0.17 g lead azide
DETONATION VELOCITY 25,400 fps (7,742 m/s) at a density of 1.7 g per ml
COMPOSITION 59.5% RDX, 39.5% TNT, 1% wax
SENSITIVITY Somewhat sensitive to heat, friction, and shock, 15% chance of detonation when struck by a .30 caliber rifle bullet
RELATIVE EFFECTIVENESS [TNT = 1.0] 1.35
USE Explosive filler for many different kinds of ordnance

COMPOSITION C2

TYPE High-explosive mixture
COLOR Brown
STATE Plastic solid
INITIATOR 0.20 g lead azide (est.)
DETONATION VELOCITY 25,000 fps (7,620 m/s) at a density of 1.6 g per ml
COMPOSITION 80% RDX, 20% explosive plasticizer composed of mononitrotoluene and a liquid mixture of dinitrotoluenes, TNT, nitrocellulose, and dimethylformamide
SENSITIVITY Relatively insensitive to friction, and shock, 40% chance of detonation when struck by a .30 caliber rifle bullet (est.), breaks down when exposed to hot conditions, leaking plasticizer and leaving sensitive crystalline RDX
RELATIVE EFFECTIVENESS [TNT = 1.0] 1.34 (est.)
USE General demolition explosive

COMPOSITION C3

TYPE High-explosive mixture
COLOR Yellow to brown
STATE Plastic solid
INITIATOR 0.20 g lead azide
DETONATION VELOCITY 25,000 fps (7,620 m/s) at a density of 1.6 g per ml
COMPOSITION 73% RDX, 23% explosive plasticizer composed of mononitrotoluene and a liquid mixture of Tetryl, TNT, dinitrotoluenes, and nitrocellulose
SENSITIVITY Less sensitive to heat, friction, and shock than TNT, 40% chance of partial (low order) detonation when struck by a .30 caliber rifle bullet
RELATIVE EFFECTIVENESS [TNT = 1.0] 1.34
USE General demolition explosive

COMPOSITION C4

TYPE High-explosive mixture
COLOR White
STATE Plastic solid
INITIATOR 0.20 g lead azide
DETONATION VELOCITY 26,500 fps (8,077 m/s) at a density of 1.6 g per ml
COMPOSITION 91% RDX, 2.10% Polyisobutylene, 1.60% SAE 10 motor oil, 5.30% Di-(2-ethylhexyl) sebacate
SENSITIVITY Insensitive to heat, friction, and shock, 0% chance of detonation when struck by a .30 caliber rifle bullet
RELATIVE EFFECTIVENESS [TNT = 1.0] 1.34
USE General demolition explosive

HBX-1 (HIGH BLAST EXPLOSIVE, TYPE 1)

TYPE High-explosive mixture
COLOR Slate gray
STATE Grainy solid
INITIATOR 13.5 grains RDX or PETN (special blasting cap)
DETONATION VELOCITY 23,700 fps (7,224 m/s) at a density of 1.75 g per ml
COMPOSITION 40.4% RDX, 37.8% TNT, 17.1% aluminum, 4.7% wax and lecithin

SENSITIVITY Slightly sensitive to heat, friction, and shock, 75% chance of detonation when struck by a .30 caliber rifle bullet

RELATIVE EFFECTIVENESS [TNT = 1.0] 1.48 in air, 1.68 underwater

USE Underwater ordnance (torpedoes, mines, depth charges), general demolition charges

HBX-3 (HIGH BLAST EXPLOSIVE, TYPE 3)

TYPE High-explosive mixture

COLOR Slate gray

STATE Grainy solid

INITIATOR 13.5 grains RDX or PETN (special blasting cap)

DETONATION VELOCITY 22,700 fps (6,920 m/s) at a density of 1.86 g per ml

COMPOSITION 31.3% RDX, 29.0% TNT, 34.8% aluminum, 4.9% wax and lecithin

SENSITIVITY Slightly sensitive to heat, friction, and shock, 80% chance of detonation when struck by a .30 caliber rifle bullet

RELATIVE EFFECTIVENESS [TNT = 1.0] 1.48 in air, 1.88 underwater

USE Underwater ordnance (torpedoes, mines, depth charges), general demolition charges

H-6

TYPE High-explosive mixture

COLOR Gray

STATE Grainy solid

INITIATOR

DETONATION VELOCITY 23,590 fps (7190 m/s) at a density of 1.71 g per ml

COMPOSITION 41.5% RDX, 29.2% Aluminum, 21.0% Wax and lecithin

SENSITIVITY Slightly sensitive to heat, friction, and shock

RELATIVE EFFECTIVENESS [TNT = 1.0] 1.48 in air, 1.68 underwater

USE Demolition charges Mk 70 Mod 0 and Mk 36 Mod 1 and various underwater explosive devices

DETASHEET C (DUPONT)

TYPE Flexible explosive

COLOR Olive drab

STATE Flexible rubberlike solid

INITIATOR 6.8 grains PETN (#8 detonator)

DETONATION VELOCITY 23,000 fps (7,000 m/s) at a density of 1.48 g per ml

COMPOSITION 63% PETN

SENSITIVITY Very insensitive to heat, friction, and shock, 0% chance of detonation when struck by a .30 caliber rifle bullet

RELATIVE EFFECTIVENESS [tnt = 1.0] 1.14

USE General demolitions

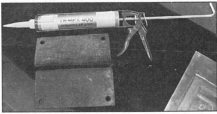

Source: Kevin Dockery

DEMEX 400

TYPE Extrudable high explosive

COLOR Light green

STATE Plastic solid

INITIATOR Standard military blasting cap

DETONATION VELOCITY 26,200 fps (8,000 m/s) at a density of 1.6 g per ml

COMPOSITION 86% RDX, 14% plasticizer/binder

SENSITIVITY Very insensitive to heat, friction, and shock, 0% chance of detonation when struck by a .30 caliber rifle bullet

RELATIVE EFFECTIVENESS [TNT = 1.0] 1.40 (est.)

USE Issued in a 1.1 lb (0.5 kg) caulking-gun cartridge or 0.55 lb (0.25 kg) and 0.28 lb (0.125 kg) tubes. Extremely flexible

DEMOLITION CHARGES

½, 1, AND 8 LB TNT BLOCKS

TYPE General demolition bulk explosive charges

IDENTIFYING COLOR CODE Olive drab container w/yellow markings

CONTAINER MATERIAL ½ & 1 lb blocks—Cardboard w/sheet metal end caps; 8 lb block—Waterproof barrier material

FILLER TNT

PACKAGING ½ lb blocks—100 per wooden box; 1 lb blocks—50 per wooden box; 8 lb—8 per wooden box

METHOD OF ACTUATION Blasting cap or primacord

WEIGHTS

Package ½ & 1 lb blocks—71.5 lbs (32.43 kg); 8 lb blocks—85 lbs (38.56 kg)

LENGTHS

Length ½ lb block—3.63 in (9.2 cm); 1 lb block—7 in (17.8 cm); 8 lb block—12 in (30.5 cm)

Width ½ & 1 lb blocks—1.88 in (4.8 cm), 8 lb block—6 in (15.2 cm)

Height ½ & 1 lb blocks—1.88 in (4.8 cm); 8 lb block—2 in (5.1 cm)

USE All forms of general demolitions especially as a cutting or breaching charge. Usable in underwater operations without special preparation

40 LB CRATERING DEMOLITION CHARGE

TYPE Packaged demolition charge

IDENTIFYING COLOR CODE Olive drab container w/yellow markings

CONTAINER MATERIAL Sheet steel

FILLER Ammonium nitrate w/TNT booster

PACKAGING 1 per wooden box

METHOD OF ACTUATION Military blasting cap or primacord

WEIGHTS

Unit 43 lbs (19.5 kg)

Filler Ammonium nitrate 30 lbs (13.61 kg); TNT 10 lbs (4.54 kg)

Package 70 lbs (31.75 kg)

EFFECTS

Effect Breaks up and moves earth and rock with a heaving rather than shattering force

Area of effect One charge buried 4 feet deep will make a crater 6 feet deep and approximately 20 feet across

LENGTHS

Length 17 in (43.2 cm)

Width (diameter) 8.25 in (21 cm)

USE Cratering, earth moving, and quarrying

M112 DEMOLITION CHARGE

TYPE General demolition bulk explosive

IDENTIFYING COLOR CODE Olive drab or clear (old mfg) w/black markings

CONTAINER MATERIAL Mylar plastic w/adhesive strip

FILLER C4

PACKAGING M112 charge—One 1.25 lb block of C4 in a mylar plastic bag w/covered adhesive strip on one side; 30 M112 charges per wooden box or; M183 Demolition charge—16 M112 blocks per M85 canvas satchel w/four M15 priming assemblies (62.0 in [157.5 cm] Primacord with a blasting cap on each end), two M183 charges per wooden box

METHOD OF ACTUATION Military blasting cap or primacord

WEIGHTS

Unit M112 block—1.25 lbs (0.57 kg); M183 Demolition charge—23 lbs (10.43 kg)

Filler M112—1.25 lbs (0.57 kg); M183 Demolition charge—20 lbs (9.07 kg) w/o priming assemblies

Package M112 blocks—47 lbs (21.32 kg); M183 Demolition charges—57 lbs (25.85 kg)

LENGTHS

Length M112 block—11.25 in (28.6 cm);
M183 Demolition charge—10.25 in (26 cm)

Width (diameter) M112 block—2.06 in (5.2 cm); M183 Demolition charge—4.88 in (12.4 cm)

Height M112 block—1.06 in (2.7 cm); M183 Demolition charge—12.75 in (32.4 cm)

USE All forms of general demolitions especially as a cutting or breaching charge. Usable in underwater operations without special preparation

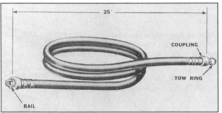

Source: U.S. Navy

MK 8 MODS 0 & 3 FLEXIBLE LINEAR DEMOLITION CHARGE (EXPLOSIVE HOSE)

TYPE General demolition charge

IDENTIFYING COLOR CODE Black hose

CONTAINER MATERIAL Flexible rubberized fabric hose w/metal end pieces

FILLER Mod 0—Flexed (broken) TNT
Mod 3—70/30 mixture of Composition A-3 & aluminum

PACKAGING Mod 3—The body is made up of a length of fabric reinforced rubber hose filled with Composition A-3/aluminum. The metal cap on the male end of the hose is a snap ring/ball joint fitted with a towing ring. Inside the male end is a Mk 12 Mod 0 TNT booster. At the opposite end is an snap ring/ball female joint fitted with a metal cap with an activator well. The activator well will accept a blasting cap or other standard firing device. The female end of the hose contains a Mk 8 Mod 0 TNT booster. Mod 0—Effectively the same

as the Mod 3 except the end caps are externally (male) and internally (female) threaded rather than fitted with snap ring/ball quick-action joints; Mod 0—packaged in bundles of 3; Mod 3—packaged 7 per wooden box

METHOD OF ACTUATION Military blasting cap or Primacord

WEIGHTS

Unit 75 lbs (34 kg)

Filler Main charge 50 lbs (22.68 kg); Mk 8 Mod 0 booster 0.17 lbs (0.08 kg); Mk 12 Mod 0 booster 0.17 lbs (0.08 kg)

Package Mod 0—225 lbs (102 kg)

LENGTHS

Length 25 ft (7.62 m)

Width (diameter) 2 in (5.1 cm)

USE General demolitions and obstacle clearing especially clearing channels through coral reefs

Source: Kevin Dockery

FLEXIBLE EXPLOSIVE SHEET DEMOLITION CHARGE (DETASHEET)

TYPE General demolition explosive

IDENTIFYING COLOR CODE Olive drab w/black markings

FILLER PETN or RDX depending on manufacturer

PACKAGING PETN or RDX explosive bound

with a rubber binder to make a flexible sheet; 10 (25.4 cm) by 20 (50.8 cm) inch sheets or 10-inch-wide rolls, length dependent on thickness

METHOD OF ACTUATION Military blasting cap or primacord

RELATIVE EFFECTIVENESS [TNT = 1.0] 1.14

WEIGHTS & LENGTHS

THICKNESS	WT PER 20 IN (50.8 CM)	ROLL LENGTH
0.043 in (1.09 mm)	0.44 lbs (0.20 kg)	76 ft (23.16 m)
0.083 in (2.11 mm)	0.88 lbs (0.40 kg)	50 ft (15.24 m)
0.125 in (3.18 mm)	1.38 lbs (0.63 kg)	38 ft (11.58 m)
0.166 in (4.22 mm)	1.75 lbs (0.79 kg)	19 ft (5.79 m)
0.208 in (5.28 mm)	2.25 lbs (1.02 kg)	15 ft (4.57 m)
0.250 in (6.35 mm)	2.69 lbs (1.22 kg)	13 ft (3.96 m)
0.291 in (7.39 mm)	3.13 lbs (1.42 kg)	11 ft (3.35 m)
0.333 in (8.46 mm)	3.56 lbs (1.61 kg)	9 ft (2.74 m)

USE General demolitions especially precision metal cutting using saddle, diamond, and ribbon charges. Cut sections can be attached to a target or other explosive sections with adhesive. Detasheet may be easily cut with a fixed-blade knife but the use of scissors is not recommended.

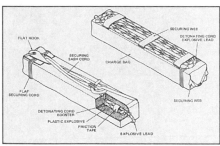

Source: Kevin Dockery

MK 20 MODS 0 & 1 DEMOLITION CHARGE (HAGENSEN PACK)

TYPE General underwater demolition charge

IDENTIFYING COLOR CODE Gray cloth bag

CONTAINER MATERIAL Canvas (cotton) treated to be waterproof, fireproof, and mildew resistant

    ̃ Mod 0—C3 (C2 in early WWII pro-
      ̃n charges) Mod 1—C4

PACKAGING Mk 20 charge—One 2 lb C2, C3, or C4 block, in a canvas bag w/11 feet (3.35 m) of Primacord. 5 ft of primacord is looped to make a 1 ft booster core, the remaining 6 feet are loose making an explosive lead. Each charge has a 3.5 ft length of sash cord with a flat steel hook for securing the charge to an obstacle. The sash cord and Primacord lead are secured to opposite sides on the outside of the charge under webbing loops

METHOD OF ACTUATION Military blasting cap or primacord

WEIGHTS

Unit 2.97 lbs (1.35 kg)

Filler 2 lbs (0.91 kg)

LENGTHS

Length 12 in (30.5 cm)

Width (diameter) 2.25 in (5.7 cm)

Height 1.5 in (3.8 cm)

USE General underwater demolition especially against obstacles during combat. Component part of Mk 127 and Mk 135 Demolition charges

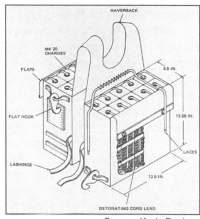

Source: Kevin Dockery

MK 127 MOD 0 DEMOLITION CHARGE

TYPE General underwater demolition charge assembly

IDENTIFYING COLOR CODE Gray haversack bag w/black markings

CONTAINER MATERIAL Cotton canvas treated to be waterproof, fireproof, and mildew resistant

FILLER C2 (early WWII production only) or C3

PACKAGING Mk 1 Mod 0 cloth haversack w/chest and back pockets. Each pocket holds ten Mk 20 Mod 0 charges (20 charges total). Each pocket of the haversack has a 10 foot (3.05 m) length of cotton sash cord and a metal flat hook for securing the charge.

Two Mk 127 assemblies per wooden box

METHOD OF ACTUATION Military blasting cap or Primacord

WEIGHTS

Unit 51 lbs (23.13 kg)

Filler 40 lbs (18.14 kg) C2 or C3 (20 Mk 20 charges)

Petn 1.54 lbs (0.70 kg) from 220 ft Primacord (20 × 11 ft)

Package

LENGTHS

Length 13.5 in (34.3 cm) each pocket

Width (diameter) 3.5 in (8.9 cm) each pocket

Height 13.25 in (33.7 cm) each pocket

USE General demolitions where the charge will not be submerged in water for more than 3 hours. This is the original assembly used with the Mk 20 Mod 0 charge (Hagensen pack)

MK 135 MODS 0 & 1 DEMOLITION CHARGE

TYPE General underwater demolition charge

IDENTIFYING COLOR CODE Gray cloth bag w/black markings

CONTAINER MATERIAL Cotton canvas treated to be waterproof, fireproof, and mildew resistant

FILLER C2 or 3 (Mod 0), C4 (Mod 1)

PACKAGING Mk 3 Mod 0 canvas field pack w/charge pocket and flotation bladder

pocket holding one Mk 1 Mod 0 or Mod 1 flotation bladder. The charge pocket contains ten Mk 20 Mod O charges (Mod 0) or ten Mk 20 Mod 1 charges (Mod 1). The Mk 3 Mod 0 field pack has an adjustable shoulder strap with a snap hook. The pack is equipped with a length of sash cord with a flat hook for securing the charge. At the bottom of the pack is a tow ring. Straps from multiple packs can be strung together in a single row to allow the charges to be towed in the water by a swimmer. Packed two charges per wooden box

METHOD OF ACTUATION Military blasting cap or Primacord

WEIGHTS

Unit 24.5 lbs (11.11 kg)

Filler 20 lbs (9.07 kg) C2 or C3 (Mod 0), or C4 (Mod 1) PETN 0.77 lbs (0.35 kg) from 110 ft Primacord

Package 67 lbs (30.39 kg)

LENGTHS

Length 11.88 in (30.2 cm)

Width (diameter) 6.88 in (17.5 cm)

Height 13.88 in (35.3 cm)

USE General underwater demolitions where the charge will not be submerged underwater for more than 3 hours

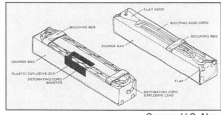

Source: U.S. Navy

MK 34 MODS 0 & 1 DEMOLITION CHARGE

TYPE General underwater demolition charge

IDENTIFYING COLOR CODE Gray body

CONTAINER MATERIAL Cotton duck treated to be waterproof, fireproof, and mildew resistant

FILLER Mod 0—C3; Mod 1—C4

PACKAGING Mk 34 charge—one 2.5 lb C3 (Mod 0) or C4 (Mod 1), block in a cloth bag w/9 feet (2.74 m) of Primacord. 3 ft of Primacord is looped to make a 1 ft booster core the remaining 6 ft are loose making an explosive lead. Each charge has a 3 ft length of sash cord with a flat steel hook for securing the charge to an obstacle. The sash cord and Primacord lead are secured to opposite sides on the outside of the charge under webbing loops

METHOD OF ACTUATION Military blasting cap or primacord

WEIGHTS

Unit 3.43 lbs (1.56 kg)

Filler 2.5 lbs (1.13 kg)

USE General underwater demolition especially against obstacles during combat. Component part of Mk 137 Demolition charge

MK 137 MODS 0 & 1 DEMOLITION CHARGE

TYPE General underwater demolition charge

IDENTIFYING COLOR CODE Gray cloth bag w/black markings

CONTAINER MATERIAL Cotton canvas treated to be waterproof, fireproof, and mildew resistant

FILLER C3 (Mod 0), C4 (Mod 1)

PACKAGING Mk 4 Mod 0 canvas field pack w/charge pocket and internal flotation bladder pocket holding one Mk 1 Mod 1 flotation bladder. The Mod 1 charge uses the Mk 4 Mod 1 canvas field pack with a charge pocket and a plastic flotation bladder sewn into the cover flap. The charge pocket contains ten Mk 34 Mod O charges (Mod 0) or ten Mk 34 Mod 1 charges (Mod 1). The Mk 4 Mod 0 & 1 field pack has an adjustable shoulder strap with a snap hook. The pack is equipped with a 17 ft length of sash cord with a flat hook for se-

curing the charge on one side and a snubber assembly on the opposite side. At the bottom of the pack is a tow ring. Straps from multiple packs can be strung together in a single row to allow the charges to be towed in the water by a swimmer. Packed two charges per wooden box

METHOD OF ACTUATION Military blasting cap or Primacord

WEIGHTS

Unit 27.7 lbs (12.56 kg)

Filler 25 lbs (11.34 kg) C3 (Mod 0), or C4 (Mod 1); PETN 0.63 lbs (0.29 kg) from 90 ft Primacord

Package 72 lbs (32.65 kg)

LENGTHS

Length 13.5 in (34.3 cm)

Width (diameter) 5.31 in (13.5 cm)

Height 13.75 in (34.9 cm)

USE General underwater demolitions where the charge will not be submerged underwater for more than 3 hours

MK 35 MODS 0 & 1 DEMOLITION CHARGE

TYPE General underwater demolition charge

IDENTIFYING COLOR CODE Gray body

CONTAINER MATERIAL Cotton duck treated to be waterproof, fireproof, and mildew resistant

FILLER C4

PACKAGING Mk 35 charge—One 2.5 lb C4 block in a cloth bag w/9 ft (2.74 m) of primacord. 3 ft of Primacord is looped to make a 1 ft booster core the remaining 6 ft are loose making an explosive lead. Each charge has a 3 ft length of sash cord with a flat steel hook for securing the charge to an obstacle. The sash cord and Primacord lead are secured to opposite sides on the outside of the charge under webbing loops

METHOD OF ACTUATION Military blasting cap or Primacord

WEIGHTS
Unit 3.43 lbs (1.56 kg)
Filler 2.5 lbs (1.13 kg)
USE General underwater demolition especially against obstacles during combat. Component part of Mk 138 Demolition charge

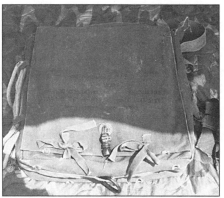

Source: Kevin Dockery

MK 138 MODS 0 & 1 DEMOLITION CHARGE

TYPE General underwater demolition Charge
IDENTIFYING COLOR CODE Gray cloth bag w/black markings
CONTAINER MATERIAL Cotton canvas treated to be waterproof, fireproof, and mildew resistant
FILLER C4
PACKAGING Mk 4 Mod 0 canvas field pack w/charge pocket and internal flotation bladder pocket holding one Mk 1 Mod 1 flotation bladder. The Mod 1 charge uses the Mk 4 Mod 1 canvas field pack with a charge pocket and a plastic flotation bladder sewn into the cover flap. The charge pocket contains ten Mk 35 Mod O charges (Mod 0) or ten Mk 35 Mod 1 charges (Mod 1). The Mk 4 Mod 0 and 1 field pack has an adjustable shoulder strap with a snap hook. The pack is equipped with a 17-foot length of sash cord with a flat hook for securing the charge on one side and a snubber assembly on the opposite side. At the bottom of the pack is a tow ring. Straps from multiple packs can be strung together in a single row to allow the charges to be towed in the water by a swimmer. Packed two charges per wooden box

METHOD OF ACTUATION Military blasting cap or Primacord
WEIGHTS
Unit 27.7 lbs (12.56 kg)
Filler 25 lbs (11.34 kg); PETN 0.63 lbs (0.29 kg) from 90 ft Primacord
Package 72 lbs (32.65 kg)
LENGTHS
Length 13.5 in (34.3 cm)
Width (diameter) 5.31 in (13.5 cm)
Height 13.75 in (34.9 cm)
USE General underwater demolitions where the charge will not be submerged underwater for more than 3 hours. This is the most recent issue explosive charge that can trace its design directly to the Hagensen pack used on the beaches at Normandy.

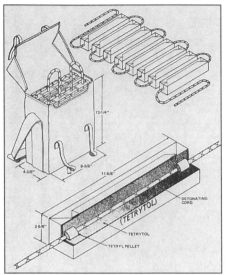

Source: U.S. Navy

M1 CHAIN DEMOLITION CHARGE
TYPE General underwater demolition charge
IDENTIFYING COLOR CODE Gray cloth bag w/black markings
CONTAINER MATERIAL Cotton canvas treated to be waterproof, fireproof, and mildew resistant
FILLER M1—Cast Tetrytol blocks on Primacord
PACKAGING Cloth haversack holding one M1 demolition chain made of eight 2.5 pound (1.13 kg) Tetrytol blocks. Each of the explosive blocks are enclosed in olive drab, asphalt-impregnated paper wrappers and are cast onto a 16-foot Primacord line spaced 8 inches apart. There is a 2-foot Primacord lead at each end of the charge chain. The haversack has an adjustable shoulder strap. Packed two charges per wooden box
METHOD OF ACTUATION Military blasting cap or Primacord
WEIGHTS
Unit 22 lbs (9.98 kg)
Filler 20 lbs (9.07 kg) Tetrytol PETN 0.11 lbs (0.05 kg) from 16 ft Primacord

Package 62 lbs (28.12 kg)
LENGTHS
Length 16 ft (4.88 m) explosive chain; 9.38 in (23.8 cm)
Width (diameter) 4.38 in (11.1 cm)
Height 12.25 in (31.1 cm)
USE General underwater demolitions, the charge has remained submerged for 24 hours without appreciably affecting its explosive characteristics.

Source: U.S. Navy

MK 133 MODS 0, 1, & 2 DEMOLITION CHARGE
TYPE General underwater demolition charge
IDENTIFYING COLOR CODE Gray cloth bag w/black markings
CONTAINER MATERIAL Cotton canvas treated to be waterproof, fireproof, and mildew resistant
FILLER Mod 0 & 1—Cast TNT blocks on Primacord (Mk 23 Mod 1 demolition chain); Mod 2— HBX-1 blocks w/50/50 Pentolite boosters on Primacord
PACKAGING Mk 2 Mod 0 haversack w/charge pocket and flotation bladder pocket (Mod 1 does not have the flotation

bladder) holding one Mk 1 Mod 0 or Mod 1 flotation bladder. Each of the explosive blocks are cast onto a Primacord line spaced 1 foot apart. There is a 5-foot Primacord lead at each end of the charge chain. The Mk 2 Mod 0 haversack has an adjustable shoulder strap with a snap hook. The haversack is equipped with a length of sash cord with a flat hook for securing the charge. At the bottom of the haversack is a tow ring. Straps from multiple packs can be strung together in a single row to allow the charges to be towed in the water by a swimmer. Packed two charges per wooden box

METHOD OF ACTUATION Military blasting cap or Primacord

WEIGHTS

Unit 23.5 lbs (10.66 kg)

Filler 20 lbs TNT or HBX-1; PETN 0.18 lbs (0.08 kg) from 25 ft Primacord

Package 65 lbs (29.48 kg)

LENGTHS

Length 25 ft (7.62 m) explosive chain; 9.88 in (25.1 cm)

Width (diameter) 8.88 in (22.6 cm)

Height 12.25 in (31.1 cm)

USE General underwater demolitions where the charge will not be submerged underwater for more than 3 hours

MK 36 MOD 1 DEMOLITION CHARGE

TYPE Underwater demolition charge

CONTAINER MATERIAL Sheet aluminum

FILLER H-6 w/boosters

PACKAGING Flanged metal canister containing an explosive core and two booster charges. There is an external activator well that accepts the Mk 39 Mod 0 Safety and Arming device. An off-center cavity inside the charge accepts the Mk 24 Mod 2 Firing device with an antidisturbance fuze. Around the outside of the charge, held by the flange, are six curved permanent magnets. The magnets hold the charge firmly against any ferrous target.

METHOD OF ACTUATION Mk 39 Mod 0 Safety and Arming device w/various firing devices

WEIGHTS

Unit 10.5 lbs (4.76 kg) in air; 6.5 lbs (2.95 kg) in water

Filler 4.2 lbs (1.91 kg)

LENGTHS

Width (diameter) 9.5 in (24.1 cm)

Height 3 in (7.6 cm)

USE This is the explosive component and main body of the Mk 1 Mods 2, 3, and 4 limpet mine

MK 70 MOD 0 EXPLOSIVE CHARGE

TYPE Underwater demolition charge

IDENTIFYING COLOR CODE Olive drab body w/white markings

CONTAINER MATERIAL Sheet metal

FILLER H-6

PACKAGING Metal canister containing an explosive core surrounded by and annular flotation chamber. The chamber provides the charge with neutral buoyancy in seawater. The module is capped by a cover held in place by a clamping band. Once the cover is removed, the band is used to clamp the modules together. A breakaway nut is used to tighten the band that can then be broken off, preventing the explosives from being removed when the Mk 5 limpet is in place on a target. Two per metal drum

METHOD OF ACTUATION Mk 47 Mod 1 Timing Firing device when used as a part of the Mk 5 limpet. Mk 114 Mod 0 Firing device adapter with a Mk 39 Mod 0 Safety and Arming device and a Mk 48 Mod 0 Firing device is used when the Mk 70 Mod 0 is used by itself as a demolition charge

WEIGHTS
Unit 74 lbs (33.57 kg)
Filler 50 lbs (22.68 kg)
LENGTHS
Length 12 in (30.5 cm)
Width (diameter) 16.5 in (41.9 cm)

USE Explosive component of the Mk 5 Mod 0 modular limpet mine assembly. Each Mk 70 charge can attack a ship of roughly 1,500 tons displacement, i.e. 6 charges, assembled as part of a Mk 5 limpet, to attack a ship displacing 7,000 tons.

EXPLOSIVE DEVICES

Source: Kevin Dockery

M7 SPECIAL NONELECTRIC BLASTING CAP

TYPE Flame or impact fired explosive initiator
IDENTIFYING COLOR CODE Unpainted
CONTAINER MATERIAL Aluminum or copper
FILLER Lead styphnate and barium chromate ignition charge, lead azide priming charge, RDX or PETN base charge
PACKAGING Aluminum or copper (early production) tube with one closed end and a flared open end. Earlier (WWII) production J1 caps did not have the flared end and were made of either aluminum or copper. Pressed into the cap is the base charge of RDX or PETN topped with a priming charge and then an ignition charge. The charges only partially fill the tube leaving about a 0.75 in (1.9 cm) space to accept the fuse, Primacord, or other initiator. The soft metal of the cap is easily crimped around the initiating material or snout. 6 caps packed per paperboard box and sealed in a barrier bag, 50 bags per card-

board container (250 caps), 12 containers (3600 caps) per wooden box, or 32 bags (192 caps) per M19A1 metal ammunition can
METHOD OF ACTUATION Time fuze, Primacord, or firing device coupling base (percussion cap)
WEIGHTS
Filler 19.3 grains (1.25 g) total explosive weight; 13.5 grains (0.87 g) base charge
Package 3,200 cap wooden box 114 lbs (51.71 kg)
EFFECTS
Effect Initiates all presently used military explosives
LENGTHS
Length 2.35 in (6 cm)
Width (diameter) Closed end—0.24 in (6.1 mm); Flared end 0.26 in (6.6 mm)
USE Primary nonelectric initiator of all military demolitions. The M7 cap is replacing the earlier straight J1 cap. The cap is not sealed against moisture and when used in wet locations must be waterproofed. Extremely sensitive to shock and heat. A drop of only a few inches onto a hard surface can set the cap off.

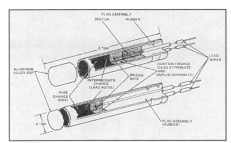

Source: U.S. Army

M6 SPECIAL ELECTRIC BLASTING CAP

TYPE Electrically fired explosive initiator

IDENTIFYING COLOR CODE Unpainted, contrasting colors on the two lead wires

CONTAINER MATERIAL Aluminum w/plastic insulated copper wires

FILLER Special smokeless powder mix ignition charge, lead azide priming charge, RDX or PETN base charge

PACKAGING Aluminum tube with one closed end. Pressed into the tube is the base charge of PETN or RDX, then the lead azide priming charge, and the ignition charge. Buried in the ignition charge is an electric bridge of high-resistance wire. When an electric current of sufficient strength crosses the bridge wire it heats and fires the ignition charge. The bridge is attached to two 12-foot (3.66 m) lead wires. The lead wires pass through a rubber filler plug or a cast sulfur and rubber plug assembly that seals off the mouth of the cap waterproofing the charge. The end of the lead wires are shorted with a safety clip that is removed just before firing. Six caps packed per paperboard box and sealed in a barrier bag, 25 bags per fiberboard carton (150 caps), 6 cartons per wooden box (900 caps)

METHOD OF ACTUATION 0.5 ampere electric current

WEIGHTS

Filler 19.3 grains (1.25 g) total explosive weight; 13.5 grains (0.87 g) base charge

Package 113 lbs (51.26 kg)

EFFECTS

Effect Initiates all presently used military explosives

LENGTHS

Length 2.35 in (6 cm) cap; 4 yds (3.66 m) lead wires

Width (diameter) 0.241 in (6.1 mm)

USE Primary electric initiator of all military demolitions. Extremely sensitive to physical shock, heat, and electricity. The cap assembly must be kept away from all radio transmitters to protect it from induced electric charges. The minimum safe distances are:

TRANSMITTER POWER (WATTS)	MINIMUM SAFE DISTANCE
0—30	33 yds (30 m)
30—50	55 yds (50 m)
50—100	120 yds (110 m)
100—250	175 yds (160 m)
250—500	252 yds (230 m)
500—1000	334 yds (305 m)
1000—3000	525 yds (480 m)
3000—5000	667 yds (610 m)
5000—20,000	1001 yds (915 m)
20,000—50,000	1673 yds (1530 m)
50,000—100,000	3336 yds (3050 m)

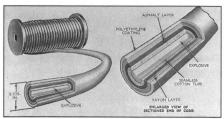

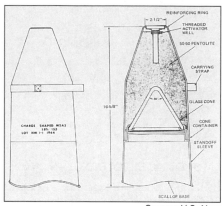

Source: U.S. Army

PRIMACORD (DETONATING CORD)

TYPE "Instant" explosive fuse

IDENTIFYING COLOR CODE Olive drab or yellow (commercial) exterior

CONTAINER MATERIAL Varies

FILLER PETN

PACKAGING Present construction consists of an explosive core with a weight of 49 grains per foot (10.4 grams per meter). Surrounding the core is a seamless cotton tube. Surrounding the cotton tube is a layer of asphalt waterproofing. Next is a layer of rayon with the entire cord covered with a polyethylene coating. Construction has varied over time and the layers can include wax, wire, paper liners, and other braided textiles. 500 feet (152.4 m) per spool, 1 spool per metal can, 8 cans per wooden box

METHOD OF ACTUATION Military blasting cap

TIME DELAY None, cord detonates at a rate of 21,000 (6,400 m) to 23,000 (7,010 m) feet per second

WEIGHTS

Unit 9 lbs (4.08 kg) per 500 ft (152.4 m)

Filler 7 lbs (3.18 kg) per 1,000 feet (304.8 m)

Package 11.7 lbs (5.31 kg) 127 lbs (57.61 kg) per box

Width (diameter) 0.203 in (0.5 cm)

USE Instantaneous initiation of several explosive charges. Can be used to connect an unlimited number of charges to a single initiator.

Source: U.S. Navy

M2A3 SHAPED DEMOLITION CHARGE

TYPE Armor/concrete penetrating demolition charge

IDENTIFYING COLOR CODE Olive drab body w/yellow markings

CONTAINER MATERIAL Molded fiber

FILLER Pentolite or Composition B with a Pentolite booster. WWII production used the Pentolite filler, present production uses the Composition B filler.

PACKAGING Conical fiber container holds a shaped charge of explosive with a glass cavity liner. A sleeve (standoff) is supplied that fits on the bottom of the charge and is set for the optimum standoff distance 5.32 inches (13.5 cm). Packaged two charges to a wooden box

METHOD OF ACTUATION Military blasting cap or Primacord

WEIGHTS

Unit 15 lbs (6.80 kg)

Filler 11.5 lbs (5.22 kg) Pentolite; 9.4 lbs (4.26 kg) Composition B w/2.1 lbs (0.95 kg) Pentolite booster

Package 57.8 lbs (26.22 kg)

EFFECTS

Effect Penetrates 12 in (30.5 cm) steel, penetrates 32 inches (81.3 cm) reinforced concrete with a tapering hold reducing from 3.5 inches (8.9 cm) at the mouth to 2 inches (5.1 cm) at the base.

LENGTHS

Width (Diameter) 7 in (17.8 cm) w/o standoff cone; 7.75 in (19.7 cm) w/standoff cone

Height 11.96 in (30.4 cm) w/o standoff cone; 16.43 in (41.7 cm) w/standoff cone

USE Primary use is for blasting holes in concrete especially for the insertion of additional charges. The glass liner allows a second charge to be placed immediately over the hole blasted by the first charge. The material of the cone forms a glass slug in the bore hole that can be shattered and removed, leaving the bore hole cool enough to accept a second charge

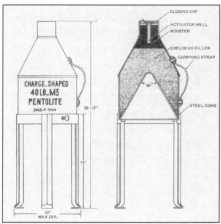

Source: U.S. Navy

M3 SHAPED DEMOLITION CHARGE

TYPE Armor/concrete penetrating demolition charge

IDENTIFYING COLOR CODE Olive drab body w/yellow markings

CONTAINER MATERIAL Sheet steel

FILLER Pentolite or Composition B with a Pentolite booster. Present production of the M3 uses the Composition B filler

PACKAGING Conical container holds a shaped charge of Composition B with a metal cavity liner. A removable tripod (standoff frame) is supplied with the charge that is set for the optimum standoff distance of 15 inches (38.1 cm). Packaged one charge to a wooden box

METHOD OF ACTUATION Military blasting cap or Primacord

WEIGHTS

Unit 40 lbs (18.14 kg)

Filler 29.5 lbs (13.38 kg) Pentolite; 28.3 lbs (12.84 kg) Composition B w/1.7 lbs (0.77 kg) Pentolite

Package 65 lbs (29.48 kg)

EFFECTS

Effect Penetrates 20 in (50.8 cm) steel, penetrates 5 feet (1.52 m) reinforced concrete with a tapering hold reducing from 5 inches (12.7 cm) at the mouth to 2.5 inches (6.4 cm) at the base.

LENGTHS

Width (diameter) 9.5 in (24.1 cm) w/o standoff frame; 10.8 in (27.4 cm) w/standoff frame

Height 15.44 in (39.2 cm) w/o standoff frame; 29.55 in (75.1 cm) w/standoff frame

USE Primary use is for blasting holes in concrete especially for the insertion of additional charges

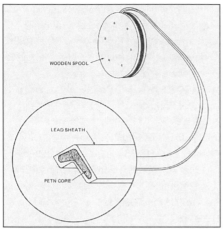

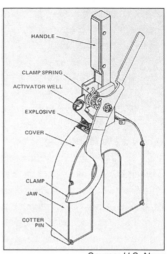

Source: U.S. Navy

FLEXIBLE LINEAR SHAPED CHARGE

TYPE Explosive cutting charge

IDENTIFYING COLOR CODE Gray body

CONTAINER MATERIAL Lead

FILLER PETN

PACKAGING V-shaped angular seamless lead sheath containing a central core of PETN; Packaged in 20 foot (6.1 m) or 30 foot (9.14 m) spools, two spools per wooden box

METHOD OF ACTUATION Military blasting cap or Primacord

WEIGHTS

Filler 300 grains (19.44 g) per foot (.305 m)

Effects

Effect The charge will penetrate a 2 inch (5.1 cm) steel plate to a minimum depth of .25 inch (6.4 mm) when used with a stand-off distance of 0.31 in (7.9 mm)

USE Used in part to cut passages through blocked doors and walls as well as cutting up debris and blockading wrecks or structures.

Source: U.S. Navy

MK 1 MOD 1 CABLE & CHAIN CUTTER

TYPE Shaped charge explosive line cutter

IDENTIFYING COLOR CODE Olive drab body

CONTAINER MATERIAL Corrosion-resistant sheet steel

FILLER C3 or C4

PACKAGING The device is issued empty with the explosive filling added in the field. The horseshoe-shaped main body contains an 80 degree V-liner facing a built-in stand-off chamber. In the open outside portion of the horseshoe is a space for the plastic explosive filling. The explosive space is protected with a removable cover. A hook-shaped clamp is spring loaded and will hold the cutter in position on a proper-sized cable or chain. Squeezing the handle of the clamp against the handle of the cutter opens the clamp for placement. Next to the handle is an activator well that accepts a standard blasting cap. Packaged 25 empty units to a wooden box

METHOD OF ACTUATION Military blasting cap or primacord

WEIGHTS

Unit 2.5 lbs (1.13 kg) w/o explosives

Filler 1.25 lbs (0.57 kg)

Package 125 lbs (56.7 kg)

EFFECTS

Effect Cuts steel cable up to 2 inches (5.1 cm) in diameter and anchor chain up to 1.5 inches (3.8 cm) thick

LENGTHS

Length 6.25 in (15.9 cm)

Width (diameter) 1.31 in (3.3 cm)

Height 15.13 in (38.4 cm)

USE Cutting chain, cable, or rod in air or underwater to a depth of 20 feet (6.1 m)

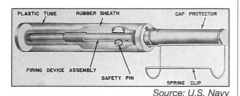

Source: U.S. Navy

MK 136 MODS 0 AND 1 DEMOLITION OUTFIT W/DESTRUCTORS DEMOLITION MK 1 MODS 0 AND 1

TYPE Water mine destruction kit

IDENTIFYING COLOR CODE Mod 0 Destructor—Green rubber sheath, solid end of translucent plastic transportation tube is green; Mod 1 Destructor, White rubber sheath, solid end of translucent transportation tube is white

CONTAINER MATERIAL Plastic transportation tube and cap protector

FILLER PETN

PACKAGING The Mk 136 Demolition outfit is a 2 foot (0.61 m) long 6 inch (15.2 cm) wide nylon belt with ten elastic pockets. The belt is equipped with two elastic straps and two commercial buckles than allow the belt to be wrapped and secured around the waist of a swimmer. Each of the belt's pockets holds one Mk 1 Mod 0 or 1 Destructor. The plastic transportation tube of the destructor fits completely inside the pocket on the belt. The cap protector extends out of the top of the pocket allowing easy removal by the swimmer. The Mk 1 Destructor is a waterproofed firing device assembly with a blasting cap attached. The device is adapted from the Army M1 Delay firing device. The blasting cap is surrounded by a plastic cap—muffler tube that cushions the effect of the cap. Around the protector is a spring wire clip that allows the destructor to be attached to the chemical horn of a mine. The muffling action of the cap protector allows the horn of the mine to be crushed and not destroyed or ruptured, this detonates the mine is a controlled manner.

The firing device assembly is contained within a rubber sheath. Removing the plastic transportation tube exposes the firing device assembly. A safety pin can be removed from the firing device by hand manipulation through the rubber, maintaining the watertight integrity of the device. Squeezing the upper half of the firing device crushes the tube, breaking an acid ampule inside. The acid eats through a restraining wire releasing a spring-loaded firing pin. Packaged 10 belts w/destructors per wooden box, separate blasting caps are attached in the field before use

METHOD OF ACTUATION 15 lbs force or greater crushing the upper half of the firing device assembly

TIME DELAY

Mk 1 Mod 0

WATER TEMP		DELAY IN HOURS	
DEGREES F	MIN.	NOMINAL	MAX.
80	1.5	3	4.5
70	2	4.25	6.75
60	2.75	5.75	9
50	4	8	12.25

Mk 1 Mod 1

WATER TEMP		DELAY IN HOURS	
DEGREES F	MIN.	NOMINAL	MAX.
80	0.25	1	1.75
70	0.5	1.5	2.5
60	0.75	1.75	3.25
50	1	2.75	4.5

WEIGHTS
Unit 3 lbs (1.36 kg) Belt w/destructors; Destructor 0.25 lbs (0.11 kg)
Filler 13.5 grains (0.88 g)
Package 50 lbs (22.68 kg)
EFFECTS
Effect Detonates Japanese JG or JE type mines, will detonate other chemical-horn type mines if the destructor can be attached to the horn.
LENGTHS
Length 9.25 in (23.5 cm) Destructor w/transportation tube
Width (diameter) 0.75 in (1.9 cm) Destructor w/transportation tube
USE Designed specifically for use by UDT swimmers in detonating antiboat mines after a delay

Source: Kevin Dockery

MK 1 MODS 2, 3, & 4 LIMPET MINE
TYPE Antiship hand-emplaced underwater demolition charge
IDENTIFYING COLOR CODE Olive drab body
CONTAINER MATERIAL Sheet aluminum
FILLER H-6 w/boosters
PACKAGING The Mk 1 Mod 2 limpet is made up of the Mk 36 Mod 1 Demolition charge with the Mk 39 Mod 0 Safety and Arming device fitted with the Mk 23 Mod 1 Firing device. Inside the mine is fitted the Mk 24 Mod 2 antidisturbance firing device.

The Mk 1 Mod 3 limpet is made up of the Mk 36 Mod 1 Demolition charge and the Mk 39 Mod 0 Safety and Arming device fitted with the Mk 48 Mod 0 Firing device. Inside the mine is fitted the Mk 24 Mod 2 antidisturbance firing device.

The Mk 1 Mod 4 limpet is made up of the Mk 36 Mod 1 Demolition charge with just the Mk 39 Mod 0 Safety and Arming device fitted with the Mk 23 Mod 1 Firing device.

A black foam-plastic float is issued that fits snugly over the Mk 1 limpet covering all but the base of the mine and the fuze assembly. With the float attached and strapped in place, the limpet has neutral or slightly positive buoyancy for ease in underwater transportation by a combat swimmer.
METHOD OF ACTUATION Mods 2, 3, and 4—Expiration of time delay; Mods 2 and 3—Disturbance of mine
TIME DELAY Arming delay 10 to 15 minutes; Various time delay settings according to firing device—see proper firing device
WEIGHTS
UNIT Mk 1 Mod 2—12.95 lbs (5.87 kg); Mk 1 Mod 3—13.55 lbs (6.15 kg); Mk 1 Mod 4—12.15 lbs (5.51 kg)
Filler 4.2 lbs (1.91 kg)
LENGTHS
Length Mk 1 Mod 2—15.75 in (40 cm) w/firing device assembly; Mk 1 Mod 3—18 in (45.7 cm) w/firing device assembly; MK 1 Mod 4—15.75 in (40 cm) w/firing device assembly
Width (diameter) 9.5 in (24.1 cm)
Height 3 in (7.6 cm)
USE Swimmer attack of ships. One Mk 1 limpet may be transported by a combat swimmer using the Mk 46 Mod 0 backpack kit. When the additional trailer is attached to the Mk 46 Mod 0 backpack, two Mk 1 limpets can be easily transported by a single combat swimmer. The mines are held to the backpack base by their integral magnets where they can be easily detached by the swimmer or his partner.

Source: Kevin Dockery

MK 5 MOD 0 MODULAR LIMPET MINE ASSEMBLY

TYPE Hand-emplaced underwater antiship/antimaterial modular demolition charge

IDENTIFYING COLOR CODE Olive drab body w/white markings

CONTAINER MATERIAL Sheet metal

FILLER H-6

PACKAGING The Mk 5 limpet mine is a group of modules that can be assembled in the field according to the size of the target. The explosive component is the Mk 70 Mod 0 Explosive charge. Any number of Mk 70 charges can be assembled to attack a target. A curved end fairing with integral handles is placed on both ends of the assembled mine. The end fairings have internal flotation chambers with water-flood valves that allow the mine to be trimmed for neutral buoyancy by the operators.

Between one end fairing and the explosive module(s) is the Mk 126 Mod 0 control unit. The control unit contains the Mk 47 Mod 1 Timer device and the Mk 156 Mod 0 power supply. Also part of the control unit is the arming handle and target sensing probe. When the arming handle is activated, the target sensing probe is released and the power supply begins charging the system 15 minutes after the arming cycle begins. When the arming cycle is completed, the sensing probe will detonate the charge if there is any movement between the mine and the target.

The Mk 47 Mod 1 timer is made up of solid-sate timing and firing circuits and has two settings for detonation, CONTACT and STANDOFF. The firing mode is set before the mine is emplaced. At the time the firing mode is selected, the delay time is set from 1 to 99 hours. If the CONTACT firing mode is used, the charge fires after the expiration of the delay time. In the STANDOFF mode, a separation bolt is fired at the end of the delay time. The separation bolt allows the unit to sink to a proper standoff depth. Four seconds after the separation bolt is fired the detonators are fired setting off the main charge.

The wing-and-yoke assembly is used to stabilized the weapon for underwater handling by the swimmer. The assembly is formed of aluminum filled with polyurethane foam and has 25 lbs (11.34 kg) of positive buoyancy in seawater. The assembly is attached to the control unit by the explosive separation bolt. The two wings have inflatable bladders that are filled with CO_2 by the operator at the target. The positive buoyancy of the wing bladders hold the limpet firmly to the target

The MK 5 may also be used as a modular demolition charge. In the demolition charge only the end fairings and explosive modules are used. Fuzing is accomplished by using a firing assembly consisting of the Mk 114 Mod 0 firing device adapter along with the Mk 39 Mod 0 safety and arming device as well as a proper timer. Once the Mk 114 Mod 0 firing device adapter is inserted into the fuze well of the end fairing it cannot be easily removed.

METHOD OF ACTUATION Expiration of timer delay or disturbance of mine

TIME DELAY Mk 47 Mod 1 Timing device—45 minute arming delay, timer delay 1 to 99 hours in 1 hour increments

WEIGHTS

Unit 253 lbs (114.76 kg) Mk 5 assembly w/2 explosive modules; 74 lb (33.57 kg) Mk 70 Mod 0 Explosive charge; 6 lb (2.72 kg) End fairing (2 required); 55 lbs (24.95 kg) Mk 126 Mod 0 Control unit; 0.75 lbs (0.34 kg) Mk 47 Mod 1 Timing firing device; 2.3 lb (1.04 kg) Mk 156 Mod 0 Power supply; 38 lbs (17.24 kg) wing-and-Yoke assembly 162.85 lbs (73.87 kg) Mk 5 Demolition charge w/2 Explosive modules; 74 lb (33.57 kg) Mk 70 Mod 0 Explosive charge; 6 lb (2.72 kg) End fairing (2 required); 2.85 lbs (1.29 kg) Firing device assembly w/Mk 48 Mod 0 firing device; 0.6 lbs (0.27 kg) Mk 114 Mod 0 Firing device adaptor; 0.75 lbs (0.34 kg) Mk 39 Mod 0 Safety and Arming device; 0.9 lbs (0.41 kg) Mk 23 Mod 1 Firing device; or the 1.5 lb (0.68 kg) Mk 48 Mod 0 Firing device

Filler 100 lbs (45.36 kg) for 2 modules; 50 lbs (22.68 kg) per Mk 70 module

LENGTHS

Length 45.25 in (114.9 cm) Mk 5 w/2 Mk 70 modules; 7 in (17.8 cm) End fairing; 7.25 in (18.4 cm) Mk 126 Mod 0 Control unit; 12 in (30.5 cm) Mk 70 Explosive charge

Width (diameter) 16.5 in (41.9 cm); 50 in (127 cm) w/wings open

USE Attacking various sized ships and for use as an underwater demolition charge

Source: Kevin Dockery

M18A1 CLAYMORE MINE

TYPE Directional antipersonnel fragmentation mine

IDENTIFYING COLOR CODE Olive drab body

CONTAINER MATERIAL Fiberglass filled polystyrene plastic

FILLER C4

PACKAGING The front half of the plastic body contains 700 steel balls embedded in a plastic matrix. Molded on the front face of the body are the words "FRONT—TOWARD ENEMY" in raised letters. The body of the mine is convexly curved toward the back to direct the outward spread of the fragmentation. The top and bottom of the mine curve towards each other concavely to minimize the upward spread of the shot. The back portion of the mine is filled with the main charge of C4 and also has raised letters spelling out the words "BACK—M18A1 APERS MINE."

On the top of the mine is molded a plastic slit to act as an aiming aid when setting up the mine. Also in the top are two threaded cap wells to accept a standard military blasting cap. The cap wells are plugged with a shipping plug that can also act as a priming adaptor, holding a blasting cap in place. On the bottom of the mine are two pairs of pivoting scissor-type folding metal legs that can be opened to secure the mine in the ground.

The mine is packaged in the M7 bandoleer which has a sheet of instructions for the mine folded as part of the bandoleers cover. Also in the bandoleer is an M57 firing device and an M4 electric blasting cap. One bandoleer in every case (6) also contains an M40 test set.

The mine can be set up with the M4 blasting cap inserted into either of the cap wells and secured in place. The 100 feet (30.48 m) of firing wire attached to the cap is unwound from its spool out to the firing position. At the position, the shorting plug is removed from the firing wire and the wire's end plugged into the M57 firing device, also called the "clacker." Moving the safety bale on the firing device allows the handle to be squeezed, firing the mine. By placing the M40 test set into the circuit, the firing system can be tested by squeezing the firing device. If the circuit is sound, a visible light will flash in the test set without setting off the cap. Packaged one M18A1 mine w/accessories per bandoleer, 6 bandoleers per wooden box

METHOD OF ACTUATION Military blasting cap or Primacord. Command detonated with the M57 firing device and M4 electric blasting cap. Remote detonated with a military blasting cap or Primacord and a suitable firing device

WEIGHTS
Unit 3.5 lbs (1.59 kg) M18A1 Mine; 0.75 lbs (0.34 kg) M57 Firing device; 0.5 lb (0.23 kg) M40 Test set
Filler 1.5 lbs (0.68 kg)
Package 6.7 lbs (3.04 kg) M18A1 Claymore w/M7 bandoleer, M4 electric blasting cap, and M57 firing device; 53 lbs (24.04 kg) 6 mine case

EFFECTS
Effect Blast drives seven hundred 10.5 grain (0.68 g) steel spheres out in a 60 degree fan-shaped sheaf (arc) from the point of detonation
Area of effect (16 m) Blast radius from C4 explosion; highly effective fragmentation in an area 55 yds (50 m) wide by 2.7 yds (2.5 m) high, 55 yds (50 m) in front of the point of detonation

LENGTHS
Length 8.5 (21.6 cm) M18A1 Mine; 4 in (10.2 cm) M57 Firing device; 100 feet (30.48 m) firing wire M4 blasting cap
Width (diameter) 1.38 in (3.5 cm) M18A1 Mine; 1.35 in (3.4 cm) M57 Firing device
Height 3.25 in (8.3 cm) M18A1 Mine w/legs folded; 3.25 in (8.3 cm) M57 Firing device
EFFECTIVE RANGE 109 yds (100 m)
MAXIMUM RANGE 273 yds (250 m) Forward danger radius
USE Local defense of fixed installations and forward areas. Antipersonnel/antivehicular ambushes and directional minefields

MK 57 MOD 0 EXPLOSIVE SHEET CHARGE KIT

TYPE Flexible directional fragmentation explosive charge
FILLER Detasheet explosive
PACKAGING The Mk 56 charge is a lightweight fragmentation composite sheet with an explosive core of sheet explosive. Glued with rubber cement to the back of the explosive sheet is a layer of 0.25 in (6.4 mm) foam rubber. On the front surface of the explosive sheet is glued a single layer of steel fragments. The fragments are cut from cold-rolled steel sheet and each one measures 0.063 in (1.6 mm) thick by 0.25 in (6.4 mm) square. The fragments are glued to the explosive sheet with rubber cement and are additionally secured

with an outside layer of nylon mosquito netting.

Issued in the Mk 57 kit are M57 firing devices and M4 electric blasting caps. Set up and used in the same way as for the M18A1 Claymore, the system can be command detonated.

Rolls of 2 inch (5.1 cm) wide olive drab ordnance tape are also in the kit and are used to secure the flexible charge to any backing that is 6 inches (15.2 cm) or greater in diameter.

The Mk 57 kit consists of a steel container 36 inches (91.4 cm) long by 12 inches (30.5 cm) high by 9 inches (22.9 cm) wide. Inside the container are:

- 4—Mk 56 Mod 0 Explosive charges
- 4—M57 Firing devices
- 1—M40 Test set
- 16—M4 Electric blasting caps
- 4—M7 Bandoleers
- 4 rolls Pressure sensitive waterproof adhesive tape

METHOD OF ACTUATION Military blasting cap or primacord; command detonated with the M57 firing device and M4 electric blasting cap; remote detonated with a military blasting cap or primacord and a suitable firing device

WEIGHTS

Unit 8.92 lbs (4.05 kg) Mk 56 charge

Filler 2.48 lbs (1.12 kg) per Mk 56 charge

Package 125 lbs (56.69 kg) Mk 57 kit

EFFECTS

Effect Blast and fragmentation, 5760 fragments per Mk 56 sheet

LENGTHS

Length 36 in (91.4 cm) Mk 56 charge; 4 in (10.2 cm) M57 Firing device; 100 feet (30.48 m) firing wire M4 blasting cap

Width (diameter) 0.44 in (1.1 cm) Mk 56 charge; 1.35 in (3.4 cm) M57 Firing device

Height 10 in (25.4 cm) Mk 56 charge; 3.25 in (8.3 cm) M57 Firing device

USE Antipersonnel charge for both offensive and defensive applications. The charge is waterproof and may be used underwater as well as on dry land.

BOOBY TRAPS
Booby Trapped Ammunition

CHINESE 82MM TYPE 53 HE (BOOBY TRAPPED)

CARTRIDGE High explosive fragmentation mortar bomb (booby trapped)

CALIBER 82mm

IDENTIFYING COLOR CODE Black body w/white lettering

FILLER TNT

FUSE TYPE Initiates on setback (firing)

WEIGHTS

Round 8.6 lbs (3.90 kg)

Filler 0.84 lbs (0.38 kg)

EFFECTS

Effect Blast and fragmentation along with destruction of the mortar tube and crew

LENGTHS

Lengths 12.8 in (32.5 cm)

Width (diameter) 3.23 in (8.2 cm)

CHICOM TYPE 56—7.62 INTERMEDIATE (BOOBY TRAPPED)

CALIBER 7.62x39mm

IDENTIFYING COLOR CODE Copper washed steel case

FILLER PETN

FUSE TYPE Percussion cap

WEIGHTS

Round 244 gr (15.8 g)

Filler 25.3 gr (1.64 g)

EFFECTS

Effect Blast and fragmentation over a small area, weapon's operator would be seriously wounded or killed

LENGTHS

Lengths 2.18 in (5.5 cm)

Width (diameter) 0.44 in (11.2 mm) cartridge rim

FLASHLIGHT KIT (BOOBY TRAP)

TYPE Manufactured booby trap

FILLER C4

PACKAGING Standard double D-cell straight flashlight body. Unit came in a kit form and explosive was installed by the user. Either a trembler switch contained in a small disk could be inserted into the flashlight for initiation or the kit used the standard switch on the light itself

METHOD OF ACTUATION Electrically fired blasting cap

FUZE TYPE Antidisturbance switch or integral ON/OFF switch

USE Would be placed in areas where enemy forces were known to frequent

COMMERCIAL, POCKET CAMERA KIT (BOOBY TRAP)

TYPE Manufactured boobytrap

FILLER C4

PACKAGING A popular type of pocket camera often used by American forces. A duplicate camera body was manufactured with integral fuzing. The body would be filled with C-4 explosive by the user. Once the back had been closed, opening it again would fire the charge. In the film indicator window a portion of a film roll with a number exposed was shown indicating there was film in the camera. The film advance lever would not operate to prompt the enemy soldier into opening the device

METHOD OF ACTUATION Military blasting cap

FUZE TYPE Pressure release

USE Would be placed in areas where enemy forces were known to frequent

DEMOLITION EQUIPMENT AND FIRING DEVICES

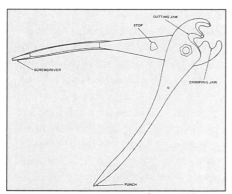

Source: U.S. Army

M2 CAP CRIMPER W/FUSE CUTTER

TYPE General demolition multi-use tool

MATERIAL Nonsparking alloy

WEIGHTS

Unit 0.30 lbs (0.14 kg)

LENGTHS

Length 7 in (17.8 cm)

Width 1.63 in (4.1 cm)

USE Crimping blasting caps to the snout of a firing device base, time fuze, or Primacord with a "cutthroat" type water resistant crimp. A stop on the handle of the crimpers prevents too much pressure from being applied to a cap crimp. Behind the crimping jaws is a pair of cutting jaws used to cut Primacord or fuze with a clean, square cut. The end of one handle of the pincers is shaped like a flat screwdriver blade and the other handle end is a sharp punch for punching holes in explosive charges when preparing the charges for priming.

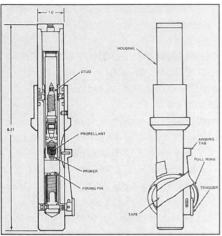

Source: U.S. Navy

MK 22 MOD 0 POWDER ACTUATED PROJECTILE UNIT DRIVER

TYPE Single-shot underwater explosive-driven fastener

PACKAGING Sealed housing containing the spring-loaded, cocked firing mechanism and a cartridge-type ammunition assembly (Mk 2 Mod 0 Powder actuated stud). The safety ring and arming tab are removed the push-button trigger can be depressed firing the device. The Mk 2 Mod 0 Stud cartridge used the captured-piston principal limiting the noise of firing and the release of gas bubbles. 3 drivers—carrying pouch, 2 pouches—M19 ammunition can

METHOD OF ACTUATION Pull ring safety w/push-button trigger

WEIGHTS

Unit 1 lb (0.45 kg) in air; 0.5 lb (0.23 kg) in water

Package 3.25 lbs (1.47 kg) per loaded pouch; 10.16 lbs (4.61 kg) per M19 can

EFFECTS

Effect Attaches demolition charges to various targets and obstacles above or below the water. Will operate on wood, metal, or cement surfaces and operates underwater to a depth of 200 feet (61 m)

LENGTHS

Length 8.31 in (21.1 cm)

Width (diameter) 1 in (2.5 cm)

USE Instantly drives a stud into the target material with a minimum of noise, can be easily operated with one hand.

Source: U.S. Navy

MK 12 & MK 15 DEMOLITION FIRING DEVICES

TYPE Clockwork time-delay nonelectric firing devices

IDENTIFYING COLOR CODE Black body w/white timer markings

CONTAINER MATERIAL Plastic

FILLER Percussion cap

PACKAGING Sealed housing containing a wound clock movement and a cocked firing pin. Rotating the head of the device sets the time desired and removing the pull ring releases the arming pin starting the action. Once the pull ring is removed the action is started and cannot be stopped. When the time delay has expired, a firing pin is released which penetrates a waterproof diaphragm and fires the percussion cap. The spit of flame will detonate a blasting cap attached to the firing device by the user

METHOD OF ACTUATION Pull ring w/cotter pin

TIME DELAY Mk 12—5 to 92 seconds delay; Mk 15—0.25 to 11.5 hours delay

LENGHTS

Length 3.66 in (9.3 cm)

Width (diameter) 1.74 in (4.4 cm)

USE Initiating explosive charges and Primacord leads on land or underwater after an operator-adjustable or preset time delay.

Source: Kevin Dockery

MK 23 MOD 1 DEMOLITION FIRING DEVICE

TYPE Clockwork time-delay nonelectric firing device

IDENTIFYING COLOR CODE Black body w/red markings

CONTAINER MATERIAL Anodized aluminum

FILLER Mk 125 Mod 1 Percussion primer w/coupling base

PACKAGING The aluminum housing is waterproofed good to a depth of 200 feet (61 m). Contained within the housing is a wound clockwork mechanism and a cocked firing pin assembly. Through a transparent window in the top of the device the luminescent timer markings can be seen. By turning the time selector knob, the delay can be set by the operator. Indents click at each time setting allowing the device to be set even in zero visibility conditions. Removing the arming pin starts the clockwork delay. Once removed, the arming pin cannot be reinserted. When the delay had expired, the firing pin is released, penetrating the waterproof seal firing the percussion primer. At the base of the device is a coupling base for crimping on a blasting cap or attaching the device to additional materials.

Packed one firing device per sealed metal can, 20 cans per Mk 1 Mod 0 Small Arms Box.

METHOD OF ACTUATION Pull ring w/arming pin

TIME DELAY Twenty-five settings indicated by detents;

- Setting 0-15 to 18 minutes
- Setting 0.-30 to 36 minutes
- Setting 1-60 to 72 minutes
- Setting 1.-90 to 108 minutes
- Setting 2-120 to 144 minutes
- Setting 2.-150 to 180 minutes

Each greater setting increases the delay by a block of 30 minutes to a maximum setting of 12—720 to 750 minutes (12 to 12.5 hours)

WEIGHTS

Unit 0.90 lbs (0.41 kg)

LENGTHS

Length 4.88 in (12.4 cm)

Width (diameter) 2.12 in (5.4 cm)

USE Initiating explosive charges and primacord leads on land or underwater after an operator-adjustable or preset time delay. Used with the Mk 39 Mod 0 Safety and Arming device as part of the Mk 1 Mods 2 and 4 limpet mine.

Source: Kevin Dockery

MK 48 MOD 0 DEMOLITION FIRING DEVICE

TYPE Electronic time-delay nonelectric firing device

IDENTIFYING COLOR CODE Black body
w/red markings

CONTAINER MATERIAL Metal

FILLER M96 detonator

PACKAGING Metal container holds an electronic delay mechanism. Prior to use, the
device is assembled with an 8.1 vdc mer-
curic oxide battery installed. Attached to
the top and bottom plates of the device
are EMR (electromagnetic radiation) rings
to protect the M96 detonator from any
stray electromagnetic radiation (radio
transmitters, etc,). The time delay is set by
use of the setting knob at the top of the
device, Pulling the knob out and rotating
the arrow to the desired delay setting prepares the time delay. Removing the arming
pin initiates the device. The arming pin can
be removed and reinserted to test the device prior to use. A base coupling allows
the device to be attached to other demolition devices or charges.

Packaged one per ammunition box with all
accessories for use

METHOD OF ACTUATION Pull ring/lanyard

TIME DELAY Delay in hours, settings for
0.25, 0.5, 1, 2, 3, 4, 8, 18, 24, 48, and 72
hours. Time tolerances are 0%, 20%, i.e.
72 hour delay can be up to 86 hours 24
minutes

WEIGHTS

Unit 1.5 lbs (0.68 kg) in air; 0.75 lbs (0.34 kg)
in water

LENGTHS

Length 6.12 in (15.5 cm)

Width (diameter) 2.12 in (5.4 cm)

USE Used with the Mk 39 Safety and Arming
device to initiate demolitions. Used with
the Mk 39 S&A device and Mk 24 Mod 2
antidisturbance device as part of the Mk 1
Mod 3 limpet mine

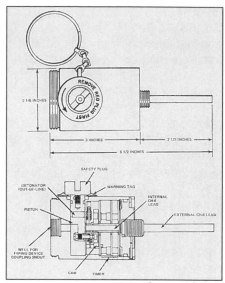

Source: U.S. Navy

MK 39 MOD 0 SAFETY AND ARMING DEVICE

TYPE Time-delay arming nonelectric explosive initiation device

IDENTIFYING COLOR CODE Black body
w/red marking and red safety plug

CONTAINER MATERIAL Anodized aluminum

FILLER Mk 43 detonator w/H-6 booster lead

PACKAGING The casing is threaded at one
end to accept either a firing device directly
or a standard firing device coupling. The
opposite end of the casing has a threaded
coupling base and a 2.5 inch (6.4 cm) external lead. Inside the casing is a piston
that holds the Mk 96 detonator out of line
with the firing device well and explosive
lead. A clockwork timer cams the detonator into line with the firing device well and
explosive lead after a preset arming delay.
Removing the safety plug allows the detonator piston to move enough to start the
delay mechanism. Once removed, the
safety plug cannot be reinserted.

The Mk 39 S&A device must be activated at
a depth of less than 60 feet (18.29 m) to

assure proper functioning. After actuation, the device may be used at depths to 240 feet (73.15 m)

METHOD OF ACTUATION Standard base coupling firing device

TIME DELAY 10 to 15 minutes

WEIGHTS

Unit 0.75 lbs (0.34 kg) in air; 0.25 lb (0.11 kg) in water

LENGTHS

Length 3 in (7.6 cm) body only; 5.5 in (14 cm) with external H-6 lead

Width (diameter) 2.13 in (5.4 cm)

USE Adds an additional out-of-line safety to an explosive train with a variety of demolition firing devices that would otherwise lack such positive safety. Used as part of the Mk 1 Mods limpet mine and as additional fuzing for the Mk 5 Modular limpet mine

Source: U.S. Navy

MODEL 3081-308-4 REMOTE FIRING DEVICE

TYPE Coded radio transmitter/receiver stand-off firing device

PACKAGING Transmitter and receiver are each packaged in watertight cases, waterproof to 60 feet. The receiver unit is issued with a code plug that must be installed in the transmitter prior to use. An operator adjustable variable time delay is part of the receiver's arming system. Once the

delay has expired, the receiver will fire up to 10 electrical caps wired in series upon receiving a proper coded signal. Batteries in the receiver give it an active field life of 14 days.

METHOD OF ACTUATION One of 2,048 possible codes

TIME DELAY 1 to 60 minutes for receiver arming time delay

WEIGHTS

Unit Transmitter 7.8 lbs (3.54 kg); Receiver 3.15 lbs (1.43 kg)

Effectie range 5 miles (8.05 km) ground-to-ground, line-of-sight, longer ranges possible from aircraft

USE Remote initiation of demolitions with electric blasting caps

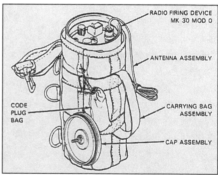

Source: U.S. Navy

MK 30 MOD 0 RADIO FIRING DEVICE

TYPE Coded radio receiver stand-off firing device

CONTAINER MATERIAL Anodized 6061-T6 aluminum

PACKAGING The receiver is packed in a watertight case waterproof to 240 feet (73.15 m). The receiver unit is issued with a 2.13 in (5.4 cm) by 0.265 in (6.7 mm) by 0.83 in (2.1) code plug that must be installed in the Mk 100 transmitter for use. A ten-position operator adjustable variable time delay is part of the receiver's arming system. Once the delay has expired, the receiver will fire up to 10 M6 electrical caps wired in series through 1,000 feet (304.8 m) of No. 18 AWG blasting wire upon receiving a proper coded signal. The receiver is powered by four BA-3030/U D-cell batteries with an active field life of more than 14 days. A nylon carrying bag assembly 12 inches (30.5 cm) long and 5 inches (12.7 cm) in diameter is issued to carry the Mk 30 receiver or Mk 100 transmitter. The bag assembly is fitted with D-rings and a carrying handle for attachment to a belt or hand carrying.

METHOD OF ACTUATION Coded transmission from the Mk 100 Radio firing device control transmitter

TIME DELAY Safety time delays of 1, 2, 4, 8, 12, 16, 32, 64, 96, and 192 minutes with an interval tolerance of 0%, 20%

WEIGHTS

Unit 5.4 lbs (2.45 kg); 1.5 lbs (0.68 kg) packaged for underwater transport

LENGTHS

Length 7.25 in (18.4 cm) w/o case; 8.96 in (22.1 cm) w/case; 5 ft (1.52 m) antenna wire

Width (diameter) 3.25 in (8.3 cm) w/o case; 3.75 in (9.5 cm) w/case

Maximum range 600 feet (183 m) to 5 miles (8.05 km) ground-to-ground, line-of-sight

USE Remote initiation of demolitions with electric blasting caps

Source: U.S. Navy

MODEL 308-5 FIRING DEVICE

TYPE Booby trap and antidisturbance self-contained electric firing device

IDENTIFYING COLOR CODE Black body

CONTAINER MATERIAL Plastic w/metal screw posts

PACKAGING The plastic container holds the battery and electronics of the device. With the self-contained battery, the device has an operational armed life of two months. During its field use, the device will fire up to 4 electric caps wired in series or parallel. A built-in test circuit indicates the proper operation of the device and the case is waterproof to a depth of 70 feet. The device cannot be used underwater and must operate in a dry condition. Once the arming switch is thrown, a built-in delay starts. After the delay has expired, the device will fire on any disturbance or if the trigger circuit is opened. An assortment of pressure switches and spools of various-sized fine wire are issued with the device for use

METHOD OF ACTUATION Circuit interruption by pressure switch or broken wire, Disturbance of device

TIME DELAY Arming delay 75 to 85 seconds

WEIGHTS

Unit 0.34 lbs (0.15 kg)

LENGTHS

Length 3 in (7.6 cm)

Width (diameter) 1.5 in (3.8 cm)

Height 1.25 in (3.2 cm)

USE Initiation of booby trap demolitions with electric blasting caps

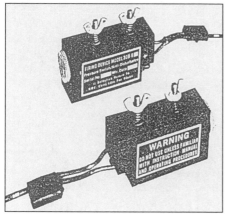

Source: U.S. Navy

MODEL 308-6 FIRING DEVICE

TYPE Booby trap, time-delay, and antidisturbance self-contained electric firing device

IDENTIFYING COLOR CODE Black body w/white markings

CONTAINER MATERIAL Plastic w/metal screw posts

PACKAGING The plastic container holds the battery and electronics of the device. With the replaceable internal battery, the device has an operational armed life of two years depending on temperature exposure. During its field use, the device will fire up to 4 electric caps wired in series or parallel. A built-in test circuit indicates the proper operation of the device and the case is waterproof to a depth of 70 feet. The device cannot be used underwater and must operate in a dry condition. Once the arming switch is thrown, a built-in delay starts. After the delay has expired, the device will fire on any disturbance or if the trigger circuit is opened, in addition a 24-hour mechanical clockwork switch can be used to operate the device as a delay detonator with an antidisturbance capability. An assortment of pressure switches, spools of various sized fine wire, and the clockwork timer are issued with the device for use

METHOD OF ACTUATION Circuit interruption by pressure switch or broken wire; clockwork timer; disturbance of device

TIME DELAY Arming delay 75 to 85 seconds, clockwork timer 5 minutes to 23.5 hours in 1 minute increments

WEIGHTS

Unit 0.34 lbs (0.15 kg)

LENGTHS

Length 3 in (7.6 cm)

Width (diameter) 1.5 in (3.8 cm)

Height 1.25 in (3.2 cm)

USE Electric blasting cap initiation of explosive charges and Primacord leads on land after an operator-adjustable or preset time delay. Initiation of booby trap demolitions.

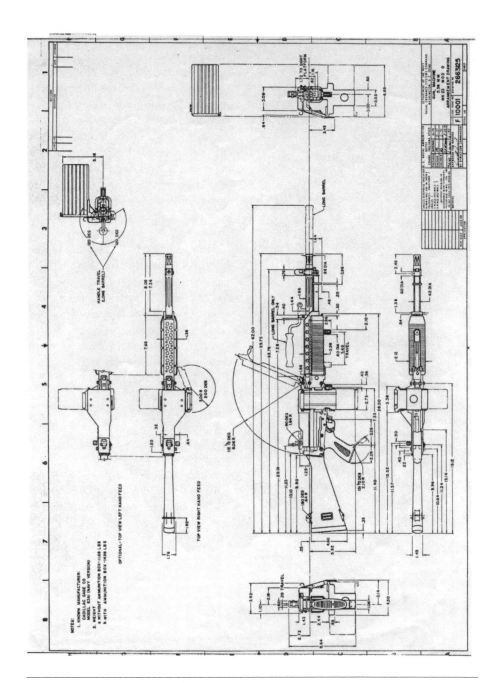

MG057—MACHINE GUNS—STONER MK 23 MOD 0 NAVY ARRANGEMENT DRAWING

A fully dimensioned arrangement drawing for the Mark 23 Mod 0 machine gun as produced by the Naval Ordnance Systems Command in 1970. This drawing shows the official version of the Mark 23 Stoner with the short barrel, right-hand feed mechanism, and 100-round box hanger. The optional long barrel and left-hand feed system are also shown. At the upper left corner of the drawing, the weapon is identified as the Cadillac Gage Co. Model 63A1 (Navy Version).

Index